1981
The Supreme Court Review

1981
The

"Judges as persons, or courts as institutions, are entitled to
no greater immunity from criticism than other persons
or institutions . . . [J]udges must be kept mindful of their limitations and
of their ultimate public responsibility by a vigorous
stream of criticism expressed with candor however blunt."
—*Felix Frankfurter*

". . . while it is proper that people should find fault when
their judges fail, it is only reasonable that they should recognize the
difficulties. . . . Let them be severely brought to book,
when they go wrong, but by those who will take the trouble
to understand them."
—*Learned Hand*

THE LAW SCHOOL

THE UNIVERSITY OF CHICAGO

Supreme Court Review

EDITED BY

PHILIP B. KURLAND

GERHARD CASPER

AND DENNIS J. HUTCHINSON

 THE UNIVERSITY OF CHICAGO PRESS

CHICAGO AND LONDON

INTERNATIONAL STANDARD BOOK NUMBER: 0-226-46434-2

LIBRARY OF CONGRESS CATALOG CARD NUMBER: 60-14353

THE UNIVERSITY OF CHICAGO PRESS, CHICAGO 60637

THE UNIVERSITY OF CHICAGO PRESS, LTD., LONDON

To
DIANE, KATY, AND DAVID

CONTENTS

HENRY PAUL MONAGHAN

OVERBREADTH

I. INTRODUCTION

The concern in constitutional law with "overbreadth" is generally understood to denote a conscious departure from conventional standing concepts in free-expression cases.[1] Assertedly justified by the special vulnerability of protected expression to impermissible deterrence,[2] overbreadth doctrine invites litigants to attack the facial validity of rules which burden expressive interests. A litigant whose expression is admittedly within the constitutionally valid applications of a statute[3] is permitted to assert the sta-

---

Henry Paul Monaghan is Professor of Law, Boston University.

[1] *E.g.*, United States v. Raines, 362 U.S. 17, 22 (1960); Ulster County Court v. Allen, 442 U.S. 140, 154–55 (1979). Any use of standing concepts is troublesome at the outset. A defendant in an enforcement proceeding or a prospective defendant who initiates a suit for prospective relief has standing in the constitutional sense: These litigants are threatened with injury in fact from application of the act. What is at stake in overbreadth challenges is the *scope* of the issues open to these litigants, and, as will be shown, distinctions can be drawn between actual defendants and prospective defendants initiating actions for anticipatory relief.

Overbreadth challenges have also been entertained on behalf of litigants suffering injury in fact but not readily viewed as either defendants or prospective defendants. Southeastern Promotions, Ltd. v. Conrad, 420 U.S. 546, 562 (1975) (denial of a permit to use municipal theater). See also Bogen, *First Amendment Ancillary Doctrines*, 37 MD. L. REV. 679, 706–07 (1978) (overbreadth analysis used in area of statutes imposing civil disabilities, such as denials of licenses and of public employment.)

[2] Overbreadth challenges are typically said to rest on a "judicial prediction or assumption that the statute's very existence may cause others not before the court to refrain from constitutionally protected speech or expression." Broadrick v. Oklahoma, 413 U.S. 601, 612 (1973).

[3] While the discussion in this paper is generally applicable to administrative regulations and orders as well as common law rules, I shall for convenience generally confine my discussion to statutes.

tute's potentially invalid applications with respect to other persons not before the court[4] and with whom the litigant stands in no special relationship.[5] Judicial focus is not on the protected character, *vel non*, of the litigant's expression[6] but on the terms of the statutory rule being invoked to regulate that expression.[7]

Overbreadth methodology has its charms. Avowedly speech protective, it simultaneously fosters at least the illusion of comparative judicial restraint because it holds out the prospect that other means may exist to achieve legislative objectives.[8] But charm is not its only attribute. Overbreadth's facial scrutiny approach has been seen as "strong medicine,"[9] and both the Court and commentators have struggled with various limiting conceptions. The result of these efforts is a body of doctrine widely perceived to be erratic and confusing. It seems appropriate, therefore, to take stock. What does overbreadth analysis entail? Specifically, how does its analytic structure differ from that of the "conventional" constitutional challenge with which it supposedly stands in contrast? Examined from this perspective, an increasingly wide gap appears between the

---

[4] A "litigant whose own activities are unprotected may nevertheless challenge a statute by showing that it substantially abridges the First Amendment rights of other parties not before the court." Village of Schaumburg v. Citizens for a Better Environment, 444 U.S. 620, 634 (1980).

[5] Unlike *ius tertii* standing, *e.g.*, Craig v. Boren, 429 U.S. 190, 194–97 (1976), no requirement exists of an identifiable third party with whom the overbreadth litigant stands in a special relationship. See Note, *Standing to Raise Constitutional Jus Tertii*, 88 HARV. L. REV. 423, 438–44 (1974).

[6] "The claim that a statute is bad on its face because overbroad does not turn on evaluation of factual data generated by a particular application." Note, *The First Amendment Overbreadth Doctrine*, 83 HARV. L. REV. 844, 863 (1970) (hereinafter cited as Harvard Note).

[7] If "the statutory line includes conduct which the judicial line protects, the statute is overbroad. . . ." TRIBE, AMERICAN CONSTITUTIONAL LAW, §12-24, p. 710 (1978). Thus a statute regulating pornography must track or fall on the safe side of the applicable constitutional standards on obscenity. Miller v. California, 413 U.S. 15, 24 (1973).

Of course, if the statute is held to be overbroad, the "statute" is not thereby erased from the statute books. The judgment runs against named officials, who cannot enforce the statute (at least not against the same litigants) unless it is rehabilitated along constitutionally acceptable lines. See note 134 *infra*.

[8] By "holding out the prospect that narrower means may be available to achieve legislative objectives, [overbreadth methodology] conveys the appearance of intervening in legislative choices more marginally than outright 'balancing' would." GUNTHER, CONSTITUTIONAL LAW, CASES AND MATERIALS, 1188 (10th ed. 1980); SHAPIRO, FREEDOM OF SPEECH 141–42 (1966); Professor Gunther has been critical of the Court's frequent refusal to articulate what those alternatives are. *Id.* at 1187 n. 7; Gunther, *Reflections on Robel* . . . , 20 STAN. L. REV. 1140, 1147–48 (1968). But see Harvard Note at 916–17 (court under no duty to discuss alternatives).

[9] Broadrick v. Oklahoma, note 2 *supra*, at 613.

views of the commentators and holdings of the Court, a gap
obscured by the rhetoric accompanying the doctrine.

Judicial and academic fascination with overbreadth standing
tends to obscure an important point: Overbreadth is, in fact, a label
that has been utilized to cover not one but two doctrines.[10] One is
concerned with the content of the substantive constitutional
standards for determining the validity of a statute affecting expression. This substantive dimension of overbreadth methodology is
most frequently concerned with matters of regulatory precision; the
means chosen by the legislature must be no broader than necessary
to achieve legitimate governmental purposes.[11] The other, more
dramatic aspect of overbreadth analysis is the procedural
dimension—a supposed special First Amendment standing rule
permitting litigants to raise the rights of "third parties." In this
essay, I propose to show that, for the Court at least, overbreadth
doctrine does not in fact possess a distinctive standing component;
it is, rather, the application of conventional standing concepts in the
First Amendment context. Accordingly, overbreadth analysis is
simply an examination of the merits of the substantive constitutional claim.

Under "conventional" standing principles, a litigant has always
had the right to be judged in accordance with a constitutionally
valid rule of law. Put differently, a litigant could make a facial
challenge to the constitutional sufficiency of the rule actually
applied to him, irrespective of the privileged character of his own
activity. To be sure, the litigant's challenge is to the statute in
operation, including the interpretive gloss placed on it; and in general the interpretive process can operate to narrow the statute to
appropriate constitutional dimensions. But however narrowed,
the boundary line of the rule actually invoked must either track or
fall on the safe side of the relevant rule of constitutional privilege,

---

[10] This dual aspect of the overbreadth label is recognized in ELY, DEMOCRACY AND
DISTRUST 100–01, 229 n.1 (1980).

[11] This test necessarily also involves, at least at the margins, some form of fact-dependent
balancing. Thus the governmental interest must be sufficiently substantial to support the
infringement on expression. E.g., ELY, note 10 supra, at 105–06; LOCKHART, KAMISAR, &
CHOPER, CONSTITUTIONAL LAW, CASES-COMMENTS-QUESTIONS 735–38 (5th ed. 1980).
For illustrative balancing decisions, see United States v. Robel, 389 U.S. 258, 268 n.20
(1967), despite its balancing disclaimer, and Procunier v. Martinez, 416 U.S. 396 (1974).
Compare Struve, The Less Restrictive Alternative Principle and Economic Due Process, 80 HARV.
L. REV. 1463, 1480–88 (1967).

that is, the judicially prescribed boundary line separating protected from unprotected activity.[12]

Viewed as a special "standing" concept, overbreadth theory is, therefore, not unique in permitting facial challenges to rules. Rather, for academic writers its distinctive aspect is the formulation of constitutionally based limits on the traditional judicial power to truncate statutes to constitutionally satisfactory boundaries in the process of applying them. The theoretical and practical difficulties with such a "standing" doctrine are considerable, and judicial doctrine has not evolved in this manner.

For the Court, its doctrinal difficulties notwithstanding, overbreadth is simply a disposition on the merits of the litigants' First Amendment claim. The litigant's right to insist on the application of a constitutionally valid rule translates into a requirement of congruence between the boundaries of the statute and the Constitution. This congruence requirement is of central importance not only in the First Amendment context but wherever any standard of review other than the rational basis test is mandated by the applicable substantive constitutional law. Overbreadth challenges are, therefore, not confined to First Amendment adjudication. Nor does an overbreadth litigant invoke the rights of third parties; as "a theoretical matter the [overbreadth] claimant is asserting his own right not to be burdened by an unconstitutional rule of law, though naturally the claim is not one which depends on the privileged character of his own conduct."[13]

II. Facial Challenges in the Conventional Context: The Litigant's Right to Challenge Unconstitutional Rules

"Conventional" constitutional challenges are widely assumed to involve distinctive characteristics. Generally, a litigant may raise only his "own" rights, not those of others; thus he can challenge a statute only "as applied" to him.[14] Formulations of this character can suggest that a conventional constitutional challenge can be completely reduced to a claim of substantive constitutional

---

[12] Bator, Mishkin, Shapiro, & Wechsler, Hart & Wechsler's The Federal Courts and the Federal System 212 (2d ed. 1973) (hereinafter cited as Hart & Wechsler).

[13] Harvard Note at 848.

[14] United States v. Raines, note 1 *supra*.

privilege; that is, the litigant must demonstrate that the conduct established by the evidence is, as a matter of substantive constitutional law, simply immune from regulation. Professor Gunther, for example, says that in as-applied review, "the Court asks simply whether the challenger's activities are protected."[15] A litigant, of course, can always make such a challenge, and that contention can be framed either in privilege terms, or alternatively, as a challenge to the statute "as applied."[16] However phrased, the challenge is wholly fact dependent: Do the determinative facts shown by the evidence fall on the protected side of the applicable rule of constitutional privilege?[17]

In their efforts to identify the distinctive standing aspects of overbreadth methodology, many commentators assume that conventional constitutional challenges are invariably restricted to such fact-dependent claims of privilege.[18] This conclusion seems to be entailed by the fact that courts can narrow the literal sweep of statutes to fit governing constitutional standards. In other words, in the process of applying a statute, courts can narrow the legislative prescription to a set of criteria which (a) are constitutionally permissible and (b) fit the general facts of the litigant's conduct as established by the evidence.[19]

Inherent in the narrowing process is a judicial conclusion that the challenged statute is "separable"; that is, the legislature intended the statute to be applied whenever it validly could be, with any invalid applications excised in the application process.[20] Volumes of judicial decisions attest to the fact that courts are thoroughly

---

[15] GUNTHER, note 8 *supra*, at 1187.

[16] "Whenever the application point has merit, the party who asserts it could forego the challenge to the statute [as applied], asserting his federal right or immunity on the determinative facts, . . ." HART & WECHSLER at 591.

[17] In this context, the only consequence of casting the constitutional contention in as-applied rather than privilege terms relates to the technical difference between seeking Supreme Court review by way of appeal rather than certiorari. Casting the point as a challenge to the statute as applied makes an appeal available under 28 U.S.C. § 1257. *E.g.*, McCarty v. McCarty, 101 S. Ct., 2728, 2734 n.12 (1981). The distinction between those two modes of review has become increasingly blurred. HART & WECHSLER'S 1981 Supplement at 160–63; see also Metromedia, Inc. v. City of San Diego, 101 S. Ct. 2882 (1981).

[18] *E.g.*, Shaman, *The First Amendment Rule against Overbreadth*, 52 TEMPLE L. Q. 259, 261 (1979).

[19] *E.g.*, United States v. Raines, note 1 *supra*, at 21–22.

[20] In this context, the policy of implementing presumed legislative intent is, of course, strongly reinforced by the policy counseling avoidance of constitutional questions. United States v. Raines, note 1 *supra*.

familiar with the separability technique;[21] indeed, the normal judicial course is to approach the issue of constitutional validity with a presumption of separability. That presumption inclines the reviewing court toward reducing the broad legislative command to a permissible subrule general enough to cover the facts of the case before it.[22] Vagueness challenges are no exception to this process; ordinarily the Court considers such a challenge in terms of the statute as construed.[23]

Moreover, in reviewing state court decisions, the Supreme Court will presume that the state statute is separable unless the contrary otherwise clearly appears. *Yazoo & Mississippi Valley R.R. v. Jackson Vinegar Co.*[24] is the paradigm. There a railroad company challenged the constitutionality of an award of actual damages and a $25.00 penalty for a partial loss of a shipment of vinegar. The state court had made the award under a statute that "required [the railroad] to settle all claims for lost or damaged freight within a specified time period. The state court made no effort to explicate the reach of the statute; the court simply held that it embraced (and constitutionally could embrace) defendant's refusal to settle. In the Supreme Court, the railroad argued that, as written, the statute also re-

[21] Stern, *Separability and Separability Clauses in the Supreme Court*, 51 HARV. L. REV. 76 (1937). See also, for example, United States v. Raines, note 1 *supra*.

[22] The narrowing process is, of course, circumscribed by fair-warning requirements. See Dombrowski v. Pfister, 380 U.S. 479, 491 n.7 (1965) (limiting construction "may be applied to conduct occurring prior to the construction, . . . provided such application affords fair warning . . ."). Narrowing of criminal statutes at the appellate stage may come too late. Ashton v. Kentucky, 384 U.S. 195, 198 (1966). Finally, the narrowing process may itself on occasion render the statute impermissibly vague. See, for example, Smith v. Cahoon, 283 U.S. 553, 563–65 (1931); Winters v. New York, 333 U.S. 507 (1948). Compare the cases cited in note 23 *infra*.

[23] "For the purposes of determining whether a state statute is too vague and indefinite to constitute valid legislation 'we must take the state statute as though it read precisely as the highest court of the state has interpreted it.' " Wainright v. Stone, 414 U.S. 21, 22–23 (1973), quoting Minnesota ex rel Pearson v. Probate Court, 309 U.S. 270, 273 (1940). ". . . [A]lthough it is usual to conceive of the void-for-vagueness cases as cases in which the Supreme Court passes upon the 'face' validity of statutes, in fact what the Court is far more frequently reviewing is a state court's reading of the statute.' " Amsterdam, *The Void for Vagueness Doctrine in the Supreme Court*, 109 U. OF PENN. L. REV. 67, 68 (1960). See also United States v. National Dairy Product Corp., 372 U.S. 29, 31–33 (1963), and United States v. Powell, 423 U.S. 87, 92–94 (1975), rejecting vagueness attacks to federal statutes "as applied." Cf. Palmer v. City of Euclid, 402 U.S. 544 (1971), where the Court sustained a vagueness attack as applied, while a concurring opinion, *id.* at 546, "would go further and hold that the ordinance is unconstitutionally vague on its face." See generally Brache v. Co. of Westchester, 658 F.2d 47 (2d Cir. 1981).

[24] 226 U.S. 217 (1912).

quired settlement of frivolous claims and thus violated the due-process clause. The Court rejected the contention in these terms:[25]

> As applied to [this] case, we think the statute is not repugnant to [the Fourteenth Amendment] . . . .
>
> Although seemingly conceding this much, counsel for the railway company urges that the statute is not confined to cases like the present, but equally penalizes the failure to accede to an excessive or extravagant claim; in other words, that it contemplates the assessment of the penalty in every case where the claim presented is not settled within the time allotted, regardless of whether, or how much, the recovery falls short of the amount claimed. But it is not open to the railway company to complain on that score. It has not been penalized for failing to accede to an excessive or extravagant claim, but for failing to make reasonably prompt settlement of a claim which upon due inquiry has been pronounced just in every respect. Of course, the argument to sustain the contention is that, if the statute embraces cases such as are supposed, it is void as to them, and, if so void, is void *in toto*. But this court must deal with the case in hand, and not with imaginary ones. It suffices, therefore, to hold that, as applied to cases like the present, the statute is valid. How the state court may apply it to other cases, whether its general words may be treated as more or less restrained, and how far parts of it may be sustained if others fail, are matters upon which we need not speculate now [citations omitted]. . . .

Yazoo, it should be noted, came to the Supreme Court without any authoritative construction of the statute by the state courts. In these circumstances, the Supreme Court will presume that the state statute is separable; that is, that the state court *has* fixed the statute's boundary at or within a clearly ascertainable line separating legitimate from illegitimate exercises of state power.[26] This means that, in subsequent cases, the state court is expected to excise any invalid applications. Just last term, for example, the Court applied the separability presumption to reject an overbreadth challenge to a statute requiring parental notification of a minor's decision to have

---

[25] *Id.* at 219–20, See also Smily v. Kansas, 196 U.S. 447, 454–55 (1905).

[26] Indeed, the state court's decision is unintelligible on any other premise. If, for example, in the *Yazoo* context the state court subsequently holds the statute inseparable, the initial application of the statute to the railroad in *Yazoo* cannot be justified. See Metromedia, Inc. v. City of San Diego, note 17 *supra*, at 2899 n.26. Perhaps, however, in a civil context notions of finality and reliance by the plaintiff might operate so as to bar restitutionary recovery by the railroad; such notions support a holding that the decision with respect to inseparability is to have prospective application only.

an abortion. In *H. L. v. Matheson*,[27] the minor argued that the statutory requirement was impermissibly "overbroad"[28] insofar as it required a notification for "mature and emancipated" minors. Despite a broad class certification by the trial court, the state supreme court, consistent with the pleadings and the evidence, considered the statute only insofar as it reached unemancipated minors living with their parents, and it upheld the statute. The Supreme Court affirmed, stating that: "We cannot assume that the statute, when challenged in a proper case, will not be construed also to exempt demonstrably mature minors."[29]

Quite plainly, the more a statute is cut down to state a permissible subrule general enough to cover the facts of the litigant's case, the more the substance of the litigant's claim becomes that of a fact-dependent claim of constitutional privilege. But this is not invariably so. A fundamental principle of our system of constitutional law lies behind the proclivity of courts to narrow the sweeping reach of statutory language. The operative rule, either as enacted or construed, must conform to the Constitution. Thus, in addition to a claim of privilege, a litigant has always been permitted to make another, equally "conventional" challenge: He can insist that his conduct be judged in accordance with a rule that is constitutionally valid.[30] In sharp contrast to a fact-dependent privilege claim, a challenge to the content of the rule applied is independent of the specific facts of the litigant's predicament. Rather, it speaks to the relationship between the facial content of the rule being applied to the facts and the applicable constitutional law, and it insists that the rule itself be valid.

Considerable decisional law demonstrates that a sanction imposed under a facially invalid rule cannot be saved by fact-dependent references to the nonprivileged character of the litigant's

---

[27] 101 S.Ct. 1164 (1981).

[28] *Id.* at 1169.

[29] *Ibid.*

[30] A "defendant in a coercive proceeding . . . always has standing to challenge the validity of the statute in the terms in which it is applied to him." HART & WECHSLER'S 1981 Supplement at 88. But the position of a prospective defendant bringing an action for declaratory relief need not be assimilated to that of an actual defendant. To be sure, any litigant is entitled to be free from the application of an unconstitutional rule of law if the court reaches the merits of the case and its judgment has preclusive effect. See Federated Department Stores, Inc. v. Moitie, 101 S. Ct. 2424 (1981); Shapiro, *State Courts and Federal Declaratory Judgments*, 74 NW. L. REV. 759 (1979). But that right does not mean that he can *insist* on the scope of the rule being adjudicated in advance of its actual application. See text at pp. 33–36.

conduct. (To be sure, many of the cases involve judicial efforts to avoid deciding the ultimate question of whether the litigant's conduct is constitutionally privileged. But fact-independent evaluation of the rule employed is available to the litigant even if it be assumed, *ex ante*, that no constitutionally privileged conduct is involved.) Vagueness cases illustrate the point. A litigant can challenge the terms of the rule applied without showing that his own conduct is privileged against conviction under a statute giving better notice of what constitutes the offense.[31] Similarly, one could not be denied equal protection of the laws simply because the conduct at issue is not independently privileged.[32]

The same principle is applicable with respect to right-based claims. The validity of the rule invoked is at issue, wholly apart from the character of the litigant's conduct. Suppose, for example, that dancing by oneself in a barroom is constitutionally privileged activity, unless the dancer has bare feet. Even if the evidence showed that the defendant was dancing in his bare feet, a conviction could not be sustained under a statute which, as construed, makes criminal *only* the act of barroom dancing *per se*.[33] A litigant has always had the right to be free from being burdened by an unconstitutional rule, whatever the state of the evidence.[34] This is

---

[31] See the cases cited in note 23 *supra*. Bouie v. City of Columbia, 378 U.S. 347 (1964), is a particularly apt illustration of the point that facial attacks are not dependent on the quality of defendant's conduct. The Court there reversed a "sit-in" conviction of black defendants for violating a state's trespass statute prohibiting "entry" without the owner's consent. In so doing, the Court did not rule that defendant's conduct was constitutionally privileged; it simply held that the rule actually applied was rendered impermissibly vague when statutory prohibition of unconsented "entry" was judicially enlarged to include remaining after consent has been withdrawn. *Id.* at 352–55.

[32] *Cf.* Michael M. v. Superior Court of Sonoma County, 101 S. Ct. 1200 (1981) (by implication). Few cases of selective enforcement of criminal statutes are accompanied by a meaningful independent claim of constitutional privilege. See generally Note, *The Right to Nondiscriminatory Enforcement of State Penal Law*, 61 COLUM. L. REV. 1103 (1961); Givelber, *The Application of Equal Protection Principles to Selective Enforcement of the Criminal Law*, 1973 U. Ill. L. F. 88.

[33] See Thompson v. City of Louisville, 362 U.S. 199 (1960), discussed in HART & WECHSLER at 615: "... *Thompson* ... does not say that Kentucky could not prohibit a person from dancing alone publicly in a cafe." As will be apparent from the discussion that follows, the state court's decision that the statute makes criminal *only* the act of dancing may, in effect, be a holding that the statute is inseparable; as a matter of state law, it cannot be truncated to constitutionally accepted limits. If the state court is clear about that, no room for the *Yazoo* presumption exists.

[34] *E.g.*, Williams v. North Carolina, 317 U.S. 287, 292 (1942); Bachellar v. Maryland, 397 U.S. 564, 569–71 (1970). See also New York R.R. v. White, 243 U.S. 188, 197 (1917); Illinois Cent. R.R. v. McKendree, 203 U.S. 514, 528–30 (1906); United States v. Ju Toy, 198 U.S. 253, 262–63 (1905); Montana Co. v. St. Louis Mining and Milling Co., 152 U.S.

made particularly clear by the "inseparability" cases. Many statutes are susceptible to both valid and invalid applications. Sometimes, as a matter of construction, the statute is held to be "inseparable"—that is, a nullity unless good in all its reasonable and foreseeable applications. This occurs, most typically, where the court concludes that, given the nature or range of the act's invalid applications, the legislature would not want the statute to stand, or that the court simply cannot sever the valid from the invalid applications. In *United States v. Reese*,[35] for example, the Supreme Court sustained a demurrer to an indictment against a state official for a racially discriminatory refusal to receive and count a vote in a state election contrary to a Congressional enactment. While application of the act to the defendant was clearly valid given the Fifteenth Amendment's prohibition of such state action, the Court stressed that, facially, the act also prohibited racially motivated private interference with voting in state elections. The Court said: "We are not able to reject a part [of the statute] which is unconstitutional, and retain the remainder, because it is not possible to separate that which is unconstitutional, if there be any such, from that which is not."[36]

Salient examples of direct challenges to the constitutional adequacy of rules impinging on rights without regard to the quality of defendant's conduct appeared in First Amendment adjudication long before the flowering of overbreadth doctrine in the 1960s. These decisions, it should be noted, cannot fairly be viewed as

---

160, 169–70 (1894); Trade-Mark Cases, 100 U.S. 82, 98–99 (1879). See also Ulster County Court v. Allen, note 1 *supra*, at 160 (. . . the Court has held it irrelevant in analyzing a mandatory presumption, . . . that there is ample evidence in the record other than the presumption to support a conviction"). See generally Note, *Supreme Court Judgment of State Statute as Unconstitutional on Its Face*, 31 NOTRE DAME LAWYER 684 (1956).

[35] 92 U.S. 214 (1876).

[36] *Id.* at 221. See also Trade-Mark Cases, 100 U.S. 82, 98–99 (1880) (defendants were indicted for counterfeiting trademarks which, apparently, were actually used in interstate or foreign commerce; nonetheless, the Court upheld the defense that the statute was beyond Congressional power, because the act was not so limited and its language could not be narrowed by construction). In the Employers' Liability Cases, 207 U.S. 463, 500–02 (1908), the Court invalidated an employers' liability act in an action by employees engaged in interstate commerce at time of injury. The Court said that, in terms, the act applied whenever the employer was engaged in interstate commerce regardless of the nature of the employee's activity.

See also the extensive collection of cases in Stern, note 21 *supra*. See also Note, 47 HARV. L. REV. 677, 680–81 (1934). The cases cited in note 34 *supra* are all ultimately premised on a holding that the statutes involved were inseparable. See, *e.g.*, *Metromedia*, note 17 *supra*, at 2890 n.26.

unacknowledged applications of a special First Amendment standing doctrine. Quite to the contrary; the Court simply applied conventional doctrine to permit the litigant to challenge the content of
the rule applied to him. In *Terminiello v. Chicago*,[37] for example, the
Court reversed a disorderly conduct conviction based on a violently
racist, anti-Semitic speech, even though the protected character of
the speech itself was at least doubtful under the then existing constitutional doctrine.[38] Over objection that only the privilege issue
was properly before it,[39] the Court focused entirely on the terms of
the rule actually applied.[40] And the Court held that the state court's
statutory construction, which permitted conviction for speech
which "stirs the public to anger, invites dispute, [or] brings about a
condition of unrest. . . ,"[41] rendered the rule constitutionally impermissible.

An even more graphic illustration is the fountainhead of the
overbreadth doctrine itself, *Thornhill v. Alabama*.[42] *Thornhill* involved review of a state conviction for labor picketing. The statute
prohibited anyone "without a just cause" to "go near to or loiter
about" any business for the purpose of "hindering, delaying, or
interfering with or injuring" the business. The state courts made no
effort to narrow the sweep of the statute and sustained a conviction
based on a charge framed substantially in terms of the statutory
language. The Supreme Court reversed. After first concluding that
peaceful picketing generally constituted "speech" within the ambit
of the constitutional guarantee, the Court turned its attention to the
constitutional sufficiency of the rule applied, rather than to a fact-
oriented review to determine whether the circumstances of the particular picketing involved rendered it unprotected.[43] The Court
advanced two justifications in defense of this approach, the second
of which gave birth to the overbreadth doctrine.[44] Prior to its over-

---

[37] 337 U.S. 1 (1949).

[38] Compare Beuharnais v. Illinois, 343 U.S. 250 (1952).

[39] Note 37 *supra*, at 8–12 (Frankfurter, J., dissenting).

[40] *Id.* at 5–6.

[41] *Id.* at 3.

[42] 310 U.S. 88 (1940).

[43] *Id.* at 106 n.23. ("The fact that the activities for which petitioner was arrested and
convicted took place on the private property of the Preserving Company is without
significance. . . .")

[44] *Id.* at 97–98. See *infra* at 44–45.

breadth discussion, however, the Court made plain that conventional analysis included a perusal of the facial validity of the rule applied:[45]

> The finding against petitioner was a general one. It did not specify the testimony upon which it rested. The charges were framed in the words of the statute and so must be given a like construction. The courts below expressed no intention of narrowing the construction put upon the statute by prior State decisions. In these circumstance[s], there is no occasion to go behind the face of the statute or of the complaint for the purpose of determining whether the evidence, together with the permissible inferences to be drawn from it, could ever support a conviction founded upon different and more precise charges. . . .
> The State urges that petitioner may not complain of the deprivation of any rights but his own. It would not follow that on this record petitioner could not complain of the sweeping regulations here challenged.

The foregoing cases make plain that a litigant has long possessed the right to question the validity of the rule actually applied and to insist that it "is invalid upon its face."[46] This is but a corollary of the proposition that the "constitutional validity of the law is to be tested not by what has been done under it, but what may, by its authority, be done."[47] The doctrine is a general one, in no way limited to either First Amendment or criminal cases. In *Wuchter v. Pizzutti*,[48] for instance, the Court permitted a nonresident motorist to challenge a statutory scheme governing service of process on nonresidents. The statute imposed no requirement of notice, and the state court imposed none by way of construction. Even though the defendant had in fact received notice, the Court found a constitutional violation in these circumstances. "[Notice not] having been directed by the statute it can not, therefore, supply constitutional validity to the statute or to service under it."[49]

---

[45] *Id.* at 96. See also Bachellar v. Maryland, note 34 *supra*, at 569–71.

[46] Smith v. Cahoon, note 22 *supra*, at 562.

[47] Montana Co. v. St. Louis Mining and Milling Co., note 34 *supra*, at 169–70, quoting Stuart v. Palmer, 74 N.Y. 183, 188 (1878).

[48] 276 U.S. 13 (1928).

[49] *Id.* at 24. The decision is vulnerable to criticism for ignoring the "*Yazoo* presumption." Compare National Equipment Rental, Ltd. v. Szukhent, 375 U.S. 311, 315–18 (1964).

Many of the foregoing cases may be conceptualized as testing a rule in terms of its impact on "third parties."[50] Be that as it may, the underlying reality remains: Faced with a challenge to the validity of the rule ultimately extracted from a statute, a court tests that rule, consciously or not, by imagining relatively standard instances of its application. On that basis it determines whether the content of the rule is valid.[51] Moreover, these decisions illustrate that *overbreadth doctrine cannot be viewed as uniquely concerned with the facial content of the rule applied to the litigant.*[52] Rather, as the next section shows, the core of overbreadth standing theory is elsewhere: It inheres in an assertion of constitutionally imposed limits on the power of courts to narrow statutes in the process of applying them. I will argue that, academic theorists notwithstanding, courts have refused to impose such limits; instead, they have applied conventional separability doctrine to narrow statutes in the face of overbreadth attacks. Viewed most comprehensively, therefore, overbreadth methodology is now best understood not as a special standing doctrine but as simply an expression of the underlying substantive constitutional law. Given the content of that law, how-

---

[50] The Court apparently now treats these cases as "exceptions" to the various formulation of the rule that a litigant can assert only his "own" rights:

> And the rules' rationale may disappear where the statute in question has already been declared unconstitutional in the vast majority of its intended applications, and it can fairly be said that it was not intended to stand as valid, on the basis of fortuitous circumstances, only in a fraction of the cases. See Butts v. Merchants & M. Transp. Co., 230 U.S. 126. The same situation is presented when a state statute comes conclusively pronounced by a state court as having an otherwise valid provision or application inextricably tied up with an invalid one, see Dorchy v. Kansas, 264 U.S. 286, 290; or possibly in that rarest of cases where this Court can justifiably think itself able confidently to discern that Congress would not have desired its legislation to stand at all unless it could validly stand in its every application.

United States v. Raines, note 1 *supra*, at 23 (footnotes omitted).

[51] These hypothetical applications may, of course, be grounded in past examples of enforcement of the statute or in agency interpretations of the statute's reach.

[52] I express no opinion on whether facial scrutiny of the rule applied is constitutionally required—whether, for example, the Congress could restrict the Court to considering whether the conduct shown by the evidence is constitutionally privileged. I once indicated such a view. See Monaghan, *Foreword: Constitutional Common Law*, 89 HARV. L. REV. 1, 43 (1975), but I now doubt the soundness of that position. The Supreme Court has intimated that at least in the criminal context a challenge to the content of the rule cannot be foreclosed. *E.g.*, De Jonge v. Oregon, 299 U.S. 353, 362 (1937) ("Conviction upon a charge not made would be sheer denial of due process.") See also, for example, Bachellar v. Maryland, note 34 *supra*. It is hard to see any relevant differences between civil and criminal proceedings in this respect. Wuchter v. Pizutti, note 48 *supra*, and accompanying text.

ever, the conventional standing principle that a litigant can always insist on application of a valid rule takes on considerable importance.

III. Overbreadth as a Federally Mandated Inseparability Rule

Consideration of overbreadth doctrine in the First Amendment context is best prefaced by a brief, albeit oversimplified, account of the operative substantive law. First Amendment law treats content-based regulations as presumptively invalid.[53] Indeed, not long ago content-based governmental regulation appeared to be automatically invalid unless confined to one of a few narrowly defined categories of unprotected speech: incitement, fighting words, obscenity, defamation, etc.[54] Recent decisions increasingly indicate, however, that these categories may state only the minimum, not the maximum, extent of governmental regulatory power; speech not falling within an unprotected category may be regulated if the compelling state interest or some other balancing test is satisfied.[55] And, in any event, some form of balancing must be employed to assess the validity of non–content-based restrictions on expression.[56]

Thornhill v. Alabama[57] must be evaluated against this general background. In *Thornhill*, the Court suggested that, in free-speech cases, courts are shorn of their general power to narrow statutes in

[53] By "content-based" rules, I mean, following Ely, rules that regulate speech because the evils sought to be controlled flow from the communicative content of the speech. See Ely, *Flag Desecration: A Case Study in the Roles of Categorization and Balancing in First Amendment Analysis*, 88 HARV. L. REV. 1481, 1497–98 (1975). See generally TRIBE, note 7 *supra*, § 12-2.

[54] ". . . only expression fairly assignable to one of an increasingly limited set of narrowly defined categories could be denied constitutional protection." Ely, note 53, *supra*, at 1491. See also ELY, note 10 *supra*, at 109–16.

[55] *E.g.*, Haig v. Agee, 101 S. Ct. 2766 (1981); F.C.C. v. Pacifica Foundation, 438 U.S. 726 (1978); Elrod v. Burns, 427 U.S. 347, 360 (1976); Buckley v. Valeo, 424 U.S. 1, 24–25, 66 (1976); Procunier v. Martinez, note 11 *supra*, at 410–14. See also Central Hudson Gas & Electric Corp. v. Public Service Comm'n of New York, 447 U.S. 557 (1980); Metromedia, Inc. v. City of San Diego, note 17 *supra*.

[56] *E.g.*, Heffron v. International Society for Krishna Consciousness, 101 S. Ct. 2559 (1981); United States Postal Service v. Council Greenburg Civic Ass'n. 101 S. Ct. 2676, 2686 (1981) ("This Court has long recognized the validity of reasonable time, place and manner regulations on such a [public] forum so long as the regulation is content neutral, serves a significant governmental interest, and leaves open adequate alternative channels for communication"). ELY, note 10 *supra*, at 110–16.

[57] Note 42 *supra*, at 88.

the application process. In launching the overbreadth doctrine, the Court said,[58]

> There is a further reason for testing the [statute] on its face. . . .
> Where regulations of the liberty of free discussion are concerned
> there are special reasons for observing the rule that it is the
> statute, and not the accusation or the evidence under it, which
> prescribes the limits of permissible conduct and warns against
> transgression.

Thornhill seems to posit an extraordinary, constitutionally based limitation on the traditional judicial power to truncate statutes to constitutionally acceptable limits. It seems, in other words to create a federally mandated rule with respect to the inseparability of statutes affecting expression and thereby forces consideration of the statutory rule "as written."[59]

Any federally imposed limitation on the power of the *state* courts to narrow state statutes in the application process generates evident difficulties.[60] Constraints on separability judgments undermine the role of the state courts as expositors and shapers of state law, and thus they cut against the general grain of "Our Federalism." This objection, however, must be evaluated in light of the broader ways in which federal constitutional prohibitions confine the authority of all state institutions, including the state courts. And it is particularly clear that the constitutional guarantee of free speech generates procedural and remedial limitations on the ways in which the states structure their decision-making processes.[61] Thus, a doctrine that the Constitution imposes limits on the authority of the state courts in the construction of state statutes cannot be rejected *a priori*. Indeed, much *ius tertii* standing may, on analysis, prove to be such a doctrine; it limits, as a matter of federal constitutional law, the power of state courts to sever statutes if certain relationships exist between the litigant and identifiable third parties.[62] In an over-

---

[58] *Id.* at 97–98.

[59] See Comment, *Inseparability in Application of Statutes Impairing Civil Liberties*, 61 HARV. L. REV. 1208, 1211 (1948). The assertion, Harvard Note at 894, that the inseparability point is "question begging" is both unexplained and mystifying.

[60] Apart, that is, from satisfaction of the traditional requirement of fair warning. See note 22 *supra*.

[61] Monaghan, *First Amendment "Due Process,"* 83 HARV. L. REV. 518 (1970).

[62] This seems true at least in those cases where the statute imposes duties directly upon the third party claimant. *E.g.*, Griswold v. Connecticut, 381 U.S. 479, 481 (1965); HART & WECHSLER'S 1981 Supplement at 82–83. See also note 5 *supra*. Perhaps some *ius tertii* cases

breadth challenge, no identifiable third party and no special relationship exist. Still, it can be and has been argued that some limits
on the power of state courts to truncate state statutes impinging on
expression are desirable. This conception might be thought to follow from the deterrence rationale supposedly underlying the overbreadth doctrine—the statute's "very existence" may deter
others.[63] Accordingly, the most sensible and refined approach is
one which properly accommodates the traditional interpretive autonomy of state courts with the values promoted by the First
Amendment.

Despite significant differences among overbreadth theorists, the
crucial feature of overbreadth analysis can be viewed as centered on
this problem of accommodation; that is, the core task becomes the
identification, *ex ante*, of those situations in which, as a matter of
constitutional law, truncating is not permitted. The commentator's
efforts display considerable variety. Some writers interpret *Thornhill* as a "clear holding" that a statute regulating speech which
"embraces permissible as well as impermissible applications is void
on its face and inseparable. . . ."[64] Stated in this form, overbreadth
doctrine is completely hostile to any notion of accommodation, and
it constitutes a strong antiseparability doctrine. Judicial attention
is, quite literally, directed to the face of the statute; having been
found to include prohibited applications, the statute becomes, in
effect, a dead letter, incapable of even prospective resuscitation by
narrowing construction. This view of the overbreadth doctrine
gives us everything but the why. No convincing explanation is
proffered as to why a state statute, if acceptably narrowed, cannot
be applied thereafter within its new confines. It would appear, after
all, that the deterrence rationale underlying the overbreadth doc-

---

can be reconceptualized as resting on a premise that the constitutional right of the third-party
right holder implies a corollary constitutional right in the litigant.

[63] Broadrick v. Oklahoma, note 2 *supra*, at 612 [". . . the possibility that protected
speech or assertive activity may be inhibited by the overly broad reach of the statute"].
Village of Schaumburg, note 4 *supra*, at 634 [". . . persons whose expression is constitutionally protected may well refrain from exercising their rights for fear of criminal sanctions by a
statute susceptible of application to protected expression"]. Gooding v. Wilson, 405 U.S. 518,
521 (1972). See generally Harvard Note. For recent challenges to the deterrence rationale,
see note 150 *infra*.

[64] Wormuth and Mirkin, *The Doctrine of the Reasonable Alternative*, 9 UTAH L. REV. 254,
274 (1964). See also Shaman, note 18 *supra*, at 260–61, 277–80 (judicial narrowing
inconsistent with premises of overbreadth doctrine). See also Note, *Inseparability in Application of Statutes Impairing Civil Liberties*, 61 HARV. L. REV. 1208 (1948) (state courts cannot
narrow statute).

trine is fully spent once a substantively acceptable narrowing construction has been provided.

Other, less sweeping but more sophisticated, versions of overbreadth have surfaced. These accounts do not deny a general authority in the state court to narrow statutes in the application process even where First Amendment interests are implicated. Rather, they seek to specify the circumstances in which that course is improper. Two general lines have emerged.

1.   The mildest form of overbreadth doctrine insists that the narrowing is improper when the surviving remnants of the rule is itself unconstitutional. That form of the doctrine is saved from utter triviality only by its emphasis on the special vagueness concerns in the First Amendment area.[65] Professor Tribe rightly argues that all too frequently judicial narrowing "simply exchanges overbreadth for vagueness."[66] Tribe offers as an example a hypothetical statute which on its face makes criminal all public speech but which has been "construed" so as not to reach constitutionally protected activity.[67] The illustration reinforces his point, but it is of little analytic aid; such wholly indeterminate statutes are seldom enacted and reach the Court yet more infrequently.[68] In any event, this formulation of overbreadth doctrine draws upon no uniquely speech-based constitutional principle. It has been long clear in "conventional" constitutional challenges that an attempted saving construction may patch one constitutional difficulty while simultaneously resulting in the different but equally impermissible vice of indefiniteness.[69] Thus, the overbreadth-vagueness axis simply

---

[65] See, e.g., Smith v. Gougen, 415 U.S. 566 (1974); Hynes v. Mayor of Oradell, 425 U.S. 610 (1976). See generally Harvard Note at 871–75. Professor Freund long ago emphasized this aspect of overbreadth analysis. FREUND, THE SUPREME COURT OF THE UNITED STATES, 67–68 (1961).

[66] TRIBE, note 7 *supra*, at § 12–26, p. 716.

[67] *Ibid.*

[68] Thornhill v. Alabama, note 42 *supra* and accompanying text, could have reached the Court in that posture if the state court had held that its antipicketing statute applied to bar all picketing "except where the federal constitution required otherwise."

[69] "The decision thus aims to remove the constitutional objection of invalid application only by creating another constitutional objection of lack of appropriate certainty. Had the legislature written into the statute itself that it was binding . . .' only so far as the provisions are legally applicable,' it would have transcended the permissible limits of statutory indefiniteness." Smith v. Cahoon, note 22 *supra*, at 565. It should be noted that state statutes made operative "to the extent constitutionally permissible" are not uncommon in the fields of state taxation and "long arm" services of process. Vagueness is of greater concern with respect to such statutes when criminal liability is at issue. Compare Monroe v. Pape, 365 U.S. 167 (1961), with Screws v. United States, 325 U.S. 91 (1945).

becomes expressive of the demands of the relevant substantive constitutional law, not a distinctive aspect of either free-speech or standing doctrine.

Moreover, this vagueness facet of overbreadth methodology seems to be waning. Recent Supreme Court cases illustrate a diminishing judicial enthusiasm for vagueness analysis in the First Amendment context. *Arnett v. Kennedy*[70] is the paradigm. Acting under statutory authority to dismiss employees for "such cause as will promote the efficiency of the service," the federal government discharged a civil service employee for speech critical of his superior. The Court rejected, *inter alia*, his overbreadth claim, stating, "We hold the [such cause . . .] language . . . excludes constitionally protected speech and that the statute is therefore not overbroad."[71] Perhaps the *Arnett* approach should be confined to statutes that in terms of ordinary applications are not focused on speech content; "just cause" discharges will, in the normal run, turn on the nonexpressive rather than the expressive features of the employee's conduct. But the Court evinces no disposition to so confine its holding,[72] and while vagueness challenges are, of course, still sustained in the First Amendment context, the Court seems far less inclined than formerly to find such a transgression.

2. A more intriguing form of overbreadth methodology would bar judicial narrowing of statutes even if the statute, as narrowed, would not thereby be rendered unconstitutionally vague. Narrowing would be prohibited in settings which lack a clear, bright line separating unprotected from protected expression.[73] Stated affirmatively, saving constructions would be permitted only in those contexts in which a "determinative rule of privilege"[74] exists to constrain the statute.

---

[70] 416 U.S. 134 (1974).

[71] *Id.* at 162. The plurality opinion was joined on this point by other justices. *Id.* at 164 (Powell and Blackmun, J.J.); *id.* at 177 (White, J.).

[72] See, *e.g.*, Hamling v. United States, 418 U.S. 87, 114–15 (1974), sustaining against a vagueness attack the federal obscenity statute as judicially restricted to accord with the requirements of Miller v. California, note 7 *supra*; Buckley v. Valeo, note 55 *supra*, at 44, 76–80, narrowing construction given to parts of the Federal Election Campaign Act; United States Civil Service Comm'n v. National Ass'n of Letter Carriers, 413 U.S. 548, 569–80 (1973), sustaining Hatch Act on the basis of prior administrative interpretations.

[73] TRIBE, note 7 *supra*, at § 12–26, pp. 714–16. The foundation for this approach is the much admired but, on close inspection, vague and abstract analysis of overbreadth doctrine in Harvard Note, note 6 *supra*, at 883–90.

[74] Harvard Note at 883.

A rule of privilege, it will be recalled, is simply the relevant line separating constitutionally protected from constitutionally unprotected activity. Whenever the categorization approach states the relevant substantive First Amendment law, the unprotected categories ("incitement, obscenity, fighting words, etc.") constitute the relevant privilege rules. In Section II, I have argued that, under conventional principles, a litigant could always insist on the application of a valid rule, and accordingly, statutes, to be valid, must track, either expressly or by construction, the relevant rule of privilege. Overbreadth theory would, of course, be entirely empty of *distinctive* content if it simply required conformity of the statute to the relevant First Amendment privilege rule. Sophisticated overbreadth theory is *not* empty. Emphasizing "determinative," advocates of this form of overbreadth methodology do not equate "determinative rules of privilege" with the judicially established categories delineating unprotected speech. Rather, effort is made to distinguish among the various unprotected categories.

The unprotected categories are, *ex hypothesi*, not unconstitutionally vague. Nevertheless, overbreadth theorists maintain that some of these categories involve a constellation of fact-dependent variables too numerous in range and too unpredictable in application to be regarded as sufficiently determinative for the purpose of slicing a statute to acceptable constitutional limits.[75] Professor Tribe, for example, rejects the "fighting words" exception as a satisfactory constraining limitation; it is, he says, not "precise and focused enough to give advance warning of the exact reach of the statute punishing offensive speech, since decisions under the standard turn on the facts particular to the speaker, the audience, and their interaction."[76] The result is curious: A statute prohibiting "fighting words" in the terms defined by the Supreme Court could be validly applied to any litigant, while a statute prohibiting some form of "offensive speech" but readily constrained by a court to reach identically defined "fighting words" could not be so applied, even prospectively.

Attempts to draw lines between acceptable and unacceptable constitutional privileges for purposes of allowing narrowing statu-

---

[75] The Harvard Note finds the Court's defamation and obscenity privilege rules "sufficient" but not the rules with respect to sedition. Compare 83 HARV. L. REV. at 883–90 with *id.* at 897–907.

[76] TRIBE, note 7 *supra*, at 714–16.

tory constructions are fundamentally flawed. The defect inheres in the impossibility of drawing principled distinctions, for these purposes, among the various rules of First Amendment privilege. The entire effort posits a sharp contrast between two types of privilege rules: (*a*) privilege rules which are subject-matter specific and which "elevate a few factors to per se status,"[77]—for example, the actual malice rule of the defamation cases and the obscenity criteria;[78] and (*b*) other First Amendment privilege standards which assertedly focus in an *ad hoc* manner on a combination of a much larger set of variables, some outside the actor's control—for example, the "fighting words" and Brandenburg[79] incitement standards which, *inter alia*, focus "on the propensity of defined conduct to bring about concrete harms. . . ."[80] This distinction between the two types of privileges seems to me to rest, in part, on a distortion of the substantive content of the "acceptable" privileges,[81] and, in part, on a thinly disguised rejection of the constitutional adequacy of the disfavored privileges.[82]

Most important, however, the asserted distinction between the two types of privilege rules cannot bear the weight placed on it. Admitting that certain kinds of harm justify some content-based regulation, the categorization approach seeks to identify those harms "at wholesale in advance, outside the context of specific

---

[77] Harvard Note at 884.

[78] "It is important to notice the analytical focus of the *Sullivan* and *Roth-Memoirs* tests. The former does not aim at the amount of tangible harm wrought by defamatory statements, but at the culpability of the speaker in abstraction from consequences. *Roth-Memoirs* aims not only at any harm to social interests which obscene materials might induce but also at the supposed worthlessness—hence unprotectedness—of such materials." *Id.* at 886–87.

[79] Brandenburg v. Ohio, 395 U.S. 444, 447 (1969) (". . . the constitutional guarantees of free speech and free press do not permit a State to forbid or proscribe advocacy of the use of force or of law violation except where such advocacy is directed to inciting or producing imminent lawless action and is likely to incite or produce such action").

[80] Harvard Note at 887.

[81] The characterization of obscenity, note 78 *supra*, seems to assume that obscenity is limited to hard-core pornography which is self-demonstratingly worthless material of the "I-know-it-when-I-see-it" variety. Perhaps that was accurate prior to Miller v. California, note 7 *supra*. But now more attention must be paid to such elusive matters as community standards. Jenkins v. Georgia, 418 U.S. 153 (1974).

The defamation privilege cannot be reduced to a state-of-the-mind question. The issue of truth is centrally important, both in and of itself, but also as bearing on the actor's state of mind. Moreover, inquiry into the actor's state of mind may itself involve a relatively broad-ranged, fact-dependent inquiry. Herbert v. Lando, 441 U.S. 153 (1979).

[82] *E.g.*, Harvard Note at 905–06.

cases."[83] This avoids the danger of distortion brought about by the pull of specific facts and particular litigants. But the categories having been established, *ex ante*, the problem of application occurs. At that stage, *no* privilege rule is or can be completely independent of the underlying factual circumstances to which it is applied, nor is there any reason to suppose that any adjudication under one set of privilege rules is materially more immune from the risk of speech-punishing mistake than under other privilege rules.[84] The system of privilege rules, real or imagined, varies only in degree of adjudicative predictability. No subset of these rules can be identified, *ex ante*, for purposes of distinguishing in a principled way between those privilege rules which can tolerably be utilized for statute narrowing and those which cannot. Once state court power to apply separability doctrine to statutes which touch expression is acknowledged in any form, no coherent limitation on that power can be developed.

Recent authority is completely consistent with this analysis. *Arnett* and its progeny represent a decisive rejection of any contention that overbreadth is a special separability rule requiring that overbroad statutes can be given a saving construction only if it is possible to specify some "satisfactory" category of privileged conduct. Indeed, apart from *Thornhill* itself, Supreme Court opinions provide little support for the commentators' view that the overbreadth doctrine *in any way* limits the power of state courts to narrow statutes to constitutionally specified boundaries in the application process.[85] In reviewing any case involving free expression the Court invariably accepts the gloss the highest state court has placed on a state statute.[86] To be sure, the statute, however narrowed in

---

[83] ELY, note 10 *supra*, at 110.

[84] Professor Ely seems to assume that *all* privilege rules are relatively free of inquiry into audience reaction. *Id.* at 110. I think that assertion implausible (Compare Ely's treatment of *Brandenburg* in the text at 115 with *id.* 232–33 n.24.) See Schauer, *Categories and the First Amendment: A Play in Three Acts,* 34 VAND. L. REV. 265, 302 (1981): ". . . 'incitement', for example, still involves an individualized assessment." But even if Ely is right, commentators like Tribe who seek to distinguish among privilege rules are wrong.

[85] The first important decision after *Thornhill* accepted the state court narrowing construction. Cox v. New Hampshire, 312 U.S. 569, 576–78 (1941). For the argument that the narrowing came too late, see Monaghan, note 61 *supra*, at 539–43.

[86] See Ward v. Illinois, 431 U.S. 767, 773–76 (1977) (state court construes obscenity statute in accordance with the specificity requirements of Miller v. California, note 7 *supra*); Colten v. Kentucky, 407 U.S. 104, 110–11 (1972) (disorderly conduct statute); Shuttles-

the state system, may still be constitutionally infirm;[87] but any such defect is the product of substantive First Amendment principles rather than a special nonseparability restriction imposed on the state courts by the First Amendment.

Contrary to the view of Professor Tribe, *Gooding v. Wilson*[88] is fully consistent with these principles. Georgia had convicted the defendant under a statute forbidding any person "without provocation, to use to or of another, and in his presence . . . opprobrious words or abusive language, tending to cause a breach of the peace." While defendant's speech arguably constituted unprotected "fighting words,"[89] the Supreme Court focused entirely on the terms of the rule applied:[90]

> [The statute] punishes only spoken words. It can therefore withstand appellee's attack upon its facial constitutionality only if, as authoritatively construed by the Georgia courts, it is not susceptible of application to speech, although vulgar or offensive, that is protected by the First and Fourth Amendments. . . . Only the Georgia courts can supply the requisite construction, since of course, "we lack jurisdiction authoritatively to construe state legislation." It matters not that the words appellee used might have been constitutionally prohibited under a narrowly and precisely drawn statute.

---

worth v. City of Birmingham, 382 U.S. 87, 91–92 (1965) (prospective narrowing valid).

Even if the Supreme Court could insist on making its own independent determination of the content of the state law, as in Indiana ex. rel. Anderson v. Brand, 303 U.S. 95, 100 (1938), it is still state law that is being interpreted, and thus the Court must cut the state statute down to size if it concludes that was what the state law required. See Metromedia, Inc. v. City of San Diego, note 17 *supra*, at 2899, n.26.

[87] Winters v. New York, note 22 *supra*, 519–20. (State court interpretation fixes the meaning of the statute in this case, but even so constrained the statute is unconstitutionally vague.)

[88] Note 63 *supra* at 518.

[89] Justice Blackmun wrote in dissent (p. 534):

> It seems strange, indeed, that in this day a man may say to a police officer, who is attempting to restore access to a public building, "White son of a bitch, I'll kill you" and "you son of a bitch, I'll choke you to death," and say to an accompanying officer, "You son of a bitch, if you ever put your hands on me again, I'll cut you all to pieces," and yet constitutionally cannot be prosecuted and convicted under [the] state statute. . . .

The unprotected character of this speech seems very arguable even on the general premise that a policeman is under a duty to exercise greater restraint than the general members of the public in reacting to provocative language. *Cf.* Gunther, ". . . *The Case of Justice Powell*," 24 STAN. L. REV. 1001 (1972), with the Court's subsequent decision in Lewis v. New Orleans, 415 U.S. 130 (1974).

[90] Note 63 *supra* at 520. On my analysis nothing of importance turns on the fact that the statute "punishes only spoken words."

The Court then concluded that, even as narrowed by the state courts, the statute still reached more than unprotected fighting words and hence was facially defective.

Professor Tribe seems in error in reading *Gooding* and other "offensive-speech" decisions as limiting the power of the state court to reconstruct statutes so as to reach only unprotected fighting words.[91] The *Gooding* Court simply emphasized the impermissibly expansive scope of the rule actually employed by the state court. Had the Georgia courts tailored the statute to a constitutionally acceptable size—that is, to fit only "fighting words"—the Supreme Court would have been compelled to face one of two very different and much thornier questions: whether defendant's speech was in fact constitutionally protected[92] or whether the fighting words category should be either abandoned or restructured.[93]

Finally, it might be argued that overbreadth's inseparability analysis is at least justified where *no* privilege rule exists to constrain the statute. The suggestion will not work. I think that analysis will show that in these situations the controlling substantive law is necessarily compelling state interest or some other balancing test. In these circumstances, overbreadth inquiry is essentially the means-focused, least restrictive alternative inquiry.[94]

IV. THE CONTOURS OF OVERBREADTH ANALYSIS

A. CONTENT-BASED RESTRICTIONS

The Court, apparently confused about the nature of the overbreadth doctrine, has formulated various limiting devices. Opportunity to press overbreadth challenges has been denied to litigants falling within the "hard core" of a statute's valid sweep,[95] to liti-

---

[91] TRIBE, note 7 *supra*, at § 12–26, pp. 715–16.

[92] The relevant cases on state power to control "offensive" speech are collected in GUNTHER CONSTITUTIONAL LAW, CASES AND MATERIALS note 8 *supra*, at 1229–43. See also White, J., dissenting from the denial of certiorari in Gormley v. Director, Connecticut State Dep't of Adult Probation, 101 S. Ct. 591 (1980) (annoying telephone call).

[93] Schauer, note 88 *supra*, at 269 n.19 (1981); Gard, *Fighting Words as Free Speech*, 58 WASH. U. L. Q. 531 (1980).

[94] Sometimes, however, the relevant substantive inquiry will generate elaboration of a different set of categories, *e.g.*, whether the speech took place in a "public forum."

[95] See, Haig v. Agee, note 55 *supra*, at 2783 n.61, citing Parker v. Levy, 417 U.S. 733, 755–56 (1974). See also Dombrowski v. Pfister, note 22 *supra*, at 479, 491–92; Brown v.

gants contesting regulations of commercial speech,[96] and to litigants challenging conduct-focused statutes unlikely to generate an
appreciable range of invalid applications to expressive conduct.[97]
These "exceptions" are evidence of the doctrinal disorder surrounding overbreadth analysis. Quite plainly, the "exceptions" do
not contradict the point that overbreadth doctrine does not restrict
judicial power to truncate statutes to constitutionally prescribed
boundaries. Nor, conversely, do they somehow license courts to
apply substantively invalid rules because of the nature of the regulatory rule or of the litigant's conduct. Consider, for example, the
suggestion that a litigant who falls within the "hard core" of a
statute cannot complain of overbreadth as to others. The meaning
of this statement is hardly plain as overbreadth theory now stands.
To be sure, such a litigant is unlikely to be able to object on vagueness grounds to a narrowing construction. And the decision to
constrain the statute by an applicable rule of privilege is a decision
that the statute is separable, so that any unconstitutional applications are to be excised in the application process. But the litigant is
still entitled to the application of a valid rule of law, his "hard-core"
status notwithstanding.

Overbreadth simply expresses that requirement of a substantively valid rule in the context of First Amendment substantive law.
That expression is, however, affected by the tension within substantive First Amendment doctrine between categorization and
balancing as distinct approaches to the validity of content-based
restrictions. Where the categorization approach is relevant, the
statute may not reach beyond the relevant unprotected category.[98]
By contrast, in cases in which the compelling state interest or other
balancing test is triggered, the Court must address the weight of the
governmental interest and matters of regulatory precision.[99] In
cases in which a balancing approach is operative, the probability of

---

Louisiana, 383 U.S. 131, 147–48 (1966) (Brennan, J., concurring). But see Gooding v.
Wilson, note 63 *supra*.

[96] Bates v. State Bar of Arizona, 433 U.S. 350, 381 (1977); Village of Schaumburg, note 4
supra, at 634. *Cf.* Central Hudson Gas Co. v. Public Service Comm'n of New York, note 55
supra.

[97] Broadrick v. Oklahoma, note 2 *supra*, at 615–16.

[98] *E.g.*, Lewis v. New Orleans, 415 U.S. 130 (1974) ("opprobrious language"); Communist
Party of Indiana v. Whitcomb, 414 U.S. 441 (1974) (oath).

[99] *E.g.*, Central Hudson Gas & Electric Corp. v. Public Service Comm'n of New York,
note 55 *supra*. See also note 11 *supra*.

a saving construction is, perhaps, less than where the categorization approach obtains because the state court may not be in an appropriate institutional position to truncate a statute to satisfy the least restrictive alternative analysis.

Whether the categorization or the balancing approach is appropriate, the important point is that the litigant is entitled to the application of a constitutionally valid rule. *Schad v. Borough of Mount Ephraim*[100] is recent confirmation of that point. In *Schad*, the wares of an adult bookstore included a coin-operated mechanism permitting the customer to watch a live nude dancer performing behind a glass panel, and the store's owner was charged with violating a zoning ordinance prohibiting any live entertainment in a commercial zone. Some forms of nude dancing may fall with the protection of the First Amendment,[101] although my inclinations are with the dissenting opinion of the Chief Justice on this predominantly prurient variety. But I think the Chief Justice is wrong in putting the decisive question in these terms:[102]

> As applied, [the ordinance] operates as a ban on nude dancing in appellants' "adult" book store, and for that reason alone it is here. Thus, the issue *in the case that we have before us* is not whether Mount Ephraim may ban traditional live entertainment, but whether it may ban nude dancing, which is used as the "bait" to induce customers into the appellants' book store. When, and if, this ordinance is used to prevent a high school performance of "The Sound of Music," for example, the Court can deal with that problem.

Contrary to the Chief Justice's view, the defendant—whatever he did—is, as the Court recognized, entitled to a judicial evaluation of the facial constitutionality of a blanket ban against live entertainment in a commercial zone. That prohibition may or may not be valid, but the issue cannot be reduced, as the Chief Justice thought, to a question of the protected character of defendant's expression.[103]

---

[100] 101 S. Ct. 2176 (1981).

[101] Indeed, I so argued as counsel in the *Hair* case, Southeastern Promotions, Ltd v. Conrad, note 1 *supra*, at 546 (1975).

[102] Note 100 *supra*, at 2191–92 (italics in original).

[103] The court framed the issue in these terms (*id.* at 2181):

As the Mount Ephraim code has been construed by the New Jersey courts—a construction that is binding upon us—"live entertainment," including nude dancing, is "not permitted use in any establishment" in the Borough of Mount Ephraim.

Nor can the Supreme Court decline to entertain a facial challenge by itself supplying a saving construction to an otherwise impermissible state statute. The contrary suggestion of cases like *Erznoznik v. City of Jacksonville*[104] is unsound. *Erznoznik* correctly sustained a facial attack to a content-based ordinance which the state court had failed to narrow to the appropriate constitutional boundary line.[105] In so doing, however, the Court added that "the possibility of a limiting construction appears remote."[106] This concern is appropriate in the setting of a suit in the federal courts seeking to restrain enforcement of a state statute on grounds of facial invalidity.[107] But it is wholly misplaced in *Erznoznik*. That case had arisen in the state courts and the ordinance had been given an authoritative construction by the state courts—thus excluding the possibility of a "*Yazoo* presumption*." Facial scrutiny by the Supreme Court in such cases does not extend beyond a consideration of whether the state rule, as authoritatively construed by the state courts, satisfies relevant constitutional standards.[108]

By excluding live entertainment throughout the Borough, the Mount Ephraim ordinance prohibits a wide range of expression that has long been held to be within the protections of the First and Fourteenth Amendment. Entertainment, as well as political and ideological speech, is protected; motion pictures, programs broadcast by radio and television and live entertainment such as musical and dramatic works, fall within the First Amendment guarantee. [Citations omitted.] Nor may an entertainment program be prohibited solely because it displays the nude human figure.

Whatever First Amendment protection should be extended to nude dancing, live or on film, however, the Mount Ephraim ordinance prohibits all live entertainment in the Borough: no property in the Borough may be principally used for the commercial production of plays, concerts, musicals, dance or any other form of live entertainment. Because appellants' claims are rooted in the First Amendment, they are entitled to rely on the impact of the ordinance on the expressive activities of others as well as their own.

See also Doran v. Salem Inn, Inc. 422 U.S. 922, 933 (1974) upholding a grant of a preliminary injunction in a challenge by bar owners to an ordinance that prohibited females from appearing topless not just in bars but "in any public place." Compare New York State Liquor Authority v. Bellanca, 101 S. Ct. 2599, 2601 (1981) (upholding prohibition of topless dancing in a barroom).

[104] 422 U.S. 205 (1975).

[105] *Id.* at 216. The ordinance prohibited exhibition of any "motion picture . . . in which the human male or female bare buttocks, human female bare breasts, or human bare pubic areas are shown if such motion picture . . . is visible from any public street or public place." *Id.* at 206–07.

[106] *Id.* at 216.

[107] *E.g.*, Cameron v. Johnson, 390 U.S. 611, 615–16 (1968); Cole v. Richardson, 405 U.S. 676 (1972).

[108] HART & WECHSLER'S 1981 Supplement at 87–88. See also, *e.g.*, Talley v. California, 362 U.S. 60, 63–64 (1960).

B. OVERBREADTH AND NON–CONTENT-BASED STATE STATUTES

If facial challenges are permissible with respect to any rule impinging on constitutionally protected speech, what facial review methodology is appropriate for ordinary criminal statutes, such as prohibitions against trespass and theft? While generally regulating "nonspeech," these statutes will on occasion be applied to "speech," a term which, substantively, embraces a diverse range of activities with many different qualities: solicitation and contribution of money, picketing, mass demonstrations, expressive conduct, etc.[109] In *Broadrick v. Oklahoma*,[110] the Court, in the course of an elaborate effort at restating the overbreadth standing doctrine,[111] sought to confine facial condemnation of statutes of this sort. Positing a general distinction between "pure speech" and conduct, including "expressive conduct," the Court said that overbreadth concerns attenuate[112]

> as the otherwise protected behavior that it forbids the State to sanction moves from "pure speech" toward conduct and that conduct—even if expressive— falls within the scope of otherwise valid criminal laws. . . . To put the matter another way, particularly where conduct and not merely speech is involved, we believe that the overbreadth of a statute must not only be real, but substantial as well, judged in relation to the statute's plainly legitimate sweep.

The analytic framework suggested in *Broadrick* contained considerable ambiguity and uncertainty, including, *inter alia*, whether the focus of the Court's distinction between "pure speech" and conduct relates to the terms of the statute or to the litigant's activity;[113] whether the "exceptions" recognized by the Court to its general distinction are potentially engulfing;[114] and, finally, whether a dis-

---

[109] *E.g.*, Village of Schaumburg, note 4 *supra* (solicitations); Buckley v. Valeo, note 55 *supra* (contributions); Cox v. Louisiana, 379 U.S. 559 (1965) (mass demonstration); United States v. O'Brien, 391 U.S. 367 (1968) (expressive conduct).

[110] Note 2 *supra*, at 601.

[111] *Id.* at 609–16.

[112] *Id.* at 615.

[113] Professor Tribe apparently reads the Court's language as focusing on the statute. TRIBE, note 7 *supra*, at § 12–25, p. 713, referring to the Court's "troublesome distinction between 'pure speech' regulations and 'conduct' regulations." For a heroic effort to explicate the decision, see Note, *Overbreadth Review and the Burger Court*, 49 N.Y.U.L. REV. 532, 538–43 (1974).

[114] Note 2 *supra*, at 612–13:
  Such claims of facial overbreadth have been entertained in cases involving stat-

tinction between "pure speech" and conduct has any useful content.[115] However these questions are resolved, the core point remains—the Court will be hostile to facial condemnation of statutes whose central focus is prohibition of tangible harms unrelated to the content of the expression generated by the production of those harms. This hostility, moreover, is not mitigated merely because such statutes can be applied to a rather disparate variety of constitutionally protected expression.[116]

Although the Court's general conclusion is sound, its underpinnings are, I think, quite different from those advanced by the Court. The question is *not* whether a defendant can raise an overbreadth challenge to an "ordinary" criminal statute; the facial validity of the rule actually invoked is always theoretically open to challenge. General criminal statutes, however, are potentially applicable in a wide variety of settings which, in turn, implicate a correspondingly wide range of First Amendment principles. No single determinative First Amendment privilege rule exists for the purpose of statutory narrowing; nor is the compelling state interest test a meaningful litmus test against which to evaluate the statute. Consider, for example, the wide range of applications of an ordinary trespass statute in the context of expression: leafletting in a company town, interruption of a judicial proceeding to make a protest, demonstrating in the curtilage of a jail, etc. Plainly, the statute cannot be evaluated, *ex ante*, in a vacuum, as it sits on the statute books. Nor should it. "The pinch of the statute is in its

---

utes which, by their terms, seek to regulate 'only spoken words.' Gooding v. Wilson, 405 U.S. 518, 520 (1972). . . . Overbreadth attacks have also been allowed where the Court thought rights of association were ensnared in statutes which, by their broad sweep, might result in burdening innocent associations. . . . Facial overbreadth claims have also been entertained where statutes, by their terms, purport to regulate the time, place, and manner of expressive or communicative conduct, . . . and where such conduct has required official approval under laws that delegated standardless discretionary power to local functionaries, resulting in virtually unreviewable prior restraints on First Amendment rights. . . .

[115] See Kalven, *The Concept of the Public Forum: Cox v. Louisiana*, 1965 SUP. CT. REV. 1. See also Henkin, *Foreword: On Drawing Lines*, 82 HARV. L. REV. 63, 79–80 (1968): "The meaningful constitutional distinction is not between speech and conduct, but between conduct that speaks, communicates, and other kinds of conduct. If it is intended as expression, if in fact it communicates, especially if it becomes a common comprehensible form of expression, it is 'speech.'" See also Ely, note 53 *supra*, at 1495.

[116] "Equally important, overbreadth claims, if entertained at all, have been curtailed when invoked against ordinary criminal laws that are sought to be applied to protected conduct." Note 2 *supra*, at 613.

application."[117] Thus the point at which to determine whether any statute is facially defective is *at the time and in the terms in which it is applied to a litigant*. But when a trespass statute is in fact applied to anything embraced within the constitutional definition of speech, the contextually specific construction given to the statute must be valid.[118] If it is not, the statute is to that extent—and to that extent only—invalid as a matter of constitutional law.

The requirement of an acceptable, contextually specific construction ordinarily will mean that the relevant constitutional principles must be sufficiently elaborated by the state court to ensure that the statute's reach is sufficiently constrained.[119] An elaboration requirement leaves little scope for application of the *Yazoo* separability "presumption"[120] in the First Amendment context. If, for example, the state court simply holds that its general trespass statute validly applies to the expression shown by the evidence, the decision is vulnerable. In this context, the decisive question is whether any plausible basis exists for a fear that the state court failed to apply a permissible rule in sustaining the conviction. This inquiry will require some inspection, however cursory, of the evidence, because the evidence will enable the reviewing court to categorize the case properly among the potentially relevant First Amendment contexts. In *Coates v. City of Cincinnati*,[121] for example, the sparse record showed little more than that the defendants had been involved in activities frequently, albeit not invariably, constitutionally privileged: a student demonstration and labor dispute picketing. They had been convicted under an ordinance which

---

[117] Terminiello v. Chicago, note 37 *supra*, and accompanying text.

[118] *E.G.*, Cox v. Louisiana, note 109 *supra*. The cases cited by the Court in Broadrick, note 2 *supra*, at 613–14, show this. Cantwell v. Connecticut, 310 U.S. 296 (1940), for example, involved a conviction for the common law crime of inciting a breach of the peace. The Court noted that this offense "embraces a great variety of conduct destroying or menacing public order and tranquility." *Id.* at 308. Whether this definition suffices for a conviction for throwing beer cans at windows, it is not sufficient in the area of freedom of speech.

[119] In this context, elaboration will often be in a negative form, for example: "Defendant's trespass conviction is affirmed because the first amendment does not include a right to interrupt a judicial proceeding to make a protest."

If the court held, however, that "defendant's trespass conviction is affirmed because the first amendment does not include a right to talk in any public place," the result would be different. That rule of state law is inconsistent with the constitutional guarantee of free speech.

[120] See the text and notes at pp. 6–8 *supra*.

[121] 402 U.S. 611 (1971).

made it unlawful "for three or more persons to assemble, . . . on any of the sidewalks, street corners . . . and there conduct themselves in a manner annoying to persons passing by. . . ."[122] It may be, as the dissent argued, that this is like an "ordinary criminal statute"[123] and that, as the Court recognized, it "is broad enough to encompass many types of conduct clearly within the city's constitutional power to prohibit."[124] Nevertheless, the Court correctly sustained a facial attack for overbreadth (and vagueness). The judgment of the state court amounted to little more than a conclusion that the ordinance applied, and validly so, to defendants' conduct.[125] Once it appeared from the record that defendants' conduct arguably fell within a category of First Amendment concern, the judgment was properly reversed, since the Court could not safely conclude that a constitutionally sufficient rule has been applied by the state court. And, as a matter of substantive First Amendment law, the state bears the duty to make precisely that showing.[126]

C.   OVERBREADTH AND FEDERAL STATUTES

In situations in which a federal statute or regulation touching expression can be authoritatively construed to accord with an applicable rule of constitutional privilege, the function of overbreadth standing is significantly limited.[127] To be sure, institutional constraints exist on the Court's authority to restructure federal statutes; at some point, such judicial efforts will exceed the bounds of what legitimately can pass as statutory "construction."[128] But the case law makes plain that this limitation, rooted in the separation-of-powers concepts, is not a significant inhibition.[129] The Court

---

[122] *Id.* at 611 n.1.

[123] *Id.* at 620 (White, J., dissenting).

[124] *Id.* at 614.

[125] *Id.* at 613–14.

[126] *E.g.*, Speiser v. Randall, 357 U.S. 513, 525–26 (1958); see also Cooper v. Mitchell Bros.' Santa Ana Theatre, 102 S. Ct. __ (1981). Justice White's dissent in *Coates* overlooks this point when in the penultimate sentence of the dissent he argues that the ordinance is not invalid on its face and the deficiencies in the record leave the Court "in no position" to judge the ordinance as applied. 402 U.S. at 620–21.

[127] HART & WECHSLER at 212.

[128] "It is true . . . that it is for Congress, not this Court, to rewrite the statute." United States v. Thirty-seven Photographs, 402 U.S. 363, 369 (1971). See generally TRIBE, note 7 *supra*, at § 12–27.

[129] United States v. Thirty-seven Photographs, note 128 *supra*, provides a particularly apt illustration that this limitation does not impose serious constraints. The Court there

now seems thoroughly committed to truncating federal statutes in light of the applicable rules of constitutional privilege.[130] Thus, overbreadth holdings of facial invalidity should disappear in cases challenging federal authority, save for those instances involving unreconstructible statutes, rules, or orders[131] or where the Court is plainly condemning the statute on the merits because of its failure to satisfy the least restrictive alternative requirement.

Argument can be mounted that overbreadth methodology should have a larger, rather than a smaller, role in review of federal enactments. So long as fair-warning requirements have been satisfied, the Court cannot oversee the interpretive ingenuity of state courts in their efforts to confine state statutes to the area of constitutionally unprotected activity.[132] But the Court labors under no similar disability with respect to federal statutes, and the deterrence rationale underlying the overbreadth doctrine might therefore dictate a special canon of federal statutory construction counseling against judicial narrowing. Such a canon might be justified on either institutional or substantive grounds. The institutional argument would contend that the Court has a unique responsibility to educate the other federal branches in the need for sensitivity to free-speech interests. A holding of invalidity for overbreadth would, in effect, "remand" the problem to the relevant branch for more finely tuned attention to speech concerns and a judgment about whether the governmental interest being pursued demanded regulation of speech to the constitutional limit, a place beneath that limit, or not at all. Forcing attention to these matters by the nonjudicial branches, moreover, might generate sensitivity to speech interests in a more generalized and systematic way, reducing thereby the

---

upheld a federal statute prohibiting importation of obscene materials and providing for their seizure. In so doing, the four-member plurality rejected on the merits an objection that the statutory standard was substantively overbroad but went on to note that in any event "the proper approach . . . was not to invalidate the section in its entirety, but to construe it narrowly. . . ." *Id.* at 375 n.3. And a majority of the Court then proceeded to read in constitutionally required procedural safeguards. *Id.* at 368–75 (plurality opinion); *id.* at 377, 378 (concurring opinions).

[130] See the text and notes at p. 18 *supra*.

[131] Aptheker v. Secretary of State, 378 U.S. 500 (1964) might be rationalized on this ground. The principal kind of statute that probably cannot be rehabilitated in the application process is a scheme that was administered in an open-ended, unbridled fashion. Shuttleworth v. City of Birmingham, 394 U.S. 147 (1969). See Monaghan, note 61 *supra*, at 518, 539–43.

[132] United States v. Thirty-seven Photographs, note 128 *supra*, at 369–70.

need for future judicial interventions. The substantive justification for such a canon of federal statutory construction is that discussed in Section II above, that is, that certain privilege rules provide inadequate guidance to enforcement officials and speakers[133] and hence should not be judicially "penciled in" to save federal statutes from holdings of unconstitutionality.

The substantive argument is no more potent here than it was in relation to the constitutional limits on separability of state statutes. If a privilege rule is constitutionally adequate to guide a legislature in drafting a statute, it is equally adequate to guide a court in creating a saving construction. Only on the assumption that the privilege rules running against the federal government should be different from those against the states could the substantive case be made for special limitations on the power of federal courts to rescue federal statutes by construction. Any such assumption seems to me implausible, and, not surprisingly, it has never been one embraced by the Court.

The institutional argument is somewhat more difficult to meet but is vulnerable, on inspection, to powerful institutional counterarguments. Although increasing sensitivity to speech interests across the federal branches is no doubt a constitutional "good," fostering that goal by way of a judicial refusal to save overbroad federal statutes generates serious countervailing costs. First, invalidation of a federal statute would leave some unprotected and presumably harmful speech or conduct wholly unregulated while Congress or the executive struggles to formulate a valid rule.[134] Given the heavy agenda of government, the matter might remain without attention for a substantial time period, a particularly serious matter with respect to matters subject to exclusive federal authority. Second, "remands" to other branches for a more speech-

---

[133] *E.g.*, TRIBE, note 7 *supra*, at § 12–26, p. 715 (advocating overbreadth approach "where the validity of the first amendment privilege must be decided in terms of the factual circumstances in which the claim is raised. . . ." Professor Tribe, it should be noted, does not distinguish here between federal and state statutes in this respect.

[134] State statutes held defective on overbreadth grounds can be rehabilitated by the state courts prospectively. *E.g.*, Dombrowski v. Pfister, note 22 *supra*, at 491; Shuttlesworth v. Birmingham, note 86 *supra*, at 153–55; Monaghan, *Constitutional Adjudication: The Who and When*, 82 YALE L. J. 1363, 1387 (1973). By contrast, if a federal statute is found facially defective it "is void *in toto*, barring all further actions under it, in this, and every other case." United States v. Petrillo, 332 U.S. 1, 6 (1947). Perhaps this point has more theoretical than practical significance—given the fact that someone will have to invoke the state court's jurisdiction and questions of issue preclusion will arise. See Shapiro, note 30 *supra*.

sensitive response may produce little future speech sensitivity. The nonjudicial branches respond to various political pressures, and little evidence exists that judicial refusals to tolerate repression are likely to produce substantially more refined political responses to the need to accommodate speech when future censorial urges develop. To the extent that this is true, it is not evident that the present hiatus costs in the exercise of federal power are justified by any countervailing gain in future speech sensitivity within the political branches of the federal government.

Finally, both the substantive and institutional arguments for a special canon of federal statutory construction leave me with the suspicion of a "double counting" of speech values. The premise of the Court's obscenity holdings, for example, is that the boundary separating obscene and nonobscene material is sufficient so as not to deter protected speech at an unacceptable level. It is hard to see why this premise should be completely abandoned at the level of statutory construction. Invocation of inseparability principles as a canon of federal statutory construction is, therefore, tantamount to a direct attack on the adequacy of what has been adjudicated to be a constitutionally sufficient dividing line.[135]

V. Broadrick v. Oklahoma: The Complexities of Overbreadth Analysis

Broadrick v. Oklahoma[136] is a graphic illustration of the difficulties inherent in thinking about overbreadth as a special inseparability doctrine. *Broadrick* involved a statute specifically directed at activity within the general ambit of the First Amendment—partisan political activity by state civil service employees.[137] The Court assumed that the statutory provisions, though generally valid,[138] embraced some constitutionally protected acts, such as wearing campaign buttons and displaying bumper stickers.[139] On the premise that the overbreadth of statutes

---

[135] Herbert v. Lando, 441 U.S. 153, 175–77 (1979) (constitutionally prescribed limits on defamation suits do not justify an additional evidentiary privilege for press).

[136] Note 2 *supra*.

[137] The statute is set out in note 1 of the Court's opinion, *id.* at 603–04.

[138] A companion case, United States Civil Service Commission v. National Association of Letter Carriers, note 72 *supra*, had sustained similar federal legislation.

[139] 413 U.S. at 609–10.

regulating expressive conduct "must not only be real, but substantial as well, judged in relation to the statute's plainly legitimate sweep,"[140] the Court upheld the statute against facial attack. *Broadrick*'s holding, albeit not all of its language, squares with a view that the overbreadth doctrine does not restrict judicial authority to narrow statutes to appropriate constitutional boundary lines.

Broadrick arose in the district court as a suit to enjoin proceedings before a state administrative agency charging the plaintiffs with various violations of the state statute. The charges did not include wearing buttons or displaying bumper stickers. In fact, no state court had authoritatively concluded that the Oklahoma statute reached those acts.[141] Ignoring the obvious abstention possibilities,[142] the Court focused on the facial challenge. Even if, however, the Court correctly assumed that the act reached this protected expression, plaintiff's suit should fail. The act was not being enforced in these respects against the plaintiffs. Plaintiffs could only prevail on a demonstration that the invalid applications could not be severed from the valid ones—an issue, I have argued, controlled by state law. The state supreme court could not rationally be expected to invalidate the entire act on inseparability grounds simply because of a few marginal invalid applications. Thus the Court was right in not permitting the offending aspects of the statutory scheme to condemn the statute in its entirety.

Broadrick is particularly instructive in illustrating the need to think clearly about the meaning of overbreadth analysis. The conventional setting for overbreadth theorists usually involves a test of the facial sufficiency of a "single" prohibition—for example, a statute prohibiting "offensive or indecent language"—judicially evaluated by viewing it in terms of some obvious, standard instances of its application. *Broadrick* demonstrates the unusual difficulty of comprehending the focus of a "facial" attack when its subject is a

---

[140] *Id.* at 615. For the argument that the decision is incorrect, even on its own terms, see Note, note 113 *supra*, at 542: ". . . the wearing of buttons and bumper stickers would appear to merit the same consideration as pure speech. . . ."

In effect, the Court "treated the state's regulation of political activity the way an ordinary trespass or theft statute might be treated." TRIBE, note 7 *supra*, at § 12–25, p. 713.

[141] The state administrative agency charged with enforcement of the act had so held. 413 U.S. at 610 n.10. Compare Law Students Civil Rights Research Council v. Wadmond, 401 U.S. 154, 162–63, 165 (1971) (agency construction "entitled to respectful consideration").

[142] The state act expressly exempted from its reach the employee's right to vote and his right to express privately his political beliefs (expansively defined). 413 U.S. at 617–18.

complex, interrelated statutory scheme (or administrative regulation or order) that impinges on a wide range of expressive behavior.
It illustrates, too, the particular difficulties of such a challenge in
the context of a suit for *anticipatory* relief in the federal district
courts. There is need for adequate integration of overbreadth doctrine with the constitutional and prudential doctrines, particularly
ripeness and abstention, which govern the timing and scale of constitutional challenges. Surely conventional doctrines governing access to the federal courts have a function in the free-speech context,
as elsewhere. Abstention doctrine has a legitimate role to play in
defining the contours of the statute.[143] Moreover, the lack of a
concrete threat of enforcement of various discrete provisions of a
broad, complex act gives rise to concerns as to whether a challenge
to them is ripe either constitutionally or prudentially.[144]

If overbreadth is viewed as a special First Amendment standing doctrine—or, to be more precise, a special inseparability
doctrine—it renders unintelligible much of the theorizing underlying the constitutional and prudential restrictions on federal "judicial power." If, by contrast, overbreadth is simply understood as a
disposition on the merits, it can be fitted into these conventional
notions. Thus, for example, a court might decline to pass on the
overbreadth challenge in a declaratory judgment action brought by
a litigant whose clearly unprotected expression falls within the hard
core of a statute readily constrained by an applicable rule of
privilege.[145] This is true even though the same litigant could insist
on his overbreadth challenge being decided if he were a defendant
in an enforcement proceeding. In the declaratory judgment action,
the litigant would, in substance, be asking whether the courts will,
as a matter of statutory construction, refuse to narrow the statute to
constitutional boundaries, thereby rendering the statute invalid. If
the litigant's expression is clearly unprotected and within the hard

---

[143] See, *e.g.*, Babbitt v. United Farm Workers Nat'l Union, 442 U.S. 289, 308–12 (1979).
Not surprisingly, the ascendancy of overbreadth methodology was accompanied by a corresponding decline of abstention doctrine. Harvard Note at 901–07.

[144] See Babbitt v. United Farm Workers Nat'l Union, note 43 *supra*, at 298–305; Socialist
Labor Party v. Gilligan, 406 U.S. 583, 586–88 (1972). See generally HART & WECHSLER at
133–49; 1981 Supplement at 45–52; Shapiro, note 30 *supra*.

[145] Consider, *e.g.*, a suit by the publisher of a book clearly constituting hard-core pornography challenging a state obscenity statute on the ground that it is invalid for failure to
comply with the specificity requirements of Miller v. California, note 7 *supra*, a defect
which can be cured by judicial construction. Ward v. Illinois, note 86 *supra*.

core of the statute, it is at least arguable that "Our Federalism" might warrant a denial of such an advance determination without any consideration of "Pullman abstention" possibilities.[146]

Most important, *Broadrick* illustrates that simply because one or several provisions of a complex act or regulation are involved in litigation, that cannot mean that every potential subsection of the act or regulation is thereby implicated on some constitutionally based inseparability premise. Any such result would wreak havoc with complex regulatory schemes, some small part of which might be constitutionally infirm. More generally, I submit that overbreadth simply cannot be sensibly understood to denote a special rule against restructuring complex regulatory provisions to accord with applicable constitutional rules of privilege. *Metromedia, Inc. v. City of San Diego*[147] is a recent illustration of this point. At issue was the validity of a complex, partially content-based ordinance that imposed substantial prohibitions on the erection of outdoor advertising displays within the city. The state supreme court had sustained the entire ordinance against a facial attack. A divided Supreme Court affirmed in part and reversed in part. The prevailing four-man plurality opinion remanded the case to the state court to determine whether, as a matter of state law, the entire ordinance was now void on inseparability grounds or was to be applied in accord with the limiting constitutional restrictions.[148] No suggestion was advanced in any of the opinions that the ordinance was void in toto as a matter of federal constitutional law simply because part of its prohibitions were invalid.

VI. CONCLUSION

Advocates of a special overbreadth "standing" rule in free-speech cases have developed an elaborate theory, one that purports

---

[146] Railroad Comm'n of Texas v. Pullman Co., 312 U.S. 496 (1941). See Shapiro, note 30 *supra*, at 768–70. Chapters 7 of HART & WECHSLER and its 1981 Supplement collect the relevant materials on the range of issues open to a prospective state defendant who initiates a federal court suit for anticipatory relief. My own general bias is to permit a prospective defendant to raise by way of anticipatory challenge an issue properly open to him in an enforcement proceeding. See Note, *Declaratory Relief in the Criminal Law*, 80 HARV. L. REV. 1490 (1967). Moreover, in the First Amendment context, there may be some constitutional requirement of anticipatory relief. See Monaghan, note 61 *supra*, at 543–51. But I hope that I am not insensitive to appropriate federalism barriers to federal anticipatory relief. Monaghan, *The Burger Court and "Our Federalism,"* 43 LAW AND CONTEMPORARY PROBLEMS 39, 43–49 (1980).

[147] 101 S. Ct. at 2882.

[148] *Id.* at 2899 n.26.

to be grounded in special First Amendment concerns. Its premises are that overbroad statutes deter protected speech at an unacceptable rate, and that the conventional judicial technique of excising unconstitutional applications is insufficient to cure that defect.[149] These premises have become the subject of increasing skepticism, both off and on the Court.[150] Recent Supreme Court decisions seem to provide little support for viewing overbreadth as a special, speech-protective standing doctrine. Rather, viewed in standing terms, overbreadth methodology simply applies the conventional principle that any litigant may insist on not being burdened by a constitutionally invalid rule. What is different from the conventional run-of-the-mill case is not standing but the substantive content of the applicable constitutional law.

As an expression of substantive constitutional principles, overbreadth is, of course, concerned with the weight of the governmental interest justifying any regulation.[151] But the dominant idea it evokes is serious means scrutiny. Wherever that law mandates strict or intermediate scrutiny, a requirement of regulatory precision is involved; a substantial congruence must exist between the regulatory means (the statute, as construed) and valid legislative ends.[152] Thus the Court has reacted interchangeably to "overbreadth" and "least restrictive alternative" challenges both inside[153] and outside[154] the First Amendment context. This observation would be particularly unsurprising to writers who have focused on the long and varying use of least restrictive alternative analysis in Supreme Court adjudication; without exception, their surveys include a discussion of First Amendment overbreadth cases.[155] This

---

[149] The major theoretical piece is the elaborate Harvard Note, note 6 *supra*. The main lines of that analysis appear in summary form in TRIBE, note 7 *supra*, at §§ 12–24 to 12–28.

[150] Professor Cox asserts that the deterrence rationale rests on pretense. COX, THE ROLE OF THE SUPREME COURT IN AMERICAN GOVERNMENT (1976). On the increasing judicial skepticism toward the doctrine, see TRIBE, note 7 *supra*, at § 12–25; GUNTHER, note 8 *supra*, 1189–95 (1980).

[151] See note 11 *supra*.

[152] The issue generally is framed in terms of the availability of less restrictive alternatives; whenever the necessary congruence is lacking, the statute is overbroad. In the First Amendment area we speak of overbreadth, but fashions in the use of language cannot disguise the substantive identity of the two inquiries, as the Court occasionally explicitly recognizes. Cameron v. Johnson, note 107 *supra*, at 616–17.

[153] *E.g.*, Cameron v. Johnson, note 107 *supra*.

[154] *E.g.*, Jones v. Helms, 101 S. Ct. 2434, 2442–43 (1981). South Carolina v. Katzenbach, 383 U.S. 301, 331 (1966).

[155] *E.g.*, Wormuth & Mirkin, note 64 *supra*, at 270–86, characterizing "the excessive

is as it should be;[156] wherever the Supreme Court is serious about judicial review—wherever, that is, the minimum rationality standard does not prevail—the Court will be concerned with the matter of least restrictive alternatives, with overbreadth.[157] By contrast, whenever the rational basis standard governs, substantive constitutional scrutiny is virtually nonexistent. Despite occasional judicial and academic protestations to the contrary,[158] that review is essentially "toothless." In all cases subject to that standard, statutory "overbreadth" is not a meaningful objection as a matter of substantive constitutional doctrine. A central feature of rational basis review is that it accords wide latitude to the states to structure their social and economic programs as they see fit. As long as the legislative scheme can be perceived as designed to promote some common good, the overbreadth of the statutory scheme does not render it constitutionally infirm.[159]

---

breadth of the statute" as the equivalent of "the doctrine of the reasonable alternative." *Id.* at 278. See also, Note, *The Less Restrictive Alternative in Constitutional Adjudication: An Analysis, a Justification, and Some Criteria*, 27 VAND. L. REV. 971, 1011–16 (1974), stating that "the principle of less drastic means has found its most frequent application due primarily to the popularity of the overbreadth technique. *Id.* at 1011. For the argument that overbreadth analysis has its historical roots in the tightening of the clear-and-present danger test, see Strong, *Fifty Years of "Clear and Present Danger": From Schenck to Brandenburg—and Beyond*, 1969 SUP. CT. REV. 41, 68–69.

[156] But see Central Hudson Gas & Electric Corp. v. Public Service Comm'n of New York, note 55 *supra*, at 565 n.8, attempting to distinguish between the two concepts. See also Moose Lodge No. 107 v. Irvis, 4076 U.S. 168 (1972) (overbreadth challenges restricted to First Amendment).

[157] We ordinarily do not consider the least restrictive alternative cases as presenting any departure from conventional standing principles. Nor should we when that same concept appears in the First Amendment context. Judicial conclusions of overbreadth or of the availability of less restrictive alternatives are equivalents. They are simply different statements that other, more finely tuned means exist to vindicate any presumably valid state policies. Cameron v. Johnson, note 107 *supra*; Note, *Less Drastic Means and the First Amendment*, 78 YALE L. J. 464, 470 (1969). Overbreadth analysis plays a different role when the relevant First Amendment law focuses on whether the regulated speech is within an unprotected category. It is frequently clear, *ex ante*, that defendant's speech is unprotected. But this is by no means invariably true. *E.g.*, Erznoznik v. City of Jacksonville, 422 U.S. 205 (1975). In either event, the litigant simply invokes the traditional right to insist on application of a valid regulating rule. Here, too, overbreadth simply expresses the applicable substantive First Amendment law, not a special First Amendment rule of standing.

[158] See, for example, Bice, *Rationality Analysis in Constitutional Law*, 65 MINN. L. REV. 1 (1980); Bennett, *Abortion and Judicial Review: Of Burdens and Benefits, Hard Cases and Some Bad Law*, 75 NW. L. REV. 978, 980–89 (1981).

[159] Williamson v. Lee Optical Co., 348 U.S. 483 (1955). See also, *e.g.*, Massachusetts Bd. of Retirement v. Murgia, 427 U.S. 307 (1976); New York City Transit Auth. v. Beazer, 440 U.S. 568 (1979); Minnesota v. Clover Leaf Creamery Co., 101 S. Ct. 715, 722–27 (1981); Schweiker v. Wilson, 101 S. Ct. 1074, 1080–85 (1981). In the "old days" things may have been different. Struve, note 11 *supra*, at 1479–80.

Jones v. Helms[160] provides a recent illustration of these principles. At issue was the validity of a Georgia statute that set harsher criminal penalties for parents who abandon children and leave the state than for those abandoners who remain within it. After rejecting a claim that the statute infringed on the defendant's constitutionally protected right to travel, the Court addressed the equal protection claim:[161]

> The characterization by the Court of Appeals and appellee of the Georgia statute as "overbroad" does not affect our conclusion. Appellee contends, and the Court of Appeals found, that Georgia has available less restrictive means to serve the legitimate purposes furthered by the felony [statute]. . . . However, because we have concluded that [the statute] does not infringe upon appellee's fundamental rights, this reasoning is inapplicable. In the context of this case, the State need not employ the least restrictive, or even the most effective or wisest, means to achieve its legitimate ends.
>
> . . . [T]he statute may well be unnecessarily broad. This is a matter, however, that relates to the wisdom of the legislation. It raises no question with respect to the uniform and impartial character of the State's law. It therefore does not implicate the fundamental principle embodied in the Equal Protection Clause of the Fourteenth Amendment.

In sum, overbreadth analysis is concerned with the substance of constitutional review; it does not rely on any distinctive standing component.

---

[160] 101 S. Ct. at 2434.

[161] *Id.* at 2442–43.

D A V I D   P .   C U R R I E

MISUNDERSTANDING STANDING

"[A]part from Art. III's minimum requirements," wrote Justice Powell in *Warth v. Seldin* in 1975, the essence of the question of standing to sue "is whether the constitutional or statutory provision on which the claim rests properly can be understood as granting persons in the plaintiff's position a right to judicial relief."[1] This is the soundest sentence the Supreme Court has uttered on this troublesome subject within human memory. Unfortunately, the Court has generally ignored its own good counsel.

The case-or-controversy requirement of Article III, the Court has made clear, forbids suit only by those who have suffered no "threatened or actual injury resulting from the putatively illegal action. . . ."[2] Yet the Court has often refused to entertain challenges made by persons plainly alleging a constitutionally sufficient injury.

The stated justifications for refusing to hear such claims have varied over the years. The TVA cases in the 1930s denied electric companies standing to attack allegedly unconstitutional competition on the ground that they had no "legal right" to be free from

---

David P. Currie is Harry N. Wyatt Professor of Law, The University of Chicago.

[1] 422 U.S. 490, 500.

[2] The quoted language is taken from Linda R. S. v. Richard D., 410 U.S. 614, 617 (1973), a case denying standing. Among decisions upholding standing of parties with nothing more than statutory authorization and actual injury is FCC v. Sanders Bros. Radio Station, 309 U.S. 470 (1940). The recently enunciated "second prong" of the constitutional test, "a 'substantial likelihood' that the relief requested will redress the injury claimed," Duke Power Co. v. Carolina Environmental Study Group, Inc. 438 U.S. 59, 75 n. 20 (1978), is implicit in the simpler formulation quoted in the text.

competition.[3] The *Data Processing* case in 1969, rejecting the "legal right" test, declared in apparently general terms that an injured party had standing only if the interest he sought to protect was "arguably within the zone of interests to be protected or regulated by the statute or constitutional guarantee in question."[4] The dominant theme today, as stated in *Warth v. Seldin*, is that even an injured party generally has no standing to litigate a " 'generalized grievance' shared in substantially equal measure by all or a large class of citizens," or to assert the "rights or interests of third parties."[5] Thus in *Warth* itself, assuming that both residents of the town of Penfield and taxpayers of the city of Rochester had been injured by the town's allegedly unconstitutional refusal to allow the construction of low-cost housing, the Court denied them standing on the ground that they were asserting the rights of others.[6] Conversely, in the *Duke Power* case the Court allowed neighbors subject to everyday power-plant radiation to contest the constitutionality of a limitation on liability for nuclear accident because they were "champion[ing their] own rights" and their injury was "particularized."[7]

No one can sue, I should have thought, unless authorized by law to do so; yet despite Justice Powell's admonition in *Warth* that the issue was whether some law granted the plaintiffs "a right to judicial relief," neither in that case nor in *Duke Power* did the Court indicate what law gave the plaintiffs a right to sue.

Numerous statutes expressly confer the right to sue: The Communications Act, for example, authorizes any "person who is aggrieved or whose interests may be adversely affected" to challenge the grant of a broadcast license,[8] and the 1968 Civil Rights Act permits suit by "any person who claims to have been injured by a discriminatory housing practice."[9] In other cases, the Court has

---

[3] Alabama Power Co. v. Ickes, 302 U.S. 464 (1938); Tennessee Electric Power Co. v. TVA, 306 U.S. 118 (1939).

[4] Association of Data Processing Service Organizations v. Camp, 397 U.S. 150, 153 (1970).

[5] 422 U.S. at 499.

[6] *Id.* at 512–14, 508–10.

[7] 438 U.S. at 80.

[8] 47 U.S.C. § 402(b)(2). See FCC v. Sanders Bros. Radio Station 309 U.S. 470 (1940).

[9] 42 U.S.C. § 3610(a). See Trafficante v. Metropolitan Life Ins. Co., 409 U.S. 205 (1972).

inferred an implicit right to challenge administrative action from a statute silent on the subject: "[W]hen the particular statutory provision invoked does reflect a legislative purpose to protect a competitive interest," wrote Justice Black in 1968, "the injured competitor has standing to require compliance with that provision" even in the absence of an explicit grant of standing.[10] This reasoning is precisely analogous to that by which the Court inferred private rights of action for damages from substantive statutory or constitutional provisions in the familiar *Borak* and *Bivens* cases,[11] and rightly so: Whether the answer is labeled "standing" or "cause of action," the question is whether the statute or Constitution implicitly authorizes the plaintiff to sue. Decisions recognizing implicit standing on the basis that the plaintiff is in the class protected by the substantive provision, therefore, have been placed under a cloud by the Court's recent retrenchment of the *Borak* doctrine.[12] In any event, neither in *Warth* nor in *Duke Power* did the Court make an effort to derive a right to sue from the Equal Protection Clause or from the other substantive provisions the plaintiffs had invoked.[13]

At least three federal statutes arguably confer a right to sue that is broader than that given by the specific provisions already considered. The first is § 10(a) of the Administrative Procedure Act (APA): "A person suffering legal wrong because of agency action, or adversely affected or aggrieved by agency action within the meaning of a relevant statute, is entitled to judicial review thereof."[14] There is some judicial support for Professor Davis's view, based on a paraphrase in the legislative history, that this provision confers standing on any person "in fact adversely affected" by federal agency action.[15] The contemporaneous *Attorney General's Manual*, however, convincingly explained that the refer-

---

[10] Hardin v. Kentucky Utilities Co., 390 U.S. 1, 6 (1968).

[11] J. L. Case Co. v. Borak, 377 U.S. 426 (1964); Bivens v. Six Unknown Named Agents, 403 U.S. 388 (1971).

[12] *E.g.*, Touche Ross & Co. v. Redington, 442 U.S. 560 (1979); Transamerica Mortgage Advisors, Inc. v. Lewis, 444 U.S. 11 (1979).

[13] Application of the precedents on implied rights might well have led to the conclusion that these provisions gave the plaintiffs no right to sue, either because they were silent on the subject, or because the plaintiffs were not their intended beneficiaries.

[14] 5 U.S.C. § 702.

[15] Davis, *The Liberalized Law of Standing*, 37 U. CHI. L. REV. 450, 466–67 (1970); S. Doc. No. 248, 79th Cong. 2d Sess. 212, 276 (1946) ("This section confers a right of review upon any person adversely affected in fact by agency action or aggrieved within the meaning of any statute"); Scanwell Laboratories, Inc. v. Shaffer, 424 F.2d 859 (D.C. Cir. 1970).

ence to persons affected or aggrieved "within the meaning of a relevant statute" was meant only to incorporate provisions of particular statutes, such as the Communications Act, that gave standing to persons "adversely affected or aggrieved," not to create new rights of its own;[16] and early decisions tended to support this interpretation.[17] The *Data Processing* case,[18] as later summarized by the Court, held "that persons had standing . . . under § 10 of the APA where they had alleged that the challenged action had caused them 'injury in fact,' and where the alleged injury was to an interest 'arguably within the zone of interests to be protected or regulated' by the statutes that the agencies were claimed to have violated."[19] In reaching this conclusion the Court relied on decisions inferring standing from particular substantive provisions for the benefit of the protected class.[20] *Data Processing* can thus be read consistently with the original view of the APA: A person is "adversely affected or aggrieved . . . within the meaning of a relevant statute" only when that statute provides an express or implicit remedy. A more recent decision, however, seems to reject the Attorney General's interpretation without discussing either it or *Data Processing*: Despite finding "no intent to create a private right or action" in a criminal statute protecting confidential information, Justice Rehnquist without explanation held the complaining party " 'adversely affected or aggrieved' within the meaning of § 10(a)."[21] Thus the Court may have backed into the position that the APA is a broad grant of standing indeed; but it did not suggest that the APA authorized suit by any of the plaintiffs in *Warth* or in *Duke Power*.[22]

---

[16] Attorney General's Manual on the Administrative Procedure Act 95–6 (1947).

[17] *E.g.*, Kansas City Power & Light Co. v. McKay, 225 F.2d 924, 931–32 (D.C. Cir. 1955). This reading is consonant with numerous other provisions of the APA. *E.g.*, "Agency subpenas *authorized by law* shall be issued to a party on request . . ."; "Agency action *made reviewable by statute* . . . [is] subject to judicial review." 5 U.S.C. § 555(d), 704 (emphasis added).

[18] See Association of Data Processing Service Organizations v. Camp, note 4 *supra*.

[19] Sierra Club v. Morton, 405 U.S. 727, 733 (1972).

[20] 397 U.S. at 153–56, citing, *inter alia*, Hardin v. Kentucky Utilities Co., note 10 *supra*.

[21] Chrysler Corp. v. Brown, 441 U.S. 281, 317–18 (1979). Apparently it had not been argued that Chrysler was not "adversely affected or aggrieved . . . within the meaning of a relevant statute"; the Court discussed only whether the challenged action was committed to agency discretion.

[22] It could hardly have done so in *Warth*, which was a challenge to state rather than federal action; and while *Duke Power* questionably entertained a claim against the Nuclear Regulatory Commission as well as against a private utility, there was no challenge to any "action" of the federal agency.

Two other general statutes arguably conferring a right to sue, however, were relevant to *Warth v. Seldin*. The first, which the plaintiffs specifically relied on, was the familiar § 1983:[23]

> [Every person who, under color of any statute, ordinance, regulation, custom, or usage, of any State or Territory, subjects . . . any . . . person . . . to the deprivation of any rights, privileges, or immunities secured by the Constitution or laws, shall be liable to the party injured in an action at law, suit in equity, or other proper proceeding for redress.]

This statute plainly authorizes suit by anyone alleging that he has been deprived of rights under the Constitution or federal law, and by no one else. It thus incorporates, but without exceptions, the Court's "prudential" principle that the plaintiff may not assert the rights of third parties; on the Court's view that the provisions in question gave no substantive rights to Penfield residents or to Rochester taxpayers, therefore, § 1983 did not give them a right to sue. Yet the Court did not seem to think it relevant to consider the statute under which the suit had been brought.

The final general provision arguably conferring standing is the Declaratory Judgment Act, which was relevant to both *Warth* and *Duke Power*:[24]

> [In a case of actual controversy within its jurisdiction, . . . any court of the United States . . . may declare the rights and other legal relations of any interested party seeking such declaration.)
> . . . [25]

The implications of this provision for the standing question are obscure. On the one hand, the reference to "a case of actual controversy" might be taken to suggest that the Act confers a right to sue on anyone satisfying the constitutional injury requirement derived from the "controversy" language of Article III. On the other hand, the court is empowered to declare only the "rights" of the "party seeking such declaration," and he must be "interested"; these terms seem both to forbid litigation of third-party rights absolutely and to impose an additional and unfamiliar "interest" requirement

---

[23] 42 U.S.C. § 1983.

[24] 28 U.S.C. § 2201.

[25] The plaintiffs asked the Court in *Warth* to "declare" the ordinance invalid and in *Duke Power* for a "declaration" that the Price-Anderson Act was unconstitutional. 422 U.S. at 496; 438 U.S. at 67.

that goes beyond the constitutional minimum. Finally, in accord
with the phrase "within its jurisdiction," the Supreme Court has
held that the Act "enlarged the range of remedies available in the
federal courts but did not extend their jurisdiction";[26] while standing in the nonconstitutional sense is not strictly speaking a jurisdic-
tional matter,[27] a brief glance at the legislative history suggests the
Act was designed merely to affect the timing and party alignment
of controversies otherwise litigable,[28] not to confer standing on
anyone who otherwise would be without it. In neither *Warth* nor
Duke Power did the Court address the question whether the Declaratory Judgment Act, under which both suits were evidently
brought, gave the plaintiffs a right to sue.

If no statute or constitutional provision authorized the plaintiffs
in *Warth* or *Duke Power* to sue, the sole remaining possibility is the
common law. In the States the doctrine that the injured beneficiary
of a legislative enactment may sue without statutory authorization
has an impressive pedigree.[29] Since the *Erie* decision interpreted the
reference to state "laws" in the Rules of Decision Act[30] to encompass judge-made rules,[31] the lawmaking powers of the federal
courts have been severely limited; the extension of this Act to
equity cases and the repeal of the provision that "the forms and
modes of proceedings in suits of equity . . . shall be according to the
principles, rules, and usages which belong to courts of equity"[32]

[26] Skelly Oil Co. v. Phillips Petroleum Co., 339 U.S. 667, 671 (1950), suggesting that realignment of the parties did not allow evasion of the principle that a case arises under federal law only if that law is the basis of the plaintiff's own claim.

[27] Bell v. Hood, 327 U.S. 678 (1946) (question whether victim of unlawful search may sue for damages goes to merits); Gladstone, Realtors v. Village of Bellwood, 441 U.S. 91, 109, n. 21 (1979) (because not properly raised, "the question whether Bellwood is a 'private person' entitled to sue under § 812 is not properly before us . . .").

[28] "The procedure has been especially useful in avoiding the necessity, now so often present, of having to act at one's peril or to act on one's own interpretation of his rights, or abandon one's rights because of a fear of incurring damages." S. Rep. No. 1005, 73d Cong., 2d Sess. 2 (1934).

[29] See Restatement, Torts § 286 (1934): "The violation of a legislative enactment . . . makes the actor liable for the invasion of an interest of another if: (a) the intent of the enactment is . . . to protect the interest of the other as an individual, and (b) the interest invaded is one which the enactment is intended to protect. . . ."

[30] 28 U.S.C. § 1652: "The laws of the several States, except where the Constitution or treaties of the United States otherwise require or provide, shall be regarded as rules of decision in civil actions in the courts of the United States, in cases where they apply." Contrary to popular rumor, nothing in this section limits its applicability to diversity cases.

[31] Erie R. R. v. Tompkins, 304 U.S. 64 (1938).

[32] 28 U.S.C. § 723 (1934). See Guffey v. Smith, 237 U.S. 101 114 (1915), holding a

seem to remove the basis of the former practice of developing judge-made federal equitable remedies independent of the implications of particular statutes. In any case, neither in *Warth* nor in *Duke Power* did the Court suggest that federal common law gave the plaintiffs a right to sue; nor did it investigate, as the Rules of Decision Act seems to require in the absence of contrary federal legislation, whether the law of any appropriate State did so.[33]

In summary, it is by no means clear that any law gave the plaintiffs in our two cases the right to sue, yet the Court in *Duke Power* upheld a statute on its merits, and in *Warth* ordered a dismissal partly on "prudential" grounds, without ever addressing the threshold question. These are by no means isolated instances; they represent typical Supreme Court practice. Yet if no law gave the plaintiffs the right to sue in *Duke Power*, the Court had no business entertaining the case; and if some statute or constitutional provision did authorize the plaintiffs to sue in *Warth*, one must echo Justice Brennan's doubts as to the right of the Court to invoke its own "prudential" notions to refuse to hear them.[34]

In short, Justice Powell was right that the proper inquiry in nonconstitutional standing cases is whether the law grants the plaintiffs "a right to judicial relief"; but unfortunately the Court failed to pursue this inquiry even in the case in which it was announced.[35]

---

federal injunction available in a diversity case despite state law limiting relief to damages, on the basis of an earlier version of this provision.

[33] A right to sue under state law for violation of a federal right would not, under some persuasive decisions, arise under federal law. See Moore v. Chesapeake & Ohio Ry., 291 U.S. 205 (1934).

[34] "[C]ourts cannot refuse to hear a case on the merits merely because they would prefer not to. . . ." 422 U.S. at 520 (dissenting opinion). See also Thermtron Products, Inc. v. Hermansdorfer, 423 U.S. 336 (1976). It is true that the word "may" in the Declaratory Judgment Act has been taken to make the declaratory remedy to some degree "discretionary," A. L. Mechling Barge Lines, Inc. v. United States, 368 U.S. 324, 331 (1961), and that statutes authorizing injunctive relief can be construed to incorporate traditional equitable limitations such as the need to show irreparable harm. Neither *Warth* nor *Duke Power*, however, attempted to relate the "prudential" standing limitations to traditional equitable principles or to limit them to declaratory actions.

[35] Views similar in some respects to those here expressed can be found in Albert, *Standing to Challenge Administrative Action: An Inadequate Surrogate for Claim for Relief*, 83 YALE L. J. 425 (1974).

RICHARD A. POSNER

RETHINKING THE FOURTH AMENDMENT

This paper, amplifying a brief suggestion in an earlier paper in this series,[1] argues for a new way of looking at the Fourth Amendment prohibition against unreasonable searches and seizures.[2] I start from the premise that the interest a criminal has in avoiding punishment for his crime is not protected by the Fourth Amendment, and argue that if this point is accepted—together with the distinction that I shall emphasize between optimum and maximum deterrence—the objections to relying on tort remedies rather than on the exclusionary rule to enforce the Fourth Amendment are

Richard A. Posner is a Judge of the United States Court of Appeals for the Seventh Circuit.

I am grateful to Frank Easterbrook for discussions of the subject matter of this paper, to Easterbrook, Richard Epstein, Dennis Hutchinson, William Landes, John Langbein, Bernard Meltzer, Geoffrey Stone, Cass Sunstein, and James White for their very helpful comments on previous drafts, and to James Finberg, Patrick Longan, and Edward Wahl for research assistance.

The views expressed in this article (which was, incidentally, completed prior to my appointment to the Seventh Circuit) are, of course, personal rather than official.

[1] See Posner, *The Uncertain Protection of Privacy by the Supreme Court*, 1979 SUP. CT. REV. 173, 185 n.30, reprinted in revised form in POSNER, THE ECONOMICS OF JUSTICE 310, 319 n.20 (1981).

[2] The Fourth Amendment provides: "The right of the people to be secure in their persons, houses, papers, and effects, against unreasonable searches and seizures, shall not be violated; and no Warrants shall issue, but upon probable cause, supported by Oath or affirmation, and particularly describing the place to be searched, and the persons or things to be seized." In Wolf v. Colorado, 338 U.S. 25 (1949), the Supreme Court held that the Fourteenth Amendment applies the prohibitions of the Fourth Amendment to the states. In Mapp v. Ohio, 367 U.S. 643 (1961), the Court held that the judge-made rule that evidence obtained in violation of the Fourth Amendment is inadmissible in a criminal prosecution against the victim of the violation (the "exclusionary rule") also was applicable to the states.

greatly weakened. (Tort remedies are not the only possible alternative to the exclusionary rule, although they are the one I stress in this paper. I shall touch briefly on some others and also explain why I think tort law and the exclusionary rule really are alternative rather than additive.)

The literature on the merits of the exclusionary rule and its tort alternatives is, of course, vast, and it is with diffidence that I add to it. My excuse is that I approach the Fourth Amendment not from the usual directions—that is, not from a background in constitutional law or criminal procedure—but from an interest, heavily economic, in privacy,[3] in remedies,[4] and in tort law.[5] Approaching the Fourth Amendment in this way enables me, I believe, to offer a fresh perspective on the old debate over the exclusionary rule and also on some substantive issues in Fourth Amendment law, notably the meaning of reasonableness (which in my view can be fruitfully explicated in cost-benefit terms) and the relationship between the two clauses of the Fourth Amendment. I conclude by applying my suggested approach to the principal Fourth Amendment cases decided by the Supreme Court last term.

I may seem in this paper to be advocating radical changes in the way in which the Supreme Court interprets and applies the Fourth Amendment. Such changes do indeed seem to me desirable—in principle. But the qualification needs to be stressed. Whether the Court should change direction as sharply as suggested here depends not only on the intrinsic merits of the proposed changes but also on institutional factors, notably the weight to be given the principle of *stare decisis*, that the paper does not discuss.

I. What Interests Does the Fourth Amendment Protect?

The first clause of the Fourth Amendment indicates the interests that the draftsmen wanted to protect. It states: "The right of the people to be secure in their persons, houses, papers, and effects, against unreasonable searches and seizures, shall not be violated. . . ." This right appears to include both (1) property interests of the sort traditionally protected by tort actions for con-

---

[3] See POSNER, THE ECONOMICS OF JUSTICE, pt. III (1981).

[4] See POSNER, ECONOMIC ANALYSIS OF LAW, chs. 6–7, 22 (2d ed. 1977).

[5] See *id.*, ch. 6.

version and for trespass to real and personal property; and (2) interests in bodily integrity, mental tranquillity, and freedom of movement traditionally protected by tort actions for assault, battery, false arrest, false imprisonment, and, more recently, for intentional, reckless, or negligent infliction of mental distress and for invasion of that branch of the right of privacy which protects people against physically intrusive surveillance.[6] The old-fashioned (that is to say, preelectronic) search, or arrest or other seizure, threatens these interests, and the simplest way to read the first clause of the Fourth Amendment is as limiting the defense of legal process for torts committed pursuant to a search or seizure to those cases where the search or seizure was reasonable. Where the search or seizure is done under warrant, the second clause of the Fourth Amendment sets forth the requirements that must be satisfied for possession of the warrant to constitute a defense to a tort action.

This seems to me the minimum content of the Fourth Amendment, but it may also protect, by the same (*i.e.* tort) remedies, a distinct interest: the privacy of information.[7] It is not important to my analysis whether it does—whether, that is, *Katz* is right and *Olmstead* wrong.[8] What is important is that the Fourth Amendment not be seen as protecting the criminal's interest in avoiding punishment. It is a real interest—if the criminal is punished he incurs a cost—but not a lawful interest. This proposition seems to me self-evident, but if evidence is needed I point to two things. First, nowhere does the language of the Fourth Amendment suggest a

---

[6] As in Galella v. Onassis, 487 F.2d 986 (2d Cir. 1973). See POSNER, note 3 *supra*, at 266.

[7] "[T]he word 'privacy' seems to embrace at least two distinct interests. One is the interest in being left alone—the interest that is invaded by the unwanted telephone solicitation, the noisy sound truck, the music in elevators, being jostled in the street, or even an obscene theater billboard or shouted obscenity. This interest is invaded even if the invader is not seeking and does not obtain any information, private or otherwise, about the individual whose peace or quiet—whose seclusion in the broad sense in which I use the term here—is invaded. . . . The other privacy interest, concealment of information, is invaded whenever private information is obtained against the wishes of the person to whom the information pertains. Whether or not the invasion impairs the individual's peace and quiet is irrelevant. Sometimes it will, as where the police stop and search a man for evidence of a crime; sometimes it will not, as where a telephone tap is installed without any entry on the premises of the telephone subscriber. . . ." POSNER, note 3 *supra*, at 272–73.

[8] Olmstead v. United States, 277 U.S. 438 (1928), held that wiretapping was outside the scope of the Fourth Amendment; it was overruled in Katz v. United States, 389 U.S. 347 (1967). The difference between the old-fashioned "barging in" search and electronic surveillance, I argue in POSNER, note 3 *supra*, at 311–12, is the difference between privacy as seclusion in the sense defined in note 7 *supra*, which is not invaded by wiretapping or other unobtrusive surveillance, and privacy as secrecy.

purpose to confer rights on criminal defendants; yet we know from other provisions of the Bill of Rights that when the framers intended to create such rights they expressed their purpose plainly. Second, the English cases that inspired the Fourth Amendment were not criminal cases, in which a defendant was seeking to escape conviction; they were tort cases in which the victims of unreasonable searches were seeking damages for invasion of their lawful interests.[9]

This is not to say that criminals may not invoke the Fourth Amendment. But they may invoke it only on behalf of a lawful interest, that is, an interest distinct from their interest in not being punished for their crimes. Suppose police search a man's house in violation of the Fourth Amendment, and the search uncovers incriminating evidence. He should have no right to prevent the use of that evidence in a criminal proceeding against him; but if in the course of the search the police use force against him, trespass on his land, damage his property, or frighten him, then the search has invaded his lawful interests and he is entitled to a remedy.

In other words, the cost to a criminal of being punished for his crime is not to be considered either in deciding whether the Fourth Amendment has been violated or in devising an appropriate remedy. Detention, apprehension, bodily harm, disruption of routine, invasion of property rights, embarrassment—these are the kinds of insecurity that the Fourth Amendment was intended to protect against; the security of the criminal in being able to commit crimes with impunity is not a protected interest.

Most supporters of the exclusionary rule agree. The rule is usually defended as a method of deterring violations of the Fourth Amendment rather than as an integral part of the Fourth Amendment. Judges and commentators do not—at least usually do not—say that illegally obtained evidence must be excluded because a criminal defendant has a right not to be punished on the basis of such evidence; they say that exclusion is the only sanction that will deter the police from violating the Fourth Amendment.[10]

Even the judicial-integrity rationale of the rule, which stems from Holmes's "dirty business" opinion in *Olmstead*,[11] asserts not

---

[9] See, *e.g.*, TAYLOR, TWO STUDIES IN CONSTITUTIONAL INTERPRETATION 29–35 (1969).

[10] This distinction is sharply drawn in United States v. Calandra, 414 U.S. 338, 347–48 (1974), and Stone v. Powell, 428 U.S. 465, 495 n.37 (1970), among other cases.

[11] 277 U.S. at 470 (dissenting opinion).

that the Fourth Amendment entitles the criminal to prevent illegally obtained evidence from being used against him but that it is unseemly for the courts to use such evidence. Sometimes it is argued that there is a Fourth Amendment right to exclude,[12] but the argument has no support in the text or history or nearly two centuries of judicial interpretation of the Fourth Amendment. And the view that such a right can be derived not from the Fourth but from the Fifth Amendment—the view perhaps implied in *Boyd v. United States*[13]—is discredited.[14] The Fourth Amendment was not intended to give criminals a right to conceal evidence of their crimes.

II. THE APPROPRIATENESS OF RELYING ON TORT REMEDIES TO ENFORCE THE FOURTH AMENDMENT

A. IN PRINCIPLE

If the Fourth Amendment is intended to protect only lawful interests of the kind mentioned in Part I, then tort law would appear to be the first place to look for remedies for violations of the Fourth Amendment. Tort law is the natural avenue for redressing invasions of lawful interests other than breaches of contract; and actions for the torts listed earlier—conversion, false arrest and imprisonment, trespass to land and to chattels, assault, battery, infliction of emotional distress, and invasion of the right of privacy[15]— are the natural avenue for recovering damages for impairment of lawful interests through unreasonable searches and seizures. These actions are available to criminal and noncriminal alike, although naturally a criminal could not hope to recover, as part of his damages, the cost to him of being punished for a crime of which he was guilty; nor should he be compensated for this cost, if the analysis in Part I of this paper is correct.

---

[12] See, *e.g.*, Schrock & Welsh, *Up from Calandra: The Exclusionary Rule as a Constitutional Requirement*, 59 MINN. L. REV. 251 (1974).

[13] 116 U.S. 616 (1886).

[14] See, *e.g.*, TAYLOR, note 9 *supra*, at 59–64. The holding in *Boyd* that the Fifth Amendment shields a person from the use of his documents in evidence against him is no longer good law. See Fisher v. United States, 425 U.S. 391, 408–14 (1976); Andresen v. Maryland, 427 U.S. 463, 471–77 (1976).

[15] Unlawful surveillance, even if unobtrusive, is a tortious invasion of the right of privacy. See POSNER, note 3 *supra*, at 266. Thus the common law torts embrace invasions of every sort of interest that might reasonably be thought protected by the Fourth Amendment.

To this it may be replied that the exclusionary rule is a more potent deterrent to violations of the Fourth Amendment than any tort remedy. No one actually knows how effective the exclusionary rule is as a deterrent,[16] but the issue is in any event immaterial to my analysis. If the exclusionary rule is not an effective deterrent, that is reason enough to abandon it since, as mentioned earlier, deterrence is the *raison d'être* of the rule. If it is a more powerful deterrent than the tort remedy, an anomaly is produced: an innocent person who is injured as the result of an unreasonable search or seizure has only the lesser, the tort remedy; only the criminal gets the benefit of the greater remedy. True, the innocent derive an indirect benefit from the exclusionary rule. The rule deters some police searches, and some of these might be searches of people who turned out not to be criminals. But the worst kind of police search is not deterred at all: the search of the known innocent for purposes purely of harassment. The innocent are not the primary beneficiaries of a remedial system that puts its main emphasis on the exclusionary rule.

More importantly, while the tort remedy can be adjusted, through the rules (discussed below) relating to assessment of damages, to yield the optimum level of deterrence, the exclusionary rule has no readily apparent mechanism for adjustment. It deters too little or too much; only by accident would it deter optimally. And if it deters too much it is just as bad as if it deterred too little. The tort remedy thus seems preferable (at least in principle), even from a deterrent standpoint, once the concept of optimum, as distinct from maximum, deterrence is introduced.

Optimum deterrence is the subject of an extensive economic literature which teaches that the penalty for an offense should be set at the level that imposes on the offender a cost equal to the harm caused, as raised to reflect the possibility of his escaping punishment.[17] The punishment must not be milder than this, but neither

---

[16] See Oaks, *Studying the Exclusionary Rule in Search and Seizure*, 37 U. CHI. L. REV. 665 (1970).

[17] The analysis, which goes back to Bentham, received its classic modern statement in Becker, *Crime and Punishment: An Economic Approach*, 76 J. POL. ECON. 169 (1968). Somewhat oversimplified, the formula for the optimum penalty is $f = C/p$, where f is fine, C is the cost to victims of the offense, and p is the probability of apprehension and conviction. Thus, if the probability of apprehending some offender were .1, and the cost of the offense $1,000, the optimum fine would be $10,000. Since the chance of its being imposed would be only one in ten, the prospective offender would face an expected punishment cost of $1,000, just equal to the cost of the offense to the victim. For "fine" one can read "damages" without loss of meaning.

should it be more severe. It is true that if the forbidden conduct were defined with perfect clarity and precision the optimum severity of the sanction would be limited only by the cost of imposing it. Since the threat of sanction would deter 100 percent, the sanction itself would never be imposed—its severity would just magnify the threat and not be a cost actually incurred by anyone. But because unlawful conduct can never be defined with perfect clarity and precision, savage penalties will deter lawful as well as unlawful conduct—will lead people to forgo socially valuable activities near the uncertain boundary.[18]

This analysis is pertinent to violations of the Fourth Amendment. A standard of reasonableness is inherently rather vague. If policemen and their employers were punished savagely for infractions of the Fourth Amendment, much lawful and proper police work would be deterred. The police would be too careful; they would steer far clear of the Fourth Amendment rather than stay just outside its (vague) boundaries. Now the exclusionary rule does not impose savage penalties on policemen and other law-enforcement personnel, but it imposes penalties that often exceed the social costs of their Fourth Amendment violations. Consider the following example. Because of some oversight a search warrant is invalid and, as a result, evidence essential to the conviction of a dangerous criminal is suppressed. The cost to the criminal of this Fourth Amendment violation is $100 (a valid warrant would have limited the scope of the search and so avoided a minor interference with the criminal's possessions and repose), while the cost to the community of letting him go free is $10,000. The sanction in this case is excessive, unless only one percent of Fourth Amendment violations are caught, which seems unlikely. In the long run, the threat of such sanctions will overdeter searches and seizures by the police.

The numbers in the example are arbitrary, but the disparity between the actual costs of the unlawful search to the victim and the social costs of the sanction, exclusion, is real; and it is real even where the evidence that is excluded is not essential to the prosecution's case, but merely helpful to it. The example assumes, of course, that the exclusionary rule does deter. But if it does not,

---

[18] This point has been emphasized in discussions of the economics of tort law. See, *e.g.*, Landes & Posner, *An Economic Theory of Intentional Torts*, 1 INT'L REV. L. & ECON. 127, 135–36 (1981).

then, to repeat a previous point, the rule cannot be defended as a superior deterrent, and that is the principal defense offered of it.

I am trying to give some precision to the widely shared intuition that the exclusionary rule is an exceptionally crude deterrent device. It is not merely crude; to the extent obeyed, it systematically overdeters, because it imposes social costs that are greatly disproportionate to the actual harm to lawful interests from unreasonable searches and seizures.[19] The tort remedy can be calibrated to yield optimum deterrence; the exclusionary rule cannot be.

It is no answer that substituting a tort remedy for the exclusionary rule would encourage the police to violate the Fourth Amendment whenever it paid to do so. Go back to my example of the search that imposes a cost of $100 on the criminal because the warrant is invalid, but excluding the unlawfully obtained evidence and letting him go free would impose a cost on the community of $10,000. Assume (points to be amplified in Part III of this paper) (1) that the warrant clause of the Fourth Amendment is designed to particularize the standard of reasonableness set forth in the first clause, and (2) that here, as in tort law generally, "reasonable" is at least a rough synonym for "cost-justified." It follows that the $100 injury to lawful interests brought about because the warrant was invalid could have been avoided at a cost of less than $100. If so, having to pay damages of $100 will give the police an incentive to obtain valid warrants—provided the tort remedy is a meaningful one, an issue taken up in the next section.

The distinction between deterrence *per se* and optimum deterrence that is at the heart of my analysis in this section of the paper has often eluded commentators on constitutional torts. Consider the following comment by Professor Whitman: "*Carey*[20] also ac-

---

[19] The element of disproportionality in the exclusionary rule has been remarked frequently. "The disparity in particular cases between the error committed by the police and the windfall afforded a guilty defendant by application of the rule is contrary to the idea of proportionality that is essential to the concept of justice." Stone v. Powell, 428 U.S. 465, 490 (1976). See also Allen, *Federalism and the Fourth Amendment: A Requiem for Wolf*, 1961 SUP. CT. REV. 1, 35–37. But my analysis is based on the concept of optimum deterrence rather than on the idea of justice as proportionality. In the antitrust area, it should be noted, the Court has recognized the "possibility of overdeterrence; salutary and procompetitive conduct lying close to the borderline of impermissible conduct might be shunned by businessmen who chose to be excessively cautious in the face of uncertainty regarding possible exposure to criminal punishment for even a good-faith error of judgment." United States v. United States Gypsum Co., 438 U.S. 422, 441 (1978).

[20] [Carey v. Piphus, 435 U.S. 247 (1978); see note 38 *infra* and accompanying text.— Auth.]

cepted the proposition that, in a procedural due process case, a defendant could defeat a claim for damages by demonstrating that the plaintiff would have suffered these damages in the absence of a due process violation—for instance, that a dismissed employee would have been fired even if a proper hearing had been held. This rule makes sense if the purpose of the action is compensation for injuries incurred; it makes less sense if the action is to serve a significant role as a deterrent."[21] But if the employee would have been fired anyway, the violation of his rights imposed no cost on him; hence an award of damages would overdeter. The relevant distinction is not between compensation and deterrence but between the right amount of deterrence and too much deterrence. Only if seemingly harmless violations of constitutional rights are somehow harmful after all—a possibility considered in the next section of this paper—does it make any sense to divorce damages awarded from damages sustained.

Commentators ignore the distinction between simple and optimum deterrence in another way. I have never read a discussion of the Fourth Amendment in which the author expressed concern that a combination of the exclusionary rule and an effective tort remedy might produce overdeterrence. But it would. Suppose, as is indeed the case under existing law, that a criminal could both bar the use of unconstitutionally obtained evidence against him and obtain damages for the invasion of his lawful interests by the search. He would clearly be overcompensated. This does not trouble advocates of the exclusionary rule, and this can only be because they do not understand that there can be such a thing as too much deterrence of violations of constitutional rights.

There is still another point. When the sanction for a violation of the Fourth Amendment takes the form of a money judgment, there is a transfer of wealth from the violator (or the government agency that employs him) to the victim of the violation, but there is no net reduction in the wealth or welfare of society. When the sanction takes the form of suppressing probative evidence, there is a net social cost. Either the police must expend resources to obtain other and equally good evidence, or the probability of convicting a guilty criminal is reduced (for there is no doubt that most criminal defendants who move to suppress evidence are guilty—usually it is the

---

[21] Whitman, *Constitutional Torts*, 79 MICH. L. REV. 5, 49 n.221 (1980).

fruits or instrumentality of crime that they are trying to exclude).
The increase in administrative costs and reduction in the probability of convicting the guilty (and consequent impairment in the deterrent, incapacitative, and retributive efficacy of criminal punishment) are, in the economist's language, "deadweight losses" caused
by the exclusionary rule. These losses would be avoided by the tort
approach. Thus, not only does the exclusionary rule overdeter; for
any given level of deterrence it is a more costly deterrent device
than tort damages would be.

B. IN PRACTICE

There are many tort remedies for violation of the Fourth
Amendment. The *Bivens* case held that federal officers may be sued
in tort directly under the Fourth Amendment.[22] The agency employing them may be sued under the Federal Tort Claims Act.[23]
State officers may be sued in federal court under 42 U.S.C. § 1983,
one of the federal civil rights acts,[24] and so (in some circumstances)
may the municipalities employing them.[25] The officers and their
municipal employers may also be suable directly under the Fourteenth Amendment.[26] The entire array of common law torts listed
earlier in this paper—assault, battery, false arrest, false imprisonment, trespass to land and to chattels, conversion, infliction of emotional distress, and invasion of the right of privacy—is also available to victims of Fourth Amendment violations suing state or
municipal officers in state courts,[27] and if the officer raises a defense

---

[22] See Bivens v. Six Unknown Named Agents of Fed. Bureau of Narcotics, 403 U.S. 388
(1971).

[23] As amended in 1974 to impose liability on the United States for intentional torts by its
law-enforcement officers. See 28 U.S. C. § 2680(h); Norton v. United States, 581 F.2d 390
(4th Cir. 1978).

[24] See, *e.g.*, Monroe v. Pape, 365 U.S. 167 (1961); Davis v. Murphy, 559 F.2d 1098 (7th
Cir. 1977). Section 1983, so far as pertinent here, provides damages and injunctive remedies
to people who are deprived of their constitutional rights under color of state law.

[25] See Monell v. New York City Dept. of Social Services, 436 U.S. 658 (1978); Owen v.
City of Independence, 445 U.S. 622 (1980). For a municipality to be liable under section
1983, however, the plaintiff must show a municipal policy of constitutional
infringement—that is, he must show that the municipality violated the Constitution, not
merely that it employed someone who violated the Constitution in the course of his employment. See, *e.g.*, *Monell*, *supra*, 436 U.S. at 691–94.

[26] See, *e.g.*, Nix v. Sweeney, 573 F.2d 998 (8th Cir. 1978); Classon v. Krautkramer, 451 F.
Supp. 12 (E.D. Wis. 1977).

[27] See, *e.g.*, Whirl v. Kern, 407 F.2d 781 (5th Cir. 1968); Jenkins v. Averett, 424 F.2d 1228
(4th Cir. 1970); Prahl v. Brosamle, 98 Wis. 2d 130, 295 N.W.2d 768 (1980). Notice that these

of legal process, the plaintiff can set up the Fourth Amendment to bar that defense. In states that have waived their immunity to tort liability, the state or municipal agency employing the officer also is liable for his torts, if committed in furtherance of his official duties.[28]

But ever since Foote's classic article[29] it has been argued that tort remedies for Fourth Amendment violations are inadequate in practice. Three main points are made. First, the damages awarded, even if computed fairly, are apt to be too small to deter; in fact, they may be too small to motivate the plaintiff to sue even if he has a good claim. Second, damages will not be computed fairly, because the jury will be unsympathetic to a plaintiff who is, as in most cases he will be, a criminal. Third, the officer who violates the Fourth Amendment is unlikely to have the means to pay a large damage judgment, while his employer, a state or federal agency, may be shielded from liability for his torts by the doctrine of sovereign immunity. Furthermore, the officer himself may have an immunity defense, and it may be imputed to the agency employing him if the agency is sued.

These points are related. They amount to saying that the plaintiff in the average Fourth Amendment tort action will not collect a large judgment. This is true but it is not necessarily a criticism of the tort remedy. The goal is not simply to deter violations of the Fourth Amendment; it is optimum deterrence. Simple deterrence would argue for sanctions of unlimited severity; optimum deterrence scales the sanction to the violation, and if the costs of the violation are slight, so should be the sanction.

This is a telling point against the first two objections to the tort remedy. The typical violation of the Fourth Amendment does not impose substantial costs on the victim. If only because the police have limited resources which they try to conserve, the typical violation consists not of harassment of the innocent but of overzealous enforcement against the guilty. As I said earlier, while the criminal is not an outlaw with no rights under the Fourth Amendment, the only interests for the invasion of which he is entitled to damages are

---

cases are frequently brought in federal court as pendent claims to a section 1983 claim, thus giving the plaintiff two strings to his bow.

[28] See, *e.g.*, Reeves v. City of Jackson, 532 F.2d 491 (5th Cir. 1976). The tangled issue of immunities is considered in greater detail below.

[29] *Tort Remedies for Police Violations of Individual Rights*, 39 MINN. L. REV. 493 (1955).

lawful interests—interests in property, bodily integrity, reputation, and mental repose. Of course these interests, especially the
last two, are apt to be valued at a rather low rate when a criminal is
asserting them. Suppose the police break into a drug peddler's
house unlawfully and find contraband drugs. The drug peddler
could seek damages for the fright or emotional upset caused him by
the illegal entry, but probably the damages awarded would be
small; a person engaged in a dangerous, illegal business is likely to
have greater emotional fortitude than the average person. We do
not consider it anomalous that a thick-skulled man involved in an
automobile accident will probably have a smaller damage claim
than a thin-skulled man. It is no more anomalous that a criminal,
especially an experienced one, should on average receive a smaller
damage award for emotional distress caused by an illegal search
than a person of ordinary sensitivity—and so with injury to reputation.

The argument with respect to the jury's probable lack of sympathy with a criminal plaintiff is parallel. If lack of sympathy reflects simply a healthy skepticism that the average criminal really
suffers a serious injury from an illegal search, well and good; such
skepticism is the sensible attitude to bring to the task of computing
damages in such a case. Experience in other areas of tort law
suggests that a criminal who is seriously injured in an illegal search
or seizure will be able to convince a jury to award him substantial
damages.[30] If the jury's prejudice against criminals prevents it from
computing damages fairly, it is the judge's duty to set aside the
jury's verdict. Incidentally, if it is true that juries are incapable of
rendering justice to a litigant who does not engage their sym-
pathies, and judges incapable of correcting these injustices, this is a
condemnation of the jury system that cannot be limited to the
context of defending the exclusionary rule. Yet one doubts that
many defenders of the exclusionary rule would support a radical
curtailment of the jury's role in our legal system.

But to all this the reply may be made that even if the damage
caused by a violation of the Fourth Amendment usually is slight, so

---

[30] For example, in Katko v. Briney, 183 N.W.2d 657 (Ia. 1971), a jury verdict of $20,000
in compensatory damages and $10,000 in punitive damages was upheld in an action brought
by a thief, Katko, against the victims of his thefts, the Brineys. Mr. Briney had set a spring
gun which wounded Katko. For a good discussion of damages calculation in Fourth Amendment actions see Rhoads v. Horvat, 270 F. Supp. 307 (D. Colo. 1967).

that it is appropriate from a tort-law perspective that the damages awarded in Fourth Amendment tort cases should usually be small, the perspective is all wrong. Damage remedies come into play only if someone is injured. What if we want the Fourth Amendment to be obeyed even if its violations cause no harm to anyone? A tort remedy will not induce compliance in these circumstances. But the text and history of the Fourth Amendment do not evince a purpose beyond protecting the specific right, declared in the first clause, to be secure in one's person and property against unreasonable searches and seizures; and if that right is not impaired, a violation of the Fourth Amendment really is harmless. The Fourth Amendment was intended to limit the defense of legal process in tort suits against public officers or agencies; that intention presupposes the tort suit as the basic method of remedying violations.

The Fourth Amendment differs in this respect from the First Amendment. The latter protects among other things the dissemination of unpopular opinions ("freedom for the thought that we hate," as Holmes put it),[31] which makes the problem of jury prejudice especially acute. Moreover, it protects the dissemination of such opinions in the interest not only of the people propagating them but also of the intended audience and of the vitality of the political order as a whole. Society could not rely entirely on tort law to protect these interests.

Another example of a right that cannot be effectively enforced through tort actions alone is the right to vote. Damages have been awarded in actions for denial of the right to vote,[32] but it would be impractical to rely solely on the tort system to enforce that right. The injury to someone who is prevented from voting is usually negligible, since in very few elections does a single vote change the result. The real cost is not to the person who is denied the vote but to the democracy and stability of the political order—that is, to the rest of us. This cost cannot be quantified, or its bearers even identified.

Some may argue that the Fourth Amendment, too, protects interests that cannot be vindicated in tort actions; that, for example, rampant police violations of the Fourth Amendment would create a climate of fear affecting millions of people each too slightly to sup-

---

[31] United States v. Schwimmer, 279 U.S. 644, 655 (1928) (dissenting opinion).

[32] See, *e.g.*, Nixon v. Herndon, 273 U.S. 536 (1927).

port a tort action, even if they had standing to sue. But the individual who will have a tort action if he is subjected to an illegal search or seizure has nothing to fear from the police unless the tort remedy is ineffective. If his lawful interests are invaded, he will be compensated. More likely, there will be no invasion; the threat of tort liability will deter.

The idea that only the exclusionary rule stands between us and a reign of police terror, or at least a wave of official lawlessness that will sap faith in the Constitution and the Rule of Law, is parochial. There are other civilized countries in the world, and none excludes unlawfully obtained evidence to the extent we do.[33] Before the *Mapp* decision imposed it on the states, few states in this country had the exclusionary rule; yet it is hard to believe that faith in the Constitution and the Rule of Law was less robust before *Mapp* was decided than it is today.

All this is not to deny the difficulties of formulating tort remedies that will deter violations of the Fourth Amendment effectively. Some of the difficulties have been indicated, but there are others; for example, some people may fear reprisals if they sue the police. Other difficulties are discussed below. But still there is a fundamental difference between the use of tort law to enforce the right to vote or freedom of speech on the one hand, and to enforce the Fourth Amendment on the other. The problems with the Fourth Amendment tort remedy are real, but they hardly seem insoluble. In contrast to the right to vote and freedom of speech, the nature of the right protected by the Fourth Amendment invites the private-law perspective of this paper.[34]

Before turning to the question of immunities, I want to discuss briefly two other aspects of the tort remedy. First, where a violation is concealable, then, as mentioned earlier, merely compensatory damages will not produce optimum deterrence; the damage award should be increased to reflect the probability that offenders will escape punishment. This can be done by awarding punitive damages. They are frequently awarded in cases of intentional tort, and the torts committed in the course of a search or seizure—trespass,

---

[33] But in Germany, for example, compliance with the legal restrictions on searches and seizures is obtained by administrative and criminal sanctions rather than by tort liability. See LANGBEIN, COMPARATIVE CRIMINAL PROCEDURE: GERMANY 68–70 (1977).

[34] *Cf.* Epstein, *Private-Law Models for Official Immunity*, 42 LAW & CONTEMP. PROB., Winter 1978, at 53.

false arrest, etc.—are intentional torts (though in some cases the victim of an illegal search might bring an action for negligent rather than intentional infliction of emotional distress). Thus, there is no doctrinal obstacle to awarding punitive damages in appropriate cases of Fourth Amendment violation. They would be especially appropriate where a pattern of deliberate concealment of such violations was proved.[35]

Second, what is to be done if a Fourth Amendment violation that inflicts too little damage to justify the expenses of suing is part of a pattern of violations that in total impose substantial costs on the community? If the police of some city adopted a policy of illegal searches in a particular neighborhood and the result was to impose costs, but small costs, on each of thousands of people, no one would have a strong incentive to bring a damage suit. The expected damages probably would be less than the plaintiff's cost of suit, for, even if his direct expenses were trivial because they would be borne by legal aid or would be recoverable from the defendant,[36] there would still be a time cost to the plaintiff. Yet the total damages, aggregated across all the victims of the police misconduct, might be large. However, in such a case either a class action could be brought or injunctive relief—which would require only that one of the many victims of the wrong be willing to bear a part of the expenses of the suit—could be sought.[37]

Another possibility, though one the Supreme Court properly rejected in a recent section 1983 case,[38] is to award "general" damages, unrelated to any provable harm, in Fourth Amendment cases. The model is the award of general damages in defamation cases. But defamation injures a thing of real, though hard to measure,

---

[35] Punitive damages have, of course, been awarded in Fourth Amendment tort actions. See, e.g., Rhoads v. Horvat, 270 F. Supp. 307 (D. Colo. 1967), and cases discussed there. In a more recent case, Zarcone v. Perry, 572 F.2d 52 (2d Cir. 1978), an award of $61,000 in punitive damages was upheld where a judge and a deputy sheriff had handcuffed, tongue-lashed, and threatened legal action against a coffee vendor because the judge thought a cup of coffee he bought from the vendor "putrid."

[36] As under the Civil Rights Attorney's Fees Awards Act of 1976, 42 U.S.C. § 1988. See, e.g., Milwe v. Cavuoto, 653 F.2d 80 (2d Cir. 1981).

[37] The class-action route is illustrated by Sullivan v. Murphy, 478 F.2d 938 (D.C. Cir. 1973), the injunctive route by the same case and also by Wheaton v. Hagan, 435 F. Supp. 1134 (M.D. N.C. 1977). But the Supreme Court has placed tight limitations on the exercise of the equity power in these circumstances, see Rizzo v. Goode, 423 U.S. 362 (1976), and rightly so, lest the injunctive route create the same overdeterrence as the exclusionary rule.

[38] See Carey v. Piphus, 435 U.S. 247 (1978), and, for criticism, Note, *Damage Awards in Constitutional Torts: A Reconsideration after* Carey v. Piphus, 93 HARV. L. REV. 966 (1980).

value to the plaintiff—his reputation—while if a Fourth Amendment violation does not impair the bodily integrity or freedom of movement or mental repose of the victim—all staple items of compensatory damage calculation in tort suits—it injures nothing (except that reputation is one of the lawful interests that a search might invade, and in an appropriate case, therefore, general damages might be allowed for loss of reputation caused by an unconstitutional search). The general-damages approach has little to recommend it even in the case of the large but diffuse injury caused by a pattern of illegal searches and seizures. Class actions and injunctions are a much better solution to that problem because they are designed, as general damages are not, to deal with it and are therefore less likely than general damages to produce the characteristic vice of the exclusionary rule—overdeterrence—in a different form.

The concern of the critics of the tort solution with the probable small size of the average Fourth Amendment tort claim implicitly acknowledges the premise of my argument, which is that the criminal's interest in not being punished for his crime is not protected by the Fourth Amendment. If it were a protected interest, there would be no problem with the size of the tort claim. The principal item of damage would be the costs to the criminal of the deprivation of liberty resulting from his conviction and would ordinarily be substantial. That no one thinks such costs recoverable in a tort action, even in principle, is further evidence that the Fourth Amendment does not create a right not to be convicted on the basis of illegally obtained evidence.

It would be a mistake to dwell too long on the problem of the small claim. Substantial harms resulting from illegal searches and seizures should be readily remediable in tort actions (subject to resolution of the immunities question discussed next), and this offers promise that at least the worst violations of the Fourth Amendment can be fully compensated, and so deterred, through the tort system.

A major problem with the tort approach is immunities.[39] Both the immunity of the officer (official immunity) and the immunity of the government agency that employs him (governmental or sovereign immunity) must be considered. Within these categories, fur-

---

[39] For a helpful discussion see Bermann, *Integrating Governmental and Officer Tort Liability*, 77 COLUM. L. REV. 1175 (1977).

ther distinctions—between the states and the federal government, and at the state level between the state and its municipalities—are necessary.

Under standard tort doctrine, public officers at the searching and arresting level are immune from personal liability for torts committed by them in the course of their employment, so long as they are acting in good faith.[40] This qualified immunity has been held applicable to Fourth Amendment tort suits,[41] for reasons that can be put into economic terms along lines recently suggested for the closely related tort defense of public necessity.[42] The key concept is that of "external benefit." A benefit is said to be externalized if the person conferring it does not receive the full value of the benefit to society. The external character of the benefit does not, of course, lessen its value; it just makes it hard to get people to produce external benefits. One way to encourage their production is by externalizing some or all of their costs. This makes them cheaper to produce and increases the likelihood they will be produced despite the lack of payoff to the creator. That is why, if someone pulls down a house in the path of a fire and saves the city, we do not make him compensate the owner of the house for its destruction; we do not want the prospect of such liability to deter what is after all a merely altruistic, so presumably only weakly motivated, public good. The principle applies to law enforcement. The police are paid a salary, and little or no effort is made to vary it in accordance with results actually achieved. A successful police officer will rise faster in his profession than an unsuccessful one and hence will be compensated indirectly for his successes, but the link between compensation and performance is a loose one. If he is made personally liable for his mistakes he will be too cautious, because he will be liable for the full social costs of mistakes resulting from excessive zeal but will not reap the full social gains of the successes that zeal produces.[43]

---

[40] See PROSSER, HANDBOOK OF THE LAW OF TORTS 989 (4th ed. 1971).

[41] See, *e.g.*, Bivens v. Six Unknown Named Agents of the Fed. Bureau of Narcotics, 456 F.2d 1339 (2d Cir. 1972); Bryan v. Jones, 530 F.2d 1210 (5th Cir. 1973); DAVIS, ADMINISTRATIVE LAW OF THE SEVENTIES 579–84 (1976).

[42] See Landes & Posner, *Salvors, Finders, Good Samaritans, and Other Rescuers: An Economic Study of Law and Altruism*, 7 J. LEGAL STUD. 83, 128 (1978).

[43] See Mashaw, *Civil Liability of Government Officers: Property Rights and Official Accountability*, 42 LAW & CONTEMP. PROB., Winter 1978, at 8, 26–27.

Notice that this is the opposite of the argument sometimes given for the good-faith immunity, which is that only willful or negligent misconduct is deterrable.[44] That is not a persuasive argument. If the penalty for a violation of the Fourth Amendment is large enough, officers will take steps to reduce the probability of committing even innocent violations. Such violations are not unavoidable; they can be avoided by steering far clear of the forbidden zone.

Whatever should be the precise scope of the official immunity for Fourth Amendment torts, the general principle seems valid. At the same time, it is (or would be, were it not for the possibility, discussed below, of imputing the officer's immunity to the agency employing him) largely of academic interest, because the average policeman will be judgment proof except where the damages are too small to make the suit worth bringing.[45] The standard solution to this problem in the tort law is to make the employer liable for the torts of his employees committed in furtherance of their employment and thereby give the employer an incentive, which the tort law cannot impart directly to the (judgment-proof) employee, to prevent tortious conduct.[46] This principle (respondeat superior) ought to be applied to Fourth Amendment as well as ordinary torts. If the city or state or federal government is liable for the costs that its officers' Fourth Amendment violations impose on society, it will have an incentive to reduce the incidence of those violations by more careful screening, training, and supervision of its law-enforcement personnel. No doubt monetary incentives are less effective in the case of public than in the case of private enterprises, but they cannot be completely ineffectual, especially in the present era of profound concern with the expenses of government at all levels. And if law-enforcement agencies do not respond to incentives, the deterrent rationale of the exclusionary rule collapses as well.

There are, however, two doctrinal obstacles to using respondeat superior in Fourth Amendment tort actions. One is the principle of

---

[44] See, e.g., Michigan v. Tucker, 417 U.S. 433, 447 (1974); United States v. Williams, 622 F.2d 830, 840, 842 (5th Cir. 1980).

[45] But see Sexton v. Gibbs, 327 F. Supp. 134 (N.D. Tex. 1970), awarding $750 in damages in an action against police officers. However, plaintiff had sought $5,000.

[46] For an economic formulation of this rationale, see Landes & Posner, *The Positive Economic Theory of Tort Law*, forthcoming in GEORGIA LAW REVIEW.

governmental immunity; the other is the possibility of treating the liability of the government agency as purely derivative from the liability of the individual officer and thereby making the officer's qualified immunity from suit a defense in an action against the agency as well.

The federal government has waived its immunity in the Federal Tort Claims Act, which, as noted earlier, now allows damage suits against the United States for violations of the Fourth Amendment by federal officers. The situation with regard to states and municipalities is more complicated. The Eleventh Amendment to the Constitution guarantees the states immunity from damage actions, although apparently only in suits brought in federal court.[47] And while almost all the states have waived their governmental immunity to some extent, the waiver is not always broad enough to assure complete relief in an action for a Fourth Amendment violation.[48] The Supreme Court could cure any inadequacies in state immunity rules either by deciding that the Fourteenth Amendment requires the states to provide effective tort remedies for violations of the Fourth Amendment, an approach suggested by *Wolf v. Colorado*,[49] or by announcing that it will abandon the exclusionary rule only in states that provide an effective tort remedy for Fourth Amendment violations. Either solution, however, would inject the Court deeply into the tort systems of the states, and such an intrusion seems unwarranted at this time given that the trend in the states is against governmental immunity.

A problem remains if, as the Fourth Circuit has held in regard to the Federal Tort Claims Act, the government agency's liability is viewed as purely derivative from the individual officer's, so that any defense he could assert in a suit against him the agency can assert in a suit against it.[50] The approach has a certain logical appeal: Respondeat superior is a doctrine of vicarious or derivative liability; therefore the employing agency cannot be liable unless the officer

---

[47] The language of the Eleventh Amendment, which refers to the judicial power of the United States, so suggests, and Nevada v. Hall, 440 U.S. 410 (1978), so holds.

[48] See Bermann, note 39 *supra*, at 1177. For a general discussion of governmental tort immunity today, see Davis, note 41 *supra*, ch. 25. And for a proposal to broaden governmental liability for constitutional torts, see Schuck, *Suing Our Servants: The Court, Congress, and the Liability of Public Officials for Damages*, 1980 SUP. CT. REV. 281, 346–60.

[49] See 338 U.S. at 28, 31.

[50] See Norton v. United States, 581 F.2d 390 (4th Cir. 1978).

would have been liable in a suit against him directly; therefore the agency should be allowed to assert any defense he could have asserted. But as Holmes said, a syllogism cannot wag its tail.[51] The reason for official immunity does not apply in a suit against the agency rather than the officer. The liability of the agency is corporate rather than personal, so there is no prospect of crushing liability to induce excessive caution. Liability is desirable because it gives the agency an incentive to minimize the "good faith" unconstitutional errors of its police through more careful selection, training, and supervision. This, incidentally, is why attempting to calibrate the exclusionary rule by recognizing a good-faith exception would be the wrong approach: it would swing the pendulum of the exclusionary rule from overdeterrence to underdeterrence by removing the incentive of law-enforcement agencies to take measures to minimize good-faith violations of the Fourth Amendment.

If the principle of *Norton* is rejected, if punitive damages are awarded in proper cases, if judges deal firmly with jury prejudice, if imagination is used in valuing intangible items of damage such as loss of mental repose, and if class-action treatment and injunctive relief are granted in appropriate cases, then, I believe, the tort remedy will bring us closer to optimum deterrence of Fourth Amendment violations than the exclusionary rule. Some may think it a choice merely between underdeterrence and overdeterrence. But there is a crucial difference. It is conjectural that the tort remedy will underdeter; it is certain that the exclusionary rule, to the extent enforced, overdeters—it is calculated to overdeter. And if there is a danger that the tort remedy will underdeter, it is much less acute than when Foote wrote his famous criticism of the remedy more than twenty-five years ago. Since that time, as every tort lawyer knows but constitutional lawyers may be unaware, tort liability has exploded, and in every area of tort law the balance has shifted in favor of plaintiffs in regard both to liability and to damages. Besides this general trend, which favors all tort plaintiffs, the proliferation of constitutional tort remedies, the provision for awarding attorneys' fees to successful plaintiffs in section 1983 actions, and the decline in governmental immunity have lightened the burden of the Fourth Amendment tort plaintiff specifically.

---

[51] See Letter to John C. H. Wu, in THE MIND AND FAITH OF JUSTICE HOLMES 419 (Lerner ed. 1943).

A word should be said about other remedies for Fourth Amendment violations besides the tort remedy and the exclusionary rule. They range from better selection and training of police officers to administrative and even criminal sanctions against them when they violate the Fourth Amendment. I offer just three observations. First, to the extent that the tort remedy is workable, it should accomplish the objectives of the other approaches and make them superfluous: for example, the threat of liability should give enforcement agencies incentives to institute procedures for screening and training officers that minimize violations. Second, the danger of overdeterrence through cumulation of remedies is a serious one: for example, subjecting the police to both civil and criminal remedies for unlawful searches may make them too cautious. Third, if we cannot, therefore, just keep piling on remedies for Fourth Amendment violations willy-nilly, but must choose among them, the choice should be made on the basis of cost-benefit analysis. The question should be: Which remedy produces the greatest benefit in compliance with the Fourth Amendment at the least cost to other objectives? This question cannot be answered without a full examination, which I have not attempted, of all possible remedies.

A final point of contrast between the tort remedy and the exclusionary rule should be noted: the former has a firmer constitutional basis. Once it is conceded that the exclusionary rule is not a part of the Fourth Amendment itself, as most courts and commentators do, a question arises as to its source in the Constitution; the answer is not obvious. There is no similar problem with the tort approach. Remedies for assault, battery, false arrest, and other torts that may be committed in the course of a search or seizure are available under state law and under 42 U.S.C. § 1983; they do not have to be created by the Supreme Court. Even if there were no federal-court remedy against federal officers under the Fourth Amendment, either directly (as held in *Bivens*—itself an example of questionable judicial creativity) or indirectly under section 1983, federal officers would be suable in state court. Any effort of the federal government to immunize them beyond the qualified immunity traditionally recognized by tort law would violate the Fourth Amendment, the central purpose of which was to ensure the availability of state remedies for unreasonable searches and seizures even where the defendant was a federal officer acting under the authority of a federal warrant or statute.

C. SOME EFFECTS OF THE TORT APPROACH

An obvious, but still interesting, effect of substituting the tort approach for the exclusionary rule should be noted: there would be many fewer cases, at all levels of the state and federal judicial systems, involving the Fourth Amendment. If every victim of a trivial tort were entitled to actual damages plus $100,000, the courts would be flooded with trivial tort cases. A comparable situation has been created by the exclusionary rule. Although the actual damages caused by most Fourth Amendment violations are slight, the (criminal) victim of such a violation has an incentive to litigate his rights to the hilt, because if he prevails he may get a tremendous windfall—he may avoid criminal punishment. It is a windfall because, as I have emphasized, the Fourth Amendment does not give criminals a right not to be convicted on the basis of illegally seized, but probative, evidence. By scaling down the sanction for Fourth Amendment violations to a level where it is proportional to the actual costs of those violations, courts will be freed from having to adjudicate claims of criminal defendants seeking these windfalls.[52]

This analysis also has implications for the judicial-integrity argument for the exclusionary rule. It is widely assumed that if the rule were abandoned the result would be the unseemly spectacle of courts regularly convicting people on the basis of evidence procured unconstitutionally. But this is unlikely to happen with great frequency if the tort approach works. The reason is that the Fourth Amendment is not a strict-liability law.

The economic analysis of tort law draws a sharp distinction between strict liability and negligence as grounds of tort liability.[53]

---

[52] A recent study estimates that 32.6 percent of all federal criminal defendants who actually go to trial file motions, based on the Fourth Amendment, to suppress evidence, and that nearly all of these motions are decided in formal hearings. See IMPACT OF THE EXCLUSIONARY RULE ON FEDERAL CRIMINAL PROSECUTIONS: REPORT OF THE COMPTROLLER GENERAL OF THE UNITED STATES 10 (U.S. Gov't Accounting Office, Rep. No. GD-79-45, April 19, 1979). Although most of these motions are denied, see ibid., when a motion to suppress is granted the result is greatly to reduce the probability of convicting the defendant—from about 84 percent to about 52 percent, see id. at 13. Search and seizure problems also result in decisions to decline to prosecute a certain number of potential defendants; and although the percentage is small, it translates into several hundred federal criminal cases a year that because of the exclusionary rule are not being brought (estimated from a comparison of id. at 13–14 with U.S. DEP'T OF JUSTICE, BUREAU OF JUSTICE STATISTICS, SOURCEBOOK OF CRIMINAL JUSTICE STATISTICS—1980, at 427 [1981] [tab. 5.21]). All these are just federal data. It seems clear, in sum, that the administrative burdens, and the reduced effectiveness of criminal law enforcement, resulting from the exclusionary rule are not trivial.

[53] See, e.g., Landes & Posner, note 46 supra.

Under a strict-liability standard, one is liable for harm caused even if the harm is cost justified, that is, even if the expected cost of the harm was less than the cost of avoiding it; therefore a potential injurer will sometimes prefer to inflict harm and pay damages rather than take (more costly) steps to avoid inflicting harm. Such cases will be rare under a negligence standard. Negligence is, at least approximately, a failure to take cost-justified precautions. The costs of harm are balanced against the costs of avoiding harm and only if the former preponderate is liability imposed. In a perfect negligence system negligence would be completely deterred because it would not pay to be negligent: the costs of inflicting an injury negligently, brought to bear on the defendant in the form of a damages judgment, would by definition exceed the costs of being careful and avoiding the injury.

The balancing approach characteristic of the negligence standard is followed not only in negligence cases as such but in other tort cases, notably nuisance cases, where the standard is unreasonableness rather than negligence.[54] Unreasonableness is also the standard in the Fourth Amendment. As spelled out more fully in the next part of this paper, only if the costs of a particular method of search are disproportionate to the benefits in more effective law enforcement is a search unreasonable. Hence, if the tort remedy for violations of the Fourth Amendment operated perfectly, it would deter all violations, and a court would never base a conviction on illegally seized evidence. No human institution works perfectly, and certainly no tort remedy for Fourth Amendment violations will; its tendency, however, will be to deter violations, so convictions based on illegally seized evidence need not become a common sight in our courts.

III. Other Implications of the Suggested Approach

An economic approach to the Fourth Amendment has additional implications unrelated to the merits of the exclusionary rule. It implies a narrower reading of the warrant clause than has become conventional; and, as already suggested, it implies using cost-benefit analysis to give meaning to the standard of reasonableness in the first clause of the Fourth Amendment.

---

[54] See, e.g., Prosser, note 40 supra, at 596–602.

Both the text and history of the Fourth Amendment suggest a different view of the warrant clause from that adopted by the Court in recent years, notably in the *Payton* case.[55] The Fourth Amendment does not in terms require that a warrant be obtained in any case. The natural reading of the amendment is that unreasonable searches and seizures are forbidden (clause 1), and specifically (clause 2) that a search (or arrest) warrant is invalid unless it complies with the specific requirements (probable cause, etc.) spelled out in the second clause. The natural reading is not that the framers wanted to encourage the use of warrants but that they wanted to discourage their use by imposing stringent requirements on their issuance. The history of the Fourth Amendment bears out this interpretation. The principal abuse at which the Fourth Amendment was aimed was the general warrant, and the warrant clause outlawed it. The Fourth Amendment does not reflect mistrust of searches made without warrants issued by magistrates; it reflects a concern, consistent with the general mistrust of officialdom in the Constitution and Bill of Rights, that magistrates might issue unreasonably broad warrants.[56]

The framers' distrust of bureaucracy is congenial to the way in which the economic analyst approaches tort law. Economists are interested in tort law in part because it embodies a market or quasi-market approach to the control of socially costly activity

---

[55] Payton v. New York, 445 U.S. 573 (1980), held that in the absence of an emergency an officer may not arrest a suspect in his home without a warrant.

[56] See Taylor, note 9 *supra*, for a lucid summary of the historical materials. As he concludes, "Our constitutional fathers were not concerned about warrantless searches, but about overreaching warrants." *Id.* at 41. (At the last minute, the text of the Fourth Amendment was changed to its present wording from a draft in which immediately after the words "shall not be violated" appeared the words "by warrants issuing" without probable cause, etc. See LASSON, THE HISTORY AND DEVELOPMENT OF THE FOURTH AMENDMENT TO THE UNITED STATES CONSTITUTION 101 [1937].)

LANDYNSKI, SEARCH AND SEIZURE AND THE SUPREME COURT: A STUDY IN CONSTITUTIONAL INTERPRETATION 43 (1966), caricatures this as the view that "the first clause confers a search power of independent potency, one that is not restricted by the specific requirements of the second clause." But the Fourth Amendment nowhere "confers" any power of search or seizure. All it does is restrict that power. The first clause uses a reasonableness standard to restrict searches not under warrant; searches under warrant are limited by the second clause. This reading does not make the second clause superfluous, on the ground that the police can avoid its restrictions simply by conducting every search and seizure without a warrant. They still would need a legal basis, common law or statutory, to conduct a search or make an arrest without a warrant. And even if they had such a basis, in the absence of the second clause they might still seek a warrant in order to have a more secure defense of legal process if sued for torts committed in the course of the search. The second clause prevents this.

rather than a licensing approach. The individual who unreasonably injures another is made to pay the costs of the injury, and the threat of this liability gives him an incentive to avoid injuring people unless the costs of avoiding injury are greater than the expected costs to the victim. The warrant procedure, in contrast, is an example of licensing: activity is not permitted unless an official is persuaded in advance that it is socially beneficial. From an economic standpoint the tort remedy is a more appealing method of controlling official misconduct than a warrant requirement that shifts control over searches from an incentives system based on monetary liability to a bureaucratic system based on getting the permission of an official (and in an *ex parte*—*i.e.* noncompetitive—setting). If the economic approach sketched in this paper is the correct approach, then as a corollary the warrant clause should be restored to its original meaning.

This change in the current interpretation of the Fourth Amendment could broaden rather than narrow its protections. It is only a small step from insisting that searches not be made without a warrant (unless a warrant is infeasible) to using the fact that a magistrate has issued a warrant as a defense either to the application of the exclusionary rule or to tort liability by the officers carrying out the search.[57] The use of the magistrate as a shield against liability would be the opposite of what the draftsmen of the warrant clause intended. Had they not been particularly concerned about magistrates issuing warrants that police would hide behind, they would have had no reason to include a separate warrant clause.

The suggested reading of the warrant clause could strengthen the protections of the Fourth Amendment in another way, by putting firmer ground under the application of the Fourth Amendment to wiretapping and other electronic surveillance. If the framers really intended to require a warrant in all but emergency circumstances, it would seem to follow that they did not intend to regulate nonintrusive surveillance at all, because the language of the warrant clause ("particularly describing the place to be searched, and the persons or things to be seized") clearly has reference just to conventional searches or seizures. But once the warrant clause is interpreted as an additional limitation on searches pursuant to warrant, the first

---

[57] A step properly rejected in United States v. Karanthanos, 531 F.2d 26, 32–34 (2d Cir. 1976). See also Franks v. Delaware, 438 U.S. 154 (1978).

clause of the Fourth Amendment is available to bar unreasonable searches accomplished through electronic or other surveillance.

A second corollary of the economic approach involves the meaning of the reasonableness standard in the first clause. I have already suggested that the natural meaning to assign this standard is an economic one. A reasonable search is a cost-justified search. The most important cost of a search is the cost to the lawful interests that the search invades. That cost, a function of the intrusiveness of the search, must be weighed against the benefits of the search. The benefits are a function of the probability that the search will turn up incriminating evidence or leads and of the value to law enforcement of such evidence or leads; this value in turn is a function of the gravity of the crime and the importance of the evidence to conviction. Thus, the less intrusive the search, the higher the probability that it will be fruitful, the more vital the evidence obtained, and the graver the crime being investigated, the likelier it is that the search is reasonable.

I do not suggest that the framers of the Fourth Amendment thought explicitly in economic terms. But in the absence of any evidence of what exactly they meant by the term "unreasonable" in the first clause of the Fourth Amendment, the economic reading is attractive. And it has support in cases in which the courts have allowed a lower degree of probability than implied by the term (from the second clause of the Fourth Amendment) "probable cause" to justify a police procedure less intrusive than the standard search or seizure.[58]

The Supreme Court, to be sure, recently rejected a "multifactor balancing test of 'reasonable police conduct under the circumstances' to cover all seizures that do not amount to technical arrests."[59] It did so because such a test "would threaten to swallow

---

[58] See 1 LaFave, Search and Seizure 450–59 (1978), for a discussion of cases using a "balancing" approach akin to the economic approach that I am advocating here. The Court decided one such case, United States v. Cortez (which I do not discuss in this paper), last term. See note 61 *infra*. One court has stated explicitly that "what is an unreasonable search depends upon the nature and importance of the crime suspected. . . ." Nueslein v. District of Columbia, 115 F.2d 690, 696 (D.C. Cir. 1940). See also Justice Jackson's dissenting opinion in Brinegar v. United States, 338 U.S. 160, 180 (1949). The extent of the intrusion and the probability that the search will turn up incriminating evidence or leads—the other elements in the economic analysis of a reasonable search—are mentioned frequently in the cases.

[59] Dunaway v. New York, 442 U.S. 200, 213 (1979).

the general rule that Fourth Amendment seizures are 'reasonable' only if based on probable cause."[60] There is no such general rule. Probable cause, a phrase from the second clause of the Fourth Amendment, is a limitation on the issuance of warrants; it is not part of the definition of reasonableness.

It may be argued that a reasonableness standard defined in economic terms would be too difficult for police officers to understand and obey. But cost-benefit analysis, at least in the very simple form in which it is being used here, is intuitive—more so than the elaborate casuistry that, as we shall see in the next section, is the modern law of the Fourth Amendment.

The economic approach is also helpful in answering a related question: What should be the bearing on reasonableness of whether or not a search turns up incriminating evidence or leads? The exclusionary rule has made this inquiry virtually disappear from Fourth Amendment law. Most Fourth Amendment cases arise out of motions to suppress evidence, so the starting point in assessing reasonableness necessarily is that the search did yield incriminating evidence or leads. In a tort perspective informed by economic analysis, it is clear that the result of the search is relevant, to damages of course but also to liability. The fact that a search is successful does not prove that it is a reasonable search, because its costs may exceed its benefits; but it is relevant to the question of reasonableness. Compare the following cases. In case 1, the police, in the course of a search for a small quantity of marihuana, beat up the defendant and damage his property. The search might well be considered unreasonable even though it yielded evidence of a crime, evidence which, under the approach suggested here, could be used against the defendant in a criminal proceeding. In case 2 the police, hot on the trail of a murderer, again cause substantial damage in the course of a search, but turn up nothing; such a search might again be ruled unreasonable, although this is a closer case than the first because the expected—though not realized—gains from searching were greater. In case 3 the facts are as in 2 but the search does turn up the crucial evidence that enables the police to solve the murder. Here a comparison of costs and benefits may well show that the search is reasonable.

---

[60] *Ibid.*

IV. Last Term's Cases Assessed under the Proposed Approach

I want to give some further concreteness to my suggested approach by examining how the four principal search and seizure cases decided by the Supreme Court last Term should have been decided if brought as tort cases.[61] I begin with two automobile search cases, *New York v. Belton* and *Robbins v. California*,[62] decided on the same day.

Belton and three companions were in a car that was stopped by a policeman for speeding. Upon approaching the car the policeman smelled marihuana and on the floor of the car saw an envelope of a type in which marihuana is commonly sold. He ordered the men out of the car and arrested them for unlawful possession of marihuana. He then searched the passenger compartment of the car and, in a jacket belonging to Belton, found cocaine. The Supreme Court held that the search of the passenger compartment and of the jacket found in it was lawful; hence Belton was not entitled to prevent the cocaine from being used in evidence against him.

Robbins was stopped by police officers because he was driving in an erratic fashion. Again the officers smelled marihuana and again they searched the passenger compartment, where they found marihuana and equipment for using it. They then searched the recessed luggage compartment in the back of the station wagon and found two opaque packages, each containing fifteen pounds of marihuana. The Supreme Court held that these packages could not be opened without a warrant.

Imagine these as tort cases litigated in conformity with the analysis in this paper. Belton could not have established liability. The search of the passenger compartment and of the jacket found in it was reasonable, for once the arresting officer discovered marihuana, the probability that a search of the car would uncover further evidence of crime was substantial, while the cost of that search to the lawful interests of the occupants was trivial—a slight extension of the period in which they were held in custody pursuant to the

---

[61] I omit three cases: Colorado v. Bannister, 101 S. Ct. 42 (1980), decided *per curiam* and without plenary hearing; Allen v. McCurry, 101 S. Ct. 411 (1980), which involved only a procedural issue; and United States v. Cortez, 101 S. Ct. 690 (1980), a unanimous decision involving an investigative "stop" (not an arrest) by Border Patrol officers.

[62] 101 S. Ct. 2860 (1981); 101 S. Ct. 2841 (1981).

arrest. Even if the search was unlawful, Belton's damages would have been trivial; they would be limited to the cost to him of the slight prolongation of the period of custody brought about by the search.

Robbins would have had no stronger case. Once marihuana was found in the passenger compartment, the probability that more marihuana or other drugs would be found in the packages in the luggage compartment was substantial. Again the cost of the added search—a slight extension in the period of custody—was trivial (in fact, it probably took longer to search Belton's jacket than to open Robbins' packages). And again even if the search was unlawful, the damages would have been slight.

In neither case would the absence of a warrant have been material if the warrant clause is indeed a limitation on the issuance of warrants rather than a requirement that warrants be obtained in order to conduct searches. And in both cases the fact that the search produced evidence of crime reinforces the conclusion that it was a reasonable search.

This discussion is not intended to suggest that the Fourth Amendment places no limits on searches of automobiles. Let me give a hypothetical case on the other side of the line. Police set up a roadblock for no better reason than that they think that if they search enough cars they will find some evidence of crime, and they stop a hundred cars, search each one painstakingly, and in one find a quantity of marihuana. Each driver would be entitled to recover tort damages (perhaps they would join together in a class action to economize on litigation expenses) for any inconvenience, embarrassment, or anxiety caused by the searches. Each would be entitled to recover damages, though in the case of the driver discovered to be carrying marihuana in his car the jury might be unsympathetic to his claim. He could also be prosecuted for illegal possession of drugs, and the marihuana seized in the illegal search could be introduced in evidence against him. But the total damages in all suits would no doubt exceed the gains to the community from one more drug conviction, so this kind of unreasonable police activity would usually be deterred by the availability of the tort remedy.

Of the other search and seizure cases that the Court decided last Term the most interesting is *Steagald v. United States*.[63] A confiden-

---

[63] 101 S. Ct. 1642 (1981).

tial informant provided federal drug officers with information concerning the whereabouts of a federal fugitive, Ricky Lyons. Armed with a warrant for the arrest of Lyons, the officers went to the address where he was believed to be. They searched at that address for Lyons, but he was not there. In the course of searching for him they noticed cocaine belonging to Steagald, apparently one of the occupants of the house. Steagald was arrested and charged with a drug offense. He moved to suppress the use in evidence of the cocaine discovered in the search. The Supreme Court held the search illegal. The officers could have obtained a search warrant—there was no emergency since the "raid" on the house had been planned days in advance—and therefore they were, in the Court's view, required to obtain one.

The Court's result was foreordained by an approach that asked whether it was feasible to obtain a warrant rather than whether the search was reasonable. Noting that the officers had entered the house occupied by Steagald on the basis of "their belief that Ricky Lyons might be a guest there," the Court stated: "Regardless of how reasonable this belief might have been, it was never subjected to the detached scrutiny of a judicial officer."[64] But if Steagald had moved to suppress the evidence obtained in the search not because there was no search warrant but because the search was unreasonable, the issue of reasonableness would have been "subjected to the detached scrutiny of a judicial officer"—that of the judge deciding the motion. And so if Steagald had proceeded by way of a tort action. The magistrate who issues a "telephonic search warrant,"[65] of course *ex parte*, is not a more detached and effective judicial officer than a judge and/or jury deciding the reasonableness issue in an adversary proceeding.

The Court rejected the government's argument that motions to suppress and actions for damages are adequate checks against unreasonable searches by stating that the Fourth Amendment "'is designed to prevent, not simply to redress, unlawful police action.'"[66] But deterrence is a mode of prevention, and damage actions a mode of deterrence.

In a tort suit conforming to the principles suggested in this paper,

---

[64] *Id.* at 1648.

[65] *Id.* at 1652.

[66] *Id.* at 1649.

Steagald would not have had much chance of prevailing. The evidence recited in the Court's opinion, though sketchy, suggests that the drug officers had a reasonable basis for believing that Lyons was at the house occupied by Steagald. They therefore had a reasonable basis for searching the house for Lyons, for they did not have to take the word of the occupants that he was not there. The cocaine was discovered, lying in plain view, as a by-product of the search for Lyons; it was not found by opening drawers or compartments too small for Lyons to have secreted himself in. Moreover, so far as appears, no damage at all was caused to any lawful interest of Steagald's, so his damages would have been zero even if the search really had been unlawful.

The last case is *Michigan v. Summers*.[67] As police officers were about to enter a house to execute a search warrant they encountered Summers leaving the house, detained him, and, after finding narcotics in the house and ascertaining that Summers was the owner of the house, arrested and searched him and found a quantity of heroin in his coat pocket. The Supreme Court held that the search was lawful; that it is lawful to detain the occupant of a house while it is being searched. The result is sensible, but is it consistent with *Steagald*? The Court in *Steagald* reasoned that if the police had time to get an arrest warrant they had time to get a search warrant. The converse is equally true. In *Summers*, if the police had time to get a search warrant they had time to get a warrant to arrest the owner of the premises to be searched, and by the reasoning of *Steagald* they should have done so if they had reason to believe that the owner of the premises was guilty of a crime. Oddly, the dissenting Justices in *Summers* did not cite *Steagald*.

If Summers had brought a tort case under the principles proposed in this paper, he would have fared poorly. The fact that he was the owner of premises in which narcotics were found created a substantial probability that a search of his person would turn up incriminating evidence or leads, as it did. He was detained only briefly for the search of his person and was not roughed up in any way. Thus the costs of the search were low relative to both the expected and the realized gains to law enforcement. If the search was unlawful, once again the damages awarded would have been trivial.

---

[67] 101 S. Ct. 2587 (1981).

The cases I have discussed show the need for a fresh approach to the Fourth Amendment. In two of the four cases the Court held that evidence had been obtained in violation of the Fourth Amendment, but those cases are not consistent with the two cases in which the Court held that there was no violation of the Fourth Amendment. In none of the cases was there a serious invasion of any lawful interest protected by the Fourth Amendment; that two of the defendants should nonetheless have prevailed is concrete evidence that the exclusionary rule does overdeter. The Court's textually unsupported and ahistorical emphasis on whether or not a warrant could have been obtained deflected the Court from the central issue, which in all of the cases should have been the reasonableness of the search. Probably none of the cases would even have been litigated if tort law were used rather than the exclusionary rule to enforce the Fourth Amendment, and that is not the least that can be said on behalf of the tort approach.

ROBERT F. NAGEL

FEDERALISM AS A FUNDAMENTAL VALUE: NATIONAL LEAGUE OF CITIES IN PERSPECTIVE

> In examining the Constitution of the United States . . . one is startled at the variety of information and the excellence of discretion which it presupposes in the people whom it is meant to govern. The government of the Union depends entirely upon legal fictions; the Union is an ideal nation which only exists in the mind, and whose limits and extent can only be discerned by the understanding. [ALEXIS DE TOCQUEVILLE*]

A. INTRODUCTION

After almost forty years of sanctioning the growth of the congressional power to regulate commerce,[1] the Supreme Court in *National League of Cities v. Usery*[2] held that the extension of the wage and hour provisions of the Fair Labor Standards Act to most state employees was unconstitutional as a violation of the principle of federalism. Although some serious commentary had suggested that the Court's record prior to *Usery* verged on abdication of constitutional responsibilities,[3] *Usery* precipitated criticism that was ex-

---

Robert F. Nagel is Professor of Law, University of Colorado School of Law.

* I Democracy in America 152 (Arlington House ed. 1970).

[1] For a history, see NOWAK, ROTUNDA & YOUNG, CONSTITUTIONAL LAW 150–56 (1978).

[2] 426 U.S. 833 (1976).

[3] The basic constitutional "test" (whether the regulation "affected" commerce) was immediately understood to provide no limitation on national power. "Almost anything—

© 1982 by The University of Chicago. All rights reserved.
0-226-46434-2/82/1981-0022$01.00

81

traordinary both for its breadth and severity. Justice Brennan, a respected and unapologetic practitioner of judicial power and imaginative constitutional analysis when the issues involve individuals' rights, labeled the decision "an abstraction without substance" and a "patent usurpation."[4] Three prominant scholars reacted to the decision extremely critically. Professors Tribe and Michelman, both resourceful at constitutional interpretation, professed themselves totally unable to understand the explanation offered by the Court in *Usery* and proposed that the decision could make sense only as an inchoate statement of a right to the provision of certain state services.[5] Professor Choper reacted with a forceful argument that, even if *Usery* were constitutionally correct on the merits, the Court should have held such matters to be nonjusticiable in order to save its resources for—that phrase again—the protection of individual rights.[6] Many others also criticized *Usery*,[7] and those who were at all supportive of the decision were muted or ambivalent.[8]

The harsh reaction to *Usery* is one aspect of a widespread pattern that inverts the priorities of the framers: an obsessive concern for using the Constitution to protect individuals' rights. This fascination with rights reinforces a form of instrumentalism that is too

---

marriage, birth, death—may in some fashion affect commerce." National Labor Relations Board v. Jones & Laughlin Steel Corp., 301 U.S. 1, 99 (1937) (McReynolds, J., dissenting). By 1959 Professor Wechsler could refer to "the virtual abandonment of limits [to the federal commerce power]." *Toward Neutral Principles of Constitutional Law*, 73 HARV. L. REV. 1, 23–24 (1959). *Cf.* McCloskey, *Economic Due Process and the Supreme Court: An Exhumation and Reburial*, 1962 SUP. CT. REV. 34.

⁴ 426 U.S. at 858, 860. (Brennan, J., dissenting).

⁵ Tribe, *Unraveling National League of Cities: The New Federalism and Affirmative Rights to Essential Government Services*, 90 HARV. L. REV. 1065, 1066 (1977) ("I make no claims about what the Justices intended. . . . I haven't a clue what that might have been, but I doubt that the conclusion of this article was it."); Michelman, *States' Rights and States' Roles: Permutations of "Sovereignty" in National League of Cities v. Usery*, 86 YALE L. J. 1165, 1166 (1977) ("The only interpretation that is compatible with the decision taken as a whole, I shall argue, is a surprising one that leads in directions the Justices do not seem to have intended or anticipated.").

⁶ Choper, *The Scope of National Power Vis-a-Vis the States: The Dispensability of Judicial Review*, 86 YALE L. J. 1552 (1977).

⁷ *E.G.*, ELY, DEMOCRACY AND DISTRUST 224 n. 44 (1980); Barber, *National League of Cities v. Usery: New Meaning for the Tenth Amendment?* 1976 SUP. CT. REV. 161; Cox, *Federalism and Individual Rights under the Burger Court*, 73 NW. U. L. REV. 1 (1978); Tushnet, *The Dilemmas of Liberal Constitutionalism*, 42 OHIO ST. L. J. 411, 420–421, (1981).

⁸ *E.g.*, Stewart, *Pyramids of Sacrifice? Problems of Federalism in Mandating State Implementation of National Environment Policy*, 86 YALE L. J. 1196, 1224–25, 1271 (1977); Kaden, *Politics, Money, and State Sovereignty: The Judicial Role*, 79 COLUM. L. REV. 847 (1979).

confining to be an adequate way to think about constitutional law. If *Usery* is viewed without these intellectual constraints, a rather plain and defensible explanation for the decision emerges. My major purpose is not to insist that *Usery* was ultimately "correct," but to suggest that the inability to understand *Usery* demonstrates the extent to which the capacity to appreciate some important constitutional principles is being lost.

I.

Judicial decisions generally reflect a priority in favor of protecting individuals' rights over the structural principles of separation of powers and federalism. Decisions directly resting on these structural principles are rare compared with decisions involving individual rights.[9] Issues of federalism and separation of powers are usually analyzed in terms of nonconstitutional doctrines. For example, they are frequently reduced to matters of statutory construction[10] The scope of the judicial power over states is often discussed in amorphous, discretionary terms—such as equitable discretion, standing, justiciability, and comity.[11] Even when structural principles are treated as fully constitutional matters, their main influence is on the definition of individual rights.[12] Those decisions that do deal unambiguously with structural values for their own sake demonstrate less explanatory creativity than do decisions dealing with rights, a fact that suggests a relative lack of

---

[9] No doubt this is in part justifiable because of the special capabilities and responsibilities of the other branches of government in resolving such disputes. See Choper, note 6 *supra*, at 1560–77 (as to federalism); see Frohnmayer, *The Separation of Powers: An Essay on the Vitality of the Constitutional Idea*, 52 ORE. L. REV. 211 (1973) (as to separation of powers). Whatever the reasons, the reluctance of the Supreme Court to rule on cases involving structural values is often dramatic. See, *e.g.*, McArthur v. Clifford, 393 U.S. 1002 (1968); Holmes v. United States, 391 U.S. 936 (1968); Velvel v. Nixon, 396 U.S. 1042 (1970); Massachusetts v. Laird, 400 U.S. 886 (1970); DaCosta v. Laird, 405 U.S. 979 (1972). See also Goldwater v. Carter, 444 U.S. 996 (1979).

[10] *E.g.*, United States v. Five Gambling Devices, 346 U.S. 441 (1953); Scarborough v. United States, 431 U.S. 563 (1977); National Cable Television Association v. United States, 415 U.S. 336 (1974).

[11] As to equitable discretion, compare Milliken v. Bradley, 418 U.S. 717 (1974) with Columbus Board of Education v. Penick, 443 U.S. 449 (1979). As to standing, compare Warth v. Seldin, 422 U.S. 490 (1975) with Duke Power Company v. Carolina Environmental Study Group, 438 U.S. 59 (1978). As to comity, compare Younger v. Harris, 401 U.S. 37 (1971) with Steffel v. Thompson, 415 U.S. 452 (1974).

[12] *E.G.*, Milliken v. Bradley, 418 U.S. 717(1974); San Antonio Independent School District v. Rodriguez, 411 U.S. 1 (1973); Labine v. Vincent, 401 U.S. 532 (1971).

judicial interest in structural matters if not lower quality opinions. Missing from decisions involving structural values is any use of the doctrinal innovations used so often in decisions involving rights. There are no analyses of motive, no dissections of legislative purpose, no demands that less drastic means be used, no tiers of judicial scrutiny.[13] Instead, decisions having to do with structure frequently rest on the baldest forms of "balancing"[14] and on undeveloped references to such generalities as "undue impairment" of the states' functions.[15] Finally, cases in which rights are articulated are frequently followed by a series of decisions that are designed to "actualize" the original right, and in the process the right is often recast in even more ambitious terms.[16] Important cases that articulate structural values tend quickly to be limited and then largely abandoned.[17]

---

[13] As to analyses of motive and legislative purpose, compare, *e.g.*, Eisenstadt v. Baird, 405 U.S. 438 (1972); or Trimble v. Gordon, 430 U.S. 762 (1977); or Craig v. Boren, 429 U.S. 190 (1976) with Hoke v. United States, 227 U.S. 308 (1913); United States v. Sullivan,.332 U.S. 689 (1948); Perez v. United States, 402 U.S. 146 (1971); United States v. Kahriger, 345 U.S. 22 (1953); Katzenbach v. McClung, 379 U.S. 294 (1964). With respect to the less drastic means requirement, see Katzenbach v. McClung and compare, *e.g.*, Roe v. Wade, 410 U.S. 113 (1973) (states' method of protecting potential life sweeps unnecessarily broadly when protecting fetuses prior to viability) with Nixon v. Administrator of General Services, 433 U.S. 425 (1977) (statute that provides for the storage and screening of 42 million pages of presidential documents and 880 presidential tape recordings does not unnecessarily subordinate presidential requirements of confidentiality).

[14] On balancing, see South Carolina State Highway Department v. Barnwell Brothers, Inc., 303 U.S. 177 (1938); Southern Pacific Co. v. Arizona, 325 U.S. 761 (1945); Bibb v. Navajo Freight Lines, Inc., 359 U.S. 520 (1959); Raymond Motor Transportation, Inc. v. Rice, 434 U.S. 429 (1978); Kassel v. Consolidated Freightways Corp., 101 S.Ct. 1309 (1981); Minn. v. Clover Leaf Creamery Co., 101 S.Ct. 715 (1981); National League of Cities v. Usery, 426 U.S. at 856 (Blackmun, J., concurring). See also Nixon v. Administrator of General Services, note 13 *supra*, at 425.

[15] New York v. United States, 326 U.S. 572, 587 (1946) (Stone, concurring). Similarly, the Court has said that "Congress may not exercise power in a fashion that impairs the States' integrity. . . ." Fry v. United States, 421 U.S. 542, 547 n.7 (1975). "[N]either government *may destroy* the other nor curtail *in any substantial manner* the exercise of its powers." Metcalf and Eddy v. Mitchell, 269 U.S. 514, 523 (1926) (emphasis added).

[16] *E.g.*, compare Brown v. Board of Education, 347 U.S. 483 (1954) with Keyes v. School District No. 1, 413 U.S. 189 (1973); and Swann v. Charlotte-Meckleburg Board of Education, 402 U.S. 1 (1971); and Green v. County School Board, 391 U.S. 430 (1968). Or compare Roe v. Wade, note 13 *supra*, with Planned Parenthood of Central Missouri v. Danforth, 428 U.S. 52 (1976); and Bellotti v. Baird, 443 U.S. 622 (1979); and Colautti v. Franklin, 439 U.S. 379 (1979).

[17] Compare United States v. Nixon, 418 U.S. 683 (1974) with Nixon v. Administrator of General Services, note 13 *supra*. Compare National League of Cities v. Usery, 426 U.S. at 833, with City of Lafayette v. Louisiana Power & Light Co., 435 U.S. 389 (1978); City of Los Angeles v. Manhart, 435 U.S. 702 (1978); Massachusetts v. United States, 435 U.S. 444 (1978); North Carolina v. Califano, 435 U.S. 962 (1978); Hodel v. Virginia Surface Min. & Reclam. Association, 101 S.Ct. 2352, 2360, 2365–67 (1981).

Modern judges work diligently at redesigning local educational programs and at defining the acceptable number of square feet in a prison cell. They void a multiplicity of laws relating to hair length, sexual preference, and abortion. But they deal rarely and, for the most part, gingerly with the great issues of power distribution that were faced so ambitiously and successfully by the framers.

Academic writing generally reflects the same priority. Scholarly discussion of constitutional structure often falls back on the more familiar issues of individual rights. For example, Professor Black's *Structure and Relationship in Constitutional Law* illuminates the possibilities of argument based on structure only to apply quickly that potential to the definition of individual rights.[18] Professor Ely's *Democracy and Distrust* emphasizes the central importance of democratic self-government in the constitutional design, but this insight is enlisted chiefly in support of rationalizing the Warren Court's creative definition of individual rights.[19] (The book is then criticized, not for overemphasizing the dependence of democratic processes on individual rights, but for attempting to define rights by reference to considerations other than the needs of individuals.)[20] Many books and articles appear on the injunctive devices that lower federal courts are using against states in an effort to implement individuals' constitutional rights. Much of this commentary seeks to conceptualize individuals' rights and the judicial function in ways that permit significant aspects of self-government to be assumed by the courts for the sake of remaking the world to suit some ideal suggested by values implicit in certain rights.[21] Much of the rest of the commentary emphasizes the practicalities of judicial enforcement and largely assumes that, if courts are able to implement individual rights effectively, implementation must have prior-

---

[18] BLACK, STRUCTURE AND RELATIONSHIP IN CONSTITUTIONAL LAW (1969).

[19] ELY, DEMOCRACY AND DISTRUST (1980).

[20] Tribe, *The Puzzling Persistence of Process-based Constitutional Theories*, 89 YALE L. J. 1063 (1980). See also Benedict, *To Secure These Rights: Rights, Democracy, and Judicial Review in the Anglo-American Constitutional Heritage*, 42 OHIO ST. L. J. 69 (1981); Grano, *Ely's Theory of Judicial Review: Preserving the Significance of the Political Process*, id. at 167; Richards, *Moral Philosophy and the Search for Fundamental Values in Constitutional Law*, id. at 319. But see Maltz, *Federalism and the Fourteenth Amendment: A Comment on Democracy and Distrust*, id. at 209.

[21] E.g., Chayes, *The Role of the Judge in Public Law Litigation*, 89 HARV. L. REV. 1281 (1976); Fiss, *The Supreme Court 1978 Term, Foreword: The Forms of Justice*, 93 HARV. L. REV. 1 (1979); Eisenberg and Yeazell, *The Ordinary and the Extraordinary in Institutional Litigation*, 93 HARV. L. REV. 465 (1980).

ity over other values.[22] Those that examine the remedial role of the
federal courts as an aspect of constitutional structure are quickly
urged to return to the proper business of legal scholars, which is
expressly defined as arguing about rights.[23]

Scholarly preoccupation with rights is also evident in the tolerant
and highly imaginative approaches frequently taken in the definition of rights. Scholars commonly argue that it ought to be no bar
to a constitutional claim that there is ambiguity about whether the
framers intended a certain interpretation or that they did not consider a possible interpretation of a constitutional right.[24] The argument is extended in such important areas as school desegregation
to include definitions of rights that are rather clearly in conflict with
historical intent.[25] It is not uncommon for sophisticated scholars to
make unembarrassed arguments for an interpretation of a right
based largely on the personal values of the proponent of the right.[26]
What more than this can be meant by assertions about "goodness"[27]
or "minimal standards of human dignity"[28] or "personhood"?[29]
Such argumentation, even if it involves more than private values,
demonstrates how wide and free the scope of acceptable constitutional argument about rights is. Indeed, scholarship indulges almost any amount of philosophical or psychological vagueness and
complexity when the goal is defining rights. We ponder how "just
wants"[30] or the "mediation of liberal conversation"[31] or "equal

---

[22] *E.g.*, Chayes, note 21 *supra*. Diver, *The Judge as Political Power Broker: Superintending Structural Change in Public Institutions*, 65 VA. L. REV. 43 (1979).

[23] Eisenberg & Yeazell, note 21 *supra*, at 467. *Cf.* Ely, *Foreword: On Discovering Fundamental Values*, 92 HARV. L. REV 5, 18 n.62 (1978); Fiss, note 21 *supra*, at 53.

[24] *E.g.*, Brest, *The Misconceived Quest for the Original Understanding*, 60 B. U. L. REV. 204 (1980); Cover, *Book Review*, NEW REP. Jan. 14, 1978 at 26, 27; Munzer & Nickel, *Does the Constitution Mean What It Always Meant?* 77 COLUM. L. REV. 1029 (1977). See also TRIBE, AMERICAN CONSTITUTIONAL LAW 816 (1978).

[25] *E.g.*, Bickel, *The Original Understanding and the Segregation Decision*, 69 HARV. L. REV. 1 (1955).

[26] For a general discussion, see Ely, note 23 *supra*, at 16–22.

[27] Wright, *Professor Bickel, the Scholarly Tradition, and the Supreme Court*, 84 HARV. L. REV. 769, 797 (1971).

[28] Eisenberg & Yeazell, note 21 *supra*, at 517.

[29] TRIBE, AMERICAN CONSTITUTIONAL LAW 914.

[30] Michelman, *The Supreme Court, 1968 Term—Foreword: On Protecting the Poor through the Fourteenth Amendment*, 83 HARV. L. REV. 7 (1969).

[31] ACKERMAN, SOCIAL JUSTICE IN THE LIBERAL STATE 311 (1980).

respect and concern"[32] or the ideas of Roberto Unger[33] might bear on the definition of rights.

In contrast, scholars often exhibit a kind of intellectual crabbedness when structural claims are made. Consider the scholars who were content to rest a defense of expanded institutional rights on an assertion about "fostering minimal standards of dignity." They had just tested federalism and separation of power claims about institutional injunctions by demanding to see evidence that the framers actually foresaw and opposed judicial operation of public institutions.[34] Almost any slight ambiguity about historical intent is urged to help defeat structural claims.[35] Similarly, arguments based on concepts such as separation of powers[36] or democratic accountability[37] are termed hopelessly indeterminate. The same scholar who demands specificity in the concept of "state sovereignty" would ground interpretations of individual rights on values such as "a meaningful opportunity [for individuals] to realize their humanity."[38]

In short, the hostile reaction to *Usery* is part of a broader pattern: Many jurists and scholars tend to envision constitutional values mainly in terms of individuals' rights and to undervalue judicial protection of principles that allocate decision-making responsibility among governmental units. This tendency may be largely a consequence of the influence of the lawsuit in shaping views of the Constitution. Lawsuits, of course, are discrete arguments, usually in-

---

[32] DWORKIN, TAKING RIGHTS SERIOUSLY 149, 227 (1977). For other elaborate efforts to conceptualize equal protection, see Alexander, *Modern Equal Protection Theories: A Metatheoretical Taxonomy and Critique*, 42 OHIO ST. L. J. 3 (1981); Simson, *A Method for Analyzing Discriminatory Effects under the Equal Protection Clause*, 29 STAN. L. REV. 663 (1977).

[33] Tushnet, *Darkness at the Edge of Town: The Contributions of John Hart Ely to Constitutional Theory*, 89 YALE L. J. 1037, 1057–62 (1980).

[34] Eisenberg & Yeazell, note 21 *supra*, at 497 ("Nor do the records of the constitutional convention or the debate surrounding consideration of the Constitution counsel specifically against judicial decisions affecting institutions traditionally regulated by executive officials.").

[35] *E.g.*, Choper, note 6 *supra*, at 1588–90 (arguing that the intent of the framers with regard to judicial enforcement of federalism limitations was ambiguous because, despite some clear statements supporting such judicial responsibility, Federalists at times pointed to other protections for the principle as well).

[36] Diver, note 22 *supra*, at 91–92; Chayes, note 21 *supra*, at 1307. See generally the discussion in Nagel, *Separation of Powers and the Scope of Federal Equitable Remedies*, 30 STAN. L. REV. 661, 686–88 (1978).

[37] Tribe, note 20 *supra*, at 1063, 1069–79; Tushnet, note 33 *supra*, at 1037, 1045–57.

[38] Tribe, note 20 *supra*, at 1077.

volving an individual, and they are often resolved by labeling the interests of one side as "rights"; thus, the lawsuit itself tends to convert even organizational matters into individual concerns. But to see the purposes of judicial review almost entirely in terms of securing individual rights is to invert the priorities of the framers and ultimately to trivialize the Constitution. The framers' political theory was immediately concerned with organization, not individuals. Their most important contributions had to do with principles of power allocation—with the blending and separation of power among the branches of government and with the bold effort to create a strong national government while maintaining strong state governments. This structure itself was to be the great protection of the individual, not the "parchment barriers" that were later (and with modest expectations) added to the document.[39] Even the danger of local majoritarian excess—so frequently cited today as a justification for vigorous protection of individual rights—cannot reconcile the modern emphasis on rights with the priorities of the framers. Although aware of the threat posed by "faction," the Federalists proposed social heterogeneity and layered government as the protection,[40] not the Bill of Rights, which, after all, was originally thought to restrain only the national government.

The modern priority on individuals' rights is striking in light of the common assumption that judicial review allows for some con-

---

[39] Apparently the idea of a bill of rights "never entered the mind of many of [the framers]" until three days before adjournment of the Constitutional Convention. SCHWARTZ, A DOCUMENTARY HISTORY OF THE BILL OF RIGHTS (1971) 627. A common argument for the exclusion of a bill of rights was that specific protections were unnecessary, since the federal government had been granted only enumerated powers. *Id.* at 634. When Madison proposed the Bill of Rights to Congress, its importance for preserving freedom was not emphasized. He argued that it would be "neither improper nor altogether useless." *Id.* at 1028. See, generally, Rumble, *James Madison on the Value of the Bill of Rights*, in NOMOS XX: CONSTITUTIONALISM 122 (Pennock & Chapman, eds., 1979). The general defense of the proposed Constitution offered in THE FEDERALIST PAPERS continually emphasizes governmental structure as the basic source of protection against tyranny: "In the compound republic of America, the power surrendered by the people is first divided between two distinct governments, and then the portion allotted to each subdivided among distinct and separate departments. Hence a double security arises to the rights of the people." THE FEDERALIST PAPERS, No. 51 at 323 (Mentor, ed., 1961). See, generally, Diamond, *The Federalist's View of Federalism*, in ESSAYS IN FEDERALISM 21, 53, 61 (Institute for Studies in Federalism, 1961). It is true, of course, that the Bill of Rights was eventually adopted, and its importance in the constitutional scheme may have been magnified both by the adoption of the Fourteenth Amendment and by modern experience with judicial enforcement of rights. But neither consideration justifies losing sight of the framers' original scheme.

[40] On the importance of size and heterogeneity, see Diamond, note 39 *supra*, at 55–59. See also Choper, note 6 *supra*, at 1617.

tinuity in the articulation of our most basic principles. In adopting a viewpoint and a vocabulary that focuses on individuals, modern judges and scholars have tended to shut themselves off from full participation in the great debates about governmental theory begun by the framers. The writings of Professor Choper, the bluntest and most extreme critic of judicial enforcement of structural values, provide a more specific understanding of how this participation has been limited.

II.

Although the priority in favor of judicial protection of rights rather than structure is widespread, it is often muted or qualified.[41] In Choper's writings, it is forthright. He argues that the two basic structural principles—the enumeration of a limited number of subjects as proper for congressional legislation and the separation of the national government into three distinct branches—ought to be left to the accommodations made in the political process.[42] Courts should preserve their political "capital" for the protection of individual rights.[43]

Choper argues that a court misallocates its efforts when it attempts to enforce constitutional limitations on congressional power, because the judiciary has no special competence to decide such issues. "The functional, borderline question posed by federalism disputes is one of comparative skill and effectiveness of governmental levels: in a word, an issue of practicability."[44] Judicial attempts to influence such practical decisions are often futile and make the courts unpopular politically—all for no important pur-

---

[41] Professor Wechsler, for example, was careful not to exclude altogether a role for judicial review in enforcing limitations on Congress (*The Political Safeguards of Federalism: The Role of the States in the Composition and Selection of the National Government*, in FEDERALISM, MATURE AND EMERGENT 97, 108–09 [MacMahon, ed., 1955]). See also Freund, *Umpiring the Federal System, id.*, 159. See also text accompanying notes 9–38 *supra*.

[42] Both arguments are contained in CHOPER, JUDICIAL REVIEW AND THE NATIONAL POLITICAL PROCESS, A FUNCTIONAL RECONSIDERATION OF THE ROLE OF THE SUPREME COURT (1980). The argument with respect to separation of powers is discussed in Monaghan, *Book Review*, 94 HARV. L. REV. 296 (1980). Here I shall deal only with Choper's argument with respect to federalism, and references will be to the article on which this aspect of the book was based. Choper, note 6 *supra*, at 1552.

[43] Choper, note 6 *supra*, at 1556, 1581, 1583.

[44] *Id.* at 1556.

pose, since the political branches are able and inclined to preserve an adequate level of power at the state level.[45]

On the other hand, Choper argues that questions of individual substantive rights are matters of "principle"—a term that is not fully explained[46]—on which the courts do have special competence.[47] These matters of principle cannot be entrusted to the majorities in the political process, apparently because it takes judicial skills to determine what they are.[48] Furthermore, federalistic disputes cannot be squeezed into this substantive-rights mold by focusing on the individuals' rights that might be served by decentralization. There is "no solid historical or logical basis" for the "assertion that federalism was meant to protect, or does in fact protect, individual constitutional freedoms."[49] Federalism, Choper asserts, was designed to protect states, not individuals, for the purpose of achieving governmental efficiency in a large heterogenous land.[50] Insofar as the existence of state power was designed to protect individuals from governmental restrictions on their liberty (in a general sense), such protections are less important than substantive constitutional freedoms because the right "to choose in smaller political units whether and how some activities would be regulated," is "not for the ultimate security of defined liberties."[51] In contrast, "the essence of the individual rights claim is that no

---

[45] *Id.* at 1560, *et seq.*

[46] Choper contrasts federalism to matters of principle by suggesting that principles are enforced without regard to immediate social costs because enforcement protects "the dignity of the individual." Choper, note 6 *supra*, at 1555. But it seems unlikely that he means by this that the definition of rights or their protection is never compromised because of practical trade-offs. Nor is it clear why federalism, as a constitutional requirement, might not have content independent of "practical" considerations and sometimes be enforced despite immediate costs. He denies that principles exclude policy considerations that require complex factual determinations (*ibid.*). Much of his discussion implies that principles have independent intellectual content which involves "technical considerations" and judicial expertise (*id.* at 1574). In contrast, federalism is often treated as meaning little more than that States must exist (see note 62 *infra*). However, in places Choper acknowledges that federalism might involve content independent of the practical accommodations made in the political process. *Id.* at 1599–1600. *E.g.*, he concedes that Congress might make constitutional errors with regard to what federalism requires. *Id.* at 1574.

[47] *Id.* at 1554. *cf. id.* at 1556.

[48] Choper, note 6 *supra*, at 1555, 1556.

[49] *Id.* at 1611.

[50] *Id.* at 1614.

[51] *Id.* at 1616.

organ of government, national or state, may undertake the challenged activity."[52]

Choper is right, of course, that the principle of federalism determines only the level of government that may restrict a liberty. But to the extent that decentralized government permits decisions to be made by local officials who might differ from national decision makers in their accessibility or sensitivity, the principle does serve "the ultimate security of a defined liberty" and is not on this ground inferior to constitutional rights. Choper appears to acknowledge this, although—true to the intellectual habits of the time—he insists on referring to self-determination as a "freedom," as if a principle cannot be taken seriously unless conceived of as attached to individuals.[53] Choper explains the inferior status of the most basic interest served by the principle of federalism with this remark:[54]

> [It is] equally likely that the withdrawal of judicial review will result in more fastidious concern for states' rights by the federal political branches [and] [m]ore important, continuing jurisdiction over states' rights claims can . . . undermine [the Court's] ability to perform the critical task of protecting all individual liberties.

In the end, Choper's argument largely begs the question. Individual rights should be protected in preference to the interest in self-determination because judicial efforts to protect this interest might be unnecessary and might conflict with the "critical" task of protecting individuals' rights. But as Choper acknowledges,[55] judicial protection of any right might reduce congressional concern over

---

[52] *Id.* at 1555.

[53] His acknowledgment is somewhat ambivalent (*id.* at 1620). It is a further sign of the widespread preoccupation with rights that Choper was criticized for not analogizing states' rights sufficiently to individuals' right and for underestimating how far the latter depends on the former. Benedict, note 20 *supra*, at 75–76. Compare note 20 and accompanying text.

[54] *Id.* at 1620–21. The discussion of this issue in the book is fuller but not significantly different. There Choper adds, but does not rely on, the argument that "the federalism principle has simply outlived its usefulness." CHOPER, note 42 *supra*, at 255–56. He also drops the adjective "critical," thus emphasizing the quantitative aspect of his argument that judicial protection of federalism threatens the capacity to protect a wide array of individual rights. But the protection of any single principle or right will naturally seem to be less weighty than the protection of all others, so in this respect the argument proves nothing that is specific to federalism. In short, the book, like the article, does not successfully escape the need to show why self-determination (while difficult to protect) is not worth protecting. See text accompanying notes 55–56 *infra*.

[55] Choper, note 6 *supra*, at 1604.

the subject. And Choper does not mean that judicial protection of substantive, individual rights—the right to work more than a ten-hour day comes to mind—at times has not significantly reduced the court's prestige and political power. Nor is an answer to the question supplied by the adjective "critical." Why the protection of rights is more critical than the protection of the principle of federalism was the question at the outset.

Although Choper's specific treatment of the interest is self-determination does not explain the inferior status of structural values, the direction and emphasis throughout his argument is suggestive of an explanation. Consider again Choper's striking and repeated assertion that the interests protected by federalism are "not for the ultimate security of defined liberties."[56] This assertion is not strictly relevant to self-determination because local control is "ultimate" in the sense that no decision maker would be permitted to remove certain decisions from the local level. Nevertheless, requirements as to decision-making processes do not provide any ultimate security with respect to outcomes. Indeed, local decision making can be used to achieve very unfair outcomes—a realization that was of constant concern to framers.[57] The interest in local decision making might be thought less significant than individuals' constitutional rights to the extent that the protection of rights requires the realization of some substantive vision of a moral world. While it may be a moral good to have some decisions made locally, that value might not seem as important as an absolute constitutional protection that restricts and prescribes outcomes, at least to the extent that the values implicit in such rights are morally compelling.[58] And Choper, of course, does assume that these values are compelling and asserts that their realization serves "the dignity of the individual."[59]

It might be objected that it is possible (if not likely) to approve morally of the decentralization of power to the same extent as one might approve of a world where the values implicit in individual constitutional rights are realized. But can a world of decentralized authority be morally compelling to this degree if no specific version

---

[56] E.g., id. at 1555, 1560, 1616, 1617.

[57] See, generally, WOOD, THE CREATION OF THE AMERICAN REPUBLIC 608–609 (1969).

[58] On Choper's concern about outcomes, see Choper, note 6 supra, at 1555, 1617–18.

[59] Id. at 1555.

of decision-making allocation is constitutionally mandated? Choper suggests throughout his argument that questions of individual rights have specific, intellectual content.[60] Matters of federalism are said not to be matters of principle and, thus, are not subject to specific intellectual elaboration. Federalism is a process that is elaborated by self-interest.[61] The only certainty provided by the Tenth Amendment is that states must not be totally destroyed or rendered ineffective.[62] An enormous range of power allocations is consistent with the abstract requirement that some degree of state sovereignty be maintained. Hence, Choper and others can argue that the principle is sufficiently devoid of content that it can safely be entrusted to the political process.

Aspects of Choper's argument, then, suggest that the priority of rights over structure rests on a preference for constitutional values that can be concretely implemented.[63] To be implemented, a value must be measurable. To be measurable, it must be determinate and specific. To the extent they are more concrete (a matter I will return to shortly), rights may generally seem more important than processes. Any specific, morally compelling outcomes that are required by rights can easily seem more important than vague processes. Indeed, the basic premise of Choper's argument—that the courts should allocate their efforts to the areas where they can achieve the greatest payoff—attests to the profoundly instrumentalist[64] view that accompanies the preference for rights. Under this view, a major criterion for assessing legal rules is their capacity to produce measurable changes in the real world.

While the other major criticisms of *Usery* are different from Choper's, they generally share this same basic orientation.[65] Tribe

---

[60] See note 46 *supra*.

[61] Choper, note 6 *supra*, at 1560–67, 1571, 1574, 1576, 1620.

[62] Or "trampled" as Choper puts it (*id.* at 1560). Or "swallow the states whole" (*id.* at 1594). See also *id.* at 1563–68, 1570. See also text accompanying note 149 *infra*.

[63] Choper does briefly recognize that judicial review serves such nonspecific purposes as "nourishment of constitutional understanding" (*id.* at 1605). In suggesting that his federalism proposal would not damage public understanding and the court's role in sustaining that understanding, Choper is at his least convincing. See Monaghan, note 42 *supra*, at 306–7.

[64] The term "instrumentalism" has various meanings. Here I use it to denote those intellectual habits and inclinations described in Summers, *Naive Instrumentalism and the Law* in LAW MORALITY AND SOCIETY, ESSAYS IN HONOUR OF H.L.A. HART (Hacker & Raz, eds., 1977).

[65] A different sort of attack was also made: that *Usery* violated *stare decisis*. For example, Professor Cox summarized his criticism this way: "The short of the matter, therefore, is that

and Michelman convert a decision that is apparently aimed at protecting the organizational principle of state sovereignty into a decision that would establish an individual right to some level of state services. The daring of this reformulation itself attests to how strong is the instrumentalist urge to speak the language of rights rather than the more abstract language of organization. And, although they deny that their interpretations of *Usery* would justify a court to require some specific level of state services,[66] both arguments depend on a judicial determination at some point of an acceptable level of concrete state services. The instrumentalist inclination to use law to achieve tangible changes in the world is reflected in these efforts to define structural values by reference to some level of individual welfare.

The sorts of justifications that Tribe and Michelman offer for rushing past[67] organizational matters to settle on their more far-fetched interpretations[68] are also consistent with the instrumentalist orientation underlying Choper's arguments. For example, *Usery* is criticized for not relying on specific evidence as to the effect of the wage and hour provisions on state governments—for not looking to the "actual impact of the regulations."[69] The opinion is criticized for protecting the state as a private agent but not as sovereign lawgiver and enforcer.[70] It is criticized for protecting the government's apparatus but not its policy-making prerogatives.[71] And it is criticized for protecting the exercise of its traditional functions but not the sovereign prerogative to decide what new

---

although the decision in *National League of Cities* is almost surely consistent with the original conception of the federal union and might not have surprised any constitutional scholar prior to the 1930s, it is thoroughly inconsistent with the constitutional trends and decisions of the past forty years." Cox, *Federalism and Individual Rights under the Burger Court*, 73 Nw. U. L. Rev. 1, 22 (1978). In this essay I do not dispute the accuracy of Cox's revealingly complacent assessment, but I do inquire into how the modern decisional law (as well as the concerns of scholars) could have come to depart so significantly from the constitutional design.

[66] Michelman, note 5 *supra*, at 1190; Tribe, note 5 *supra*, at 1088–90.

[67] Both authors deal briefly with the issue of local self-determination. Michelman, note 5 *supra*, at 1191 n.86 ("Further investigation of this sensitivity to community self-determination, its role in the cited decisions, its theoretical significance, and its relationship to the issues in *NLC*, must await another article."). Tribe, note 5 *supra*, at 1093 n.109 ("Political accountability . . . poses a problem not only for state and local governments, but also for Congress.").

[68] See note 5 *supra*.

[69] Tribe, note 5 *supra*, at 1072.

[70] Michelman, note 5 *supra*, at 1168. Tribe, note 5 *supra*, at 1074.

[71] Michelman, note 5 *supra*, at 1168. Tribe, note 5 *supra*, at 1074–75.

functions ought to be assumed by the state.[72] In short, as Justice Brennan complained, *Usery* created an "abstraction without substance."[73] Or, as Michelman put it with understated relish, it is "no easy matter to ascribe operational content to that notion [of sovereignty]."[74]

In focusing on the difficulties of making the abstract concept of federalism operational, the major criticisms of *Usery* are all strongly instrumentalist. The belief that judicial protection of rights is more valuable than judicial protection of structural principles may, then, have become widespread because structural values are not easily assimilated into the instrumentalist assumptions that underlie so much of modern legal thought.[75] However, the precise relationship between this operationalism and the critics' common emphasis on individuals' rights remains somewhat mysterious. Their lack of enthusiasm for structural values is more understandable than their vigorous commitment to judicial protection of constitutional rights. Why is it, after all, that the values implicit in constitutional rights are thought of as being sufficiently specific to fit comfortably with the instrumentalist demands of the major critics of *Usery*? If it is difficult to identify when a federal statute interferes with some "essential" level of state functioning, it is difficult to identify when the provision of state services has dropped below some "minimally adequate level."[76] If a state's "sovereignty" is an abstract idea, so is an individual's "humanity."[77]

A principle like state sovereignty might, however, be thought to be different from a principle such as free speech in that almost no conceivable statute could impair the value behind the existence of state governments. In contrast, it has become easy and customary to think that specific statutes impair the values behind, for example, the First Amendment. And it is possible to define the value protected by the Tenth Amendment in such a way that its impairment

---

[72] Tribe, note 5 *supra*, at 1074. Michelman, note 5 *supra*, at 1172.

[73] 426 U.S. at 860.

[74] Michelman, note 5 *supra*, at 1166.

[75] See Summers, *Professor Fuller's Jurisprudence and America's Dominant Philosophy of Law*, 92 HARV. L. REV. 433 (1978).

[76] A matter that is acknowledged by both Tribe and Michelman (see note 66 *supra*).

[77] Tribe, note 20 *supra*, at 1077 ("The crux of any determination that a law unjustly discriminates against a group . . . [is] that the law is part of a pattern that denies those subject to it a meaningful opportunity to realize their humanity.").

by any one statute is improbable. The Court, for instance, has said that the commerce power may not be used in a way that centralizes all power in the national government.[78] No statute other than one that abolished the states could do that. But no conceivable statute threatens the larger purposes behind the First Amendment either. Whether these purposes are defined systemically ("the maintenance of open public debate for the sake of democratic decision making") or personally ("the protection of access to and use of information for the sake of autonomous individuals"), these large values are not threatened by any discrete act. A statute that prohibits the reading of pornographic books in one's home will not destroy autonomy unless accompanied by a wide array of other restrictions that destroy other sources of personal autonomy.[79] Even a major instance of prior restraint over the publication of political news could not by itself destroy the level of debate generally necessary for the democratic system to operate.[80] Discrete governmental restrictions do threaten these larger values cumulatively and in the long run. Rights *can be* made operational, then, not so much because the values they serve are specific or concrete, but because they *must be*. Rights must be made operational precisely because their purposes are remote and general and can be undercut only gradually and insensibly. But that, of course, is also true of the exercise of federal power as it gradually diminishes state sovereignty.

Although rights are not innately more concrete or measurable than structural values, concentration on rights does lead to instrumentalist habits of thought. This is because noninstrumentalist justifications for decisions that protect rights are never fully satisfactory. Even Judge Hans Linde's well-known effort to emphasize noninstrumental justifications for major Warren era cases demonstrates the difficulty of severing rights from instrumentalism. He asked, "What would be the implications for the Constitution, in its role as primary national symbol, of a decision saying that a bit of organized public prayer never hurt anyone?"[81] This question was designed to suggest that compliance with judicial decrees—concrete alterations of actual behavior—is less important than the

---

[78] National Labor Relations Board v. Jones & Laughlin Steel Corp., 301 U.S. at 37.

[79] *Cf.* Stanley v. Georgia, 394 U.S. 557 (1969).

[80] *Cf.* New York Times Co. v. United States, 403 U.S. 713 (1971).

[81] Linde, *Judges, Critics, and the Realist Tradition*, 82 YALE L. J. 227, 238 (1972).

sense of understanding and reassurance that the Court's statement of principle creates.[82] As important as this argument is in supplementing the instrumentalists' narrower understanding, emphasizing as it does the immediate and tangible consequences of decisions,[83] it is not fully satisfying. To the extent that a court can make compelling the normative premise in its decision regarding an individual right, the court has stated reasons for realizing that right in actual situations. Parties who have convincingly been labeled "wronged" may be reassured by their abstract vindication, but they will also want the matter righted. And what is good for one individual is morally compelling for others in analogous situations. Thus, the vindication of a constitutional "right" localizes the moral claim in an individual and thereby creates an inevitable insistence on "actualization."[84] In short, the constant impulse to define rights in measurable ways derives from the fact that, as Choper emphasized, constitutional rights are individuals' rights. Rights are specified—the percentage of each race that should attend public schools, the extent of acceptable governmental participation in parochial education, the number of square feet required in prison cells—to give some assurance that each individual can receive whatever moral benefit is inherent in the right.

Because structural values need not be immediately localized in individuals, noninstrumental justifications may be more fully satisfying when applied to matters of governmental organization than when applied to matters of right. Such justifications, because not linked to concrete alterations of the world, would not be credited or even noticed by those absorbed in matters of individual rights. Such justifications satisfactorally explain *Usery*.

III.

The Court's decision in *National League of Cities v. Usery* is understandable and admirable once the intellectual habits associated with thinking about constitutional rights are set aside. The Court did not attempt to limit congressional power by a restrictive definition of "commerce among the States." Such a tactic was

---

[82] *Id.* at 232, 237, 238, 239.

[83] See Summers, note 64 *supra*, and Linde, note 81 *supra*, at 229–30.

[84] See Fiss, note 21 *supra*.

employed by the Court prior to 1937 when, for example, it attempted to distinguish such local matters as "manufacture" from the national concern, "commerce."[85] This approach, like present-day efforts to actualize rights, involved the Court in efforts to create and maintain a concrete, identifiable "constitutional" condition—a condition that then consisted of a "proper" division of substantive areas of regulation between the state and nation. The effort, of course, is now discredited. The *Usery* Court, instead, emphasized the abstract concept behind the principle of federalism; it spoke of states as being "coordinate elements" and as needing "separate and independent existence."[86] This language does not require some tangible, static system of power allocation, a fact that was emphasized by the unwillingness of the Court to rest its decision on any specific measurement of the burden imposed on the states by the Fair Labor Standards Act (FLSA).[87] The Court's language is true to the idea of federalism, in that it describes a process rather than an edifice.[88]

In applying these abstractions to the facts of *Usery*, the Court first distinguished those cases that involved the exercise of federal authority over individuals from those over states "as states."[89] It emphasized the importance of the employment relationship for the effective exercise of state functions[90] and (in general terms) the sorts of burdens created by the FLSA for important programs carried on by state and local governments.[91] It described the burdens as affecting broad areas of governmental activity,[92] including areas where states have traditionally delivered services.[93] These factors, I believe, can be shown to define state sovereignty in a way that is entirely consistent with the Federalists' political theory. Although the Court in *Usery* did not specifically refer to this theory, the main

---

[85] *E.g.*, Carter v. Carter Coal Co., 298 U.S. 238 (1936).

[86] 426 U.S. at 849, 851.

[87] *Id.* at 851.

[88] See Wechsler, note 41 *supra*, passim. See also Freund, note 41 *supra*, at 159–61; FRIEDRICH, TRENDS OF FEDERALISM IN THEORY AND PRACTICE 3–11 (1968).

[89] 426 U.S. at 845.

[90] *Id.* at 845, 847–48, 851.

[91] *Id.* at 846–51.

[92] *Id.* at 847, 848, 850.

[93] *Id.* at 851.

elements of the opinion are protective of the purposes that the framers intended the states to serve in the "federal" system.[94]

Those purposes, although not reducible to anything concrete or measurable, are well known and important. Proponents of the proposed constitution who, like Madison and Hamilton, argued for a strong national government had to answer the fears of those who thought that the new national government would consolidate all power at the national level.[95] The reasons that the anti-Federalists feared this possibility were varied. They feared that regional interests would be undervalued in a legislature so small and so physically remote[96] and, more generally, that the quality of political accountability would suffer because the national leadership would become culturally and psychologically alienated from localities.[97] They argued that national authority would not be sufficiently responsive to elicit voluntary compliance, so that force would become the mechanism of government.[98] They were concerned that the opportunity for participation and identification with government would be too limited, ultimately threatening devotion to liberty itself.[99] Such fears were sufficient to threaten the adoption of the proposed constitution and to force not only the adoption of the first ten amendments, but also the creation of a theory of federalism that explained and justified the proposed system of power allocation.[100]

This theory turned the anti-Federalists' emphasis on the size and heterogeneity of the country into a powerful argument for adopting the Constitution. It was, the Federalists argued, the size and variety

---

[94] I am using the modern nomenclature which nearly reverses framers' usage. See Diamond, note 39 *supra*.

[95] Apparently there was at least some basis for the anti-Federalist fear that some Federalists wished literally to abolish the states. See MAIN, THE ANTI-FEDERALISTS, CRITICS OF THE CONSTITUTION 121 (1961); SCHWARTZ, note 39 *supra*, at 597. More generally, however, the anti-Federalists feared that the proposed constitution provided inadequate safeguards against the enlargement of federal power beyond the enumerated powers. See, *e.g.*, SCHWARTZ, note 39 *supra*, at 572, 592–93, 653, 526.

[96] See MAIN, note 95 *supra*, at 129; KENYON, THE ANTI-FEDERALISTS xli (1966).

[97] KENYON, note 96 *supra*, at xl, li, liii.

[98] *Id*. at 210, xl.

[99] *Id*. at 388. Subsequent writings attest to the importance of such arguments. See, *e.g.*, DAHL & TUFTE, SIZE AND DEMOCRACY (1973); McCONNELL, PRIVATE POWER AND AMERICAN DEMOCRACY 190 (1966); TOCQUEVILLE, II DEMOCRACY IN AMERICA 79, 148, 307–11 (1970) (Arlington House).

[100] See, *e.g.*, LEWIS, ANTI-FEDERALIST V. FEDERALIST 28 (1967).

within the nation that would reduce the likelihood of overreaching by the national government.[101] Because state governments would remain alternative power centers, the national government would be in constant competition with state governments.[102] This would curtail the tendency of the national government toward un-responsiveness and would prevent excessive centralization of power. Thus, the anti-Federalists' argument that state governments were more responsive was turned on its head: The very efficiency and responsiveness of local governments would enable them to act as a "counterpoise"[103] to national authority. The existence of states could, then, make practical what at the time seemed a contradiction in terms—a large country with a strong national government that would not degenerate into a "tyranny."[104]

The theory of the proponents of the new national government, in short, depended on assurances that effective state governments could continue to exist. As modern writers also argue,[105] the states' influence on the national political process was identified as a major protection for state sovereignty, and this influence was thought to depend in part on how the electoral process was organized.[106] However, unlike the modern writers, the Federalists understood and emphasized that influence through electoral politics presupposes that state governments would exist as alternative objects of loyalty to the national government.[107] Unless the residents of the states and their political representatives understand that states are entitled to claim governmental prerogatives and unless they perceive states as legitimate, separate governments, there will be no impulse to use political influence to protect the interests of states as governmental entities. It is, as Madison put it, "the existence of subordinate governments *to which the people are attached* [that] forms a barrier against the enterprises of ambition. . . ."[108]

---

101 THE FEDERALIST PAPERS, Nos. 10, 51.

102 See text accompanying notes 108, 117–24, 133 *infra*.

103 THE FEDERALIST PAPERS, No. 17 at 9, 20.

104 See MAIN, note 95 *supra*, at 130; DAHL & TUFTE, note 99 *supra*, at 4–11; THE FEDERALIST PAPERS, Nos. 9, 10.

105 See WECHSLER, note 41 *supra*; CHOPER, note 6 *supra*, at 1560–65.

106 THE FEDERALIST PAPERS, No. 45.

107 See text accompanying notes 117–24 *infra*. See generally DIAMOND, note 94 *supra*, at 46.

108 THE FEDERALIST PAPERS, No. 46 at 299 (emphasis added).

The justifications offered in *Usery* for limiting congressional power over commerce are directly relevant to preserving those preconditions necessary for the states to act as a counterpoise to national authority. The factors emphasized by the Court all define state sovereignty in the sense relevant to the Federalists' theory, because they all preserve the capacity of state governments to elicit enough respect and loyalty to act as legitimate competitors to the central government. These sources of legitimacy[109] can be grouped into four categories: symbolic, regulatory, communicative, and organizational. All can be shown to be inherent in the Federalists' theory and all connect *Usery* to existing case law.

1. *Symbolism as a source of legitimacy.* The framers of the Constitution were acutely aware of the emotional underpinnings of governmental authority. Madison referred to "that veneration which time bestows on every thing, and without which perhaps the wisest and freest governments would not possess the requisite stability."[110] Similarly, Hamilton spoke of "impressing upon the minds of the people affection, esteem, and reverence towards the government."[111] Supreme Court decisions have reflected the same sensitivity, holding that the national government could not control the location of a state capital,[112] suggesting that the statehouse would be exempt from federal taxation,[113] and, after some hesitation, protecting state court proceedings from interruptions by federal courts.[114] None of these decisions can be explained on the basis of actual impact on the functioning of states. The business of state government can go on once the capital city has been located, a tax on a state operation might be greater in amount and consequence than a tax on the statehouse, and state courts would not dry up because of occasional interruptions by federal injunctions. All these decisions are explicable only as efforts to protect the symbolism of

---

[109] "Legitimacy" has been defined as the capacity to engender and maintain the belief that the existing political institutions are "appropriate," (see LIPSET, POLITICAL MAN 64 [Anchor ed. 1963]), "rightful," or "entitled to rule" (FRIEDRICH, TRADITION AND AUTHORITY 89 [1972]). I treat the effectiveness of a government in meeting the needs of its citizens as one source of legitimacy. Compare Lipset, *supra*, ch. 3, with Friedrich, *supra*, at 89.

[110] THE FEDERALIST PAPERS, No. 49 at 314.

[111] *Id.*, No. 17, at 120.

[112] Coyle v. Oklahoma, 221 U.S. 559 (1911).

[113] New York v. United States, note 15 *supra*, at 582.

[114] Younger v. Harris, note 11 *supra*.

the states as sovereign governments and, therefore, their capacity to sustain emotional attachments.

The symbolism of a state that is unable to control the wages and hours of its own employees is stark. The *Usery* Court's repeated emphasis on the effect of the federal rules on the states, as states, can be understood in this light. The apparatus of government may not be a special aspect of sovereignty in some exalted philosophical sense,[115] but psychologically the apparatus does represent the government's authority to the people. The Court's reliance on the impact of the FLSA on such traditional areas of state control as police and fire protection is also responsive to the requirements of symbolic authority. Again, as *Usery's* critics maintain, "sovereignty" might be equally involved in innovative functions as in traditional ones, but the longer an area has been subject to state control the more symbolic of state authority that area becomes. Psychologically, a federal burden on a state water bottling operation, for example, simply does not threaten the legitimacy of a state government in the same way as would federal burdens on public education or police protection.[116]

2. *Regulatory authority as a source of legitimacy.* The Federalists understood that any government "must be able to address itself immediately to the hopes and fears of individuals; and to attract to its support those passions which have the strongest influence upon the human heart."[117] They argued repeatedly that states would have a natural advantage over the national government because of "the nature of the objects" of state regulation.[118] States, Hamilton thought, would control the "variety of more minute interests . . . which will form . . . many rivulents of influence running through every part of the society. . . ."[119] Not only would state control be pervasive but it would also involve[120]

---

[115] See note 71 *supra*.

[116] *Cf.* New York v. United States, note 113 *supra*. In many other cases, the Supreme Court has shown an inclination to protect "traditional" areas of state governmental activity from federal encroachment. See, *eg.*, Rizzo v. Goode, 423 U.S. 362 (1976); Milliken v. Bradley, 418 U.S. 717 (1974); San Antonio Independent School District v. Rodriguez, note 12 *supra*; Labine v. Vincent, note 12 *supra*.

[117] THE FEDERALIST PAPERS, No. 16 at 116.

[118] *Id.*, No. 17, at 119.

[119] *Id.* at 119–20.

[120] *Id.* at 120.

all those personal interests and familiar concerns to which the sensibility of individuals is more immediately awake . . . impressing upon the minds of the people affection, esteem, and reverence towards the government.

Madison echoed these arguments[121] and added to them by appealing to a widely held assumption that states could be expected to deliver services effectively.[122] In contrast to all these resources available to state governments, the powers granted the national government were "few and defined."[123] That is,[124]

[R]elating to more general interests, they will be less apt to come home to the feelings of the people; and, in proportion, less likely to inspire an habitual sense of obligation and active sentiment of attachment.

Many of the Federalists' arguments regarding the natural advantages of state power sound quaint today and might have been somewhat disingenuous at the time.[125] Certainly, the Federalists cannot be read as predicting or guaranteeing the primary of state power.[126] But the underlying idea in these reassurances cannot be dismissed lightly because it is a necessary part of the Federalists' larger theory: to be able to protect themselves in the political process states would need (and were assured under the proposed Constitution) the capacity to elicit loyalty by providing for the needs of their residents. Consequently, there is nothing improper or unusual in judicial sensitivity to the need to preserve traditional areas of

---

[121] "The powers delegated by the proposed Constitution to the federal government are few and defined. Those which are to remain in the State governments are numerous and indefinite. The former will be exercised principally on external objects, as war, peace, negotiation, and foreign commerce; with which last the power of taxation will, for the most part, be connected. The powers reserved to the several States will extend to all the objects which, in the ordinary course of affairs, concern the lives, liberties, and properties of the people, and the internal order, improvement, and prosperity of the state." THE FEDERALIST PAPERS, No. 45, at 292–93; see also No. 46 at 294–95.

[122] ". . . [I]t is only within a certain sphere that the federal power can, in the nature of things, be advantageously administered." THE FEDERALIST PAPERS, No. 46, at 295.

[123] *Id.*, No. 45, at 292.

[124] *Id.*, No. 17, at 120; see also Nos. 45 at 292, 46 at 295.

[125] See Diamond, note 94 *supra*.

[126] *Ibid.*

primary control for state authority. Such sensitivity is commonplace in areas like education[127] or family law.[128]

Nevertheless, a fundamental fear of *Usery*'s critics was that the principle of the case could not be restricted to protecting the states' governing apparatus but would necessarily be extended to protect state control over policies regarding private citizens as well.[129] Why, they asked, is state control over employees more a sovereign matter than state control over citizens? But *Usery* does not require that any particular area of policy necessarily be reserved for state control. The Federalists' reassurances make clear that the basic idea behind enumerating federal powers was to reserve to the states the capacity for a pervasive relationship with their citizenry—to require that federal control over citizens be exceptional and specially justified.[130] The extension of the FLSA to state employees would have insinuated a federal presence into nearly every activity carried on by the state, which would have seriously undermined the role of the states as the governments with broad primary contact with the citizenry.[131]

Moreover, the Court's emphasis on the importance of the services affected by the FLSA extension—"fire prevention, police protection, sanitation, public health . . ."[132]—tracks the framers' assumption that states would control most policies of personal importance to people. And Madison's acknowledgement of the importance to state sovereignty of effective delivery of such services is echoed in the Court's concern that the wage and hour provisions would disrupt what the states had regarded as useful methods of administration. In short, the FLSA was threatening to *all* the ele-

---

[127] *E.g.*, San Antonio Independent School District v. Rodriguez, note 12 *supra*; Brown v. Board of Education (II), 349 U.S. 294 (1955).

[128] *E.g.*, Labine v. Vincent, note 12 *supra*. I do not mean to imply, of course, that the Court consistently honors the tradition of state control over such matters. See, *e.g.*, Carey v. Population Services, 431 U.S. 678 (1977); Zablocki v. Redhail, 434 U.S. 374 (1978). But such intrusions are made against a backdrop of the acknowledged propriety of general state authority over such matters. See, *e.g.*, Griswold v. Connecticut, 381 U.S. 479, 499 (Harlan, concurring) (1965).

[129] *E.g.*, 426 U.S. at 833, 875 (Brennan, J., dissenting).

[130] See notes 121, 122 *supra*. See also Wechsler, note 41 *supra*, at 98: "National action has thus always been regarded as exceptional in our polity, an intrusion to be justified by some necessity, the special rather than the ordinary case."

[131] Federal control over state employees who perform general functions, then, is analogous to general federal common law in that both, almost by definition, are at odds with the concept of enumerated powers. *Cf.* Erie Railroad Co. v. Tompkins, 304 U.S. 64 (1938).

[132] 426 U.S. at 851.

ments of what the framers thought were the special characteristics of state regulatory authority. When a single federal statute compromises the states' authority to respond effectively and pervasively to the ordinary concerns of personal importance to the people, the Court is justified in sensing an incompatibility with the assumptions behind the constitutional design.

3. *Communication as a source of legitimacy.* How did the Federalists think that states might resist encroachments of federal power? One answer was that the states would provide a constant method of measuring whether federal policy had strayed too far from the popular will:[133]

> Either the mode in which the federal government is to be constructed will render it sufficiently dependent on the people, or it will not. On the first supposition, it will be restrained by that dependence from forming schemes obnoxious to their constituents. On the other supposition, it will not possess the confidence of the people, and its schemes of usurpation will be easily defeated by the State governments, who will be supported by the people.

A second sort of answer was that the states would organize resistance both within their respective borders and among the other states.[134] The states would "sound the alarm."[135] The national government might then be faced with "the disquietude of the people; . . . the frowns of the executive magistracy of the State; the embarrassments created by legislative devices. . . ."[136] In the first of these roles, states require a formal capacity to articulate possible alternates to federal policy. In the second, states require the capacity to express dissatisfaction with federal policies officially. Such considerations must underlie judicial reluctance to expose official state legislative acts to federal injunctions[137] or to supplant the state appointment process.[138]

---

[133] THE FEDERALIST PAPERS, No. 46 at 300.

[134] *Id.* at 296–99.

[135] *Id.* Nos. 44–46.

[136] *Id.*, No. 46 at 297.

[137] For example, typically courts threaten to raise funds themselves but do not directly order state legislatures to raise taxes. *E.g.*, Wyatt v. Stickney, 344 F. Supp. 373 (M.D. Ala. 1972), *aff'd in part sub. nom.* Wyatt v. Aderholt, 503 F.2d 1305 (5th Cir. 1974).

[138] *Cf.* Mayor of Philadelphia v. Educational Equality League, 415 U.S. 605 (1974); Carter v. Jury Comm'n., 396 U.S. 320 (1970); Lance v. Plummer, 384 U.S. 929 (1966) (Black, J., dissenting from denial of certiorari).

Usery is responsive to the need to protect the capacity of state governments to represent and articulate opposition to federal power. The Court properly noted the special and fundamental character of the power to set wages and hours,[139] for federal control over basic working conditions would be a major way of shifting the loyalty of state employees to the national government. To the extent that opposition to federal policies must be expressed through the state employees who have daily and immediate contact with the citizenry, the capacity for opposition would be compromised. Moreover, the Court's emphasis on the impact of the FLSA on the states, as states, has widely been understood to insulate from congressional control such formal elements of governance as the adoption of legislation or the promulgation of regulations.[140] To the extent that *Usery*'s principles protect these formal elements of policy articulation, the decision protects the capacity of states— governments rather than individual leaders—to endorse (if not implement) policies that can stand as potential alternatives to national policy.

4. *Organizational authority as a source of legitimacy.* The Federalists thought that the states would draw loyalty from the people on the same principle that "a man is more attached to his family than to his neighborhood, to his neighborhood than to the community at large. . . ."[141] Physical proximity would be reinforced by immediate opportunities for participation in local government:[142]

> Into the administration of [the governments of the states] a greater number of individuals will expect to rise. From the gift of these a greater number of offices and emoluments will flow. By the superintending care of these, all the more domestic and personal interests of the people will be regulated and provided for. With the affairs of these, the people will be more familiarly and minutely conversant. And with the members of these will a greater proportion of the people have ties of personal acquaintance and friendship, and of family and party attachments; on the side of these, therefore, the popular bias may well be expected most strongly to incline.

---

[139] 426 U.S. at 845, 851.

[140] EPA v. Brown, 431 U.S. 99 (1977).

[141] THE FEDERALIST PAPERS, No. 17 at 119.

[142] *Id.*, No. 46, at 294–95.

The capacity of states to elicit participation in government depends in large part on their authority to organize and control the units of local government.[143] It is by determining the appropriate amount of decentralization over such matters as taxation or public education that states can attempt to match local control to local interest, and the resulting political participation serves to give people a stake in public decisions and a sense of identification with their government. The Court has repeatedly recognized the special importance to state governments of control over such organizational decisions.[144]

The Court in *Usery* was sensitive to the impact of the wage and hour provisions on local participation. It noted, for example, that the provisions would lead to "a significant reduction of traditional volunteer assistance which has been in the past drawn on to complement the operation of many local governmental functions."[145] The decision insulated political subdivisions from the wage and hour provisions on the ground that these "derive their authority and power from their respective States."[146] At least one critic somehow found this protection of state authority proof that *Usery* was not aimed at protecting "the state as object of political loyalty."[147] The framers understood the sources of loyalty more realistically. In their scheme, it is important that the emotional referent of local governments continue to match their legal referent, so that the states derive full advantage from self-government at the local level. Federal control over wages and hours of employees of political subdivisions would begin to displace to the national government the allegiance and identification of those who are part of local government.

In summary, the Court in *Usery* displayed a sure feel for protecting the "essential role of the States in our federal system of government" as the framers defined that role. Despite the Court's

---

[143] Evidence suggests that the sense of identification and participation is possible to a far greater extent in very small units of government. See DAHL & TUFTE, note 99 *supra*, at 60, 63, 84. On the relationship between state authority and local authority, see TOCQUEVILLE, I. 45, 51, 52, 79, 148; II, 109. For a detailed account of the advantages of localism and of the legal status of cities, see Frug, *The City as a Legal Concept*, 93 HARV. L. REV. 1057 (1980).

[144] *E.g.*, San Antonio Independent School District v. Rodriguez, note 12 *supra*; Milliken v. Bradley, 418 U.S. 717 (1974).

[145] 426 U.S. at 850–51.

[146] *Id.* at 855–56.

[147] Michelman, note 5 *supra*, at 1169.

failure to refer specifically to the role of the states as political competitors to the national government, the tracking of the Federalists' theory was not coincidental. The case law that informed and shaped the Court's assumptions about federalism was no doubt influenced by the framers' ideas, and, in any event, the *Usery* Court, like the framers, focused on what is necessary for the states' "separate and independent existence."[148]

Usery, then, was not incomprehensible to its critics because its holding and explanation were unrelated to the Constitution. It was incomprehensible because of the critics' intellectual habits which had developed out of long concern for questions of individuals' rights.

Decisions like *Usery* that protect constitutional structure are different from the more familiar efforts of courts to protect rights. Structural principles such as federalism are intended to maintain a rough system of power allocation over long periods of time. There is no analogy to the adjudication of rights where, at some point in time, desegregation must be achieved or enough services must be provided. Structure is a process that is maintained, not achieved. The courts' function in matters of structure is largely to sustain (or at least not undercut) the understandings, the attitudes, and the emotional ties that underlie the system of power allocation. These objectives may be intangible, but they are directly relevant to preserving the constitutional system, since that system presupposes divided loyalties and complex attitudes toward authority. Structural decisions are not necessarily based on the injustice of depriving a single individual of a particular allocation of authority. Hence, the assertion of structural values is not essential in every case where they are potentially implicated; nevertheless, their assertion in especially appropriate cases like *Usery* is important because of the indirect, long-run consequences to the whole political system of ignoring the underpinnings of constitutional structure. These consequences are not adequately described by images of states as "empty vessels" or "gutted shells."[149] Such metaphors are more expressive of the critics' urge to render the issues tangible (and therefore more familiar) than of the values at stake in a dispute

---

[148] 426 U.S. at 845 (quoting from Lane County v. Oregon, 74 U.S. [7 Wall.] 71 [1869]).

[149] *E.g.*, Tribe, note 5 *supra*, at 1072 ("empty vessels"), 1071 ("gutted shell"); Choper, note 62 *supra*.

about federalism. In the Federalists' scheme, the states were to be maintained partly for their own sakes and partly as a tool for assuring adequate levels of political responsiveness, competition, and participation.[150]

Much of the scholarly and judicial attention to the definition of individual rights is aimed at achieving these same goals by more direct means. Definitions of free speech, equal protection, procedural due process, privacy, and other rights are grounded on the belief that such protections will produce the kind of independent individuals who can participate vigorously in the political process. And it may be that these rights are ultimately important to the potential for self-government. But, quite aside from the familiar charge that enforcement of such rights centralizes too much power at the national level, excessive attention to rights can be a threat to self-government. A subtle conflict exists between rights, taken too seriously, and structure. The frame of mind that is created by concentration on the direct, tangible protection of individuals does not easily appreciate the less determinate requirements of constitutional structure. A judicial system deeply engaged in achieving immediate justice for all individuals will not be sensitive to, or much interested in, the intellectual and emotional preconditions for political competition between sovereigns. The "constitutional law" that develops in such a system will be more attuned to the demands of measurement and the excitement of accomplishment than to the full range of the framers' concerns.

Suppose for a moment that divided and limited loyalties are not as important as the right to contraceptives for preserving the capacity for self-government in the modern world. At least, a decision like *Usery* that presumed there might be some small usefulness in promoting the framers' organizational theory ought not to have been dismissed as *constitutionally* incomprehensible. That the decision was so widely unappreciated ought to be unsettling to anyone who is not certain that the framers' structural principles are worthless today.

---

[150] THE FEDERALIST PAPERS, No. 45 at 289. See also text at notes 94–104 *supra*.

LOUIS MICHAEL SEIDMAN

THE SUPREME COURT, ENTRAPMENT, AND OUR CRIMINAL JUSTICE DILEMMA

In 1932, the Supreme Court announced that a federal criminal conviction could not be sustained when "the criminal design originates with the officials of the Government, and they implant in the mind of an innocent person the disposition to commit the alleged offense and induce its commission in order that they may prosecute."[1]

Two remarkable facts emerge from the study of our fifty-year experience since this first authoritative articulation of a federal entrapment defense.[2] First, although members of the Court have con-

---

Louis Michael Seidman is Associate Professor of Law, Georgetown Law Center.

AUTHOR'S NOTE: John Gomperts and Susan Donner provided valuable research assistance and copious moral support during the preparation of this article. Warren Schwartz, Steven Cohen, Steve Goldberg, Joel Handler, Thomas Krattenmaker, Deirdre Golash, Mark Tushnet, Silas Wasserstrom, Peter Tague, Katherine Klein, Geoffrey Stone, and Yale Kamisar graciously gave of their time to read and criticize an earlier version of this paper.

[1] Sorrells v. United States, 287 U.S. 435, 442 (1932).

[2] Five years before *Sorrells*, in Casey v. United States, 276 U.S. 413 (1928), the Court seemed to acknowledge the theoretical possibility of an entrapment defense. The Court rejected the claim on the facts before it, however, because no record had been made on it below and because there was no evidence that the defendant "was induced to commit the crime beyond [a] simple request . . . to which he seems to have acceded without hesitation and as a matter of course." 276 U.S. at 419. See also Grimm v. United States, 156 U.S. 604, 610 (1895).

The defense seems to have been well established in the lower federal courts some years before receiving the Supreme Court's imprimatur. See, *e.g.*, Woo Wai v. United States, 223 F. 412 (6th Cir. 1915). For collections of the early cases, see 18 A.L.R. 146 (1922); 66 A.L.R. 478 (1930).

ducted a sporadic debate concerning the origin and scope of the defense,[3] not a single Justice has written to question whether it should exist at all.[4] Second, no member of the Court—and none of the numerous commentators on its work—has advanced a defense of the doctrine that is satisfactory.[5]

How can one account for such unanimity coupled with such reticence? It is barely possible that entrapment doctrine is no more than an analytical mutation—a fluke in the judicial process preserved and nurtured by the forces of *stare decisis*. Indeed, if one takes seriously the function supposedly served by judicial opinions, the

---

[3] From the beginning, the Justices have divided on the question whether the defense should focus on the defendant's "predisposition" or on the wrongfulness of the government's conduct. Compare, *e.g.*, Sorrells v. United States, 287 U.S. 435, 451 (1932), with *id.* at 458–59 (separate opinion of Roberts, J.). See also Hampton v. United States, 425 U.S. 484, 496–97 (1976) (Brennan, J., dissenting); United States v. Russell, 411 U.S. 423, 441 (1973) (Stewart, J., dissenting); Sherman v. United States, 356 U.S. 369, 383 (1958) (Frankfurter, J., concurring). There has been a parallel dispute over whether the defense derives from the unexpressed intent of Congress, see, *e.g.*, Sorrells v. United States, 287 U.S. 435, 446–49 (1932), or from the Court's supervisory powers. See, *e.g.*, Sherman v. United States, 356 U.S. 369, 380 (1958) (Frankfurter, J., concurring). More recently, this second dispute has been complicated by the argument that certain forms of police encouragement may violate the Due Process Clause of the Fifth Amendment. See United States v. Russell, 411 U.S. 423, 431–32 (1973); Hampton v. United States, 425 U.S. 484, 492–93 (1976) (Powell, J., concurring).

[4] Although the *Sorrells* Court divided sharply over the appropriate test for entrapment, only Justice McReynolds dissented from the proposition that the trial court's failure to give an entrapment instruction was reversible error. See 287 U.S. at 453. Since Justice McReynolds wrote no opinion, it is unclear whether he rejected the concept of an entrapment defense or believed that the facts before him were insufficient to raise the issue. In the six cases since *Sorrells* in which the Court has adjudicated entrapment claims, no Justice has written to suggest that the entrapment defense should not be permitted. See Hampton v. United States, 425 U.S. 484 (1976); United States v. Russell, 411 U.S. 423 (1973); Osborn v. United States, 385 U.S. 323 (1966); Lopez v. United States, 373 U.S. 427 (1963); Sherman v. United States, 356 U.S. 369 (1958); Masciale v. United States, 356 U.S. 386 (1958).

Moreover, although the states are largely free to formulate their own entrapment doctrine, state courts have also been all but unanimous in embracing some version of the entrapment defense. See Park, *The Entrapment Controversy*, 60 MINN. L. REV. 163, 164 n.1 (1976) [hereinafter cited as "The Entrapment Controversy"]. This unanimity is all the more puzzling when one realizes that most of the rest of the civilized world manages to survive quite well without an entrapment defense. See, *e.g.*, FLETCHER, RETHINKING CRIMINAL LAW 541 (1978); Barlow, *Entrapment and the Common Law: Is There a Place for the American Doctrine of Entrapment*, 41 MOD. L. REV. 266 (1978).

[5] For the most part, commentators have been preoccupied with the appropriate test for entrapment and procedural issues surrounding the defense. See, *e.g.*, *The Entrapment Controversy*; Goldstein, *For Harold Lasswell: Some Reflections on Human Dignity, Entrapment, Informed Consent and the Plea Bargain*, 84 YALE L.J. 683 (1975); Groot, *The Serpent Beguiled Me and I (Without Scienter) Did Eat—Denial of Crime and the Entrapment Defense*, 1973 U. ILL. L. F. 254; Orfield, *The Defense of Entrapment in the Federal Courts*, 1967 DUKE L. J. 39; Donnelly, *Judicial Control of Informants, Spies, Stool Pigeons and Agent Provocateurs*, 60 YALE L.J. 1091 (1951) [hereinafter cited as "Judicial Control of Informants"].

doctrine's survival may crucially depend upon the failure of the Justices to focus on the necessity for providing a rationale for it.

Still, that failure itself remains a puzzle. On the face of it, it seems unlikely that Justices of the intellectual caliber of Hughes, Frankfurter, Brennan, and Rehnquist[6]—all of whom have written and thought about entrapment—would have simply overlooked the troubling nature of the defense. And surely it is doubtful that *stare decisis* alone would have supported a fundamentally erroneous doctrine through a half century of extraordinary volatility in criminal procedure.

My thesis is that something more important and troubling explains the survival of the entrapment defense: entrapment doctrine is one of a number of adaptive mechanisms which compensate for our failure to develop a coherent theory of blame and choice to regulate the imposition of criminal punishment. More fundamentally, the doctrine is a consequence of the inherent limits on the ability of government to distribute the social cost of deterring crime in an equitable fashion.

These are large claims, and I want to qualify them immediately in two ways. First, although I am reasonably confident in my conclusion that the customary arguments in favor of an entrapment defense are flawed, I wish to be more tentative in advancing my own explanation for the defense. In particular, I make no claim about the actual thought processes or motivations of the Justices who have written about, and voted for, the doctrine. My argument, instead, is that, objectively considered, the entrapment defense serves certain functions which are important to the maintenance of the criminal justice system. The otherwise puzzling survival of the defense, in the absence of any alternative justification for it, suggests a causal link between these functions and the defense. But whether such a link actually exists is an empirical question that cannot be answered by legal analysis.

Second, I do not wish to overstate the practical importance of entrapment doctrine. The doctrine illustrates the pervasive limitations on the power of government to impose criminal sanctions—limitations that are supremely important. But the doctrine itself

---

[6] See Sorrells v. United States, 287 U.S. 435 (1932) (Hughes, C.J.); Sherman v. United States, 356 U.S. 369, 378 (1958) (Frankfurter, J.); United States v. Russell, 411 U.S. 423 (1973) (Rehnquist, J.); Hampton v. United States, 425 U.S. 484 (1976) (Rehnquist, J.); *id.* at 495 (Brennan, J).

plays a minor role in enforcing those limitations. There are few entrapment defenses mounted,[7] and fewer still that are successful. If the cases establishing the defense were overruled tomorrow, we would hardly notice the difference.

Thus, if the defense is worthy of study, it is not because of what it does, but because of what it represents. I believe that our commitment to an entrapment defense demonstrates in especially graphic fashion a weakness at the heart of our criminal justice system—a weakness which is systematically reflected in areas as divergent as police enforcement patterns, sentencing discretion, our elaborate network of legal justifications and excuses, and the very definition of substantive criminal offenses.

Before examining how entrapment relates to this more general problem, however, it is first necessary to understand more precisely the content of the entrapment defense.

I. Predisposition, Inducement, and the "Unwary Criminal"

Superficially, the "black letter" of federal entrapment law seems easy enough to comprehend. As a matter of statutory construction, the Supreme Court has read federal criminal statutes to prohibit punishment of a defendant, not previously disposed to commit a crime, who is induced to commit it by a government agent.[8] Although the defendant has the burden of production on the issue,[9] once he introduces some evidence that he was "in-

---

[7] See, e.g., The Entrapment Controversy 267–68 n.339; Hardy, The Traps of Entrapment, 3 AM. J. CRIM. L. 165, 188–90 (1974). The defense apparently had more practical significance at the time of its initial formulation. See Judicial Control of Informants 1099. Of course, there is no necessary correlation between the frequency with which the defense is raised and the frequency with which police pursue some form of entrapment strategy. Compare The Entrapment Controversy 238 (little evidence that police utilize entrapment strategy) with Marx, The New Police Undercover Work, 8 URBAN LIFE 399, 400–01 (1980) (police use of entrapment and undercover activity expanding). Nor does the paucity of successful entrapment defenses necessarily prove that police would not make much more frequent use of this technique if the legal restraints on their doing so were removed. See text at notes 144–45 infra.

[8] See, e.g., Sorrells v. United States, 287 U.S. 435, 451 (1932). One consequence of the statutory construction theory of the defense is that it need not attach to all statutes. See ibid.

[9] See, e.g., United States v. Watson, 489 F.2d 504, 509 (3d Cir. 1973); The Entrapment Controversy 262. But see United States v. Braver, 450 F.2d 799, 801–803 (2d Cir. 1971) (defendant has both production and persuasion burden on issue of inducement). Cf. Lopez v. United States, 373 U.S. 427, 435 (1963) (entrapment not raised when defendant fails to show any evidence of inducement). Some courts require more than a showing of a bare solicitation to establish inducement. See, e.g., United States v. DeVore, 423 F.2d 1069, 1071 (4th Cir. 1970).

duced," the government must then demonstrate beyond a reasonable doubt that the defendant was in fact predisposed[10]—a burden that it can meet by introducing evidence of the defendant's reputation, character, prior convictions, and prior bad acts.[11] Except in the very rare case where the government can offer no evidence of predisposition, the defense then goes to the jury.[12]

Although its position has been roundly criticized in the literature,[13] the Supreme Court has adhered to the view that the success of the defense does not depend on the reasonableness of the inducement which the government offers. Even if the government offers an "excessive" inducement, the defendant will not prevail if he is in fact predisposed.[14] Conversely, a quite ordinary and proper inducement is enough to trigger the defense if it has the effect of leading a nondisposed defendant into crime.[15]

The defense is thus subjective; its focus is on the defendant's preinducement state of mind.[16] A bare majority of the Supreme

---

[10] See, *e.g.*, United States v. Webster, 649 F.2d 346, 347 (5th Cir. 1981); United States v. Mosely, 496 F.2d 1012, 1014–15 (5th Cir. 1974); *The Entrapment Controversy* 264.

[11] See generally *The Entrapment Controversy* 200–16, 247–62. *Cf.* Sherman v. United States, 356 U.S. 369, 373 (1958); Sorrells v. United States, 287 U.S. 435, 451 (1932).

[12] Professor Parks calls entrapment "a quintessentially jury issue [which is] easy to raise and supremely difficult to establish as a matter of law." *The Entrapment Controversy* 178. In his exhaustive study of federal entrapment decisions for the five-year period beginning in 1970, he found only two cases where convictions were reversed because entrapment had been established as a matter of law. *Ibid.* at 178 n. 44. But see Sherman v. United States, 356 U.S. 369 (1950).

[13] The commentators have overwhelmingly favored an objective approach focusing on the propriety of the government's conduct. See, *e.g.*, Goldstein, *For Harold Lasswell: Some Reflections on Human Dignity, Entrapment, Informed Consent, and the Plea Bargain* 84 YALE L.J. 683 (1975); Williams, *The Defense of Entrapment and Related Problems in Criminal Prosecution*, 28 FORD. L. REV, 399 (1959); *Judicial Control of Informants*. But see *The Entrapment Controversy*. Both the American Law Institute and the Brown Commission have endorsed versions of the objective approach. See AMERICAN LAW INSTITUTE, MODEL PENAL CODE § 2.13 (Official Draft 1962); NATIONAL COMMISSION ON REFORM OF FEDERAL CRIMINAL LAWS, A PROPOSED NEW FEDERAL CRIMINAL CODE § 702(2)(1971).

[14] See, *e.g.*, Hampton v. United States, 425 U.S. 484, 488–89 (1976); United States v. Russell, 411 U.S. 423, 429 (1973).

[15] See, *e.g.*, Sorrells v. United States, 287 U.S. 435, 451–52 (1932). The lower federal courts have consistently interpreted Supreme Court authority to permit the defendant to raise the defense despite the absence of evidence of impropriety by government agents. See, *e.g.*, United States v. Webster, 649 F.2d 346, 351 (5th Cir. 1981); United States v. Watson, 489 F.2d 504, 509 (3d Cir. 1973); *Cf.* United States v. Licursi, 525 F.2d 1164, 1168 (2d Cir. 1975). See generally *The Entrapment Controversy* 180–83.

[16] Or at least so the courts claim. I argue below that it is logically impossible to make meaningful statements about the defendant's subjective propensity for crime without assessing the objective forces making a particular criminal act attractive or unattractive. See text at notes 27–8 *infra*.

Court has maintained, however, that the defense should be supplemented by objective, constitutionally based restrictions. When truly outrageous government conduct is proved, the due process clause apparently prohibits conviction of even predisposed defendants.[17] Because the Court has never reversed a conviction on this ground, we can only guess at the kind of activity that would strike the Justices as "truly outrageous." But we do have some indications of the sort of tactics that will survive constitutional attack. Due process principles seem to prohibit neither government initiation of criminal activity,[18] nor government provision of an item essential to the successful completion of the offense,[19] nor the offering of substantial inducements by government agents.[20]

---

[17] In United States v. Russell, 411 U.S. 423 (1978), the Court held that the entrapment defense was unavailable to the defendant because he was predisposed. Justice Rehnquist, writing for the Court, noted in dicta, however, that "[W]e may some day be presented with a situation in which the conduct of law enforcement agents is so outrageous that due process principles would absolutely bar the government from invoking judicial processes to obtain a conviction." 411 U.S. at 431–32. Three years later, Justice Rehnquist apparently changed his mind. Writing for a plurality of the Court in Hampton v. United States, he stated that "the remedy of the criminal defendant with respect to the acts of Government agents, which, far from being resisted, are encouraged by him, lies solely in the defense of entrapment. But . . . petitioner's conceded predisposition rendered this defense unavailable to him." 425 U.S. 484, 490 (1976). This time, however, Justice Rehnquist was unable to hold a court for his views. Writing for himself and Justice Blackmun, Justice Powell agreed that the facts before the Court did not establish a due process violation, but was "unwilling to join the plurality in concluding that, no matter what the circumstances, neither due process principles nor our supervisory power could support a bar to conviction in any case where the government is able to prove predisposition." 425 U.S. at 495. The three dissenting Justices would have reversed Hampton's conviction on due process grounds. See 425 U.S. at 497 (Brennan, J., dissenting). For an account of post-*Hampton* reliance on due process theory in the lower courts, see Abramson and Lindeman, *Entrapment and Due Process in the Federal Courts*, 8 AM. J. CRIM. LAW 139 (1980).

[18] In Hampton v. United States, on the defendant's version of the facts, which the Court apparently accepted as true, see 425 U.S. at 487, the illegal transaction was initiated by government agents. See *id.* at 486–87. Yet the Court rejected his due process claim. But *cf.* United States, v. Twigg, 588 F.2d 373 (3d Cir. 1978).

[19] See United States v. Russell, 411 U.S. 423, 431–32 (1973). However, the *Russell* court left open the possibility that due process might be violated by the provision of an essential item that would be otherwise unavailable. See *id.* at 431.

[20] Because the Court has remained scrupulously silent as to the content of its due process test, it is possible that the offering of a huge inducement might be found to "shock the conscience." But it cannot be that due process is violated whenever the government offers an inducement large enough to risk attracting nondisposed defendants, since such a holding would make the Court's insistence on a subjective entrapment test pointless. *Cf.* Hampton v. United States, 425 U.S. 484, 495 n.7 (1973) (Powell, J., concurring) (cases where predisposition not dispositive "will be rare").

The depth of our confusion concerning the proper limits on government power in this area is illustrated by comparing the intuitions of Justice Powell with those of the authors of the Model Penal Code. Justice Powell hints that his objective, due process test would be violated

For the most part, the commentators have accepted all this at face value. Their attention has focused primarily on the seemingly endless dispute between those Justices preferring a subjective approach, which depends on the defendant's predisposition, and those preferring an objective approach, which depends on the propriety of the government inducement.[21] The intensity of this argument has tended to obscure two puzzles of considerable significance. First, it is unclear what the practical difference is between the two approaches. Second, it is uncertain how the core concepts underlying each of them—predisposition and improper inducement—should be defined.

A. THE SUBJECTIVE APPROACH

In theory, once the threshold requirement of an inducement is satisfied, the subjective approach focuses exclusively on the defendant's preinducement state of mind. Unfortunately, the Court has been rather vague in defining the state of mind on which we are to focus.

In *Sorrells v. United States*, the first Supreme Court decision recognizing the defense, Justice Hughes wrote that the defense was established when "the criminal design originates with the officials of the Government," who implant it "in the mind of an innocent person."[22] At first blush, this test might be taken to mean that a defendant must be acquitted when the intent to commit the particular criminal acts in question originates with a government agent. This reading is untenable, however, because the fact that the government solicited the specific criminal act demonstrates that the defendant did not originate the intent to commit it.[23] Making government origination the sole element of the defense thus reads out the further requirement that the defendant be "otherwise innocent" or nondisposed.

Accordingly, the "criminal design" to which Justice Hughes re-

---

if the government induced beatings or armed robberies. See Hampton v. United States, 425 U.S. 484, 493 n.4 (1973) quoting United States v. Archer, 486 F.2d 670, 676–77 (2d Cir. 1973) (Friendly, J.). Yet the Model Penal Code makes an entrapment defense unavailable in precisely those cases where the defendant causes or threatens bodily injury. See AMERICAN LAW INSTITUTE, MODEL PENAL CODE § 2.13(3) (Proposed Official Draft 1962).

[21] See notes 5 & 13 *supra*.

[22] 287 U.S. 435, 442 (1932).

[23] See *The Entrapment Controversy* 244–45.

ferred must be a more general intent to commit crimes similar to the one the government proposes.[24] This is presumably the sense behind Chief Justice Warren's oft-quoted aphorism that "a line must be drawn between the trap for the unwary innocent and the trap for the unwary criminal."[25] It is also the notion behind the standard federal jury instruction which asks the jury to decide whether "the defendant was ready and willing to commit crimes *such as* are charged in the indictment, whenever opportunity was afforded, and that government officers or their agents did no more than offer the opportunity."[26]

On closer analysis, this test also turns out to be unhelpful. The test is premised on the notion that it is possible to isolate the class of "unwary criminals" who are "ready and willing" to engage in crime apart from the inducements offered by the government. But whether a person is "ready and willing" to break the law depends on what the person expects to get in return—that is, on the level of inducement.[27] Like the rest of us, criminals do not generally work for free. Their willingness to take the risks of crime varies with the incentive which is provided. To be sure, the less cynical among us may believe that there is still a class of people who "have no price" and would remain law abiding regardless of temptation. But even if one concedes that such people can be found somewhere, they are, by definition, not among the ranks of entrapped defendants, since such defendants must have succumbed to some inducement in order to be entrapped.

Consequently, so long as one equates "predisposition" with a readiness to commit crime, no definition of "predisposition" can be complete without an articulation of the level of inducement to which a "predisposed" defendant would respond.[28] Furthermore,

---

[24] See Sherman v. United States, 356 U.S. 369, 382 (1958) (Frankfurter, J., concurring).

[25] *Id.* at 372.

[26] I DEVITT & BLACKMAR, FEDERAL JURY PRACTICE AND INSTRUCTIONS § 13.09, at 364 (3d ed. 1977) (emphasis added). The instruction has been generally accepted by the lower federal courts. See, *e.g.*, United States v. Gardner, 516 F.2d 334, 347–48 (7th Cir. 1975); United States v. Penz-Ozuna, 511 F.2d 1106 (9th Cir. 1975).

[27] Because the Court has attempted to define predisposition without regard to the level of inducement to which the defendant would respond, it is hardly surprising that the commentators have found the definition baffling. See, *e.g.*, TIFFANY, McINTYRE & ROTENBERG, DETECTION OF CRIME 267–68 (1967); Mikell, *The Doctrine of Entrapment in the Federal Courts*, 90 U. PA. L. REV. 245, 250–52 (1942).

[28] Of course, if "predisposition" is intended to refer to some other aspect of a defendant's personality, it can be separated from the level of inducement. See text at notes 45–8 *infra*.

the "predisposed" cannot be distinguished from the "nondisposed" without focusing on the propriety of the government's conduct— the very factor that the subjective approach professes to ignore. This is true because a defendant who responds favorably to a "proper" inducement has thereby conclusively demonstrated that he is disposed to crime when such an inducement is offered. It would seem, then, that so long as government agents restrict themselves to "proper" inducements, they run no risk of violating the entrapment rules. The entrapment test is "subjective" only in the sense that even if the government offers an "excessive" inducement, the defendant may nonetheless be convicted under such a test if he would have responded favorably to a proper one.

B. THE OBJECTIVE APPROACH

Even this formulation, however, overstates the distinction between the objective and subjective approaches for two reasons.

First, the objective test in theory avoids analysis of the defendant's predisposition and focuses, instead, exclusively on the propriety of the inducement.[29] That question, in turn, is determined "by the likelihood, objectively considered, that it would entrap only those ready and willing to commit crime."[30] But plainly that likelihood depends in large measure on the group to whom the inducement is targeted.[31] So long as the police direct their attention toward only those likely to be predisposed, the risk of entrapment,

---

[29] See, e.g., Sherman v. United States, 356 U.S. 369, 382 (1958) (Frankfurter, J., concurring).

[30] Id. at 384. Similarly, the Model Penal Code would prohibit "methods of persuasion or inducement which create a substantial risk that . . . an offense will be committed by persons other than those who are ready to commit it," AMERICAN LAW INSTITUTE, MODEL PENAL CODE § 2.13 (Official Draft 1962). The Brown Commission proposal also follows this pattern. See U.S. NATIONAL COMMISSION ON REFORM OF FEDERAL CRIMINAL LAWS, A PROPOSED NEW FEDERAL CRIMINAL CODE § 702(2) (1971) (prohibits "using persuasion or other means likely to cause normally law-abiding persons to commit the offense").

[31] Thus, Justice Frankfurter emphasized that the objective approach, which he advocated, did "not mean that the police may not act so as to detect those engaged in criminal conduct and ready and willing to commit further crimes. . . . It does mean that in holding out inducements they should act in such a manner as is likely to induce to the commission of crime only these persons and not others." 356 U.S. at 383–84. See also 1 U.S. NATIONAL COMMISSION ON REFORM OF FEDERAL CRIMINAL LAWS, WORKING PAPERS 322–23 (1970) (reasonable suspicion of target's predisposition helps to justify officer's conduct under objective test); Grossman v. State, 457 P.2d 226, 231 (Ala. 1969) (defendant's prior conduct relevant to propriety of inducement under objective test). See generally The Entrapment Controversy 201–10.

objectively considered, is small, and the inducement is, therefore, presumably permissible. Thus, in most cases, both the objective and subjective approaches would permit an inducement, so long as the defendant is predisposed. The two approaches would reach different results only in the rare case where the police reasonably, but incorrectly, believe the defendant to be predisposed at the time the inducement is offered.[32]

Second, most courts adopting an objective approach have supplemented it with a causation requirement.[33] This requirement means that the defendant must demonstrate not only the impropriety of the inducement, but also that the inducement caused him to commit the crime. If the requirement is taken literally, the distinction between the objective and subjective approaches collapses completely. A defendant who is predisposed and who would have responded to a proper inducement cannot claim that his conduct was caused by an improper inducement, because he would have committed the same crime even if the inducement had been proper.[34] He therefore fares no differently under the objective and subjective tests.[35] Conversely, if the defendant responds favorably to a proper inducement, he cannot claim that he was not predisposed, because his favorable response *ipso facto* demonstrates predisposition. The result is, therefore, again the same whether an objective or subjective standard is utilized.

C. PREDISPOSITION AND INDUCEMENT

In virtually every case, therefore, the objective and subjective tests produce the same results, and those results turn on the defendant's predisposition. Predisposition, in turn, seems inextricably linked to the level of inducement to which the defendant can be

---

[32] See *The Entrapment Controversy* 215–16.

[33] See, *e.g.*, Grossman v. State, 457 P.2d 226, 229 (Ala. 1969) (misconduct by government must be shown to have induced crime); State v. Mullen, 216 N.W. 2d 375, 382 (Iowa 1974) (same).

[34] See, *e.g.*, 1 U.S. NATIONAL COMMISSION ON REFORM OF FEDERAL CRIMINAL LAWS, WORKING PAPERS 320 (1970) (causation requirement rejected because it "of necessity, must treat the question of the accused's criminal predisposition"). But *cf. The Entrapment Controversy* 210–11 (Model Penal Code should not be read as requiring proof of causation, since this would defeat its purpose of avoiding examination of defendant's predisposition).

[35] It would be possible, of course, to restrict the causation inquiry to whether the inducement as a whole caused the crime without investigating whether the improper segment of the inducement was the causal factor.

expected to respond. But how are we to distinguish a "proper" inducement, which a nondisposed defendant will resist, from an "excessive" one, to which he will respond?

At this point, the analysis necessarily becomes more tentative. Because the Court's opinions proceed on the premise that it is possible to define "predisposition" without regard to the level of inducement, the Justices have never felt called upon to address what type of inducement triggers the defense. We are left, therefore, with the dubious task of extrapolating general rules about the defense from the facts of the cases in which it has been recognized.

We can begin this process by eliminating what might seem to be the most promising possibility. One might think that an inducement should be defined as "proper" if it is likely to be replicated in the real world. Conversely, the inducement is "excessive" if it is so large as to constitute a temptation which the defendant would be unlikely to face but for the government's intervention. Under this approach, a predisposed defendant is "ready" to commit crimes in the sense that he is prepared to accept inducements that are very likely to be forthcoming.

There may be some sense to this approach, although I attempt to demonstrate below that there are also significant problems with it. But for present purposes, it is enough to observe that, whatever its merits, it is not the Supreme Court's approach. This is clear from examination of the facts in the two cases in which the Court has reversed convictions on entrapment grounds. In *Sorrells v. United States*,[36] the defendant was convicted of selling one-half gallon of whiskey in violation of the National Prohibition Act. The Court held that an entrapment defense was properly raised when the defendant showed that the crime had been induced by "repeated and persistent solicitation in which [the government agent had] succeeded in taking advantage of the sentiment aroused by reminiscences of their experience as companions in arms in the World War."[37] In *Sherman v. United States*,[38] the Court went further and held that entrapment was established as a matter of law when a government agent, posing as a drug addict, induced the defendant,

---

[36] 287 U.S. 435 (1932).

[37] *Id.* at 441.

[38] 356 U.S. 367 (1958).

a former addict enrolled in a rehabilitation program, to resume his habit and supply the agent with drugs. The defendant succumbed only after the agent, who claimed to be suffering withdrawal pains, appealed to the defendant's sympathy and made repeated requests for drugs.[39]

In neither *Sorrells* nor *Sherman* could it plausibly be argued that the inducement offered was "excessive," in the sense of being more attractive than those which the defendant might otherwise encounter. Appeals to friendship and to shared experience are frequent occurrences, and many addicts seeking treatment must resist temptations created by associates still mired in the drug culture. Surely, it would hardly shock us to learn that Sorrells and Sherman were confronted with real associates seeking a drink "for old time sake" or drugs to relieve withdrawal symptoms.[40] What disturbs us about these inducements is not that they are unrealistically large, but that, whether realistic or not, they would appeal to a "reasonable" or "average" person. Because an average person might well be moved by the type of sentimental or humanitarian pleas made to Sorrells and Sherman, it seems in some sense unjust to punish them.

Perhaps, then, an "improper" inducement is one that would cause an average person to succumb.[41] Yet this formulation also fails to capture the cases precisely. An average person might well have been sympathetic to the appeals directed to Sorrells and Sherman, but it is doubtful, at best, that such a person would have been moved to break the law, even if he had been in a position to do so.[42] Moreover, the average person would not have been in a posi-

---

[39] See 356 U.S. at 371, 373.

[40] The lower federal courts have consistently read *Sorrells* and *Sherman* to mean that an entrapment defense is available even in cases where the government inducement is not unreasonably large. See, *e.g.*, Johnson v. United States, 17 F.2d 127 (D.C. Cir. 1963) (provision of funds for purchase of narcotics and transportation to location of purchase sufficient to raise defense); United States v. Harell, 436 F.2d 606 (5th Cir. 1970) (friendly conversation with government agent sufficient to raise defense); United States v. Gilmore, 436 F. Supp. 187, 191 (W.D.N.Y. 1977) (offer of $300 to participate in heroin sale sufficient to raise defense).

[41] *Cf.* U.S. NATIONAL COMMISSION ON REFORM OF FEDERAL CRIMINAL LAWS, A PROPOSED NEW FEDERAL CRIMINAL CODE § 702(2) (1971) ("Entrapment occurs when a law enforcement agent induces the commission of an offense, using persuasion or other means likely to cause normally law-abiding persons to commit the offense").

[42] The "average-person" test seems particularly difficult to reconcile with the result in *Sherman*, where the Court found entrapment as a matter of law. Under the average-person

tion to do so. Only a person with special ties to bootleggers or the drug culture—with a special "predisposition" to these offenses—would be likely to have immediate access to the contraband.

Thus, to account for *Sorrells* and *Sherman*, the "average person" standard must be modified to test the defendant's conduct against that of an average person who found himself in the defendant's situation. But this amendment immediately embarks us upon the most famous and well-traveled slippery slope in the criminal law.[43] The average person cannot be placed in precisely the defendant's situation, because he would then become the defendant and, by definition, would respond as the defendant responded. One must therefore distinguish between the aspects of the defendant's situation that are significant and those that are not. One might attribute to the average person all aspects of the defendant's situation, except for the defendant's weakness of will, because this is the very aspect of the defendant's personality that the law is attempting to control. But there are two difficulties with this solution. First, it assumes that it is possible to disentangle a person's will from the circumstances in which it is exercised. Even if such a separation were possible in principle, the test would still leave us with the task of defining the circumstances that are properly thought to determine a person's will. Second, and more fundamentally, the test once again fails to account for the cases. It was not mere happenstance that Sorrells had access to liquor and Sherman to drugs. These defendants posed a special danger because of previous failures of will which brought them into contact with forbidden substances. In-

---

test, the Court's holding would mean that a reasonable jury could not have found that the average person would have resisted the agent's plea for drugs.

For the most part, the lower federal courts have not required the defendant to prove that an average or normal person would have succumbed to the inducement in order to raise the defense. See, *e.g.*, United States v. Licursi, 525 F.2d 1164, 1168 (2d Cir. 1975); United States v. Armocida, 515 F.2d 49, 55 (3d Cir. 1975); United States v. Watson, 489 F.2d 504, 509 (3d Cir. 1973). *Cf.* Lopez v. United States, 373 U.S. 427, 437 (1963) (unnecessary to decided whether "entrapment should turn on the effect of the government's conduct on "men of ordinary firmness' ").

[43] See, *e.g.*, Keenan v. Commonwealth, 44 Pa. 55, 58–59 (1862)· "[M]easured by this rule, the crimes of a proud, or captious, or selfish, or habitually ill-natured man, or of one who eats or fasts too much, or of one who is habitually quarrelsome, covetous, dishonest, or thievish, or who, by any sort of indulgence, fault, or vice, renders himself very easily excitable, or very subject to temptation, are much less criminal than those of a moderate, well-tempered and orderly citizen. . . . [I]f we admit [this] and carry it out logically, we shall abolish law entirely as a compulsory rule of civil conduct; for we shall measure all crime and all duty by the conscience of the individual, and not by the social conscience."

deed, the very factor that seems to have most offended the *Sherman* court was the government's deliberate exploitation of the defendant's special weakness of will with regard to drug offenses.[44] But such exploitation cannot possibly provide Sherman with a defense under a test designed to focus punishment on those with this very weakness.

It seems clear, then, that when the Court speaks of nondisposed defendants, it means neither harmless individuals responding only to inducements unlikely to be replicated, nor blameless individuals responding only to inducements likely to attract the average person. A third possibility remains, however. It is possible that the Court is using the word "disposition" as a synonym for "temperament" or "character" rather than for "tendency."[45] In everyday life, we sometimes categorize individuals in terms of the specific acts they perform. But more frequently, we categorize them in terms of the general demeanor that they present. There is no specific act that qualifies an individual as a "hippie." A member of the "brie and chablis set" need neither eat brie nor drink chablis. Nor need a person belong to the formal organization to be a member of "The Moral Majority." These terms refer to ways of life or thought rather than to specific acts. So, too, when we say that a person has a "criminal disposition," we may mean that his general life-style and pattern of behavior are associated with criminality. This association, based on stereotypic notions of how criminals behave, may exist independently of the specific criminal acts which the individual performs. Conversely, a seemingly ordinary, upstanding citizen occasionally surprises us by committing a crime. When such an event occurs, we are likely to attribute it to an external source, sometimes even isolating the person's character flaw from the rest of his personality.[46] This odd bifurcation is necessary, because we

---

[44] The Court pointed out that Sherman "was trying to overcome the narcotics habit at the time" and condemned the government for "play[ing] on the weaknesses of an innocent party." 356 U.S. at 376.

[45] Webster's New International Dictionary defines "disposition" as both "[a] relatively permanent tendency to act in any certain way" and a "[n]atural or prevailing spirit, or temperament of mind."

[46] Our use of the label "kleptomania" to distinguish "ordinary" people who commit property crimes from criminals who perform identical acts provides a familiar example of this phenomenon. See Cressy, *The Differential Association Theory and Compulsive Crimes*, 45 J. CRIM. L.C. & P.S. 29, 35–36 (1954).

know that, at the core, the person does not have a "criminal disposition."[47]

Of course, the Court never says that it is using "disposition" in
this manner, and it therefore cannot be proved that this is the test
that is being applied. Still, this test explains much that is mysterious in the cases. At a minimum, it explains the Court's otherwise
baffling insistence on separating the concept of predisposition from
that of inducement. As I have argued above, it is meaningless to
speak of "disposition" in the sense of "tendency" without assessing
the strength of the inducement producing the tendency. But there
is no similar problem in considering "disposition" in the sense of
"temperament" in isolation. Because one's temperament is not determined by specific conduct, it can be defined without reference to
the external forces that help mold conduct.[48] One can therefore
meaningfully say that a defendant was "nondisposed" in this sense,
even though he responded to a very modest inducement which was
both likely to be replicated and could easily have been spurned by
an average person.

Defining "disposition" in terms of "temperament" also helps to
explain the kind of evidence that the Court has thought relevant to
the issue. In *Sorrells*, for example, the Court characterized the defendant as an "industrious" citizen[49] and apparently thought it relevant that he was gainfully employed and had been "on his job
continuously without missing a day since March, 1924."[50] Similarly, if one were to judge Sherman solely by his acts, there is no
doubt that he was a criminal. Not only did the government succeed
in inducing him to break the law; he had repeatedly broken it
before the government agent arrived on the scene.[51] Yet, despite

---

[47] I do not mean to argue that there is no relationship between a person's acts and his
disposition. Obviously, conduct is evidence of disposition. If a person committed many
crimes over a long period of time, we might, at some point, revise our opinion of his
disposition. But the corollation between disposition and conduct is only a loose one, and our
judgment about a person's disposition can easily survive one or more specific acts more
usually committed by persons of a different disposition.

[48] *Cf. Judicial Control of Informants* 1108.

[49] 287 U.S. at 441.

[50] *Id.* at 440.

[51] The Court held that entrapment had been established as a matter of law in the face of
government evidence showing that Sherman had twice been convicted of narcotics offenses.
See 356 U.S. at 375.

these acts, the Court was able to find that Sherman's disposition was "innocent," based on evidence that he was seeking medical help for his addiction and was not profiting from the distribution of drugs.[52] These facts are not relevant to the kinds of acts Sherman was likely to perform. They obviously had no bearing on his ultimate willingness to break the law. They are relevant, instead, to the kind of person Sherman was, apart from those acts. Although he continued to commit crimes, he was not a "criminal," because "criminals" do not respond to humanitarian appeals, or try to change their ways.

Moreover, even if the Court does not intend "predisposition" to be understood in this way, there can be little doubt that this is what it means in practice. The Court has insisted from the beginning that, except in extraordinary circumstances, entrapment is a jury question.[53] Even in ordinary cases, juries are sometimes influenced by a defendant's general life-style apart from the acts he performs.[54] The decision to commit the entrapment issue to the jury means that, however it is instructed and whatever evidence it hears, there is considerable risk that its verdict will be influenced by this factor.

This likelihood becomes a near certainty when one examines the special nature of the decision the jury must make in entrapment cases, the standard it is instructed to utilize in making it, and the evidence to which it is exposed. The jury in an entrapment case does not have the luxury of deciding an issue as concrete as what the defendant did, or even what he was thinking when he did it. Rather, it must speculate on what the defendant would have done under a set of circumstances that never occurred. As noted above, the judge tells them how to make this decision in a series of instructions that are impossible of principled application.[55] Moreover, once the defendant raises an entrapment defense, special rules of evidence apply. The prosecution is permitted to undertake a broad-scale

---

[52] See *ibid.*

[53] See Sorrells v. United States, 287 U.S. 435, 452. *Cf. id.* at 457 (separate opinion of Roberts, J.) (entrapment issue should be decided by judge rather than jury).

[54] See generally KLAVEN & ZEISEL, THE AMERICAN JURY 193–218 (1966).

[55] The judge instructs the jury to decide whether the defendant was "ready and willing" to commit the crime. The jury is somehow supposed to decide this question in the abstract without reference to any particular level of inducement which might make the defendant "ready and willing." See text at notes 27–28 *supra.*

inquest into the defendant's character and reputation.[56] Normally, of course, such evidence is inadmissible, precisely because it distracts the jury from the task of deciding what acts the defendant performed and causes it to focus instead on the kind of person the defendant is.[57] Can it be doubted, then, that when such evidence is admitted on a question as nebulous as entrapment under a test as confused as predisposition that even the most conscientious juror ends up making a "seat of the pants" judgment as to the defendant's general character?[58] Indeed, the interesting question is not *whether* juries decide entrapment cases on this basis, by *why* we insist on a doctrine which encourages them to do so.

II. RATIONALES FOR THE ENTRAPMENT DEFENSE

I have argued that the entrapment defense serves to shield defendants from punishment when their crimes are induced by government agents and when their general character, life-style, or nature is not "criminal." What remains to be considered are the reasons why we have such a doctrine. For the most part, the Justices have treated the matter as too obvious to require further explication. Entrapment should not be permitted, because it "falls below the standards, to which common feelings respond, for the proper use of governmental power."[59] It is "a gross abuse of authority,"[60] which is "as objectionable . . . as the coerced confession and the unlawful search"[61] and deserving of "the severest condemnation."[62]

If one has the temerity to push beyond this rhetoric and ask why this seemingly effective law enforcement tool should be outlawed, the answer is confused and contradictory. Sometimes, the Justices suggest that the defense is necessary because the entrapped defen-

---

[56] See text at note 11 *supra*.

[57] See, *e.g.*, Michelson v. United States, 335 U.S. 469, 475–76 (1948).

[58] Even some advocates of an entrapment defense seem to concede this point. See, *e.g.*, *The Entrapment Controversy* 257: "The argument that testimony about prior criminal conduct is 'prejudicial' because the jury may punish the defendant for being a bad man instead of committing the specific act charged is based upon a misleading analogy of entrapment cases to cases in which the defendant has denied committing the criminal act. . . . [In entrapment cases, t]he issue is precisely whether he was a 'bad man' who was predisposed to commit the type of crime charged."

[59] Sherman v. United States, 356 U.S. 369, 382 (1958) (Frankfurter, J., concurring).

[60] Sorrells v. United States, 287 U.S. 435, 441 (1932).

[61] Sherman v. United States, 356 U.S. 369, 372 (1958).

[62] Sorrell v. United States, 287 U.S. 435, 441 (1932).

dant is in some sense "innocent" and unworthy of punishment.[63] At other times, the Court suggests that the defense is unrelated to the defendant's guilt, but is instead necessary either to deter the police from engaging in objectionable behavior or to preserve the integrity of the courts.[64] In fact, as others have demonstrated,[65] the version of the defense actually fashioned by the Court is supported by neither of these arguments. It can hardly be maintained that entrapment doctrine is necessary to vindicate the innocent, so long as we continue to treat as guilty nondisposed defendants induced to commit crime by private, rather than by governmental, temptors.[66] Because governmental conduct is a necessary predicate for the defense, it might therefore be thought that we allow a defendant to raise it in order to deter such conduct. But the defense is also inconsistent with this goal, since its success is unrelated to the wrongfulness of the government's actions.

Entrapment doctrine thus represents neither a consistent judgment as to the culpability of entrapped defendants nor an effective strategy for deterring unwanted police behavior. Although this simple observation has dominated academic discussion of the defense, the point should not be overstated. If that were all there were to the matter, entrapment would be no different from a score of other uneasy compromises in the law.[67] The fact that such a compromise is not fully justified by any of the competing theories motivating it should neither surprise nor puzzle us.[68]

---

[63] See, *e.g.*, United States v. Russell, 411 U.S. 423, 434–36 (1976); Sherman v. United States, 356 U.S. 369, 372 (1958).

[64] See, *e.g.*, Sorrells v. United States, 287 U.S. 435, 446 (1932).

[65] See, e.g., Kelman, *Interpretive Construction in the Substantive Criminal Law*, 33 STAN. L. REV. 591, 644–45 (1981); Rotenberg, *The Police Detection Practice of Encouragement*, 49 VA. L. REV. 871, 897 (1963).

[66] See, *e.g.*, *Judicial Control of Informants* 1109. It is clear that the entrapment defense is unavailable when the inducement comes from a private source. See, *e.g.*, Holloway v. United States, 432 F.2d 775, 776 (10th Cir. 1970). *Cf.* United States v. Twigg, 588 F.2d 373, 376, 381–82 (3d Cir. 1978) (due process but not entrapment claim available when inducement comes from private source).

[67] The predisposition requirement for the entrapment defense is analogous to the standing limitations on the Fourth Amendment exclusionary rule, for example. The exclusionary rule, like one version of the entrapment defense, is designed to deter police misconduct and is unrelated to the culpability of the defendant who benefits from it. See, *e.g.*, Stone v. Powell, 428 U.S. 465, 486 (1976). Yet the Court has been willing to accept some diminution of its deterrent impact by permitting only those defendants whose rights were violated to assert it. See, *e.g.*, Rakas v. Illinois 439 U.S. 128 (1978).

[68] Thus, Professor Parks quite sensibly defends the Supreme Court's entrapment test by arguing that its purpose is to deter police misconduct, but that the Court is unwilling to effectuate that purpose at the price of releasing a guilty person when the defendant is

But that is far from all there is to the matter. What should surprise and puzzle us is that each of these competing theories is itself incoherent. Moreover, while some anomalies result from the way the Court has defined predisposition and the special version of the entrapment defense it has thereby created, the problems are mostly intrinsic to the defense and cannot be remedied however it is reformulated.

A. THE CULPABILITY THEORY

Although we are not close to an agreement on why it should be so,[69] there is a consensus that culpability is a necessary predicate for imposition of criminal sanctions.[70] For the moment, at least, it is unnecessary to explore precisely what one means by this term.[71] Nor need we address whether the establishment of moral blameworthiness is the central goal of the exercise or simply a constraint on our ability to reach other goals.[72] It is sufficient to note that our willingness to pursue a policy of crime prevention has historically been limited by a recognition that punishment of the "innocent" is out-of-bounds.

Consequently, if a nondisposed defendant induced to commit a crime by another is "innocent," he should not be punished. But why should such a defendant be viewed as innocent? Ordinarily, one would expect to look to the statutory definition of a particular crime to discover the boundaries between guilt and innocence. Perhaps in response to this expectation, the Supreme Court has always treated the entrapment defense as somehow implicit in federal statutory law.[73] But it is painfully obvious that the statutory

---

predisposed. See *The Entrapment Controversy* 242–43. Alternatively, it might be argued that the purpose of the defense is the exculpation of innocent defendants, but that this purpose must be subordinated in the case of private inducements because of the increased risk of collusion and fraud. *Id.* at 241.

[69] Compare, *e.g.*, Rawls, *Punishment*, in PHILOSOPHY OF LAW (Feinberg & Gross. eds. 1975) with Ross, ON GUILT, RESPONSIBILITY, AND PUNISHMENT 87–93 (1975).

[70] Of course, consensus is not the same thing as unanimity. See generally WOOTON, SOCIAL SCIENCE AND SOCIAL PATHOLOGY (1959). But as Professor Gross has pointed out, "Condemning one who is blameless is universally abhorred as an injustice, and it is astonishing that those who advocate criminal liability regardless of culpability do not perceive this abhorrence as an insurmountable obstacle to the adoption of their program." GROSS, A THEORY OF CRIMINAL JUSTICE 414–15 (1979).

[71] See text at notes 135–41 *infra*.

[72] Compare, *e.g.*, KANT, THE METAPHYSICAL ELEMENTS OF JUSTICE 100–01 (Ladd trans. 1965) with HART, PUNISHMENT AND RESPONSIBILITY 11–13 (1968).

[73] See, *e.g.*, Sorrells v. United States, 287 U.S. 435, 446–52 (1932).

basis for the defense is wholly fictional.[74] An entrapped defendant has, by definition, committed an act made criminal by positive law, and he has done so with the requisite state of mind.[75] One looks in vain through the United States Code for any indication that Congress meant to condition culpability on the defendant's predisposition, however that term is defined.[76] Indeed, Congress has consistently declined to codify any of the versions of the entrapment defense presented to it.[77]

It is, of course, true that the criminal law has traditionally recognized a series of defenses to what would otherwise be criminal acts, and that not all of these have been codified.[78] In general, such defenses fall into two categories: claims such as duress, necessity, and self-defense, relating to external pressures brought to bear on

---

[74] Indeed, even those Justices defending the majority view of entrapment appear to have all but conceded this point. In *Russell*, the Court noted that the criticisms of the "implied intent of Congress" rationale were "not devoid of appeal" and seems to have rejected them only because they "[had] been twice previously made to this Court, and twice rejected by it." 411 U.S. at 433–34.

Professor Park argues that congressional silence for the half century since *Sorrells* constitutes implied endorsement of the defense. See *The Entrapment Controversy* 247. But the argument suffers from all the weaknesses inherent in inferences from silence. It assumes that members of Congress focused on the problem and consciously chose not to act, that Congress has a general duty to scan the United States Reports for erroneous decisions to correct, and that congressional silence is an endorsement of the specific holding in a case rather than of judicial power to develop the law. See generally HART & SACKS, THE LEGAL PROCESS: BASIC PROBLEMS IN THE MAKING AND APPLICATION OF LAW 1381–1401 (Tent. ed. 1958).

[75] There are occasionally situations where the Government's participation in the offense does negative one of the statutory elements. See, *e.g.*, United States v. Berrigan, 482 F.2d 171 (3d Cir. 1973). But the entrapment defense exculpates the defendant even in circumstances where the elements are satisfied.

[76] I do not mean to suggest that Congressional silence should be taken to preclude the courts from formulating an entrapment defense if the defense can be shown to be desirable on some other ground. My only point is that Congress has not mandated the defense and that supporters of the defense must therefore look elsewhere to justify it.

It might still be contended that this approach puts the burden of proof in the wrong place. Since most forms of entrapment would be illegal if undertaken by private persons, one might argue that Congress must specifically authorize law enforcement officers to entrap before the tactic can be lawful. For a discussion of this argument, see note 106 *infra*.

[77] Congress has enacted neither the Brown Commission nor the Model Penal Code recommendation on entrapment. See note 13 *supra*. An early version of the proposed federal criminal code revision contained a statutory entrapment defense. See Criminal Justice Reform Act of 1975, S. 1, 94th Cong., 1st Sess. § 551 (1976) (committee print). The provision was removed in later versions, however, and the development of entrapment doctrine was explicitly left to the courts. See Criminal Code Reform Act of 1979, S. 1722, 96th Cong., 1st Sess. § 501 (1979). See generally Report of the Committee on the Judiciary, United States Senate, to Accompany S. 1722, 96th Cong., 1st Sess., at 87–125 (1980).

[78] As Professor Donnelly has pointed out, "The application of common law defenses to statutory crimes is one of the commonest examples of non-literal interpretations of statutes." *Judicial Control of Informants* 1110.

the defendant; and claims such as insanity, infancy, and mistake, relating to the defendant's internal thought processes. Regardless of the categorization, each defense proceeds from the premise that a defendant should not be blamed for an act when he has done what we want him to do under the circumstances, in which case we say that he is justified, or when he lacked meaningful freedom to act differently, in which case we say that he is excused.[79]

Superficially, the entrapment defense might be thought quite consistent with these firmly established limits on culpability. Indeed, the doctrine seems to fit comfortably in both the external and internal categories: it looks, on the one hand, to external pressure which in some sense explains or mitigates the defendant's conduct, and, on the other, to the defendant's innocent state of mind prior to committing the offense. Upon closer analysis, however, entrapment doctrine is consistent with neither type of defense.

1. *External pressure.* The Court has occasionally suggested that we have an entrapment defense to prevent the punishment of a person whose conduct is the product of external forces. When the defendant is not predisposed, the argument goes, the government inducement in effect creates a crime in order to punish it.[80] In the words of Justice Hughes, it is improper for the government "to punish [a person otherwise innocent] for an alleged offense which is the product of the creative activity of its own officials."[81]

It is true, of course, that when a government agent entraps a defendant, the agent may cause a crime to be committed in the "but for" sense. Depending on the facts, it may be unwise on policy grounds for the government to pursue this course.[82] But it is far from clear why this type of government causation should be thought to bear on culpability. As noted above, entrapment doctrine presently requires the acquittal of a nondisposed defendant regardless of the attractiveness of the inducement. Thus, the doctrine exculpates a defendant who succumbs to a temptation that a person of reasonable moral fortitude would easily spurn.[83] It is

---

[79] See, *e.g.*, FLETCHER, RETHINKING CRIMINAL LAW 759–62 (1978).

[80] See, *e.g.*, Sorrells v. United States, 287 U.S. 435, 444 (1932), quoting Butts v. United States, 273 F. 35, 38 (8th Cir. 1921).

[81] *Id.* at 451.

[82] See text at notes 122–24 *infra*.

[83] See text at notes 41–44 *supra*.

hard to imagine a culpability principle which requires the acquittal of such a defendant.[84]

Entrapment doctrine might be made more consistent with culpability principles by changing the definition of predisposition to exculpate only those defendants who succumb to inducements that the average person would be unable to resist. But the existence of such a hypothetical doctrine which could be justified on culpability grounds hardly justifies or explains the doctrine that has in fact developed. More fundamentally, even this modified entrapment defense would not be fully consistent with our culpability principles. We know that there is no generally held normative principle precluding punishment of defendants succumbing to even very attractive inducements, because a defendant offered such an inducement by a private person has no defense to the resulting charge.[85] Such a defendant's blameworthiness is not somehow diminished because, unbeknownst to him, his temptor happens to be a government agent.

One might still argue that it is this failure to exculpate defendants offered large private inducements that is inconsistent with our culpability principles. But extending entrapment doctrine to private inducements would work a revolutionary change in our law of excuse. From a culpability perspective, there would be no way to confine this change to situations in which the inducement comes from other persons. It would be necessary to exculpate defendants whenever circumstances of any kind made the lure of crime difficult to resist.[86]

---

[84] A normal entrapment strategy should be distinguished from situations, sometimes loosely termed entrapment, where a government agent deliberately misleads a defendant into believing that his conduct is legal. See, *e.g.*, Cox v. Louisiana, 379 U.S. 559 (1965); Raley v. Ohio, 360 U.S. 423 (1959). If the government's representations would cause a reasonable person to believe that his conduct was legal, this fact might be thought to negate culpability. But in the more usual entrapment situation, the defendant knows that he is violating the law, and often does so in response to an inducement which he should have resisted.

[85] See note 66 *supra*.

[86] Sometimes, for example, police decoys disguise themselves as drunks, handicapped, or otherwise defenseless persons in an effort to induce robberies. See, *e.g.*, Marx, note 7 *supra*, at 404–05. From a culpability perspective, this strategy seems no different from offering large sums of money to perform criminal acts. In both cases, the police have attempted to make the crime more attractive—in one situation by seeming to increase the return, while in the other by seeming to decrease the risk. Since the decision to perform a criminal act presumably involves some assessment of return discounted by risk, both techniques might cause a person to perform a criminal act. Yet it is an odd culpability principle indeed which holds a person less blameworthy because he preys solely upon the weak and defenseless.

An argument that defendants should be exculpated in these circumstances confuses the fundamental distinction between an offer
and a threat.[87] If a person's will is overborne by a threat, duress or
self-defense may well provide him with a defense.[88] Because these
doctrines are presumably fully applicable to government agents, a
defendant who commits a crime because of a threat by a government agent has no need to rely upon an entrapment claim. In
contrast, when another actor *expands* the defendant's range of
choice, we say that the defendant has received an offer, and we
generally hold him to that choice.[89] For example, a homeowner
using force against a burglar may have a defense because he is the
victim of a threat. The burglar, on the other hand, can hardly
maintain that he should be acquitted because the homeowner
"threatened" to withhold the property in the house from him. The
presence of an unlocked house waiting to be burglarized may well
be a substantial temptation, but it is in the nature of an offer rather
than a threat,[90] and the burglar is therefore fully responsible for the
act he commits.

This analysis suggests that principles of excuse do not in fact rest

---

[87] For a systematic effort to examine the implications of this distinction, see Nozick,
Coercion in PHILOSOPHY, SCIENCE AND METHOD: ESSAYS IN HONOR OF ERNEST NAGEL 440,
447–53 (Morgenbesser, Suppes and White eds. 1969). See also Bayles, *A Concept of Coercion*,
14 NOMOS (Coercion) 16, 22–23 (Pennock & Chapman eds. 1972).

[88] It does not follow that these defenses are available whenever a defendant's will is
overborne by a threat. The law of duress is somewhat confused because of our ambivalence
as to whether it rests on principles of justification or excuse. To the extent that it rests on
justification theory, the defendant should be exculpated only when otherwise illegal conduct
avoids a greater harm than it inflicts. Compare LaFAVE & SCOTT, HANDBOOK ON CRIMINAL
LAW 374–75 (1972) with FLETCHER, RETHINKING CRIMINAL LAW 831 (1978). See text at
notes 94–96 *infra*.

[89] See Bayles, *A Concept of Coercion*, XIV NOMOS: COERCION 16, 26 (Pennock & Chapman eds. 1972). Professor Nozick argues that offered conduct would improve the recipient's
situation from that which is expected or morally required, while threatened conduct would
worsen it. Both offers and threats can be so large that we cannot reasonably expect the
recipient not to respond to them. It is nonetheless proper to hold a person to acceptance of an
offer, but not a threat, because in the pre-offer/pre-threat situation, a rational person would
want an offer, but not a threat, to be made. See Nozick, *Coercion*, note 87 *supra*, at 458–65.
Even if one accepts the structure of this argument, however, its utility depends on our ability
to determine what situation is expected or morally required—*i.e.*, what the person's rights
were before the offer or threat was made. See text at notes 91–93 *infra*. *Cf.* Kronman,
Contract Law and Distributive Justice, 89 YALE L.J. 472, 480–83 (1980).

[90] It admittedly strains language to say that the homeowner has "offered" his property,
since he is in fact unwilling to have it taken. As noted above, however, there is no culpability
distinction between a defendant responding to an offer from a person and a defendant
responding to an "offer" in the form of a situation which makes certain conduct seem
unusually desirable. See text at note 85 *supra*. The unlocked house constitutes an "offer" in
the second sense.

on the coercive impact of the defendant's situation, but, rather, on a determination of the defendant's rights against which offers and threats should be measured.[91] The homeowner and burglar discussed above may have precisely the same need for the property, and their desire for it may produce the same impact on their will. Indeed, it is possible that the burglar's need is much greater and that it requires a more heroic act of will for him to refrain from breaking into the house than for the homeowner to refrain from defending it. The burglar is nonetheless guilty and the homeowner is not, because the homeowner, but not the burglar, has a right to the property.

There may, of course, be cases where the question of rights is more controversial. Suppose, for example, that A is bleeding to death on the street when B approaches him and tells him that he will save A's life if A agrees to rob a bank upon his recovery.[92] Whether B's proposal is treated as an offer to take A to the hospital, or as a threat not to, depends on the kind of treatment A has a right to expect. While we may disagree on the answer to that question, the crucial point is that A's liability for bank robbery turns on a determination of A's right, rather than upon the effect of B's conduct on his will.[93]

In certain exceptional situations, we exculpate a defendant even though he has invaded what we normally consider to be the rights of others. Specifically, the necessity doctrine allows a defendant to disregard a criminal statute when necessary to avoid a greater evil.[94] But an analogy between necessity and entrapment confuses

---

[91] See Kronman, *Contract Law and Distributive Justice*, note 89 *supra*, at 483–89.

[92] For a closely analogous hypothetical, see Nozick, *Coercion*, note 87 *supra*, at 449–50.

[93] In most American jurisdictions, B would have no duty to take A to the hospital in this situation and, therefore, A would have no right to expect such treatment. See PROSSER, LAW OF TORTS 338–43 (1971). If my analysis is correct, it would follow that A would have no defense to the bank robbery, since he responded to an offer rather than a threat. I suspect that our intuitive dissatisfaction with this result stems from a dissatisfaction with the way the law has stated A's background rights in this situation. If we feel that A's conviction is unjust, it is not because his will was overborne, but because he should be accorded the right to be taken to the hospital. See generally Weinrib, *The Case for a Duty to Rescue*, 90 YALE L.J. 247 (1980).

[94] See generally LAFAVE & SCOTT, HANDBOOK ON CRIMINAL LAW 381–88 (1972). At common law, necessity and duress were distinct defenses. Duress exculpated the defendant when he was subjected to an unlawful threat from another person. Necessity, in contrast, traditionally arose in situations where nonhuman forces beyond the actor's control made the criminal conduct the lesser of two evils. See *Id.* at 384; United States v. Bailey, 444 U.S. 394,

the distinction between a justification and an excuse. Necessity provides no solace to an individual who breaks the law because circumstances make obedience unattractive to him. As the doctrine has been formulated in this country, it rests on the belief that in unusual situations overall social welfare will be maximized by disobedience. Thus, a defendant acting out of necessity is innocent because, under the circumstances, he has done the right thing, rather than because we are prepared to excuse him for doing the wrong thing.[95] The doctrine provides no support for the view that it is morally defensible for a person to impose a net social loss in order to benefit himself.[96] An expanded entrapment defense, in contrast, would require just such a judgment, because the entrapped defendant cannot maintain that society is improved by his commission of the crime.

Accordingly, the existence of external pressure neither justifies nor excuses an entrapped defendant. If such defendants are nevertheless deserving of exculpation, it must be because something about their internal behavior controls limits their ability to resist the pressure.

2. *Internal behavior controls.* If one could show that nondisposed defendants were somehow congenitally less capable of resisting criminal offers, this might be a basis for exculpating them, since it would be unfair to hold such defendants to a standard devised for those better equipped to resist pressure. The Supreme Court's re-

---

409 (1980). Modern cases have tended to blur this distinction. See United States v. Bailey, *supra.*

[95] See, *e.g.*, LAFAVE & SCOTT, HANDBOOK ON CRIMINAL LAW, note 94 *supra*, at 382. This proposition is not uncontroversial. Some have argued that the necessity defense should be treated as an excuse—*i.e.*, that even a defendant who chooses the greater evil should be relieved of liability if his will has been overborne. See FLETCHER, RETHINKING CRIMINAL LAW 818–29 (1978). *Cf.* United States v. Bailey, 444 U.S. 394, 409–10 (1980). But even if the defense is an excuse, it does not benefit the entrapped defendant, since it would then be unavailable when the defendant succumbed to an offer rather than a threat. See text at notes 87–90 *supra.*

[96] There may be situations when the desirability of the criminal act to the defendant outweighs the overall social cost of the act. When this is true, a utilitarian calculation would suggest that the act should occur. Normally, however, the criminal punishment for the act is designed to make the defendant internalize the cost of his act so that he will accurately perform this calculation. Allowing the defendant to raise a necessity defense in this situation would defeat this effect. It follows that the necessity defense should be restricted to cases where the social benefit of the otherwise criminal conduct falls on people other than the defendant or where the situation is so unusual that we can say that the legislature did not anticipate it and miscalculated the social cost of the criminal act when it established the penalty for it. But the entrapment defense would exculpate the defendant even if neither of these two conditions were satisfied.

peated references to victims of entrapment as "innocent"[97] might be read as endorsing such a view.

But this defense of entrapment doctrine once again founders on the Court's definition of "predisposition." There is no reason to suppose that a person lacking a criminal disposition or character is less able to control his behavior and, therefore, is less culpable. Indeed, from a culpability perspective, the predisposition requirement is perverse. An individual with an ordinary, "upstanding" life-style has presumably been thoroughly socialized to resist deviant behavior. The very reason we are surprised when such an individual commits a crime is because we "expect more" of him than of a person leading a dissolute life.

The argument cannot be salvaged by redefining "predisposed" to focus on the danger posed by the defendant. There is no culpability reason to acquit a defendant simply because he responded to an inducement unlikely to be replicated and therefore posed little danger. The culpability question is not *whether* the defendant is likely to commit a crime, but *why* he is likely to commit it. A defendant likely to respond to a small inducement may be disposed toward crime precisely because of a weakness in his behavior controls which reduces his culpability. Conversely, a defendant responding to only very large inducements may be able to resist smaller ones because of behavior controls which make him fully responsible for his conduct.

B. THE GOVERNMENT DETERRENCE THEORY

The inability to formulate a convincing argument that an entrapped defendant should be considered "innocent" strongly suggests that the defense does not in fact exist for his protection. If entrapment doctrine results in the release of culpable defendants, this must be because this cost is thought worth bearing to mold government conduct in desirable ways. This justification for the defense finds ample support in opinions of the Justices advocating both the subjective and objective versions of the defense. The *Sorrells* majority, for example, thought an entrapment defense was necessary "to stop the prosecution in the interest of the government

---

[97] See, *e.g.*, United States v. Russell, 411 U.S. 423, 428–29 (1973) quoting Sorrells v. United States, 287 U.S. 435, 448 (1932); Sherman v. United States, 356 U.S. 369, 376 (1958).

itself, to protect it from the illegal conduct of its officers and to preserve the purity of its courts."[98] And Justice Frankfurter, concurring in *Sherman*, agreed that "[i]nsofar as they are used as instrumentalities in the administration of criminal justice, the federal courts have an obligation to set their face against enforcement of the law by lawless means or means that violate rationally vindicated standards of justice, and to refuse to sustain such methods by effectuating them."[99]

As already noted, this view of entrapment is not easy to square with the actual defense, because the ability of the prosecution to convict the defendant does not depend on the wrongfulness *vel non* of its conduct. But even if the defense were reformulated so as to meet this objection, its proponents would still have the burden of demonstrating why the government conduct should be deemed wrongful.

Several arguments can be quickly dismissed. First, it might be asserted that the offering of inducements by government agents is undesirable because such conduct creates the risk that innocent people will be corrupted. But this argument obviously depends upon the characterization of those responding to the inducements as innocent—a characterization which is untenable.

Second, some Justices have suggested that government participation in a criminal venture is wrongful because it is illegal.[100] These Justices analogize entrapment to violations of the Fourth and Fifth Amendments[101] and rely on the classic dissents of Holmes and Brandeis in *Olmstead v. United States*.[102] It would, of course, end the argument if we chose *a priori* to define entrapment as out-of-bounds. But since the point of the discussion is to determine whether entrapment should be made illegal, it rather spoils the fun to adopt this proposition as an initial premise.[103] Nor are propo-

---

[98] 287 U.S. at 446.

[99] 356 U.S. at 380.

[100] See, *e.g.*, Sherman v. United States, 356 U.S. 369, 380 (1958) (Frankfurter, J., concurring). See also Goldstein, *For Harold Lasswell, Some Reflections on Human Dignity, Entrapment, Informed Consent, and the Plea Bargain*, 84 YALE L.J. 683, 688 (1973).

[101] See United States v. Russell, 411 U.S. 423, 442–43 (1973) (Stewart, J., dissenting); Sherman v. United States, 356 U.S. 369, 380 (1958) (Frankfurter, J., concurring).

[102] 277 U.S. 438, 469, 471 (1928).

[103] The circularity of the government illegality argument is illustrated by Professor Donnelly's treatment of it. At one point, he suggests that officers should be prohibited from entrapping defendants because this conduct is illegal. *Judicial Control Informants* 1111. Yet

nents of the defense assisted by the observation that undercover agents seeking to entrap a defendant may engage in conduct that would be illegal if undertaken by a private citizen. Such arguments reflect a basic misunderstanding of Justice Brandeis's point in *Olmstead*. The Fourth and Fifth Amendments, as well as Washington state law as interpreted by Justice Brandeis, outlawed government wiretapping.[104] It was in that sense that "the Government [had become] a lawbreaker."[105] But it hardly follows that the government always acts illegally whenever it engages in conduct prohibited to private citizens. Surely, the collection of taxes, seizure of evidence, and use of military force do not, in themselves, "breed[] contempt for law" or "invite[] every man to become a law unto himself."[106] The issue raised by entrapment is not whether the government ought to obey the law, but what the law ought to be.[107]

---

later he contends that the legality of an officer's conduct depends upon whether or not it constitutes entrapment. *Id.* at 1117.

[104] See 277 U.S. at 475–76, 479 (Brandeis, J., dissenting).

[105] *Id.* at 485 (Brandeis, J., dissenting).

[106] *Ibid.*

These cases might be distinguished on the ground that in each of them the legislature has specifically authorized the government conduct, whereas entrapment has not been so authorized. Since the conduct of an entrapping officer might well be an illegal solicitation if undertaken by a private person, and since no explicit statutory provision makes it legal for the officer, it might be argued that entrapment does involve government illegality. See note 76 *supra*.

There are several responses to this contention. First, it once again fails to justify present entrapment doctrine. If the argument were taken seriously, it would mean that any government participation in or inducement of a criminal venture would be impermissible. Yet no Justice on either side of the entrapment dispute, and none of the commentators, is prepared to defend that position.

The argument proves too much in a second way as well. No one would suggest that an officer seizing contraband from a suspect could himself be convicted of illegally possessing the illicit substance simply because there was no specific statutory exemption covering his conduct. Nor need the officer rely upon such an exemption from assault statutes when he uses reasonable force to effect the seizure. We have traditionally interpreted criminal statutes to confer upon the police discretion to utilize reasonable means to enforce them. While it may be that entrapment is not a reasonable means, that contention must be independently established.

Finally, even if the point is conceded, it simply shifts the focus of discussion to a different forum. Even if we assume arguendo that the police should be forbidden to entrap without legislative authorization, entrapment opponents must then explain why, in the absence of other objections to the tactic, such authorization should not be forthcoming.

[107] Oddly, Justice Brandeis himself seems to have grasped the distinction which those who rely upon his opinions have missed. Dissenting from the court's refusal to recognize an entrapment defense in Casey v. United States, he wrote: "I am aware that courts—mistaking relative social values and forgetting that a desirable end cannot justify foul means—have, in their zeal to punish, sanctioned the use of evidence obtained through criminal violation of

Nor is it persuasive to argue that entrapment should be prohibited as invasive of individual privacy. This argument actually encompasses two separate objections to entrapment which must be separately addressed. Sometimes, critics of entrapment refer to privacy in the sense of personal autonomy. Their objection then is that the government has impermissibly manipulated the behavior of its citizens.[108] But this argument is no more than a reformulation of the culpability objection. If government agents utilized force or threats of force, the target's free will has, of course, been invaded. But, as noted above,[109] entrapment generally takes the form of offers that expand the target's range of choice rather than threats that narrow it.

Other entrapment critics use the privacy rubric to refer to matters that the targetted individual wishes to keep secret. Their objection, then, is to the use of government deception to learn of the target's secret criminal tendencies.[110] This objection is serious and might well prevail were we writing on a clean slate. But the Supreme Court has repeatedly held in nonentrapment contexts that a person who reveals his criminal disposition to a supposed confederate assumes the risk that the confederate is a government agent and has no reasonable expectation of privacy in the information revealed.[111] So long as these decisions remain on the books, it is hard to see what additional privacy concerns are implicated by entrapment.[112]

A more troubling argument against pursuit of an entrapment strategy is that it stimulates antisocial conduct that would not

---

property and personal rights or by other practices of detectives even more revolting. *But the objection here is of a different nature. It does not rest merely upon the character of the evidence or upon the fact that evidence was illegally obtained. The obstacle to the prosecution lies in the fact that the alleged crime was instigated by officers of the Government.*" Casey v. United States, 276 U.S. 413, 423 (1928) (Brandeis, J., dissenting) (emphasis added).

[108] See *e.g.*, Goldstein, *For Harold Lasswell: Some Reflections on Human Dignity, Entrapment, Informed Consent, and the Plea Bargain*, 84 YALE L.J. 683, 685 (1975). Dix, *Undercover Investigation and Police Rulemaking*, 53 TEX L. REV. 203, 247 (1975).

[109] See text at notes 87–89 *supra*.

[110] See, *e.g.*, Dix, *Undercover Investigations and Police Rulemaking*, note 108 *supra*, at 211–12.

[111] See, *e.g.*, United States v. White, 401 U.S. 745 (1971); On Lee v. United States, 343 U.S. 747 (1952).

[112] There may be some cases where the mere act of proposing a criminal violation constitutes an affront implicating additional privacy concerns. See, *e.g.*, Dix, *Undercover Investigation and Police Rulemakings*, note 108 *supra*, at 247 ("straight" solicited for purposes of homosexual conduct may experience discomfort). In more usual situations, however, the target can fully protect his privacy by declining the offer.

otherwise occur and, therefore, serves no legitimate end.[113] "The function of law enforcement," the Court held in *Sherman v. United States*, "is the prevention of crime and the apprehension of criminals. Manifestly, that function does not include the manufacturing of crime."[114]

Proponents of this view are surely correct in asserting that entrapment does manufacture some antisocial activity. It produces this effect in at least three ways. First, the government may offer an inducement to a person who would never have been so tempted, and thereby create a crime that would not otherwise occur.[115] Second, when the government buys illegal conduct, it competes with real purchasers, thereby increasing the demand for crime and, so, stimulating more supply.[116] Third, in order to maintain their cover, government agents may be forced to engage in the very sort of antisocial conduct they are seeking to prevent.[117]

The observation that entrapment creates crime hardly ends the analysis, however. It is also true that we would have no prison breaks if we tore down penitentiaries, and that assaults on policemen would decline dramatically if officers were kept off the streets. Obviously, the question is not whether a particular law enforcement strategy creates crime, but whether it creates more crime than it prevents. That question is hard with respect to entrapment, because, while the strategy unquestionably creates crime, it may also be an effective tool for stopping it.

Entrapment may reduce crime in two ways. First, it serves as a means of identifying and incapacitating dangerous individuals likely to commit crime in the future if not apprehended. Indeed, in the case of "victimless" crime, where the technique is most often utilized, entrapment may be the only effective means of ap-

---

[113] See *id.* at 214, 246.

[114] 356 U.S. at 372.

[115] For some examples of cases where the police have succeeded in generating their own crime wave through use of an entrapment strategy, see Marx, *The New Police Undercover Work*, note 7 *supra*, at 412–14.

[116] For example, when the police compete with real fences in the market for stolen goods, they may drive up prices and so stimulate theft. See *id.* at 414.

[117] In addition to these costs, entrapment also produces what might be called the keystone-kop effect. When one can no longer tell the "good guys" from the "bad guys," there is an inevitable risk that undercover agents will be attacked by irate citizens, be arrested by their own or other police forces, or become a part of the criminal life they are supposedly merely simulating. See *id.* at 418–23. Occasionally, two undercover officers may even attempt to entrap each other. See *id.* at 423 & n.22.

prehending law violators.[118] The argument that a nondisposed defendant is not dangerous because he lacked the disposition to commit the offense before the government intervened is not convincing. As cases such as *Sherman* prove, a person lacking a criminal disposition may nonetheless be quite likely to commit crimes. Indeed, the very fact that an entrapped defendant accepts an inducement conclusively proves that he poses a risk of committing the offense whenever a similar inducement might be offered in the future. True, such an inducement might never be offered. But all predictions of dangerousness are contingent and uncertain. The case of the entrapped defendant, moreover, is crucially different from that of a person incarcerated for an inchoate crime or a presumed disposition to commit crimes. In the latter situations, the defendant has not yet performed a criminal act, and we therefore must speculate whether, if left alone, he will ever violate the law. But the entrapped defendant *has* violated the law. He has performed an act that the law condemns, and incapacitating him for reasons of dangerousness is no different in principle from incapacitating any other criminal on this basis.

Second, even if the entrapped defendant is not dangerous, his incarceration may nonetheless reduce crime by deterring others.[119] Potential criminals who know that police are utilizing an entrapment policy will realize that there is a greater risk that they will be apprehended and so will be less tempted to commit crime.[120] Put in

---

[118] See, *e.g.*, United States v. Sherman, 200 F.2d 880, 882 (1952) (Hand, J.) ("Indeed, it would seem probable that, if there were no reply [to the claim of inducement], it would be impossible ever to secure convictions of any offences which consist of transactions that are carried out in secret").

[119] There are a few cases where an entrapment strategy has been spectacularly successful in deterring crime. For example, several years ago the FBI mounted "Operation Lobster" designed to combat truck hijacking in the Northeast corridor. Undercover officers posed as brokers of stolen merchandise and succeeded in convicting fifty individuals and recovering $3 million in stolen property. For the next six months, there was only one reported hijacking. The decline was apparently at least partially attributable to the uncertainty of potential hijackers as to the genuineness of the fences with whom they would have to deal. See Testimony of Philip Heymann, Asst. Attorney General, Criminal Division, before the Subcommittee on Civil and Constitutional Rights, Committee on the Judiciary, March, 4, 1980, at 137. See also Marx, *The New Undercover Police Work*, note 7 *supra*, at 411.

[120] Paradoxically, entrapment serves as an effective deterrent only to the extent that police efforts to maintain their cover are not fully effective. Potential criminals can only be deterred by the entrapment strategy if they know that the police may be employing it. This fact produces an ironic relationship between the effectiveness of the strategy as a deterrent and the risk that the strategy will entice otherwise harmless people into crime. If all potential criminals know of the entrapment strategy and are deterred by it, the police will only attract those who would not have engaged in crime but for the strategy. *Cf. id.* at 413.

concrete terms, the few well-publicized cases of Arab sheikhs who turned out to be FBI agents are likely to make members of Congress think twice before accepting a bribe.[121]

Unfortunately, these observations leave us with an uncomfortable sense of indeterminacy as to the utility of the entrapment strategy. About all that can be said is that the strategy creates some crime, stops other crime, and that it is hard to generalize about which effect is predominant. To be sure, there may be certain forms of entrapment that are likely to be inefficient. For example, when government agents engage in very harmful conduct to detect very minor offenses, the strategy is difficult to defend. Most of us would agree that narcotics agents should not commit murders to preserve their cover when investigating marijuana offenses. This observation explains the dicta, now supported by a majority of the Court, establishing due process limits on the extent to which government agents can engage in antisocial conduct in order to fight crime.[122] Although the Court has been extremely vague in defining those limits, they presumably involve some balance between the social cost of the crime on the one hand and the means used to combat it on the other. But the existence of these constitutional limits does not explain the need for an additional entrapment defense in situations where government agents have not imposed severe social costs.

If the Court were to adopt one of the competing definitions of "predisposition," entrapment doctrine might be somewhat easier to justify on efficiency grounds. It makes some sense to acquit defendants who succumb only to very large or attractive inducements which are either unlikely to be replicated or likely to cause the average person to succumb. If the inducement is unlikely to be replicated, then a defendant responding to it poses little danger, and the enforcement costs are largely wasted. If the inducement is unusually attractive, then the possibility of deterring those tempted

---

[121] My point is not that entrapment can necessarily be shown to be an effective deterrent against crime over the long term. In fact, the empirical data on this question are sketchy and inconclusive. See *id.* at 411. My point is, rather, that a rational person might suppose that an entrapment strategy would serve as an effective deterrent. In the absence of strong evidence to the contrary, it is therefore difficult to understand why we should have a judicial doctrine premised on the assumption that entrapment does not deter crime. See text at notes 124–28 *infra.*

[122] See text at notes 17–20 *supra.*

to succumb is small, and the effort to deter them may again produce
a less than optimal allocation of resources.

Thus, an entrapment doctrine different from the one we have
might not be altogether senseless. Yet the case for even this
hypothetical doctrine is at best uneasy. The efficiency argument
explains why a sensible police department might want to forgo an
entrapment strategy in some cases, but not why we should have a
formal, judicially enforced doctrine incorporating that judgment.[123] Illustrating the flaws of an entrapment strategy by limiting cases tends to mask the complexity of the analysis in the more
usual situation when the cases are closer. Of course, government
agents should not commit murders to catch pot smokers. But in a
closer case, how is the court to measure the social cost of a particular enforcement decision against the cost of the crime it is designed
to combat? Without some *a priori* unit of conversion, it is difficult to
see how this calculation can be performed even in principle.

Similarly, everyone would agree that no purpose is served by
offering an inducement so large or so unusual that there is no risk of
replication or possibility that anyone would resist it. But in the real
world, the risk of replication and possibility of deterrence are almost never zero. As one moves away from this extreme, the utility
of offering any particular inducement depends upon the value assigned *a priori* to avoiding an incidence of the particular crime
involved. If one believed, for example, that even a single sale of
drugs to a minor were a catastrophe, one could justify the use of
extraordinarily attractive inducements to avoid this event.

The real mystery is why courts and juries should be thought the
proper bodies to make these difficult law enforcement judgments.[124] Surely they have no special expertise or legitimacy with
regard to such matters. The *ad hoc* quality of jury judgments makes
them especially inappropriate for the formulation of consistent law

---

[123] It is significant, for example, that Professor Dix's argument for restrictions on police
utilization of an entrapment strategy is couched in terms of suggestions for internal police
department regulations. See Dix, *Undercover Investigations and Police Rulemaking*, note 108
supra. Cf. testimony of Louis Seidman before the subcommittee on Civil and Constitutional
Rights of the House Judiciary Committee, February 19, 1981 (Congress should restrict
entrapment strategy on efficiency grounds).

[124] Of course, this objection would be overcome if the legislature mandated an entrapment
defense. But, as noted above, the statutory construction justification for the defense is an
obvious fiction. See text at notes 100–107 *supra*.

enforcement policy.[125] And it is hard to see why we should allow judges shielded from political responsibility the power to make the value choice implicit in deciding on the level of inducement to be offered.

Judicial intervention to enforce entrapment rules is significantly different from judicial enforcement of other limitations on police conduct, such as the exclusionary rules of the Fourth and Fifth Amendments. These rules are premised on the assumption that the police are primarily interested in fighting crime and that they may therefore undervalue privacy concerns which obstruct the apprehension of criminals.[126] But to the extent that entrapment doctrine rests on efficiency grounds, one would expect the police themselves to be motivated to use scarce resources in a manner that maximizes the number of criminals apprehended.

Of course, this argument may rest on an oversimplified model of police motivation. It is conceivable, for example, that the police are in fact interested in maximizing arrests rather than minimizing crime on the view that as arrests increase, police appropriations increase as well. But even if one adopts this cynical assumption, the value of an entrapment defense remains unclear, because police officers uninterested in minimizing crime are less likely to be deterred by the eventual acquittal of the defendants they entrap.[127]

Moreover, the possibility that police departments may inaccurately reflect public desires concerning the allocation of law enforcement resources proves only the obvious point that wherever

---

[125] See Sherman v. United States, 356 U.S. 369, 385 (1958) (Frankfurter, J., concurring); Dix, *Undercover Investigations and Police Rulemaking*, note 108 *supra*, at 248. Indeed, the commitment of entrapment decisions to juries, which need not give reasons or reach consistent results, may serve as a mechanism by which we obscure the underlying incoherence of the doctrine. See CALABRESI & BOBBIT, TRAGIC CHOICES 57–58 (1978).

[126] A classic statement of this argument appears in Justice Jackson's opinion for the Court in Johnson v. United States, 333 U.S. 10, 13–14 (1948):

The point of the Fourth Amendment, which often is not grasped by zealous officers, is not that it denies law enforcement the support of the usual evidence. Its protection consists in requiring that those inferences be drawn by a neutral and detached magistrate instead of being judged by the officer engaged in the often competitive enterprise of fereting out crime.

[127] Generally, an officer's career advancement is determined by his success in effecting arrests, whether or not they ultimately culminate in conviction. See, *e.g.*, Oaks, *Studying the Exclusionary Rule in Search and Seizure*, 37 U. CHI. L. REV. 665, 727–28 (1970). Thus, an officer unconcerned with reducing crime is likely to have little additional reason to worry about entrapment rules. *Cf. id.* at 721–22, 726–27.

power is vested, it may be abused. It is also true that courts may err in assigning an *a priori* value to the avoidance of certain types of crime and that the rigidity of any doctrine which is judicially manageable may make it unresponsive to constant shifts in the pattern of crime and need for deterrence.

For precisely these reasons, we have traditionally relied upon the executive to decide how to deploy the forces available to combat crime.[128] No doubt, those forces are sometimes squandered. There are those among us who think it a scandal to prosecute bookies and prostitutes while murders go unsolved and armed robbers unpunished. But no one suggests that, therefore, such decisions should be subjected to comprehensive judicial oversight. On the contrary, the law is clear that, except in the narrowest of circumstances, police and prosecutorial enforcement decisions are immune from judicial review.[129] In the words of Justice Rehnquist, the federal judiciary does not have "a 'chancellor's foot' veto over law enforcement practices of which it [does] not approve. The execution of federal laws under our Constitution is confided primarily to the Executive Branch of the Government."[130] Unfortunately, Justice Rehnquist nowhere explains why this language appears in an opinion reaffirming an entrapment defense entailing just such a veto.

There is, however, one distinction between an entrapment strategy and other uses of law enforcement resources. Entrapment might be thought especially dangerous, because it places in the hands of the executive the power to make criminals. If the government can offer inducements that no one would refuse, it can pick and choose the persons who will obey the law. The risk that this power might be used to punish disfavored groups is obvious.[131]

---

[128] I argue below that limitations on the executive's freedom to allocate law enforcement resources are more pervasive than they first appear. But these limitations do not relate to efficiency. On the contrary, they stem from inherent problems with the criminal sanction which cause inefficient outcomes. See text at notes 145-54 *infra*.

[129] See, *e.g.*, Inmates of Attica Correctional Facility v. Rockefeller, 477 F.2d 375 (2d Cir. 1973); United States v. Cox, 342 F.2d 167 (5th Cir. 1965).

[130] United States v. Russell, 411 U.S. 423, 435 (1973).

[131] Of course, there are other legal doctrines which control the power of the executive to single out disfavored groups for overtly discriminatory prosecution. See, *e.g.*, Yick Wo v. Hopkins, 118 U.S. 356 (1886); United States v. Falk, 479 F.2d 616 (7th Cir. 1973). The evidentiary problems in establishing discriminatory prosecution are severe, however. See, *e.g.*, Butler v. Cooper, 554 F.2d 645 (4th Cir. 1977); United States v. Kelly, 556 F.2d 257 (5th Cir. 1977). It might therefore be thought that a prophylactic rule is necessary to minimize the risk of discrimination. But this argument fails to explain why a doctrine limiting the

I suspect that this fear of the government's power to create criminals provides the ultimate answer to the entrapment puzzle. It is not an obvious answer, however. It will not do to claim that entrapment is necessary to prevent the executive from engaging in selective application of the criminal sanction, because within broad limits,[132] we tolerate precisely this risk when the universe of potential criminals consists solely of persons acting without government inducement.[133] When the government chooses which shoplifters, pickpockets, and drug users to prosecute and to jail, we regularly rely upon political checks to guard against abuse. Why do these checks become suddenly inadequate when the class of potential criminals is broader?

III. Entrapment and Our Criminal Justice Dilemma

The entrapment defense neither protects the innocent nor conserves scarce law enforcement resources. The defense allows the punishment of persons on the basis of general life-styles without regard to specific criminal acts, while vindicating persons clearly worthy of punishment. It empowers ad hoc decision-making bodies, largely immune from political control, to decide basic social policy issues, while depriving the executive of an effective means of reducing the social cost of crime.

This analysis is not yet complete, however, because it fails to respond to two deeply seated and widely shared intuitive judgments. The first is that a person is somewhat less culpable if tempted into crime by certain kinds of inducements. The second is that it is extremely dangerous to allow government the power to stress test the morality of ordinary citizens by dangling substantial inducements before them.

The existence of these intuitions no doubt explains the creation and survival of the entrapment defense. But where do the intuitions come from? No answer to that question can be offered with certainty. In the end, we can only guess at the ultimate source of our moral and political sensibilities. Still, I believe an understanding of

---

government's power to prosecute persons with mainstream life-style serves to discourage discriminatory prosecution of disfavored groups. See text at note 134 *infra*.

[132] See note 131 *supra*.

[133] See, *e.g.*, Oyler v. Boles, 368 U.S. 448 (1962).

what entrapment objectively accomplishes—how it operates and who benefits from it—provides some useful insights.

A. ENTRAPMENT AND RISK DISTRIBUTION

The police conduct prohibited by our entrapment doctrine is best understood as a technique that shifts the risk of becoming a criminal to a group on which it would not otherwise fall. Each of us on occasion is subject to the temptation to commit a criminal act. Since none of us is perfect, we all run the risk that we will someday succumb to this temptation, be caught committing the act, and so be subject to punishment. But the risk of this misfortune is not spread equally throughout the society. Some of us are subject to temptations more frequently and more intensely than others. Many of us go through a lifetime without being asked to commit a serious crime. If we were asked, our relatively comfortable status means that the inducement would have to be very large indeed to offset the risk of the endeavor. But in certain subcultures, armed robbery is a daily option, and pimps, pushers, and hustlers are daily temptors.

When the government pursues an entrapment strategy, it artificially generates similar pressures to commit crime. Of course, this fact alone does not demonstrate that an entrapment strategy shifts the risk of becoming a criminal. In fact, if the government were totally unfettered in the use of an entrapment strategy, it is probable that it would concentrate its efforts on deviant subcultures which already bear most of the risk. The police are hardly immune from the stereotypic judgments that the rest of us make, and it is therefore likely to make sense to them to concentrate enforcement on those with life-styles we disapprove of in any event. Indeed, it is possible that this strategy is rational and that potential criminals are in fact disproportionately represented among these groups.

Accordingly, an outright ban on the entrapment strategy might actually benefit disfavored groups. But the crucial point is that we have no such outright ban. Rather, entrapment is prohibited only when it induces the nondisposed—that is, those with ordinary, rather than disfavored, life-styles.[134] This partial ban has the effect of prohibiting entrapment if, but only if, the government attempts to shift the risk of criminality. By discouraging the offering of

---

[134] See text at notes 45–58 *supra*.

inducements to those who are nondisposed, the entrapment doctrine assures that the risk distribution which exists in the private sphere will not be upset.

Why do we have a formal legal doctrine that restricts the government in this fashion? The short answer is that the inherent difficulty in using the legal system to shift the risk of criminality is merely one example of the difficulty in utilizing it to shift benefits and burdens more generally. If a legal system is responsive to the culture from which it emerges, it should already reflect the relative political power of the groups affected by it. It is therefore no more than a tautology that groups disadvantaged by the system will have difficulty generating the political power to change it. A more complete answer, however, requires an understanding of the special limits on the power of government when it attempts to impose a criminal sanction.

B. ENTRAPMENT AND THE DECLINE OF WILL AND RIGHTS

According to the dominant utilitarian tradition, the criminal sanction inflicts pain on a few individuals so as to avoid greater pain which would otherwise be inflicted on others. A few people are made to bear intense discomfort so as to avoid the greater social loss caused by crime—albeit a loss which may be spread more broadly throughout society.[135]

For a society that has adopted this strategy, the mode of selection of the few people required to bear this intense loss is an issue of some moment. Most of criminal law consists of the doctrines that govern this selection and limit the size of the group subject to the risk of selection. As a formal matter, we profess to have two criteria for membership in this group: the person must have performed an act previously made illegal by the criminal law, and we must be able to say that, given the circumstances, we could reasonably expect him to have acted differently.

It is worth noting at the outset that we pay a price for respecting these limits.[136] At least short-term utilitarian gains could be

---

[135] See, e.g., BENTHAM, AN INTRODUCTION TO THE PRINCIPLES OF MORALS AND LEGISLATION 158–59 (Burns & Hart eds. 1970); POSNER, ECONOMIC ANALYSIS OF LAW 163–77 (2d ed. 1977).

[136] Most of the discussion in the next two paragraphs is drawn from H. L. A. Hart's classic essay Legal Responsibility and Excuses in HART, PUNISHMENT AND RESPONSIBILITY

realized by punishing people who have not yet acted or who could not have acted differently. There would be an immediate savings in the process and error costs presently associated with establishing blame. Moreover, because there is no necessary correlation between blame and dangerousness, the criminal sanction might profitably be used to isolate individuals who, although blameless, are likely to inflict social harm. Finally, punishing the blameless could produce important benefits in terms of general deterrence. To be sure, a person who cannot choose cannot be deterred. But potential criminals do not necessarily accurately predict the category in which they will ultimately be placed. Thus, a potential criminal might be emboldened to commit a crime by the belief that, if caught, he could prove blamelessness and so escape punishment.

There are nonetheless utilitarian reasons for resisting the lure of immediate gains to be derived from a "no-fault" theory of criminal justice.[137] It is perfectly rational to accept some increase in crime to reduce the risk of becoming a criminal.[138] If a blameless person could be punished, we would all live in constant fear of getting caught up in the criminal justice system. To be sure, the risk of this misfortune cannot be reduced to zero without also destroying the deterrent force of the criminal law, thereby creating a much greater risk of becoming a victim. It is therefore necessary to balance the desirability of deterring crime against the desirability of avoiding punishment. The requirement of an act and a meaningful choice constitutes the method by which we have struck that balance. These requirements ensure that we need not be subject to the risk of punishment unless we wish to bring it on ourselves.[139] Because

28–53 (1968). See also Rawls, *Punishment in* PHILOSOPHY OF LAW (Feinberg & Gross eds. 1975); PACKER, THE LIMITS OF THE CRIMINAL SANCTION 66–69 (1968).

[137] In addition to the reasons discussed in text, punishment of the blameless may actually reduce the deterrent efficacy of the criminal law by reducing the difference between the treatment of those who choose to obey and disobey the law. *Cf.* POSNER, ECONOMIC ANALYSIS OF LAW 430–32 (2d ed. 1977).

[138] This point is made more elegantly and in far more detail in Goetz and Schwartz, *"Unequal" Punishment for "Equal" Crimes: An Economic Rationale* (unpublished paper on file with author). Professors Goetz and Schwartz propose a model whereby individuals calculate their own preferred level of punishment for criminal offenses. These individual solutions are then aggregated by the political process. See *id* at 2. The authors suggest that in making their individual calculations, people will be motivated in part by the fear that they will commit an act prohibited by the criminal law. An individual will therefore support a level of punishment which minimizes the sum of the possible costs to him as a victim of crime and the possible value of the losses to him caused by punishing the crime. *Id.* at 20–21.

[139] See GROSS, A THEORY OF CRIMINAL JUSTICE 415 (1979).

people do not readily vote for self-condemnation, it is hardly surprising that our political institutions have insisted on limiting the criminal sanction in this fashion.

Given this important role that blameworthiness plays in our system, one might suppose that we would have a well-developed, consistent theory of choice and blame. But in fact, the necessary predicates for such a theory have been under a double-barreled assault for much of this century. The story is a familiar one and need not be recounted here in great detail. A theory of choice requires one to distinguish between a person's will and the external forces that act on the will. But various determinist theories have undermined our confidence that we can extricate an independent will from the forces that act upon it.[140] The concept of blameworthiness could perhaps survive this determinist onslaught if it were buttressed by a theory of rights. We might then say that a person was not responsible in situations where he had a right not to have certain sorts of forces determine his actions.[141] But what we once thought of as natural rights now increasingly appear to be temporary accommodations of conflicting interests which we are free to manipulate in order to produce desired social outcomes.

Entrapment doctrine is a symptom of the decline of blameworthiness as a meaningful concept. If we really still believed that each of us were free agents, able to reject the path of crime and therefore blameworthy if we choose that path, there would be no need for an entrapment defense. We would be happy to allow the government to offer any inducement it chose, secure in the knowledge that the blameless among us would reject temptation. It is only because we do not believe this—because we believe instead that many of us would succumb to the temptation to which only some of us are daily subjected—that the defense is necessary. If we really still believed that individuals had a right to lead their lives free from certain types of external pressures, then entrapment doctrine would look quite different. The doctrine would define the kinds of pressures that were out-of-bounds and exculpate defendants subject to those pressures. It is only because we do not believe this—because

---

[140] Thus, as noted above, the applicability of our law of excuse does not generally depend upon whether external forces have overpowered the defendant's will. See text at note 91 *supra*.

[141] See text at notes 91–93 *supra*.

we believe instead that there are no inherent limits on government power to manipulate the individual for social ends—that we have a doctrine that exculpates on the basis of the kind of person the defendant is, rather than the kind of forces to which he has succumbed.

Entrapment doctrine is more than a symptom, however. It is also representative of the adaptive mechanisms to which we have resorted in order to maintain a criminal justice system without an adequate theory of blame. The partial demise of that theory leaves the balance between the gain from deterring crime and the loss from incurring punishment in disequilibrium. If one no longer believes that he has a choice not to commit criminal acts, then the risk of engaging in such conduct and being punished for it may loom large. And, of course, it looms larger still if one has reason to fear that the government is sytematically offering temptations designed to lure people into crime.

But choice is not the only way to limit the criminal sanction. Entrapment doctrine is an example of an alternative means for limiting the class potentially subject to punishment. Even if we cannot agree on a theory of blame, the great majority of us can remain secure if we agree on a limited class of people to be blamed. Even if we can no longer define this class by the acts they choose to commit, we can still define it by their life-style, character, and status.

This mechanism seems closely linked to the intuitive judgments that support the entrapment defense.[142] Is it not possible that defendants succumbing to certain temptations seem less culpable because we can imagine persons with our life-styles making a similar choice? Is not our fear of government power to make criminals really a fear that it will make the wrong people criminals? Is not entrapment doctrine simply a means of regaining our distance from those suffering punishment so that we can avoid the politically impossible task of self-condemnation?

---

[142] It may also explain why almost all entrapment problems arise in cases of peripheral and "victimless" crimes, such as drug, liquor, and prostitution offenses. *Cf.* AMERICAN LAW INSTITUTE, MODEL PENAL CODE § 2.13(3) (Official Draft 1962) (entrapment defense not available for offenses involving threat of bodily harm). On the one hand, these are crimes which "ordinary" people can imagine themselves or their friends committing. On the other, the reduced deterrent efficacy which recognition of the defense entails imposes only small social costs.

IV. Conclusion: Entrapment and Crime

What impact does all this have on our ability to control
crime at reasonable social costs? If one means by this question,
what do we pay for recognition of an entrapment defense, the
answer is some—but not much. As argued above, it is at least
possible that more vigorous utilization of an entrapment strategy
would deter some additional crime and incapacitate some additional
dangerous offenders.[143] But the infrequency with which the entrapment defense is raised[144] makes it implausible in the extreme
that the restrictions it places on law enforcement are significant.[145]
Entrapment doctrine, standing alone, is no more than a curiosity,
of more use to legal academics seeking tenure than to criminals
seeking acquittals.

But obviously, entrapment doctrine is only one of a wide variety
of rules, institutions, and practices that limit the extent to which we
punish socially harmful conduct. It seems at least possible that
these other limitations are also related to the substitution of status
for culpability as a limiting principle for the criminal law. For
example, our relatively lenient treatment of whole classes of demonstrably dangerous conduct, like drunk driving or air and water
pollution, may be related to our inability to use the criminal law
when people think that the cost to them as potential victims of the
crime is outweighed by the advantages as potential perpetrators or
beneficiaries of the conduct. Other defenses, which cut across the
definitions of crime, like infancy and insanity, as well as mitigating
factors like provocation, may also be a product of our reluctance to
punish when we can imagine ourselves, or people like us, committing crimes while suffering from similar disabilities. And on a less
formal level, practices like unstructured sentencing and prosecutorial discretion, parole, and jury nullification all allow at least
the possibility of mitigating or avoiding the punishment of those
who remind us too much of ourselves.

---

[143] See text at notes 118–21 *supra*.

[144] See note 7 *supra*.

[145] I do not mean to suggest that the entrapment strategy plays an unimportant role in
reducing crime. In fact, there is reason to believe that police reliance on entrapment is
growing. See Marx, *The New Undercover Police Work*, note 7 *supra*, at 400. Rather, my point
is that the legal restrictions on entrapment are relatively insignificant.

Each of those phenomena is complex, and it would be wrong to suppose that any of them can be explained fully by a single theory.[146] Clearly, much more work needs to be done. Some of our most perceptive criminal law scholars have already begun to demonstrate the inconsistency between the ways in which we limit punishment and our traditional theories of culpability and deterrence.[147] But we need to ask more questions about the source and persistence of exculpatory doctrines now that choice and blame no longer effectively restrain government power.

I think that more work needs to be done as well on the link, if any, between these doctrines and the level of crime. No assertion on this subject can be made with much confidence in the absence of detailed empirical investigation. But the analysis above suggests, as a working hypothesis, that we may be generating a level of punishment that is at once too low and too high to produce a socially acceptable level of crime.

The level of punishment is too low because our squeamishness about punishing people who closely resemble ourselves leaves large classes of harmful conduct substantially underdeterred. Every doctrine or practice which reduces our ability to apprehend or punish criminals reduces the risk for those tempted to engage in a criminal conduct, and thereby produces more crime.[148] This increase, in turn, generates political pressure to compensate for the loss of deterrent impact by punishing more severely the remaining defendants who are left unprotected by these exculpatory or mitigating principles.[149]

---

[146] For example, it does not seem to be true that a failure of identification is the only predicate for punishment. On the contrary, the urge to punish may in some measure be linked to the repression of our own darker desires, so that some degree of identification with a criminal is also necessary to make punishment seem appropriate. Thus, some exculpatory doctrines may be based on the fact that the defendant's conduct is too bizzare or irrational to permit identification rather than too ordinary or familiar to avoid it. We seem to reserve punishment for the class of people falling between those on one side who are too conventional to be "criminals" and those on the other who are too strange to be "responsible."

[147] For one such demonstration which is especially compelling and provocative, see Kelman, *Interpretive Construction in the Substantive Criminal Law*, 33 STAN. L. REV. 591 (1981).

[148] See text at notes 136–37 *supra*.

[149] This effect does not result from the lenient treatment of whole categories of harmful conduct. There is no reason to suppose that leniency toward drunk drivers produces political pressure to lock up more armed robbers. But as noted above, we mitigate punishment not only by lenient treatment of classes of criminal conduct, but also by leniency toward criminals within a given class. Thus, our insistence on lightly punishing some armed robbers with whom we identify probably results in more armed robbery, which in turn produces pressures to treat the remaining armed robbers more harshly.

But there is reason to believe that this pressure produces a level of punishment that is also too high. At this point, one's conclusions must be very tentative indeed. Despite much theorizing, we really know very little about what causes people to avoid crime. It is doubtful, however, that people remain law abiding solely because of the risk of criminal punishment. Indeed, the most sophisticated deterrence theorists concede that the deterrent effect of the criminal law is most potent when it serves to reinforce preexisting moral inhibitions.[150]

If this observation is correct, the dissociation of crime and blame may have an impact on the deterrent force of the criminal law. Society regularly inflicts pain on individuals without blaming them—by taxing them, for example, or requiring them to risk their lives during wartime. Private conduct is no doubt influenced to some extent by the desire to avoid such misfortunes. But the criminal law has traditionally gained its special ability to mold conduct from the fact that similar pain is linked to a group declaration of blameworthiness.[151] This power is fragile indeed. When criminals and potential criminals believe that the criminal law is operating unjustly or unequally, they see those punished as victims to be pitied—or perhaps even martyrs to be emulated—rather than outcasts to be condemned.[152] It hardly matters whether this perception is correct, or even reasonable. The perception itself is a reality which disables society from stigmatizing those convicted of crime and so deprives the criminal law of an important part of its deterrent impact.

It is once again impossible to know the importance of this effect, if, indeed, it exists at all. But if it is important, we may caught up in a vicious cycle with no obvious way out. The understandable public anger and frustration at crime produces irresistible pressures to

---

[150] See, e.g., ANDENAES, PUNISHMENT AND DETERRENCE 8–9, 110–26 (1974).

[151] See ROSS, ON GUILT, RESPONSIBILITY AND PUNISHMENT 90–91 (1975).

[152] Professor Gross has argued that "A system that routinely disregards the rudiments of exculpation insisted upon by common justice can no longer preserve the effectiveness of the law as a force for social control, since allegiance to its rules is bound to disappear and is certain to be replaced by artifice and guile as citizens make every effort to protect themselves against the hazards of the law." GROSS, A THEORY OF CRIMINAL JUSTICE 416–17 (1979). Both he and Professor Ross, see note 151 supra, address the consequences which would be produced if society as a whole viewed the criminal justice system in this way. But if this view were widely shared, society would presumably change the system. The situation is much more serious when most people think the system is fair and are unwilling to change it for the benefit of a minority which regards itself as victimized.

strengthen criminal sanctions. As the sanctions become stiffer, their application must also be narrowed, because we are increasingly unwilling to risk imposition of such draconian measures against ourselves or people like us. Yet the narrowing and intensification of punishment may actually weaken its deterrent efficacy, both by making more people immune from punishment and by making those who are punished seem like victims rather than criminals.[153] This effect produces still more crime, thereby generating pressure for still harsher punishment.

Entrapment doctrine is but a small part of this problem. But the remarkable fervor with which Justices of widely varying ideological views have defended the doctrine implies that we have much less ability to deal with the problem than might be supposed. Our experience with entrapment suggests that we simply will not tolerate proposals to broaden the class of potential criminals, even when the resulting change is likely to be inconsequential.[154] Yet we may in the end be faced with an unavoidable choice between having more criminals and having more crime. The ambivalence of our political institutions before this dilemma has contributed to the present difficulties in our courtrooms and in our streets.

---

[153] The point is hardly new. Blackstone understood that "punishments of unreasonable severity, especially when indiscriminately inflicted, have less effect in preventing crimes, and amending the manners of the people, than such as are more merciful in general, yet properly intermixed with due distinctions of severity. . . . [T]hough . . . we may glory in the wisdom of the English law, we shall find it more difficult to justify the frequency of capital punishment to be found therein, inflicted (perhaps inattentively) by a multitude of successive independent statutes upon crimes very different in their natures. . . . So dreadful a list, instead of diminishing, increases the number of offenders. The injured, through compassion, will often forebear to prosecute; juries, through compassion, will sometimes forget their oaths, and either acquit the guilty or mitigate the nature of the offence; and judges, through compassion, will respite one half of the convicts, and recommend them to the royal mercy. Among so many chances of escaping, the needy and hardened offender overlooks the multitude that suffer: he boldly engages in some desperate attempt to relieve his wants or supply his vices, and, if, unexpectedly, the hand of justice overtakes him, he deems himself peculiarly unfortunate in falling at last a sacrifice to those laws which long impunity has taught him to condemn." 4 BLACKSTONE, COMMENTARIES *16–19.

[154] As noted above, abolition of the entrapment defense would have little practical effect in broadening the class of persons subject to criminal punishment, since the police are likely to use the strategy primarily against disfavored groups in any event. The stubborness with which we have resisted even this marginal broadening of the criminal sanction is therefore even more remarkable.

CHARLES E. ARES

CHANDLER v. FLORIDA: TELEVISION, CRIMINAL TRIALS, AND DUE PROCESS

In *Chandler v. Florida*,[1] the Supreme Court decided that televising criminal trials does not, *per se*, violate due process.[2] Doctrinally, the case adds little, if anything, to developments in the so-called fair trial–free press controversy. Practically, the decision probably will result in somewhat greater public familiarity with what actually goes on in courtrooms. But the major significance of the decision lies in its recognition that a criminal trial is not simply a deadly little piece of combat between an individual and the state, the sole purpose of which is to determine whether the accused committed a crime and must be punished. The trial is more than that; it is an act of government of considerable social and political importance to people who have no direct concern with the specific events that led to the prosecution. Of course, the administration of the criminal law has always had broad social significance, but, until the advent of television, only a few spectators could participate in an im-

Charles E. Ares is Professor of Law, University of Arizona College of Law.

AUTHOR'S NOTE: I have profited much from discussion with my colleague, Joseph Livermore. Arthur Andrews and Jean Ares read an earlier draft and made many valuable suggestions. I am also grateful for the valuable research assistance of Roberta Schulte, second-year law student at the University of Arizona.

[1] 101 S.Ct. 802 (1981). The vote was 8–0. Justice Stevens did not participate.

[2] The issues discussed here include not only television coverage but still photography and radio broadcasting as well. For simplicity, I will refer generally to television coverage on the understanding that still photography and radio broadcasting present similar, but less troublesome, issues. Also, it is obvious that civil trials should be treated no differently from criminal trials.

mediate way. Since *Chandler*, it is at least possible for vastly larger numbers of people to witness a hearing, or a trial, or a sentencing exactly as it occurs.

The decision permitting state courts to open trials to an extent reflects a change in the perception of the criminal process. In 1976, *Nebraska Press Association v. Stuart*[3] held that a trial court could not prevent the press from publishing information about an upcoming trial, even information about the accused or evidence that might prejudice prospective jurors. Coupled with the Court's reluctance to reverse convictions because of prejudicial pretrial publicity, save in the most egregious cases,[4] the right of the press to publish large amounts of information about crime and criminal trials has become to a large degree unchecked. In *Gannet v. DePasquale*,[5] in an apparent attempt to reduce the amount of prejudicial publicity, the Court upheld the power of a state court to close a pretrial hearing to the public and the press. But in light of the Court's decision the next term in *Richmond Newspapers, Inc. v. Virginia*,[6] it may be doubtful that even the *Gannett* closure device will be very effective in the long run.

The press is free to publish information about crime and criminal cases largely as it pleases, within the bounds of its own sense of taste and its awareness that excesses may cause a miscarriage of justice or jeopardize a conviction.[7] And in *Richmond Newspapers* the Court confirmed that the public and the press have a First Amendment right to attend and report the events of a trial even though the defendant and the prosecutor might prefer to close the proceedings to public scrutiny.[8] Now, the Court in *Chandler v. Florida* has

---

[3] 427 U.S. 539 (1976). The Court held that the doctrine of prior restraint precluded a so-called gag order except in the rarest circumstances.

[4] Compare Stroble v. California, 343 U.S. 181 (1952) with Irvin v. Dowd, 366 U.S. 717 (1961).

[5] 443 U.S. 368 (1979).

[6] 448 U.S. 555 (1980). For a discussion of the relation between these cases and the possible future impact of *Gannett*, see Lewis, *A Public Right to Know about Public Institutions: The First Amendment as Sword*, 1980 SUP. CT. REV. 1.

[7] See, *e.g.*, Sheppard v. Maxwell, 384 U.S. 333 (1966).

[8] 448 U.S. 555, 560 (1980). Open trials have been a tradition in Anglo-American law, thus accounting for the fact that not until 1980 was the Court required to decide whether the Constitution required that trials be open at the public's demand. But see In Re Oliver, 333 U.S. 257 (1948) (witness testifying in secret before "one man judge-grand jury" summarily charged and convicted of contempt by perjury; secrecy of trial and conviction violated due process.)

permitted the states, if they wish to do so, to extend public access by televising court proceedings to members of the public who can "attend" in their own homes simply by flipping a television switch.

The new emphasis on the *public* dimensions of the criminal trial reflected by these decisions has troubling implications in the television age. To the extent that public considerations compete with concern for individual rights, courts may tend to slight protection of the defendant. *Chandler* is particularly troubling, because virtually nothing is known about the effects of television on trials, and it is difficult to see how anything very definite is going to be learned about some of those effects.

In *Chandler*, the Court was careful to point out that the case did not involve any claim that the First Amendment required television access to trials. Florida had granted that access, and the question for the Court was whether the defendant's due process rights had been thereby infringed. After reciting a history of dire predictions of prejudice if cameras were allowed in courtrooms and acknowledging uncertainty about what the consequences might be, the Court offered practically no discussion of the reasons that would justify allowing the states to take such risks with criminal trials. And none of those reasons mentioned rested on First Amendment–type considerations.

The note that dominates the *Chandler* opinion is the Chief Justice's assertion that, although television may "adversely affect the conduct of the participants and the fairness of the trial, yet leave no evidence of how the conduct or the trial's fairness was affected,"[9] notions of federalism required the states to be allowed to experiment.[10] This deference to the states which rings so harmoniously to ears tuned to rejecting claims of "substantive due process" seems strangely jolting when offered as a response to a claim that a state's criminal procedure has violated due process. The recitation of Justice Brandeis's familiar statement of federalism in *New State Ice Co. v. Liebmann*[11] hardly seems an adequate justification.

The feeling of unease one gets upon reading the opinion may stem from the almost total absence of any discussion of the First Amendment values that necessarily lie beneath the surface of the

---

[9] 101 S.Ct. at 811.

[10] *Id.* at 812.

[11] 285 U.S. 262, 311 (1932).

case. One would think that only interests at least similar to those protected by the First Amendment would justify running the risks of prejudice to the defendant that the Court acknowledged are created whenever trials are televised.

The arguments to be developed here will be that, although it reached the right result in *Chandler*, the Court failed to justify that result in a persuasive way. Moreover, its decision inevitably means that it will have to face a series of troublesome questions relating to televising witnesses and jurors. The Court will necessarily face the difficult question of whether television has a First Amendment right of access to governmental proceedings. Finally, I will suggest that television coverage emphasizes a public aspect of the trial which shifts its focus away from individualized justice and toward a view of the trial as a governmental event with profound public effects.

I. The Case

Chandler stemmed from a petty burglary that would never have achieved national attention except for the fact that the trial was televised.

In an early morning in May 1977, John Sion could not sleep, so he switched on his ham radio for company while he read a book. Hearing what sounded like a suspicious conversation, he turned on his tape recorder and produced what proved to be sensational evidence of the burglary of a restaurant in Miami Beach. The burglars were two policemen, and the conversation Sion overheard had taken place over their walkie-talkie radios. At the time Florida, as an experiment, permitted trials to be televised and photographed pursuant to a temporary relaxation of Canon 3A(7) of its Code of Judicial Conduct. Both defendants objected to the cameras on due process grounds, but the court permitted coverage without their consent. Apparently the publicity surrounding the case was not so pervasive as to interfere with securing an unbiased jury, and so far as *voir dire* revealed, the prospect of having television cameras in the courtroom seemed not to bother any prospective jurors. The trial jury was not sequestered, but the jurors were told to avoid reading anything about the case in the newspapers or watching local television news. The trial itself was uneventful, and the television coverage was a good deal less than total. One camera was present during the afternoon when the ham radio operator testified. It was absent when the defense presented its case but returned during closing arguments. There were no allegations of physical distraction by television personnel, and the televising of the *Chandler* trial was about as unobtrusive as it could be. The defendants made no attempts to show that because of the presence of the cameras they had been prejudiced in fact.

The Florida District Court of Appeals rejected attacks on the television rule, facially and as applied, and affirmed the convictions.[12] The Supreme Court of Florida declined review.[13]

II. The History of Cameras in Courts

The controversy over cameras in the courtroom is generally traced to the 1935 New Jersey prosecution of Bruno Hauptmann for the kidnap-murder of the Lindbergh baby. The trial, held in the small town of Flemington, was a shambles—an international event which drew huge crowds to the little town and into the overcrowded courtroom. Reporters clambered on press tables, runners darted in and out with stories to file, film and still cameras were installed in the courtroom, although apparently they were used only surreptitiously. Noise from spectators frequently interfered with the proceedings. Counsel for both sides carried on a regular campaign of press conferences, and the trial judge seemed unable to control the participants.[14] Hauptmann was convicted,[15] but reactions to the excesses of the trial ultimately led to the adoption by the ABA of Canon 35 of the Canons of Judicial Ethics and to the almost total exclusion of cameras from American courtrooms for almost the next half-century.[16]

---

[12] Chandler v. State, 366 So. 2d 64 (D.C.A. Fla. 1978).

[13] Chandler v. State, 376 So. 2d 1157 (Fla. 1979).

[14] The proceedings are fully described in Hallam, *Some Object Lessons on Publicity in Criminal Trials*, 24 MINN. L. REV. 453 (1940). Dean Hallam was the chairman of a 1936 ABA Special Committee on Publicity in Criminal Trials. Its creation was a reaction by the organized bar to the excesses evident in the Hauptmann case. Ironically, the most serious disruptions in Hauptmann apparently were created not by photographers but by the print reporters and the spectators. And the circus atmosphere of the trial was first created *before* the trial. The report of the Hallam Committee fully details the events of the trial and is attached as an appendix to the cited article.

[15] State v. Hauptmann, 115 N.J. Law 412, 180 A 809 (1935), *cert. den.* 296 U.S. 649.

[16] A summary of the history of Canon 35 is set out in an appendix to the opinion of Justice Harlan, concurring in Estes v. Texas, 381 U.S. 532, 596 (1965). The adoption of the Canon

The Canons, and the successor Code of Judicial Conduct, do not, of course, have any legal force until adopted by a state, generally as rules of court. Exact numbers are difficult to pin down, but by 1965, Chief Justice Warren noted that apparently thirty states had adopted Canon 35, and that, with two or possibly three exceptions, no states affirmatively permitted televised trials.[17] The press never became reconciled to Canon 35 and made repeated but unsuccessful efforts to persuade the ABA to modify or repeal it.[18]

A few states dissented. In 1956, the Colorado Supreme Court, after hearings at which demonstrations were conducted, issued an order permitting televised trials with the consent of the trial

---

in 1937 apparently came as a surprise to newspaper members of a joint bar-press committee that had been working on the problem. Their sense of betrayal may have contributed to the relatively hostile relations that have existed between press and the law in the ensuing years. On the adoption of Canon 35, see *Report of the Special Committee on Cooperation between Press, Radio and Bar, as to Publicity Interfering with Fair Trial of Judicial and Quasi-judicial Proceedings,* 62 A.B.A. REP. 851 (1937); Kielbowitz, *The Story behind the Adoption of the Ban on Courtroom Cameras,* 63 JUDICATURE 14 (1979).

The Canon originally prohibited the taking of photographs in the courtroom, whether court was in session or not, because they were "calculated to detract from the essential dignity of the proceedings, degrade the court and create misconceptions" in the minds of the public. 62 A.B.A. REP. 1134–35 (1937). Over the years the wording has been modified, particularly to include television in the prohibition. In 1972, the Canons of Judicial Ethics were replaced by the Code of Judicial Conduct. Canon 3A(7) of the Code, which replaces old Canon 35, provides:

(7) A judge should prohibit broadcasting, televising, recording, or taking photographs in the courtroom and areas immediately adjacent thereto during sessions of court or recesses between sessions, except that a judge may authorize:
   (a) the use of electronic or photographic means for the presentation of evidence, for the perpetuation of a record, or for other purposes of judicial administration;
   (b) the broadcasting, televising, recording, or photographing of investitive, ceremonial, or naturalization proceedings;
   (c) the photographic or electronic recording and reproduction of appropriate court proceedings under the following conditions:
      (i)   the means of recording will not distract participants or impair the dignity of the proceedings;
      (ii) the parties have consented, and the consent to being depicted or recorded has been obtained from each witness appearing in the recording and reproduction;
      (iii) the reproduction will not be exhibited until after the proceeding has been concluded and all direct appeals have been exhausted; and
      (iv) the reproduction will be exhibited only for instructional purposes in educational institutions.

For a discussion of 3A(7) see THODE, REPORTER'S NOTES TO CODE OF JUDICIAL CONDUCT 56–59 (1973).

[17] Estes v. Texas, 381 U.S. at 581 n.39 (concurring opinion).

[18] In 1952, a committee chaired by John W. Davis, whose concerns were apparently triggered by the televised Kefauver crime hearings, insisted that television was incompatible with a sober search for the truth. 77 A.B.A. REP. 607 (1952). In 1962 and 1963, the Association again rejected changes in Canon 35. 87 A.B.A. REP. 457 (1962); 88 A.B.A. REP. 305 (1963).

judge.[19] Texas, and perhaps Oklahoma, also permitted television of trials in the discretion of the trial court.[20] A survey conducted at about that time showed that while cameras were permitted in a few courtrooms, they were not admitted to most, and the vast majority of lawyers and judges who responded to a questionnaire were opposed to any change in the rule.[21]

Most of the professional discussion of the issue has been strongly polemical.[22] In a 1960 address at the University of Colorado Law School,[23] Justice William O. Douglas summed up the objections to televised trials. They would exacerbate the tendencies of the press to make fair trials impossible in sensational cases. Cameras would affect the participants in unpredictable ways. Trials would become sources of entertainment rather than searches for truth. They would be exploited by lawyers and judges with political ambitions. Commercial sponsorship would vulgarize the proceedings. And he sounded a political note not found much in the literature. There is a danger, he thought, that those who control the communications media, and who have their own ideas about what justice is and how it should be administered, would use this new access to courtrooms to indoctrinate their viewers.[24] The power to select and edit trial coverage, one supposes, was the power he feared.

For its part, the federal judiciary has been uncompromising about cameras in the courtroom.[25] Moreover, many courts have adopted rules that prohibit photography not only in courtrooms but in their "environs" as well.[26]

---

[19] *In re* Hearings Concerning Canon 35 of the Canons of Judicial Ethics, 296 P.2d 465 (Colo. 1956).

[20] See Estes v. Texas, 381 U.S. at 580–581 n.38.

[21] Geis and Talley, *Cameras in the Courtroom*, 47 J. CRIM. L., C. & P. S. 546 (1956).

[22] Much of the literature is collected in a useful bibliography, ELECTRONICS AND PHOTO-GRAPHIC MEDIA COVERAGE OF COURT PROCEEDINGS: AN ANNOTATED BIBLIOGRAPHY (National Center for State Courts, 2d ed. 1980).

[23] Douglas, *The Public Trial and the Free Press*, 33 ROCKY MT. L. REV. 1 (1960).

[24] Compare *id.* at 1–2 with a description of Colorado's experience by a member of the Colorado Supreme Court in Hall, *Colorado's Six Years' Experience without Judicial Canon 35*, 48 A.B.A.J. 1120 (1962). For an eloquent statement of the traditionalist's view, see Griswold, *The Standards of the Legal Profession: Canon 35 Should Not Be Surrendered*, 48 A.B.A.J. 615 (1962).

[25] F. R. Cr. P. 53. It is also clear that the prohibition includes television cameras. 1962 ANNUAL REPORT OF THE PROCEEDINGS OF THE JUDICIAL CONFERENCE OF THE UNITED STATES 10.

[26] Federal courts have supplemented Rule 53 with local rules that protect the traditional

III. Fair Trial–Free Press

The struggle over photography and television in courtrooms, though it has flared into new prominence, is an outgrowth of a long-standing contest between the press and the courts. The press, following its natural instincts, digs up and publishes all the information it can about notorious crimes and pending cases. The courts, following equally natural instincts of their own, have sought ways to control pretrial publicity.

One method of controlling the press, the contempt power, was largely taken away from trial judges by the Supreme Court's decisions in *Bridges v. California*,[27] *Pennekamp v. Florida*,[28] and *Craig v. Harney*.[29] Other methods exist, such as careful *voir dire* of the jury, continuances, and changes of venue, but, for a variety of reasons, they frequently seem inadequate.[30]

An indirect alternative, reversal of a conviction on grounds of prejudicial publicity, is strong medicine, and courts are reluctant to use it except in egregious cases. For example, in *Stroble v. California*,[31] the defendant was charged with the gruesome murder of a small girl and was variously referred to in the newspapers as a "werewolf," a "fiend," a "sex mad killer," and, by the district attorney, as guilty and mentally responsible. Nevertheless, the Supreme Court found that it had not been shown that this publicity, which had moderated by trial time, had so aroused the community as to deny the defendant a fair trial. But in *Irvin v. Dowd*[32] the Court found that pervasive and virulent pretrial publicity had created

quiet of the courthouse. Mazzetti v. United States, 518 F.2d 781 (10th Cir. 1975) ("environs" in local rule defined to include the courthouse and parking areas); compare Dorfman v. Meiszner, 430 F.2d 558 (7th Cir. 1970) ("environs" in local rule defined to include entire floor on which courtrooms were situated, as well as area around elevators, but not including floors of federal building where there were no courtrooms or the lobby and plaza surrounding the building.) See also Seymour v. United States, 373 F.2d 629 (5th Cir. 1967); Tribune Review Publishing Co. v. Thomas, 254 F.2d 883 (3d Cir. 1958); In re Acuff, 331 F. Supp. 819 (D.C. N. Mex. 1971). See generally 1 WRIGHT, FEDERAL PRACTICE AND PROCEDURE, CRIMINAL, §861 (1969).

[27] 314 U.S. 252 (1941).

[28] 328 U.S. 331 (1946).

[29] 331 U.S. 367 (1947).

[30] We now know that some publicity could have been deterred by closing pretrial proceedings to the public and press. Gannett v. DePasquale, note 5 *supra*.

[31] 343 U.S. 181 (1952).

[32] 366 U.S. 717 (1961).

such a "pattern of deep and bitter prejudice" that, as indicated by the *voir dire*, a fair trial could not be had, and the conviction was reversed. The problem was becoming more common, as Justice Frankfurter noted in his concurring opinion.[33] In *Rideau v. Louisiana*,[34] where the defendant's pretrial confession had been televised and broadcast to the community, the Court reversed without even examining the record for signs of actual prejudice.

The issue crystalized as the result of the assassination of President Kennedy in 1963. The Warren Commission's report noted that the press was essentially unrestrained by the public authorities immediately following the shooting of the President and had contributed to a chaotic condition not conducive to effective investigation or the protection of the prisoner.[35] It recommended that the bar, law enforcement groups, and the press develop corrective measures for similar events.[36] The American Bar Association, as a part of its Project on Minimum Standards for Criminal Justice, issued the Reardon Report, which became a focus of controversy between press and bar.[37] And *Estes v. Texas*,[38] which involved both wide-

---

[33] For the Justice this appeared a deeply troubling problem and his opinion contained some ominous hints. "Not a Term passes without this Court being importuned to review convictions, had in States throughout the country, in which substantial claims are made that a jury trial has been distorted because of inflammatory newspaper accounts—too often, as in this case, with the prosecutor's collaboration—exerting pressures upon potential jurors before trial and even during the course of trial, thereby making it extremely difficult, if not impossible, to secure a jury capable of taking in, free of prepossessions, evidence submitted in open court. Indeed such extraneous influences, in violation of the decencies guaranteed by our Constitution, are sometimes so powerful that an accused is forced, as a practical matter, to forego trial by jury. See Maryland v. Baltimore Radio Show, 338 U.S. 912, 915. For one reason or another this Court does not undertake to review all such envenomed state prosecutions. But, again and again, such disregard of fundamental fairness is so flagrant that the Court is compelled, as it was only a week ago, to reverse a conviction in which prejudicial newspaper intrusion has poisoned the outcome. [citations omitted] This Court has not yet decided that the fair administration of criminal justice must be subordinated to another safeguard of our constitutional system—freedom of the press, properly conceived. The Court has not yet decided that, while convictions must be reversed and miscarriages of justice result because the minds of jurors or potential jurors were poisoned, the poisoner is constitutionally protected in plying his trade." 366 U.S. at 730.

[34] 373 U.S. 723 (1963).

[35] REPORT OF THE PRESIDENT'S COMMISSION ON THE ASSASSINATION OF PRESIDENT JOHN F. KENNEDY 20 (1964).

[36] *Id.* at 27. For an excellent review of the press-trial implications of the Report, see Jaffe, *Trial by Newspaper*, 40 N.Y.U. L. REV. 504 (1965).

[37] The technical title of the Committee was the Advisory Committee on Fair Trial and Free Press. Professor Franklin noted that feelings on the issue ran so high that lawyers and journalists could not agree on the correct title of the controversy. To the former it was "fair trial–free press"; to the latter it was "free press–fair trial." Franklin, *Untested Assumptions and Unanswered Questions*, 29 STAN. L. REV. 387 (1977).

[38] 381 U.S. 532 (1965).

spread pretrial publicity and television cameras in the courtroom, and that most extreme of all prejudicial publicity cases, *Sheppard v. Maxwell*,[39] were both reversed by the Court.

IV. A NEW TURN

It is not too much to say that, in 1976, the Court's decisions regarding press influence on criminal trials took a new turn. A Nebraska judge issued an order prohibiting the publication of information about an accused's confession or statements and other incriminating evidence, even though it had been obtained outside of court, as well as from a public preliminary hearing. When *Nebraska Press Association v. Stuart*[40] reached the Supreme Court, the so-called gag order was struck down with that most potent of First Amendment protective devices—the doctrine against prior restraint.[41] While the several opinions of the Court reflected continuing controversy about the burden that must be carried by one seeking a pretrial restraining order against the press,[42] the effect of the decision was to stem the tide of such restraining orders.[43]

In *Nebraska Press Association*, the press won an important victory. But there was lurking in the background a method of choking off sources of information that had not yet been tested. As the Reardon Report had suggested,[44] trial courts or magistrates could sometimes

---

[39] 384 U.S. 333 (1966).

[40] 427 U.S. 539 (1976).

[41] Near v. Minnesota, 283 U.S. 697 (1931) is, of course, the seminal case.

[42] Chief Justice Burger, writing the opinion of the Court, appeared to resurrect the "clear and present danger test." 427 U.S. at 562. Justice White, concurring, indicated grave doubt that prior restraints of pretrial publications could ever be valid. 427 U.S. at 570–71. Justice Powell would also have stated a more rigorous standard ("high likelihood of preventing . . . the impaneling of a jury meeting the Sixth Amendment requirement of impartiality"). 427 U.S. at 571. Justice Brennan, speaking also for Justices Stewart and Marshall, would hold that under no circumstances could such a prior restraint as here ever be issued. 427 U.S. at 588. See generally, Schmidt, *Nebraska Press Association: An Expansion of Freedom and Contraction of Theory*, 29 STAN. L. REV. 431 (1977).

[43] The ABA has now adopted a Standard that expressly prohibits any order preventing the publication or broadcast of any information about a criminal case. ABA Standard 8-3.1 (2d ed. 1978).

[44] ABA STANDARDS FOR FAIR TRIAL AND FREE PRESS, Standard 3.1 and discussion at 112–18 (Approved Draft, 1968). The ABA has now changed its standard relating to closing pretrial hearings so as permit closure only if the court finds a clear and present danger that a fair trial will be prevented and that no alternative means of protecting the trial will suffice. ABA STANDARDS FOR CRIMINAL JUSTICE, FAIR TRIAL AND FREE PRESS, Standard 8-3.2. (2d ed. 1978).

close preliminary hearings to the public and press and thereby prevent the dissemination of information that might bias prospective jurors. In *Gannett v. DePasquale*,[45] the Supreme Court upheld such a closure on the ground that the Sixth Amendment right to a public trial belonged to the defendant, not the public or the press. The Court assumed, but did not decide, that the First Amendment gave the public and press a right of access to the hearing. But it held that the right had been sufficiently recognized when the magistrate balanced it against the probable effects of publication.[46] The uproar was instantaneous and widespread.[47]

The most important case here is *Richmond Newspapers, Inc. v. Virginia*, decided the very next term.[48] There, the Court held that the First Amendment guarantees the public and the press the right to attend criminal trials, and that the Virginia trial court could not close the trial at the mere request of the defendant with the concurrence of the prosecution. *Gannett* was distinguished on the ground that it had involved a pretrial proceeding, not a trial. *Richmond Newspapers* provides the basis on which it is possible to assess the real importance of *Chandler v. Florida*.

V. The Decision in Chandler

The first order of business in *Chandler* was to deal with *Estes v. Texas*,[49] the only prior case in which the question of televising trials had been directly confronted by the Court. *Estes* was puzzling. In addition to a great deal of pretrial publicity, there had been a televised pretrial hearing to determine whether the trial itself would be televised. After two days during which virtually all the horrors of courtroom photography and disruption were permitted to occur, the judge agreed to admit the cameras. The trial, a month later, was, as Justice Stewart described it, "a most mundane affair."[50]

---

[45] 443 U.S. 368 (1979).

[46] *Id*. at 392.

[47] See Lewis, note 6 *supra*, at 1. See also the catalog of responses to the decision in Justice Blackmun's concurring opinion in Richmond Newspapers, Inc. v. Virginia, 448 U.S. at 602 ns. 1, 2 (1980).

[48] Note 6 *supra*. The Court's position is that the press has no greater right of access than the public. Blanchard, *The Institutional Press and Its First Amendment Privileges*, 1978 Sup. Ct. Rev. 225.

[49] 381 U.S. 532 (1965).

[50] *Id*. at 614 (Stewart, J., dissenting).

Filming was done through a slot in a specially constructed partition, and the activities of photographers were carefully controlled. Nevertheless, the Supreme Court reversed the conviction, holding that the defendant had been deprived of due process by the televising and broadcasting of his trial. However, the scope of the Court's decision was far from clear.

Justice Clark wrote the "opinion of the Court," but it was joined totally only by Chief Justice Warren and Justices Douglas and Goldberg. This plurality took the position that the televising of a criminal trial was a *per se* violation of due process.[51] The dissenters, Justices Stewart, Black, Brennan, and White, on the other hand, rejected such a categorical rule and took the position that the *Estes* trial, viewed separately from the pretrial hearing, had not been unfair.[52]

The swing vote then was Justice Harlan's, and, in truth, his concurring opinion was not one of that fine craftsman's clearest. First, he insisted on deciding the case only on the basis of what happened at the trial itself, where television was "relatively unobtrusive." He also pointed out that the record showed no "isolatable prejudice" resulting from the use of television. Nevertheless, he voted to reverse, although he did not join the plurality's opinion fully. He relied on the fact that *Estes* was a "heavily publicized and highly sensational affair," and his opinion cataloged all the undetectable ways television could distort the judicial process in such a case. He was reluctant, he said, to stifle the opportunity of the states to experiment, and he did not agree to a categorical rule that would apply to more routine—that is, unpublicized—cases than the one before him.[53]

Although recognizing that Justice Harlan's fears of the inevitable effects of television on the trial could have supported a *per se* rule, Chief Justice Burger in *Chandler* gave Harlan's opinion a narrower reading. He concluded that Harlan had found television to violate due process only in the particular circumstance of *Estes*. Therefore,

---

[51] *Id.* at 535, 552. Justice Clark's opinion contains an ambiguity that suggests that, if television technology improved in the future, he might view the matter differently. 381 U.S. at 551–52. But the Chief Justice's concurring opinion is clear and uncompromising. He wrote to "agree that the televising of trials is inherently a denial of due process." 381 U.S. at 552. Justice Douglas's view that television had no place in courtrooms had previously been expressed in *The Public Trial and Free Press*, note 23 *supra*.

[52] 381 U.S. at 601 (Stewart, J., dissenting).

[53] *Id.* at 587–96 (Harlan, J., concurring).

only a plurality of the Court in *Estes* had erected a *per se* rule, and the Court in *Chandler* could address unencumbered the more limited question whether the televising of a routine trial would violate due process.[54]

With *Estes* to one side, the Court was confronted with two factors that must have influenced its decision. First, it is commonly agreed that the technology of television and photography has so improved that, with proper equipment, there need be no physical disruption due to its mere presence in the courtroom. Miniaturized, sound-proofed television cameras requiring no distracting lighting, not even the little red light on the top, are now in common use, and virtually inaudible still cameras are available.[55] The second factor arises from a remarkable change in attitudes of state courts toward cameras in courtrooms. No doubt the increasing pervasiveness of television in our society has much to do with the change. However, one cannot discount the political acumen and power of the press. Years ago, lawyers had detected that, thwarted in its attempts to persuade the ABA to repeal Canon 35, the press had organized a campaign to persuade state courts, many of whose judges are elected, to open their courts to television.[56] The campaign has been phenomenally successful. In 1965, at most three states explicitly approved televised trials. By the time *Chandler* reached the Court, it was reported that some twenty-three states permitted television in trial or appellate courts, either experimentally or on a permanent basis.[57] And in 1978, the Conference of State Chief Justices re-

---

[54] 101 S.Ct. at 807. The Chief Justice took the hard line that if Justice Harlan had in fact joined his four brethren in finding television a *per se* due process violation, the Court in *Chandler* would "be obliged to apply that holding and reverse the judgment under review." Justices Stewart and White thought Harlan had found a *per se* violation in *Estes* and therefore the case should have been overruled. 101 S.Ct. at 814, 816. The only other present member of the Court who sat in *Estes*, Justice Brennan, had expressly noted in a concurring opinion in that case that Harlan did not join unreservedly in the *per se* holding of the plurality. 381 U.S. at 617 (Brennan, J., dissenting.)

The Chief Justice noted in *Chandler* that the Court itself had several times referred to *Estes* as a case in which the entire trial had been tainted by prejudicial publicity and television coverage. 101 S.Ct. at 809 n.8. And, of course, the state courts that approved television coverage after *Estes* did not read the case as erecting an insurmountable barrier. See, *e.g.*, Petition of Post-Newsweek Stations, Florida, Inc., 370 So. 2d 764, 774.

[55] 101 S.Ct. at 810 n.11.

[56] See *Report of the Special Bar-Media Conference Committee on Fair Trial–Free Press*, 83 A.B.A. REP. 790 (1958); Douglas, note 23 *supra*; REPORT, CAMERAS IN THE COURTROOM, HOW TO GET 'EM THERE (Associated Press Managing Editors Association Freedom of Information, undated.)

[57] 101 S.Ct. at 805 n.6, citing Joint Brief of Amici Curiae of Radio Television News

solved, 44 to 1, that Canon 3A(7) should be changed to permit state courts to allow televising of judicial proceedings.[58] Even within the ABA, there were movements to relax the prohibitions against television coverage, but, while gaining considerable support, they were rejected by the House of Delegates.[59] It was evident, however, that a fairly massive movement away from the ABA position was underway.

It was also important that *Chandler* was tried in a state in which the supreme court had done a particularly careful and well-documented job of devising standards for televised trials. Acting on a petition of local television stations, the Florida court, in 1976, had authorized an experimental program to determine whether electronic coverage of trials was feasible.[60] At the conclusion of the program, the state supreme court, in a lengthy opinion, canvassed experiences in its own trial courts, as well as those in other states. It also had the benefit of two surveys of the opinions of participants in Florida trials that had been televised. As a consequence, the court ordered Canon 3A(7) amended to permit television coverage of judicial proceedings under careful guidelines laid down in the opinion. The rules did not require the consent of trial participants, but the presiding judge was given broad discretion to "control the conduct of the proceedings."[61] It was under this regime that *Chandler* was tried.

A number of *amici curiae* filed briefs in the Supreme Court. The

---

Directors Association. CARTER, MEDIA IN THE COURTS (1981) reports that in the spring of 1981 the figure had reached thirty.

[58] The resolution, adopted in Burlington, Vt., on August 2, 1978, is attached as an appendix to the Florida court's opinion in Petition of Post-Newsweek Stations, Florida, Inc., 370 So. 2d 764, 791 (1979).

[59] Goodwin, *A Report on the Latest Rounds in the Battle over Cameras in the Courts*, 63 JUDICATURE 74 (1979).

[60] The program went through several stages. The initial order required that the "parties to the litigation, jurors and witnesses must consent to the television of their participation in the trial." Petition of Post-Newsweek Stations, Florida, Inc., for Change in Code of Judicial Conduct, 327 So. 2d 1, 2 (Fla. 1976). No cases could be found in which all the participants would consent, so the court dispensed with that requirement and ordered the experiment to continue for one year. 347 So. 2d 402, 403 (Fla. 1977). At the end of the experimental period, the court required reports of all participants. 358 So. 2d 1360 (Fla. 1978).

[61] 370 So. 2d 764, 781 (Fla. 1979). The guidelines permit no more than one soundproofed portable film or videotape camera operated by one camera person, no artificial light, and no more than one still photographer using cameras producing no distracting sound. Access to television transmission must be pooled by the media representatives and all personnel must take places assigned by the presiding judge and remain there while court is in session. 370 So. 2d at 792–93.

American College of Trial lawyers, various public defenders associations, and the American Bar Association urged reversal. The
Conference of Chief Justices, the attorneys general of several states,
a public television organization, and representatives of several print
and electronic news media supported affirmance.

The Supreme Court acknowledged that television might pose
serious risks to the criminal defendant but could not say that television would inevitably cause an unfair trial. Faced with this uncertainty, the plurality in the *Estes* case would have chosen a categorical definition of due process that prohibited televised trials. In
Chandler, on the other hand, the Court chose an *ad hoc* rule that
leaves the question of due process to a case-by-case determination.[62]

The contrast between the approaches of the *Estes* plurality and
the *Chandler* Court is dramatic.[63] In Justice Clark's opinion, there is
much talk of inherent prejudice that would be powerful but unprov-
able. Jurors, knowing they were involved in a *cause celebre*, might
be inclined to bias against the defendant, particularly if they knew
that the community, and their friends and neighbors watching,
wanted a guilty verdict. At the very least, they would be distracted
by the cameras and might even see on television at night evidence
that had been excluded from the trial during the day. Witnesses
would likewise be distracted, perhaps intimidated or embarrassed,
by the large audience, and their testimony could thereby be distorted. Pressure would be exerted on the judge, who would have a
more difficult time controlling the courtroom. Moreover, Justice
Clark mentioned a fact that has run throughout much of the bar's
resistance to television—the fact that most state judges are popu-
larly elected and might therefore play to the cameras, or at the least
be subjected to irresistible political pressure from the press in deciding whether to allow television coverage in a particular case.
Finally, Justice Clark observed that television coverage of the defendant already undergoing the ordeal of a criminal trial would

---

[62] One must not read too much into this facet of the case, but the Court does turn away
from establishing strict national requirements for televising state criminal trials. *Cf.*
WECHSLER, THE NATIONALIZATION OF CIVIL LIBERTIES AND CIVIL RIGHTS (1969).

[63] One cannot distinguish neatly here between the Warren Court and the Burger Court
even though the two Chief Justices took different paths to a solution. Justices Stewart, Black,
Brennan, and White dissented from the categorical view of the plurality in *Estes*. And, of
course, Justices Brennan, Stewart, White, and Marshall were part of the unanimous Court in
Chandler.

subject him to harassment and scrutiny that "might well transgress his personal sensibilities, his dignity and his ability to concentrate on the proceedings before him—sometimes the difference between life and death—dispassionately, freely and without the distraction of wide public surveillance."[64] Chief Justice Warren's concurrence emphasized that television was simply irrelevant to the fact-finding purpose of the trial, as well as inherently prejudicial to the dignity and integrity of the process. "The prejudice of television may be so subtle that it escapes the ordinary methods of proof, but it would gradually erode our fundamental conception of trial."[65]

In contrast, Chief Justice Burger in *Chandler* stressed that, although many of the risks so persuasive to five justices in *Estes* were no doubt possibilities, the Court could not find a constitutional violation in the absence of empirical evidence that television would always have harmful effects. Unlike the totality of circumstances in *Estes*, the *Chandler* trial apparently had not been tainted in fact by either pretrial publicity or courtroom television, or a combination of both.[66]

The premise of *Chandler* is that the empirical evidence available does not justify the finding of a *per se* due process violation. In fact, the evidence is at the very least inconclusive. Such data as exist are almost entirely posttrial surveys eliciting the reactions of participants to their experiences. For example, the admittedly "non-scientific" results of the survey conducted by the Florida court administrator's office tended to show that television did not produce the horrendous impact many had feared.[67] In fact, they indicated the participants were only slightly to moderately conscious of the cameras' existence and none professed to be distracted from their tasks to any substantial degree.[68]

---

[64] 381 U.S. at 549.

[65] *Id.* at 578 (Warren, C. J., concurring).

[66] 100 S.Ct. at 812.

[67] A SAMPLE SURVEY OF ATTITUDES OF INDIVIDUALS ASSOCIATED WITH TRIALS INVOLVING ELECTRONIC MEDIA AND STILL PHOTOGRAPHY COVERAGE IN SELECTED FLORIDA COURTS BETWEEN JULY 5, 1977 AND JUNE 30, 1978 (copy available from National Center for State Courts).

[68] 370 So. 2d at 767–69. The trial judges of Florida also conducted a survey of their own members. Their chairman reported that they opposed allowing television cameras in the courtroom, largely on the grounds of greater work loads for trial judges and unwarranted invasions of the privacy of jurors. But as the Florida Supreme Court noted, the results of their survey did not seem to support the conclusions of the Report. REPORT OF THE FLORIDA CONFERENCE OF CIRCUIT JUDGES, JULY 18, 1978 (copy available from National Center for

The small accumulation of data from state experiments was not given much attention by the Court in *Chandler;* it rated a footnote in which the Chief Justice found grounds for optimism about the ability of state courts to manage the potential problems of electronic coverage. He found that none of the data supported the *Estes* position that television coverage inherently undermines due process,[69] even though the dangers could not be entirely discounted.

Given the risks of unfair trials outlined by the plurality in *Estes,* what persuaded the *Chandler* Court to permit Florida to televise trials? The major consideration, said the Chief Justice, is the concept of federalism, the same notion that influenced Justice Harlan's position in *Estes.* But, as suggested at the outset, Justice Brandeis's belief that the states should be allowed to function as laboratories and conduct "social and economic experiments,"[70] even foolish ones, does not make a compelling case for experimentation in criminal cases where the possibilities of due process violations are not fanciful. As Justice Black suggested in *Duncan v. Louisiana,*[71] it seems strange to suggest that the demands of federalism are that powerful.

VI. A First Amendment Case?

If the claims of federalism are not enough to justify permitting televised trials, perhaps there are values of greater weight that support the decision in *Chandler.* Those values must lie elsewhere than in what we know about what television does to trials. We are

---

State Courts). Other similar surveys are found in Prior, Strawn, Buchanan, and Meeke, *The Florida Experiment: An Analysis of on-the-Scene Response to Cameras in the Courtroom,* 45 So. Speech Comm. J. 12 (1979). A valuable collection of such materials is found in Netteburg, *Does Research Support the Estes Ban on Cameras in the Courtroom?* 63 Judicature 467 (1980). (He finds that it does not.) See also Cameras in the Courtroom: A Two Year Review in the State of Washington (copy available from National Center for State Courts). One of the few attempts to determine by controlled research whether cameras impair witnesses' ability to testify is found in Hoyt, *Courtroom Coverage: The Effects of Being Televised,* 21 J. of Broadcasting 487 (1977). Three small groups of college students were shown a short film after being told they would then be asked certain questions. One group was questioned before a visible camera, another before a hidden but known camera and the third without a camera. Not surprisingly, the researcher found that those who knew they were being filmed, especially those who could see the camera, performed best. Concededly, the test proves little with respect to television of real witnesses in a courtroom setting.

[69] 101 S.Ct. at 810 n.11.

[70] New State Ice Co. v. Liebmann, 285 U.S. 262, 311 (1932) (Brandeis, J., dissenting).

[71] 391 U.S. 145, 170 (1968) (Black, J., concurring).

not within that "middle range" that Harry Kalven described,[72] where empirical evidence can tell us what the policy about cameras in the courtroom ought to be. The only interests our institutional structure suggests, and that are sufficiently compelling, are those that inhere in the desirability of the public's knowing what goes on in courtrooms. Justice Stewart put his finger on it in *Estes* when he worried that the Court there failed to appreciate that First Amendment interests were involved. He put it even more strongly in suggesting that some of the opinions in the case struck him as "disturbingly alien to the First and Fourteenth Amendments guarantees against federal or state interference with free communication of information and ideas. The suggestion that there are limits upon the public's right to know what goes on in courts causes me deep concern."[73]

Television in the courtroom expands public access to public institutions both qualitatively, because of its immediacy, and quantitatively, because of its reach. It is reported that a majority of Americans acquire their news primarily from television rather than from newspapers.[74] To exclude the most important source of information about the workings of courts without some compelling reason cannot be squared with the First Amendment.

The so-called Abscam cases illustrate the interests at stake. In those federal prosecutions, videotapes of various government officials, predominently congressmen, discussing or taking bribes, were introduced in evidence. There is an established, but not very well-known, common law right of access to inspect and copy public records, including judicial records.[75] The television networks applied to the district courts for permission to copy and broadcast the tapes. Three federal courts of appeals[76] have upheld the right of

---

[72] Kalven, *The Quest for the Middle Range: Empirical Inquiry and Legal Policy*, in LAW AND A CHANGING AMERICA (Hazard, ed. 1968).

[73] 381 U.S. at 614–15 (Stewart, J., dissenting).

[74] ROPER ORG., PUBLIC PERCEPTION OF TELEVISION AND OTHER MASS MEDIA: A TWENTY YEAR REVIEW, 1959–1979.

[75] Nixon v. Warner Communications, Inc., 435 U.S. 589, 597–603 (1978).

[76] In re Application of National Broadcasting Co., Inc., 653 F.2d 609 (D.C. Cir. 1981); United States v. Criden, 648 F.2d 814 (3d Cir. 1981); In re Application of National Broadcasting Co., Inc., 635 F.2d 945 (2d Cir. 1980). Technically, the copying can be done simply by attaching one wire to the videotape recorder and running it inconspicuously to recording equipment in another room. The original tape will be unaffected. See description in 635 F.2d 945, 948.
Watergate produced a similar application to copy the "White House" audiotapes after they

access, and, although they make it clear that the decision is within the discretion of the trial judge, the description of the grounds on which judges might deny access are almost indistinguishable from discussions of limitations on First Amendment rights. In *United States v. Criden*, the Third Circuit spoke of the "same policy considerations" supporting open trials and a right to copy trial materials.[77] The Second Circuit spoke of a presumption in favor of access to the record that only the "most compelling circumstances" should overcome.[78] Significantly, both courts relied on *Richmond Newspapers*, where the First Amendment was involved, in finding that the right of access rests on the tradition of open trials and on the strong public interest in knowing what goes on in courts.

It is quite true that the Abscam cases, unlike *Chandler*, involve a common law right of access, a right that could not be imposed as such on the states by the Supreme Court. But similar considerations were at work in the *Chandler* case, even though the Court there had no occasion to determine whether the First Amendment, through the Fourteenth, made them fully applicable to the states. Justice Stewart's dissent in *Estes* correctly suggested that First Amendment values were at stake when television cameras were excluded from a state court.

No court has yet held that television (or television journalists) have a First Amendment right of access to trials, and the Court in *Chandler* was not faced with the question. However, the Chief Justice did pointedly refer to the Court's rejection, in *Nixon v. Warner Communications, Inc.*,[79] of a claimed right to copy White House tapes that were in evidence. Justice Powell's reasoning in that case was that the press was free to publish what they legitimately learned about a trial, but that, inside the courtroom, it has no greater constitutional rights than the general public. The general public attending the trial had listened to the tapes but did not have

---

had been introduced in evidence. In United States v. Mitchell, 551 F.2d 1252 (D.C. Cir. 1976), the Court of Appeals reversed a denial of the application. The case was reversed on other grounds *sub. nom.* Nixon v. Warner Communications, Inc., 435 U.S. 589 (1978). But *cf.* Belo Broadcasting Corp. v. Clark, 50 U.S.L.W. 2134 (5th Cir., Aug. 28, 1981), rejecting the reasoning of the Abscam cases and holding that the district court properly exercised its discretion in denying the right to copy audiotapes where another defendant had not yet been tried.

[77] 648 F.2d at 820.

[78] 635 F.2d at 952.

[79] 435 U.S. 608–10.

physical access to them. The press had no constitutional right to more than that. As for Justice Powell's statement in *Nixon* that there is no right to broadcast a trial live or on tape, the reference there was as to a *Sixth Amendment* right to do so, an issue not presented in *Chandler*. Any future claims by the press to televise trials will rest on the First, not the Sixth, Amendment. In any event, Justice Powell's opinion in *Nixon* preceded *Richmond Newspapers*. His dictum there is obviously subject to reconsideration in light of the more recent cases.

Given the historic attitudes that only spectators, or reporters who conduct themselves as spectators, are appropriate visitors to courtrooms, it is not surprising that existing cases are not particularly hospitable to a constitutional claim of access by television. Moreover, the acceptance of such a claim invests with constitutional dimensions a number of issues now treated as being within the discretion of trial judges. Courts may well be reluctant to impose a greater burden on the trial judge in this respect, but it is worth noting that even in the context of this discretion, at least two courts have seemed to create presumptions in favor of television coverage—the presumption to be overcome only by factual findings of a strong need to exclude cameras.[80]

To this point, the television people have been successful in gaining access to courtrooms, at least under some conditions, and so may lack an incentive to push the constitutional claim very soon.

---

[80] *E.g.*, State ex rel. Grinnell Communications Corp. v. Love, 62 Ohio St. 2d 399, 406 N.E. 2d 809 (1980). Reversing a trial judge who excluded television cameras from the courtroom, the Supreme Court of Ohio held that its Canon 3A(7) was mandatory and that "A failure to make a specific determination of the existence of a disqualifying factor falling within the purview of Canon 3A(7)(c)(ii) or (iii) dictates that media coverage be permitted." 406 N.E. 2d at 811. (The disqualifying factors are that the broadcasting would "distract the participants, impair the dignity of the proceedings, or otherwise materially interfere with the achievement of a fair trial or hearing" or that a victim or witness has a "reasonable cause" to object to coverage. 406 N.E. 2d at 810.) In a subsequent case the Ohio court has held that television representatives must be given notice of any hearing on trial coverage and have the right to offer evidence and cross-examine witnesses. State ex rel. Miami Valley Broadcasting Corp. v. Kessler, 64 Ohio St. 2d 165, 413 N.E. 2d 1203 (1980). *Cf.* State v. Palm Beach Newspaper, Inc., 395 So. 2d 544 (Fla. 1981). The Florida court held that television coverage may be excluded only upon a finding that it would have some harmful effect on the trial and that ordinarily a hearing should be held before making such a finding. But, stressing that no First Amendment claim was involved, the court held that such hearing should not be allowed to disrupt the trial of the principal issue, guilt or innocence. While the trial judge must be satisfied of the need to exclude cameras, if the choice is between television coverage and, as in that case, witnesses who would refuse to testify before cameras for fear of their lives, the trial court could legitimately deny television coverage.

Nevertheless, it is not difficult to foresee such an argument. Maryland has adopted a statute prohibiting the televising of criminal trials,[81] and a constitutional challenge to this, or a similar statute, or to an order by a trial court excluding cameras from a particular case, is tempting to predict.

When and if such a claim is faced directly, it is hard to see how television can be treated as constitutionally different from other forms of the press. It is quite true that the Court has said that each medium of expression, for First Amendment purposes, must be treated in terms of its own nature and the unique problems it creates.[82] In *Chandler*, the Court found that television does not inherently violate due process. Given that decision and the powerful role television plays in disseminating information to the public, there do not seem to be any grounds on which television can be denied the same rights of access that *Richmond Newspapers* upholds for the public and the print press. Doubtless there will be occasions, as developed below, when the special effects on particular witnesses will indicate that television cameras should be excluded from the courtroom, even though spectators and print reporters are allowed to remain. But those instances will illustrate the principle that First Amendment guarantees must be tailored to the medium and its effect, not that they are wholly inapplicable.

One argument should be mentioned only because it seems no longer to have any force since *Chandler*. In *Estes*, Justice Clark asserted that television reporters in fact have the same access to courts as other reporters. They simply cannot bring their cameras in with them, even as print reporters cannot bring in their typewriters. The argument had some validity so long as television equipment was disruptive, because of its bulkiness, trappings, and noise. Once such physical disruption is no longer a problem, the argument only begs the question whether television reporters with their cameras may attend trials on the same basis as other news people. If cameras do not cause special problems, the justification for treating this medium differently from the others seems to disappear.

The point is neatly illustrated by the increasingly familiar artist

---

[81] Ch. 748, Laws of Md., 1981. See also Ill. Rev. Stat. ch. 51, §57 (1975), which prohibits requiring a person to testify before television cameras.

[82] Metromedia, Inc. v. City of San Diego, 101 S.Ct. 2882, 2889 (1981).

who sketches the participants in a judicial proceeding and broadcasts the result on television. The Fifth Circuit held a ban on such
sketching unconstitutionally overbroad unless there was some
showing that the sketching was disruptive of the proceedings.[83]

VII. Protection of Witnesses and Jurors

One of the more troublesome consequences of televised
trials is the wider publicity it will give to participants, jurors, and
witnesses, who have not voluntarily sought the public limelight.
The Court in *Chandler* noted with satisfaction that Florida explicitly
requires the trial courts to provide special protection for particular
witnesses such as "children, victims of sex crimes, some informants
and even the very timid witness or party."[84] Historically, courts
have exercised the power to clear the courtroom of spectators in a
variety of cases, for example, when young witnesses are to testify
about lurid matters,[85] sometimes where the witness is an adult
victim of a sex crime,[86] when a witness is shown to be in fear of his
or her life,[87] when testimony would concern trade secrets,[88] or
when there is a need to protect the identity of undercover agents or
informants.[89]

---

[83] United States v. CBS, 497 F.2d 102 (5th Cir. 1974). The district judge had barred both
in-court sketches and those made outside court from memory of a visit to the court. For a
discussion of the implications of the case, see Note, *United States v. CBS: When Sketch Artists
Are Allowed in the Courtroom, Can Photographers Be Far Behind?* 1975 DUKE L. J. 188.

[84] 101 S.Ct. at 811. It will be remembered that the Florida rule does not require consent of
any of the participants but leaves the matter in the discretion of the trial judge. 370 So. 2d at
781–82. The standard for the exercise of the court's discretion was also set out: "The
presiding judge may exclude electronic media coverage of a particular participant only upon a
finding that such coverage will have a substantial effect upon the particular individual which
would be qualitatively different from the effect on members of the public in general and such
effect will be qualitatively different from the coverage by other types of media." 370 So. 2d at
779.

[85] State v. Sinclair, 274 S.E. 2d 411 (So.Car. 1981).

[86] People v. Latimore, 33 Ill. App. 3rd 812, 342 N.E. 2d 209 (1975), *habeas corpus denial
aff'd. sub. nom.* United States ex rel. Latimore v. Sielaff, 561 F.2d 691 (7th Cir. 1977).

[87] United States v. Herold, 368 F.2d 187 (2d Cir. 1966).

[88] Stamicarbon, N.V. v. American Cyanamid Co., 506 F.2d 532 (2d Cir. 1974).

[89] People v. Cantone, 73 A.D. 2d 936, 423 N.Y.S.2d 507 (1980). In United States ex. rel.
Lloyd v. Vincent, 520 F.2d 1272 (2d Cir. 1975), *cert. den.* 423 U.S. 937 (1975) the court, while
upholding the exclusion of the public during the testimony of undercover agents, noted that
the exclusionary power should be used sparingly in light of the importance of the right to a
public trial. 520 F.2d at 1274. While the closing of a trial during the testimony of certain
witnesses does not necessarily violate the right to public trial, some courts have given
considerable weight to the protection the defendant derives from requiring the victim to

Closure orders have always had to be squared with the defendant's right to a public trial. But since *Richmond Newspapers*, it seems reasonable to suggest that the standards for closure should take on even more rigorous First Amendment dimensions. There are, to be sure, problems here. The opinions in *Richmond Newspapers* send out confusing signals. The issue was not directly presented, because the trial proceedings had long since been concluded. But in reversing the exclusion of the public and press, the Chief Justice, for himself and for Justices White and Stevens, said the trial must remain open "absent an overriding interest articulated in findings."[90] Justice Brennan, with Justice Marshall, noted that the Court need not concern itself with "[W]hat countervailing interest might be sufficiently compelling" to justify closure.[91] Justice Stewart thought the trial judge might impose "reasonable limitations on the unrestricted occupation of the courtroom" by the press and public, and he went so far as to suggest that not all considerations for closure, such as trade secrets and the need to protect the sensibilities of rape victims, need be of constitutional proportions, so long as the defendant's Sixth Amendment right to a public trial is protected.[92] Justice Blackmun, lamenting the Court's refusal to ground the public right of access to trials in the Sixth Amendment, rather than the First, pointed to uncertainty in the standard of closure as a consequence of the Court's choice.[93]

A second problem with the argument that closure orders against television cameras should now be required to meet constitutional standards, whatever they may be, is that *Richmond Newspapers* did

---

testify in public. For example, in Lexington Herald Leader Co., Inc. v. Tackett, 601 S.W. 2d 905 (Ky. 1980), the Kentucky Supreme Court held that, in a sodomy prosecution involving victims under the age of twelve years, the trial court should not have closed the courtroom to the entire public and press during the victim's testimony. The court's result rested on the very high value placed on open trials. 601 S.W. 2d at 906.

[90] 448 U.S. at 581.

[91] *Id.* at 598.

[92] *Id.* at 600, particularly n.5.

[93] *Id.* at 603. For a good discussion of the general problem, see Note, *The First Amendment Right of Access to Sex Crime Trials*, 22 B. C. L. REV. 361, 374–75 (1981). The Supreme Court will have an early opportunity to revisit this problem. It vacated and remanded Globe Newspaper Co. v. Superior Court, ____ Mass. ____, 401 N.E. 2d 360 (1980), for reconsideration in light of Richmond Newspapers. 101 S.Ct. 259 (1980). The case involves a statute that requires the exclusion of the public from trials during the testimony of minor victims of sex crimes. On remand, the Massachusetts court has reaffirmed its previous decision that the statute is constitutional. The Supreme Court noted probable jurisdiction on Nov. 16, 1981. 102 S.Ct. ——.

not involve television access, and, of course, the Court in *Chandler* made it clear that it was not dealing with a television claim of a right of access. In fact, the Court seems to have gone out of its way to discourage such claims.[94]

At the moment, the decision to admit television cameras to courts at all, or whether to exclude coverage of certain witnesses, lies in the discretion of the trial judge. It is on this basis that a number of states, even though permitting television of trials generally, have frequently required the consent of all parties,[95] or have prohibited the televising of any witness or party who objects.[96] Jurors are frequently given special consideration through rules that prohibit televising members of the jury in such a way that they would be recognized publicly,[97] and perhaps subjected to threats or pressure.

In the not too distant future, the Court will probably have to face a claim by television of a right of access to the courtroom. The need to protect witnesses and jurors does not seem an insurmountable barrier to recognizing such a claim. First Amendment rights of access, as *Richmond Newspapers* suggests, are not absolute, and one foresees little difficulty in regarding the protection of innocent participants as compelling reasons to exclude cameras.

VIII. TELEVISION AND PRIVACY

Perhaps the major reason why televising trials has met with an instinctively negative reaction is that the broadcasting of one's image to a large audience seems to involve a much greater invasion of the personal freedom than simply requiring one to testify in open court. This feature of television coverage is frequently treated under the rubic of privacy.[98] However, the common understanding is that one who is a participant in a public event has no common law

---

[94] 101 S.Ct. at 807. Justice White observed that, in his view, the states are as free after *Chandler* as before to bar cameras from the courtroom. *Id.* at 817.

[95] Colorado Code of Judicial Conduct, Canon 3A(7)–(10).

[96] CARTER, note 57 *supra*, at 82; Canon 3A(7), Code of Judl. Conduct, Washington Court Rules (1977).

[97] *Id.* at 84; Wis. Sup. Ct. Rule 61.11.

[98] In re Petition of Post-Newsweek Stations, Florida, Inc., 370 So. 2d 764, 779 (1979); Note, *Television and Newsreel Coverage of a Trial*, 43 IOWA L. REV. 616, 623 (1958); Comment, *In the Wake of Chandler v. Florida: A Comprehensive Approach to the Implementation of Cameras in the Courtroom*, 33 FED. COM. B. J. 117, 125 (1981).

right of privacy.[99] Constitutional privacy, in the sense of freedom
from press intrusion, appears to offer no greater protection. *Cox
Broadcasting Co. v. Cohn*[100] explicitly held that a statutorily based
claim of privacy by the father of a rape victim could not overcome
the free press right to publish the name of that victim as recorded
on an open public record.

But a privacy claim in the context of televised trials may carry
greater weight, at least in some circumstances. It is important to
make it clear that I do not argue here that a claim of privacy should
have produced a different result in *Chandler*. Nor is it even
suggested that any witness should have a constitutional right not to
be televised against his or her will.[101] I do suggest, however, that,
under some circumstances, the televising of a witness during testimony could well be regarded as an invasion of privacy, even
though the witness might still be required to testify before spectators, including members of the press. The paradigm case is that of
the young rape victim. While some jurisdictions would permit the
exclusion of all spectators, including the press, others would not
and it would seem that such total exclusions rarely ought to be
upheld.[102] Even if spectators and reporters are present, it still
seems to be an unreasonable intrusion in some cases to televise the
victim, and such an intrusion far outweighs any public interest in
observing the victim testify. The need to test the witness's veracity
by subjecting her to public testimony is amply satisfied by the
presence of spectators and newspeople. Thus, there is a compelling
interest in turning off the television cameras temporarily.

The interest advanced here is not a claim of secrecy but only an

---

[99] "It seems to be generally agreed that anything visible in a public place can be recorded
and given circulation by means of a photograph, to the same extent as by a written description, since this amounts to nothing more than giving publicity to what is already public and
what anyone present would be free to see." PROSSER, HANDBOOK OF THE LAW OF TORTS
811 (4 ed. 1971). See also discussion of lack of right of privacy of persons caught up in
criminal cases as victims, witnesses, or even innocent bystanders. *Id.* at 825.

[100] 420 U.S. 489 (1975). See Generally, Posner, *The Uncertain Protection of Privacy by the
Supreme Court*, 1979 SUP. CT. REV. 173.

[101] But see United States v. Kleinman, 107 F. Supp. 407 (D.D.C. 1952) in which the
court, on unclear ground, held a witness before a congressional committee could not be
televised against his will. The Rules of the House now prohibit televising a witness who
objects. Rules of the House of Representatives, Rule XI, c.3.

[102] For an excellent discussion of the difficult problem of preventing further trauma to the
rape victim while honoring the defendant's right to a public trial, see Berger, *Man's Trial,
Woman's Tribulation: Rape Cases in the Courtroom*, 77 COL. L. REV. 1, 88–95 (1977).

interest against unreasonable intrusion. Professor Alfred Hill has made a similar point in criticizing *Cox*. The Court's mistake in that case, he suggests, was that it treated the rights of the press and of individual privacy in absolute terms. Anything on the public record may be published, regardless of the justification for the publication. There must be, he thinks, some limit to this. The limitation he suggests, which is drawn from some common law privacy cases, is that one's right of privacy should be regarded as violated if the publication even of a public record would involve "revelations so intimate and unwarranted as to outrage the community's notions of decency."[103] As a standard for tort liability for invasion of privacy, Hill's submission may be unwarrantedly chilling to freedom of the press. But as a device for determining whether there is a compelling interest against televising a witness, especially when spectators and other members of the press are still in the courtroom, it states a useful idea.[104]

IX. The Defendant

One of the arguments pressed most strongly in *Chandler* was that to display the defendants on television during trial is itself a denial of due process and a form of punishment. The Chief Justice related the point to an argument made by Chief Justice Warren in *Estes*, that selective television coverage "singles out certain defendants and subjects them to trials under prejudicial conditions not experienced by others."[105] Chief Justice Burger transformed this into the question whether television coverage will subject an accused to humiliation in such a random way as to evoke Justice Stewart's metaphor in the first death penalty cases of being struck

---

[103] Hill, *Defamation and Privacy under the First Amendment*, 76 COL. L. REV. 1205, 1258–68 (1976).

[104] The standard has been applied in what was regarded as a non-First Amendment setting in In re Application of KSTP Television, 504 F.Supp. 360 (D. Minn. 1980). There, in a kidnapping case, a videotape of the victim held in captivity prior to a rape was introduced in evidence. In denying the application to copy and broadcast the tape, the district judge held that to do so would serve only sensationalism and would impinge on the victim's interest in privacy.

[105] 381 U.S. at 565 (Warren, C.J., concurring). There is in Justice Warren's statement, of course, an assumption that televised trials are necessarily prejudicial, a proposition the Court now rejects.

by lightning.[106] It is hard to know what the word "random" means in this context. In *Furman*, Justice Stewart was referring to the lack of any legal standard by which those convicted of capital offenses were selected to receive the death penalty. But here, as the Chief Justice notes, the choice whether to televise a trial, or a part of it, will be made by the broadcasters on the basis of newsworthiness. It is impossible to see how courts can impose standards of choice on the broadcasters without trenching on freedom of the press.[107] Apparently, Chief Justice Burger had in mind the possibility that a notorious televised trial might be turned into a "Yankee Stadium" display of a particularly despised defendant. But the problem there would not be randomness but the denial of a fair trial, and, if it were allowed to happen, it could easily be handled on the authority of *Estes*, which to that extent still stands.

But a serious problem might be created if a court permitted the media to telecast only defendants charged with certain types of crimes, or to televise only defendants of identifiable racial groups. If such cases should occur, convictions might be overturned on equal protection grounds.[108]

Another argument against televising defendants stems from what some have seen as an eagerness to use television as a political weapon.[109] Justice Douglas asserted that theme in his Colorado speech. He feared the power of the press to impose the ideologies of its owners on the communities it dominates and its power to whip up hostility toward particular defendants.[110] His reference to the Castro trials in a stadium in Cuba calls to mind other trials staged in Russia and China for political purposes.[111]

One cannot entirely dismiss the possibility that the government

---

[106] 101 S.Ct. at 812, citing Justice Stewart, concurring in Furman v. Georgia, 408 U.S. 238, 309 (1972).

[107] Miami Herald Publishing Co. v. Tornillo, 418 U.S. 241, 256 (1974); *Cf.* Pittsburgh Press Co. v. Pittsburgh Commission on Human Relations, 413 U.S. 376, 391 (1973).

[108] United States v. Falk, 479 F.2d 617 (7th Cir. 1973); See Oyler v. Boles, 368 U.S. 448, 456 (1962).

[109] Arnold, *Mob Justice and Television*, 12 FED. COM. B. J. 4 (1951). See generally TAYLOR, GRAND INQUEST: THE STORY OF CONGRESSIONAL INVESTIGATIONS (1955).

[110] Douglas, note 23 *supra*, at 2.

[111] Berman, *The Powers Case*, 191 NATION 103 (Sept. 3, 1960) (Moscow trial of American pilot of U-2 spy plane); Clubb, *A Revolution on Trial*, 232 NATION 110 (Jan. 31, 1981) (Peking show trial of so-called gang of four).

would televise a so-called political trial for its own purposes. But to try to prevent such trials by closing out one form of news medium seems fundamentally at odds with the notion of free dissemination of information.

On a less cosmic political level, it was the notorious case in which the community's interest had been whipped up by the press and public officials that concerned Justice Harlan in *Estes* and led him to hold that the trial there had been fatally tainted by the addition of television coverage.[112] The Court now appears to have answered Justice Harlan's concern by suggesting in *Chandler* that, even in the highly publicized case, the defendant will have to make a showing that the trial took place in a "circus" or "Yankee Stadium" atmosphere as in *Estes*, or that an "unsequestered" jury had been tainted by prejudicial publicity.[113] Thus, even the notorious case could be televised if the trial court has utilized all the devices for the protection of a fair trial, such as changes of venue, continuances, careful *voir dire* of the jury, and sequestration after selection and has carefully controlled the television coverage of the trial. In any event, the argument against televising such trials has a sort of Alice in Wonderland ring to it, because the media will usually be interested in televising only the notorious trial, and the trial will be notorious because the media have helped to make it so.

Some of the concerns expressed about the effects on the defendant of subjecting him to a wide audience through television are serious. The Chief Justice pointed out in *Chandler*, however, that these effects can be guarded against by the exercise of careful discretion. For example, the Florida Supreme Court has held that where there is evidence that the presence of television cameras might render an unstable defendant incompetent, the trial court should exclude cameras from the courtroom.[114]

Beyond all this, there is a bedrock objection to televising defendants that inheres in the very process. Its rejection by state and lower federal courts reflects the view that a criminal trial has public functions beyond deciding guilt or innocence of the individual defendant. The objection was best expressed by the district judge in

---

[112] 381 U.S. at 590. Justice Harlan conceded that the line between a notorious case such as *Estes* and a "non-notorious" one might not prove workable, but his suggestion seems to have been that televising even the latter case might deny due process.

[113] 101 S.Ct. at 813.

[114] State v. Green, 395 So. 2d 532 (Fla. 1981).

one of the Abscam cases previously discussed. In *United States v. Criden*,[115] the district judge's most strongly stated reason for refusing to permit the broadcast of the videotapes was his revulsion at the idea that, to the natural humiliation and anguish visited on a defendant and his family by the ordeal of prosecution, there is now to be added the further degradation of having his misconduct graphically portrayed "in every living room in America."[116] We would not, he said, tolerate parading the defendant, even a convicted one, through the streets or exhibiting him in a "cage or in the stocks." What the networks proposed to do seemed to him little different. But the district judge spoke alone and was shortly reversed by the Third Circuit in an opinion that relied on the Court's decision in *Chandler* and flatly rejected the notion that the broadcast of evidence of wrongdoing violates "accepted notions of decency."[117]

In fact, the Watergate and Abscam episodes have produced a series of opinions that highlight the public role criminal trials are expected to play in our society, a role that reaches its ultimate when trials are televised.

In *United States v. Mitchell*,[118] the question was whether the so-called White House audiotapes could, after admission in evidence at the former Attorney General's trial, be copied and broadcast. In holding that the trial judge should have allowed the copying, the Court of Appeals noted that the right to inspect and copy is "fundamental to a democratic state" and likened the public interests served by it to those values of public knowledge about the workings of government protected by the First Amendment.[119] In *Application of NBC* (Jenrette),[120] *United States v. Criden*,[121] and *Application of NBC* (Myers),[122] the District of Columbia, and the Second and Third Circuits emphasized that the right to access to judicial documents has its footings, as Judge Newman put it, in the "high public

---

[115] United States v. Criden, 501 F.Supp. 854 (E.D. Pa., 1980).

[116] *Id.* at 860.

[117] United States v. Criden, 648 F.2d 814, 825 (3d Cir. 1981).

[118] See note 76 *supra*.

[119] 551 F.2d at 1258, 1261, particularly n.39. ("The interests served by the common law right of access to judicial proceedings are closely related to First Amendment interests.")

[120] 653 F.2d 609 (D.C. Cir. 1981).

[121] 648 F.2d 814 (3d Cir. 1981).

[122] 635 F.2d 945 (2d Cir. 1980).

interest in the full opportunity to know whatever happens in a courtroom."[123] As a consequence, these courts have assumed that copying is to be permitted and that the burden will be placed on an objector to show strong reasons why the court should decide to the contrary.

The conclusion to be drawn from these cases is that the justification for the right of access to judicial records and the right to televise trials has become virtually indistinguishable from First Amendment considerations. At the very least they are further evidence of the increasing emphasis placed on the *public* role of criminal trials.

Perhaps the clearest way to demonstrate the now dominant perspective on criminal trials is to compare some of the opinions in *Estes* and *Richmond Newspapers*.

Chief Justice Warren's concurring opinion in *Estes* captures the essence of the traditional notion of the trial. It is a proceeding with a clear, primary purpose—to reach ". . . a fair and reliable determination of guilt, and no procedure or occurrence which seriously threatens to divert it from that purpose can be tolerated."[124] He believed that the presence of television cameras in the courtroom was, at best, irrelevant to the purpose of a trial, and, at worst, a "desecration of the courtroom." For him, the profound changes television works in human behavior meant that it impaired the reliability of the trial, and, therefore, denied due process.[125] The Chief Justice was aware that there had been a time when trials were a form of local entertainment.[126] But he thought those days were gone.

A sharp contrast appears in two of the opinions in *Richmond Newspapers*. Chief Justice Burger, building on the traditional openness of Anglo-American trials, stressed not only the function of such openness in reassuring the people of fair procedure but of the "prophylactic purpose [of] providing an outlet for community concern, hostility and emotion."[127] A trial is a community exercise, a

---

[123] 635 F.2d at 951.

[124] 381 U.S. at 564–65 (Warren, C.J., concurring).

[125] *Id.* at 569–70.

[126] *Id.* at 570 n.27, citing WIGMORE, A KALEIDOSCOPE OF JUSTICE 487 (1941).

[127] 448 U.S. at 571. See also 6 WIGMORE, EVIDENCE 435 (Chadbourn rev., 1976). A useful discussion of this aspect of *Richmond Newspapers* is found in CHOPER, KAMISAR, & TRIBE, THE SUPREME COURT: TRENDS AND DEVELOPMENTS 145 *et seq.* 1979–80.

way of demonstrating that the law does in fact function to provide
safety and security. Justice Brennan put the matter in somewhat
more traditional First Amendment terms—the courts are institutions of our republican form of government, and it is axiomatic that
in a democracy the people must debate their performance, and, to
do that, they must be informed:[128]

> While individual cases turn upon the controversies between par-
> ties or involve particular prosecutions, court rulings impose offi-
> cial and practical consequences upon members of society at
> large. Moreover, judges bear responsibility for the vitally im-
> portant task of construing and securing constitutional rights.
> Thus, so far as the trial is a mechanism for judicial factfinding, as
> well as the initial forum for legal decisionmaking, it is a genuine
> governmental proceeding.

Chandler, of course, furthers the aspect of the criminal trial
stressed in *Richmond Newspapers*. As a matter of fact, the Florida
court rested its decision to admit cameras to its courts primarily on
the state's commitment to "open government."[129] To the extent
that the newly sanctioned right to televise trials is exercised by state
courts, the institutional functions of criminal trials will be emphasized; whether protection of the defendant's rights will suffer in
the process will depend on how carefully the state courts control
this new participant in the courtroom.

Beyond its possible effect on the trial itself, television may
exacerbate the possible prejudice created by pretrial publicity generally. For example, pretrial hearings may be kept open, and if
those proceedings are televised, the problem of securing an unbiased jury may be aggravated. Thus, the decision whether to close
such a hearing, or to allow television if it is left open, will be more
difficult. To the extent that television coverage implicates First
Amendment values, it would seem that *Nebraska Press*, *Gannett*, and
Richmond Newspapers would require coverage, except in the face of at
least substantial reasons for closure. Fortunately, except where a
confession or evidence of a defendant's prior criminal record is
involved, such publicity is not likely to prevent a fair trial, if the
proper protective measures are taken.[130] There is even some ex-

---

[128] 448 U.S. at 595–96 (Brennan, J., concurring).

[129] Petition of Post-Newsweek Stations, Florida, Inc., 370 So. 2d at 780 (1979).

[130] Simon, *Does the Court's Decision in Nebraska Press Association Fit the Research Evidence on the Impact on Jurors of News Coverage?* 29 STAN. L. REV. 515, 526 (1977).

perience, growing out of Watergate, with the effect of pretrial television coverage on prospective jurors. Despite the saturation of the airwaves with the various televised hearings, two people prominently involved, John Mitchell and Maurice Stans, were acquitted of related charges in the federal court in New York.[131] And, despite the same coverage, the district court in the District of Columbia, by proceeding carefully, was able to select a jury to try the Watergate principals.[132] In one of the Abscam cases, the Second Circuit noted that, despite the heavy publicity about those bizarre events, "about half of those summoned for jury selection had no knowledge of Abscam, and only a handful had more than a cursory knowledge."[133]

It is also noteworthy that, in two of the Abscam cases, the networks were allowed to broadcast the videotapes, even though some defendants to whose cases the tapes would be relevant had not yet been tried. The courts reasoned that the tapes had already been admitted in evidence in the first trial. It was speculative to suggest that their broadcast would make it impossible to secure a fair jury in the subsequent cases. This certainly seems justifiable, because the print media, and indeed television newscasters, had already described the tapes in detail for their readers and viewers.[134]

One more problem deserves brief mention. It is the converse of the usual claim of a defendant that television will infringe his due process rights. There may be cases in which the defendant desires television coverage, perhaps to put pressure on a witness.[135] Such a case would seem to trigger the power of the court to decide how to reconcile the defendant's public trial rights, the press's First Amendment rights, and the witnesses' privacy interest discussed above.

It is also possible that defendants may desire television coverage for political purposes of their own. To the extent that no disruption

---

[131] Graham, *From the Press*, in THE JURY SYSTEM IN AMERICA: A CRITICAL OVERVIEW 202 (Simon, ed. 1975).

[132] United States v. Haldeman, 559 F.2d 31 (D.C. Cir. 1976), *cert. den.* 431 U.S. 933 (1977).

[133] Application of NBC, Inc., 635 F.2d 945, 953 (2d Cir. 1980).

[134] United States v. Criden, 648 F.2d 814 (3d Cir. 1981); Application of NBC (Myers) 635 F.2d 945 (2d Cir. 1980).

[135] See, *e.g.*, Cody v. State, 361 P.2d 307 (Okla. Cr. App. 1961) (defendant's demand for television coverage of very sordid rape trial denied).

of the trial would result, there seem to be no grounds on which to deny the coverage. But if the result would be to turn the courtroom into a theater, as it might have in the Chicago Seven trial,[136] surely the court's power to control its proceedings would support exclusion of the cameras.

X. CONCLUSION

The Supreme Court made clear in *Chandler* that it did not hold that there is a First Amendment right of access to televise trials.[137] Predictions of a change in that position would be foolhardy, since the Court will undoubtedly let the problems percolate until some pattern develops. Some lower courts will avoid the issue by construing their television rules so as to create a presumption in favor of such coverage.[138] But is hard to see how the Court, once it directly faces the question, can hold that properly controlled television reporters do not have the same constitutional right of access to the courts as do other news people. Having opened the courtroom to cameras, it is difficult to find a defensible stopping place.

One stopping place seems particularly inappropriate. Virtually all the concern with the impact of television on judicial proceedings centers on the trial court where jurors and witnesses may be influenced by cameras. There is no basis whatever for believing that televising appellate proceedings would in any way affect the nature of those proceedings or the quality of the end product. If a major purpose of admitting television cameras to courtrooms is to

---

[136] In re Dellinger, 461 F.2d 389 (7th Cir. 1972); for a suggestion about this problem, see Kalven, *"Please, Morris, Don't Make Trouble": Two Lessons in Courtroom Confrontation*, in LAW, JUSTICE AND THE INDIVIDUAL IN SOCIETY 325 (Tapp and Levine, eds. 1977).

[137] In fact, the Court declined either to endorse or invalidate television in the courtroom. There is something of an irony here. The federal courts have been among the most stubborn of opponents of cameras in or even near courtrooms. Fed. R. Cr. P. 53 states: "The taking of photographs in the courtroom during the progress of judicial proceedings or radio broadcasting of judicial proceedings from the courtroom shall not be permitted by the court." The Judicial Conference has been adamant that cameras will not invade the courtroom and has recommended that district courts adopt local rules that bar cameras from courtrooms and their "environs." See letter from Chief Justice Warren indicating the views of the Judicial Conference in 1962, as reported in 87 A.B.A. REP. 793; the later history of the Conference's attitude is reported in WRIGHT, FEDERAL PRACTICE AND PROCEDURE, CRIMINAL, Sec. 861, 376–80 (1969).

[138] See note 80 *supra*.

educate the public about the way major governmental institutions function, one can hardly imagine a better example than a dignified telecast of appellate arguments or of opinion day in cases of major public interest. In fact, the Supreme Court seems to be the most logical candidate for television coverage.[139]

The press has been eminently successful in ensuring public access to judicial proceedings.[140] One can only respond to *Richmond Newspapers* with loud applause. The notion that the public and press should not have a constitutional right to attend criminal trials now seems nothing short of odd. But applause for *Chandler v. Florida* must be a good deal more restrained. There are risks to defendants in being subjected to televised trials. Television will tempt society to use criminal trials for public catharsis and reassurance, and that will only exacerbate those risks.

---

[139] Justice Potter Stewart, announcing his retirement, is quoted as saying: "Our courtroom is an open courtroom: the public and the press are there routinely, and since today television is a part of the press, I have a hard time seeing why it shouldn't be there too, so long as it is not a disruptive influence. Now in the early days of television before the technical advancement we have seen, I think perhaps the noise and the lights and so on would have distorted and disrupted the proceedings. But as I understand the present technology, that hardly is a threat anymore, and I think it is difficult to make an argument to keep television out when you allow everyone else in." 67 A.B.A.J. 954 (1981). To the same effect, see Wright, *A Judge's View: The News Media in Criminal Justice*, in SELECTED READINGS: FAIR TRIAL–FREE PRESS 22 (Winters, ed. 1971).

[140] *Chandler* should also give impetus to efforts to gain television coverage of those nonjudicial events that are already open to the public. In CBS, Inc. v. Lieberman, 439 F.Supp. 862 (N.D. Ill. 1976) the district court declined to require the Illinois Commerce Commission to admit television cameras to its public, nonadjudicatory proceedings. The court found the precedents against the network on its First Amendment claim. In addition the judge thought the potential dangers of cameras in the hearing room, where no one but the examiner objected, were imponderable and might be profound. Of course, this was a case in which a federal court was asked to order access to a state administrative proceeding. *Chandler* does not touch that problem, but it is hard to see how policymakers can continue to resist television on grounds now so widely rejected in criminal cases. For an example of an effort to deal with the problem before *Chandler*, see Bennett, *Broadcast Coverage of Administrative Proceedings*, 67 NW. U. L. REV. 528 (1972). Coupled with open meeting laws, *Chandler* ought to generate considerable change in the availability of public proceedings to the viewing audience. See Note, *The Government in the Sunshine Act: An Overview*, 1977 DUKE L. J. 565; Note, *Open Meeting Statutes: The Press Fights for the "Right to Know,"* 75 HARV. L. REV. 1199 (1962). *Cf.* Garrett v. Estelle, 556 F.2d 1274 (5th Cir. 1977), cert. den. 438 U.S. 913 (1978), which reversed a district judge's decision that a television news cameraman had a First Amendment right to televise a state execution. A limited number of people, including press pool representatives, had been admitted to the execution chamber. The Fifth Circuit held that any right of access extended only to the right to attend, not the right to photograph. An interesting feature of this intriguing case is that the state was willing to provide closed circuit television of the execution for members of the press who could not be admitted to the execution chamber, but public broadcast was not permitted. 556 F.2d at 1277.

Moreover, it is not at all clear just what television will teach society about crime and the administration of justice. One of the earliest fears expressed by leaders of the bar about photographic coverage of trials was that the public would get the wrong impression of the way the judicial process actually works.[141] Except for rare documentaries, what the public will usually get, as it did in *Chandler*, is a few seconds of pictures on the evening news, accompanied by some less than expert commentary.[142] This, it is said, will create in the public mind a misconception of the courts. But fears that the public would learn the wrong lessons about courts may only be lawyers' elitism. Anyway, those fears were generated in the first place by the abuses in uncontrolled cases such as *Hauptmann* and *Estes*. Presumably, those excesses will now be prevented. Moreover, it is difficult to see how any more distortion of the proceedings can come from actual pictures, however fragmentary, than comes, deliberately or subconsciously, through the writing and editing of a newspaper story of the same event.[143]

---

[141] In fact, Canon 35 originally asserted that the taking of photographs, and later the televising, of court proceedings would not only "degrade the court but create misconceptions with respect thereto in the mind of the public." See *Report of Special Committee on Televising and Broadcasting Legislative and Judicial Proceedings*, 77 A.B.A. REP. 607, 610 (1952).

[142] See generally TYRELL, THE WORK OF THE TELEVISION JOURNALIST 13–14 (1972); WOOD, ELECTRONIC JOURNALISM 31 (1967). There is, of course, the possibility that documentaries will provide more complete and edifying coverage. Relatively few have yet been broadcast, no doubt because they are expensive and have unpredictable commercial appeal. Moreover, they would require extensive editing because trials, like war, contain long stretches of boredom punctuated by short bursts of excitement. Public television stations have on occasion undertaken virtually full-length coverage. The murder trial of the young Florida defendant who claimed to have been stimulated by television to commit a crime received twenty-seven hours of videotape coverage and was later broadcast nationally. Zamora v. State, 361 So. 2d 776 (D.C.A. Fla. 1978). In fact, the extent of coverage of Florida courts by public television stations suggests that public television will play a major role in conveying to the public much useful information about the workings of courts. See *amici curiae* brief of Public Television Stations et al, filed in Florida v. Chandler.

[143] It is often said that sentiment against the Vietnam war grew as Americans saw the violence of the war on their television screens. An argument has been made, however, that the real effect of such sensationalism was to distract the public from the more subtle political issues at stake and thus to distort the picture of the war. Even so-called documentaries were hardly more than reiteration of "the company line." ARLEN, LIVING ROOM WAR, 6–9, 45–50 (1969). One of the more active opponents of televised coverage of trials has made a somewhat similar point: "A review of research on the impact of television on American institutions shows that it has reshaped politics, changed the nature of sports and business, transformed family life and the socialization of children, and affected public security and the enforcement of laws. The debate over cameras in the courts may be our last opportunity to consider the evidence already available on the influence of television on public images of law and the courts, and to halt the rush toward televised trials until we can take a fresh look at the

Television is in the courts to stay. However unsettling it may seem, it is right for it to be there. As Justice Blackmun said in *Virginia Board of Pharmacy*,[144] the choice between the danger of public ignorance and that of freedom of information has already been made for us.

---

problem." Gerbner, *Trial by Television: Are We at the Point of No Return?* 63 JUDICATURE 416, 418 (1980).

[144] 425 U.S. 748, 770 (1976).

JOHN H. GARVEY

FREEDOM AND EQUALITY IN
THE RELIGION CLAUSES

The Supreme Court has been extremely puzzled about how to treat the distribution of public benefits when the pattern of distribution may cause individuals to alter their preferences in making constitutionally protected choices. When dealing with the freedom to choose an abortion, for example, the Court held that the Hyde Amendment was constitutional because the government did not interfere with freedom when all it did was offer money to make the option *it* preferred (childbirth) more attractive.[1] In free speech cases, the Court has said that when the government opens up public property or offers financial incentives to speakers it must treat all options *equally*—it may not favor a particular subject or position.[2] Last term, in *Thomas v. Review Board*,[3] the Court held that when freedom of religion is at stake, the government has an independent obligation to fund the option which the *individual* finds more attractive. The case directed the state of Indiana to pay unemployment compensation to one who quit his job for religious reasons, even though the state paid nothing to those who quit for other personal reasons. The allocation of public funds has created similar

John H. Garvey is Law Alumni Professor of Law, University of Kentucky College of Law.

AUTHOR'S NOTE: I would like to thank Thomas P. Lewis for his careful reading and generous criticism of an earlier draft of this paper.

[1] Harris v. McRae, 448 U.S. 297 (1980). *Cf.* Maher v. Roe, 432 U.S. 464 (1977).

[2] Carey v. Brown, 447 U.S. 455 (1980); Police Dept. of the City of Chicago v. Mosley, 408 U.S. 92 (1972). *Cf.* Speiser v. Randall, 357 U.S. 513 (1958).

[3] 101 S. Ct. 1425 (1981).

problems with regard to other constitutional freedoms, such as travel,[4] voting,[5] and parental choices about their children's education.[6] I think that all these cases present questions of equality rather than freedom, and that the free exercise and abortion decisions err on different sides of the correct principle. The proper approach is to say, as the Court has regarding freedom of speech, that the government need not fund protected choices, but if it does, it must do so in a neutral fashion. If that is correct, then the question *Thomas* poses is not whether Indiana had prohibited the freedom to exercise religious belief but whether the Court, by awarding benefits, violated the equality principle inherent in the Establishment Clause.

I. THE THOMAS CASE

A. THE FACTS AND PROCEEDINGS BELOW

Eddie Thomas, a Jehovah's Witness, was hired to work at the Blaw-Knox Foundry and Machinery Company in the roll foundry, which fabricated sheet steel for a variety of uses. After he had worked there about a year, the roll foundry was closed, and he was transferred to a department which made turrets for military tanks. Thomas shortly concluded that his new position required him to work directly in the production of armaments in a way that conflicted with religious principles he found in scripture. An examination of the other departments in the plant convinced him that he would face a similar conflict at any other job Blaw-Knox might offer him, the roll foundry having been closed. He asked to be laid off, was denied, and quit after a few weeks in the turret department.[7]

Thomas then applied for unemployment compensation and stated in his claim that he had voluntarily quit his job because of religious convictions. Under the Indiana Employment Security Act, benefits are denied to "an individual who has voluntarily left

---

[4] Memorial Hospital v. Maricopa County, 415 U.S. 250 (1974); Shapiro v. Thompson, 394 U.S. 618 (1969).

[5] Buckley v. Valeo, 424 U.S. 1, 94–95 (1976).

[6] Norwood v. Harrison, 413 U.S. 455, 462 (1973).

[7] Thomas v. Review Bd., 391 N.E.2d 1127, 1128–29 (Ind. 1979).

his employment without good cause in connection with the work."[8] The phrase "good cause in connection with the work" is understood to mean a provocation attributable to the employer which makes the decision to quit objectively justifiable.[9] One forced to work under conditions hazardous to his health has good cause to quit;[10] one who quits because of parental obligations or transportation difficulties does not.[11] Thomas contended that the responsibility for his termination really lay with Blaw-Knox, since it had closed the roll foundry, into which he had been hired on the recommendation of a fellow church member. He supported that claim by pointing out that his application for employment stated that he was a Jehovah's Witness and that his hobby was reading the Bible.[12] Both the appeals referee and the Employment Security Review Board rejected his claim. Since the circumstances of Thomas's hiring did not show that he had imposed contractual conditions on his employment, Blaw-Knox was entitled to require him to work anywhere in the plant.[13] The only relevant cause of Thomas's decision to quit was his personal religious objection to working on weapons.

Even if Thomas could not squeeze within the language of the statute, he might win by showing that the interpretation of the "good cause" provision was unconstitutional. *Sherbert v. Verner*[14] offered considerable help on that score. State law there had provided that one already unemployed who refused without good cause to accept a job could not get unemployment compensation.[15] The Supreme Court had held that it was unconstitutional to use that provision to deny benefits to a Seventh Day Adventist who refused to accept Saturday work for religious reasons. Such a burden on free exercise could only be justified by a compelling state

---

[8] Indiana Code § 22-4-15-1 (Burns Code Ed. 1974, Supp. 1978).

[9] See, *e.g.*, Gray v. Dobbs House, Inc., 357 N.E.2d 900, 903–05 (Ind. Ct. App. 1976); Lewis v. Review Board, 282 N.E.2d 876, 882–83 (Ind. Ct. App. 1972); Geckler v. Review Board, 193 N.E.2d 357, 359 (Ind. 1963).

[10] Evans v. Enoco Collieries, 96 N.E.2d 674 (Ind. App. 1951).

[11] Gray v. Dobbs House, Inc., note 9 *supra*.

[12] Thomas v. Review Bd., 381 N.E.2d 888, 889 (Ind. Ct. App. 1978).

[13] *Id.* at 890. It would be hard to blame the company for not foreseeing the turn Thomas's conscience would take. His friend, a Jehovah's Witness, who had helped him get the job, had no scruples about working in the turret department. *Ibid.*

[14] 374 U.S. 398 (1963).

[15] S.C. Code § 68-114(3)(a), quoted in 374 U.S. at 400 n.3.

interest,[16] and the review board in *Thomas* had conceded that it could not meet that test.[17] The Indiana Court of Appeals found the analogy to *Sherbert* persuasive and overturned the review board's decision.[18]

The Indiana Supreme Court reversed and reinstated the board's decision. It found *Sherbert* inapplicable because Thomas's decision to quit was a "personal philosophical choice rather than a religious choice."[19] According to the court, the line between fabricating steel in the roll foundry and using the fabricated steel to make turrets was a rather fine one, and Thomas had neither articulated the religious basis for the distinction nor shown that other members of his congregation subscribed to it.[20] The court also held that payment of benefits to Thomas would violate the Establishment Clause because the purpose and effect of such action would be protection of religious belief.[21]

B. THE SUPREME COURT'S OPINION

The Chief Justice began his opinion for the Court by saying that Thomas's reasons for quitting were unquestionably religious in the sense required for protection by the free exercise clause. It did not matter that Thomas found a difference of principle between two different stages in the production of weapons. "[R]eligious beliefs need not be acceptable, logical, consistent, or comprehensible to others in order to merit First Amendment protection."[22] Nor was it significant that his interpretation of scripture was not shared by other members of his faith. The guarantee of free exercise is not limited to doctrines that command universal assent within a sect; and where there is disagreement, courts are not competent to say who is right.

Up to that point, the Court was on safe ground. The trouble started when it addressed the second issue: whether the mere denial of unemployment compensation to one who quit his job for reli-

---

[16] 374 U.S. at 406.

[17] 381 N.E.2d at 890–93.

[18] *Id.* at 888.

[19] 391 N.E.2d at 1131.

[20] *Id.* at 1131–33.

[21] *Id.* at 1134.

[22] 101 S. Ct. at 1430.

gious reasons counted as a prohibition of freedom of religion. The Chief Justice began with the unimpeachable observation that "the Indiana law does not *compel* a violation of conscience."[23] But having said that, he went on to find a[24]

> coercive impact on Thomas . . . indistinguishable from *Sherbert*. . . . Where the state conditions receipt of an important benefit upon conduct proscribed by a religious faith, or where it denies such a benefit because of conduct mandated by religious belief, thereby putting substantial pressure on an adherent to modify his behavior and to violate his beliefs, a burden upon religion exists. While the compulsion may be indirect, the infringement upon free exercise is nonetheless substantial.

He even quoted the parallel that *Sherbert* found most apt to describe the nature of the coercion:[25]

> "Governmental imposition of such a choice puts the same kind of burden upon the free exercise of religion as would a fine imposed against [her] for her Saturday worship."

The outcome of the case followed inexorably, once that problematic assumption was made. If the mere failure to pay benefits was "coercive," an "indirect compulsion" indistinguishable from a fine, then the state would need compelling reasons to justify such a severe restriction of free exercise. The board had offered no proof that the number of people who voluntarily quit jobs for religious reasons would be sufficiently great to imperil the solvency of the state's unemployment fund. Nor was there any showing that the number would be large enough to prompt employers to probe the religious beliefs of their job applicants and hire only those whose principles were compatible with the nature of the employer's business.

Having concluded that Indiana's law restricted religious freedom, the Court faced a third issue: whether paying benefits to Thomas while denying them to those who quit jobs for personal but nonreligious reasons would foster religion in violation of the Establishment Clause. That contention, too, had been advanced and rejected in *Sherbert v. Verner*, and the majority found no reason to disturb its earlier holding that an accommodation of religious free-

---

[23] *Id*. at 1431.

[24] *Id*. at 1432.

[25] *Id*. at 1431, quoting Sherbert v. Verner, 374 U.S. at 404.

dom did not amount to an impermissible involvement of religious with secular institutions.[26]

Justice Rehnquist dissented. He concluded that the Court's broad reading of the Free Exercise Clause created an irreconcilable conflict with the Establishment Clause. If *Sherbert* and *Thomas* stand for the principle that the government cannot put pressure on religious belief by withholding monetary benefits, it might equally be argued that "a State may not deny reimbursement to students who choose for religious reasons to attend parochial schools."[27] On the other hand, if we adhere to the three-part test currently used to enforce the Establishment Clause, Indiana would be constitutionally forbidden to legislate the result that *Sherbert* and *Thomas* require. In the first place, a law allowing benefits to those who quit jobs for religious reasons (while denying them to those who quit for other personal reasons) would serve a religious, not a secular, purpose. Second, the primary effect of such a law would be to advance religion by funding the exercise of religious choices. Third, the law would invite entanglement, because it would require the state to investigate the religious nature and sincerity of a claimant's belief.

II. The Limits of Freedom: Restriction of Choice

The basic mistake that the Court made in both *Thomas* and *Sherbert* was to assume that the failure to pay unemployment compensation burdened the free exercise of religion. In fact, a proper understanding of the freedom protected by the Constitution shows that neither case involved any restriction on liberty at all.

A. A COMMON SENSE LOOK AT FREEDOM, CHOICE, AND MOTIVE

What distinguishes constitutional freedoms (such as speech and religion) from other constitutional rights (such as the right to a jury trial and the protection against cruel and unusual punishment) is that freedoms give protection to choices. Freedom of speech protects the choice to praise the president, the choice to condemn him, and the choice to keep silent. The Seventh Amendment, in contrast, does not protect the choice to try one's case without a jury.

---

[26] 101 S. Ct. at 1433. Justice Blackmun concurred in the opinion on the first two points and in the result on the third—the establishment question. *Ibid.*

[27] *Id.* at 1435 n.2 (Rehnquist, J., dissenting).

The government may act in a number of ways to affect the outcome of the process of choice.[28] (1) It might compel an individual to choose the option that the government prefers, under the threat of fine or imprisonment for noncompliance.[29] (2) It might forbid or deter choice of the option that the individual prefers, either by making that option a criminal offense or by increasing the cost of the preferred option without making it illegal.[30] (3) The government might try to induce (rather than compel) choice of the option that it prefers by offering a monetary reward or similar bait to those who comply.[31] (4) Finally, the state might discourage (rather than forbid or deter) choice of the option that the individual prefers by withholding monetary or other benefits that the individual desires to receive. The last was the type of state action involved in *Sherbert* and *Thomas*.[32]

---

[28] In addition to the four examples which are discussed in text, the government may also, though it seldom does, simply prevent exercise of a preferred choice by making it impossible. One example might be locking the individual up in advance of his action. A second example outside the free exercise context might be laws which prevent a candidate's name from appearing on the ballot, thereby preventing the voter's freedom to choose that individual as his representative and the candidate's freedom to run for office. See text at notes 46–48 *infra*. In these cases the individual's action (going to jail, staying off the ballot) is not voluntary, much less free, see text at note & note 33 *infra*, because he could not choose to do otherwise.

[29] Wisconsin v. Yoder, 406 U.S. 205 (1972), is an example. The state of Wisconsin required parents to send their children to public or private school until they reached age sixteen. Violation was punished by fine or imprisonment. High school attendance violated the tenets of the Old Order Amish religion. See also West Virginia State Board of Education v. Barnette, 319 U.S. 624 (1943).

[30] An example of a law forbidding a choice preferred by the individual is the federal bigamy statute upheld in Reynolds v. United States, 98 U.S. 145 (1878). The law made bigamy a criminal offense; the defendant, a Mormon, was required by his religion to practice polygamy. An example of a law deterring a preferred choice without making it illegal is the license tax invalidated in Murdock v. Pennsylvania, 319 U.S. 105 (1943). The ordinance there required religious colporteurs to pay a flat fee for doing what they thought was a religious duty. *Cf.* Braunfeld v. Brown, 366 U.S. 599 (1961).

The essential difference between case 1 (compelling) and case 2 (forbidding or deterring) is that in the former the individual must undertake the specific activity favored by the government (go to school, salute the flag) or be subjected to sanctions. In the latter case the individual is free to pursue any option except the one disfavored by the government. Reynolds was free, as far as the government was concerned, to remain unmarried or to get married only once. Murdock was free in the same sense to distribute tracts free of charge, to convey his message orally, and so on.

[31] The Hyde Amendment is a good example. See note 1 *supra*. A challenge to it on free exercise grounds was dismissed in Harris v. McRae for lack of standing, note 1 *supra*, at 320–21.

[32] The difference between case 3 (the Hyde Amendment) and case 4 *(Thomas)* is that a pregnant woman can, by the choice she makes, control whether she will get benefits or not. Thomas, on the other hand, had no choice open to him which would produce governmental benefits. He could only elect between keeping his job (and drawing wages paid by Blaw-

In cases 1 and 2, the individual will do what the government wants him to voluntarily but not freely. His action is voluntary in the sense that he chooses to do it; it is unfree in the sense that his choice results from a motive that he wishes were not affecting him. Suppose it is a religious holy day and I want to go to church.[33] I may nevertheless choose not to if (1) the state will penalize me for skipping school; or if (2) the state will penalize me for going to church, though I may do whatever else I want. In either case, I could do otherwise, if I chose to. My decision not to go to church is not a reflex action such as a knee jerk, or a simply physical reaction such as being pushed into someone in front of me, but one I have willed to do after weighing my distaste for sanctions against my desire to conform to my religious obligations. In that sense, my action is voluntary. But it is unfree because the state has influenced the outcome of my choice of *actions* by supplying me with a *motive* (fear of sanctions) which I would not choose.

From a common sense way of speaking, however, in cases 3 and 4 the individual acts both voluntarily and freely. In both cases, his action results from choice, so it is voluntary. In both cases, his action is also free, because it either proceeds from a motive that he was happy to have the state supply (case 3), or it proceeds from motives that are unaffected by state action (case 4).[34] Suppose that I want to go to the movies this afternoon. I may choose not to go because (3) you offer me a free ticket to the Cubs game, or because (4) I have used up all my paid vacation and would have to take the

---

Knox) and quitting (without compensation of any kind). To use the standard metaphor, the government influences the pregnant woman's choice by offering her a carrot; it influences Thomas's choice by failing to offer him a carrot.

[33] My use of the word "voluntary" follows MOORE, ETHICS 12–16 (1912). In using the word "motive" I refer to the individual's disposition or desire to achieve or avoid a certain end. The desire to acquire money and the fear of going to jail are two types of motives, which the state may cause to arise in an individual by inducement or threat. Though motives may determine one's choices, so that he generally does what he *wants* to do, a motive itself may be one he does *not* desire. My use of "motive" also parallels Plamenatz's usage in his CONSENT, FREEDOM AND POLITICAL OBLIGATION 111–13, 118, 122 (2d ed. 1968). With this stipulation I hope I can avoid the controversy about the respective meanings of "reason," "motive," and "intention." For an introduction to the literature on that subject, see RAZ, PRACTICAL REASONING (1978); H. MORRIS, FREEDOM AND RESPONSIBILITY 158–230 (1961).

[34] *Cf.* Bayles, *A Concept of Coercion*, XIV NOMOS: COERCION 16 (1972); Gert, *Coercion and Freedom*, *id.* at 30; PLAMENATZ, note 33 *supra*, at 122. For a contrary view that enticement may be coercive, and hence restrict freedom, see Held, *Coercion and Coercive Offers*, XIV NOMOS: COERCION at 49. The fault of Held's analysis is that she relies on examples which may be explained more appropriately as denials of equality than as limitations of freedom. *Id.* at 56–57. See text at notes 53–66 *infra*.

afternoon off without pay. In case 3, the motive that determines my choice not to go to the movies is one that I want to have affecting me. I value a movie for which I have to pay at less than I value a free baseball game, and if it were in my control I would choose to have you offer me a ticket to the game. I may be unhappy that you did not *also* offer me a free movie pass (since I might then have gone to the movies rather than to the game), but I undoubtedly see myself as, if anything, more free than I would have been if you had done nothing. In case 4, my choice would not be affected by the fact that other employees still had vacation coming to them and could take the afternoon off with pay. The question for me would still be whether I valued a movie more or less than I valued an afternoon's wages. I might be unhappy that I too could not get paid while going to the matinee, but the reason I do not have that option is that I have just spent a week at the beach.

What is true of that innocuous illustration is equally true if we adapt it to religious choices. Thomas is no less free if he wants to go to church (instead of the movies) and the government offers him $100 to do something else. He is also no less free to do what his conscience directs if he wants to quit and others who have "good cause" to quit get unemployment benefits (instead of paid vacation). He is free in the former situation because a bounty of $100—unlike a tax, a fine, or a jail term—provides a motive he wants to have affecting him. His choices are enhanced, rather than restricted, by the government's action. He is free in the latter situation because his choice to exercise his belief is unaffected by the fact that the state pays benefits to others who quit for good cause. The government has neither restricted his choices nor supplied him with any motive that affects his decision.

There are several points about the problem in *Thomas* that seem to distinguish it from the moviegoer in case 4. One obvious difference is Thomas's need for unemployment benefits. It is certainly easier to take off an afternoon without pay than it is to quit one's job with no assurance of another source of income. And as Franklin D. Roosevelt once said, "Necessitous men are not free men."[35] But that suggests that Indiana would violate Thomas's freedom of religion if it had no unemployment compensation system whatsoever—or, to turn it around, that the state must act to make

---

[35] Message to Congress, 90 Cong. Rec. 57 (1944).

people free by assuring the satisfaction of their basic needs. That suggestion, for all its humanitarian appeal, is one I am sure the Court did not intend to make.

A second argument—one which makes *Thomas* look more like case 2 (in which the state increases the cost of the individual's preferred option)—might be that Thomas was more entitled than was the hypothetical moviegoer to income while he was not working. As one's entitlement becomes more secure, the state's refusal to pay looks more like a debit than a lost opportunity. And one who holds a job against his religious principles then is not free in the sense that his action is determined, as in case 2, by a motive that he does not desire: loss of "his" benefits if he quits. The Court would then be correct in saying that "Governmental imposition of such a choice puts the same kind of burden upon the free exercise of religion as would a fine imposed aginst appellant. . . ."[36]

Of course, in a positivistic sense, Thomas had no more claim to benefits than I would have to an extra vacation day to attend the movies. Had he asked a good lawyer before quitting whether his reason satisfied Indiana's "good cause" requirement, he would have been told no. On the other hand, Blaw-Knox's contribution to the unemployment fund was made possible by the value of Thomas's services and might in other circumstances have passed to him in the form of higher pay and resultant higher private savings to sustain himself after he quit. Thus, it could be argued that by operating its unemployment compensation program, Indiana took away from Thomas money that he needed to exercise his religious belief. Now that he has quit, Indiana has to give it back.

That sort of argument will not work for a number of reasons. One is that it rests on an inaccurate factual assumption. Indiana's unemployment compensation scheme was an insurance program, and the size of the premiums paid in on Thomas's behalf might be considerably smaller than the amount of benefits he was claiming.[37] A second reason is that the argument rests on assumptions of causation that in many cases will prove unjustified: if Indiana had not enacted an unemployment insurance program, Blaw-Knox may

---

[36] 101 S. Ct. at 1431, quoting Sherbert v. Verner, note 14 *supra*, at 398, 404.

[37] *Cf.* Fleming v. Nestor, 363 U.S. 603, 610 (1960). ("To engraft upon the Social Security system a concept of 'accrued property rights' would deprive it of the flexibility and boldness in adjustment to ever-changing conditions which it demands.")

have kept the extra money rather than passed it on, or the job market may have been so changed by the lack of employment security that Thomas would have gone to work somewhere else in the first place. In case 2, the state's action is keyed to the protected choice; an effect on motives is guaranteed by the way the law is designed to operate. The state says, for example, that if you want to ring doorbells to sell religious literature (or pots and pans), you must pay a fee for a license.[38] In *Thomas*, the state's act of collecting unemployment insurance may not play any role at all in Thomas's later choice about quitting.

B. A CONSTITUTIONAL PERSPECTIVE ON FREEDOM, CHOICE, AND MOTIVE

If what the preceding section says were to be reflected in constitutional law, one would be left with the uneasy feeling that the state could rid itself of Hare Krishnas, Moonies, and, for that matter, Jehovah's Witnesses by an appropriately cunning fiscal policy. In this section, I would like to make two points: first, that the common sense view of freedom (choice proceeding from a motive which either is actively desired or is unaffected by state action) finds support in cases defining constitutional freedoms; and second, that cases that seem to reject that view in fact point toward a different limit on the government's power to buy out Jehovah's Witnesses—the principle of equality.

/Support for the common sense view of freedom is most frequently found in cases, like case 3 above, in which the government attempts to induce choice of the option that it prefers by offering a monetary reward or similar bait to those who comply. Funding for childbirth, but not for abortion, is the best current example. Like the freedoms of speech and religion, the aspect of due-process liberty recognized in *Roe v. Wade*[39] offers protection for choice—in this case the choice whether to bear a child. Yet in *Harris v. McRae*, the Supreme Court said that that freedom of choice was not impinged on by a Medicaid system which paid for childbirth but not abortion, because a woman's choice was not restricted.[40] The foun-

---

[38] Murdock v. Pennsylvania, note 30 *supra*, at 105.

[39] 410 U.S. 113 (1973).

[40] 448 U.S. at 316–18.

dation for that conclusion was laid three years earlier in *Maher v. Roe*, which found[41]

> a basic difference between direct state interference with a protected activity and state encouragement of an alternative activity consonant with legislative policy. Constitutional concerns are greatest when the State attempts to impose its will by force of law; the State's power to encourage actions deemed to be in the public interest is necessarily far broader.

That difference between case 1 (compelling) or case 2 (forbidding), on the one hand, and case 3 (inducing), on the other, exists because in the case of inducement the woman acts from a motive she desires. The state has influenced the woman's decision by "ma[king] childbirth a more attractive alternative, . . . but it has imposed no restriction on access to abortions that was not already there."[42] The pregnant woman might be happier if the state *also* offered to fund abortions, but "it simply does not follow that a woman's freedom of choice carries with it a constitutional entitlement to the financial resources to avail herself of the full range of protected choices."[43]

The common sense view of freedom is also reflected in cases, like case 4 above, in which the state discourages choice of the option the individual prefers by withholding benefits the individual desires to receive. Consider the challenge to public financing of presidential election campaigns in *Buckley v. Valeo*.[44] The plaintiffs complained that Subtitle H of the Internal Revenue Code,[45] by restricting the public subsidy available to minor and new parties in primary and general election campaigns, infringed various freedoms that have

---

[41] 432 U.S. 464, 475–76 (1977) (footnote omitted).

[42] *Id.* at 474.

[43] *McRae*, note 1 *supra*, at 316. The Court reached a similar conclusion in Norwood v. Harrison, note 6 *supra*, at 455, regarding another aspect of due process liberty. Pierce v. Society of Sisters, 268 U.S. 510 (1925), held that the Fourteenth Amendment protected a parent's freedom to choose private, rather than public, education for his child. Obviously the state makes choice of a public education more attractive by paying the bill. The appellees in *Norwood* argued that such an inducement violated the Equal Protection Clause by discriminating against those who exercised the freedom recognized in *Pierce*, and that Mississippi was constitutionally required to provide free textbooks to private school students. The Court said, "It is one thing to say that a State may not prohibit the maintenance of private schools and quite another to say that such schools must, as a matter of equal protection, receive state aid." Note 6 *supra*, at 462.

[44] 424 U.S. 1 (1976).

[45] 26 U.S.C. §§ 9001–12, 9031–42 (1970, Supp. IV). Section 6096 provided for designation of income tax payments to the Presidential Election Campaign Fund.

been secured in voting cases under the Equal Protection Clause: the voter's freedom to choose a representative of his interests, the voter's freedom of political association,[46] and the candidate's freedom to run for office.[47] The Supreme Court held that there was a difference between withholding benefits (case 4), on the one hand, and laws that actually prevented a candidate's name from appearing on the ballot.[48]

> [The latter are] direct burdens not only on the candidate's ability to run for office but also on the voter's ability to voice preferences regarding representative government and contemporary issues. In contrast, the denial of public financing to some Presidential candidates is not restrictive of voters' rights and less restrictive of candidates'. Subtitle H does not prevent any candidate from getting on the ballot or any voter from casting a vote for the candidate of his choice; the inability, if any, of minor-party candidates to wage effective campaigns will derive not from lack of public funding but from their inability to raise private contributions.

Such cases suggest that the common sense view of what counts as a restriction on freedom is one the Supreme Court has adopted when enforcing constitutional liberties.[49] There are, though, even more decisions that seem to point in the opposite direction—to say that the distribution of public benefits either to induce or to discourage a particular result of a protected choice counts as an interference with constitutional freedom. Let me refer to three groups of such cases, all like *Thomas* (and case 4 above), in which the state has

---

[46] See Williams v. Rhodes, 393 U.S. 23 (1968); Storer v. Brown, 415 U.S. 724, 729 (1974); Lubin v. Panish, 415 U.S. 709, 716 (1974); *Developments in the Law, Elections*, 88 HARV. L. REV. 1111, 1134–36 (1975). The right to vote itself, though not explicitly denominated a "freedom" in the Constitution, offers protection for choice. A voter may not only vote for the candidate he chooses but is free (unlike voters in Belgium, for example) not to vote at all.

[47] *Buckley*, note 5 *supra*, at 94. The candidate's interest is not of a stature sufficient to provoke a strict standard of review. Bullock v. Carter, 405 U.S. 134, 142–43 (1972).

[48] 424 U.S. at 94–95 (footnote omitted). Keeping a candidate's name off the ballot is a case of preventing, see note 28 *supra*, rather than compelling (case 1) or forbidding (case 2). It is a more drastic interference with freedom than either of those cases since the individual's action is involuntary.

[49] One possible difference between *Thomas* and cases like Harris v. McRae and *Buckley* might be that in *Thomas* the choice favored by the petitioner is seen as a matter of duty, whereas the choice to have an abortion, to run for office, and so on are not usually viewed in that light. There surely is something morally repugnant about intentionally tempting someone to violate or discouraging someone from following a moral or religious obligation. *Cf.* Bayles, *Limits to a Right to Procreate*, in HAVING CHILDREN 13, 15 (O'Neill & Ruddick eds. 1979).

discouraged choice of the option the individual prefers by withholding public benefits the individual desires. First are the so-called
right-to-travel cases, which in fact involve the freedom to migrate
from one state to another.[50] The Supreme Court has blocked state
efforts to discourage migration by withholding such public benefits
as welfare[51] and medical care.[52] Second is a cluster of cases involving government employees, in which the state affects choices concerning free speech, association, or even free exercise[53] by refusing
to put on the public payroll people who will not take a loyalty
oath[54] or subscribe to some other orthodoxy.[55] In all of the cases
referred to, the Court has invalidated the conditions on public employment. Third are the public forum cases, in which the Court has
forbidden states to fiddle with religion[56] or speech[57] by closing the
streets, parks, and so on to advocates of disfavored positions or
subjects.

I want to suggest that, far from undermining the concept of
freedom for which I have been arguing, these cases show that the
manipulation of public benefits produces problems of equality, not
freedom. In the first place, each of the three groups of cases (travel,
conditions on employment, public forum) resolves an issue that

---

[50] Memorial Hospital v. Maricopa County, note 4 *supra*, at 250, 254; Shapiro v.
Thompson, note 4 *supra*, at 618, 629, 630.

[51] Shapiro v. Thomson, note 4 *supra*. *Cf.* Vlandis v. Kline, 412 U.S. 441 (1973).

[52] Memorial Hospital v. Maricopa County, note 4 *supra*.

[53] Torcaso v. Watkins, 367 U.S. 488 (1961). *Cf.* McDaniel v. Paty, 435 U.S. 618 (1978).

[54] Whitehill v. Elkins, 389 U.S. 54 (1967); Keyishian v. Board of Regents, 385 U.S. 589
(1967); Elfbrandt v. Russell, 384 U.S. 11 (1966); Baggett v. Bullitt, 377 U.S. 360 (1964);
Cramp v. Board of Public Instruction, 368 U.S. 278 (1961).

[55] Perry v. Sindermann, 408 U.S. 593, 597 (1972); Pickering v. Board of Education, 391
U.S. 563, 568 (1968).

[56] Niemotko v. Maryland, 340 U.S. 268 (1951). *Cf.* Fowler v. Rhode Island, 345 U.S. 67
(1953); Kunz v. New York, 340 U.S. 290 (1951). Last term, in Heffron v. International
Society for Krishna Consciousness, 101 S. Ct. 2559 (1981), the Court upheld a time, place,
and manner regulation of religious solicitation at the Minnesota state fair, relying heavily on
the "nondiscriminatory" nature of the rule. See *id.* at 2562, 2564.

[57] Shuttlesworth v. City of Birmingham, 394 U.S. 147 (1969); Cox v. Louisiana, 379 U.S.
536 (1965); Edwards v. South Carolina, 372 U.S. 229 (1963).
If there is such a thing as an absolute right to some minimum access to the public forum,
these cases resemble case 2, text at note 30 *supra*, rather than case 4—the state does not
simply withhold something the individual desires but deprives him of something he has. To
date, the Supreme Court has kept its own counsel about the degree to which access is
unconditionally guaranteed. See Carey v. Brown, note 2 *supra*, at 455, 459 n.2 (1980); Cox v.
Louisiana, note 57 *supra*, at 555. *Cf.* United States Postal Service v. Council of Greenburgh
Civic Associations, 101 St. Ct. 2676, 2683–87 (1981).

does not fit the traditional legal (and common sense) view of freedom. The roots of the freedom to migrate are found in older cases outlawing taxes and criminal penalties (case 2) imposed to inhibit interstate travel.[58] But, as Justice Rehnquist pointed out, a durational residence requirement[59]

> raises no comparable barrier. Admittedly, some indigent persons desiring to reside in Arizona may choose to weigh the possible detriment of providing their own nonemergency health care during the first year of their residence against the total benefits to be gained from continuing location within the State, but their mere entry into the State does not invoke criminal penalties. To the contrary, indigents are free to live within the State. . . .

Similarly, the Court for a long time resolved government employee cases by saying that imposing conditions on employment did not interfere with constitutional freedoms. In Justice Holmes's epigram:[60]

> The petitioner may have a constitutional right to talk politics, but he has no constitutional right to be a policeman. There are few employments for hire in which the servant does not agree to suspend his constitutional rights of free speech as well as of idleness by the implied terms of his contract. The servant cannot complain, as he takes the employment on the terms which are offered him.

Holmes resolved the public forum cases in the same way, upholding the conviction of a preacher who spoke on the Boston Common without getting a permit from the mayor:[61]

---

[58] See Crandall v. Nevada, 73 U.S. (6 Wall.) 35 (1868); Edwards v. California, 314 U.S. 160 (1941).

[59] Memorial Hospital v. Maricopa County, note 4 *supra*, at 250, 283 (Rehnquist, J., dissenting).

[60] McAuliffe v. Mayor of New Bedford, 155 Mass. 216, 220, 29 N.E. 517, 517–18 (1892). For later adoptions of the position, see Adler v. Board of Education, 342 U.S. 485, 492 (1952) ("If they do not choose to work on such terms, they are at liberty to retain their beliefs and associations and go elsewhere. Has the State thus deprived them of any right to free speech or assembly? We think not."); Bailey v. Richardson, 182 F.2d 46, 59 (D.C. Cir. 1950), *aff'd by an equally divided Court*, 341 U.S. 918 (1951) ("The First Amendment guarantees free speech and assembly, but it does not guarantee Government employ.").

[61] Commonwealth v. Davis, 162 Mass. 510, 511, 39 N.E. 113, 113 (1895), *aff'd*, 167 U.S. 43 (1897). *Cf.* U.S. Postal Service v. Council of Greenburgh Civic Associations, note 57 *supra*, at 2676, 2685 ("The State, no less than a private owner of property, has power to preserve the property under its control for the use to which it is lawfully dedicated.") (quoting Adderly v. Florida, 385 U.S. 39, 47 [1966]).

> For the Legislature absolutely or conditionally to forbid public speaking in a highway or public park is no more an infringement of the rights of a member of the public than for the owner of a private house to forbid it in his house.

In the second place, the Court's recent opinions condemning the manipulation of public benefits make clear that the evil of the practice is not that it restricts freedom but that it constitutes a denial of equal protection. That conclusion is most evident in the right-to-travel cases, in which the basis for decision was the Equal Protection Clause. The principle at stake was nondiscrimination: "Ye shall have one manner of law, as well for the stranger, as for one of your own country."[62] The same is true of the public forum cases, where the Court has recently made explicit what was implicit from the beginning: that "under the Equal Protection Clause, not to mention the First Amendment itself, government may not grant the use of a forum to people whose views it finds acceptable, but deny use to those wishing to express less favored or more controversial views."[63] Even before that doctrinal shift, it was well understood that the vice of vagueness in a permit system was the invitation it offered for discriminatory enforcement.[64] One finds less conscious recognition that the equality principle is at work in the government employment cases, although there are clear signals.[65] Just as revealing is the frequent reliance here, as in the public forum cases, on

---

[62] *Memorial Hospital*, note 4 *supra*, at 261 (quoting Lev. 24:22); *Shapiro*, note 4 *supra*, at 627 (the statute "creates a classification which constitutes an invidious discrimination denying them equal protection of the laws").

[63] Police Department of Chicago v. Mosley, note 2 supra, at 92, 96; Carey v. Brown, note 2 *supra*, at 455. *Cf.* Cox v. Lousiana, note 57 *supra*, at 557–58 (opinion of the Court), 581 (Black, J., concurring); Fowler v. Rhode Island, note 56 *supra*, at 67, 70 (Frankfurter, J., concurring); Niemotko v. Maryland, note 56 *supra*, at 268, 272 (opinion of the Court), 284 (Frankfurter, J., concurring).

[64] Shuttlesworth v. City of Birmingham, note 57 *supra* at 153; Cox v. Louisiana, note 57 *supra*, at 557–58; Edwards v. South Carolina, note 57 *supra*, at 236–37; Kunz v. New York, note 56 *supra*, at 293. *Cf.* Heffron v. International Society for Krishna Consciousness, note 56 *supra*, at 2564 ("Nor does Rule 6.05 suffer from the more covert forms of discrimination that may result when arbitrary discretion is vested in some government authority.").

[65] Cramp v. Board of Public Instruction, note 54 *supra*, at 288 ("exclusion . . . is patently . . . discriminatory"); Torcaso v. Watkins, 367 U.S. at 492–94 (Establishment Clause); Wieman v. Updegraff, 344 U.S., 183, 191–92 (1952) ("Congress could not 'enact a regulation providing that no Republican, Jew or Negro shall be appointed to federal office, or that no federal employee shall attend Mass or take any active part in missionary work.' . . . We need not pause to consider whether an abstract right to public employment exists. It is sufficient to say that constitutional protection does extend to the public servant whose exclusion pursuant to a statute is patently arbitrary or discriminatory.").

the doctrines of vagueness and overbreadth.[66] Once again, the concern over such defects is prompted by the opportunity they provide for discriminatory enforcement—the appropriate sin for statutes nearly always aimed at political minorities.

III. EQUALITY, AFFIRMATIVE ACTION, AND THE ESTABLISHMENT CLAUSE

I have argued in Section II that when the government influences constitutionally protected choices by the way it distributes benefits, the problem is one of equality, not freedom.[67] Taking that perspective on the *Thomas* case, obviously I suggest a different outcome: Jehovah's Witnesses were treated no differently under Indiana's scheme than were any other employees who voluntarily quit, so Thomas had no greater claim to unemployment compensation than did anyone else who quit for personal reasons. Not only did the case involve no interference with freedom, but also there was no issue of inequality that would justify judicial intervention.

In fact, by deciding *Thomas* as it did, the Court engaged in a kind of "affirmative action" which may have violated the brand of equality demanded by the Establishment Clause.[68] I would like to

---

[66] Whitehill v. Elkins, note 54 *supra*, at 62 ("overbreadth . . . makes possible oppressive or capricious application"); Keyishian v. Board of Regents, note 54 *supra*, at 597–604 (vagueness), 609 (overbreadth); Baggett v. Bullitt, note 54 *supra*, at 369–74 (vagueness); Cramp v. Board of Public Instruction, note 54 *supra*, at 286–87.

[67] In concluding as I do that the public forum and public employment cases present problems of equality rather than freedom, I do not mean to suggest that they can be resolved by resort to the Equal Protection Clause alone. If we had no First Amendment, the level of scrutiny that would be given classifications disfavoring some speakers would approximate that given classifications disfavoring some recipients of AFDC benefits. See Dandridge v. Williams, 397 U.S. 471, 484–85 (1970). My point is, rather, that the Court has felt compelled to talk in terms of equality, and indeed to invoke the Equal Protection Clause explicitly, because its consistent understanding of the term "freedom" in the First Amendment (choice proceeding from a motive that is not undesired) does not provide sufficient protection for the values it sees underlying individual and political expression. "Freedom" so defined would allow the government to buy unanimous support for orthodox opinions despite the obviously unhealthy social consequences of such a program. See text at notes 86–88 *infra*.

[68] In referring throughout this section and Sec. IV to the "neutrality" (or "equality") principle, I do not wish to be understood as suggesting that neutrality is an adequate description of the jurisprudence that the Supreme Court has adopted in Establishment Clause cases. I make clear (*e.g.*, text at notes 99, 113 *infra*) that it is not, though the state of the law might be considerably improved if it were. It is enough for my purposes that neutrality is a baseline principle which the Court has consistently reaffirmed. Roemer v. Maryland Public Works Board, 426 U.S. 736, 746–47 (1976) (opinion of Blackmun, J.); Committee for Public Education & Religious Liberty v. Nyquist, 413 U.S. 756, 788 (1973); Tilton v. Richardson, 403 U.S. 672, 677 (1971) (opinion of Burger, C. J.); Walz v. Tax Commission, 397 U.S. 664,

explore that question here by looking at parallel types of affirmative action that the Court has approved. One is benign racial classification, a phenomenon to which *Thomas* bears obvious similarities, for not only there, but in most recent cases, the Free Exercise Clause "has functioned primarily to protect what must be counted as discrete and insular minorities, such as the Amish, Seventh Day Adventists, and Jehovah's Witnesses."[69] The other is government sponsorship of speech, a kind of "affirmative action" which the Court has occasionally countenanced despite the general principle of free-speech neutrality. That, too, has a family resemblance to the unique support the Court gave religious objections in *Thomas* despite the general neutrality principle of the Establishment Clause.

A. BENIGN DISCRIMINATION

In one way, the affirmative action that the Court took on behalf of religious employees in *Thomas* is more radical than the benign discrimination at stake in *Bakke*[70] and *Fullilove*.[71] *Thomas* does not simply say, as those cases did, that government *may* act to aid a particular disadvantaged group; it says instead that government *must* afford a special advantage to religious voluntary quitters. Such mandatory affirmative action makes sense if withholding benefits actually restricts free exercise,[72] but as I assert in Section II, it does not. If Indiana's law did not violate anyone's constitutional rights, the decision about affirmative aid to religious minorities, just as the decision about affirmative action on behalf of racial minorities, should, as an institutional matter, be left to the discretion of the legislature. That was the solution preferred by Justice Rehnquist in

---

669 (1970); Epperson v. Arkansas, 393 U.S. 97, 103–04 (1968); Abington School Dist. v. Schempp, 374 U.S. 203, 215 (1963); Zorach v. Clauson, 343 U.S. 306, 314 (1952); Everson v. Board of Education, 330 U.S. 1, 18 (1947).

[69] ELY, DEMOCRACY AND DISTRUST 100 (1980).

[70] University of California Regents v. Bakke, 438 U.S. 265 (1978).

[71] Fullilove v. Klutznick, 448 U.S. 448 (1980).

[72] An example of such a case is Wisconsin v. Yoder, note 29 *supra*. The Court there concluded that the state's compulsory-education law restricted the free exercise rights of the Amish and ordered that the Amish be allowed a religious exemption. In so doing the Court consciously overrode the Establishment Clause principle that the government must give equal treatment to religion and nonreligion. *Id.* at 220–21. See also Kurland, *The Supreme Court, Compulsory Education, and the First Amendment's Religion Clauses*, 75 W. VA. L. REV. 213, 236–37 (1973). I suggest in Sec. IV that the neutrality principle of the Establishment Clause may be stated in such a way that it is consistent with the outcome in *Yoder* though not with the results in *Thomas* and *Sherbert*.

Thomas[73] and by Justice Harlan in *Sherbert*.[74] I think, however, that by awarding benefits to Thomas, the Court not only undertook a legislative task but also violated the Establishment Clause—just as the State of Indiana would have done had it voluntarily enacted the religious exemption which the Court said was constitutionally required.

If the Establishment Clause in fact states a kind of equality principle, the Rehnquist-Harlan position assumes that it tolerates benign legislative intervention just as the Equal Protection Clause does regarding racial classifications. But the arguments that support affirmative action in the latter case simply do not wash when applied to religion.

One such argument, which goes to the substance of the harm ca. ;ed by discrimination, maintains that the evil of racial classifications is that they stigmatize the disfavored class. Because that does not occur when whites are disadvantaged vis-à-vis blacks, we need not demand exceptional reasons to uphold benign classifications.[75] A second argument, really an evidentiary presumption, is that we need not be unusually suspicious of classifications that disfavor the political majority because its members are unlikely to hurt themselves without good reason.[76] A third argument, defensive in nature, is that even if we look equally hard at benign and malign discrimination, we can on occasion find compelling enough reasons for approving the former.

One is tempted to leap at the first two as support for Indiana's hypothetical religious exemption. After all, most Hoosiers will feel no psychic or moral affront if Jehovah's Witnesses are given special consideration. And it is hard to believe that a legislature in which the Witnesses are hardly represented at all is gearing up for an offensive on behalf of the Kingdom. But both those suggestions ignore the fact that the exemption carved out by the Court favored

---

[73] 101 S. Ct. at 1435.

[74] 374 U.S. at 422.

[75] *Bakke*, note 70 *supra*, at 357–58, 374–75 (opinion of Brennan, J.); Dworkin, *Why Bakke Has No Case*, NEW YORK REVIEW OF BOOKS 11, 15–16 (November 10, 1977); Greenawalt, *Judicial Scrutiny of 'Benign' Racial Preference in Law School Admissions*, 75 COLUM. L. REV. 559, 570–71 (1975).

[76] See Ely, *The Constitutionality of Reverse Racial Discrimination*, 41 U. CHI. L. REV. 723 (1974). That argument is what underlay Justice Brennan's emphasis in *Bakke* on the fact that "whites as a class [do not] have any of the 'traditional indicia of suspectness . . . .'" Note 70 *supra*, at 357.

religions generally. The same would be true of any modification that Indiana might make in its Employment Security Act. That makes the second argument, the evidentiary presumption, untenable: we may not be suspicious of classifications benefiting fringe sects, but the collective forces of religion are another matter. It is a rare legislator who has the temerity to disclaim a belief in God. The general nature of the exemption also undercuts the first argument by making the individual harm more substantive: the Establishment Clause, no less than the Equal Protection Clause, is worried about the psychic and moral affront from discrimination,[77] and that evil is likelier to ensue from general favoritism of religion than it is from special consideration of a distinct minority like Jehovah's Witnesses. The audience is more adult, but apart from that, the problem is not too different from *Engel v. Vitale*,[78] the Regents' Prayer Case. In each situation, the state purposefully uses its resources in a noncoercive and denominationally neutral fashion to favor its religious

---

[77] I find it odd that this point has not received more attention than it has. That there is such a stigmatic effect seems to me self-evident. Consider the trial testimony of Edward Schempp, explaining why he did not have his children excused from voluntary school-prayer services: "He said that he thought his children would be 'labeled as "odd balls"' before their teachers and classmates every school day; . . . that today the word 'atheism' is often connected with 'atheistic communism,' and had 'very bad' connotations, such as 'un-American' or 'anti-red,' with overtones of possible immorality." Abington School District v. Schempp, note 68 *supra*, at 203, 208 n.3. See also *id.* at 290 (Brennan, J., concurring) ("even devout children may . . . continue to participate in exercises distasteful to them because of an understandable reluctance to be stigmatized as atheists or nonconformists"); Illinois ex rel. McCollum v. Board of Education, 333 U.S. 203, 232–33 (1948) (Jackson, J., concurring) ("The complaint is that when others join and he does not, it sets him apart as a dissenter, which is humiliating."). Such an impact makes perfectly understandable what has been seen as a unique standing rule for Establishment Clause cases laid down in *Schempp*, note 68 *supra*, at 224 n.9. See Brown, *"Quis Custodiet Ipsos Custodes?—The School-Prayer Cases,"* 1963 SUP. CT. REV. 1, 15–31. In fact, the rule is no different from that which we apply in equal protection cases. In either instance, discrimination need not amount to coercion, that is to say, to an interference with freedom, to provide a basis for standing. Suppose, *e.g.*, that instead of a prayer the class chanted "White is right" and blacks were allowed to leave the room. That violates no constitutional freedom that I know of, but is certainly a denial of equal protection, and a black student would undoubtedly have standing to complain. What is more, in an action for injunctive relief, he would not have to prove harm to himself as a factual element of his case. It is a fact of which a court could take judicial notice. Compare Black, *The Lawfulness of the Segregation Decisions*, 69 YALE L.J. 421, 426–28 (1960), *with* Brown, 1963 SUP. CT. REV. at 30–31.

The psychic and moral affront from discrimination may also help explain the complementary standing rule applied in school aid cases. Flast v. Cohen, 392 U.S. 83 (1968). The problem of state aid to sectarian schools is structurally like the problem of state aid to private segregated schools, and in the latter case no one has doubted the standing of black students even though they were not taxpayers. See Norwood v. Harrison, 340 F. Supp. 1003, 1007 (N.D. Miss. 1972), *aff'd*, note 6 *supra*.

[78] 370 U.S. 421 (1962).

citizens over the nonreligious. In *Engel*, the state actually conducted a religious exercise, whereas our hypothetical amendment funds the performance of religious obligation. But, as the Court has argued in a related context, the distinction between state conduct and state funding is "a formalistic dichotomy that bears . . . little relationship . . . to common sense."[79]

The third argument for sustaining benign racial discrimination, defensive in nature, has been to look for compelling state interests that will satisfy even the strictest scrutiny. The striking feature of this approach is that the interests advanced are always in the service of a longer-range equality. The claim is that race-conscious action is necessary to achieve some end that pervasive societal discrimination frustrates,[80] and that such tactics will be unnecessary in a future, more egalitarian, society.[81] Neither contention can be made about a religious exemption in Indiana's unemployment scheme. There is simply no such thing as societal discrimination against religion generally,[82] or even any suggestion in the Court's opinion that it was saving Jehovah's Witnesses from the effects of a more focused and local prejudice.[83] More important still, the institution of a religious exemption is not aimed at any future goal to make religion, like race, irrelevant to decisions about labor relations. On the contrary, it sets up the pursuit of religious options[84] as a substantive good

---

[79] Committee for Public Education and Religious Liberty v. Regan, 444 U.S. 646, 658 (1980).

[80] Thus, Justice Powell in *Fullilove* argued that the minority business set-aside "serves the compelling governmental interest in eradicating the continuing effects of past discrimination identified by Congress." Note 71 *supra*, at 496. In Minnick v. California Department of Corrections, 101 S. Ct. 2211 (1981), the department contended that it had a compelling state interest in increasing the number of minority correction officers in order to cope with racial tensions in its prisons. *Id.* at 2215 & n.11. Even Justice Powell's argument in *Bakke* that the state had a compelling interest in pursuing the academic goal of a racially diverse student body addresses a problem—the homogeneity of medical student bodies—which is the product of past discrimination. Note 70 *supra*, at 369–73 (opinion of Brennan, J.).

[81] *Bakke*, note 70 *supra*, at 403 (opinion of Blackmun, J.); Dworkin, note 75 *supra*, at 11.

[82] "We are a religious people whose institutions presuppose a Supreme Being." Zorach v. Clauson, note 68 *supra*, at 313.

[83] As far as the record shows, Thomas may have been the only Jehovah's Witness with a complaint against the law. Thomas v. Review Board, note 7 *supra*, at 1128–29. Indeed, there is a fair argument that the effect of the decision in *Thomas* will be to make employers less willing to hire Jehovah's Witnesses then they were before. 101 S. Ct. at 1432.

[84] I say "the pursuit of religious options" rather than "religious liberty" because, as Sec. II makes clear, the latter is not affected by the Indiana Employment Security Act. What the Court's decision does is to make more attractive one option—the religious one—which Thomas was already free to pursue. See also text at notes 100–01 *infra*.

which it will be no less important for the state to promote in the future than it is now. But that is precisely what the Establishment Clause is intended to prevent.[85]

B. PROTECTING FREEDOM AND PROMOTING CHOICES

The comparison with benign racial discrimination suggests not only that the Court was wrong in *Thomas* and *Sherbert*, but that the dissenters in those cases were also wrong to say that the state had a wide zone within which it could act to accommodate religion. A look at an even closer parallel—the companion Free Speech Clause of the First Amendment—provides no better support for the Harlan-Rehnquist proposal. The equal protection theory of those free speech cases discussed in Section II is anchored in a belief that it is possible to reach a satisfactory equilibrium in a free speech market. In part, the principle of governmental neutrality is grounded on the trust that uninhibited discussion of public issues will lead to informed decision making, avoid standardization of ideas, and make government responsive to the will of the people.[86] In part, it is thought to allow a healthy type of social conflict productive of consensus and stable change.[87] Debate free from government influence is also crucial if scholarship is to flourish, science to advance, and culture to build.[88] Each of those objectives can be frustrated, as well, when the government offers or withholds financial inducements as when it engages in outright regulation. I argue in Section II that fiscal manipulation did not interfere with freedom of choice. That is not to say, however, that it does not affect the outcome of choices. If every person has his price, then for a suitable aggregate figure, the government can buy unanimity for any posi-

---

[85] "The 'establishment of religion' clause of the First Amendment means at least this: Neither a state nor the Federal Government . . . can pass laws which aid one religion, aid all religions, or prefer one religion over another. . . . That Amendment requires the state to be a neutral in its relations with groups of religious believers and nonbelievers. . . ." Everson v. Board of Education, 330 U.S. at 15, 18.

[86] Carey v. Brown, note 2 *supra*, at 462–63, 466–67; Pickering v. Board of Education, note 55 *supra*, at 571–72; Cox v. Louisiana, note 57 *supra*, at 551–52; Baggett v. Bullitt, note 54 *supra*, at 372 n.10; Edwards v. South Carolina, note 57 *supra*, at 237–38; Cramp v. Board of Public Instruction, note 54 *supra*, at 287–88.

[87] Baggett v. Bullitt, note 54 *supra*, at 372 n.10; Edwards v. South Carolina, note 57 *supra*, at 237–38; Cramp v. Board of Public Instruction, note 54 *supra*, at 287–88.

[88] Police Dept. of Chicago v. Mosley, note 2 *supra*, at 95–96; Whitehill v. Elkins, note 54 *supra*, at 59–60; Keyishian v. Board of Regents, note 54 *supra*, at 603; Shelton v. Tucker, 364 U.S. at 486–87.

tion it favors, regardless of the loss to science, scholarship, culture, or informed and creative political decision-making.

There is, however, somewhat more latitude permitted the government when it enters the market as a participant rather than as a regulator.[89] That is particularly true when the state's entry into the market is designed to preserve or enhance political expression within a democratic system, though the same may be said of efforts to expand the quality, range, and depth of freedom of expression generally.[90] To take an example considered in *Harris v. McRae*[91] and *Maher v. Roe*,[92] it is improper for a state to prevent parents from sending their children to private schools, but there is no restriction on the state's ability to favor public education by funding it,[93] and it would be fatuous to suggest that in designing public school curricula the state could not include civics courses which teach the virtues of democracy and the evils of facism. A similar explanation may be given for the holding in *Buckley v. Valeo* concerning public financing of presidential election campaigns.[94] The funding provisions sustained there allow the distribution of unequal shares of the Presidential Election Campaign Fund to "major," "minor," and "new" parties. The practical effect of Chapter 95 is that a Republican or a Democratic candidate will receive better than $20 million, while a Communist or Nazi party candidate will receive nothing.[95]

---

[89] There is a curious parallel to this aspect of free speech doctrine in the free trade theory of the Commerce Clause. There, as with speech, discriminatory state regulation must meet exacting state-interest and least-restrictive-alternative requirements. But when the state enters the commercial market as participant rather than as regulator, the Court has been more accommodating. Reeves, Inc. v. Stake, 447 U.S. 429 (1980); Hughes v. Alexandria Scrap Corp. 426 U.S. 794 (1976).

[90] An example of the latter is the legislation creating the Corporation for Public Broadcasting. 47 U.S.C.A. §§ 396 *et seq.* (Supp. 1981).

[91] 448 U.S. at 318.

[92] 432 U.S. at 476–77.

[93] Norwood v. Harrison, note 6 *supra*.

[94] 424 U.S. at 94–95.

[95] Chapter 95 of Title 26 establishes a Presidential Election Campaign Fund, 26 U.S.C. § 9006, and provides that "major party" candidates in the general election shall be entitled to $20 million, adjusted for inflation. See 26 U.S.C. § 9004(a)(1). A "major party" is defined as one whose candidate for president in the last election received 25 percent of the popular vote. 26 U.S.C. § 9002(6). A "minor party" is one whose candidate received 5 percent of the popular vote in the last election. 26 U.S.C. § 9002(7). Minor party candidates are entitled to a fraction of $20 million, determined by the ratio of the vote received by the party's candidate in the last election to the average of the major party candidates. 26 U.S.C. § 9004(a)(2)(A). "New parties" include all other political parties. Their candidates receive no money before the general election, but if they win 5 percent of the vote they are entitled to payments according to the formula applicable to minor party candidates. 26 U.S.C. § 9004(a)(3).

The Supreme Court concluded that the scheme enhanced, rather than abridged, freedom of speech and so was consistent with the First Amendment. For one thing, displacing private contributions with public funding[96] made it more likely that political candidates would be responsive to widely shared, rather than narrow but financially powerful, opinions.[97] Thus, the Act would counteract private distortions in the free speech market. And in deciding how to divide up the fund, Congress could give more money to candidates who took more popular positions, because that, like free speech itself, tended to promote a democratic consensus. To treat all candidates equally, in contrast, would spawn instability by "'artificially foster[ing] the proliferation of splinter parties.'"[98]

If the theory of such cases is that the demands of government neutrality may yield to the purpose of promoting free speech values, there is an obvious parallel in the current doctrine that the Establishment Clause must yield where necessary to protect free exercise values. As the Court said in *Wisconsin v. Yoder:*[99]

> an exception from a general obligation of citizenship on religious grounds may run afoul of the Establishment Clause, but that danger cannot be allowed to prevent any exception no matter how vital it may be to the protection of values promoted by the right of free exercise.

To say that the Court was protecting free exercise values in *Thomas* and in *Sherbert*, where there was no restriction of free exercise in the first place, is just loose talk. It is important to distinguish between protecting religious liberty, on the one hand, and promoting religious options, on the other. As I demonstrated in Section II, *Yoder*

---

[96] In order to be eligible for funds a major party candidate must certify that he will accept no private contributions except to the extent necessary to make up any deficiency in payments received out of the fund. 26 U.S.C. § 9003(b)(2). Minor and new party candidates must accept an expenditure ceiling and limit private contributions to an amount which, when added to public funds, does not exceed that ceiling. 26 U.S.C. § 9003(c).

[97] *Id.* at 91.

[98] *Id.* at 98. A related phenomenon has been the willingness to sustain rules about access to broadcast media over claims of interference with editorial discretion. See, *e.g.*, CBS, Inc. v. FCC, 101 S. Ct. 2813, 2829–30 (1981); Red Lion Broadcasting Co. v. FCC, 395 U.S. 367 (1969). In such cases the government's role is regulatory rather than participatory, though the permissibility of more active intervention is premised on the theory that the airwaves are a "part of the public domain." CBS, Inc. v. FCC, 101 S. Ct. at 2829.

[99] Wisconsin v. Yoder, note 29 *supra*, at 205, 220–21. See also Sherbert v. Verner, note 25 *supra*, at 413–17 (Stewart, J., concurring); Everson v. Board of Education, note 68 *supra*, at 17; TRIBE, AMERICAN CONSTITUTIONAL LAW 833–34 (1978); KAUPER, RELIGION AND THE CONSTITUTION 71 (1964).

was a type 1 case, in which the state compelled the Amish to choose an option (school attendance, contrary to their religious belief) that the state preferred, under threat of fine or imprisonment for non-compliance.[100] That was a clear interference with religious liberty in the sense that the state dictated the outcome of choice by supplying an undesired motive (fear of sanctions). In contrast, the Indiana Employment Security Act did not supply Thomas with any motive he did not already have for keeping his job. But the result of the Court's decision was to promote the contrary option—the religious one—which Thomas was already free to pursue.

It is on that distinction that the free speech comparison founders. In the realm of expression, the government can not only protect liberty but also promote particular options, such as preference for democracy over fascism. Not so with religion:[101]

> "Our constitutional policy . . . does not deny the value or the necessity for religious training, teaching or observance. Rather it secures their free exercise. But to that end it does deny that the

---

[100] Text at note & note 29 *supra*.

[101] Abington School Dist. v. Schempp, note 68 *supra*, at 218–19, quoting Everson v. Board of Education, note 68 *supra*, at 52 (Rutledge, J. dissenting). Note the Court's recognition of the same distinction in *Buckley*, where it rejected the suggestion that it read an Establishment Clause into the free speech guarantee. Note 5 *supra*, at 92–93 & n.127.

It may be possible to justify a statutory "religious" exemption if it is drawn in terms broad enough to cover everyone, including atheists and agnostics. Suppose that the law allows unemployment compensation to anyone who sees quitting as a choice for *or against* religion, so that an atheist whose job required her to assist in the manufacture of sacramental objects would be entitled to collect benefits if she quit. *Cf.* Young v. Southwestern Savings and Loan Ass'n, 509 F.2d 140 (5th Cir. 1975). In that instance it makes some sense to argue that the state is not promoting religious *options* but merely protecting religious *liberty* (*i.e.*, choices about religion, which might have positive or negative outcomes) against private restrictions. To put it another way, such a law would be not a species of affirmative action but simply another application of the principle of nondiscrimination. That is the aim of § 703(a)(1) of Title VII of the 1964 Civil Rights Act, 42 U.S.C. § 2000e—2(a)(1), which provides that

(a) It shall be an unlawful employment practice for an employer—
(1) to . . . discriminate against any individual with respect to his compensation, terms, conditions, or privileges of employment, because of such individual's . . . religion. . . .

The provision apparently extends to atheists, see *Young supra;* EEOC Dec. 72-1114, 4 F.E.P. Cas. 842 (1972); 110 Cong. Rec. 2607 (1964) (remarks of Rep. Celler), and the Court has been uneasy about finding in the law any duty to favor the religious over the nonreligious. See Trans World Airlines, Inc. v. Hardison, 432 U.S. 63, 85 (1977) ("we will not readily construe the statute to require an employer to discriminate against some employees in order to enable others to observe their Sabbath"). Of course, even if the law I have hypothesized would be constitutional, it does not justify the Court's decision in *Thomas*, which says that such a measure is not only permitted but required.

state can undertake or sustain them in any form or degree. For this reason the sphere of religious activity, as distinguished from the secular intellectual libèrties, has been given the two fold protection and, as the state cannot forbid, neither can it perform or aid in performing the religious function. The dual prohibition makes that function altogether private."

IV. A RECONCILIATION OF THE FREE EXERCISE AND ESTABLISHMENT CLAUSES

Taken together, Sections II and III yield what seem to be two inconsistent principles about the relation of government and religion. The conclusion of Section III is that the equality principle of the Establishment Clause forbids the government to provide any unequal benefit to religion. On the other hand, the discussion of religious freedom in Section II suggests that a law applying to all equally—like the school attendance law in *Yoder*—might violate the Free Exercise Clause if it provided an undesired motive to refrain from making a religious choice. Or, to turn it around, under some circumstances the government might be required to give special consideration to religion in order to protect free exercise. The apparent conflict of those two propositions does not affect the resolution of *Thomas*, where free exercise was not involved, but I should say a few words about the problem to show that I have not based my criticism of the case on contradictory premises about the meaning of religious freedom and equality.

Consistency depends on perspective. If one takes the perspective that the First Amendment requires government to treat people equally in all circumstances *irrespective of their religious convictions*, the principles in Sections II and III seem to be polar opposites. Such a reading of the religion clauses demands, as Philip Kurland has said,[102]

> that government cannot utilize religion as a standard for action or inaction because these clauses prohibit classification in terms of religion either to confer a benefit or to impose a burden.

The free exercise principle of Section II is inconsistent with that view because it sees some purely secular laws (like that in *Yoder*) as restrictions on freedom and calls in appropriate cases for a religion-

---

[102] See KURLAND, RELIGION AND THE LAW 18 (1962).

conscious solution. On the other hand, if we say, as Gail Merel recently suggested, that the First Amendment requires government to be neutral *with respect to religious choices*, the principles in Sections II and III come into line.[103] What the free exercise principle says about cases like *Yoder* is that government may not affect the outcome of religious choices by supplying a motive[104] for refraining from religious action. What the establishment principle says about cases like *Thomas* is that government may not affect the outcome of religious choices by supplying a motive for engaging in religious action.

The difficulty with Professor Kurland's formulation of the neutrality principle is that, in an effort to reconcile the religion clauses, it substitutes "equality" for "freedom" in the Free Exercise Clause and thereby gives that guarantee a meaning significantly more narrow than the principle stated in Section II.[105] Laws such as "All children must attend school" that make no classification along religious lines are seen as consistent with free exercise if they impose no special burden on religious objectors.[106] But when the Constitution uses the words "free," "freedom," and "liberty," what it guarantees is protection for individual choice to do or not to do a particular thing.[107] For example, a law that said "Everyone must stay home after sundown" would abridge my right to freedom of speech if I would otherwise choose to go to night school, or the theater, or to address a Nazi party rally. It would be no excuse that all people were treated alike. In the same way, requiring universal attendance at school irrespective of religious convictions is a way of treating everyone equally, but it restricts the free exercise of religion because it leaves only a Hobson's choice to those who see school attendance as a religious issue.

The second perspective—government neutrality regarding religious choices—does not completely resolve the tension between the two religion clauses, but it does reduce the area of conflict, and it

---

[103] Merel, *The Protection of Individual Choice: A Consistent Understanding of Religion under the First Amendment*, 45 U. CHI. L. REV. 805, 810–11 & nn.36, 37 (1978).

[104] A motive which the individual would not choose. See text at note 33 *supra*.

[105] *Cf.* Merel, note 103 *supra*, at 807–8.

[106] Kurland, *The Supreme Court, Compulsory Education, and the First Amendment's Religion Clauses*, 75 W. VA. L. REV. 213 (1973).

[107] See text *supra* at note & note 28.

justifies the theory of free exercise predominance[108] in cases where they cannot be reconciled. The principle eliminates conflict between free exercise and establishment in public benefits cases (like *Thomas* and *Sherbert*) by making clear that freedom is not at stake and by enforcing the proscription against government supplying a motive for engaging in religious action. But it is impossible, if we are to give *"free* exercise" its full meaning, to blink the difficulty presented by religious exemptions from laws imposing general obligations. Take *Wisconsin v. Yoder*[109] and *Reynolds v. United States*[110] by way of example. To refuse to allow an exemption from a compulsory school-attendance law or an antipolygamy law is to provide the Amish or the Mormons with an undesired motive (fear of fine and imprisonment) to make a choice which violates their religious convictions. But to allow an exemption for those with religious scruples is to provide a motive (an opportunity to skip school, a chance to get married twice) for the nonreligious to get religion. The problem dissolves under current doctrine if the state can prove a compelling interest in uniform enforcement,[111] but that solution will be rare. A second possibility is to make school attendance voluntary and repeal restrictions on multiple marriages; but to do that for every law to which someone could interpose a religious objection would be monstrously impractical. The best we can hope for, if we are still to run a government, is to minimize the effect on the outcome of

---

[108] See text *supra* at note & note 99.

[109] 406 U.S. 205 (1972).

[110] 98 U.S. 145 (1878).

[111] The principle that the government may not supply a motive for refraining from religious action is not absolute. What it means is that when the government prevents (see note 28 *supra*), compels (case 1), forbids, or deters (case 2) a particular religious choice, it must have a compelling reason to justify the restriction on religious freedom. See *Yoder*, note 29 *supra*, at 215. For example, a draft with no religious exemption might be justified by military necessity. The received learning has it that the state must also prove its law is the least restrictive alternative. *Ibid. Cf. Thomas*, 101 S. Ct. at 1432.

How *Reynolds* would fare when measured against these exacting contemporary standards is not clear. It is possible that the Court would relax the demands made on the state along the lines suggested in Braunfeld v. Brown, note 30 *supra*, at 599, 603–04: "The freedom to hold religious beliefs and opinions is absolute. . . . However, the freedom to act, even when the action is in accord with one's religious convictions, is not totally free from legislative restrictions. . . . As pointed out in Reynolds v. United States, . . . legislative power . . . may reach people's actions when they are found to be in violation of important social duties or subversive of good order, even when the actions are demanded by one's religion." But the significance of the state's interest in preventing polygamy is cast in some doubt by the Court's recent approval of nontraditional family relationships. See cases cited in *Developments in the Law, the constitution and the Family*, 93 HARV. L. REV. 1156, 1279 nn. 163–66 (1980).

religious choices by requiring the state to take the approach that has the least influence on religious choices. And that will invariably dictate a preference for protecting free exercise. One reason is that any well-written law imposing a general obligation will attach penalties which make obedience more attractive than violation. It is more unpleasant to go to jail, for example, than to go to school or to avoid multiple marriages. That means that the motive for abandoning religious convictions (fear of imprisonment) which results from uniform enforcement is stronger than the motive for adopting a religious position (dislike of school or monogamy) which results from an exemption. A second reason, contingent though it is, will also often be persuasive. It is undeniable that there is an element of self-interest in complying with most laws (going to school, avoiding polygamy), but there is none in paying a fine or going to jail; and to the degree to which complying with the law is appealing in itself, making a religious exemption will not provide a motive for people to adopt a faith they would not buy for its own merits.

The second perspective is also consistent with those Establishment Clause cases holding that the state can provide benefits to religion provided they are no different from the benefits given to competing nonreligious choices. Providing free bus transportation to parochial schoolchildren does not affect the balance of motives for choosing a religious school if free rides are also given to the public schoolchildren.[112] Of couse, the cases concerning school aid hold that there is something more at issue than neutrality under the Establishment Clause. But tacking on an entanglement codicil to the general neutrality principle does not affect what I have said about free exercise, so I can safely leave to others the decision whether that is a good idea.[113]

---

[112] See Everson v. Board of Education, note 68 *supra*, at 18. *Cf.* Walz v. Tax Commission, note 68 *supra*, at 664, 672–73; *id.* at 696–97 (Harlan, J., concurring).

[113] For suggestions that the entanglement test has not been a notable success see Choper, *The Religion Clauses of the First Amendment: Reconciling the Conflict*, 41 U. PITT. L. REV. 673 (1980); Kurland, *The Irrelevance of the Constitution: The Religion Clauses of the First Amendment and the Supreme Court*, 24 VILLANOVA L. REV. 3, 19–20 (1978).

DANIEL D. POLSBY

CANDIDATE ACCESS TO THE AIR:
THE UNCERTAIN FUTURE OF
BROADCASTER DISCRETION

I. INTRODUCTION

On July 1, 1981, the Supreme Court of the United States decided *CBS, Inc. v. FCC.*[1] Anyone walking that morning near Farragut Square in Washington, D.C., where the communications lawyers roost, or along "network row" in midtown Manhattan, would have heard the unmistakable sound of gnashing teeth and rending garments. The Court interpreted the Communications Act to grant a legally enforceable right of access to the airways to someone other than the licensee. According to the Court, a 1972 amendment to the Act, Section 312(a)(7),[2] entitled "legally qualified candidates for federal elective office" to "purchase reasonable amounts of time" from broadcast stations on behalf of their candidacies.[3] This was not the first time the Court upheld a right of

---

Daniel D. Polsby is Visiting Professor of Law, Cornell University, and Professor of Law, Northwestern University.

AUTHOR'S NOTE: Grateful acknowledgement must be made to the research assistance of Albert Bender and Tomas Szoboszlai. Useful comments on an early draft were received from Robert W. Bennett, Mayer G. Freed, John P. Heinz, Nathaniel L. Nathanson, Glen O. Robinson, and Matthew Spitzer. However, the mistakes in this article remain the sole property of the author.

[1] 101 S. Ct. 2813 (1981).

[2] 47 U.S.C. § 312(a)(7).

[3] "The Commission may revoke any Station license . . . (7) for willful or repeated failure to allow reasonable access to or to permit purchase of reasonable amounts of time for the use of a

access: the seminal case of *Red Lion Broadcasting v. FCC*[4] had declared something like it twelve years earlier. But the right announced in *Red Lion* was a right of an individual to respond in certain circumstances to a personal attack made on the air.[5] The *CBS* right of access was different, in that it was not contingent on anything that had previously occurred on the broadcast air.

The *CBS* holding was altogether unremarkable, both as an exercise of statutory construction and as an interpretation of constitutional precedent. The statute does seem to grant candidates a right of access, and it had long been understood to do so by the Federal Communications Commission, which has the legal responsibility for interpreting it, and by important members of the Congress and of the broadcast industry as well. But those who have followed the development of broadcast communications policy in the past few years may nevertheless have found the Court's holding a bit out of the ordinary. Until the *CBS* decision was handed down, broadcasters had some ground for believing that the administrative and constitutional law of broadcasting was moving tidally in the direction of their interests. The *CBS* case obviously represents a major disappointment to their hopes and presents numerous practical problems. No one can say, of course, just how these problems will develop; that depends on the future conduct of the industry, the FCC, and the courts. But it does seem a safe bet that unhappy consequences of some sort are likely. The only satisfactory way for public policy to avoid these consequences is to treat candidate access to the air waves (as well as other content-based obligations that are placed on broadcasters) precisely as these matters are treated in relation to newspapers and magazines—which is to say that they should be treated not at all.

II. The Access Wars

In the past decade, "access" in communications law has been a widely touted idea, and more than that, a populist battle flag, a rallying point for communications media reform. The basic idea of "access" is that some overarching principle of law, sometimes lo-

---

broadcasting station by a legally qualified candidate for federal elective office on behalf of his candidacy" (47 U.S.C. § 312(a)(7)).

[4] 395 U.S. 367 (1969).

[5] See text at notes 14–17.

cated in the First Amendment to the Constitution and sometimes thought to be present in the Communications Act, deprives the Federal Communications Commission of considerable legislative discretion in shaping communications policy. The FCC itself, quite understandably, was never enthusiastic about access, but writers in law reviews were,[6] and so was the United States Court of Appeals for the District of Columbia Circuit, prodded by the energetic legal staffs of several foundation-funded public interest law firms,[7] such as the Citizens Communication Center, the National Citizens Committee for Broadcasting, and the Media Access Project, whose tireless advocacy before the courts gained some important, if temporary, victories for the cause.

If there is an "original understanding" about the basic terms on which licensees of commercial broadcast stations hold their franchises, it is probably reflected in the 1940 decision of the Supreme Court in *FCC v. Sanders Bros. Radio Station*[8] that broadcast stations are not common carriers, from which it follows that they are under no obligation to yield broadcast time on demand to paying customers. The legislative history of the original Communications Act supports the notion that Congress intended to use the ether, not as an agent of moral uplift, but more prosaically to establish numerous private broadcasting businesses in communities throughout the country.[9] At the time the Communications Act was debated in

---

[6] Barron, *Access to the Press—a New First Amendment Right*, 80 HARV. L. REV. 1641 (1967), is the leading article. See also Johnson & Westen, *A Twentieth Century Soapbox: The Right to Purchase Radio and Television Time*, 57 VA. L. REV. 574 (1971); Botein, *Clearing the Airwaves for Access, 59 A.B.A.J.* 38 (1973); Canby, *The First Amendment Right to Persuade: Access to Radio and Television*, 19 U.C.L.A. L. REV. 723 (1972); Barron, *Access—the Only Choice for the Media?* 48 TEX L. REV. 766 (1970).

[7] See Schneyer, *An Overview of Public Interest Law Activity in the Communications Field*, 1977 WISC. L. REV. 619.

[8] 309 U.S. 470 (1940).

[9] For example, during the Senate debates of the Radio Act, the predecessor to the Communications Act, the question arose whether radio broadcasters ought to be forbidden to install meters on radios, which would prevent listening to them until a fee was paid. Senator Dill, one of the legislative leaders in communications policy and later the architect of the Communications Act, responded that Congress need not fear this contingency because "a broadcasting station that intended to put on such a device would immediately so limit its listeners that it would lose its chief means of support, namely its advertising. . . ." But suppose a station did opt for a "pay for play" apparatus? Senator Dill responded: ". . . [H]ave we reached the point in this country where we are going to forbid men to use radio as a means of business as well as other things? . . . I know of no reason why Congress should interfere with that kind of private business any more than it should interfere with any other kind of private business." 68 CONG. REC. 2881 (Feb 3, 1927).

Congress, there was substantial support for fastening upon broadcasters certain specific obligations to carry educational and public affairs programming,[10] but these proposals were defeated, and so was born the orthodoxy of maximum broadcaster control of its licensed frequency, subject only to the fuzzy, all-but-unenforceable duty to operate "in the public interest." The "access" movement (and it was nothing less than a movement)[11] was a heresy that sprang from this orthodoxy.

The access theory is supposed by its proponents to have one basic task: promoting freedom of speech. The greater the diversity of voices that find an outlet in the media of mass communications, the more different things the public will be able to listen to, and the more different people will have the opportunity to speak. Allowing people to demand time from licensees to air their views makes for greater diversity; restricting the number of broadcast stations to which a single broadcaster can be licensed also makes for more diversity. The First Amendment ought to enlist on the side of more diversity; that is, it should favor, if not command, the adoption of policies that are calculated to foster the expression of "a multitude of tongues."[12] During the past decade, a series of important cases were brought to test whether the diversity notion upon which the access concept is based would displace the orthodoxy of the "original understanding" with its preference for giving the discretion of broadcast licensees a heavy, practically decisive weight in deciding what material is broadcast over the air.

Although there was some preliminary rumbling in the law reviews,[13] the access wars began in earnest on June 9, 1969, when the Supreme Court decided *Red Lion Broadcasting Co. v. FCC.*[14] In that case, a broadcaster declined, on constitutional grounds, to abide by a provision of the FCC's fairness doctrine which obliges licensees to

---

[10] Senator Wagner, the leading spokesman for this point of view, proposed that the Communications Act transfer 25 percent of the available frequencies to "nonprofit" organizations of an educational, cultural, or religious character. This proposal was defeated, essentially on practical grounds. Senator Dill made the point colorfully: "[Congress or somebody else would have to determine] how much of the 25 percent should go to education, how much to religion, how much to Catholics, Protestants, Jews, Hindus. . . . [A]nd probably the infidels would want some time." 78 CONG. REC. 8843 (May 15, 1934).

[11] See Schneyer, note 7 *supra*.

[12] United States v. Associated Press, 52 F. Supp. 362, 372 (S.D.N.Y. 1943).

[13] See Barron, *Access to the Press—A New First Amendment Right*, note 6 *supra*.

[14] 395 U.S. 367.

offer people a reasonable opportunity to respond on the air when their honesty, character, or integrity have been impugned during the presentation of views on a controversial issue of public importance.[15] The Supreme Court held that no such constitutional immunity as was claimed by the broadcaster existed: as applied to broadcast stations, the fairness doctrine was not constitutionally objectionable. In the course of its opinion, the Court announced a theory of the relationship among broadcasters, the public, and the First Amendment which has fueled the fires of litigation (and the hearths of countless private lawyers) ever since. "A license permits broadcasting, but the licensee has no constitutional right to be the one who holds the license or to monopolize a . . . frequency to the exclusion of his fellow citizens. There is nothing in the First Amendment which prevents the Government from requiring a licensee to share his frequency with others. . . ."[16] The Court continued, "it is the right of the viewers and listeners, not the right of the broadcasters, which is paramount [under the First Amendment]. . . . *It is the right of the public to receive suitable access to social, political, aesthetic, moral, and other ideas and experiences which is crucial here. That right may not constitutionally be abridged either by Congress or by the FCC.*"[17]

That the Supreme Court would uphold the fairness doctrine was not, perhaps, surprising; it was an FCC "old hat," and was the sort of doctrine that could be upheld on the strength of tradition and custom without the necessity of invoking any particular theory. But the Court did have a theory, and a novel one at that;[18] and the implications of this theory were not lost on the *pro bono publico* lawyers who had begun recently to take an interest in the FCC.[19] The *Red Lion* Court's language was, after all, unambiguous, and could be fairly read, not as dicta, but as necessary to the result of

---

[15] It could be assumed even then—*pace* Professor Barron—that no such legal requirement as the fairness doctrine could be sustained as applied to a newspaper (as the Supreme Court later held in Miami Herald Publishing Co. v. Tornillo, 418 U.S. 241 (1974). See 395 U.S. at 386).

[16] 395 U.S. at 389.

[17] *Id.* at 390 (emphasis added).

[18] The *Red Lion* court's theory of free speech was evidently influenced by the works of Alexander Meiklejohn, for example, FREE SPEECH AND ITS RELATION TO SELF-GOVERNMENT (1948). See 395 U.S. at 390. See Polsby, *Buckley v. Valeo and the Special Nature of Political Speech*, 1976 SUP. CT. REV. 7–14 (1977).

[19] See Powe, *Or of the [Broadcast] Press*, 55 TEX. L. REV. 39, 46 (1976).

the case. The broadcaster cannot make a good First Amendment claim standing in its own shoes; the public has the constitutional claim here—and a claim of real constitutional stature it must be, for it holds good not only as against the administrative agency, but against the Congress as well. How does one vindicate this sort of constitutional right, except by "access"? If the broadcaster has no constitutional right to control what goes out over the frequency to which it is licensed, unmolested by public demands "to receive suitable access to social, political, aesthetic, moral, and other ideas and experiences," it is but a short step to requiring that licensees surrender at least some portion of their programming discretion to the "multitude of tongues" in the audience who are clamoring to speak and to be spoken to by others.

That short step was taken only two years after *Red Lion* by the United States Court of Appeals for the District of Columbia Circuit, in *Business Executives Move for Vietnam Peace v. FCC*,[20] which declared that as a corollary of the First Amendment (and not merely as a principle of administrative law) broadcast licensees could not decline to consider accepting editorial advertisements from organizations desiring to advocate a position on an issue of public importance. After all, if the constitutional "right" is held by the people, it must be unconstitutional to deprive the people of this right.[21]

According to the Court of Appeals, among the First Amendment interests of the public in broadcasting is "the mode or manner—as well as the content—of public debate aired on the broadcast media. The *Red Lion* court itself stated specifically that "[i]t is the purpose of the First Amendment to preserve an *uninhibited* marketplace of ideas' [in the broadcast medium]."[22] The Court of Appeals recalled a precedent of its own, which said that the FCC was under an obligation to administer the airwaves "in such a manner that . . . debate on public issues is 'uninhibited, robust, and wide open,' "[23]

---

[20] 450 F.2d 642, 650 ff. (D.C. Cir. 1971).

[21] The response that the actions of the broadcast stations in this connection were not "state action" were brushed aside by the Court of Appeals, which considered that the "reach of the First Amendment . . . depends not upon . . . technicalities, but upon more functional considerations." *Id.* at 651. As "administrators of a highly valuable communications resource, subject to First Amendment contraints," *id.* at 654, broadcast stations are required, inasmuch as they sell advertising to commercial users, not to discriminate against other advertisers merely because of the content of the advertisement.

[22] *Id.* at 655 (emphasis in original).

[23] National Association of Theatre Owners v. FCC, 420 F.2d 194, 207 (D.C. Cir. 1969).

thereby summoning up the spirit of *New York Times v. Sullivan.*[24]
The court took note of a "most important . . . First Amendment
interest. That is the interest of individuals and groups in effective
self-expression. . . . [T]he public's First Amendment interests constrain broadcasters not only to provide the full spectrum of view-
points, but also to present them in an uninhibited, wide-open fashion and to provide opportunity for individual self expression."[25]
The First Amendment could not tolerate a broadcaster's retention
of total initiative in editorial control over advertisements. "[S]uper-
vised and ordained discussion" is not enough to satisfy the Constitution;[26] there is always "a strong First Amendment interest in
opening up channels for more spontaneous, self-initiated, self-
controlled expression."[27]

It must be said of the *Business Executives' Move* case that it makes
an entirely plausible use of *Red Lion.* By stitching together the
proposition that the constitutional right belongs to the public rather
than to the broadcaster, and the proposition that "a multitude of
tongues" will make for "robust, wide-open, and uninhibited debate," a right of access quite naturally emerges. The Court of Appeals' decision in the *Business Executives' Move* case was obviously the
high-water mark for the access notion; it is difficult to imagine how
the court possibly could have gone further in vindicating this
theory. But the victory did not last long. In an opinion nearly as
unequivocal as that of the lower court, the Supreme Court reversed
under the style of *Columbia Broadcasting System, Inc. v. Democratic
National Committee.*[28] The Court repudiated the entire theory put
forth below: broadcasters' doings were not "state action," nor did
the Constitution require the broadcasters ever to accept editorial
advertising. But the *Columbia Broadcasting* Court withheld one favor
from the forces of the old orthodoxy: it did not substantially qualify
the position it had taken earlier in *Red Lion,* but, on the contrary,

---

[24] 376 U.S. 254 (1964).

[25] 450 F.2d at 655.

[26] *Id.* at 656, *citing* Tinker v. Des Moines Independent Community School District, 393
U.S. 503 (1969).

[27] 450 F.2d at 656, *citing* Keyishian v. Board of Regents, 385 U.S. 589 (1967): "the
Nation's future depends upon leaders trained through wide exposure to that robust exchange
of ideas which discovers truth 'out of the multitude of tongues, [rather] than through any
kind of authoritative selection.' "

[28] 412 U.S. 94 (1973).

treated *Red Lion* as the authority-in-chief for this entire field of law.[29] If *Red Lion* was still authoritative, then the access theory, in some form, might yet prove tenable.

Throughout the 1970s, while access battles were being fought on other fronts, the bitterest theater of conflict, and the longest lasting, was the question whether radio stations would be allowed to change their entertainment formats at their pleasure (as the FCC and the broadcasters contended they should), or rather, whether (as the Court of Appeals repeatedly insisted) the Commission had to inhibit format alterations by inquiring into the impact of a changed format on the diversity of program choices available to listeners in a particular community. The regulation of licensee discretion in the selection of programming is access in a special form: not the claim that a licensee must let somebody else use the frequency, but rather that it must use its frequency so as to accord with somebody else's judgment about how it should be used. In all, there were six such cases, stretching over a period of some ten years.[30] The Court of Appeals' theory in all of them is consistent with the access notion in *Red Lion, Business Executives' Move*, and *National Citizens Committee for Broadcasting*: the public interest standard of the Communications Act[31] (standing in for the Constitution) carries a presumption favoring diversity of program choices; when a "unique" format— for example, one featuring classical music, or "progressive" rock music (whatever that is)—is planned to be withdrawn in favor of more conventional programming, the FCC must inquire, through hearings if necessary, whether the "public interest" will indeed be served by going through with the proposed change.[32]

---

[29] See *id.* at 101, 102, 121, 130.

[30] WNCN Listeners Guild v. FCC, 610 F.2d 838 (D.C. Cir. 1979); Citizens Committee to Save WEFM v. FCC, 506 F.2d 246 (D.C. Cir. 1974) (*en banc*); Citizens Committee to Keep Progressive Rock v. FCC, 478 F.2d 926 (D.C. Cir. 1973); Lakewood Broadcasting Service, Inc. v. FCC, 478 F.2d 919 (D.C. Cir. 1973); Hartford Communications Committee v. FCC, 467 F.2d 408 (D.C. Cir. 1972); Citizens Committee to Preserve the Voice of Arts in Atlanta v. FCC, 436 F.2d 263 (D.C. Cir. 1970).

[31] Several different sections of the statute advert to this standard. See 47 U.S.C. §§ 303, 307(a), 307(d), 309(a), 310(d).

[32] All but the last of these cases arose in the context of assignment applications, but the Court of Appeals' format doctrine would appear to be equally germane in connection with any other application provided for under 47 U.S.C. § 309(a) as well, such as an application for license renewal. See Polsby, *National Citizens Committee for Broadcasting v. FCC, and the Judicious Uses of Administrative Discretion*, 1978 SUP. CT. REV. 1, 19 (1978); see also, Notice of Inquiry, Entertainment Formats, 57 FCC 2d 580, 599 (1976) (concurring statement of Commissioner Robinson).

Once the battle lines were drawn, it proved impossible for either side to disengage. Radio stations continued to want to abandon formats that proved to be losers; activist citizens groups, assisted by a cadre of increasingly experienced and confident public interest lawyers, continued to bring complaints about proposed abandonments; the Commission continued to resist implementing the Court of Appeals' format doctrine; and the Court of Appeals continued to insist that its doctrine be enforced, reversing the Commission in almost every format case. All the while, the FCC was searching for a case with an auspicious array of facts in order to get the dispute before the Supreme Court. Finally the Commission hit upon the tactic of promulgating a policy statement concerning format changes: the policy statement itself, after being quashed by the Court of Appeals, could then be presented to the Supreme Court in the simplest and most straightforward form. The tactic proved to be effective. In *FCC v. WNCN Listeners' Guild*,[33] the Supreme Court, for the second time in ten years, dealt the access principle a devastating blow. In April of last Term, the Court said that the FCC was within its power to take a laissez-faire attitude toward the format changes of radio stations, and that the Court of Appeals was not within its power in reading the public interest standard of the Communications Act to require the Commission to do otherwise.

Read together, *Columbia Broadcasting* and *WNCN Listeners' Guild* appear totally to dismantle the legal idea of access. Whatever *Red Lion* really meant, by April of 1981 it was about as clear as it could be that the old orthodoxy had made a clean sweep of the new. Neither directly nor indirectly did anyone have the right of access to a licensed frequency. Neither the Communications Act nor the Constitution compelled licensees to sanctify diversity in behalf of their audience, nor was the Commission obliged to require that the licensees do so. But the Commission in the past had been authorized to do so. The proposition for which this line of decisions fairly stands is that the FCC retains broad legislative discretion to make communications policy, free of the rigorous a priori "diversity" constraints that the Court of Appeals would have imposed. Broadcasters had some reason to hope, however, that there was at least an element in these decisions that stood up for the fundamental im-

---

[33] 101 S.Ct. 1266 (1981).

portance of their discretion as well.[34] That hope grew dimmer in the last week of the 1980 Term when the Court decided that candidates for federal elective office do indeed have a specific, noncontingent, and enforceable right of access to the air.

III. The Problem of Candidates' Access

In October of 1979, the Carter-Mondale Presidential Committee made a written request for air time to each of the three television networks. The Committee asked to purchase one half hour of time in early December, at the time President Carter's formal campaign for renomination and reelection was scheduled to begin. Even then, President Carter was being challenged for the Democratic nomination by Senator Kennedy and Governor Brown of California; it was as yet unclear how these challenges would fare, and still less clear who the Republican nominee would be. By return letter, the CBS network said that it was prepared to make ten minutes of time available to the Carter-Mondale committee, five in prime time. ABC and NBC refused to consider selling any time to the committee, at least for the time being. ABC's letter was abrupt: "The ABC Television Network has not reached a decision as to when it will start selling political time for the 1980 Presidential Campaign, and, accordingly, we are not in a position to comply with your request.[35] The reply letters from NBC and CBS were more soothing. Each of them pointed to the large number of candidates who had already announced for the Presidency and explained the difficulties that might arise in treating everyone evenhandedly if the President's request for a full half hour of prime time was granted. CBS also mentioned that two of the candidates for the Republican presidential nomination had already made similar requests for time that had been denied.

Shortly after it received the networks' responses, the Carter-Mondale committee filed a formal complaint with the Federal Communications Commission and alleged that the networks, by refusing to sell the requested time, were in violation of Section 312(a)(7) of the Communications Act.[36] Several weeks later, the

---

[34] See Columbia Broadcasting System, Inc. v. Democratic National Committee, 412 U.S. 94 (1973).

[35] The letters are reproduced in the Court's opinion, 101 S.Ct. 2813, 2818–19 (1981).

[36] 47 U.S.C. § 312(a)(7).

Commission ruled that, early as it was, the presidential campaign had in fact begun, and thus the blanket policy by licensees of refusing to sell time to candidates was a violation of the Act. The Commission gave the three respondents another week to show how they meant to fulfill their obligations under Section 312(a)(7) of the Act. The networks asked the Commission to reconsider, and, when it refused, filed petitions for review in the United States Court of Appeals for the District of Columbia Circuit.

The basic question in the case is the interpretation of Section 312(a)(7). Depending upon how that statute is understood, candidates for federal office have either a specific and legally enforceable right of access, or a "fuzzy," practically unenforceable right recapitulating the vague obligations of the "public interest" standard of the Communications Act. The FCC chose the former interpretation, and both reviewing courts agreed.

To a great degree, the dispute between the networks and the government involved only a matter of timing. The networks have always sold time to presidential candidates, and in oral argument before the Court of Appeals, counsel for one of the networks agreed that Section 312(a)(7) obligates licensees to sell time to candidates at some point in the campaign.[37] When does the campaign begin? Nothing in the statute limits the application of Section 312(a)(7) to the period of political campaigns, but the FCC had adopted this limitation interpretatively. Determining when the campaign has begun is a matter for licensee discretion. The Commission has characterized this determination as one of fact, however, and has noted the pertinence of several objective indicia: whether national fund-raising organizations have been established, whether endorsements have been sought and granted, whether the news media regard the campaign to have begun, and the progress of delegate selection.[38] Chairman Charles Ferris, writing separately, emphasized that "an individual who announces his or her candidacy for an election several years off cannot expect to capture automatically the reasonable access rights of the statute by such unilateral

---

[37] 629 F.2d at 14.

[38] 74 FCC 2d 645–47 (1979); 74 FCC 2d 665–66 (1979). The Supreme Court appears to have understood the FCC as claiming the power to say when a campaign has begun as a matter of de novo discretion. 101 S.Ct. at 2826. The Commission, however, fudges this point somewhat: it defers to licensee discretion as to when the campaign begins, 74 FCC 2d at 666; but it also will make "its own independent evaluation of the status of the campaign" and judge the licensee's discretionary choice accordingly, *id.* at 665.

action." Whether Section 312(a)(7) meant what the Commission said it meant is a matter first of statutory, and then of constitutional, interpretation. The analysis of the FCC and the two reviewing courts were similar, and may be sketched together.

A. STATUTORY INTERPRETATION

1. *The language of the statute.* The agency and both courts were persuaded that the plain meaning of Section 312(a)(7) was that candidates for federal elective office had a specific and enforceable right to a certain amount of access to the air. If the statute is viewed in the context of the law that it amended, the conclusion is compelling. Prior to the enactment of Section 312(a)(7), the Commission had long held that licensees had a duty to provide a certain amount of broadcasting about political contests. This duty was said to arise under the "public interest" standard that is supposed to govern the administration of the Communications Act.[39] But in contrast to Section 312(a)(7), this "duty" to offer time (although not necessarily on an unpaid basis) to political candidates during election campaigns was not a right that could be enforced by any candidate. It did not apply only to candidates for federal office; indeed, it did not apply to candidates at all. Rather, it applied to the coverage of political contests, federal, state, or local, which, in the opinion of the licensee, were of special public importance. (The licensee was not, in other words, required to pay attention to elections for dog catcher or chairman of the local mosquito control district.)[40] If, as the networks contended, Section 312(a)(7) had been meant only to codify the fuzzy duty of the public interest standard, it would be strange indeed for Congress to adopt language that apparently changed the scope of the duty, making it at once broader (by zeroing in on candidates, rather than on particular races) and narrower (by restricting its application only to candidates for federal office).[41] In *Columbia Broadcasting System, Inc. v. Democratic National Commit-*

---

[39] See note 36 *supra.*

[40] See Report and Order, Policy on Enforcement of Section 312(a)(7), 68 FCC 2d 1079 (1978).

[41] See Memorandum Opinion and Order, *In Re* Complaint of Carter-Mondale Presidential Committee, Inc., 74 FCC 2d 631, 662 (1979), *citing* Second Report and Order, 68 FCC 2d at 1088 (1978); CBS, Inc. v. FCC 629 F.2d 1, 11–12 (D.C. Cir. 1980); 101 S.Ct. 2813, 2820–23 (1981).

tee,[42] the Supreme Court had dropped dicta suggesting that Section 312(a)(7) "essentially codified the Commission's prior" practices with respect to political broadcasting. But Section 312(a)(7) was not before the Court in that earlier CBS case; the petitioners' heavy reliance on an obiter footnote was hardly more than grasping at straws. When the time came, the Court showed little embarrassment in shrugging off its earlier comment and went so far as to chide the petitioners for parsing the language of an opinion as though it were a statute.[43]

2. *Consistent administrative interpretation.* If the language of the statute were not enough to decide the case, there was also a history of administrative interpretation (spanning two Republican and one Democratic administrations) which had, with a basic consistency, taken the position that Section 312(a)(7) does indeed impose additional and specific obligations on broadcast licensees with respect to candidates for federal elective office.[44] In a policy statement issued shortly after the enactment of Section 312(a)(7), the Commission interpreted the provision to create an "additional specific requirement" of access, over and above the requirements arising under the public interest standard.[45] Given the Commission's consistency in its interpretation of Section 312(a)(7), the position that it took here is hardly surprising. Given the increasing emphasis that the Supreme Court has laid on judicial deference to an agency's interpretation of the provisions of its own organic statute, it is even less surprising that both the Court of Appeals and the Supreme Court found the FCC's history of consistent interpretation persuasive.[46]

3. *Legislative history.* The legislative history of Section 312(a)(7) is admittedly ambiguous; it offers a few crumbs to each side, but croissants to neither. The networks, for example, could cite the fact

---

[42] 412 U.S. 94, 113–14 n.12 (1973).

[43] 101 S.Ct. at 2824–25.

[44] See Licensee Responsibility under Amendments to the Communication Acts Made by the Federal Election Campaign Act of 1971, 47 FCC 2d 516–18 (1974); 1978 Report and Order, 68 FCC 2d 1079, 1088; Political Broadcasting and Cable-Casting, 69 FCC 2d 2209, 2286, 2290; Summa Corp., 43 FCC 2d 602, 603–05 (1973); Labor Party, 67 FCC 2d 589 (1978).

[45] See Policy Statement, Use of Broadcast and Cable-Cast Facilities by Candidates for Public Office, 34 FCC 2d 510, 537–38 (1972).

[46] See 629 F.2d at 14–15; 101 S.Ct. at 2823–24 (1981). See also FCC v. WNCN Listeners Guild, 101 S.Ct. 1266, 1275 (1981); FCC v. National Citizens Committee for Broadcasting, 436 U.S. 775 (1978).

that Section 312(a)(7), when it was enacted in 1972, was not accompanied by a committee report mentioning specific access rights. Granting candidates an enforceable access right would be a major renovation of the communications law, the sort of thing that one would expect to see mentioned in the committee report. Furthermore, two prior attempts at amending the Communications Act that had been buttressed with very explicit access arguments had failed.[47] Given a history of extreme reluctance by the Commission, the Congress, and the Supreme Court to give the Communications Act "access" properties, it is not an untenable inference that Section 312(a)(7) might not, indeed, have been "intended" to produce a specifically enforceable right of access.[48]

There is also legislative history favoring the Government. There is evidence, for example, that Senator John Pastore, the grand panjandrum of communications policy in the United States Senate during his later years there, understood Section 312(a)(7) to mean exactly what the Commission had declared it meant.[49] And although the legislative history of the statute itself is not very clear, it is highly doubtful that broadcast licensees were really in the dark about the responsibilities imposed on them by the law in respect to federal candidates. Dr. Frank Stanton, then vice chairman of CBS, had grumped on the record to a Senate committee about Section 312(a)(7), and urged its repeal, because he thought it would do precisely what the FCC had always said it did: oblige a broadcaster to "make available to candidates for a federal elective office reasonable amounts of paid time or reasonable access to free time."[50]

Ambiguous legislative history has few nontendentious uses, and analysis of the legislative history of Section 312(a)(7) would not be likely to sway the views of anyone who found stronger arguments inconclusive. But arguments based on evident meaning and administrative history are very persuasive for the Government. It remains, however, to consider whether principles of constitutional

---

[47] S. 956, § 302(c), 92d Cong., 1st Sess. (1971); H.R. Rep. No. 1347, 91st Cong., 2d Sess. 7 (1970).

[48] See 101 S.Ct. at 2830, 2832 (dissenting opinion of Justice White).

[49] See hearings before the Communication Subcommittee of the Senate Committee on Commerce, 93d Cong., 1st Sess., Ser. 93–94 at 137 (1973); 629 F.2d at 12–13.

[50] Statement of Dr. Stanton. Hearings before the Subcommittee on Communications, Senate Committee on Commerce, 93d Cong., 1st Sess., Ser. 93–94 at 190.

law can turn the tide of the argument. The short answer is that, given the precedents, they cannot.

B. CONSTITUTIONAL CONSIDERATIONS

Conspicuously absent from the opinions of the Commission and of both reviewing courts was any extended constitutional discussion. For the FCC, this is a matter of routine; the Commission, an Article I agency, does not exercise "the judicial power of the United States." If it considers that a statute's requirements are clear, it will not hesitate to act in spite of substantial constitutional doubts, leaving the resolution of such issues to Congress and the courts.[51]

The Court of Appeals considered that the *Red Lion* case essentially disposed of the constitutional arguments against Section 312(a)(7) as interpreted by the Commission.[52]

> It is settled doctrine that the government retains the power to decide how and to whom to allocate the airwaves. . . . Section 312(a)(7) represents only a congressional re-allocation of the "use" of portions of the airways from the licensee to the candidate. The broadcaster's exercise of journalistic discretion—his right to speak and editorialize—is unimpaired.

The Supreme Court basically agreed with the Court of Appeals: the principle of *Red Lion*, once swallowed, does indeed appear to give the Congress broad authority, unencumbered by constitutional theology, to promote some free-speech interests at the expense of others. Here the broadcaster suffers so that the citizenry may prosper.

Moreover, the sacrifice that the broadcaster is asked to make is only that of surrendering inventory; the broadcaster retains substantial leeway to determine how much inventory will be surrendered, and at what hours. This point was also made by the Court of Appeals. The policy announced by the FCC does not arrogate to the Commission the decision as to how much time is to be sold; that is for the licensee to decide. The Commission's role is to review the

---

[51] See 68 FCC 2d at 1094 (1978); 74 FCC 2d at 665 (1979). *Cf.* Pacifica Foundation, 56 FCC 2d 94, 103, 106 (concurring statement of Commissioner Robinson).

[52] 629 F.2d at 25, *citing Red Lion Broadcasting Co.*, 395 U.S. at 390–91.

licensee's judgment for reasonableness and good faith. The practice of allowing licensees to make initial determinations subject to agency review is based on whether the licensee's judgment was "reasonable" (a means of adjudication distinct from de novo review) and is the way that the Commission has sought to cushion the sharp constitutional corners of outright government control of the broadcast media.[53] While the Commission does have the authority to decide what factors must be taken into account by broadcasters in deciding whether and when to grant access to candidates, determination of how those standards shall apply in a particular case belongs to the licensee. "Discretion remains with the broadcaster, but *not* discretion to act without reasonable regard to the standards."[54]

IV. THE PRACTICAL EFFECTS

A. IF LOGJAMS DEVELOP

The legalities of this latest *CBS* decision are straightforward; the practical effects are somewhat more problematic. Given the Supreme Court's decision, what will television be like every election year from now on? Will the prime-time schedules devolve into a tangle of candidates' propaganda films? Will regular entertainment programming have to seep through whatever cracks it can find in the logjam of paid political announcements? Obviously, this is a possibility.[55] Candidates for federal office—and especially presidential candidates, whose campaigns are publicly subsidized[56]— will be emboldened to demand more and more network time to

---

[53] This issue is discussed *infra* in Section IVB.

[54] 629 F.2d at 18.

[55] The FCC, however, is on record as doubting it. Report and Order, Policy on Enforcement of Section 312(a)(7), 68 FCC 2d 1079, 1090–91 (1978).

[56] The Presidential Primary Matching Payment Account Act, 26 U.S.C. § 9033 *et seq.* (1976), provides that active presidential candidates may receive federal funds to match private contributions to the candidate's campaign. To be eligible for matching funds, a candidate must *inter alia*, raise $5,000, consisting of contributions no greater than $250, from residents in each of at least twenty states. 26 U.S.C. § 9033(b)(3). Candidates remain eligible for payments until they withdraw or until thirty days have passed since second consecutive primary in which the candidate failed to receive 10 percent of the vote. 26 U.S.C. § 9033(c)(1). Matching funds may not be received in excess of a prescribed limit, which in 1974 was set at $5 million, and which since 1976 is annually increased at a rate determined by the Consumer Price Index. 26 U.S.C. § 9034(b). Candidates receiving federal matching funds are also prohibited from making expenditures in excess of the Federal Election Commission limitations. 2 U.S.C. § 441a(b)(1)(A).

further their candidacies. As of 1980, one half hour of prime time
on any of the networks cost less than $200,000, well within the
means of many suitors for the nomination of a major party. During
the last election, there were more than a few such candidates for
nomination who could credibly claim national stature and following. For the Democrats, there were Edmund Brown and Edward
Kennedy as well as the President; for the Republicans, John Con-
nally, Howard Baker, Robert Dole, John Anderson, George Bush,
and Ronald Reagan.[57] So long as preconvention candidacies are
publicly subsidized, there is no reason to suppose that the pack of
contenders will be any thinner in future election years. What if
each of them demanded a half hour's time on, say, two of the three
networks in January of the election year, so as to build momentum
for the supposedly crucial New Hampshire primary? Quite possibly, serious logjams could develop. If they do, burdens will be
imposed on broadcasters and on the public-as-consumers, although
perhaps the public-as-citizens would benefit.

Counting the three networks together, there are sixty-three
prime-time hours in every week. If a dozen candidates each received a half hour of prime time from two networks during the
same week, fifty-one hours would remain free for normal entertainment use. On its face, this burden may seem manageable, but
the picture is somewhat more complex. Networks have a limited
inventory of half-hour prime-time programming and hardly any
inventory of shorter programs. Unless a half-hour program can be
matched to a candidate's needs, a half-hour broadcast by the candidate will interrupt programming for a full hour. Television viewers
are assumed to be creatures of habit who tend to fall into a pattern
of watching the same programs week after week. If one of their
favorites is displaced or canceled because Governor Sawdust has
demanded time, viewers may very well turn to another channel. If
they like what they see on the other channel, a new habit may be
born; a certain number of the people who tune Governor Sawdust
out this week will not return next week to see the program he
displaced. The problem is exacerbated for the network if the days
in which time is demanded coincide with the beginning of the
television season (September) or the "second season" (January),

---

[57] There were, in addition, a few extra long shots in the race, such as Larry Pressler and
Philip Crane, who, if implausible, nevertheless could not be dismissed as "fringe" candidates.

when the past September's dogs and cats are put to sleep and new programs are tried out. These are the seasons in which networks invest heavily in promoting new shows in order to change established viewing habits. Being required to program significant amounts of candidate promotion in January will very substantially complicate the networks' lives.

Of course, it is a long stretch to work up great sympathy for television networks, profitable as they are even when down on their luck. But fouling up an honest business cannot be counted as a social good, whether or not one has any reason to sympathize with the owners of the business. A better answer to the network programmer's legitimate concerns might be that the burdens of Section 312(a)(7) will fall more or less equally on each network; all of their lives will be complicated in approximately equal measure. But this generality needs to be qualified. Whichever network is in last place in the prime-time ratings will have a much keener need than the first-place network to cultivate favorable new viewing habits among the audience. The first-place network will already have captured the loyalty of its viewers; the last-place network, especially if its cellar dwelling has become perennial, will be the one under greatest pressure to "do something," a goal that large-scale candidate access may help to frustrate. If it is more difficult to cultivate new viewing habits than to extinguish old ones, wide-scale candidate access could cut down on effective competition among the networks: while the burdens of candidate access may fall (roughly) equally, they will not fall upon equals.

The potential gains from a greatly increased volume of political programming probably focus on the hope that the citizenry will have more information about the candidates who are seeking their votes. How much more information there is likely to be about front-runners is debatable; these candidates normally receive generous exposure on news programs and in newspapers. But dark horses, always under-covered by the media of mass communications, will be able to make an end run around the editorial judgments of news departments, to take their names, faces, and messages directly to the people—such people, that is, as have not tuned to another station.

It is easy, but maybe not wise, to get carried away when extolling the virtues of candidate-produced campaign programs as providers of information. As television watchers know from the experience of the last few elections, it is increasingly a common practice for political advertisements to mimic commercial ones. Political advertisements, that is, are often short on information and long on patriotic *montage*, emotive music, flags, eagles, and cheering crowds. But sometimes a bit of information does slip through; and in any case, who is to say that appeals for votes ought to be directed to the frontal lobe of the voter rather than to the limbic system? Besides, for many voters, the preeminent issue in a presidential campaign is the character of the candidate, and not the evanescent stands he may take on various policies. If nothing else, campaign programming is apt to give people a sense for the candidate as a person, even though this impression will be filtered by the craftsmanship of highly professional marketing consultants.

It would appear, then, that the *CBS* Court's interpretation of Section 312(a)(7) could lead to a logjam of political programs by candidates, and that this logjam, if it does occur, would be at best a mixed blessing. There would be costs to the networks and welfare losses to viewers, with offsetting gains—although not necessarily large ones—in increasing voters' knowledge about candidates. But if there is some reason to expect that logjams may develop, there is also some reason to expect that they will not. Although we may confidently look for a spate of litigation as candidates file complaints with the FCC in order to vindicate their newly affirmed right of access, neither the *CBS* opinion nor the order it upholds says that broadcasters have lost the discretion to deny access demands. Broadcasters may not always say "no," and in denying access they may give reason for the suspicion that the denial was premised on improper grounds. But on the strength of *CBS*, it cannot be said that the statutory right of access means that candidates will always, or even usually, get their way.

B. LICENSEE DISCRETION

One of the premises of the Supreme Court's conclusion that the Commission's interpretation of Section 312(a)(7) is constitutional was the fact that the licensee retains substantial discretion to determine how it will meet the obligations imposed by the statute.[58] While the Commission requires that licensees have due regard for

---

[58] See 68 FCC 2d 1079, 1089 (1978): "We continue to believe that the best method of achieving a balance between the desires of candidates for air time and the commitments of licensees to the broadcast of other types of programming is to rely on the reasonable, good faith discretion of individual licensees." See also Summa Corp., 43 FCC 2d 602, 604 (1973).

the desires of candidates—the intended beneficiaries of Section 312(a)(7)[59]—it has not laid down any hard-and-fast rules as to what a licensee must do in response to a given demand, except that licensees may not adopt any hard-and-fast policies of their own "flatly banning access by a federal candidate to any of the classes and lengths of program or spot time in the same periods which the station offers to commercial advertisers."[60] Licensees are required to treat each case on an individual basis, taking into account the needs and desires of the candidate, the claims of horizontal equity to other candidates who might ask for similar treatment, the potential for disruption in the regular broadcast schedule, and the timing of a candidate's request. But how a particular request is resolved is left to the licensee.

The agency's position that Section 312(a)(7) gives licensees a substantial residual discretion echoes a related matter of long-standing practice. In connection with the fairness doctrine, the FCC has a well-established rule of deferring to reasonable and good-faith determinations by a licensee whether it has been guilty of a violation of the fairness doctrine. The agency's refusal to accord these broadcaster determinations de novo review is not merely a rule of administrative practice, but is, as the *CBS* court implies in connection with Section 312(a)(7), understood to be a requirement of constitutional law. It is possible, of course, that the rule of deference is mere lip service and that the agency covertly exercises a broader discretion than it professes to claim. Looking at the Commission's behavior in connection with the fairness doctrine tests for this possibility, because fairness-doctrine complaints, if they are prima facie sufficient, are treated the same, as a matter of procedure, as are Section 312(a)(7) complaints. The way that fairness-doctrine complaints have been handled in the past could provide a suggestive clue as to how Section 312(a)(7) access complaints may be handled in the future and whether the reasonable and good-faith exercises of discretion by licensees will likely count for much in the resolution of future disputes. Inspection of the Commission's fairness-doctrine behavior fails to substantiate the speculation that the agency furtively exercises de novo powers.

The fairness doctrine requires that broadcasters give adequate

---

[59] 68 FCC 2d at 1089 n.14.

[60] *Id.* at 1090.

coverage to issues of public importance and that the coverage of such issues be "fair" in the sense of accurately representing various points of view that are taken concerning those issues.[61] The part of the fairness doctrine that requires licensees to identify and furnish programming on issues of great importance to the community of license has been virtually a dead letter in the law.[62] Only once has the Commission faulted a licensee for its failure to present programming on an issue of great importance to its community.[63] Virtually all of the FCC's business with the fairness doctrine has concerned either the personal attack rules or the question whether programming on controversial issues of public importance had indeed been reasonably balanced.

The Commission does not of its own initiative attempt to police licensee compliance with the fairness doctrine. It relies on complaints from the public that the fairness doctrine has been violated.[64] Many thousands of complaints are received by the Commission each year, and in the vast majority of cases, these complaints fail to meet the Commission's (relatively stiff) standards for alleging a prima facie case of violation and are dismissed.[65] In a relatively small number of cases, a complaint does allege a prima facie violation, and here the similarity between fairness doctrine and Section 312(a)(7) complaints begins. A Section 312(a)(7) complaint always

---

[61] See 1949 Report on Editorializing by Broadcast Licensees, 13 FCC 1246 (1949). The doctrine also includes a personal attack rule: when the honesty, character, or integrity of a person is impugned in the course of a presentation concerning a controversial issue of public importance, the person attacked must be given an opportunity to respond. The personal attack rules "differ from the general fairness requirement that issues be presented, and presented with coverage of competing views, in that the broadcaster does not have the option of presenting the attacked party's side himself or choosing a third party to represent that side. But insofar as there is an obligation of the broadcaster to see that both sides are presented, and insofar as that is an affirmative obligation, the personal attack doctrine and regulations do not differ from the . . . fairness doctrine." *Red Lion Broadcasting Co.*, 395 U.S. at 378.

[62] See Comment, *Enforcing the Obligation to Present Controversial Issues: The Forgotten Half of the Fairness Doctrine*, 10 HARVARD CIVIL RIGHTS–CIVIL LIBERTIES L. REV. 137 (1975).

[63] See Complaint of Representative Patsy Mink, 59 FCC 2d 987 (1976) (failure of West Virginia radio station to present programming concerning surface mining for coal, at a time when legislation was pending in Congress that would regulate this activity).

[64] See FCC Broadcast Procedure Manual, 39 FED. REG. 32288, 32290.

[65] Complaints that fail to state a case of prima facie violation are almost always handled by staff acting on authority delegated by the Commission. In order to plead a prima facie case of fairness violation, the complainant must state with specificity such things as the particular issue that was supposed to be controversial and of public importance, and a basis for the claim that the licensee's overall programming has not been adequately balanced with respect to that issue. See Fairness Primer, 40 FCC 598, 600 (1964).

makes out a prima facie case and calls for further inquiry. When a complaint alleges a prima facie violation of the fairness doctrine, the Commission sends a written inquiry to the licensee asking for its opinion whether the matter complained of was a controversial issue, or of public importance, and if so, whether its overall programming had adequately ventilated the various points of view generally entertained concerning the controversy. The answers to these questions given by the licensee, although not legally conclusive, are usually dispositive. The licensee has leeway to decide that an issue is not controversial,[66] or, if controversial, is not an issue of public importance.[67] The licensee also has wide discretion to determine whether it has presented adequately balanced programming and, indeed, to define what kind of programming constitutes adequate balance for fairness-doctrine purposes.[68] The Commission has repeatedly said that it considers such deference to licensee discretion to be required by the First Amendment.[69]

The Court of Appeals has adopted the same view. In *Straus Communications, Inc. v. FCC*,[70] the Court of Appeals held that the practice of deference to the exercise of licensee discretion (except in cases of unreasonableness or bad faith) was in effect a necessary condition of the constitutionality of the fairness doctrine. If a Commission decision to overturn the licensee's judgment that it had not violated the fairness doctrine whiffs of de novo review, the Court of Appeals does not consider itself bound by the normal rule of judicial review requiring it to defer to agency determinations:[71]

---

[66] See Club Palmach Rifle and Pistol Club, 43 FCC 2d 411, 412 (1973); Dr. Michael Kielty, 69 FCC 2d 960, 961–62 (1978); Lippitt v. WKYC-TV, 53 FCC 2d 1195, 1196 (1975); see also *in re* Applications of Rust Communications Group, Inc., 57 FCC 2d 873, 882 (1976).

[67] See Club Palmach Rifle and Pistol Club, 43 FCC 2d 411, 412 (1973); Dr. Michael Kielty, 69 FCC 2d 960, 961–62 (1978); American Broadcasting Co., 56 FCC 2d 275, 283–84 (1975); Lippitt v. WKYC-TV, 53 FCC 2d 1195, 1196 (1975); see also *in re* Applications of Rust Communications Group, Inc., 57 FCC 2d 873, 882 (1976).

[68] See Robin Ficker, 65 FCC 2d 657, 658 (1977); Aircraft Owners and Pilots Association, 25 FCC 2d 735, 736–37 (1970); Cairo Broadcasting Co., 63 FCC 2d 586, 593 (1977); WTWV, 62 FCC 2d 633, 639 (1976), *citing* Applicability of Fairness Doctrine, 40 FCC 598, 599–600 (1964).

[69] See, *e.g.*, Minnesota Clergy and Laymen Concerned, 44 FCC 2d 767, 768–69 (1974); *In Re* Application of N.B.C., 52 FCC 2d 273, 285 (1975). See also National Gay Task Force, 58 FCC 2d 1213 (1976).

[70] 530 F.2d 1001 (D.C. Cir., 1976).

[71] *Id.* at 1011 (footnotes omitted). See also National Broadcasting Co. v. FCC, 516 F.2d 1101 (D.C. Cir. 1974) (vacated as moot, July 11, 1975) (opinion of Leventhal, J.).

We are aware that "busy agency staffs are not expected to dot 'i's' and cross 't's'." And we know that courts are generally "indulgent toward administrative action to the extent of affirming an order where the agency's path can be 'discerned' even if the opinion 'leaves much to be desired.' " But here we cannot fairly discern that the agency has in fact applied the proper standard of review. And in Fairness Doctrine cases that standard is itself so closely linked to protection of broadcasters' First Amendment rights that we cannot indiscriminately apply the principle of indulgence toward agency action.

If these expressions of the rule of deference actually find their way into the practice of the agency, one would expect to find quite a low ratio of prima facie fairness complaints eventually resulting in a Commission finding of apparent liability (licensees almost never plead guilty). And sure enough, that is precisely what one does find: the published reports of the agency (the *Federal Communications Reports*, 2d ser.) indicate that the agency overturns licensee determinations of nonviolation of the fairness doctrine no more than one time out of five.[72] This ratio is consistent with the estimate of the assistant chief of the agency's Broadcast Complaints and Compliance Division, Stephen F. Sewell, for fiscal year 1980, a period too recent to be indexed by the agency's official reporter.[73]

These data are merely suggestive and can hardly support firm conclusions. How is one to know that a one-in-five rate of reversal of licensee judgments by the Commission actually does represent a high degree of deference to licensee judgments? The short answer is that one cannot know for sure. In order to be certain of that conclusion, it would be necessary first to look at every complaint that was prima facie sufficient, and then to characterize in some rigorous, widely acceptable format both the adequacy of the licensee's explanation and of the Commission's action with respect to that explanation. But if it were possible to impose rigorous, quantitative

---

[72] From volumes 40–69 of the Federal Communications Reports, Second Series—a period of about six years between 1973 and 1978—it appears that licensees were asked to comment in connection with a total of eighty-six prima facie violations of the fairness doctrine. Liability was found in sixteen cases.

[73] In a telephone interview on July 13, 1981, Mr. Sewell stated that in the 1980 fiscal year, the Commission received about 10,000 fairness-doctrine complaints concerning radio and television broadcasters. He estimated that fewer than 100—perhaps seventy-five—of these complaints successfully alleged a prima facie violation, and that at most fifteen eventually resulted in the agency's overturning the licensee's self-determination of nonviolation.

standards on these judgments, there would be no justification in the first place for ever treating them as matters of discretion.

The proposition that the Commission does indeed accord licensees considerable discretion to decide questions involving their own interests that lie in a gray area is, in the end, only an intuition guided by experience. It is not an intuition that will be universally shared by people who have an opinion on the subject. Nevertheless, there is at least a strong aroma of deference present when the agency, out of tens of thousands of complaints covering hundreds if not thousands of broadcast stations, finds a basis for affixing liability for fairness-doctrine violations in only a handful of cases. To achieve this record without the aid of a rule of deference, broadcasters would have to be holding themselves to an almost inhumanly high standard of performance in connection with their fairness obligations, and it seems appropriate to be somewhat skeptical of this explanation.[74]

Inasmuch as the Commission's review of licensee determinations concerning prima facie cases of fairness doctrine violation is identical to that followed for Section 312(a)(7) complaints, there is at least some reason to suppose that the resolution of Section 312(a)(7) complaints will follow a similar pattern of deference to exercises of licensee discretion.[75] The networks and other licensees have some chance of avoiding the feared logjam if they handle candidates' access demands precisely as they now handle prima facie fairness complaints, that is, in encyclopedic detail, making explicit reference to the matters that the Commission requires to be considered in reaching a judgment. What the networks must avoid is the impression that was unmistakably conveyed by their letters to the Carter-Mondale committee—especially the letter of ABC—that a blanket policy of some sort has produced the refusal to consider selling requested time or has placed drastic limitations on the amount of time that will be sold when a presidential campaign is already under way. The pursuit of a "blanket" policy by the licensee is not an exercise of discretion to which the Commission is obliged to defer. This follows not merely from the Commission's protestations to this effect,[76] but more strongly from a diverse and

---

[74] See Fairness Doctrine Opinion and Order, 58 FCC 2d 691, 703, 709–11 (1976) (dissenting statement of Commissioner Robinson).

[75] But see Section VB *infra*.

[76] Enforcing Section 312(a)(7), 68 FCC 2d 1079, 1090 (1978).

authoritative line of cases holding that a refusal to exercise discretion, when required by law, is not an exercise of discretion at all. Even where the decision maker has discretionary authority to choose a result identical to the result that nonexercise had produced, the blanket refusal by the decision maker to consider an option—even though it might ultimately reject it—is error.

For example, in a context analogous to that presented by FCC review of licensee discretion, Judge Frank wrote for the Second Circuit:[77]

> Courts have no power to review administrative discretion when it is reasonably exercised. But, in appropriate circumstances, they can compel . . . an official to exercise his discretion where he has obviously failed or refused to do so. Such an obvious refusal occurs, we think, when an official sets up a class of cases as to which he refuses ever to exercise any discretion, one way or the other, if that class is not rationally differentiated from other cases, not within that class, where he uses his discretion case by case.

But insisting that discretion be exercised in a case, one way or the other, is not at all the same thing as requiring that it be exercised so as to produce a particular outcome. In *Wilbur v. United States*,[78] the Supreme Court spoke of mandamus "employed to compel action, when refused, in matters involving judgment and discretion, but not to direct the exercise of judgment or discretion in a particular way. . . ."[79] Similar policies appear to be applicable in federal appellate review of the criminal sentencing of trial judges: while the Court of Appeals cannot control the discretion of the District Court, it can and does insist that no "blanket rule" be followed in passing sentence.[80]

It remains to consider what meanings, if any, can be extracted

---

[77] Mastrapasqua v. Shaughnessy, 180 F.2d 999, 1002 (1950).

[78] 281 U.S. 206, 218 (1930).

[79] Sodus Central School Dist. v. Kreps, 468 F.Supp. 884, 885 (W.D. N.Y. 1978): Mandamus is available "to compel an exercise of discretion where the applicable statute requires an exercise of discretion. Mandamus is not available to compel the exercise of discretion in a particular manner." Further authority to the same effect is copious, *e.g.*, Work v. United States, 267 U.S. 175, 184 (1925); Adel v. Shaughnessy, 183 F.2d 371, 372 (2d Cir. 1950); United States v. Nebbie, 357 F.2d 303, 305 (2d Cir. 1966); Sheppard v. National Ass'n of Flood Insurers, 520 F.2d 11, 27 (3d Cir. 1975). See also Phelps-Dodge Corp. v. NLRB, 313 U.S. 177, 197 (1941); Safir v. Gibson, 417 F.2d 972, 978 (2d Cir. 1969).

[80] *E.g.*, United States v. Hartford, 489 F.2d 652, 655 (5th Cir. 1974); United States v. McCoy, 429 F.2d 739, 743 (D.C. Cir. 1970).

from the licensees' duty to "weigh" various considerations, and what "an exercise of discretion," as distinct from "a refusal to exercise discretion," might look alike. But it appears that the networks were not so much victims of an overweening agency, but of their own clumsiness. By treating the Carter-Mondale request summarily, rather than elaborately, before denying it, the networks made certain that the first major test of Section 312(a)(7) would occur on a set of facts decidedly unfavorable to them.

V. Problems with Discretion

A. RULES OF LAW AND RULES OF ETIQUETTE

The initial responses made by the networks to the Carter-Mondale committee's request for access could fairly be characterized as somewhat peremptory. But it did not take long for the networks to catch on to the strategy that would be required in order to give them some hope of ultimate success. Following the FCC's initial order finding that Section 312(a)(7) had been violated, the networks petitioned for reconsideration. At this stage, NBC, for example, agonized in writing over the factors that the Commission had required to be taken into account by licensees in reaching a decision about candidate access.[81] It wrote:[82]

> NBC considered [in the first place] and has, since the Commission's decision reconsidered the needs of a campaign for the Presidency generally and Mr. Carter's expressed "needs" and "desires as to the method of conducting his . . . media campaign. . . ." NBC has again, and separately, in light of the Commission's

---

[81]CBS's Petition for Reconsideration was similar in tone: it noted that the network had considered the desires of the Carter-Mondale committee to purchase time and had concluded that, given the early stage of the campaign and the substantially greater audience than five-minute candidate-produced campaign programs have historically enjoyed as compared with similar half-hour programs, it was reasonable to offer five minutes in prime time. CBS also pointed to the timing of the request for time in relation to the beginning of the primary season (the first primary was not to be held until seven weeks after the period in which time had been requested)—that at the time of the request, President Carter had not announced his candidacy and, possibly most important, that the multiplicity of other presidential candidates, considering the demands they might make on the network for equal treatment, precluded offering to one what could not feasibly be offered to all. (J.A. 169). ABC's Petition for Reconsideration contains nothing similar, but relies instead on an archly worded legal argument that the Commission's first order "seriously distorts the meaning and purpose of § 312(a)(7)," usurping for the agency "a dangerous dictatorial role" in the political process. (J.A. 187, 189).

[82] J.A. at 176–77 (citation omitted).

decision, weighed these considerations against other relevant factors including [the possible obligation to grant "equal time" to other candidates]; the timing of the requested broadcast relative to the overall nomination campaign; the pool of available programming time; the number of other actual or potential candidates for nomination for the Presidency; and the extensive coverage which the NBC television network has already given to President Carter.

The Commission responded:[83]

[W]e cannot find that any of the factors that NBC "weighed" against the needs of the candidate are persuasive. Neither NBC's original response nor its Petition articulate any adequate basis for its decision. . . . NBC merely asserts in conclusory terms it has weighed all relevant factors; but it has totally failed to articulate how it reached its result.

The Commission's cryptic response raises an important question about the actual content of the licensee's discretion. Moreover, the response raises legitimate doubts about whether the analysis in the previous section is overly optimistic about the likelihood that the Commission will actually give licensee discretion wide scope. Obviously, the agency was not demanding to see the scales that the network used to weigh the factors that were supposed to be weighed. Perhaps the Commission was reluctant to allow the network's lawyers to plead extra equities for a decision already reached by the time sales department (which had sent an initial letter of rejection to the Carter-Mondale committee) without regard to the required standards. But on its face, the Commission's response appears to be a demand for a more detailed explanation, and one must accordingly wonder how any "weighing" process could possibly be verified. What does it mean to treat each case on an individual basis, or to weigh factors before coming to a conclusion? The metaphor of "weighing" can itself carry only so much weight: in the end, such a process requires a judgment, which is not, except in a very loose sense, subject to public verification.

The entire concept of deferring to licensee discretion logically includes the need to give broadcasters great leeway to improvise. Improvisation is sure to lead either to inconsistent treatment of different candidates, or to the accretion of some sort of "blanket rule" to guard against inconsistencies. In requiring that a number of

83 74 FCC 2d at 671 (1979).

factors be taken into account by licensees facing candidates' Section 312(a)(7) access requests, the Commission requires broadcasters to engage in the sort of multicriteria choice process that Professor Matthew Spitzer has shown, in a related context, to lead inevitably to unacceptable results.[84] If the FCC were not tethered by a rule of deference, it could impeach any decision a licensee might make concerning a Section 312(a)(7) request for time, for it has specifically prohibited broadcasters from following blanket rules to decide Section 312(a)(7) complaints; each case must be treated individually. At the same time the "equal treatment" provision of Section 315 of the Communications Act would seem to elevate the principle of horizontal equity among candidates to a requirement of positive law.[85] Licensees may not accord substantially different treatment to similarly situated candidates. The rule of deference, in other words, cannot be accommodated to a regulatory regime in which the broadcaster's decisions are held to high standards of both rationality and individuation. Beyond a certain point, the Commission's demand for more and more explanation of a broadcaster's discretionary choice simply dissolves into the cry of the wild goose.

How much individuation of treatment, then, will be tolerated? There are two possibilities. The first is that, contrary to my guess, licensee discretion over candidate access will turn out to be a will-o'-the-wisp, and licensees will be obliged to offer candidates approximately what they want, when they want it. If this occurs, Section 312(a)(7) begins to take on dark constitutional overtones, for the reasons suggested by the Court of Appeals in *Straus Communications*: the constitutionality of substantial, content-based government impositions on broadcasters has generally been understood to be premised on the maintenance of great residual discretion in the

---

[84] See Spitzer, *Multicriteria Choice Processes: An Application of Public Choice Theory to Bakke, the FCC, and the Courts*, 88 YALE L. J. 717 (1979).

[85] In determining equal opportunities under Section 315, primary elections and conventions are considered separately from the general election. During the primaries equal time need only be furnished to candidates within their own primary election, as candidates from different parties vying for the same office do not become "opposing candidates" until the primaries are concluded and the general campaign begins. See Kay v. FCC, 443 F.2d 638 (D.C. Cir. 1970); *Use of Broadcast Facilities by Candidates for Public Office*, 35 FED. REG. 13048, 13059 (1970). See also Georgia Socialist Workers Campaign, 48 FCC 2d 233 (1974); Badaracco v. KMOX, 54 FCC 2d 1029 (1975); Ryan v. T. V. Networks 58 FCC 2d 666 (1976); Pabst v. KTRH, 59 FCC 2d 405 (1976); Shaw v. KPOP, 59 FCC 2d 656 (1976). There seems to be little doubt, however, that licensees could not treat Section 312(a)(7) demandants differently, whether they were rivals for the same nomination or not, Section 315's narrow scope notwithstanding.

licensees. The second possibility is that the rule of Section 312(a)(7) is not at all the sort of hard-edged legal rule that can be profitably pursued to its remote logical implications but is more of a rule of etiquette: when candidates demand access time, broadcasters must sit down with them and negotiate in good faith toward a mutually satisfactory resolution of the concerns of each.

There is a suggestive analogy in the National Labor Relations Act, Sections 8(a)(5) and 8(d).[86] Section 8(a)(5) makes it an unfair labor practice for an employer to refuse to bargain collectively with the representatives of its employees; Section 8(d) defines such bargaining as "the mutual obligation of the employer and the representative of the employees to meet at reasonable times and confer in good faith . . . but such obligation does not compel either party to agree to a proposal or require the making of a concession." The statute neither compels agreement nor regulates substantive terms of an agreement,[87] but it does require that there be made " 'every reasonable effort to reach an agreement.' "[88] The duty to bargain in good faith is not, of course, capable of effortless application: "Obviously there is tension between the principle that the parties need not contract on any specific terms and a practical enforcement of the principle that they are bound to deal with each other in a serious attempt to resolve differences and reach a common ground."[89] But at least the statute is clear that employers may not refuse, directly or by subterfuge, to recognize that employee representatives have in principle a proper claim upon their attention.[90]

A similar principle, perhaps, governs the broadcaster's duty to a candidate who requests access time. The broadcaster, in other words, must recognize the interest of the candidate, and it must be prepared to hold discussions with the candidate in order to determine how the legitimate interests of both parties can be accommodated. There is nothing in the FCC's opinions, or those of the reviewing courts, that requires more than this, although, as in the labor cases, it is certain to be true under the *CBS* reading of Section 312(a)(7) that a broadcaster cannot satisfy its duty by holding dis-

---

[86] 29 U.S.C. § 158(a)(5); § 158(d).

[87] NLRB v. American National Insurance Co., 343 U.S. 395 (1952).

[88] *Ibid.*

[89] NLRB v. Insurance Agents' International Union, 361 U.S. 477, 486 (1960).

[90] See Cox, *The Duty to Bargain in Good Faith*, 71 HARV. L. REV. 1401, 1413 (1958).

cussions and simply refusing to discuss the possibility of any departure from an initial "take it or leave it" position: good faith "is
inconsistent with a predetermined resolve not to budge from an
original position. . . ."[91]

B. DEALING WITH UNCERTAINTY

It is not yet clear whether Section 312(a)(7) will develop as a
hard-and-fast rule that presumptively requires broadcasters to sell
time upon demand, or rather whether it will be seen as a legally
imposed rule of etiquette like the duty to bargain in good faith. If it
becomes a presumptive requirement that demanded time must be
sold to a candidate, First Amendment problems for the courts lie
ahead—problems quite possibly more serious than those that have
been encountered hitherto. This sort of rule would be inconsistent
with licensees' continued exercise of broad discretion over broadcasting on the licensed frequency. But even if Section 312(a)(7)
develops as a rule of etiquette similar to the duty to bargain in good
faith, there will be serious problems.

The proposed analogy between Section 312(a)(7) and the duty to
bargain in good faith breaks down completely at the remedy phase.
Employers who have been guilty of a refusal to bargain in good
faith are subject only to an order requiring them to return to the
bargaining table.[92] Under the terms of Section 312 of the Communications Act, a broadcaster guilty of "willful or repeated failure
to allow reasonable access or [the] purchase of reasonable amounts
of time" by candidates may have its broadcast license revoked. This
is a stern penalty for a breach of etiquette. If such penalties are in
the offing, broadcasters are entitled to a greater degree of certainty
to guide their conduct. The need for certainty in the administration
of Section 312(a)(7) is even more acute than in the administration of
the fairness doctrine; although a broadcaster can also lose its license
for violating the fairness doctrine,[93] the Section 312(a)(7) context is
almost certain—as a practical matter—to present a more treacher-
ous situation. Section 312(a)(7) claimants, for network time at least,

---

[91] NLRB v. Truitt Manufacturing Co., 351 U.S. 149, 154 (1956) (opinion of Frankfurter,
J., concurring in part and dissenting in part). *Cf.* 74 FCC 2d at 668 (1979).

[92] H.K. Porter Co. v. NLRB, 397 U.S. 99 (1970).

[93] Brandywine-Main Line Radio, Inc. v. FCC, 473 F.2d 16 (D.C. Cir. 1972), *cert. denied*,
412 U.S. 922 (1973).

will almost always be people of national political stature, such as incumbent Presidents, Senators, Governors, and the like. Fairness-doctrine complainants, in contrast, are seldom persons of such prominence. Putting aside the procedural formalities, it would be only human nature for the FCC to take the complaints of an influential Section 312(a)(7) claimant with above-average seriousness, which would necessarily correspond with giving licensee judgments below-average deference. The matter is most poignant, of course, when the claimant is the President, because the Chairman of the Commission is appointed by the President and can be removed from the Chair at the President's pleasure. How, then, shall a tolerable degree of certainty be obtained?

In 1978, the Commission looked toward the possibility of enhancing certainty and considered whether it should attempt to clarify the obligations of licensees under Section 312(a)(7) by making, for example, specific rules about what lengths of program time should be made available or whether candidates should be entitled to have short "spot" announcements broadcast at certain times.[94] The proposal was met with heated opposition from the broadcasting industry,[95] but its objections were raised at a time when it was not clear that Section 312(a)(7) actually added obligations to the routine "public interest" obligations of licensees, or that licensees could be blamed for refusing to sell time without an agonizing appraisal of circumstances. The *CBS* case, having put a quietus on that uncertainty, has opened the door on a whole new world of uncertainty. Now the question must be faced: how many licensees order their affairs to be certain that they will not risk losing their licenses, which, in the networks' case, are among the most valuable broadcast franchises in the United States.

There are several possible approaches. One could be implemented by the licensees themselves; they could play safe by selling time on demand. Broadcasters would never be reprimanded by the Commission for adopting this strategy, even though it surely smacks of abandoning a considerable degree of discretion to program for "the public interest"—assuming that consumer welfare (the programs that people want to see) has at least some claim to

---

[94] Notice of Inquiry, Commission Policy in Enforcing Section 312(a)(7) of the Communications Act, 43 FED REG. 12938 (1978).

[95] Report and Order: Commission Policy in Enforcing Section 312(a)(7) of the Communications Act, 68 FCC 2d 1079, 1080 (1978).

consideration in competition with candidate-produced material[96] (which ought to be broadcast whether people like it or not). If networks and other licensees sell time on demand, they run the lowest risks of Commission reprisal, but correlatively high risks with the loyalty of their viewers.[97]

The administrative agency could also use its rule-making powers to reduce uncertainty by adopting specific rules of a more or less ambitious scope. On the more ambitious side, the FCC could require that licensees set aside a certain amount of prime time in every day of the political campaign, which could be sold to candidates in half-hour (or smaller) blocks in some "neutral" fashion, for example, by lottery or on a first-come, first-served basis. Such a rule would increase certainty, at least if licensees who followed the Commission-prescribed recipe were given the presumption of having complied fully with the requirements of Section 312(a)(7). There is, moreover, a time slot that readily suggests itself for dedication to this task: the first half hour of prime time, which by Commission rule[98] has long been off limits to network programs. But existing rules also exempt from this limitation "political broadcasts by or on behalf of legally qualified candidates for public office."[99] The first half hour of prime time is the part of the evening television schedule that is least valued by TV stations and their commercial customers, but it is far from clear that this time slot would constitute second-class goods from the perspective of candidates. It is, after all, the time period that follows a news broadcast in most communities. If people who watch these broadcasts can be

---

[96] The Commission has taken the position that it does. See Summa Corp., 43 FCC 2d 602 (1973); Use of Broadcast and Cablecast Facilities by Candidates for Public Office, 34 FCC 2d 510, 536 (1972); Policy Statement on Enforcing Section 312(a)(7), 68 FCC 2d 1079, 1089 (1978).

[97] Furthermore, it is not so clear how "time on demand" would actually work. What if Governor Sawdust, a candidate for President, buys a half hour of network time from CBS just before the New Jersey primary, while Congressman Shoehorn, a candidate for U.S. Senate, buys the same half hour from a local affiliate of CBS, thus requiring that the Sawdust broadcast be bumped. The FCC has indicated that local affiliates of networks continue to have discretion not to clear their time to receive network broadcasts (74 FCC 2d at 665 (1979)): in these circumstances, would Shoehorn's program have the edge (on the theory of deferring to the discretion of local licensees), or would Sawdust's (on the theory that presidential elections are more important than senatorial elections or, more cogently, on the theory that when a licensee automatically prefers a local over a national demand for time, it is following a forbidden "blanket rule")?

[98] See 47 C.F.R. § 73.658(k).

[99] See 47 C.F.R. § 73.638(k)(2).

assumed to have a greater appetite for public affairs programming, including that which is candidate produced, than average members of the audience, political candidates receiving access in early prime time could find that a substantial portion of their potential audience had already been assembled for them by the evening news.

What this sort of access system gains in certainty, of course, it loses in flexibility. There is no way of being confident that early prime time will in fact suit the strategic needs of most candidates; indeed, it seems likely that candidates would prefer to broadcast various messages of varying lengths at different times of the day. Accommodating these desires with a highly determinate set of rules would eventually become a complex regulatory business for the Commission and, in the end, would undoubtedly prove unpopular with broadcasters and candidates alike.

A less ambitious attempt to define the obligations imposed by Section 312(a)(7), along the lines suggested by the Commission in its 1978 Notice of Inquiry on the subject, would give wider scope to licensee discretion and hence would be much more flexible. But such a regime would, in proportion to its flexibility, leave substantial uncertainties about whether the obligations of the statute had been met. There appears to be no satisfactory escape from the dilemma of discretion and uncertainty. The inherent instability of the status quo, and the evident inability of the administrative process to find an acceptable point of equilibrium, entitles one to return to the underlying policy of the statute to pose a number of well-worn but still important constitutional questions.

VI. CONCLUSION: MANAGING SCARCITY IN THE HORN OF PLENTY

The difficult problems involved in the government regulation of broadcasting come down, in the end, to one problem: how to manage a scarce resource. The argument is familiar. The luminiferous ether, the imaginary medium through which radio waves propagate, has a limited carrying capacity. Only so many broadcasters can occupy the spectrum, and the government must manage the dearth. In the first instance, the obligation of government is simply the management of a commons: engineering standards must be set, signal interference defined, and the rules must be enforced. Otherwise, there will be no radio or television for anyone. But the powers of the government over broadcasting have long been understood to extend far beyond the powers of a traffic cop to include determining the very composition of the traffic.[100] Section 312(a)(7) is a part of this tradition. It announces plainly that broadcasters, who profit from a scarce resource at the sufferance of the public, must do something (it is not yet quite clear precisely what) when a candidate for federal elective office demands access time during a campaign.

The constitutional tradition is so firmly established in the cases that it might seem pointless to dispute it any further. But its rationale is too seriously defective to permit acquiescence.[101] It is ironic that the Court would sustain a major regulatory incursion on the liberty of the broadcast press just as the theory on which the doctrine rests has fallen into ruins. Although no one seriously questions that there is a role for government to play in the regulation of broadcasting, there seems to be no persuasive basis for carrying regulation of this medium to anything like the lengths suggested by Section 312(a)(7), the fairness doctrine, or other content-based legal rules.

Before the Radio Act of 1927, broadcast licenses were almost literally free for the asking. The Secretary of Commerce had no discretion to withhold licenses from would-be broadcasters[102] or to grant them on conditions.[103] A great many commercial broadcast stations came into being, and with them a great deal of mutual signal interference and jamming. For many years, the broadcast industry—such as it was—sought public intervention in the progressively deteriorating conditions, but was stymied by the view of both the Congress and the Executive that "the industry ought to regulate itself."

The self-regulation notion, however, was ill-conceived from the beginning, for unless it carries some sort of legal sanction, self-regulation simply cannot function effectively where entry into the industry is free for the asking. If, as was not the case, the number of broadcast licenses were limited, it very well might be in the interest of all broadcasters to submit to certain limitations on their opera-

---

[100] National Broadcasting Co. v. United States, 319 U.S. 190, 215–16 (1943).

[101] Indeed, the proposition is not merely defective in its "scarcity" premise but, even granting the premise, is a non sequitur. See Coase, *The Federal Communications Commission*, 2 J. OF LAW AND ECON. 1, 20 (1959).

[102] See Hoover v. Intercity Radio Co., 286 F. 1003 (App. D.C. 1923).

[103] See United States v. Zenith Radio Corp., 12 F.2d 614 (N.D. Ill. 1926).

tions: the choice, after all, would be between a license limited by common agreement versus one that, although theoretically unlimited, was drastically devalued because of spectrum chaos. If a rational, profit-maximizing broadcaster could be shown that its assured piece of a limited resource was more valuable than the average of what it could probably salvage from the unregulated system, it might well be persuaded voluntarily to submit.[104] But, where the right to broadcast is free for the asking, as was the case before the Radio Act, the incentive for self-regulation breaks down. No licensee would be assured how large its share of the resource would be; on the other hand, every broadcaster would have an incentive to compete, including by means that would add to the chaos (e.g., by raising transmitter power or broadcasting on two or more different frequencies at once), because while each broadcaster reaps all of the additional benefits of its own behavior, it suffers only its aliquot share of the additional collective costs.[105] And as long as the right to broadcast in a chaotic spectrum was valued at more than zero, there would always be plenty of additional entrants, each one making the problem marginally worse.

Where there exists a "commons," that is, a resource that is simultaneously "free" to all comers and yet not unlimited, there is always a danger that the resource will be overconsumed and hence spoiled for everyone. Some sort of regulatory constraint is required, either by enforcing the institution of property[106] or by direct regulatory intervention. The role of "traffic cop," therefore, is one that someone has to play in one way or another. But once the "rules of the road" are established and policed, there is no strong argument for government control of what a broadcaster must do that is readily distinguishable from government control of any other medium of mass communications. Unless one is persuaded by constitutional arguments favoring "public interest" impositions on newspapers and magazines, arguments for imposing "public interest" standards on broadcasters should prove unpersuasive as well.

The "scarcity" rationale for treating broadcasting differently from other media of mass communications for purposes of substan-

---

[104] It should be recognized, of course, that horizontal industry agreements to "rationalize cut-throat competition" might suggest serious antitrust problems.

[105] See Hardin, *The Tragedy of the Commons*, 162 SCIENCE 1243 (1968).

[106] See Coase, note 101 *supra*, at 17–35.

tive regulation has worn so thin that continuing to refute it would be gratuitous. The degeneration of the factual elements of the scarcity hypothesis continues at an accelerating pace as new cable and communications satellite services rapidly enter the market.[107] Except by the Supreme Court, hardly a kind word has been written in years about the supposed scarcity of spectrum space as a tenable justification for the substantive regulation of broadcasting by the government.[108] Indeed, even the Court may be backing away from the scarcity premise.

The proposition that scarcity is still important to the Court is an inference from the weight that the *CBS* Court gave to *Red Lion*, which did clearly rely on the scarcity rationale.[109] But it may be noteworthy that the *CBS* opinion, in its last paragraph, referred to the airwaves as "an important resource," but nowhere did it refer to this resource as being "scarce." Neither was "scarcity" mentioned as a rationale for substantive regulation in *FCC v. Pacifica Foundation*,[110] although *Pacifica*, too, relied upon *Red Lion*. Accordingly, it may be fair to say that the Court is inching away from the scarcity rationale, although what it will inch *toward* as a means of distinguishing electronic from print communications remains to be seen.

There are several likely candidates for the job of making this

---

[107] The burgeoning of these services is discussed at length in CASS, REVOLUTION IN THE WASTELAND: VALUE AND DIVERSITY IN TELEVISION 73–99 (1981). See also Besen & Krattenmaker, *Regulating Network Television*, 5 REGULATION 27, 33 (May–June 1981); Geller, *Making Cable TV Pay?* 5 REGULATION 35 (May–June 1981).

[108] The leading article is Robinson, *The FCC and the First Amendment: Observations on 40 Years of Radio and Television Regulation*, 52 MINN L REV. 67, 157 (1967). See also Karst, *Equality as a Central Principle in the First Amendment*, 43 U. CHI. L. REV. 20, 49–50 (1975); Powe, note 19 *supra*, at 55–58; Bazelon, *FCC Regulation of the Telecommunications Press*, 1975 DUKE L. J. 213, 223 (1975); Schneyer, note 7 *supra*, at 619, 679; Krattenmaker & Powe, *Televised Violence: First Amendment Principles and Social Science Theory*, 64 VA. L. REV. 1123, 1124–25 (1978); Lee, *Antitrust Enforcement, Freedom of the Press and the "Open Market": The Supreme Court on the Structure and Conduct of Mass Media*, 32 VAND. L. REV. 1249, 1309–10 (1979); Lively, *Media Access and a Free Press: Pursuing First Amendment Values without Imperiling First Amendment Rights*, 58 DENV. L. J. 17, 25–26 (1980).

Even commentators who profess considerable sympathy with content-based regulation have recognized that the scarcity rationale is unpersuasive, and rest their arguments on different grounds. See Barron, *Access to the Press—a New First Amendment Right*, 80 HARV. L. REV. 1641 (1967); Canby, *The First Amendment Right to Persuade: Access to Radio and Television*, 19 U.C.L.A.L. REV. 723 (1972); Bollinger, *Freedom of the Press and Public Access: Toward a Theory of Partial Regulation of the Mass Media*, 75 MICH. L. REV. 1 (1976). But see Marks, *Broadcasting and Censorship: First Amendment Theory after* Red Lion, 38 GEO. WASH. L. REV. 974, 979–80 n.37 (1970).

[109] See 395 U.S. 367, 387–89.

[110] 438 U.S. 726 (1978); see Note, 92 HARV. L. REV. 57, 159 n.82 (1978).

distinction, none of them at all appealing. Professor Paul Freund, for example, has pointed to "[t]he distinctive impact of television . . . and its potential for powerful partisanship" as a possible reason in support of regulation.[111] No one, presumably, would quarrel with the premise that television does have a powerful impact on society, sometimes for better, sometimes for worse. But whether that premise points in the direction of curtailed freedom of speech is doubtful. It should not be lightly supposed that a condition of the freedom of expression is that it will be in great part ineffectual, or that a polished knack for subtle partisanship in the private sector should invite the government to clamp down. Television is not the first medium of communications that has exhibited a flair for producing a powerful subliminal influence on audiences: if this is the criterion, one thinks of music, poetry, and religion as equally apt candidates for government regulation. Indeed, in book 3 of *The Republic*, Plato documents the dangers of these influences, dangers he considered serious enough to invite prophylactic suppression by the philosopher king.[112]

Another potential ground for distinguishing broadcasting from printed communications is suggested by the Court's opinion in *Pacifica*. Radio signals come into the home unbidden and without a substantial opportunity for the consumer to evaluate the messages they carry. Especially where children are concerned, this is an issue of obvious concern to many people. It is facile to suggest that keeping the radio or television set turned off would be a complete remedy. But while there may be some justification for policing in behalf of people who have developed strong reliance interests in the customary decorum of broadcast speech, that reliance will not be present if people are not led to believe that they may properly rely on the inoffensiveness of everything that comes out of the tube. In the complete absence of content control, it seems inevitable that most broadcast stations would see it in their interest to maintain fairly straitlaced standards of propriety, just as daily newspapers do. There is no profit to be had in offending one's audience. Given the number of options that are likely to be available to people who are easily offended, it is by no means facile to propose that such people stay tuned to stations that will be run so as not to scandalize

---

[111] Freund, *The Great Disorder of Speech*, 44 AM. SCHOLAR 541 (1975).

[112] PLATO, THE REPUBLIC 114–44 (Trans. H.D.P. Lee, Penguin 1955).

them. Other broadcasters would undoubtedly try to cultivate different audiences, with different tastes and less fragile sensibilities. But, at least to a point, the existence of such programming would not seem intolerable if it were not seen as incongruous, any more than T-shirts with vulgar legends, or jackets with antidraft slogans, are intolerable on the streets where, as one has come to expect, they are encountered every day without creating the smallest stir.[113] In short, the rationale for content regulation to protect reliance interests of viewers is largely dependent on the existence of such reliance in the first place. The regulatory justification is caused by its own effect.

Quite apart from the notion of scarcity or any of the other theoretical premises for regulation, there is undoubtedly some appeal in the notion that the government ought to demand a fair return from broadcasters, in the form of special obligations to "the public interest," in exchange for the protection and benefits that are conferred by allowing them to monopolize a public resource.[114] But further reflection should make it seem odd to think about the ether as a "public resource" at all. As a consequence of the famous experiment of Albert Michelson and Edward Morley in 1887, it has long been recognized that there is no such thing as ether. Radio waves are not like sound waves: they do not need a "medium" in which to propagate. The scarcity of spectrum space is simply the

---

[113] Of course it is as true for broadcasting as for other media of communications that some things will be "incongruous" or otherwise unacceptable irrespective of people's expectations. This is the domain of obscenity regulation. If obscenity regulation is permissible generally, there is no good argument that would specially exempt broadcasting from its reach. But matters of lesser indignity than obscenity do indeed appear to be tied to what people expect and rely upon—something that the *Pacifica* Court's "nuisance" theory may even imply.

[114] A more hard-headed criticism of imposing "public interest" obligations on broadcasters is that this system does not seem to work very well. The FCC has not been successful in its efforts to recapture broadcaster rents through the imposition on broadcasters of public interest obligations of various kinds intended to increase diversity and cultural or informational programming. LEVIN, FACT AND FANCY IN TELEVISION REGULATION (1980); CASS, note 107 *supra*, at 68; Crandall, *Regulation of Television Broadcasting*, 2 REGULATION 31 (Jan.–Feb. 1978). This finding is consistent with the speculation advanced here that Section 312(a)(7) may not, after all, pose much of a burden on a broadcaster who is determined to go to the trouble to avoid it.

If taxing supranormal profits away from broadcasters is to be considered an important desideratum, it would be hard to improve on the suggestion first offered in Comment, *"Public Interest" and the Market in Color Television Regulation*, 18 U. CHI. L. REV. 802, 811 (1951), that the right to a broadcast license be acquired through competitive bidding. Beside enriching the Treasury, this procedure would have other desirable efficiency-tied effects as well. See also NOLL, PECK & MCGOWAN, ECONOMIC ASPECTS OF TELEVISION REGULATION, 53–54 (1973).

outcome of government decisions about the frequencies on which commercial broadcasting shall be conducted and the sensitivity that shall be required of radio and television transmitters and receivers.[115] The cruder and less discriminating this equipment is allowed to be, the more "scarcity" will result.

If one is determined to make public policy by reification, no special ingenuity is required to see that other abstractions, no less intuitive than ether, could be characterized as public resources and could just as well serve as the premise for imposing "public interest" obligations on whoever "used" or "consumed" them. For example, "interstate commerce"—surely as real a thing as ether—could easily be treated as a public resource. The Court may, indeed, already have laid down the metaphorical basis for this sort of treatment by the pervasive use of such figures as "the stream of commerce,"[116] and the proposition that Congress has power to ensure that this stream shall not be "polluted."[117]

If "interstate commerce" is a "river," as the Court repeatedly suggests, why should the businesses that navigate this river not be required to make a fair return to the citizenry, in the form of bearing "public interest" obligations, in exchange for that use? For example, where would the *New York Times* be without the federal mails, the public roads, and the United States Supreme Court to deliver it from the vengeance of Alabama juries?[118] Does it follow, then, that Congress could subject the contents of the *Times* to regulation "in the public interest"?

There is, it should be clear, no shortage of casuistry available if the idea is to impose the sort of public interest obligations borne by broadcasters upon newspapers, magazines, or anyone at all. That we do not impose such obligations, and consider it to be out of the question to do so, is a reflection of constitutional policy with thoroughly respectable philosophical underpinnings. The persistence not only of the Supreme Court, but also of the Congress, in making the broadcasting business an exception to that constitu-

---

[115] See Coase, note 101 *supra*, at 33.

[116] See, *e.g.*, World-Wide Volkswagen Corp. v. Woodson, 444 U.S. 286, 298 (1980); United States v. Orito, 413 U.S. 139, 143 (1973).

[117] NLRB v. Jones & Laughlin Steel Corp., 301 U.S. 1, 36–37 (1937); Santa Cruz Fruit Packing Co. v. NLRB, 303 U.S. 453, 464 (1938); United States v. Urbuteit, 335 U.S. 355, 357 (1948). See also Champion v. Ames, 188 U.S. 321, 356 (1903).

[118] See New York Times, Inc., v. Sullivan, 376 U.S. 254 (1964).

tional policy has, with the rapid fading of the "scarcity" rationale for substantive regulation, come to appear increasingly indefensible. If Congress will not correct the problem, it is appropriate, considering the nature of the constitutional principle involved, for the Supreme Court to take the initiative.

Having said this, however, I must also say that obligations of the kind treated by Section 312(a)(7) are the stuff of good citizenship. It is sad when broadcasters do not live up to these obligations, just as it is sad when, as sometimes happens, newspapers and magazines betray the public trust through intemperance, corruption, or misdirected zeal. There is no question that the media of mass communications ought willingly to bear the obligations of good citizenship. The only question is whether, in a free society, they should be called to account when their government considers that they have not done so.

DANIEL A. FARBER

NATIONAL SECURITY, THE RIGHT
TO TRAVEL, AND THE COURT

One of the first casualties of the Cold War was freedom of travel. Although most Americans continued to receive passports routinely, others found themselves singled out for special restrictions. For example, Arthur Miller was denied permission to see the opening of one of his plays in Brussels. His trip was said to be not in the "best interest of the United States."[1] Perhaps the most frequent targets of travel control were artists[2] and scientists,[3] but other groups, such as Unitarian ministers, also faced barriers to travel.[4] Even dissident Congressmen,[5] federal judges,[6] and congressional investigators[7] were not immune.

Daniel A. Farber is Associate Professor of Law, University of Minnesota.
AUTHOR'S NOTE: The author would like to thank Dianne Farber for her editorial assistance and Professor Yale Kamisar for his helpful suggestions.

[1] See Parker, *The Right to Go Abroad: To Have and to Hold a Passport*, 40 VA. L. REV. 853, 858 (1954).

[2] See Jaffe, *The Right to Travel: The Passport Problem*, 35 FOREIGN AFFAIRS 17, 24 (1956); Comment, *Passport Refusals for Political Reasons*, 61 YALE L. J. 171, 176–78 (1952).

[3] Comment, note 2 *supra*, 174–76, 178 n. 58. A notable example was the denial of a passport to Linus Pauling, the Nobel Laureate. Chafee, *Book Review*, 101 U. PA. L. REV. 703, 705 (1953).

[4] See Jaffe, note 2 *supra*, at 24.

[5] See Comment, note 2 *supra*, at 176. For further details, see text accompanying notes 83–90 *infra*.

[6] See Parker, note 1 *supra*, at 859. In another instance, the government refused to allow travel by a lawyer involved in international litigation. See Boudin, *The Constitutional Right to Travel*, 56 COL. L. REV. 47, 66 (1956).

[7] Parker, note 1 *supra*, at 860. The informant had been previously imprisoned and then deported by Switzerland for his activities.

This period of travel control ended in 1958 when the Supreme Court decided *Kent v. Dulles*.[8] The court held in *Kent* that the President lacked statutory authority to restrict foreign travel by Communists and other political dissidents. Some twenty-three years later, however, the Court held in *Haig v. Agee*[9] that the President could restrict travel by individuals whose conduct abroad might seriously injure the national interest.

The *Agee* Court surely did not intend to resurrect the discredited practices of the 1950s. Agee, a renegade CIA agent, presented a much different problem than the artist involved in *Kent v. Dulles*. In an earlier case, the Court had already shown its antipathy toward renegade agents by imposing harsh penalties on violators of CIA secrecy regulations.[10] Moreover, the *Agee* Court went out of its way to distinguish *Kent*, which clearly remains a bar to purely ideological restrictions on travel.[11]

Although the holding in *Agee* was clearly incorrect, the route the Court took there is more disturbing than the holding itself. It might well have been reasonable for Congress to deny passports to individuals such as Agee. Nevertheless, the President quite clearly lacked the statutory power to do so. This conclusion is required not only by *Kent* but by intervening legislative developments. To reach its result, the *Agee* Court had to go to extraordinary lengths. First, while not overruling the specific holding of *Kent*, the *Agee* Court had to distort completely the *Kent* rationale; thus, *Kent* has apparently been abandoned *sub silentio*. Second, the Court resorted to extraordinary distortions of the historical record. Even a cursory examination of the Court's sources reveals serious inaccuracies in the opinion. In particular, the Court omits any reference to crucial legislative history which was brought to its attention in the briefs.[12] The historical materials that the Court does cite are misdescribed in significant ways.[13]

These flaws in the opinion go beyond mere defects of craftsmanship and suggest rather a breakdown of principled adjudication.

---

[8] 357 U.S. 116 (1958).

[9] 101 S. Ct. 2766 (1981).

[10] Snepp v. United States, 444 U.S. 507 (1980) *(per curiam)*. *Snepp* is discussed in more detail *infra* at text accompanying notes 146–48.

[11] See *Agee*, 101 S. Ct. at 2780–81.

[12] See text accompanying notes 103–27 *infra*.

[13] See text accompanying notes 74–102 *infra*.

The Court seems to have been willing to abandon all else in its eagerness to uphold the government's national security claim. In contrast, the possible effects of the decision on the civil liberties of other travelers do not seem to have interested the Court. For instance, the Court did little to delineate the limits of executive discretion in future passport cases. This attitude is the most disturbing aspect of the case. If it simply reflects the unappealing facts of the *Agee* case, it is regrettable but perhaps not alarming. If, on the other hand, it is an indication of the Court's future performance in resolving clashes between civil liberties and national security, then the prospect is indeed gloomy.

I.

Neither *Kent* nor *Agee* can be understood without some familiarity with the history of passport regulation. Two separate, but related, lines of statutes are involved. One line of statutes has authorized the Secretary of State to issue passports to citizens who request them. The other line of statutes, known as travel control acts, has required at various times that citizens have passports in order to leave the country, except when this requirement is waived by the President. These travel control acts presuppose that the executive has authority to issue passports, but they do not themselves grant this authority or authorize denial of passports to particular individuals.

The Secretary of State has been authorized by statute to issue passports since 1856.[14] In the nineteenth century, passports were generally not required either by American law or by foreign countries.[15] They functioned as identification documents or letters of introduction rather than as travel control documents. During this period, the executive claimed unbridled discretion over the issuance of passports.[16] Passports began their metamorphosis into travel control documents[17] with the passage of the 1918 Travel Control

---

[14] See *Agee*, 101 S. Ct. at 2775–76, for an account of American passport practices in the nineteenth century.

[15] Jaffe, note 2 *supra*, at 17; Parker note 1 *supra*, at 863; Comment, note 2 *supra*, at 172 (stating that in 1897 only four countries required passports).

[16] See ASSOCIATION OF THE BAR OF THE CITY OF NEW YORK, FREEDOM TO TRAVEL: REPORT OF THE SPECIAL COMMITTEE TO STUDY PASSPORT PROCEDURES 10–11 (1958); Parker, note 1 *supra*, at 865; Comment, note 2 *supra*, at 172–73, 189.

[17] See Jaffe, note 2 *supra*, at 17.

Act, requiring a passport for entry into or departure from the country.[18] In 1926, Congress passed the current Passport Act. The 1926 Act simply authorizes the Secretary of State to issue passports under such rules as the President may prescribe. No statutory standards are provided.[19] The 1918 Travel Control Act was reactivated in 1941 for the duration of World War II.[20] After the war, the requirement of a passport for foreign travel was extended into the subsequent period of national emergency.[21] That "national emergency" did not expire until 1978.[22]

Until 1952, administrative regulations under the Passport Act contained no standards for passport denial except in wartime. Executive orders in 1928, 1932, and 1938 gave the secretary discretion to refuse to issue a passport, but provided no standards.[23] Observers agree that passports were often denied on political grounds in the postwar period.[24] This is difficult to document, however, because the secretary's customary explanation was simply that denial of the passport was "in the national interest," with no further elaboration.[25] In 1952, for the first time, the State Department adopted a regulation expressly stating a national security ground for denial. The 1952 regulation prohibited the issuance of passports to Communist Party members, individuals under the control of the Communist Party, and anyone else whose activities

---

[18] 40 STAT. 559.

[19] See 22 U.S.C.A. § 211a. The executive continued to claim total discretion over the issuance of passports until the 1950s. See Jaffe, note 2 *supra*, at 21.

[20] 55 STAT. 252.

[21] See Briehl v. Dulles, 248 F.2d 561, 570 (D.C. Cir. 1957) (en banc).

[22] See National Emergencies Act, § 101, 90 STAT. 1255 (1976).

[23] See Executive Order No. 4800, §§ 1(1), 77 (1928); Executive Order No. 5860, §§ 1(1), 117 (1932); Executive Order No. 7856, 3 Fed. Reg. 805 (1938), *codified at* 22 C.F.R. §§ 51.75, 51.77 (1949). The *Agee* Court mistakenly cites these executive orders as part of "an unbroken line of Executive Orders [and] regulations" in which "the President and the Department of State left no doubt that likelihood of damage to national security or foreign policy of the United States was the single most important criterion in passport decisions." *Agee*, 101 S. Ct. at 2777. Actually, these executive orders focus on proof of citizenship and say nothing about national security or foreign policy. See Boudin, *The Constitutional Right to Travel*, 56 COL. L. REV. 47, 55 (1956) ("[n]ot a single executive order . . . sought to impose substantive conditions" on passport issuance); Briehl v. Dulles, 248 F.2d 561, 580–81 (D.C. Cir. 1957) (Bazelon, J., dissenting). See also note 25 *infra*.

[24] See Jaffe, note 2 *supra*, at 24; Comment, note 2 *supra*, at 174.

[25] N.Y. BAR ASS'N, note 16 *supra*, at 11 ("[b]efore 1952 one could search in vain for any standards applied with sufficient consistency to be called a discernible policy"); Ehrlich, *Passports*, 19 STAN. L. REV. 129, 131 (1966); Comment, note 2 *supra*, at 173–74.

abroad would intentionally aid the Communist movement.[26] This was the regulation at issue in *Kent*.

Kent involved two plaintiffs, both of whom had been denied passports under the regulation. One was the artist Rockwell Kent, who wished to paint pictures in Europe. He also wished to attend a meeting of a group called the "World Council of Peace" in Helsinki. The other plaintiff was Walter Briehl, a physician, who wished to attend psychiatric conferences in Geneva and Istanbul.[27] In an *en banc* decision, the D.C. Circuit held that the 1952 regulation was authorized by the Passport Act.[28] A lengthy dissent by Judge Bazelon argued that the regulation exceeded the State Department's authority.[29]

The government's position underwent a significant change in the Supreme Court. In its brief, the government argued that issuance of a passport was "wholly discretionary"[30] and that this discretion was ratified by Congress in the Passport Act and various travel control statutes.[31] To his credit, however, Solicitor General Rankin had qualms about his position. At oral argument, he was clearly troubled by the civil liberties aspect of the case. He continued to argue that the Passport Act had originally granted unlimited discretion. He contended, however, that this grant of authority was valid only so long as passports were unnecessary for travel.[32] With the transformation of passports into travel control documents, the fundamental nature of the passport changed, and the permissible grounds for discretion narrowed. That is, insofar as passports were used to control travel, the source of power had to be found in the Travel Act rather than in the Passport Act.[33] The Court plainly found this line of argument somewhat confusing.

The Court nevertheless held that the regulation was unau-

---

[26] 17 FED. REG. 8013 (1952), *codified at* 22 C.F.R. § 51.135 (1958).

[27] See Kent v. Dulles, 248 F.2d 600 (D.C. Cir. 1957) (en banc); Briehl v. Dulles, 248 F.2d 561, 563 (D.C. Cir. 1957) (en banc).

[28] *Id.* at 572–73, 576.

[29] *Id.* at 596.

[30] Brief for Respondent in Kent v. Dulles at 37.

[31] *Id.* at 36–57.

[32] Tr. of Oral Arg. at 14–15 (reprinted with original pagination in 53 KURLAND & CASPER, LANDMARK BRIEFS AND ARGUMENTS OF THE SUPREME COURT OF THE UNITED STATES 1089–1123 [1975]).

[33] Tr. of Oral Arg. at 26–27.

thorized by the Passport Act and therefore invalid. The opinion, written by Justice Douglas, stressed the importance of freedom of travel. Because this right is an important component of constitutional liberty, the Court construed the delegation of power to the secretary narrowly.[34] It was willing to construe congressional approval to extend not to all the power historically claimed by the executive but only to the power actually exercised. Putting aside wartime measures which it found irrelevant,[35] the Court concluded that only two classes of practices had sufficiently "jelled" to have received meaningful congressional acquiescence: (1) denial of passports to noncitizens, and (2) denial of passports to those engaged in illegal conduct. In contrast, the Court found only scattered and inconsistent rulings respecting Communists and held these insufficient to uphold the challenged regulation.[36]

Justice Clark, joined by three other Justices, dissented. Relying largely on the travel control statutes, he argued that Congress had specifically approved denial of passports in national security cases. He also pointed to instances in which passports had been denied during peacetime on national security grounds.[37] His dissent foreshadowed the approach taken by the Court a quarter-century later in *Agee*.

A companion case to *Kent* involved rather vague accusations that a physicist was in some way associated with several espionage suspects. Based on these vague accusations, his passport application had been denied on the ground that he was "going abroad to engage in activities which will advance the Communist movement for the purpose, knowingly and willfully of advancing that movement."[38] Finding this ground for denial indistinguishable from that involved in *Kent*, the Court reversed the lower court's judgment in favor of the secretary.[39]

---

[34] *Kent*, 357 U.S. at 125–27, 129–30.

[35] *Id.* at 128. The *Agee* Court relied heavily on wartime practices. See *Agee*, 101 S. Ct. 2776–77, 2780.

[36] *Kent*, 357 U.S. at 127–28.

[37] *Id.* at 131–43.

[38] Dayton v. Dulles, 357 U.S. 144, 153 (1958). This basis for denial seems almost indistinguishable from the standard applied in Agee's case.

[39] *Id.* at 150. Justices Clark, Burton, Harlan, and Whittaker dissented. They contended that "the Secretary of State is authorized to deny a passport to an applicant who is going abroad with the purpose of engaging in activities that would advance the Communist cause." *Id.* at 154. The majority apparently disagreed.

Two Supreme Court decisions from the mid-sixties should be mentioned as a prelude to the *Agee* case. In *Aptheker v. Secretary of State*,[40] the Court struck down a statutory ban on the issuance of passports to Communists. (This ban had not been in effect at the time of the *Kent* decision.) The statute was held to be too broad an intrusion on the constitutional right to travel because it indiscriminately presumed that all travel by Communists was dangerous to the national security. In the other case, *Zemel v. Rusk*,[41] the Court upheld a ban on the use of passports for travel to Cuba. This ban was implemented through language on the passport prohibiting its use for travel to Cuba. The Court found a consistent history of such "area restrictions" on travel. The Court upheld the constitutionality of the area restrictions on the theory that they were supported by the "weightiest considerations of national security."[42] The same considerations of national security would also weigh heavily in the *Agee* case.

II.

The *Agee* litigation was an outgrowth of Philip Agee's campaign against the CIA. Agee, a former CIA agent, is an American citizen but currently resides in West Germany. In the course of his campaign, he has been responsible for producing several exposés about the agency. His actions are not only a breach of trust but also violate his secrecy agreement with the agency as well as an injunction enforcing that agreement. In 1979, as a result of these activities, the United States revoked his passport.[43] This action was

---

[40] 378 U.S. 500 (1964).

[41] 381 U.S. 1 (1965), noted in 13 U.C.L.A. L. REV. 470 (1966). *Zemel* foreshadows later cases rejecting claims of a First Amendment right of access to information. With the exception of access to criminal trials, such claims have been rejected so long as the ban on access is nondiscriminatory, as it was in *Zemel*. See Richmond Newspapers, Inc. v. Virginia, 100 S. Ct. 2814 (1980); Houchins v. KQED, 438 U.S. 1 (1978); Pell v. Procunier, 417 U.S. 817 (1974). See generally LOCKHART, KAMISAR, & CHOPER, CONSTITUTIONAL LAW 36 (1981 Supp.).

[42] 381 U.S. at 16. Between *Zemel* and *Agee*, freedom of travel was less extensively discussed in the legal literature. For discussion of the intervening developments, see Ehrlich, *Passports*, 19 STAN. L. REV. 129 (1966); Comment, *The Right to Travel and the Loyalty Oath*, 12 COL. J. TRANSNAT'L L. 387 (1973); *Developments in the Law—National Security*, 85 HARV. L. REV. 1141 (1972). Much of this discussion was directed toward the problems encountered by the State Department in attempting to enforce area restrictions.

[43] These background facts are drawn from the *Agee* opinion, 101 S. Ct. at 2769–71.

based on a 1966 regulation authorizing passport denial when a citizen's "activities abroad are causing or are likely to cause serious damage to the national security or the foreign policy of the United States."[44]

Agee immediately filed suit challenging the validity of the 1966 regulation. Affidavits filed by the government explain in some detail the charges against him. The government was primarily concerned with Agee's repeated disclosures of the names of CIA agents, which jeopardized not only their work but also their safety.[45] An affidavit by the Deputy Director for Operations conceded that American officials have been deliberately exposed as CIA agents in "numerous instances" not involving Agee.[46] The affidavit also admitted that these exposures might have damaged the effectiveness of these agents. The affidavit maintained, however, that "there is . . . an enormous difference between an allegation of CIA connection by hostile foreign governments and foreign publications on one hand, and a similar allegation by a former CIA employee such as Mr. Agee on the other."[47] A later affidavit by the Deputy Director explained the reasons for restricting Agee's travel. Agee's ability to travel was allegedly essential to finding, recruiting, and training his collaborators. Also, his public announcements had greater impact, accordingto the Deputy Director, when Agee made them in the country involved in the disclosures. As an example of the harm Agee might do, the affidavit cited newspaper reports concerning possible cooperation between Agee and the captors of the American hostages in Iran.[48] Although the record is unclear, these reports seem to have triggered the decision to revoke Agee's passport.[49] For purposes of his motion for summary judgment, Agee conceded the government's factual allegations.[50]

---

[44] 31 FED REG. 13544, codified at 22 C.F.R. § 51.70(b)(4). An earlier version of the regulation, adopted in 1956, was broader. It covered all travel "prejudicial to the orderly conduct of foreign affairs or . . . otherwise prejudicial to the interests of the United States." 21 FED. REG. 336.

[45] This is made clear, for example, in the government's petition for certiorari, pp. 4–5 and 11; see also Appendices D and E to the Petition.

[46] Affidavit of John N. McMahon, Pet. for Certiorari, Appendix E, at 111a.

[47] Id. at 111a–112a.

[48] Affidavit of John N. McMahon in Support of Motion for Stay Pending Appeal, Petition for Certiorari, Appendix F, at 114a–118a.

[49] See Agee v. Muskie, 629 F.2d 80, 81 & n.1 (D.C. Cir. 1980).

[50] See Joint Appendix at 11, 14–20.

District Judge Gesell granted Agee's motion for summary judgment. In a brief opinion, he held that the 1966 regulation was unauthorized by Congress. He stressed that the regulation had only been used on one previous occasion.[51] The government had relied heavily on broad statements of executive authority made in hearings in 1957. Judge Gesell countered by noting that, in 1958, Congress had denied a presidential request for "the precise authority sought here." "Implied authority is not," he observed, "gained in this fashion."[52]

The government appealed to the D.C. Circuit, which affirmed Judge Gesell's order.[53] The opinion was by Judge Robb. After a careful review of *Kent* and *Zemel*, Judge Robb concluded that in the absence of any express delegation of power, the government needed to show a "'sufficiently substantial and consistent' administrative practice to warrant finding the implied approval of Congress."[54] Like Judge Gesell, he found insufficient evidence of such a consistent administrative practice. Rather, he found only scattered instances in which the power was actually exercised. Except in the context of war or national emergency, which *Kent* held irrelevant to peacetime practices, the executive had rarely even asserted the existence of this power.[55] Judge MacKinnon, the Court's most conservative member, wrote a lengthy and impassioned dissent accusing Agee of high treason.[56]

The government's petition for certiorari was granted on October 6, 1980.[57] In its brief and during oral argument, the government argued for a broad discretionary power over foreign travel. The brief particularly stressed the history leading up to the 1926 Passport Act as indicating congressional understanding of the secretary's broad powers in the area.[58] The concern for civil liberties expressed in the *Kent* argument was absent from the government's argument in *Agee*. In the brief, freedom of travel was dismissed as

---

[51] Agee v. Vance, 483 F. Supp. 729, 731 (D.D.C. 1980).

[52] *Id*. at 732.

[53] Agee v. Muskee, 629 F.2d 80 (1980), noted in 22 HARV. INTERNAT'L L. J. 187 (1981).

[54] 629 F.2d at 85.

[55] *Id*. at 86–87.

[56] *Id*. at 87–117. The treason discussion is at 112–17.

[57] 101 S. Ct. 69. The Chief Justice previously had issued a stay.

[58] Brief for Petitioner at 22. See also *id*. at 35 (Congress was "aware of the Secretary's broad discretion" and ratified prior practice).

not being a fundamental right.[59] At oral argument, the government made it clear that it was asserting a broad grant of power:[60]

> QUESTION: General McCree, supposing a person right now were to apply for a passport to go to Salvador, and when asked the purpose of his journey, to say, to denounce the United States policy in Salvador in supporting the junta. And the Secretary of State says, I just will not issue a passport for that purpose. Do you think that he can consistently do that in the light of our previous cases?
> SOLICITOR GENERAL MCCREE: I would say, yes, he can. Because we have to vest these—The President of the United States and the Secretary of State working under him are charged with conducting the foreign policy of the Nation, and the freedom of speech that we enjoy domestically may be different from that that we can exercise in this context.

This far-reaching claim clearly has implications extending well beyond Agee and other violators of national security laws. Apparently, the government sought the power to halt all extraterritorial dissent.

Chief Justice Burger wrote the opinion of the Court upholding the 1966 travel regulation. He opened with a lengthy canvass of the charges against Agee and the proceedings in the lower court.[61] Turning to the statutory issue, he began by stressing the broad language of the Passport Act and the need for deference to "the consistent administrative construction of that statute."[62] As Justice Brennan pointed out in dissent, this was a glaring deviation from the test used in Kent.[63] The Chief Justice then spent a considerable time reviewing the pre-1926 history of passport controls, concluding that Congress had ratified the "longstanding administrative con-

---

[59] Id. at 53.

[60] This exchange is quoted in Justice Brennan's dissent, 101 S. Ct. at 2788 n.9. In 1958, the government specifically disclaimed any power "to deny passports to persons whose sole activity abroad would be to voice their own opinions." Hearings on the Right to Travel, Subcomm. on Const. Rights, Sen. Comm. on the Judiciary, 85th Cong., 2nd Sess., pt. 2, 380 (1957).

[61] Agee, 101 S. Ct. at 2769–73. Agee has complained that the Court's version of the facts was inaccurate. See Agree, I Don't Need a Passport, THE NEW YORK TIMES, July 27, 1981, at 15, col. 1.

[62] Agee, 101 S. Ct. at 2774.

[63] Id. at 2785–86.

struction" in 1926.[64] Again, as Justice Brennan pointed out, this was an argument considered and rejected in *Kent*.[65]

Concerning the post-1926 history, the Chief Justice made three arguments in support of the regulation. First, he argued that Congress had been put on notice concerning the 1966 regulation and a similar 1956 regulation. He pointed to 1957, 1960, and 1966 congressional documents in support of this assertion.[66] Second, he relied on a 1978 statute amending the Travel Act and the Passport Act as "weighty evidence of congressional approval."[67] Third, he pointed to three instances in which passports were revoked on national security grounds. Despite the low number of incidents, he argued that the power had been consistently exercised because few situations involving serious threats to national security had arisen.[68] These three arguments are at the heart of the Court's opinion.

The Court also rejected Agee's constitutional arguments. It held that national security was a sufficiently compelling interest to justify travel restrictions; that due process did not require a prerevocation hearing; and that Agee was not protected by the First Amendment.[69] Since Agee's disclosures had "the declared purpose of obstructing intelligence operations," the disclosures were "clearly not protected by the Constitution."[70] In any event, the Court said, revocation of Agee's passport merely inhibited his conduct, not his speech. The Court left open the question whether Americans abroad enjoy any First Amendment protection.[71] Given the impact of Agee's writing on the safety of government agents, the Court's First Amendment holding is not surprising. The Court's rationale, however, was hardly limited to the facts of the case.

---

[64] *Id*. at 2777.

[65] *Id*. at 2785–86. The pervasive inaccuracy of the Court's account of post-1926 history necessarily casts doubt on the accuracy of its account of earlier events. In addition, the *Agee* Court's argument really proves too much, for what the executive claimed prior to 1926 was unlimited discretion. See notes 19, 23, and 25, *supra*. Yet no one, including the government, takes that position today. The government's brief, as noted in the text, claims "broad" but not infinite discretion.

[66] *Id*. at 2778.

[67] *Id*. at 2779.

[68] *Id*. at 2779–80.

[69] *Id*. at 2781–83.

[70] *Id*. at 2783.

[71] *Id*. at 2782–83.

Two Justices filed separate opinions. Justice Blackmun's brief concurrence argued that the Court had indeed, and in his view properly, disavowed aspects of *Kent* and *Zemel*.[72] Justice Brennan, in dissent, argued that *Agee* was clearly governed by those cases. He called *Agee* "a prime example of the adage that 'bad facts make bad law.'"[73]

The Court's opinion rests heavily on its analysis of the post-1926 history of travel control. That analysis contains serious distortions and omissions.

ACTUAL ADMINISTRATIVE PRACTICE

As evidence of a consistent administrative practice, the Court points to three episodes from 1948 to 1978. In each case, the Court's account of the episode is distorted.

The most recent of these episodes was in 1970. The Court says only that this episode involved "two persons who sought to travel to the site of an international airplane hijacking."[74] These two persons turn out to have been the lawyers of Sirhan Sirhan, the convicted assassin of Senator Robert Kennedy. Early reports of the hijacking had indicated that the hijackers intended to negotiate for Sirhan's release. These reports were later repudiated.[75] The government nevertheless refused to allow the lawyers to travel to the scene for the announced purpose of seeking the release of the hostages.[76] Oddly enough, the government did not attempt to prevent Mrs. Sirhan from proceeding with the journey.[77] This somewhat undercuts the Court's claim that "in the cases which have arisen, the Secretary has consistently exercised his power to withhold

---

[72] *Id.* at 2783–84. Justice Blackmun's concurrence is more candid than the opinion of the Court. For reasons set forth in detail later, however, his rejection of *Kent* and *Zemel* is misguided. See text accompanying notes 129–43 *infra*.

[73] *Id.* at 2788. His dissent was joined by Justice Marshall.

[74] *Agee*, 101 S. Ct. at 2779. Thus described, the incident hardly seems to fall under the 1966 regulation. After all, hundreds of media employees must have converged on the same spot.

[75] NEW YORK TIMES, September 8, 1970, at 16, cols. 2, 6.

[76] NEW YORK TIMES, September 9, 1970, at 16, col. 3. The lawyers said that they and Mrs. Sirhan would have been in the "best position to save the lives of the passengers." The incident was the subject of unreported litigation, which terminated in the dismissal of an appeal on September 11. See *Agee*, 101 S. Ct. at 2780 n. 54.

[77] NEW YORK TIMES, September 9, 1970, at 16, col. 3.

passports."[78] Moreover, the entire episode was obscure, never getting beyond page 16 of the *New York Times*. No evidence exists that anyone in Congress ever heard of this incident, which makes for weak evidence of implicit congressional approval.

The earlier episodes are described rather less accurately by the Court. One episode involved, according to the Court, "the 1954 revocation of a passport held by a man who was supplying arms to groups abroad whose interests were contrary to positions taken by the United States."[79] This is a somewhat peculiar way to describe an entirely legal sale of arms to the government of Guatemala. The man involved was Hubert Julian, also known as the Black Eagle of Harlem for his exploits as a World War II aviator.[80] After arms shipments from Italy to Guatemala were seized, he spoke to the United States embassy in Paris. He informed the embassy that he was currently seeking arms only for friendly governments. According to Julian, the First Secretary of the embassy "scolded him for criticizing the United States Government."[81] Julian's passport was seized when he left Paris for London. Two weeks later, it was returned.[82] As in the Sirhan episode, the government's actions were not entirely consistent, nor was the episode likely to come to the attention of Congress.

The earliest episode is the most important. The Court's description of the episode merits quotation:[83]

> Perhaps the most notable example of enforcement of the administrative policy, which surely could not have escaped the attention of Congress, was the 1948 denial of a passport to a Member of Congress who sought to go abroad to support a movement in Greece to overthrow the existing government.

The facts bear little relation to this description. Congressman Isacson, an American Labor Party representative, was an outspoken critic of American support for the Greek government. In a speech on March 13, 1948, he accused the Greek Army of "brutality and

---

[78] *Agee*, 101 S. Ct. at 2779.

[79] *Ibid.*

[80] New York Times, June 18, 1954, at 7, col. 3.

[81] *Ibid.*

[82] New York Times, July 12, 1954, at 2, col. 4. The July 12 story also fills in some of the details of the revocation.

[83] *Agee*, 101 S. Ct. at 2779.

bestiality," including mass executions.[84] He also alleged (with some truth, as it turns out) that the administration was contemplating the use of American troops in Greece.[85] In April, he announced plans for a fact-finding mission abroad, which was to include visits to Paris and Palestine. In Paris, he planned to observe the meetings of a group called the American Council for Aid to Democratic Greece. He was not a delegate to the meeting, but he was hoping to get more information about human rights violations. The State Department denied him a passport. Its explanation was that issuance of the passport was "not in the interests of the Government" because the "attitude" of the American Council toward U.S. policy was "well known."[86] While denying Isacson his passport, the government made no effort to prevent the departure of two men who were actually delegates to the conference.[87] Once again, the administrative policy was inconsistently applied.

The episode did not involve any specific acts of unlawful, disloyal or otherwise improper conduct. The only apparent "threat" to U.S. interests was that Isacson would discover more human rights violations, which were proving an embarrassment to the government.[88] The standard purportedly applied by the government

---

[84] 94 CONG. REC. A2029, A2030 (1948) (remarks of Rep. Isacson). Isacson also attributed the passport denial to his criticism of Truman's policy toward Palestine. NEW YORK TIMES, April 4, 1948, at 30, col. 1.

[85] 94 CONG. REC. A2031 (1948). Although Isacson's charges were exaggerated, government documents show that the option of using American troops was under active consideration. See 4 STATE DEPT., FOREIGN RELATIONS 5, 22–23, 25, 39, 93, 95, 99 (1948) (reprinting various State Dept., Defense Dept., and National Security Council documents). For further background on the United States role in Greece in this period, see GADDIS, THE UNITED STATES AND THE ORIGINS OF THE COLD WAR, 1941–1947, 346–52 (1972); FREELAND, THE TRUMAN DOCTRINE AND THE ORIGINS OF MCCARTHYISM 88–102 (1970). Freeland links the Greek crisis and the resulting Truman doctrine with the rise of McCarthyism. See id. at 140–50, 196–200, 241–45.

[86] NEW YORK TIMES, April 3, 1948, at 1, col. 6. (The only source cited by the Court is the TIMES, but unfortunately, the Court seems to have read only the skeletal account in the "Week in Review" feature. See Agee, 101 S. Ct. at 2779 n. 52, citing N.Y. TIMES, April 11, 1948, § E, at 9.)

THE TIMES editorialized that regardless of the innocence of Isacson's intentions, his mere presence at the conference would have undermined U.S. policy. It added that "[n]o citizen is entitled to go abroad to oppose the policies and interests of his country." NEW YORK TIMES, April 1948, § E, at 8, col. 2.

[87] NEW YORK TIMES, April 9, 1948, at 6, col. 6. The two individuals were the national vice-president of the American Council for Aid to Democratic Greece and another member of the group who was a New York City councilman.

[88] Isacson's atrocity charges had struck a nerve. The State Department had been secretly cautioning the Greek government that future executions could have an adverse affect on world opinion. See Telegram of the Secretary of State to the U.S. Embassy in Greece,

(travel "not in the interests of the Government") was the same as that invoked when numerous other dissidents were denied passports.[89] Seen in historical context, the Isacson episode was merely an early example of the abuses of the McCarthy period.[90]

The *Agee* Court was able to point to only these three episodes as examples of the challenged practice over a thirty-year period. Its excuse for the scarcity of examples was that the occasions for exercise of this power were equally rare.[91] To support this claim, the Court had to make these episodes sound dramatic and highly extraordinary. In fact, scores of other travelers must have presented equal threats to American interests during the same period. For example, the *Agee* regulation never seems to have been invoked during the Vietnam War, despite notorious cases of travel to Hanoi in support of the Viet Cong.[92] Although its administration was somewhat inconsistent, the regulation struck down in *Kent* was at least applied with some frequency. Other national security restrictions on passports have been applied with extreme rarity in cases apparently chosen at random.[93] One major flaw in the *Agee* opinion

---

[89] See text accompanying note 25 *supra*.

[90] Significantly, when Congress considered legislation to override *Kent*, both supporters and opponents of the legislation were anxious to see that it could not be used to limit the travel of Congressmen. See 105 CONG. REC. 18446 (1959) (remarks of Rep. Selden); *id.* at 18612 (remarks of Rep. Porter); *id.* at 18616 (remarks of Rep. Hays). This is a strong indication that Congress believed, at least after *Kent*, that the President lacked such power without additional legislation. For further discussion of this proposed legislation, see text accompanying notes 103–14 *infra*.

[91] See *Agee*, 101 S. Ct. at 2779–80. Additional incidents may have simply disappeared into the government's files, since the files are maintained by name and not otherwise indexed. See *id.* at 2787 n.8 (Brennan, J., dissenting). Of course, as Justice Brennan points out, Congress could not very well have been aware of these episodes if even the State Department is unable to identify them.

[92] The Vietnam War episodes were extensively discussed in Congress, with Ramsey Clark and Jane Fonda being named as the most notorious offenders. See 118 CONG. REC. 33186, 33188 (1972) (remarks of Rep. Ichord); *id.* at 33189 (remarks of Rep. Zion); *id.* at 33193–33194 (remarks of Rep. Sikes); *id.* at 33195 (remarks of Rep. Montgomery). In 1980, Ramsey Clark and others went to Iran for a conference on Iranian grievances against the United States. They also met with the captors of the American hostages. This conduct was at least as much an affront to our foreign policy as Isacson's 1948 trip to Paris. Yet the passport laws were never invoked. See NEW YORK TIMES, June 8, 1980, at 8, col. 1.

[93] Like capital punishment, passport denial seems to have the same random quality as being struck by lightning, see Furman v. Georgia, 408 U.S. 238, 309 (1972) (Stewart, J., concurring).

is its attempt to convert these few scattered instances into a consistent program.

CONGRESSIONAL APPROVAL OF THE ADMINISTRATIVE PRACTICE

To show congressional awareness of the challenged practice, the Court relies on "specific presentations" to Congress. These presentations consisted of "1957 and 1966 reports by the Department of State explaining the 1956 regulation" and a 1960 Senate Staff report.[94] On inspection, none of these provides much support to the Court's position. The 1960 staff report was made to a committee with no jurisdiction over standards for passport issuance.[95] Two years earlier, another report to a committee which did have jurisdiction had given contrary information. The earlier report concluded that, except in wartime, passport restrictions must be specifically authorized by Congress.[96]

The 1957 "presentation" cited by the Court turns out to be an offhand reference in testimony explaining various passport procedures.[97] A memorandum submitted in the same hearing shows that passports were denied to non-Communists for a variety of reasons: mental incompetence, illegal activity, draft evasion, etc. One of these categories is labeled: "Persons Whose Activities Might Be Detrimental to Foreign Policy of the United States."[98] This turns out, however, to refer to actions that became grounds for expatriation in 1952, e.g., serving in foreign armies. As a result, after 1952 there was "seldom occasion to invoke the discretionary authority."[99] The memorandum also mentions that passports are sometimes denied at the request of other agencies when "individuals are engaged on highly classified projects."[100] The memo does not indi-

---

[94] *Agee*, 101 S. Ct. at 2778.

[95] Staff Report, Reorganization of the Passport Functions of the Department of State, Senate Comm. on Gov't Operations, 86th Cong., 2d Sess. (1960).

[96] Legislative Ref. Serv. of the Library of Congress, Passports and the Right to Travel: A Study of Administrative Control of the Citizen, 85th Cong., 2d Sess. 36 (1958) (printed for the use of the House Foreign Affairs Committee, also reprinted in the 1957 hearings, note 60 *supra*, at 158).

[97] Hearings, note 60 *supra*, at 59–61.

[98] *Ibid.*

[99] Nicholas, *Discretionary Refusal of Passports in Non-Communist Cases* (1955), reprinted in Hearings on the Right to Travel, note 97 *supra*, at 266.

[100] *Id.* at 266–67.

cate any general policy of screening passports for national security
or foreign policy risks.

The 1966 "presentation" cited by the Court is also an offhand
reference, no more than half a page out of thirty-eight pages of
testimony by Philip Heymann.[101] Moreover, the committee that
heard the testimony had jurisdiction over Travel Act amendments
but no jurisdiction over passport practices.[102]

Thus, the documents cited by the Court fail to lend much support to the inference of congressional approval. Congressional failure to respond to these far from forceful "presentations" seems
more indicative of inattention than approval. At best, the documents weakly support the Court's position.

A much more important episode was cited to the Court but
completely ignored in the opinion. In this episode, which followed
the *Kent* decision, Congress was informed that the government
lacked the power it later claimed in *Agee*. Despite urgent pleas from
the administration, Congress refused to supply additional legislation. Because this episode is so critical, a detailed discussion is
warranted.

Immediately following the *Kent* decision, President Eisenhower
sent an urgent message to Congress calling for legislative action:[103]

> In recent years the Secretary of State has based his limitation
> of passports on two general grounds. The first of these has been
> that an applicant's travel, usually to a specific country or coun-
> tries, was inimical to United States foreign relations. The second
> of the general grounds of denial has been that an applicant is a
> member of the Communist Party; is under Communist Party
> discipline, domination, or control; or that the applicant is
> traveling abroad to assist knowingly the international Com-
> munist movement.
>
> Recently the Supreme Court limited this power to deny
> passports under existing law. It is essential that the Government
> today have power to deny passports where their possession

---

[101] Proposed Travel Controls, Hearings on S. 3243 before the Internal Security Subcommittee of the Senate Judiciary Committee, 89th Cong., 2d Sess. 72 (1966). Although the
Court fails to cite them, there are also brief relevant discussions at pp. 37 and 70 of the
hearings. Two other aspects of Heymann's testimony are of interest. First, he indicated
concern about allowing excessive discretion to the executive branch. *Id.* at 40. Second, he
indicated that any attempt to prevent an American citizen from returning to this country
would be plainly unconstitutional. *Id.* at 56.

[102] See *id.* at 51.

[103] 104 Cong. Rec. 13046, 13062 (1958).

would seriously impair the conduct of foreign relations of the United States or would be inimical to the security of the United States. . . .

. . .

I wish to emphasize the urgency of the legislation I have recommended. Each day and week that passes without it exposes us to great danger. I hope the Congress will move promptly toward its enactment.

Legislation was immediately introduced. Supporters pressed for fast action.[104] As Senator Eastland, Chairman of the Internal Security Committee explained, the Chief Legal Officer of the Passport Division had given dramatic testimony in favor of the administration bill. According to Eastland:[105]

> Mr. Johnson said that even if the Department knew that an American Communist planned to go to Moscow and take with him important American defense secrets for delivery to Communist espionage officials, the Department would not be able to deny him a passport to make the trip.

The House committee rejected the administration bill as giving too much discretion to the executive. Instead, it reported a bill creating a rebuttable presumption that Communist Party members would engage in harmful activities abroad.[106] Supporters of the bill stressed that without it, the Secretary of State could not deny passports to persons traveling abroad in furtherance of Communist activities.[107] The bill passed the House but failed to reach the Senate floor.[108]

In the next session of Congress, the President continued to press for action, citing "the total lack of legislative authority to deny passports to really dangerous participants in the international

---

[104] Besides Senator Eastland's statement, note 105 *infra*, and the President's statement, there were other statements of the urgent need for legislation. See 104 CONG. REC. 19656 (1958) (remarks of Rep. Morgan); *id.* at 19655 (remarks of Rep. Selden); *id.* at 19656 (remarks of Rep. Gubser); 106 CONG. REC. 16413 (1960) (remarks of Sen. Hruska). See also H. R. Rep. No. 1151, 86th Cong., 1st Sess. 2 (1959).

[105] 104 CONG. REC. 13335 (1958). See Hearings, note 60 *supra*, at 379 (statement of the Under Secretary of State).

[106] See 104 CONG. REC. at 19655–19656 (remarks of Rep. Morgan).

[107] See *id.* at 19655 (remarks of Rep. Morano); *id.* at 19656 (remarks of Rep. Gubser).

[108] See 106 CONG. REC. 16076 (1960) (remarks of Sen. Lausche) (complaining of inaction by the Senate Committee on Foreign Relations). See also H. R. Rep. No. 1151, 86th Cong., 1st Sess. 2 (1959).

Communist conspiracy."[109] The House committee responded with a bill allowing denial of passports based on two concurrent findings: (1) Communist affiliation, and (2) likelihood of harm to U.S. security through foreign travel.[110] The 1966 regulation upheld by the Court in *Agee* actually goes further, by making the second finding alone sufficient. Similar legislation was approved by the Senate committee, but the Senate bill applied only during war or national emergency.[111] The reason for this restriction (also absent from the *Agee* regulation) was opposition by the State Department to broader controls. The State Department believed "it would be contrary to the traditional American dedication to the ideal of free travel to institute such controls in the absence of war or of any other national emergency. . . ."[112] Even subject to these limitations, the legislation failed to pass.[113]

The legislative history is not conclusive on the *Agee* issue. All of the proposed legislation contained findings about the dangers posed by the international Communist movement. These findings were to be used in determining the likelihood that an applicant's activities abroad would injure national security. Thus, the legislation rejected by Congress was not quite identical to the *Agee* regulation. On the other hand, few members of Congress in 1958 or 1960 would have questioned these general findings about the dangers of Communism. Consequently, this aspect of the legislation is unlikely to have been the cause of rejection. In any event, the President's original message to Congress, as well as the testimony recounted by Senator Eastland, certainly gave Congress good reason

---

[109] Quoted in H. R. Rep. No. 1151, note 108 *supra*, at 2.

[110] See *id*. at 3.

[111] S. Rep. No. 1811, Part 1, 86th Cong., 2d Sess. 16 (1960).

[112] Letter from the Assistant Secretary of State to Sen. Eastland, May 6, 1959, reprinted *id*. at 8.

[113] The bill once again passed the House. The debates in the House stress that without the bill, passports could not be denied even to persons "[who] frankly state that they are going abroad to further the cause of international communism." 105 CONG. REC. 18443 (1959) (remarks of Rep. Selden). See also *id*. at 18443–18444 (quoting a State Department memorandum to the same effect); *id*. at 18612 (remarks of Rep. Walters) (State Department completely lacks "any control on a security basis of the issuance of passports"); *id*. at 18613 (remarks of Rep. Fascell) (government needs authority to deny passports to those Communists "whose travel abroad is found to be detrimental to U.S. security").

The bill never came up for a vote in the Senate. Apparently, it was killed by the Senate leadership. See 106 CONG. REC. 16416 (1960) (remarks of Sen. Cotton); *id*. at 16493 (remarks of Sen. Lausche); *id*. at 16940 (remarks of Sen. Curtis 16940); *id*. (remarks of Sen. Williams) (all complaining about their inability to get the bill on the calender for a vote).

to think that the executive lacked the power it was later to claim in *Agee*. As Judge Gesell said in his district court opinion, "implied authority is not gained in this fashion." [114]

THE 1978 LEGISLATION

Perhaps in recognition of the weakness of its other arguments, the *Agee* Court placed its primary reliance on 1978 legislation. It found this legislation to be "weighty evidence of congressional approval of the Secretary's interpretation, particularly that in the 1966 regulations." [115] The Court refrained from explaining the relevant legislative history, which in fact showed strong hostility to the whole idea of executive travel control. The 1978 legislation contained two relevant provisions. One amended the Passport Act, and the other affected the Travel Act.

The Passport Act amendment concerned area restrictions. Under the regulations in effect in 1978, such restrictions on the use of passports to travel to certain countries were limited. Area restrictions were allowed only when "such travel would seriously impair the conduct of United States foreign affairs." [116] This is a standard almost identical to that in the *Agee* regulation, but, in 1978, Congress rejected this standard. Although broad area restrictions were upheld in *Zemel* on the basis of the "weightiest considerations of national security," [117] the 1978 legislation allows their use only to protect travelers from physical danger. [118] The Senate Report explained that "the freedom-of-travel principle is sufficiently important that it should be a matter of law and not dependent upon a particular Administration's policy." [119] The Report also explained that Congress wanted to support the Helsinki agreement on human rights, which called for greater freedom of international travel. [120]

---

[114] Agee v. Vance, 483 F. Supp. at 732.

[115] *Agee*, 101 S. Ct. at 2779.

[116] 22 C.F.R. § 51.72 (1977), *added by* 31 FED. REG. 13544 (1966).

[117] See text accompanying note 42 *supra*.

[118] Act of Oct. 7, 1978, § 707, 92 STAT. 992-993, *amending* 8 U.S.C. § 1185. Under this statute, area restrictions may only be used in cases involving war, ongoing hostilities, or public health hazards.

[119] S. Rep. No. 842, 95th Cong., 2d Sess. 14 (1978).

[120] *Id.* at 15. On the Helsinki provisions relating to travel, see HUMAN RIGHTS, INTERNATIONAL LAW AND THE HELSINKI ACCORD 172–80 (Buergenthal ed. 1977); Turack, *A Brief*

The Senate Report does contain one sentence that mildly supports the *Agee* holding. The sentence states that the President should be able to control travel which is "inconsistent with a greater government interest, such as preventing a citizen who is seeking to avoid the judicial processes of the United States."[121] In the lower court, Judge MacKinnon argued that this was an endorsement of the *Agee* regulation.[122] This argument, however, requires a series of implausible assumptions. First, the argument assumes that Congress remembered the *Agee* regulation. According to the Court, the regulation was last brought to the attention of Congress in 1966.[123] After that date, it was invoked only once, in an obscure 1970 incident.[124] It seems unlikely that by 1978 Congress recalled either the incident or the regulation itself. Second, assuming Congress did recall the regulation, the argument assumes that Congress approved of the regulation. The *Agee* regulation and the area-restriction regulation allowed travel control based on similar standards involving serious damage to U.S. policy. In view of this similarity, no reason exists to assume that Congress drew any fine distinction between the two regulations. Third, if Congress did intend to draw such a distinction, the argument assumes that the Senate committee simply neglected to mention the *Agee* regulation in its report, while using the less relevant example of persons evading judicial process. If Congress was aware of the *Agee* regulation, despite that regulation's obscurity, and if Congress did intend to distinguish that regulation from the area restriction regulation, despite their similarity, then Congress's silence on the subject is certainly baffling.

The amendment to the Travel Act is less ambiguous in its implications. The "state of emergency" declared in 1958 was about to expire, and with it the requirement of a passport for foreign travel. Representative Eilberg introduced a floor amendment to deal with this problem. His amendment, while retaining the requirement of a passport for foreign travel, actually represents a complete repudiation of the philosophy of the prior Travel Act.

Review of the Provisions in Recent Agreements Concerning Freedom of Movement Issues in the Modern World, 11 CASE W. RES. J. INT'L L. 95, 105–14 (1979).

[121] S. Rep. No. 842, 95th Cong., 2d Sess. 14 (1978).

[122] Agee v. Muskie, 629 F.2d at 108.

[123] See *Agee*, 101 S. Ct. at 2778.

[124] See text accompanying notes 74–93 *supra*.

That statute was intended to control travel in time of war or national emergency. Eilberg's purpose was quite different, as he carefully explained:[125]

> Although the continuation of the passport requirement for citizens may appear to impede travel, I believe the impediment will occur if the passport requirement is allowed to lapse. Passports permit travel with a minimum of inconvenience because most countries in the world now require travelers to be documented with passports which show both citizenship and identity. Abandoning the passport requirement for U.S. citizens and nationals may result in many cases where travelers arrive at their countries of destination only to discover that they are not allowed entry because they lack the proper documentation.
>
> . . .
>
> In my amendment, I am deleting the provisions in the administration's bill for an administrative penalty against persons who violate any provisions of section 215. The thrust of my amendment is to facilitate travel, not to obstruct it and cover it with penal overtones.

Other representatives also commented on the need for a passport requirement to facilitate travel.[126] As finally passed, the statute omitted any penalty for travel without a passport.[127] The *Agee* opinion contains no hint of this legislative history.

The *Agee* Court purported to find implicit congressional approval for travel controls based on national security. Instead, the legislative record demonstrates almost complete hostility to travel control for over twenty-five years before *Agee*. The travel control program adopted in the early years of the Cold War consisted of three elements: area restrictions, a penalty for travel without a passport, and denial of passports to subversives. In 1958, Congress refused to reinstate the last element, and in 1978 it abolished the other two. The *Agee* regulation, on the other hand, derived from a minor, late addition to the travel control program. It had been applied rarely, under peculiar and obscure circumstances. It was never brought forcefully to the attention of Congress. To infer congressional approval under these circumstances seems to surpass the bounds of credibility.

---

[125] 124 CONG. REC. H4689 (May 31, 1978) (daily ed.).

[126] *Id.* at H4690 (remarks of Rep. Zablocki); *ibid.* (remarks of Rep. Fish).

[127] Act of Oct. 7, 1978, § 124, 92 STAT. 971, *amending* 22 U.S.C. § 211a.

III.

Agee is an important case for several reasons. Its approach represents a major shift from previous travel cases such as *Kent*. Moreover, its holding will govern travel control for the future. Finally, its mishandling of the historical record raises disturbing prospects for future cases involving national security questions.

To begin with the question of analytic approach, *Agee* clearly represents a major shift in theory. *Kent* laid heavy stress on the importance of the right to travel and took a correspondingly grudging approach to discretionary travel controls. *Agee*, on the other hand, distinguishes the *right* to travel within the United States from the mere *freedom* to travel outside the United States.[128] It takes a correspondingly generous view of executive discretion. For three reasons, the *Kent* approach is preferable, even ignoring the matter of *stare decisis*.

First is the importance of the right to travel itself.[129] As the *Kent* Court said, "[f]reedom of movement is basic in our scheme of values."[130] One important aspect of international travel is its relation to freedom of speech. Without the right to travel, criticism of foreign policy is greatly impeded.[131] More generally, as Zechariah Chafee explained in a passage quoted by the Court in *Kent*:[132]

> Foreign correspondents and lecturers on public affairs need first-hand information. Scientists and scholars gain greatly from consultations with colleagues in other countries. Students equip themselves for more fruitful careers in the United States by instruction in foreign universities. Then there are reasons close to the core of personal life—marriage, reuniting families, spending hours with old friends. Finally, travel abroad enables American citizens to understand that people like themselves live in Europe and helps them to be well-informed on public issues. An American who has crossed the ocean is not obliged to form his opinions about our foreign policy merely from what he is told

---

[128] *Agee*, 101 S. Ct. at 2782. On the origins of constitutional protection for interstate travel, see NOWAK, ROTUNDA, AND YOUNG, CONSTITUTIONAL LAW 668–74 (1978).

[129] As Judge Edgerton said a quarter of a century ago, "Iron curtains have no place in a free world." Briehl v. Dulles, 248 F.2d 561, 596 (D.C. Cir. 1957) (dissenting opinion).

[130] Kent v. Dulles, 357 U.S. at 126.

[131] Indeed, this is a major reason why so many nondemocratic countries restrict foreign travel. See Comment, note 1 *supra*, at 171, 202; Parker, note 1 *supra*, at 853, 853–54.

[132] CHAFFE, THREE HUMAN RIGHTS IN THE CONSTITUTION OF 1787, 195–96 (1956), quoted in Kent v. Dulles, 357 U.S. 116, 126–27 (1958).

by officials of our government or by a few correspondents of American newspapers. Moreover, his views on domestic questions are enriched by seeing how foreigners are trying to solve similar problems. In many different ways direct contact with other countries contributes to sounder decisions at home.

The principle of free travel is embodied not only in judicial opinions but also in other guarantees of open borders, such as the statutory right of expatriation[133] and the unchallenged right of any citizen to return to this country.[134] The approach taken in *Kent* gave recognition to the importance of travel by requiring a clear delegation of authority to restrict travel.

The second reason for preferring *Kent* relates to the problem of executive discretion. *Kent's* grudging attitude toward executive discretion is amply supported by history. Several glaring examples from the Cold War period have already been considered; the Isacson episode is perhaps the worst.[135] Numerous other instances support Jaffe's observation that "[w]hat began in an alarmed concern for the country's safety concludes in routines of unmitigated gall."[136] This was true, not only in the Cold War when Jaffe wrote, but also in other periods. At various times, we have denied passports to writers whose work was not considered "constructive,"[137] to Mormons seeking to travel abroad as missionaries,[138] and to chess champions seeking to play on forbidden territory.[139] The *Agee* Court seems to have assumed that the discretion to control travel had only been exercised on a principled basis. Too many counterexamples exist to allow reliance on this assumption.

The third reason for preferring *Kent* to *Agee* is that *Kent* aligns more closely with congressional intent. Since *Kent*, Congress has strongly supported the principle of freedom of travel. Despite urgent pleas from the President, Congress refused to supply the statutory power held lacking in *Kent*. Even supporters of the override legislation were unwilling to give the President as much dis-

---

[133] See Jaffe, note 2 *supra*, at 17, 18–19; Parker, note 1 *supra*, at 856 and n.12.

[134] Even Agee was offered permission to return home. See *Agee*, 101 S. Ct. at 2773 n.16. See also note 101 *supra* (government concession that citizens cannot be denied entry).

[135] See text accompanying notes 83–87 *supra*.

[136] Jaffe, note 2 *supra*, at 28.

[137] Comment, note 2 *supra*, at 178.

[138] Jaffe, note 2 *supra*, at 22–23.

[139] *Travel and the First Amendment: Zemel v. Rusk*, 13 U.C.L.A. L. REV. 470, 481 (1966).

cretion as he requested.[140] Twenty years later, Congress abolished the other major elements of the Cold War program of travel control. In essentially abolishing area controls, the Senate committee stressed the importance of the freedom-of-travel principle and its reluctance to leave the matter to Presidential discretion. It also expressed its firm support for the Helsinki agreement favoring looser restrictions on travel everywhere in the world. In the House, penalties for travel without a passport were abolished. The reason, as the sponsor of the measure explained, was that passport rules should be used to facilitate travel, not to hinder or penalize it. With this measure, the legal basis for travel control vanished. In sum, not only the holding but also the underlying policies of *Kent* have received congressional endorsement. This is of critical importance, because both *Kent* and *Agee* proceed from the premise that the President's power flows from Congress. Indeed, even if the President did have some inherent power in the area, that power would be greatly diminished by Congressional disapproval.[141]

The *Agee* opinion is thus a misguided retreat from the *Kent* analysis. Even more important, perhaps, is the change in judicial attitude between the two cases. *Kent* is part of a series of cases using non-constitutional grounds to protect civil liberties. In *Kent* and similar cases, the Court required clear statutory authority, explicit and narrow guidelines, full procedural protection, and other safeguards before allowing the government to burden the exercise of important rights.[142] The benefits of this approach are obvious. It avoids constitutional rulings and thus averts direct confrontations between the Court and other branches of government. At the same time, it gives the other branches an opportunity for sober reconsideration before they proceed. At times, such reconsideration has led to a change in

---

[140] See 105 CONG. REC. 18445 (1959) (remarks of Rep. Selden); *id.* at 18448 (remarks of Rep. Morgan); *ibid.* (remarks of Rep. O'Hara); *id.* at 18613 (remarks of Rep. Fascell); 104 CONG. REC. 19655 (remarks of Rep. Selden) (1958); S. Rep. No. 1881, 86th Cong., 2nd Sess. 7 (1960). Opponents of the measure stressed the dangers of excessive executive discretion. See 105 CONG REC. 18612, 18618 (1959) (remarks of Rep. Porter); *id.* at 18616 (remarks of Rep. Hays); *id.* at 18623 (remarks of Rep. Fulton); *id.* at 18449–50 (remarks of Rep. Celler); 104 CONG REC. 13773–74 (1958) (remarks of Sen. Humphrey).

[141] See Youngstown Sheet & Tube Co. v. Sawyer, 343 U.S. 579, 637–38 (1952) (Jackson, J. concurring), quoted with approval in Dames & Moore v. Regan, 101 S. Ct. 2972, 2986 (1981).

[142] See, *e.g.*, Watkins v. United States, 354 U.S. 178 (1957); Service v. Dulles, 354 U.S. 363 (1957); Noto v. United States, 367 U.S. 290 (1961); Yates v. United States, 354 U.S. 298 (1957).

decision. After *Kent*, for example, Congress proved unwilling to authorize denial of passports to Communists.[143] By requiring narrow, carefully drawn regulations, the Court also helped minimize the side effects of regulation on the exercise of First Amendment rights.

The *Agee* opinion has little in common with these cases. The *Agee* opinion contains alarming distortions of both the Court's prior decisions and the historical record. At a time when a city's billboard ban requires many pages of agonizing judicial appraisal,[144] Agee's First Amendment claim is brushed aside in a few sentences.[145] In short, the opinion seems anxious to uphold the President's national security prerogatives without serious scrutiny.

Agee is not the only recent case in which the Court has taken shortcuts in its haste to defend the nation's security. The more obvious example is *Snepp v. United States*.[146] *Snepp* involved another former CIA agent who had violated his secrecy agreement with the government. The Fourth Circuit held the agreement valid, upheld an injunction against future violations, and remanded for a determination of damages.[147] Snepp petitioned for certiorari. The government filed a conditional cross-petition, asking the Court to review another aspect of the remedy if it granted Snepp's petition. The Supreme Court summarily reversed the lower court on the remedy issue and imposed an extremely harsh remedy. Because Snepp had failed to allow the CIA to check his manuscript for classified material, the Court held that the CIA was entitled to all of Snepp's book profits, even though the book concededly did not contain classified information. First Amendment problems were brushed away in a footnote.[148] Nor was the Court concerned about the complete absence of any statutory basis for this remedy. All this was done summarily, without the benefit of oral argument or full briefing.

---

[143] See note 113 *supra*.

[144] See Metromedia Inc. v. City of San Diego, 101 S. Ct. 2882, 2885–2925 (1981), in which five Justices found it necessary to write separately and at length on this issue.

[145] See *Agee*, 101 S. Ct. at 2782–83. For a brief critique of the Court's First Amendment discussion, see Kamisar, *The Agee Decision*, NEW YORK TIMES, July 28, 1981, at 21, col. 1.

[146] 444 U.S. 507 (1980) (*per curiam*).

[147] United States v. Snepp, 595 F.2d 926 (4th Cir. 1979).

[148] 444 U.S. at 513 n. 8.

Agee and *Snepp* raise disturbing prospects. Of course, the temptation is always greatest to cut a few corners when national security is at stake. Precisely for that reason, it is critical that the Court hold rigorously to its highest standards of craftsmanship in such cases, while demanding scrupulous attention to legality from the other branches of government.

IV.

Given Agee's conduct, the Court's willingness to limit his travel is not a complete surprise, especially if it thought its decision would affect only a few similar individuals. The regulation at issue in *Agee* required a finding of "serious" damage to national security or foreign policy. In its review of history, the Court found only three other instances in thirty years when this standard had been met. As we have seen, even these instances were distorted to maximize the appearance of a threat to national security.[149] Thus, the Court may well have thought its decision would affect only individuals presenting truly extraordinary threats to national security. This belief may explain the Court's lack of concern for the civil-liberties implications of its decision, because the right to travel clearly does not encompass Agee's attempt to travel abroad to disclose classified information.[150] It is not hard to understand the temptation to bend the law, just a little, in order to thwart Agee.

The Court paid a heavy price for yielding to this temptation. At considerable cost to intellectual integrity, the Court did violence both to its own precedents and to clearly manifested congressional intent. Moreover, history gives good grounds for questioning whether the narrow restrictions on travel upheld in *Agee* will long remain narrow in their application.

In exchange for this damage to the law, the Court seems to have gotten little in return. Before receiving the Court's endorsement, the *Agee* regulation was rarely used, and then under questionable circumstances involving relatively insignificant threats to national

---

[149] See text accompanying notes 74–93 *supra*.

[150] See Zemel v. Rusk, 381 U.S. 1, 26 (1965) (Douglas, J., dissenting) (right to travel is "at the periphery of the First Amendment"; peacetime restrictions on travel "should be so particularized that a First Amendment right is not precluded unless some clear countervailing national interest stands in the way of its assertion").

security.[151] Even with respect to Agee himself, the regulation seems to have been largely ineffective. Shortly after the Court's decision, Agee announced his determination to continue his campaign against the CIA and obtained a new passport from Grenada.[152]

The basic error in *Agee* was the Court's decision to bend the law to impose sanctions on a single individual. In this case, the individual involved may well have deserved some form of sanction, perhaps even the kind authorized by the Court. But in bending the law to reach this one individual, the Court has endangered the liberties of many more. Prior to *Agee*, freedom of travel was protected by the *Kent* decision and by several manifestation of congressional intent. After *Agee*, these barriers have been breached, leaving as safeguards only executive restraint in exercising discretion and judicial willingness to intervene on an ad hoc basis.

---

[151] See text accompanying notes 74–93 *supra*.

[152] Agee, note 6 *supra*, at 15, col. 1; *Philip Agee's Grenadian Passport*, NEWSWEEK, August 10, 1981, at 15.

BERNARD SCHWARTZ

THE COURT AND COST-BENEFIT ANALYSIS: AN ADMINISTRATIVE LAW IDEA WHOSE TIME HAS COME—OR GONE?

Mr. Dooley notwithstanding,[1] the Supreme Court does not always follow the election returns.

Soon after he took office, President Reagan issued Executive Order 12,291, to govern federal regulation. Under it, "Regulatory action shall not be undertaken unless the potential benefits to society for the regulation outweigh the potential costs to society."[2] Commenting upon this provision, a *New York Times* editorial declared, "That's timely common sense."[3] This is a truism. But it has not been that simple for the Supreme Court in its two recent decisions on cost-benefit analysis.

I.

Until recently, cost-benefit analysis has been part of the arsenal of esoterica with which contemporary economics has increasingly armed itself. The layman has scarcely been able to understand, much less appreciate, the abstruse discussions of the

---

Bernard Schwartz is Webb Professor of Law, New York University.

[1] BANDER, MR DOOLEY ON THE CHOICE OF LAW 52 (1963).

[2] 46 Fed. Reg. 13193 (1981).

[3] March 23, 1981, p. A16.

subject in texts by economists. But the underlying concept is as old as rational thought itself.[4]

The modern roots of cost-benefit analysis are to be found in the utilitarianism of Jeremy Bentham and John Stuart Mill. The "greatest happiness of the greatest number"[5] can scarcely be furthered by anything whose cost exceeds its benefit. Indeed, the Benthamite "felicific calculus"[6] of pain and pleasure was but a primitive way of stating the notion of costs versus benefits.

A decade after Bentham's death, Jules Dupuit, a French engineer, published *On the Measurement of the Utility of Public Works*,[7] which is considered the beginning of the literature on cost-benefit analysis.[8] In this country, use of cost-benefit analysis is usually said to have started with the Flood Control Act of 1936, where Congress provided that federal projects should be undertaken "if the benefits to whomsoever they may accrue are in excess of the estimated costs."[9] This statute, the Supreme Court has stated, indicates an "intent on the face . . . that an agency engage in cost-benefit analysis."[10]

Such a provision was until recently the rare exception in the federal statute book. In particular, cost-benefit analysis was not required in the host of regulatory laws enacted by Congress since the creation of the Interstate Commerce Commission.[11] Express provision for cost-benefit analysis was not called for in these laws because of the nature of traditional regulatory administration. With a few exceptions,[12] the ICC-type agency has regulated a specific industry. While its enabling Act has required the agency to regulate to further the public interest, the well-being of the regulated industry has also been an essential part of that interest.[13] Referring to the creation of the ICC, Landis wrote, "What was important was

---

[4] "For which of you, intending to build a tower, sitteth not down first, and counteth the cost. . . ." (Luke 14:28).

[5] 10 THE WORKS OF JEREMY BENTHAM 142 (Bowring, ed. 1962).

[6] 3 ENCYCLOPEDIA BRITTANICA 486 (1969 ed.).

[7] 2 INTERNATIONAL ECONOMIC PAPERS 83 (1952) (translated from French, 1844).

[8] SASSONE & SCHAFFER, COST-BENEFIT ANALYSIS: A HANDBOOK 3 (1978).

[9] 33 U.S.C. § 710a (1976).

[10] American Textile Manufacturers Institute v. Donovan, 101 S.Ct. 2478, 2491 (1981).

[11] Interstate Commerce Act, 24 Stat. 379 (1887).

[12] Notably, the Federal Trade Commission and National Labor Relations Board.

[13] See, *e.g.*, Federal Aviation Act, 49 U.S.C. § 1302 (1976).

the deliberate organization of a governmental unit whose single concern was the well-being . . . of a vital and national industry."[14]

An agency such as the ICC or the Civil Aeronautics Board, concerned with the totality of its regulated industry, concentrated primarily on economic factors. When it fixed rates, issued licenses, or imposed regulatory requirements, it would inevitably consider the costs its action imposed on the industry. Thus, the ICC would have to pay attention to the effects of orders fixing rates and entry for truckers under its statutory mission to ensure a trucking business that would provide adequate and economical transportation services to the public.[15] If the costs imposed by ICC action were disproportionate to the benefits secured, the statutory goal could not be met.

In addition, the private adversaries in the traditional administrative process were even more intimately concerned with costs. Whether the phenomenon of "capture" of the ICC-type agency by its industry[16] was valid or not, it was certainly true that the agency's primary "constituency" was the industry being regulated. An agency that ignored the costs it imposed on its constituency did so at its peril. The regulated industry had sufficient influence, on Capitol Hill and elsewhere, to ensure that its dominant concerns would normally be met by the agency concerned.

During the past decade and a half, however, a new generation of administrative agencies has been created. These agencies have been a direct product of the increased concern with consumer and environmental protection that has so changed our public law in recent years. The leading agencies among this newer breed are the Environmental Protection Administration, Occupational Safety and Health Administration, and the Consumer Products Safety Commission.

The jurisdiction of these agencies is not limited to a single industry. Instead, it cuts across the economic system. The newer agency also operates in a narrower sphere than the traditional regulatory agency. It is not concerned with the totality of an industry, but only with the segment of its operations that comes within its bailiwick. Thus, the EPA, like the ICC, may be concerned with

---

[14] LANDIS, THE ADMINISTRATIVE PROCESS 10 (1938).

[15] See 49 U.S.C. § 304 (1976).

[16] See SCHWARTZ, THE PROFESSOR AND THE COMMISSIONS 115 et seq. (1959).

trucking—but its interest is only in the effect of trucking operations on the environment.[17]

The new breed of EPA-type agency is established to promote social, rather than economic, goals. The traditional theory of regulation has been geared to a world where the regulators, as well as their constituency, are concerned almost entirely with business factors, such as prices and costs. The EPA-type agency is normally oblivious to these factors. That is also true of its constituency, which is not a particular industry but the public interest groups supporting its efforts. Both the agency and its constituency tend to condemn as callous any consideration of cost, or other economic factors, in decisions on product, personnel, or environmental safety.[18]

This has been particularly true under statutes providing for protection of public health. "Minimum public health requirements are often, perhaps usually, set without consideration of other economic impact."[19] The outstanding example is, of course, the so-called Delaney Clause of the Food, Drug, and Cosmetic Act.[20] Most other statutes protecting public health also contain cost-oblivious provisions.[21] Thus, in enacting the provision for national ambient air standards in the Clean Air Act,[22] Congress decided that the public has the right to the prescribed levels of air quality, regardless of what cost-benefit analysis might indicate in the matter. The same has been true in other important health-protection laws, notably the Occupational Safety and Health Act.[23]

There have, it is true, been a few statutes in which Congress has required cost-benefit analysis by a newer type regulatory agency.[24] The most important is the Consumer Products Safety Act. It authorizes the Consumer Products Safety Commission to promulgate

---

[17] See WEIDENBAUM, BUSINESS, GOVERNMENT, AND THE PUBLIC 18–21 (2d ed. 1981).

[18] See *id.* at 20.

[19] South Terminal Corp. v. EPA, 504 F.2d 646, 675 (1st Cir. 1974).

[20] 21 U.S.C. § 348(c)(3)(A)(1976). See Bell v. Goddard, 366 F.2d 177 (7th Cir. 1966).

[21] See Rodgers, *Benefits, Costs and Risks: Oversight of Health and Environment Decisionmaking*, 4 HARV. ENV. L. REV. 191, 201–04 (1980).

[22] 42 U.S.C. § 7409(b)(1)(1976).

[23] 29 U.S.C. § 651(1976).

[24] Compare National Environmental Policy Act, 42 U.S.C. § 4321(1976), which mandates the balancing of the environmental costs of a project against its economic and technological benefits. Calvert Cliffs Coord. Com. v. AEC, 449 F.2d 1109, 1123 (D.C. Cir. 1971). See Columbia Basin Ass'n v. Schlesinger, 643 F.2d 585, 594 (9th Cir. 1981).

safety standards, provided that "Any requirement of such a standard shall be reasonably necessary to prevent or reduce an unreasonable risk of injury associated with such product."[25] The House committee report stressed the "unreasonable risk" standard, stating, "It is generally expected that the determination of unreasonable hazard will involve the Commission in balancing the probability that risk will result in harm and the gravity of such harm against the effect on the product's utility, costs, and availability to the consumer."[26]

According to the Supreme Court, Congress used the "unreasonable risk" phrase, as shown by the House committee statement, "to signify a generalized balancing of costs and benefits."[27] The leading case so holding is *Aqua Slide 'N' Dive Corp. v. CPSC.*[28] The decision there set aside a CPSC standard that required warning signs for swimming pool slides. According to the court, "In weighing the 'reasonable necessity' for the signs, the crucial question then, is whether the benefit has a reasonable relationship to the disadvantages the sign requirement imposes."[29]

As explained by the court in a later case, the importance of *Aqua Slide* is that it "requires the agency to assess the expected benefits in light of the burdens to be imposed by the standard. Although the agency does not have to conduct an elaborate cost-benefit analysis, it does have to determine whether the benefits expected from the standard bear a reasonable relationship to the costs imposed by the standard."[30]

II.

The regulatory statute that put cost-benefit analysis to the Supreme Court test was the Occupational Safety and Health Act. The Act delegates broad authority to the Secretary of Labor to promulgate standards to ensure safe and healthful working condi-

---

[25] 15 U.S.C. § 2056(a)(1976).

[26] H.R. Rep. No. 92-1153, 92d Cong., 2d Sess., 33 (1972).

[27] American Textile Manufacturers Institute v. Donovan, 101 Sup. Ct. 2478, 2491 n.30 (1981).

[28] 569 F.2d 831 (5th Cir. 1978).

[29] *Id.* at 842.

[30] American Petroleum Institute v. OSHA, 581 F.2d 493, 503 (5th Cir. 1978) (citation omitted).

tions for the Nation's workers, and made the Occupational Safety and Health Administration (OSHA) the agency directly responsible for carrying out the authority. Section 3(8) of the Act defines an "occupational safety and health standard" as a standard that is "reasonably necessary and appropriate to provide safe and healthful employment." Where toxic materials or harmful physical agents are concerned, a standard must also comply with section 6(b)(5), which directs the Secretary to "set the standard which most adequately assures, to the extent feasible, on the basis of the best available evidence, that no employee will suffer material impairment of health or functional capacity." In promulgating standards limiting worker exposure to benzene,[31] as well as to cotton dust[32] and to lead poisoning,[33] the Secretary took the position that no safe exposure level could be determined and that section 6(b)(5) required him to set an exposure limit at the lowest technologically feasible level that would not impair the viability of industries regulated. The administrative view was that the very notion of cost-benefit analysis was inconsistent with the aim of the Act to provide the safest possible workplace for employees. OSHA asserted that, in a case where the harmful agent regulated was a carcinogen, the risks could not be reliably quantified and that there was no acceptable way to put a dollar value on them even if they could be.

The OSHA position was first tested in the courts in *American Petroleum Institute v. OSHA*.[34] In that case, after having determined that there is a causal connection between benzene and leukemia, the Secretary of Labor promulgated a standard reducing the permissible exposure limit on airborne concentrations of benzene from ten parts benzene per million parts of air (10 ppm) to 1 ppm, and prohibiting dermal contact with solutions containing benzene. On pre-enforcement review, the Court of Appeals held the standard invalid because it was based on findings unsupported by the administrative record. The Court concluded that the agency had exceeded its standard-setting authority because it had not been shown that the 1 ppm exposure limit was "reasonably necessary or appro-

---

[31] 43 Fed. Reg. 27962 (1978).

[32] 43 Fed. Reg. 27350 (1978).

[33] 43 Fed. Reg. 52952 (1978).

[34] 581 F.2d 493 (5th Cir. 1978), *affirmed sub nom.* Industrial Union Department v. American Petroleum Institute, 100 S.Ct. 2844 (1980).

priate to provide safe and healthful employment" as required by section 3(8), and that section 6(b)(5) did not give the agency the unbridled discretion to adopt standards designed to create absolutely risk-free workplaces regardless of cost.

Despite the difference in statutory language, the Court of Appeals followed the reasoning of the *Aqua Slide* case.[35] This meant that it was not enough for the agency to show only that the standard's goal was achievable and one that the industry could afford. The statute "does not give OSHA the unbridled discretion to adopt standards designed to create absolutely risk-free workplaces regardless of cost."[36] On the contrary, under the Act, the Secretary was under a duty to determine whether the benefits expected from the new standard bore a reasonable relationship to the costs that it imposed—that is, cost-benefit analysis was required. The agency had to estimate the extent of the expected benefit and costs in order to determine whether the relationship between the benefits and costs of the benzene standard was reasonable. Because the agency did not show that the benefits to be achieved by reducing the permissible exposure limit from 10 ppm to 1 ppm bore a reasonable relationship to the costs imposed by the reduction, it failed to show that the standard was reasonably necessary to provide safe or healthful workplaces, as required by the Act.

The Supreme Court affirmed the judgment in *Industrial Union Department v. American Petroleum Institute*,[37] but the Court avoided the cost-benefit analysis issue. They voted by a bare majority to strike down the OSHA benzene standard, but there was no majority opinion. The five Justices voting against OSHA split three ways among themselves, while a solid four-Justice minority voted to uphold the standard.

The plurality opinion of Justice Stevens (joined by Chief Justice Burger and Justice Stewart) held that the benzene standard was unenforceable since the standard was not supported by appropriate findings. Before the Secretary could promulgate any permanent health or safety standard, he must make a threshold finding that the place of employment was unsafe, in the sense that significant risks

---

[35] Note 28 *supra*.

[36] 581 F.2d at 502.

[37] 100 S.Ct. 2844 (1980).

were present and could be eliminated or lessened by a change in practices.

Only Justice Powell indicated that cost-benefit analysis was required. He concluded that the Act does require OSHA to determine that the economic effects of its standard bear a reasonable relationship to the expected benefits. A standard is neither "reasonably necessary" nor "feasible," as required by the Act, if it calls for expenditures wholly disproportionate to the expected health and safety benefits. Here, according to Justice Powell, the record contained no evidence that OSHA weighed the relevant considerations. The agency simply announced its finding of cost justification without explaining the method by which it determined that the benefits justified the costs and their economic effects.[38]

The four dissenting Justices in *Industrial Union* also addressed the cost-benefit analysis issue and "indicated that the statute did not contemplate cost-benefit analysis."[39] Indeed, the four dissenters went so far as to compare imposition of a cost-benefit mandate to the substantive due process approach followed in discredited cases like *Lochner v. New York*:[40] "But as the Constitution 'does not enact Mr. Herbert Spencer's Social Statics,' *Lochner v. New York* . . . (Holmes, J., dissenting), so the responsibility to scrutinize federal administrative action does not authorize this Court to strike its own balance between the costs and benefits of occupational safety standards."[41]

III.

Though the Court avoided the cost-benefit analysis issue in the *Industrial Union* case, the handwriting was on the wall so far as the issue was concerned. The *Industrial Union* dissenters, who had condemned imposition of a cost-benefit analysis requirement so strongly, needed only one vote from the four who had not spoken on the matter to translate their view into law. The necessary vote was secured in *American Textile Manufacturers Institute v. Donovan*.[42]

---

[38] Justice Rehnquist, one of the five-member majority, found that the statute involved an invalid delegation.

[39] 101 Sup. Ct. at 2483 n.4.

[40] 198 U.S. 45 (1905).

[41] 100 S.Ct. at 2905.

[42] 101 S.Ct. 2478.

At issue there was the cotton dust standard promulgated by OSHA.[43] After finding that inhalation of cotton dust was the primary cause of byssinosis ("brown lung" disease), the agency issued the standard, which established mandatory permissible exposure limits ranging from 200 to 500 micrograms per cubic meter of air. The standard stated that it was based on interpretation of the Act which required adoption of the most stringent standard to protect against material health impairment, bounded only by technological and economic feasibility.[44] The agency expressly found the standard to be both technologically and economically feasible, based on the evidence in the record as a whole.

An action challenging the standard was brought by the textile manufacturers trade association and individual cotton textile manufacturers. Their principal claim was that OSHA had misinterpreted the Act by refusing to engage in cost-benefit analysis. They urged that the Act required OSHA to determine that the costs of the standard bore a reasonable relationship to its benefits. The agency not only must show that a standard addressed a significant risk of material health impairment,[45] but also must demonstrate that the reduction in risk of material health impairment was significant in light of the costs of attaining that reduction. The Court of Appeals rejected petitioners' claim and held that the Act did not require the agency to compare costs and benefits. The Supreme Court affirmed.

This time the Court addressed the cost-benefit analysis issue squarely. Five Justices spoke on the issue, and they ruled that the Act did not require cost-benefit analysis. The three dissenters did not deal with the question. Justice Powell, the only one to vote for cost-benefit analysis in *Industrial Union*, did not participate, so that no Justice spoke in favor of cost-benefit analysis in the cotton dust case.

The opinion of the Court rejecting cost-benefit analysis was simple—if not simplistic—in its approach. Justice Brennan stressed the section 6(b)(5) provision that the Secretary "shall set the standard which most adequately assures, *to the extent feasible*, on the basis of the best available evidence, that no employee will suffer

---

[43] Note 32 *supra*.

[44] 43 Fed. Reg. 27361.

[45] *I.e.* the requirement imposed by the *Industrial Union* decision, note 34 *supra*.

material impairment of health or functional capacity."[46] The key phrase, said Justice Brennan, was that italicized—"to the extent feasible." Using standard dictionaries, Brennan concluded that section 6(b)(5) directed OSHA to promulgate the standard that most adequately assured that no employee would suffer material health impairment—"limited only by the extent to which this is 'capable of being done.' "[47]

In light of its ordinary meaning, the word "feasible" could not be construed to articulate Congressional intent to require cost-benefit analysis: "cost-benefit analysis . . . is not required by the statute because feasibility analysis is."[48] As the Court saw it, "Congress itself defined the basic relationship between costs and benefits, by placing the 'benefit' of worker health above all other considerations save those making attainment of this 'benefit' unachievable. Any standard based on a balancing of costs and benefits by the Secretary . . . strikes a different balance than that struck by Congress."[49]

IV.

Cost-benefit analysis has been elevated to the top of the administrative agenda by the Reagan Administration's program for regulatory reform. The Administration came to power assailing the costs created by governmental intervention in the economy, and it has tried to make comparison of costs and benefits a central element of federal regulation. On February 17, 1981, President Reagan issued Executive Order 12,291.[50] It provides detailed procedures for issuance of so-called major regulations by executive branch regulatory agencies. All such agencies are required to prepare regulatory impact analyses when they promulgate major rules.[51] They must analyze the costs and benefits of the proposed regulations, and

---

[46] Emphasis added.

[47] 101 S.Ct. at 2490.

[48] *Ibid.*

[49] *Ibid.*

[50] Note 2 *supra.*

[51] Under section 1(b) of the Reagan order, " 'Major rule' means any regulation that is likely to result in: (1) An annual effect on the economy of $100 million or more; (2) A major increase in costs or prices for consumers, individual industries, Federal, State, or local government agencies, or geographic regions; or (3) Significant adverse effects on competition, employment, investment, productivity, innovation, or on the ability of United States–based enterprises to compete with foreign-based enterprises in domestic or export markets."

they are required to "maximize the net benefits to society." If the least-cost alternative has not been selected, the agencies are required to explain why in the analysis.

Unlike prior Presidential orders on the rule-making process—notably President Carter's Executive Order 12,044[52]—the Reagan order provides an enforcement mechanism. Agencies must submit proposed major rules, with preliminary regulatory impact analyses, to the Director of the Office of Management and Budget for review prior to making them public. The agencies are also required to submit final major rules and final regulatory impact analyses to the Director for review prior to promulgation. The Director is to monitor compliance with the Executive Order, and he is empowered to refer any disagreement with the rule-making agency to the President.

The Reagan order is limited to agencies in the executive branch. Presidential power in this respect does not extend to the independent regulatory commissions, which are not subject to direct presidential control. Executive Order 12,291 recognizes this,[53] as indeed it must under the cases establishing the independence of agencies such as the Federal Trade Commission.[54]

The Department of Labor and OSHA are, of course, agencies in the executive branch and are, as such, subject to Executive Order 12,291. Two months after the Reagan inauguration, OSHA issued a notice of proposed rule making which announced that it was reexamining its cotton dust standard[55] and that it would "evaluate the feasibility and utility of relying on cost-benefit analysis in setting occupational health standards."[56] At the same time, the Solicitor General filed a memorandum informing the Supreme Court of OSHA's new position. As a result, the Solicitor General wrote, "the Court may wish to refrain from further consideration" of the cotton dust case.[57] The Government asked the Court to vacate the lower-court decision upholding the standard and send the matter back to OSHA "for further consideration and development."[58]

---

[52] 43 Fed. Reg. 12661 (1978).

[53] See Executive Order 12,291. § 1(d).

[54] Humphrey's Executor v. United States, 295 U.S. 602 (1935); Wiener v. United States, 357 U.S. 349 (1958).

[55] N.Y. Times, March 28, 1981, p. 9.

[56] Id., April 5, 1981, p. E9.

[57] Ibid.

[58] Ibid.

Soon thereafter, both OSHA and the Department of Justice took similar steps with regard to a standard designed to protect workers from lead poisoning.[59] The Occupational Safety and Health Administration announced that it was reconsidering the standard and would assess whether the cost to industry of compliance was justified by the health benefits to workers. At the same time, the Government asked the Supreme Court to vacate a Court of Appeals decision upholding the lead-exposure standard and to remand the case to OSHA "for further consideration and development."[60]

A footnote in the *Textile Manufacturers* opinion summarily rejects the Government's request to have the judgment below vacated and the case sent back to OSHA. The Court said only, "We decline to adopt the suggestion."[61] The same approach was followed in the lead-exposure case, where the Court let stand the lower-court decision that cost-benefit analysis was not necessary by denying certiorari.[62]

The Court's refusal to remand the cotton dust and lead cases to OSHA for it to reevaluate the standards under a cost-benefit analysis approach constitutes a direct rebuff to the Reagan Administration's intention to use cost-benefit analysis as the measuring rod for federal regulation. Does this mean that, as counsel for the unions in the cotton-dust case declared after the decision there, "Cost-benefit analysis is kaput?"[63]

The answer depends, first of all, upon the reach of the *Textile Manufacturers* decision. Counsel for the union saw the decision as mandating OSHA standards requiring the maximum technologically possible protection for workers, provided that the test of feasibility is met.[64] Under this view, as summarized by Justice Rehnquist, "Congress itself balanced costs and benefits when it enacted the statute, and . . . the statute *prohibits* the Secretary from engaging in a cost-benefit type balancing."[65]

Justice Rehnquist himself took a different view of the cotton-dust

---

[59] Note 33 *supra*.

[60] N.Y. TIMES, April 18, 1981, p. 9.

[61] 101 S.Ct. at 2488 n.25.

[62] Lead Industries Assn. v. Donovan, 101 S.Ct. 3148 (1981).

[63] N.Y. TIMES, June 27, 1981, p. 9.

[64] *Ibid*.

[65] 101 S.Ct. at 2508.

decision. "As I read the Court's opinion, it takes a different position. It concludes that, at least as to the 'Cotton Dust Standard,' the Act does not require the Secretary to engage in a cost-benefit analysis, which suggests of course that the Act *permits* the Secretary to undertake such an analysis if he so chooses."[66]

Both the *Textile Manufacturers* opinion and administrative law principles support the Rehnquist view. The Court indicates that OSHA was required by the statute to promulgate the standard that would provide the greatest protection from cotton dust, subject only to the feasibility requirement—which includes both technological and economic feasibility, with the latter ensuring that the standard would not drive the industry out of business. But the Court did not, in fact, hold the agency to such a strict requirement. Nor did OSHA, in setting the cotton-dust standard, go anywhere near the feasible limit of stringency.

Despite the contrary implication in the *Textile Manufacturers* opinion, the OSHA cotton-dust standard was not so much the product of administrative expertise as the result of a political tug of war between the Department of Labor and the White House. When OSHA first proposed its standard in 1976, it required exposure to cotton dust to be limited to 200 micrograms per cubic meter of air throughout a textile plant.[67] The final standard, issued two years later, was considerably more lenient, requiring 200 micrograms only for spinning, and allowing 750 micrograms for weaving and 500 micrograms for all other processes in the cotton industry.

The strict proposed standard and the less stringent final standard were both technically and economically feasible in the sense dictated by the *Textile Manufacturers* opinion. The same would have been true of an even stricter standard, because even that proposed in 1976 was not set at the limit of feasibility.[68]

The Occupational Safety and Health Administration relaxed its proposed cotton-dust standard after a bitter battle within the Carter Administration, fought out in a series of leaked memos widely reported in the press. The White House economists (particularly the Council on Wage and Price Stability) argued that the proposed standard was too stringent, urging that its costs were too high and

---

[66] *Ibid.*

[67] 41 Fed. Reg. 56498 (1976).

[68] See MacAvoy, *The Nondecision Cotton Dust Decision*, N.Y. TIMES, July 5, 1981, p. F3.

the health benefits too low when compared to alternatives. The OSHA modified its standard in response to the White House pressure. The economists pressed for further relaxation, and the final decision was made by President Carter, who sided with OSHA after initially agreeing with the White House economists.[69]

The Court in *Textile Manufacturers* deferred to the agency determination on the limitation to be imposed on cotton dust, holding that it could not reverse the Court of Appeals conclusion that it was supported by substantial evidence. The outside observer is, however, bound to be disturbed by the flimsy nature of the evidence supporting the OSHA standard and the estimates upon which it was based.[70] OSHA had before it two financial analyses. The first was prepared by Research Triangle Institute under an OSHA contract. Despite the fact that the study was by a group under contract to OSHA, its cost estimates were rejected by OSHA. The other study was prepared by industry representatives. But its estimates assumed a less stringent standard than that issued. OSHA concluded that this was an overestimate of the costs of the less stringent standard the study was assuming. Then the agency decided that it would be treated as a reliable estimate for the more costly standard finally promulgated.[71] As Justice Stewart, dissenting, noted, OSHA "never rationally explain[ed] how it came to this happy conclusion."[72] Analysis of the record leads to the inevitable conclusion that the agency's estimate was sheer guesswork— "unsupported speculation." as Justice Stewart terms it.[73]

The extent of deference shown to the agency suggests that the Court would have reached the same result had the agency promulgated a more stringent cotton-dust standard. Presumably, that would also have been true if OSHA had reached a less stringent standard by relying on cost-benefit analysis. In fact, though neither the agency nor the Court admitted it, in relaxing the stringency of its original proposed standard, OSHA was doing exactly what the Court said it did not have to do—balancing health benefits against costs. The 1976 proposed standard required the same reduced level

---

[69] See DeMuth, *The White House Review Programs*, REGULATION, Jan./Feb. 1980, 13, 19.

[70] The evidence is analyzed in 43 Fed. Reg. at 27369 *et seq.*

[71] *Id.* at 27370.

[72] 101 S.Ct. at 2508.

[73] *Ibid.*

of cotton dust throughout the mill. This would have required much more ventilating equipment[74] in some rooms than in other rooms in the same mill, depending on the work done in them. OSHA's reduction of the standard for the parts of the mill that required the most equipment was based upon unavowed cost-benefit analysis, designed to equalize equipment costs throughout the mill,[75] even though that meant protection to workers below the 200 microgram level uniformly required under the 1976 proposed standard.

It is thus erroneous to conclude that the *Textile Manufacturers* decision sounds the knell for cost-benefit analysis or the Reagan reform program based upon it. In fact, the decision leaves it up to the agency to decide whether, and to what extent, to use such analyses. From this point of view, the Court, like the Congress, declined to make the crucial policy decision itself. Congress, says Justice Rehnquist in his dissent, declined to make the decision to require or prohibit cost-benefit analysis. Instead, it passed and left the choice to OSHA.[76] The same is true of the *Textile Manufacturers* decision. It leaves OSHA free to choose whether to require the most technically sophisticated equipment possible for worker safety or to set limits on cost by using cost-benefit analysis. The Court, no less than Congress, passed on the decisive policy choice.

V.

Where does *Textile Manufacturers* leave cost-benefit analysis?

The decision there, like that in *Vermont Yankee*,[77] means only that the Court will not impose requirements on rule making in addition to those demanded by Congress. The agency is free to interpret its enabling legislation along cost-benefit analysis lines. If it does so, as the Rehnquist dissent indicates,[78] the Court will defer to its judgment that the statute permits the agency to undertake cost-benefit analysis.

OSHA itself reacted to the *Textile Manufacturers* decision by

---

[74] Up to ten times as much, according to MacAvoy, note 68 *supra*.

[75] See 43 Fed. Reg. at 27378.

[76] 101 S.Ct. at 2509.

[77] Vermont Yankee Nuclear Power Corp. v. NRDC, 435 U.S. 519(1978). See Scalia, *Vermont Yankee: The APA, the D.C. Circuit, and the Supreme Court*, 1978 SUP. CT. REV. 345.

[78] Text to note 66 *supra*.

announcing that it would not use cost-benefit analysis as the basis for setting safety standards. Instead, it intended to use a "cost-effectiveness" test in issuing standards. By cost-effectiveness, OSHA said, it meant the least expensive way of reaching a specific level of protection for workers.[79] When he learned of the new OSHA approach, the director of occupational safety and health for the American Federation of Labor–Congress of Industrial Organizations declared, "This sounds to me as though they are trying to get as close as they can to cost-benefit analysis."[80] Certainly, it would appear difficult for OSHA to determine the most cost-effective standard without coming close to cost-benefit analysis.

The Supreme Court decision also leaves it open for Congress to enact legislation requiring cost-benefit analysis. Sponsored by eighty Senators, S. 1080 extends cost-benefit analysis requirements to agency rule making, "except where the enabling statute pursuant to which the agency is acting directs otherwise."[81] Under the bill, agencies must describe and analyze the benefits and costs of each new "major" regulation[82] and publish a statement with the final rule explaining how the benefits of the rule justify its costs and why the rule is more cost-effective than the alternatives considered. The bill S. 1080 has been approved by the Senate Judiciary Committee and action, at least in the Senate, appears "very likely" in the present session of Congress.[83]

Yet, even if the *Textile Manufacturers* decision does not prove to be the last word on the use of cost-benefit analysis in regulatory administration, it will remain significant for what it tells us about the Court's relationship to the administrative process. At a time of growing dissatisfaction with administrative performance, the Court has reaffirmed its deference toward agencies. A decade ago, Judge Bazelon asserted that we stood on the threshold of a new era in the relationship between agencies and reviewing courts.[84] *Textile Man-*

---

[79] N.Y. Times, July 13, 1981, p. A 11.

[80] *Ibid.*

[81] S. 1080, § 3(c)(1)(D), 97th Cong., 1st Sess.

[82] "Major rule" in S. 1080 is defined in a manner similar to its definition in Executive Order 12,291, supra note 51.

[83] Letter to writer from Senator Strom Thurmond, Chairman, Judiciary Committee, May 21, 1981.

[84] Environmental Defense Fund v. Ruckelshaus, 439 F.2d 584, 597 (D.C. Cir. 1971).

ufacturers indicates that the new review era has not yet dawned in the Supreme Court.

The overriding theme of the *Textile Manufacturers* opinion is deference toward administrative expertise, even though close analysis of the record shows that the OSHA conclusions were based on what Justice Stewart called "unsupported speculation."[85] Perhaps, as some claim, agencies "express an intuition of experience which outruns analysis and sums up many unnamed and tangled impressions; impressions which may lie beneath consciousness without losing their worth.[86] One would have hoped, however, that the highest court would require more than the mystique of administrative devotees to support so far reaching a regulatory standard.

OSHA's cotton-dust standard suffered from what Harold Laski once termed the limitations of the expert[87]—particularly zeal in promoting the agency's own administrative policy, regardless of the cost to other, broader interests. OSHA imposed its standard without comparing costs in relation to benefits, finding only that compliance with the standard would not threaten the economic viability of the industry and hence was economically feasible.[88] In considering costs, OSHA assumed that they would be borne by employers, indicating that the protections imposed were to be without cost to the employee.[89]

The notion that the cost of the OSHA standard was to be imposed only on employers is, however, illusory. Employers may pay the compliance costs initially. But that is not the end of the matter. The cost will ultimately be passed on to consumers. But the higher prices will lead them to consume less cotton products, leading to industry contraction and to worker layoffs. Then, too, at future bargaining sessions with labor, management will be unable to grant increased wages and benefits without further industry contraction and layoffs.[90] OSHA's desire to have compliance with its standard at no cost to employees thus turns out to be administrative pursuit of the will-o'-the-wisp.

---

[85] Note 72 *supra*.

[86] Chicago, B. & Q. Ry. v. Babcock, 204 U.S. 585, 598 (1907).

[87] Laski, *The Limitations of the Expert*, 162 HARPER'S 101 (1930).

[88] 43 Fed. Reg. 27378.

[89] 29 C.F.R. § 1910, 1043.

[90] Compare NATIONAL LAW JOURNAL, July 27, 1981, p. 29.

FRANK H. EASTERBROOK

INSIDER TRADING, SECRET AGENTS, EVIDENTIARY PRIVILEGES, AND THE PRODUCTION OF INFORMATION

I. Introduction

Most things are owned by someone. The owner makes decisions on the assumption that, if he can improve the use or productivity of the property, he may claim a substantial part of the benefits. Information, in contrast, usually is unowned; at least, it is not subject to the same rules of property law that govern apples and steel mills. It is difficult too, for someone who possesses information to appropriate the benefits of knowledge. Much of the value of information depends on its employment in transactions with third parties (whether strangers or employees) who may elect to use the knowledge for their own benefit later on.[1] It is hard to detect a

---

Frank H. Easterbrook is Professor of Law, The University of Chicago.

AUTHOR'S NOTE: I thank Douglas G. Baird, Walter J. Blum, Daniel R. Fischel, Dennis J. Hutchinson, Edmund W. Kitch, Richard A. Posner, and Steven M. Shapiro for their helpful comments on an earlier draft. The Law and Economics Program of the University of Chicago Law School provided financial support for the writing of this article. David Glazer and James Talent provided valuable assistance in the research.

[1] Compare Kaiser Aetna v. United States, 444 U.S. 164, 176 (1979) (characterizing the right to exclude as "one of the most essential sticks in the bundle of rights that are commonly characterized as property"), with PruneYard Shopping Center v. Robins, 447 U.S. 74 (1980) (holding that not every limitation on the right to exclude others is a "taking" of property for which compensation must be paid).

given use and harder still to argue that the producer of the knowledge suffered a loss because of that use.

This article discusses the way in which the Supreme Court has dealt with the scope of property rights in information. I argue that many problems usually thought to be distinct—trading in stocks by those who possess "inside" information, the publication of books by former agents of the CIA, and the assertion of the attorney-client privilege, to name only a few—are simply different aspects of the question whether someone who creates new knowledge has a property right in that knowledge and, if so, whether he may use that property right to advantage in later transactions.

Legal recognition of property rights in intangible thoughts is old. Article I, section 8, clause 8 of the Constitution gives Congress power "To promote the Progress of Science and useful Arts, by securing for limited Times to Authors and Inventors the Exclusive Right to their respective Writings and Discoveries." The patent, copyright, and trademark statutes will establish property rights. The Supreme Court has held that states may recognize still broader rights in intangible property.[2] The common law of the federal courts before *Erie* contained some rather broad rights to use knowledge. Several of the older cases may be read to say that one who creates or first finds information has a right to prevent anyone else from using the knowledge for profit.[3] The principle, if it still exists,[4] confers a property right of sorts on the creators of some kinds of information.

---

[2] *E.g.*, Aronson v. Quick Point Pencil Co., 440 U.S. 257 (1979) (contractual obligation to pay perpetual royalties for information about the design of a keyholder); Kewanee Oil Co. v. Bicron Corp., 416 U.S. 470 (1974) (state trade secret law); Goldstein v. California, 412 U.S. 546 (1973) (state law against copying recordings).

[3] *E.g.*, International News Service v. Associated Press, 248 U.S. 215 (1918) (granting the AP a privilege to enjoin the unauthorized publication of events reported in the AP's dispatches); Hunt v. New York Cotton Exchange, 205 U.S. 322 (1907) (holding that the Exchange may enjoin the unauthorized use of price information produced by trading on the floor of the Exchange); Board of Trade v. Christie Grain and Stock Co., 198 U.S. 236 (1905) (same). See also E.I. duPont deNemours & Co. v. Christopher, 431 F.2d 1012 (5th Cir. 1970), *cert. denied*, 400 U.S. 1024 (1971), discussed in Kitch, *The Law and Economics of Rights in Valuable Information*, 9 J. LEGAL STUDIES 683, 696–701 (1980).

[4] None of the cases has been overruled, and *Aronson* suggests that persons who obtain information by virtue of contract must continue to pay the agreed-on price. Nonetheless, the Court has not taken the cases for their broadest principles. See, *e.g.*, Associated Press v. United States, 326 U.S. 1 (1945) (the antitrust laws require AP to sell news to papers it does not wish to serve); Chrysler Corp. v. Brown, 441 U.S. 281 (1979) (the Freedom of Information Act never requires the government to withhold from the public information created by private parties). For discussions of the extent of property rights in information under federal

In recent years, the Supreme Court has begun to recognize property rights in additional kinds of information. Several cases create property rights under the guise of recognizing a constitutional right of privacy.[5] Other cases rest uneasily between statutory analysis and common law; these cases have been especially frequent in the last two terms. The Court held, for example, that medical researchers (rather than courts) may decide whether and to whom to release their raw data;[6] that the Consumer Product Safety Commission must verify the accuracy of consumers' accident reports before releasing them, thus giving television manufacturers a right to some confidentiality;[7] and that one spouse does not have a privilege to prevent all adverse testimony by another in a criminal trial.[8] In a case arising under the Truth in Lending Act, the Court pointedly observed that the disclosure of information is not always a virtue.[9] The Court also considered rights in information under the patent laws,[10] the Freedom of Information Act,[11] Title VII of the Civil Rights Act of 1964,[12] the Travel Act,[13] and a variety of other statutes and doctrines.[14]

---

statutes such as the Freedom of Information Act, see Kronman, *The Privacy Exemption to the Freedom of Information Act*, 9 J. LEGAL STUDIES 727 (1980); Easterbrook, *Privacy and the Optimal Extent of Disclosure under the Freedom of Information Act*, 9 J. LEGAL STUDIES 775 (1980); Note, *The Freedom of Nonfree Information: An Economic Proposal for Government Disclosure of Privately Submitted Commercial Information*, 32 STAN. L. REV. 339 (1980).

[5] See Posner, *The Uncertain Protection of Privacy by the Supreme Court*, 1979 SUP. CT. REV. 173, reprinted in THE ECONOMICS OF JUSTICE 310–47 (1981).

[6] Forsham v. Harris, 445 U.S. 169 (1980).

[7] Consumer Product Safety Commission v. GTE Sylvania Inc., 447 U.S. 102 (1980).

[8] Trammel v. United States, 445 U.S. 40 (1980).

[9] Ford Motor Credit Corp. v. Milhollin, 444 U.S. 555, 568 (1980) ("*Meaningful* disclosure does not mean *more* disclosure. Rather, it prescribes a balance between . . . 'competing considerations of complete disclosure . . . and the need to avoid . . . "informational overload." ' . . . And striking the appropriate balance is an empirical process . . .") (emphasis original).

[10] Diamond v. Chakrabarty, 447 U.S. 204 (1980); Diamond v. Diehr, 450 U.S. 175 (1981).

[11] Kissinger v. Reporters Committee for Freedom of the Press, 445 U.S. 136 (1980); GTE Sylvania, Inc. v. Consumers Union of the United States, Inc., 445 U.S. 375 (1980).

[12] EEOC v. Associated Dry Goods Corp., 449 U.S. 590 (1981).

[13] Perrin v. United States, 444 U.S. 37 (1979) (holding that the Act proscribes commercial bribery—in *Perrin* itself, an employee of a minerals exploration firm was paid to reveal geophysical data created by the firm).

[14] There have been three cases under the Truth in Lending Act in addition to *Milhollin*. American Express Co. v. Koerner, 101 S. Ct. 2281 (1981); Anderson Bros. Ford v. Valencia, 101 S. Ct. 2266 (1981); Ford Motor Credit Co. v. Cenance, 101 S. Ct. 2239 (1981). The Court has held that the government may not be estopped for failure to provide accurate

The proliferation of cases about rights in information should not be surprising. As methods of production become more sophisticated, information plays a larger role.[15] A computer, for example, is composed of $100 in information costs to every $1 of silicon, and the cost of computer software (essentially a bundle of information that tells the silicon chips what to do) may exceed the cost of hardware. The computer itself processes information about other aspects of production and distribution.

I focus in this article on questions about information that are neither explicitly addressed by statute nor covered by the common law of intellectual property. They are questions, then, requiring the Court to find its own way. The three cases discussed in depth are *Chiarella v. United States*,[16] which dealt with a printer's use of confidential information about impending mergers and tender offers; *Snepp v. United States*,[17] which enforced a promise by a former employee of the CIA to submit manuscripts for prepublication review; and *Upjohn Corp. v. United States*,[18] which addressed the scope of the attorney-client and work product privileges.

The cases do not, at first glance, have much in common. The Court put them in pigeonholes having little to do with information: one was a securities case, another a national security case, the third an evidence case. My thesis is that they are grouped more naturally as information cases. In two of them an agent attempted to use information in a way not approved by his principal; in the third the government attempted to compel a loyal agent to disclose the principal's information. In each, the central question was whether the principal had a property interest sufficient to require the agent neither to use nor to disclose without the principal's consent. The superficial differences—in *Snepp*, for example, the government sought secrecy, while in *Upjohn* it sought disclosure—should not obscure the fundamental identity of the problems in these cases and many others that face the Court.

---

information, Schweiker v. Hansen, 450 U.S. 785 (1981); that former CIA employees who violate their secrecy agreements may have their passports revoked, Haig v. Agee, 101 S. Ct. 2766 (1981); and that the Due Process Clause of the Fourteenth Amendment sometimes requires states to secure blood tests for litigants who cannot afford them in paternity suits, Little v. Streater, 101 S. Ct. 2202 (1981).

[15] See SOWELL, KNOWLEDGE AND DECISIONS (1980).

[16] 445 U.S. 222 (1980).

[17] 444 U.S. 507 (1980).

[18] 449 U.S. 383 (1981).

All three cases required the Court to consider a problem that distinguishes rights in information from rights in physical property. Information may be used without being used up. Much of the cost may lie in creating information, while use is less costly, or even free.[19] There is thus a powerful tension. A rule allowing information to be used freely, once in existence, may well maximize the wealth of both the users and society. Yet the same rule would reduce the ability of those who create information to appropriate the benefits of their efforts; people would create less information and take costly precautions to keep secret what they do create.[20] In the long run the reduction in incentives to produce and the increase in the costs of preservation could swamp the gains available from the free use of information. (Imagine the effects of a rule under which a rancher needed to protect cattle from theft without the benefit of any property right in the herd or any legal rule penalizing thieves.)

The patent and copyright laws deal with the tension between creating incentives to create new information and obtaining the optimal use of existing information by limiting the duration and scope of the rights conferred. The patent laws grant the inventor full privileges to control the production and use of the invention for seventeen years but do not allow him to control the use of the idea. Trade secret laws and common law doctrines allow perpetual control and use of the idea, but only if no one else comes by the idea independently; the owner of a trade secret may not block the production of articles embodying the knowledge. Copyright laws give the author a privilege to collect royalties from copying for substantially more than fifty years, but authors may not control the use to

---

[19] George Stigler has reminded us that information cannot be used at no cost. Stigler, *An Introduction to Privacy in Economics and Politics*, 9 J. LEGAL STUDIES 623, 640–41 (1980). Colleges and graduate schools devote substantial resources to explaining what $E = MC^2$ means; high schools spend tens of millions of dollars each year transmitting principles of trigonometry that were old hat in ancient Greece. Nonetheless, it seems beyond dispute that some kinds of knowledge can be used by some persons at a cost lower than the price that would be charged by a competitive firm that sought to levy a uniform charge just high enough to recover all of the costs incurred in generating the increment to knowledge. Whether the marginal cost of using the information is zero or just lower than the competitive price is irrelevant for present purposes.

[20] See Kitch, note 3 *supra*, for an excellent discussion of the way in which information is protected and retains value with or without property rights. See also Kronman, *Mistake, Disclosure, Information, and the Law of Contracts*, 7 J. LEGAL STUDIES 1, 9–18 (1978); POSNER, note 5 *supra*, at 232–48; for discussions of the tension between principles that facilitate creation and those that facilitate use.

which their creations are put. Whenever the question of property rights in information arises, the legislature or the court must confront the tensions between principles that encourage the creation of new information and those that allow the existing stock of information to be well used. If the Court puts information cases in securities law or evidence law pigeonholes, it may overlook the need to consider the way in which the incentive to produce information and the demands of current use conflict.

II. INSIDER TRADING

A. THE CHIARELLA CASE

Vincent Chiarella was a "markup man" in the composing room of a financial printer. He also was good at deciphering codes.

Firms that had decided to make tender offers or merger proposals delivered extensive financial information to the printer, with the names of the corporations in code. Using financial tables and other aids, Chiarella broke the codes and bought the stock of the intended targets. He routinely turned a handsome profit when he resold at the premium price offered by the bidders.

Alas for Chiarella, he could not make very much money on these trades without buying a good deal of stock. Large purchases in advance of a tender offer invite attention. Chiarella, the recipient of such unwanted attention, was prosecuted for a criminal violation of the Securities Exchange Act of 1934. The jury convicted him of violating section 10(b) of the Act, which makes it unlawful to use "any manipulative or deceptive device in contravention" of rules promulgated by the Securities and Exchange Commission.[21] Rule 10b-5 in turn makes it unlawful "[t]o employ any device, scheme, or artifice to defraud, [or] . . . [t]o engage in any act, practice, or course of business which operates or would operate as a fraud or a deceit upon any person, in connection with the purchase or sale of any security."[22]

The court of appeals affirmed the conviction, thinking it antithetical to notions of risk taking in financial markets to allow Chiarella to bet on a sure thing.[23] It announced that anyone with

---

[21] 15 U.S.C. § 78 j(b) (1976).

[22] 17 C.F.R. § 240.10b-5(a) and (c).

[23] United States v. Chiarella, 588 F.2d 1358 (2d Cir. 1978).

regular access to financial information not generally available to the public is forbidden to trade without disclosing that information.[24] Chiarella's trading was fraudulent, the court thought, because Chiarella had an unavoidable informational advantage over other traders.

The courts of appeals's principle was far too broad for the SEC's good. It had won too much, and when the Supreme Court granted Chiarella's petition, the government repudiated the court of appeals's rationale.[25] It argued that Chiarella committed fraud not only because he had privileged access to information but also because that information was the property of the printer's customers. The Solicitor General's brief contended that unauthorized use of information by employees and agents "can disturb market prices and prematurely reveal acquisition plans, contrary to the interests of the acquiring companies."[26] In other words, Chiarella had defrauded the acquiring firms, not the people whose stock he purchased.

The new argument did not carry the day. The Court reversed the conviction. Justice Powell's opinion, for six Justices, explained that the government's new theory had not been considered by the jury.[27] That left the court of appeals's unequal information approach, which the Court, like the Solicitor General, rejected. Although willing to conclude that trading without disclosure of information could be fraud or deceit under the rule,[28] the Court reasoned that nondisclosure can be deceitful only if there is a duty to disclose.[29] Chiarella had no duty to disclose to the people from whom he bought stock because he had no relationship, fiduciary or otherwise, to the sellers.[30] Any other view, the Court feared, would create "a general duty between all participants in market transactions to forgo actions based on material, nonpublic information."[31]

The Chief Justice dissented. He would have adopted the Solictor

---

[24] *Id.* at 1365.

[25] No. 78-1201, Br. at 70–71 n.48.

[26] *Id.* at 16.

[27] 445 U.S. at 235–37.

[28] *Id.* at 226–30.

[29] *Id.* at 228.

[30] *Id.* at 232.

[31] *Id.* at 233.

General's argument that "a person who has misappropriated non-public information"[32] may not trade without disclosing; and because disclosure by someone in Chiarella's position would violate a duty to the acquiring firm, he thus may not trade at all.[33] The statute encompasses any fraudulent scheme; it protects business as well as casual participants in the market;[34] Chiarella's use of information would be fraud against the customer under the common law; the Chief Justice saw no reason not to proscribe the conduct, because it "quite clearly serves no useful function except [Chiarella's] enrichment at the expense of others."[35] Justice Brennan, although agreeing with the Court that this "theft" approach had not been presented to the jury,[36] indicated agreement with the Chief Justice on the merits. Justice Stevens indicated willingness to be persuaded.[37]

Justice Blackmun, in a dissenting opinion joined by Justice Marshall, was more amenable to the court of appeals's "fairness" approach. He would have found Chiarella's conduct unlawful "even if he had obtained the blessing of his employer's principles,"[38] apparently because trading on information unknown to other participants is "inherently unfair."[39] But the two Justices left unclear the scope of their principle and concluded their opinion with a statement that only people "having access to confidential material information that is not *legally* available to others generally are prohibited" from trading.[40] A footnote then hinted that "legally available" means that there must be "parity of *access* to material information"[41]—which could mean anything from the Chief Justice's focus on theft to the court of appeals's focus on information that comes to the trader by

---

[32] *Id*. at 240.

[33] Chiarella's employer posted conspicuous signs warning the staff that all information is the property of the customer and that any use of the information is criminal. Chiarella admitted that he knew of his obligation not to use the information by trading. 588 F.2d at 1369–71; 445 U.S. at 243–45 (Burger, C. J., dissenting).

[34] See United States v. Naftalin, 441 U.S. 768 (1979).

[35] 445 U.S. at 241.

[36] *Id*. at 239–40.

[37] *Id*. at 237–38.

[38] *Id*. at 246. This is a strange remark, for Justice Blackmun also said that he agreed with Chief Justice Burger's views, and those views surely allow the bidder or its agents to trade.

[39] *Id*. at 248.

[40] *Id*. at 251 (emphasis added).

[41] *Id*. at 252 n.2 (emphasis in original).

virtue of his profession. Justice Blackmun apparently thought it unnecessary to tie up loose ends; his was, after all, only a dissenting opinion.[42]

B. INSIDER TRADING AND THE SCOPE OF DUTIES

All of this is unsatisfying. It is unsatisfying as law and as an application of economics to law. Economics seems an especially appropriate tool for looking at a case such as *Chiarella*. Economists study, first and foremost, the operation of markets. The trading of stock is the operation of a market, one of especially low transactions costs and therefore one especially likely to conform to economic models.

In the pages that follow, I discuss in turn Justice Powell's opinion for the Court and Justice Blackmun's dissent. Both discussions mix economic and more traditional legal analysis, although my critique of the Court's opinion focuses on traditional legal shortcomings. Then in Part IID I turn to a more general, principally economic, treatment of the problems posed by insider trading.

1. *Statutory support.* In holding that the ban on insider trading did not reach Chiarella's conduct—at least not unless the Solicitor General's theory was to be accepted—the Court first had to conclude that there *is* a ban on insider trading. The Court did not, however, examine the language or legislative history of the 1934 statute in any detail. The Justices examined, instead, decisions of the SEC and lower courts since 1960, which they generally endorsed.

---

[42] See United States Railroad Retirement Board v. Fritz, 449 U.S. 166, 176 n.10 (1980), in which the Court replied to the dissenting arguments of Justice Brennan by remarking that "[t]he comments in the dissenting opinion about the proper cases for which to look for the correct statement of the equal protection rational basis standard, and about which cases limit earlier cases, are just that: comments in a dissenting opinion." Three months later Justice Rehnquist, who wrote for the Court in *Fritz*, filed a lengthy dissenting opinion explaining the Court's Commerce Clause cases for the benefit of Justice Brennan, who this time was in the majority, albeit one unable to agree on a single opinion. He dutifully included an apology for the exercise. Kassel v. Consolidated Freightways Corp., 450 U.S. 662, 703 n.13 (1981). The meaning of these exchanges doubtless was summed up by Justice Stevens, who explained, in a concurring opinion for himself alone, that another concurring opinion of Justice Rehnquist—again summarizing cases for the benefit of the bench and bar—was not of much moment: "As The Chief Justice, Justice Stewart, Justice Rehnquist and I noted *in our separate opinion* in Regents of the University of California v. Bakke, 438 U.S. 265, 408, n.1 (1978), 'it is hardly necessary to state that only a majority can speak for the Court' or give an authoritative explanation of the meaning of its judgments." California v. Sierra Club, 101 S. Ct. 1775, 1782 n.5 (1981) (Stevens, J., concurring) (emphasis added). Hardly necessary indeed!

As the Court saw things, "[t]he SEC took an important step in the development of § 10(b)" when in 1961 it imposed penalties on a broker-dealer for trading on inside information.[43] It recited the central language of the SEC's decision and noticed that lower federal courts, too, had "found violations of § 10(b) where corporate insiders used undisclosed information for their own benefit.[44] That, apparently, was that.

Perhaps this was an appropriate course. Chiarella did not argue that insider trading is lawful. He argued only that he was not an insider.[45] Nonetheless, the process of endorsing the work of the SEC and lower courts, without independent examination, is reminiscent of how private rights of action under Rule 10b-5 and other features of the securities rules were found by the Court.[46] Recent cases seemed to say that the days of finding securities law rules by looking in the SEC's reports were over,[47] but *Chiarella* follows the older model.

An examination of the statute might have led to a different outcome. A considerable distortion of language underlies any holding that trading in a market without issuing a press release is "fraud" or "deceit." These words ordinarily mean the uttering of false statements or, perhaps, of half-truths. The Court has used them that way before.[48] False statements and half-truths move the price of securities away from the accurate one. If I know that Acme Mfg. Co. is broke, but I lie to you about the balance sheets, I can obtain a higher price.[49] But if I know that Acme is booming or that a tender offer is imminent, and I start buying stock, my purchases may nudge Acme's price higher, in the direction it should move. Who is hurt? Surely it will not do to say that section 10(b) requires disclosure because some sort of philosophy of disclosure pervades the 1933 and 1934 Acts even if no one section addresses insider trading.

---

[43] 445 U.S. at 226.

[44] *Id.* at 229.

[45] Brief for Petitioner at 20–31.

[46] See Blue Chip Stamps v. Manor Drug Stores, 421 U.S. 723, 733 (1975); Sup't of Ins. v. Bankers Life & Cas. Co., 404 U.S. 6, 13 n.9 (1971).

[47] Teamsters v. Daniel, 439 U.S. 551, 566 n.20 (1979) (collecting cases).

[48] *E.g.*, Aaron v. SEC, 446 U.S. 680 (1980); Ernst & Ernst v. Hochfelder, 425 U.S. 185 (1976); Affiliated Ute Citizens v. United States, 406 U.S. 128 (1972). *Cf.* Santa Fe Indus., Inc. v. Green, 430 U.S. 462 (1977).

[49] See, *e.g.*, Shearson, Hammill & Co., 42 S.E.C. 811 (1965) (selling stock of a bankrupt firm with no assets at $17 per share by fraudulently misrepresenting income and profits).

The 1933 Act allows trading in the aftermarket with no disclosure by anyone; the great majority of all trades are executed with no disclosure, even of the price, in advance.

The Securities Exchange Act has a provision explicitly dealing with some insider trading, but this provision, section 16, covers only people who own 10 percent of a firm's stock or have certain control positions.[50] It is not a disclosure rule at all; quite the contrary, it allows insiders to trade but requires them to pay the profits to the corporation if they buy and sell within six months. Disclosure is unnecessary; fraud is irrelevant; and the recovery goes to the firm (and thus continuing shareholders), rather than to the people who sold stock to the insiders. If they received too little, they are out of luck.

One could argue, with fair support in the structure of the statute, that section 16 is the sole device for addressing insider trading. Certainly such *expressio unius exclusio alterius* arguments have been popular lately in securities litigation.[51] And the legislative history of section 16 seems to establish that Congress intentionally drew back from the sort of extensive insider trading rules that have since been developed under section 10(b).[52] The Court had dealt with insider trading from time to time under section 16(b) and provisions of the bankruptcy law without hinting that section 10(b) might be pertinent.[53] State fraud law, which the Court often has used as a guide for interpreting section 10(b), allowed most insider trading.[54]

---

[50] Section 16(b), 15 U.S.C. § 78p(b) (1976). Section 16(c) bans short sales by those treated as insiders, thus depriving insiders of any incentive to run the firm into the ground.

[51] *E.g.*, Transamerica Mortgage Advisors, Inc. v. Lewis, 444 U.S. 11 (1979); Touche Ross & Co. v. Redington, 442 U.S. 560 (1979). See also Middlesex County Sewerage Authority v. National Sea Clammers Ass'n, 101 S. Ct. 2615, 2622–25 (1981).

[52] See the recounting in Foremost-McKesson, Inc. v. Provident Securities Co., 423 U.S. 232, 251–60 (1976), and Reliance Electric Co. v. Emerson Electric Co., 404 U.S. 418, 422–25 (1972).

[53] *E.g.*, Wolf v. Weinstein, 372 U.S. 633 (1963); Blau v. Lehman, 368 U.S. 403 (1962). One commentary on *Wolf* pointed out the omission and presciently remarked on the importance of section 10(b) for the future. Kaplan, Wolf v. Weinstein: *Another Chapter on Insider Trading*, 1963 SUP. CT. REV. 273.

[54] *E.g.*, Goodwin v. Agassiz, 283 Mass. 358, 186 N.E. 659 (1933). State courts generally found liability only when the form of the transaction had been set up to deceive the other party. See, *e.g.*, Brophy v. Cities Service Co., 31 Del. Ch. 241, 70 A.2d 5 (Del. Ch. 1949); Freeman v. Decio, 584 F.2d 186 (7th Cir. 1978) (Indiana law does not allow the corporation to recover insiders' profits on trades made with special knowledge). The "special facts doctrine" used by the Supreme Court before *Erie* is in much the same spirit. See Strong v. Repide, 213 U.S. 419 (1909) (purchase of shares by insider through undisclosed agent in person-to-person transaction).

Academic commentary on insider trading before 1961 discussed only section 16(b) and the bankruptcy rules; when authors ventured more broadly, they did so only to bemoan the absence of any other remedies.[55]

Certainly nothing compelled the Court to hold that the SEC's revolutionary 1961 approach to insider trading comports with the statute. Justice Powell cited no legislative history and never mentioned the state law on the subject as it stood in 1934.[56] He gave no reason for thinking that a rule against insider trading would be beneficial to investors. The rule may well be beneficial; I discuss that later. Even so, that would not be sufficient to support Justice Powell's assumption in *Chiarella*; to say "it would be beneficial if X were illegal" does not make it so.[57]

The only way to reconcile the Court's disquisition on duties with the statute is to say that any fraud "touching" a sale of securities is unlawful, even if the fraud had nothing to do with the existence or price of the sale. This is not an unknown treatment of fraud under Rule 10b-5.[58] Although it is most unlikely that in 1934 Congress intended to create a federal law of fraud with a crazy-quilt pattern—woven together by the proximity of fraud to a sale of a "security"—I now assume for purposes of further discussion that it did so. The question then becomes: What *is* the new federal law of fraud? That question can be answered only with some theory about how investors gain or lose in securities transactions. I postpone theory to Part IID and ask how the Court answered the question.

2. The source and limits of duties. The Court clearly was concerned that its recognition of restrictions on insider trading would lead to a rule banning all dealing on the basis of special knowledge. It stopped short of that position, stating that a trader must disclose only when he has a "duty" to do so.

The duty language, like the general restriction on insider trading,

---

[55] *E.g.*, Cook & Feldman, *Insider Trading under the Securities Exchange Act*, 66 HARV. L. REV. 385–422, 612–41 (1953), written by the Chairman of the SEC and a member of his staff. See also Brudney, *Insider Securities Dealings during Corporate Crises*, 61 MICH. L. REV. 1 (1962).

[56] Rubin v. United States, 449 U.S. 424 (1981), provides a sharp contrast. There the Court decided that a pledge of stock is a "sale," within the meaning of the statute, by examining the treatment of pledges at common law prior to 1934.

[57] United States v. Maze, 414 U.S. 395, 404–05 & n.10 (1974).

[58] See, *e.g.*, Sup't of Ins. v. Bankers Life & Cas. Co., 404 U.S. 6 (1971); Arrington v. Merrill Lynch, Pierce, Fenner & Smith, Inc., 651 F.2d 615 (7th Cir. 1981).

came from the SEC's opinion in *Cady, Roberts & Co.*[59] But the SEC did not put much stock in duties in *Cady*. It articulated a rationale in which duty played no role. The restriction on trading arises, the Commission said, from two elements:[60]

> [F]irst, the existence of a relationship giving access, directly or indirectly, to information intended to be available only for a corporate purpose and not for the personal benefit of anyone, and second, the inherent unfairness involved where a party takes advantage of such information knowing it is unavailable to those with whom he is dealing.

The first part of this rationale is the "business property" theory espoused by the Solicitor General and the Chief Justice; the second is the fairness theory espoused by Justices Blackmun and Marshall. Neither element offers much help to the Court.

The Court's treatment of wisdom received from the SEC is highly selective, to say the least. The Court extracted a duty principle from an opinion in which duty played little role and then explicated the duty requirement in a way foreign to the SEC's approach. The Court announced that duties do not arise from unequal possession of information;[61] they come, rather, from prior dealings of the trader as a fiduciary,[62] from a "relationship of trust and confidence."[63] Chiarella had no duty to those from whom he bought, the Court held, because he had no prior dealings with them.[64] But *why* is this the call of duty? The Court did not say, and the SEC has espoused a different view. The SEC regularly uses "duty" in a conclusional way. If the SEC concludes that a person should not trade, the Commission says that he "assumed a duty" not to do so.[65] Similarly, negligence in tort law is the violation of a "duty of care"; the duty arises by virtue of legal doctrine, not because of prior dealings between tortfeasor and victim.

The SEC has not been deterred by *Chiarella* from continuing to assert that people who (in the SEC's view) ought not to trade as-

---

[59] 40 S.E.C. 907, 911 (1961), *quoted* at 445 U.S. 227.

[60] 40 S.E.C. at 912, footnote omitted.

[61] Chiarella v. United States, 445 U.S. at 228 n.10.

[62] *Id.* at 229.

[63] *Id.* at 230.

[64] *Id.* at 232.

[65] E.g., Blyth & Co., 43 S.E.C. 1037 (1969).

sumed duties not to do so.[66] The Commission's position is not wholly at odds with Justice Powell's opinion, because that opinion is not internally consistent. Although the Court was sure that Chiarella had no duty because he had no prior dealings with the target companies, the Court also recited—with apparent approval—holdings of lower courts that recipients of tips from insiders may not trade. These tippees, the Court thought, "have a duty not to profit from the use of inside information that they know is confidential."[67] Where does the duty come from? The tippees are not fiduciaries of the firm; only the tippers are fiduciaries. Did the tippees assume a duty? If so, who else assumes a duty by the very fact of trading? The Court quoted Learned Hand to the effect that people assume duties when the contrary result would be "sorry."[68]

The Court's treatment of the "duty" requirement is perfectly circular. A trader has a duty when he assumes it; he assumes a duty when he trades knowing that others, in like circumstances, have been required to disclose; a fiduciary relationship (which itself may be imposed by a court) is one source of duty but not the only one. To say that someone has a duty, therefore, is to summarize—but not to support—a conclusion reached by other means that someone ought not to trade. The obligation not to trade rests on a concealed premise, perhaps on the Court's judgment about the costs and benefits of insider trading. And this brings us back to the central problem in *Chiarella*: the Court articulated no concept of why insider trading is wrongful, of who suffers as a result, or of what costs should be borne to stamp out the practice.

Only the lack of a theory could have led the Court to assert that Chiarella's liability would be inconsistent with trading by "warehousers"—people who buy stock on the advice of the bidder before the offer is made.[69] Warehousers act as agents of the acquiring firm and make the acquisition easier; Chiarella's acts undermined the bidder's efforts.

---

[66] Raymond L. Dirks, Rel. No. 17480, Jan. 26, 1981, at 13 n.42. Dirks, a securities analyst who learned from fired employees of the Equity Funding Corp. that the firm's books were fraudulent, was barred from alerting his clients to the fraud because "Dirks—standing in their [the former employees'] shoes—committed a breach of the fiduciary duty which he had assumed in dealing with them, when he passed the information on to the traders." The SEC did not explain how or why Dirks had assumed a duty.

[67] 445 U.S. at 230 n.12.

[68] *Id.* at 228 n.8, *quoting* from Gratz v. Claughton, 187 F.2d 46, 49 (2d Cir. 1951), cert. denied, 341 U.S. 920 (1951).

[69] 445 U.S. at 234.

Only the lack of a theory could have led the Court to assert that Chiarella's liability would have implied a general duty to disclose in all transactions.[70] As cases such as *Snepp* and *Upjohn* show, the Justices know that sometimes nondisclosure is necessary to enable people to capture the value of information; to permit use without disclosure is to encourage the creation of new information. Some firms invest in learning about others in order to decide whether to acquire them; the acquisitions lead to higher-valued uses of the targets' assets.[71] Firms' ability to trade on the knowledge of their plans enables them to obtain more of the value of their efforts. Chiarella's trading, in contrast, reduced the returns available to the bidders. His trading may have alerted the market to the impending offers and so made them more difficult to consummate. Chiarella's conduct subjected his principals to uncompensated risk, and there is thus no difficulty in designing a rule that would catch the Chiarellas of the world without simultaneously impairing the ability of tender bidders to obtain a profit from their investment in information.

C. FAIRNESS AS THE SOURCE OF THE OBLIGATION TO DISCLOSE

If notions of "duties" do not supply a coherent way to discuss the obligation to disclose, what about notions of fairness? Justice Blackmun argued that insider trading is "inherently unfair"[72] and that the Court should interpret the securities laws "flexibly" in order to be at the head of a "movement" to increase fairness in the securities markets.[73]

If arguments about fairness are to be more than discussion stoppers, they must have some content.[74] Justice Blackmun did not, however, explain what he meant by fairness, or why insider trading is detrimental to fairness. Perhaps he thought the answers were

---

[70] *Id.* at 233.

[71] See Easterbrook & Fischel, *The Proper Role of a Target's Management in Responding to a Tender Offer*, 94 HARV. L. REV. 1161 (1981), for a discussion of the functions of tender offers. See also Brudney, *Insiders, Outsiders, and Informational Advantages under the Federal Securities Laws*, 93 HARV. L. REV. 322, 370–76 (1979).

[72] 445 U.S. at 248.

[73] *Id.* at 247–50.

[74] Brudney & Clark, *A New Look at Corporate Opportunities*, 94 HARV. L. REV. 997, 1020 (1981) (calling fairness "that last refuge of courts" seeking to adjust the law to the presumed expectations of the parties and observing that case law gives the term "no principled content").

324   THE SUPREME COURT REVIEW

obvious; that may be why he referred to trading as "inherently" unfair. Here the Justice is supported by distinguished commentators, who have called insider trading "manipulation,"[75] "fraught with sufficient possibility of abuse,"[76] and "unfair,"[77] all without explaining why. Without some further explanation, however, we cannot tell how far these fairness principles reach. Is it unfair for a geologist, after studying the attributes of farmland, to buy the land without revealing that the land likely covers rich mineral deposits? If the answer is yes, then fairness means that no one may appropriate the value of information he has created.[78] An assertion about "fairness" thus deals with the tension between optimal use and optimal creation of information by dispatching it at the outset through assumption rather than analysis.

I suspect that few people who invoke arguments based on fairness have in mind any particular content for the term. Justice Stewart knew obscenity when he saw it; Justice Blackmun knows unfairness when he sees it. It should be possible, though, to supply a meaning.

1. *Fairness as identical returns.* Justice Blackmun may have thought that shareholders should be treated identically. Suppose there are ten shares of Target Corp. They trade freely for $10. Chiarella knows that a tender offer will be made the next day at $15. He buys one share at $10 and sells the next day for a profit. Nine of the ten original shareholders obtain the $5 gain; the one who sold to Chiarella does not. The difference might be called unfair.

This proposed definition is unsatisfactory. Shareholder 1, who sold to Chiarella, might well have sold no matter what Chiarella did. There is no reason to think that Chiarella's "buy" order, placed through a broker, caused additional investors to sell. If Chiarella's buying did not cause shareholders to part with their shares, then it is not responsible for the difference in returns obtained by the ten shareholders.

---

[75] HERMAN, CORPORATE CONTROL, CORPORATE POWER 116 (1981).

[76] Kaplan, note 53 *supra*, at 275.

[77] Ferber, *The Case against Insider Trading: A Response to Professor Manne*, 23 VAND. L. REV. 621 (1970); Schotland, *Unsafe at Any Price: A Reply to Manne, Insider Trading and the Stock Market*, 53 VA. L. REV. 1425 (1967).

[78] See Kronman, note 20 *supra*. Professor Brudney, who supports a limited version of insider trading restrictions, has recognized this effect. Brudney, note 71 *supra*, at 339–43, 371–76.

It is conceivable that the specialist in Target Corp., interpreting Chiarella's order as a signal of news, will raise his bid and asked prices in response to the new information. Then, the argument might run, shareholders of Target Corp. will sell even though they would not have done so at a lower price. These induced sellers are the victims of unfair treatment. But this explanation does not work because it does not show why the higher price causes more stock-holders to sell.[79] There is no reason why it should do so. The stock of Target is no less attractive an investment at $11 (after Chiarella starts buying) than at $10. Even shareholders who believe they can pick stocks and beat the market will not sell reflexively when the price rises. They may sensibly treat the rise as a signal that some-one knows something they do not and that further rises may be expected as the news spreads. There is simply no reason to believe—and certainly no evidence—that shareholders are bilked by rising prices into selling too soon.[80]

But suppose this is wrong, and insider trading causes some in-vestors to sell in advance of the price rise. Insider trading then reduces the likelihood that an active trader will obtain the highest possible price. If there is a chance that they will be shortchanged as a result of insiders' purchases, shareholders will respond by bidding less for the stock in the first place. The lower price compensates them *ex ante* for the risk. Because many sophisticated buyers are acquainted with the approximate frequency of insiders' purchases, the discount will accurately reflect the odds. If the discount accu-rately reflects the odds, then it is hard to see any unfairness in the process. (Because all traders, at any given time, deal at the same price, the self-protective moves of sophisticated traders protect the unsophisticated as well.) The stockholders who lose out in one round of insider trading are compensated by the increased gains they obtain if their shares (purchased at a small discount) are not scooped up by insiders and thus appreciate more in other cases.[81]

---

[79] Many of the common law cases holding insiders liable for fraud in securities transactions involved situations in which the insider's representations caused an unsuspecting shareholder to part with the shares. See, *e.g.*, Strong v. Repide, 213 U.S. 419 (1909).

[80] See Dooley, *Enforcement of Insider Trading Restrictions*, 66 VA. L. REV. 1 (1980).

[81] See Scott, *Insider Trading: Rule 10b-5, Disclosure, and Corporate Privacy*, 9 J. LEGAL STUDIES 801, 807–09 (1980); Easterbrook, Landes, & Posner, *Contribution among Antitrust Defendants: A Legal and Economic Analysis*, 23 J. LAW & ECON. 331, 339–44 (1980); POSNER, note 5 *supra*, at 92–99.

The process of price adjustment to reflect the odds of insider trading makes investing a fair game no matter how much insiders trade. The argument that a rule against insider trading is needed to preserve "small" investors' confidence in the fairness of securities markets[82] consequently is beside the point; markets are fair whether insiders trade or not, and small investors have little to fear. Larger investors' trades set the price and protect all others. Investors who want to avoid even the fair gamble may do so by buying shares of diversified mutual funds.

2. *Fairness as the ability to trade at the right price.* In a sense, the price at which Chiarella bought his stock was "wrong." It did not reflect all of the information about the corporations. Had the market known of the impending offers, people would have offered more for the stocks. On this view, Chiarella cheated all traders in the stocks, not just those he induced to sell, because all trades took place at the wrong price.

This treatment of fairness presents one possible resolution of the tension between optimal use of knowledge and optimal incentives to produce knowledge. It is hard to take seriously, though, as a version of fair conduct. Someone always is first to use any given piece of information. Most people would accept as fair the fact that people trade on some kinds of informational advantages even though the resulting price could be called "wrong." The law of contracts permits such trading. It is called shrewd bargaining. Texas Gulf Sulfur is allowed to purchase the mineral rights to farmland without first telling the farmers what it found. And a firm may buy stock in advance of a tender offer it plans to make, even though the pre-offer price is not as high as the offer price.

If there is some ethical obligation to make the trading price "right," it naturally rests on the firm whose stock is being traded. The firm has some obligations (of uncertain dimension) to its shareholders. It certainly has obligations more extensive than those of Chiarella and other strangers. Yet it seems to be accepted that corporations need not disclose the information necessary to enable the prices of their shares to become "right."[83] Disclosure could

---

[82] See, *e.g.*, Schotland, note 77 *supra*.

[83] See, *e.g.*, State Teachers Retirement Board v. Fluor Corp., 654 F.2d 843 (2d Cir. 1981), *aff'g in part* 500 F. Supp. 278 (S.D.N.Y. 1980). See Fischel, *The Law and Economics of Dividend Policy*, 67 VA. L. REV. 699, 717–25 (1981), for an excellent discussion of the reasons why corporations do not voluntarily disclose all information and why they should not be required to do so.

expose the firm to substantial liabilities if it turned out to be misleading, and it might tip the firm's hand and prevent it from obtaining an advantage over its rivals. (Imagine the effect of a requirement that the firm disclose all of the details of new product
development as it proceeded, so that the price of the stock could
fully reflect the prospects.)

If the firm has no general obligation to release information about
itself, a disclose-or-abstain rule applied to insiders could not improve the accuracy of the pricing of securities. It would produce
abstention rather than disclosure. If the firm (or the trader) disclosed, the market price of the stock would adjust promptly and the
discloser would not profit. But if the firm or insider withheld the
information, it would avoid giving an edge of rivals and reduce the
chance that it would be found liable for making premature, and
therefore misleading, disclosures.[84] If insider trading is allowed,
in contrast, the trades will convey at least some information to the
market. Henry Manne, whose pioneering work the Court slighted,
pointed out that such trading could convey full information and
lead to the "right" price even while the firm—fearful of liability for
releasing half of the story—remains silent.[85] In other words,
perhaps we can have both optimal use and optimal production of
knowledge, a question to which I shall return. It is enough for now
to say that any "fairness" argument based on the desire to induce
people to supply more information to the market is unpersuasive.

3. *Fairness as the absence of wealth transfers.* Insiders who trade
obtain gains that otherwise would have gone to the shareholders.
Justice Blackmun might believe that the shareholders ought to receive 100 percent of the gains. The insiders, after all, receive other
compensations for their efforts.

This approach begs the question whether insider trading is a
good method of compensating people for productive activity.

---

[84] This is no small worry. Texas Gulf Sulfur Co. was held liable to its shareholders for
releasing half-truths about its spectacular discovery. SEC v. Texas Gulf Sulfur Co., 401
F.2d 833, 862–64 (2d Cir. 1968) (*en banc*), *cert. denied*, 404 U.S. 1005 (1972).

[85] Manne, *Insider Trading and the Law Professors*, 23 VAND. L. REV. 547, 565–76 (1970).
Kenneth Scott has elaborated the argument by observing that, even if a rule against insider
trading expedites the disclosure of good news, it will retard the disclosure of bad news. Why
would a firm want to disclose unfavorable information? See Scott, note 81 *supra*, at 810–11.
One reason for disclosing bad news is the firm's desire to have shareholders believe it when it
reveals good news. A firm that revealed only the best about itself would find the market
severely discounting its stories. But this incentive generates disclosures no matter what the
rule about insider trading may be. See Fischel, note 83 *supra*, at 720.

Sometimes, as in *Chiarella*, the entire value-increasing enterprise would disappear if people (there, the acquiring firms and their agents) were barred from acquiring the stock for less than it would be worth under new ownership.[86] Similarly, there would have been no discoveries of ore in Timmons, Ontario, by the Texas Gulf Sulfur Corp. unless the discoverer were allowed to use its hard-won information to appropriate much of the value of the deposits.

The view that appropriation of gains is unfair may seem more compelling as applied to employees of the firm in whose stock they trade. These traders are on salary; why is not the stated salary sufficient compensation? The answer may be that the top managers need additional compensation that varies with performance. When they do well, stock prices rise; they can gain by trading.[87] There is no general principle that all of the gains from managers' good performances belong to the shareholders. Managers may pay themselves bonuses or issue stock options exercisable at less than the market price. If firms give managers such performance-based extras, managers will accept lower base salaries. Shareholders obtain the benefits of this arrangement. The only difference between these payments and the gains from insider trading is that bonuses come from the firm's treasury and are charged *pro rata* to all stockholders, while managers' gains from insider trading come disproportionately from the stockholders who sell to the managers. But this just returns us to fairness-as-equal-returns, which has been examined above.

Perhaps, though, the no-wealth-transfer concept of fairness turns on the *secrecy* of the insiders' conduct rather than on the fact that the trading helps them to appropriate gains. Salaries, bonuses, options, and the like are public; shareholders can react if managers pay themselves too much in public. Secret trades appear to be akin to theft.

Yet the existence of trading is not secret. Many managers of public corporations must report their holdings under section 16(a) of the 1934 Act and the proxy rules. Shareholders and investment advisers thus can make reasonably accurate estimates of the total compensation of insiders. Insider trading is secret only in the sense

---

[86] See Easterbrook & Fischel, note 71 *supra*, at 1174–80.

[87] MANNE, INSIDER TRADING AND THE STOCK MARKET (1966).

that the insiders steal a march on other persons who do not know the valuable information. The compensation package may reflect this opportunity, and adjustments *ex post* may also even things out.[88]

4. *Fairness as equality of information.* The last concept of fairness I consider here is that it is unfair for one person to trade with another unless the two are equally knowledgeable about the subject of the deal. In this view, not only insider trading but also Texas Gulf Sulfur's acquisition of land is unfair. Although this view of fairness seems astonishingly broad, the "equal information" position has its share of adherents.[89]

Justice Blackmun was not among them, and for good reason.[90] One cannot resolve the optimal use–optimal production problem by wishing it would go away. If information must be equalized, there will be precious little to go around. Indeed, the fact that some people can reap rewards by creating and using information provides a great benefit to the ignorant. The informed traders will buy and sell stock until its price is appropriate in light of its risk. They cannot manipulate the price for long. If it goes too high, some informed traders will start selling short, and if it goes too low they will start buying. Solid evidence suggests that this process of equilibration is completed in a few minutes after new information becomes available.[91] The informed traders thus protect the unin-

---

[88] Fama, *Agency Problems and the Theory of the Firm*, 88 J. POL. ECON. 288 (1980).

It is not persuasive to say, in response, that the insiders have "bargaining power" and thus can appropriate wealth. If they have this ability, they can use it whether or not insider trading is banned. They are always better off arranging the *structure* of the compensation package in the most efficient way (that is, the way preferred by shareholders). The efficiency gains increase the firms' profits. A group with bargaining power prefers a larger pie to a smaller one.

[89] See, *e.g.*, Kaplan, note 53 *supra*; Loss, *The Fiduciary Concept as Applied to Trading by Corporate "Insiders" in the United States*, 33 MOD. L. REV. 34 (1970); Painter, *Rule 10b-5: The Recodification Thicket*, 45 ST. JOHN'S L. REV. 699 (1971), and his THE FEDERAL SECURITIES CODE AND CORPORATE DISCLOSURE (1979); Schotland, note 77 *supra*. Cf. FRIED, CONTRACT AS PROMISE 79–85 (1981) (thoughtful treatment of fairness in dealings between farmer and one who locates minerals). The SEC's opinions have strains of this approach. Loss, however, may have changed his mind. His commentary to the ALI's Federal Securities Code 666 (1980) remarks that "it is hard to find justification today for imposing a fiduciary's duty of affirmative disclosure on an outsider who is not a 'tippee'." In other words, there is nothing wrong with trading on superior knowledge.

[90] Chiarella v. United States, 445 U.S. at 252 n.2.

[91] Many of the studies and arguments are collected in LORIE & HAMILTON, THE STOCK MARKET: THEORIES AND EVIDENCE (1973). See also Easterbrook & Fischel, note 71 *supra*, at 1165–68.

formed. Because the price is set by the knowledgeable, it is quite safe to buy stock in ignorance. It would be a colossal waste if the information, so conveniently and cheaply embedded in prices, had to be extracted and presented to everyone who executed a trade on the market.

Justice Blackmun may have intended, however, to argue that trading becomes unfair if one person lacks *access* to information known to another.[92] Victor Brudney has developed the equality of access position with considerable skill.[93] If Justice Blackmun and Professor Brudney mean that one may not use information to which his *own* access has been barred—for example, a person who has agreed by contract not to trade—the position is identical to the "business property" argument advanced by the Chief Justice. I discuss it immediately below, and it has substantial force. To the extent an equality of access position focuses on the situation of the person who lacks information, though, it is less compelling. People do not have or lack "access" in some absolute sense. There are, instead, different costs of obtaining information. An outsider's costs are high; he might have to purchase the information from the firm. Managers have lower costs (the amount of salary foregone); brokers have relatively low costs (the value of the time they spent investigating); Sherlock Holmes also may be able to infer extraordinary facts from ordinary occurrences at low cost. The different costs of access are simply a function of the division of labor. A manager (or a physician) always knows more than a shareholder (or patient) in some respects, but unless there is something unethical about the division of labor, the difference is not unfair.

D. THE REAL CONCERNS ABOUT INSIDER TRADING

The fairness arguments get us nowhere, and duty arguments must specify a source of the duties. I turn now to some considerations that deal more explicitly with the optimal use–optimal production problem.

---

[92] 445 U.S. at 252 n.2 (dissenting opinion).

[93] Brudney, note 71 *supra*. But see Galeno, *Drawing the Line on Insiders and Outsiders for Rule 10b-5*, 4 HARV. J. LAW & PUB. POLICY 203, 227–33 (1981), for a critique of Brudney along the lines I offer in the text.

1. *Business property.* A thief may not lawfully use stolen information.[94] Disclosure of the information would reduce its value to the rightful owner, and trading on the information would do likewise if it increased the price of the securities and led the market to infer the truth. This is the basis of much trade secret law, as the Court recognized in *Perrin v. United States*[95] only three months before it decided *Chiarella*. *Perrin*, a unanimous decision written by the Chief Justice, held that the sale of confidential commercial information is a federal crime.[96] Yet no one cited *Perrin* in *Chiarella*.

The business property rationale for restrictions on insider trading carries obvious limits. It applies only when secrecy is necessary to preserve the value of information to the firm that created the knowledge, but that condition obtained in *Chiarella*. Chiarella's trading posed a threat to the profits of the tender offerors. The bidders did their utmost to prevent Chiarella and other employees of the printer from trading or disclosing. At the same time, the bidders may have been acquiring stock for their own accounts or alerting friendly institutions (warehousers) to the profits available from acquiring the targets' stock. These are the devices by which they obtain the gains from their own information; they represent one accommodation of the optimal use–optimal production problem.

Surely the shareholders of the targets have no right to be free from such purchases without disclosure. This suggests that insider trading should be permitted to the extent the firm that created the information desires (or tolerates) such trading. The firm extracts value through exploiting the knowledge itself or reducing the salary of those who exploit it. The firm's decision to allow insiders to profit through a given device is the same in principle as any ordinary compensation decision, or as any decision to license know-how in exchange for a payment. If the managers err in setting their compensation, redress lies in the market, which will reduce their future earnings.

---

[94] 445 U.S. at 240–43 (Burger, C. J., dissenting). See also Scott, note 81 *supra*, at 814–15 (an article written before the *Chiarella* decision but published after it); Dooley, note 80 *supra*, at 63–64.

[95] 444 U.S. 37 (1979).

[96] Provided that the interstate commerce and illegality-under-state-law requirements of the Travel Act are met.

2. *Perverse incentives*

a) Perhaps, however, the opportunity for profits from insider trading does not create the same incentives for employees as the opportunity to receive salaries, bonuses, and so on. The market can exact an *ex post* settling up from particular insiders only if it possesses accurate information about the circumstances of their trades. Not all insiders are covered by reporting requirements, and those who are may not always comply.

b) There is, moreover, an important difference in the actors' attitudes toward risk. Shareholders are free to hold diversified portfolios. Those who do so will be indifferent to price changes of individual stocks in the portfolio. Swings offset each other. But because managers have much of their wealth in their human capital, they are more sensitive to the volatility of their compensation. Most managers would prefer the certainty of $100,000 salary to a salary of $50,000 and a 10 percent chance of a bonus of $500,000, even though the two have the same expected value. If this is so, then insider trading is an inefficient compensation scheme. It amounts to paying managers in lottery tickets.[97] The ticket costs the shareholders the actuarial value of the payoff, but risk-average managers value the ticket at less than that. The managers receive less than the firm gives up. Both shareholders and managers could gain by abolition of insider trading.

c) The opportunity to gain from insider trading also may induce managers to increase the volatility of the firm's stock prices.[98] They may select riskier projects than the shareholders would prefer, because if the risk pays off they can capture a portion of the gains in insider trading and, if the project flops, the shareholders bear the loss.[99] Shareholders would want to eliminate insider trading in order to remove this incentive for managers to adopt risky projects that have an expected value less than that of more predictable ventures.[100]

---

[97] See Scott, note 81 *supra*, at 808.

[98] See POSNER, ECONOMIC ANALYSIS OF LAW § 14.9 (2d ed. 1977); Brudney, note 71 *supra*, at 356.

[99] There is a similar conflict between shareholders and bondholders. Elaborate covenants protect bondholders from shareholders' desire to pursue excessively risky projects. Smith & Warner, *On Financial Contracting: An Analysis of Bond Covenants*, 7 J. FIN. ECON. 117 (1979).

[100] There may be countervailing incentives. For an argument that managers conduct firms in order to minimize volatility, see Shavell, *Risk Sharing and Incentives in the Principal and Agent Relationship*, 10 BELL J. ECON. 55 (1979). Perhaps the lure of insider trading profits would

d) The prospect of insiders' gains may lead the firm to delay the release of information, and such delays lead to extra costs for the firm. The firm must safeguard the information; snoopers will expend resources trying to find the information. Prompt release shortens this period of costly protections and costly snooping.[101] This may not be a large effect. I have argued that firms have reasons other than insider trading for delaying the release of information. During the period of delay, there will be expenditures on protection and investigation. It always pays for outsiders to learn the truth in advance of its release, so expenditures of these sorts seem unavoidable. The incremental costs under a system of insider trading could be small.

These four considerations suggest that granting insiders property rights in their knowledge about the firm is not necessarily beneficial. Perhaps an adjustment of rights, under the aegis of Rule 10b-5, could increase shareholders' welfare. Yet such adjustments have costs of their own, including the costs of enforcement and the costs with deterring desirable activities that might be mistaken for prohibited ones. Because some stock ownership and trading by insiders is, in general, desirable, reducing the divergence of interest between investors and managers, the costs of a legal rule may well be substantial.

Michael Dooley asked the right question: If insider trading is undesirable, why do not firms voluntarily curtail the practice?[102] If managers and shareholders have different attitudes toward risk, both gain from restrictions on trading. If trading leads to costs from riskier projects and precautions against disclosure of information, the shareholders would willingly ban the practice, obtain the savings, and pay part of the gains to managers to obtain their cooperation. Yet almost no firms attempted to curtail insider trading before the SEC's *Cady, Roberts* decision in 1961.[103]

One possible explanation of the firms' failure to do away with insiders' trading on material information—assuming that would be

---

offset such incentives and lead the managers to be effectively risk neutral, which shareholders would prefer. It would be necessary to do some very sophisticated work to determine where the balance of incentives lay.

[101] See Kitch, note 3 *supra*, at 718–19.

[102] Dooley, note 81 *supra*, at 45–47.

[103] Some do limit trading today. Louis, *The Unwinnable War on Insider Trading*, FORTUNE 72, 74 (July 13, 1981).

beneficial—is that they lack adequate enforcement devices. One way to abolish the practice is to ban shareholding by insiders. This works quite well for institutions such as law firms, which avoid trading on clients' information by abstaining; it would be counter-productive for the firms themselves, though, for shareholding helps to induce managers to run the firm in the interest of shareholders. If managers and insiders own shares, it may be exceptionally difficult to separate proper trades from the improper ones that use material inside information. Managers might agree, *ex ante*, that they would forego improper trading; but when the opportunity presented itself they could trade anyway, knowing that they probably would avoid detection.

When most incidents of an undesirable practice escape detection, the only way to deter that practice is to impose very large penalties when the practice is detected.[104] Such penalties generally must be imposed by public prosecution. The size of the optimal penalty could exceed the wealth of the trader; in that case, only jail would be an adequate response. Even when the traders can pay the optimal fines (in a combination of reduced future income and current payment), a system of private enforcement in which such very large recoveries is available could lead to too much investment in detecting and prosecuting offenses.[105] Private plaintiffs would investigate and litigate until the last dollar spent produced just one dollar of recovery. Such a system may lead to exceedingly costly trials and to penalties imposed on innocent conduct.[106] Finally, there may be economies of scale in public enforcement, because enforcers (including the stock markets) may find it possible to program their computers to monitor unusual trading as well as to perform more mundane functions.[107]

These considerations offer support for prohibition of insider trading under some circumstances. Surely the prohibition is desirable when it protects business property. The prohibition probably is

---

[104] On the relationship between the probability of detection and the size of the necessary penalty, see Polinsky & Shavell, *The Optimal Tradeoff Between the Probability and Magnitude of Fines*, 69 AM. ECON. REV. 880 (1979); Posner, *Optimal Sentences for White Collar Criminals*, 17 AM. CRIM. L. REV. 409 (1980).

[105] See Landes & Posner, *The Private Enforcement of Law*, 4 J. LEGAL STUDIES 1 (1974).

[106] See Easterbrook, *Predatory Strategies and Counterstrategies*, 48 U. CHI. L. REV. 263, 317–33 (1981), for exploration of this problem in a slightly different setting.

[107] Chiarella was caught because the New York Stock Exchange's computer signalled unusual trading. See also Louis, note 103 *supra* (describing stock watch programs).

desirable in general, because it allows public enforcement to replace inefficient private enforcement.[108] But the conclusion is uneasy, because it depends on conjectures about the magnitude of the costs of insider trading and its prohibition. Under plausible assumptions the costs of prohibition exceed the costs of the practices. Morever, the case for a legal rule is uneasy because it does not explain why firms do not even try to restrict insider trading. It would be simple to have a legal rule saying: If any given firm adopts a rule prohibiting trading by its insiders, then such trading is a crime; and if not, not. If insider trading is indeed costly to shareholders, firms might adopt such rules, just as they adopt other internal rules that maximize their value[109] and just as the CIA adopted rules governing disclosure by agents. That firms have not adopted such rules may show that trading is beneficial on balance. It could, however, show only that the legal system is reluctant to wheel the criminal enforcement machinery into play to enforce internal corporate rules. Any judgment about the value of a general rule against insider trading ultimately must rest on assessments of these costs and considerations, assessments that do not appear in the SEC's cases or the *Chiarella* opinions.

3. *Trading and stock prices.* I have addressed only briefly the point, frequently made by those who see little wrong in insider trading, that such trading causes prices to move toward the accurate one for the stock. Trading seems to give shareholders the best of all worlds, solving the tension between optimal use and optimal production of knowledge. Their firms can maintain business secrets, thus fully exploiting the value of information, while insider trading causes stock prices to move to the level they will reach once the news is revealed.

Unfortunately, the tension will not yield so easily. Why does insider trading cause prices to change? An increase in the insiders' demand for stock will not do the trick. The stock of any one firm is only a minuscule portion of the total supply of investment oppor-

---

[108] The structure of rules under section 10(b) and Rule 10b-5 supports this observation. A violation of section 10(b) and the implementing rules is a crime; Chiarella was prosecuted criminally and sentenced to jail even after he had surrendered his trading profits. In private actions under the rule, however, recovery is limited to the trader's profits. Elkind v. Liggett & Myers, Inc., 635 F.2d 156 (2d Cir. 1980). This limit reduces expenditures on private enforcement.

[109] See WINTER, GOVERNMENT AND THE CORPORATION (1978); Easterbrook & Fischel, note 71 *supra*, at 1168–82.

tunities. People invest in stocks because they anticipate return. They will shift funds around in order to equalize the expected (and risk-adjusted) return from each part of their portfolios. The simple fact that many people start to buy AT&T stock should not affect its price; an equal number of shares are bought and sold. People who have high hopes for a firm's future buy its stock from those who are relatively pessimistic. The process damps out any substantial differences in the expectations of shareholders, who then fall into two classes: active traders who have homogeneous expectations, and passive holders who take the price set by the active traders and have no independent expectations about the firm. The upshot is that "stock of firm X" has a highly elastic supply. People can buy arbitrarily large amounts at the going price.

This might seem inconsistent with the observation that, to obtain a lot of stock, people often must pay a premium price. It is not. Purchases often convey information to the market about the prospects of the firms. If the information indicates that the firm's prospects are better than those previously perceived, the price of the shares rises. Large purchases give the market a good deal of information. Traders find out or infer why one person is buying so much, and the new knowledge causes prices to adjust. For this reason, large transactions for technical, portfolio-adjustment reasons should have no effect on price, while smaller purchases based on new information should have an effect, even a dramatic one. This seems to be the pattern in the market.

The insider's trading thus may lead to price adjustments, but only to the extent the insider's secret has leaked to the market or been inferred by traders. It is not possible for the firm's stock to trade at the optimal level while the firm keeps its information hidden;[110] better for the firm to release the information itself at the appropriate time.[111]

Because information can be conveyed to the market without a press release, it follows that insiders also may alert the market to the correct prices of the firm's stock *without* trading. Insiders' decisions

---

[110] This is another way of saying that the strong version of the efficient capital market hypothesis—that prices reflect all information, even information unknowable by traders—is not supported.

[111] And firms will do just that. See Bensten, *Required Disclosure and the Stock Market: An Evaluation of the Securities Exchange Act of 1934*, 63 AM. ECON. REV. 132 (1973); Grossman & Hart, *Disclosure Laws and Takeover Bids*, 35 J. FINANCE 323 (1980).

not to trade, in response to good or bad news, could allow others to deduce the news. Suppose managers of a firm have a pattern of buying (or selling) stock, or that they have placed orders to buy or sell at particular prices. In response to good news, the insiders might cancel all sell orders or change their reservation prices. The specialist in the stock, and even the insiders' brokers, can profit by being alert to such things. If the specialist observes managers cancel sell orders and raise their off-market selling price, he will be less willing to sell from his own portfolio. The changes in these patterns of dealing sometimes may allow the market to infer all that is necessary to a price adjustment. A rule against insider trading doubtless diminishes the efficiency of the price system in reflecting the value of firms, but this diminution will be small if the market draws appropriate inferences from inaction.

4. *Rewards for investigation.* Sometimes trading on secret information may be necessary to encourage outsiders to investigate the firm. The case of the Equity Funding Corp. supplies a vivid example. The firm perpetrated a colossal fraud on its creditors and shareholders; one of its many ploys was claiming to have written nonexistent insurance. It then made the mistake of firing some employees. The disgruntled employees told Ray Dirks, a securities analyst, who investigated further and told his clients. The clients sold in advance of the precipitous decline in the firm's stock price, and the SEC found that Dirks had violated the rule against insider trading.[112] The fired employees were "insiders," the SEC reasoned; Dirks thus was a tippee; the clients were subtippees, and all of them assumed a duty not to trade without disclosing.

Dirks did everyone a service. The sooner frauds are discovered—and the more costs a defrauder bears in deferring disclosure—the fewer frauds there will be. Dirks's efforts were costly. He had to have a network of contacts, many of which would never pay off. (After all, most employees have no news of similar importance to disclose.) The investigation following the tip was costly too. While courting contacts and following up leads, Dirks could not sit around soliciting clients' trades and earning commissions. The ability to pass secret information to clients enabled Dirks to profit from his investigation, which redounded to everyone's benefit.

---

[112] Raymond L. Dirks, Rel. No. 17480, Jan. 26, 1981.

The Equity Funding case is unusual. It does not support a principle that insider trading is desirable as a rule. It suggests, instead, that there is little point in penalizing the trading of tippees of information. When the firm is entitled to secrecy, the person who passes out a tip is the wrongdoer. He can be penalized appropriately, by his employer if not by the courts. But when the release of information was not wrongful—and certainly the former employees of Equity Funding did no wrong in telling Dirks about the fraud—there is no justification for barring the use of the information. The SEC censured Dirks for violating the law, but it refused to impose a real penalty.[113] Doubtless it knew why: because Dirks's efforts were laudable.

E. CONCLUSION

I have paraded a series of arguments, mostly economic, for and against insider trading. Trading such as Dirks's is unambiguously beneficial, Chiarella's unambiguously detrimental to shareholders. The more frequent cases of trading by managers on the basis of knowledge about their own firms are much more difficult to judge. The arguments are closely balanced. Although I think it likely that legal restrictions on such trading are beneficial, the questions ultimately are empirical. I may be singing a different tune tomorrow.

Only the Chief Justice raised any of these problems in *Chiarella*. The other Justices seemed captivated by opposite horrors: the majority by the specter that to condemn Chiarella is to condemn all trading on unequal information and thus to eliminate much of the incentive to develop knowledge, Justice Blackmun by the fear that to allow insider trading is to allow the exploitation of investors through the use of secrets. Yet to consider effects on use without considering effects on incentives to produce, or the reverse, is simplistic. As I have shown, the proper treatment of insider trading depends on a multitude of considerations and more than a few guesses about the costs of different rules. In all probability Congress never delegated to the SEC or the courts the authority to say whether insider trading is wise, fair or unseemly. The ability to trade is more like the salary and bonus provisions of the employment contract than like ordinary fraud in transactions between in-

---

[113] *Id.* at 16.

vestors. Allocating opportunities to use information under an employment contract may call for difficult decisions, as the tortuous path of the law of trade secret and no-competition agreements shows,[114] and the difficulties cannot be avoided by disregarding the problems of optimal use versus optimal incentives to create knowledge.[115]

II. SECRET AGENTS

A. THE SNEPP CASE

The *Snepp* case raised problems concerning the allocation between employer and employee of rights to use information. This time the Justices saw the use-versus-creation problem, which makes the Court's treatment all the more puzzling, for it decided *Snepp* four weeks before it decided *Chiarella*.[116]

When Snepp joined the CIA, he signed an agreement promising not to publish "any information or material relating to the Agency, its activities or intelligence activities generally"[117] without the prior approval of the CIA. He served with the CIA for some years, quit, and published a book about the CIA without seeking approval. The district court and court of appeals found that the prior submission requirement is valid. The district court ordered Snepp to pay over his profits to the government; the court of appeals reversed this portion of the order and remitted the government to a claim for punitive damages.[118] The Supreme Court, acting without briefs or oral argument, restored the district court's disposition.

The Supreme Court treated Snepp's arguments with disdain. He

---

[114] See Kitch, note 3 *supra*.

[115] The Court left open the possibility of accepting the business property arguments made by Chief Justice Burger. 445 U.S. at 236–37. One lower court has adopted the Burger approach. United States v. Newman, 664 F.2d 12 (2d Cir. 1981). But see Feldman v. Simkins Industries, Inc., 492 F. Supp. 839 (N.D. Cal. 1980) (reading *Chiarella* as holding that only one in a "fiduciary relationship to market traders" ever could be liable).

[116] It is inappropriate to blame "the Court" for this problem. Many of the Justices were quite consistent in their perceptions of the problems presented by the cases. Only Justices Stewart, White, Powell, and Rehnquist cast votes that fairly may be described as inconsistent. The inconsistent disposition of cases that a majority of the Court finds similar is one of the unavoidable consequences of the voting process and not a legitimate reason for criticizing the institution. See Easterbrook, *Ways of Criticizing the Court* 95 HARV. L. REV. ——— (Feb. 1982).

[117] *Snepp*, 444 U.S. 507, 509.

[118] United States v. Snepp, 456 F. Supp. 176 (E.D. Va. 1978, *rev'd in part*, 595 F.2d 926 (4th Cir. 1979).

had violated a promise and in the process, the district court found, did "irreparable harm" to the intelligence apparatus essential to the national security.[119] The Court abruptly dismissed Snepp's argument that the agreement he signed was unauthorized or unconstitutional. The agencies concerned with the national security have ample authority to require such submission before publication, the Court thought. The CIA's organic statute entitled it to protect its sources and methods of intelligence.[120] And because Snepp "voluntarily" signed the agreement he could not argue that it violated his First Amendment rights; indeed, the Court intimated that agencies could require prior submissions even without the employee's agreement.[121]

The government had not argued that Snepp's book contained any classified information. This was unimportant, the Court said, because Snepp's acts exposed classified information to an unnecessary "risk of disclosure."[122] Only the CIA could reliably pick out the sensitive parts of a manuscript. Because Snepp had created an unnecessary risk and because any attempt to prove in court that the book contained secret materials likely would disclose the very secrets the CIA wanted to protect, the Court thought it appropriate to require Snepp to surrender his profits. The common law routinely required such a surrender for a breach of trust, it thought.[123]

The three dissenting Justices argued that the remedy of profits is inappropriate.[124] They would have required proof of actual harm to the government as a result of the publication. In their view, it was no longer material that Snepp violated his obligation to submit the manuscript for review; if the violation did not cause any loss, there was no justification for ordering Snepp to disgorge his profits. The common law imposed a requirement to pay over the profits only for violation of the duty not to disclose information, and Snepp, the dissenters thought, had not violated this duty—or at

---

[119] 444 U.S. at 509.

[120] *Id.* at 509 n.3, *quoting* from 50 U.S.C. § 403(d)(3).

[121] *Ibid.* See also Brown v. Glines, 444 U.S. 348 (1980), decided four weeks before *Snepp*, which sustained a regulation requiring military personnel to submit writings for review before circulation on military bases.

[122] 444 U.S. at 511.

[123] *Id.* at 514–15 & n.11.

[124] *Id.* at 516–26.

least the government had not offered to prove such a violation. The dissenting Justices thought the Court's remedy would chill harmless or beneficial speech. Although they were not prepared to dispute the Court's conclusion that the submission requirement is constitutional, they were sufficiently troubled by the matter to counsel moderation in the selection of a remedy.

B. CONTRACTS AND THE CREATION OF INFORMATION

1. Voluntary transactions are generally the best way to resolve the use-versus-creation problem. The parties to a contract are likely to know the value of information and the effects of more disclosure. People routinely contract about trade secrets, and the contract Snepp signed is very similar to an agreement not to disclose trade secrets. Snepp's new career as a writer threatened harm to the prospects of a Company that discovers, guards, and uses secrets. The publication of Snepp's book doubtless reduced the value of the CIA's stock of information and discouraged "suppliers" of information as well. The rationale for secrecy here is familiar; the press routinely asserts that it cannot disclose sources, for that would make information harder to acquire. The case for nondisclosure is much stronger when a firm wants to keep the information as well as the source secret.

The CIA would survive if former agents could publish without prior submission. It would take other steps to reduce the risk of disclosure. It could, for example, parcel out information more carefully so that fewer agents knew the full details of any aspect of its operations; it could give "disinformation" to its agents, so that they would believe things that are not true.[125] But these steps are costly and reduce the value of each agent to the CIA. A prior submission agreement allows the Company to give more information to the agents; it can tolerate additional discussion among them; as a result they will be more productive.[126] They can speak in English rather than in some code among themselves. Indeed, the increased openness within the CIA could lead to more information

---

[125] See POSNER, note 5 *supra*, at 242–48; Kitch, note 3 *supra*, at 689–705, 715–16.

[126] This can be characterized as additional investment by the CIA in the human capital of its agents, who will be worth more to the agency if they possess greater skills and knowledge. Without the ability to restrict subsequent disclosures, however, the agency would not endow the agents with as much training or knowledge. Rubin & Shedd, *Human Capital and Covenants Not to Compete*, 10 J. LEGAL STUDIES 93 (1981).

ultimately reaching the public. Because each agent will know more, he could write a more interesting story without the use of classified information.

A prior submission requirement also serves a channeling function. It will be less onerous to close-mouthed people who do not want to write about their employer than it will be to budding journalists. The agreement matches people who put little value on speech with an employer that puts a negative value on speech, just as other governmental agencies try to place those who are adept at speech in their press offices.

2. Why prior review rather than scrutiny, as the dissenting Justices suggested, to determine whether the former agent actually revealed confidential information? Again the Court supplied a thoughtful answer; scrutiny only after publication entails an unacceptable *risk* of disclosure. The agent may not realize how seemingly innocuous statements in his manuscript could be used to infer secrets. Snepp was in the same position as a research engineer at IBM who desires to write an article for a scholarly journal; IBM will want to review the article before publication to ensure that it discloses no trade secrets. Lack of review may lead to disclosure unintended by all. And if an article containing trade secrets nonetheless should appear, IBM does not want to wander into court and ask for the excision of three passages; that simply identifies them as the secrets. The government's experience in the *Progressive* case[127] establishes that a suit filed to suppress the publication of secret information, after it has been written and the publication process has begun, is more likely to disclose new secrets than to shield the old from public view.

C. THE REMEDY FOR IMPROPER USE

These considerations also show that recovery of profits is a plausible remedy in cases of misuse of information. Optimal damages equal the harm an offender does to the rest of us.[128] When someone robs a bank, he must disgorge the loot and pay an addi-

---

[127] Morland v. Sprecher, 443 U.S. 709 (1979); United States v. Progressive, Inc., 467 F. Supp. 990 (W.D. Wis.), *appeal dismissed*, 610 F.2d 819 (7th Cir. 1979).

[128] This discussion is based on Gary Becker's seminal work, *Crime and Punishment: An Economic Approach*, 76 J. POL. ECON. 169 (1968). For other applications see Easterbrook, note 106 *supra*, at 317–33; Posner, note 104 *supra*.

tional penalty reflecting the harm robbery does to all of us (it forces people to take precautions, employ police, and so on), all augmented to reflect the fact that many robbers are not caught. Agents of the CIA who write books are not all caught;[129] but even if detection and punishment were certain, it would be necessary to remove the financial incentive to violate the rules.

In principle we could follow the suggestion of Justice Stevens and let most agents keep their profits but impose a greatly multiplied fine on those who both fail to submit their manuscripts and publish secrets. But such a remedy would work only if the damages could be collected from the miscreants. This is unlikely. If, for example, the appropriate fine is 10,000 times the book's profits when the publication reveals secrets and zero otherwise, few authors would be able to pay. Authors would reason: I can violate the agreement and keep the profits if I am careful, and if not, I will simply declare bankruptcy and start over. This would produce too much disclosure, because the total damages collected from the agent-authors would be less than the optimal penalty. It may be *much* less. The harm from disclosure could be very large, requiring the invention of new code systems, the recruitment of new sources, the training of new agents and protection of exposed ones, and so on. Even if the costs of disclosure could be measured, which seems unlikely, few ex-agents could pay a fine equal to these costs, let alone a fine multipled to reflect the probability that the harms will go undetected or unredressed.

Still, recovery of profits is not necessarily the best remedy. It does not contain any element reflecting the actuarial value of the harm imposed by the occasional revelation of secrets, the costs of recruiting or mollifying sources frightened by the likelihood of disclosure, or the costs of taking precautions to prevent disclosure by other agent-authors. It may therefore be too low. On the other hand, the profits may overstate the loss in many cases. The profits could reflect only a small portion of the value to society of the information in a book that does not reveal classified data. The profits are not simply a transfer payment, after the fashion of a robber's loot or a monopolist's overcharge. They reflect real value, if only entertainment, provided to those who buy the book. The

---

[129] Phillip Agee, for example, fled the country. See Haig v. Agee, 101 S. Ct. 2766 (1981) (holding that Agee's passport may be revoked).

more value society sees in the book, the more it pays and thus the more the former agent must disgorge.

Here, it seems, the tension between optimal use of information about the CIA and optimal incentives to the CIA for future action is substantial. An award of profits is a rough accommodation at best. But rough or not, it is familiar. Those who trade on inside information must repay their profits without regard to the harm their activities do;[130] trustees who trade for their own account must do likewise, even if the trust beneficiary gains from the trade. These awards of profits force the trustee or possessor of someone else's information to get express permission for his activities rather than to act first and settle up later. That channeling function of the profit award may be the best one can hope for when the true harms are incalculable and the use-versus-creation problem insoluble.

D. INFORMATION AND THE FIRST AMENDMENT

There is only one interesting difference between Chiarella's conduct and Snepp's. Chiarella extracted profits from information by trading and Snepp by disclosing. Because Snepp wrote a book, his lawyers maintained, the First Amendment prevented the CIA from doing anything about his endeavors. The prior submission required by his contract is, they argued, "a classic system of prior restraint. The would-be author must seek and obtain the censor's approval before he can publish. If he bypasses the censor, he is liable to punishment solely on the ground that he has published, regardless of what he publishes."[131] True, Snepp signed a promise to submit the writings before publishing them, but the promise is worthless: "Government employment may not 'be conditioned on an oath that one . . . will not engage in protected speech activities'. . . ."[132]

It is conceivable that Snepp was right in saying that the First Amendment answers the use-versus-creation problem, but I doubt it. The agreement did not require Snepp to abandon criticism of government. He was free to publish without submission any general criticisms he had. The agreement required submission only of intelligence-related materials and barred publication only of classified material.

---

[130] Elkind v. Liggett & Myers, Inc., 635 F.2d 156 (2d Cir. 1980).

[131] Petition for Certiorari at 7, Snepp v. United States, No. 78-1871, filed June 18, 1979.

[132] Id. at 11.

The more general point, however, is that Snepp had struck a bargain. He learned of the CIA's activities by agreeing to limit his speech about them. The situation is similar to that of an employee who receives access to trade secrets or news of impending tender offers. So long as he enters into the agreement without fraud or coercion, he has made a judgment that he is better off with the agreement (and all its restraints) than without; he can hardly complain that his rights have been reduced. He has simply decided to exercise them in a particular way.

We may assume, therefore, that Snepp has a First Amendment right to broadcast to the world anything within his knowledge, without anyone's permission.[133] The assumption makes no difference to the case if Snepp can bargain with others about how (or whether) he will exercise this privilege. If Snepp's silence, or a prior submission routine, is worth more to the CIA than speech is worth to Snepp, he will sell his speech rights to the CIA; he receives in exchange a salary higher than he could obtain in employment that did not impose conditions on publication.[134] Having taken the CIA's money for years, Snepp is in no position to claim a right to publish without approval as well. The same principles apply to Snepp and to holders of trade secrets; it is hard to design any rule that would allow Snepp to breach his contract without simultaneously allowing employees of mineral exploration firms to sell or broadcast data about the locations of ore.[135]

---

[133] The assumption may be unduly favorable to Snepp, but the matter is debatable. Compare New York Times Co. v. United States, 403 U.S. 713 (1971), and Landmark Communications, Inc. v. Virginia, 435 U.S. 829 (1978), with Brown v. Glines, 444 U.S. 348 (1980).

[134] See Coase, *The Problem of Social Cost*, 3 J. LAW & ECON. 1 (1960). Coase showed that in the absence of transactions costs parties will bargain and assign the rights to engage in particular activities to those who value them more highly. The principle may seem inapplicable to Snepp's case, because the value of information is not fully appropriable. Suppose the expected profits of a book are $45,000. Snepp might accept $50,000 to surrender his privilege to write a book, even though the public would value the book at $100,000 and the CIA would suffer only $50,000 loss on publication. Snepp would look only to the appropriable portion of the gains in making his decision. But the government would have a broader perspective. The gain not captured by Snepp could be captured by the government through taxes. The government's loss on publication of the book thus is only $5,000 (the $50,000 harm to the CIA less the $55,000 gain to the public); the CIA's maximum offer to Snepp would be $5,000; and that would not be enough to induce him to surrender his privilege to publish.

[135] See Perrin v. United States, 444 U.S. 37 (1979), holding such a sale of information unlawful. It will not do to say that such a sale involves only "commercial" information and a private transaction. Commercial speech and private speech are covered by the First Amendment. Virginia State Board of Pharmacy v. Virginia Citizens Consumer Council, 425 U.S.

There are nonetheless three arguments that might support Snepp's contention that his agreement with the CIA is ineffectual. He might say that constitutional rights cannot be bartered, that this particular bargain was coerced, or that the kind of speech contained in his book excuses compliance even if constitutional rights generally may be the subject of bargains.

1. *Rights cannot be waived.* Ronald Dworkin, arguing in support of Snepp, had adopted the position that constitutional rights cannot be waived.[136] One cannot sell oneself into slavery, the argument goes, and therefore one cannot surrender any other constitutional rights. This is a *non sequitur.* The Thirteenth Amendment has a unique history and interpretation. It hardly shows that no rights may be surrendered.

Constitutional rights are waived every day. People incriminate themselves,[137] surrender their rights to counsel, waive a bundle of rights as part of plea bargains,[138] and sign contracts surrendering a right to trial through arbitration or confession of judgment clauses.[139] A criminal defendant even has a constitutional right to waive certain constitutional rights.[140] Congress routinely makes states offers they cannot refuse; states take federal money and surrender rights to autonomous government.[141] There is nothing special about the First Amendment. Governmental employees surrender their right to run for office and to associate in political campaigns,[142] and they surrender their right to raise and expend

---

748 (1976); Givhan v. Western Line Consolidated School District, 439 U.S. 410 (1979). When the government penalizes the disclosure of trade secrets, the speech *is* the crime.

[136] Dworkin, *Is the Press Losing the First Amendment?* NEW YORK REVIEW OF BOOKS 49 (Dec. 4, 1980).

[137] See North Carolina v. Butler, 441 U.S. 369 (1979); Michigan v. Mosley, 423 U.S. 96 (1975), and all of the other cases in the *Miranda* sequence. See also Garner v. United States, 424 U.S. 648 (1976).

[138] Corbitt v. New Jersey, 439 U.S. 212 (1978); Bordenkircher v. Hayes, 434 U.S. 357 (1978).

[139] D. H. Overmeyer Co. v. Frick Co., 405 U.S. 174 (1972); Steelworkers v. Warrier & Gulf Navigation Co., 363 U.S. 574 (1960).

[140] Faretta v. California, 422 U.S. 806 (1975) (right to counsel). *Cf.* Gannett Co. v. DePasquale, 443 U.S. 368 (1979) (public trial). *But cf.* Singer v. United States, 380 U.S. 24 (1965) (rule requiring prosecutor's consent to waiver of jury trial).

[141] North Carolina v. Califano, 435 U.S. 962 (1978), *aff'g mem.* 445 F. Supp. 532 (E.D.N.C. 1977); King v. Smith, 392 U.S. 309, 333 n.34 (1968); Steward Machine Co. v. Davis, 301 U.S. 548 (1937); Massachusetts v. Mellon, 262 U.S. 447, 480 (1923). Cf. County of Los Angeles v. Marshall, 631 F.2d 767 (D.C. Cir.), *cert. denied*, 449 U.S. 839 (1980).

[142] CSC v. Letter Carriers, 413 U.S. 548 (1973); Broadrick v. Oklahoma, 413 U.S. 601 (1973).

money when they accept campaign subsidies from the government.[143] In all of these cases, people sell their constitutional rights in ways that, they believe, make them better off. They prefer the benefits of the agreement to the exercise of their rights.

If people can obtain benefits from selling their rights, why should they be prevented from doing so? One aspect of the value of a right—whether a constitutional right or title to land—is that it can be sold and both parties to the bargain made better off. A right that cannot be sold is worth less than an otherwise-identical right that may be sold.[144] Those who believe in the value of constitutional rights should endorse their exercise by sale as well as their exercise by other action.[145]

2. *Snepp waived his rights under duress.* Professors Edgar and Schmidt have argued that the CIA's secrecy agreements are unenforceable because new employees have no real choice about the terms of their employment.[146] They are presented with a package: take it or leave it. Because Snepp did not explicitly endorse or bargain for the clause about prepublication review, it does not bind him.

This line of argument, a variant of objections to contracts of adhesion, would invalidate almost all agreements concerning the use of information. Employment always entails a package of rights and duties. Yet although each package has prescribed contents, the prospective employee has ample choice among packages; Snepp could have joined Woolworth's or the Agriculture Department's Press Office instead of the CIA. Because different agencies and private employers must compete for capable employees, they adjust the terms of their offers in order to make them attractive. The CIA's offer was designed to be attractive to the taciturn. That Snepp took the deal, knowing about the prepublication submission clause, is sufficient evidence that he thought the package, clause and all, beneficial to him.

---

[143] Buckley v. Valeo, 424 U.S. 1, 57 n.65 (1976).

[144] The Court has recognized this. Andrus v. Allard, 444 U.S. 51 (1979). See also Adams v. United States ex rel. McCann, 317 U.S. 269, 280 (1942), expressing unwillingness to "imprison a man in his privileges."

[145] Dworkin appears to argue, note 136 *supra*, at 56, that property rights may be waived but personal rights may not be. The distinction is incomprehensible; the right to hold and dispose of property *is* a personal right. Lynch v. Household Finance Corp., 405 U.S. 538, 550–52 (1972); Stigler, *Wealth, and Possibly Liberty*, 7 J. LEGAL STUDIES 213 (1978).

[146] Edgar & Schmidt, *The Espionage Statutes and the Publication of Defense Information*, 73 COLUM. L. REV. 929, 1078–79 (1973).

This analysis might seem inconsistent with the doctrine of unconstitutional conditions, which asserts that the government may
not demand waiver of a constitutional right as part of the price of
benefits it confers. The Supreme Court has said that a person "must
pay no . . . price for the exercise of his constitutional privileges."[147]
I am not sure that there *is* a "doctrine" of unconstitutional conditions after *Buckley v. Valeo*,[148] which held that the government may
demand that candidates surrender part of their right to speak as a
condition of receiving campaign subsidies, and any doctrine that
draws a distinction between a price for the exercise of a right and a
reward for the nonexercise of a right probably begs all the important questions.[149]

If, nonetheless, there is a doctrine of unconstitutional conditions,
it could have a number of possible meanings. One is that the government may not force someone to elect one right or another; it may
not say: "You may exercise your First Amendment rights or your
Fourth Amendment rights; choose which you prefer." The doctrine is not plausible if stated in this fashion, for sometimes the
constitutional rights are mutually exclusive; a criminal defendant
lawfully may be required to choose between his constitutional right
to silence and his constitutional right to testify in his own defense,
and he may be told that he will be penalized if he testifies falsely.[150]
Be that as it may, Snepp was not put to a choice between rights.

Another possible meaning is that the government may not make
an "offer" of the sort ordinarily made by the Mafia—one that asks
for a choice but leaves the recipient of the offer worse off than
before, a choice of the "Your money or your life" variety. Such
offers are deemed coercive in the law of contracts as well as in
constitutional law.[151] One may take this as a minimum content of
the doctrine. Even so, it does Snepp no good, for the CIA's offer of
employment made him better off.

---

[147] Carter v. Kentucky, 450 U.S. 288, 301 (1981).

[148] 424 U.S. 1 (1976).

[149] Roberts v. United States, 445 U.S. 552, 557 n.4 (1980).

[150] McGautha v. California, 401 U.S. (1971) (choice between rights); Baxter v. Pal-
migiano, 425 U.S. 308 (1976) (same, plus adverse inference for choosing silence); Roberts v.
United States, 445 U.S. 552 (1980) (penalty for testifying falsely). See generally Westen,
Incredible Dilemmas: Conditioning One Constitutional Right on the Forfeiture of Another, 66 IOWA
L. REV. 741 (1981), for a thoughtful treatment of the problem.

[151] See FRIED, note 89 *supra*.

The third possibility, and the most plausible one, is that the doctrine serves to control cases of externalities and monopoly, problems that would cause contracts to lead to less-than-desirable results. Contracts for wheat are, presumably, value increasing, because there are thousands of wheat producers, and buyers have ample choice. If there were only one seller of wheat, however, the terms of the deal would not necessarily be beneficial to buyers or society. The same is true when, as frequently occurs, the government has monopoly power. If it requires everyone to pay taxes for schools and requires children to attend school, it has monopoly power over education even though it does not suppress private schools. Consequently, the government may not make prayer a condition of public education. Similarly, the argument would run, the government may not demand that Snepp surrender a constitutional right to speak.

But imposing terms and conditions on the CIA's employment contract surely does not represent an exercise of monopoly power. The CIA employs only a trivial portion of all members of the labor force. There might be cause for substantial concern when the government dominates a larger fraction of all opportunities—for example, when it imposes conditions such as the Hatch Act on all public employment, or when it collects in taxes a substantial part of the national income and then offers money back to the states and private parties with strings attached. When the government monopolizes a particular market, perhaps the Constitution demands that the conditions it imposes on its deals serve some rational purpose. In other words, the conditions would be treated as if they were coercive legislation and subjected to the usual constitutional scrutiny.[152] If this is the appropriate standard, again Snepp has no case; the CIA has no market power, and the conditions of Snepp's deal unquestionably were rationally related to the purposes for which the CIA hires agents.

3. *Snepp's agreement violates the rights of others.* Snepp's book is a

---

[152] Many of the recent unconstitutional conditions cases appear to adopt an approach similar to this one, although they do not explicitly articulate a monopoly power standard. See, *e.g.*, Western & Southern Life Ins. Co. v. State Board of Equalization, 101 S. Ct. 2070, 2077–83 (1981) (discussing earlier cases). See also Westen, note 150 *supra*, at 749–51. The school teacher cases such as Pickering v. Board of Education, 391 U.S. 563 (1968), have much the same focus in holding that the government may penalize a school teacher for speaking, contract or no, when the speech is closely related to, and adversely affects, the teacher's employment relations or teaching effectiveness.

form of political speech, a challenge to the way in which the government does business. Perhaps a challenge to the government is entitled to special protection; perhaps the public has a right to know what Snepp thinks about the CIA. Both Archibald Cox and Ronald Dworkin have advanced arguments of this sort on Snepp's behalf.[153]

That the book criticizes the CIA offers little help to Snepp; he is free under the agreement to publish criticism, so long as the critique contains no classified information.[154] The fact that the CIA's activities are of concern to the public is both a reason for publication and a source of the CIA's concern that classified information not be disclosed. The CIA had to pay Snepp more in return for Snepp's promise than the Board of Tea Tasters would pay for a similar agreement by one of its employees. Unless something prevents Snepp from taking the compensation, there is no reason to distinguish political criticism from trade secrets or information about the stock market.

This leaves the argument that the public has a right to know about the CIA, a right Snepp cannot surrender. The public's "right to know" first appeared in the Court's cases more than 170 years after the First Amendment was adopted, which may be taken as a sign that it is based on invention rather than interpretation.[155] It has had a checkered history at best, coming to the fore when corporations want to speak[156] and when the press wants access to trials,[157] but vanishing when a politician wants the press to print his reply to a personal attack,[158] the press wants entrance to a jailhouse,[159] or a Belgian communist wants a visa.[160]

---

[153] Cox, *Foreward: Freedom of Expression in the Burger Court*, 94 HARV. L. REV. 1, 8–11, (1980); Dworkin, note 136 *supra*.

[154] Snepp has encountered no obstacle to criticism. His play about the CIA was approved by the agency without deletions. N. Y. TIMES, p. 19, col. 1 (July 1, 1981) (Midwest ed.).

[155] The first case is Zemel v. Rusk, 381 U.S. 1 (1965). Zemel attacked restrictions on travel to Cuba, arguing that they interfered with the right of citizens to learn about conditions there. The Court thought the ban a restriction on "the flow of information" but concluded: "we cannot accept the contention of appellant that it is a First Amendment right which is involved." *Id.* at 16.

[156] First National Bank of Boston v. Bellotti, 435 U.S. 765, 777–83 (1978).

[157] Richmond Newspapers, Inc. v. Virginia, 448 U.S. 555 (1980).

[158] Miami Herald Publishing Co. v. Tornillo, 418 U.S. 241 (1974).

[159] Pell v. Procunier, 417 U.S. 817 (1974); Saxbe v. Washington Post Co., 417 U.S. 843 (1974); Houchins v. KQED, Inc., 438 U.S. 1 (1978).

[160] Kleindienst v. Mandel, 408 U.S. 753, 762–70 (1972).

If there is a "right to know," perhaps the repeal of the Freedom of Information Act would be unconstitutional, and the "public" had a right to compel Snepp to write a book. Nonsense. The "right to know" is a mere by-product of the First Amendment right to speak. If one person has a right to speak, others learn. It is quite inappropriate to take a by-product and convert it into a right of independent standing.[161]

At all events, a right to know is one held by the community at large and may be waived by the community at large, just as Snepp may waive the rights he holds personally. Interests held in common are singularly appropriate for the legislative process. Dworkin put the point well:[162]

> [I]t is bizarre to say that even if the community, acting through its legislators, wishes to [allow some aspect of secrecy] because it believes that the integrity of such [secret governmental action] is more important than the information it gives up, it must not do so because of its right to have the information.

A legal doctrine preventing the CIA from contracting with Snepp harms everyone by stripping all of the power to have a CIA protected by a cloak of secrecy—that is, of the power to choose. There is no reason to think that those who want to "know" are a powerless minority. The Freedom of Information Act and other statutes illustrate the effectiveness of Congress in imposing disclosure rules on the Executive Branch.[163]

Having established that there is no public right to know, Dworkin immediately asserts that Snepp's contract is ineffective because it violates "the rights of those who want to listen to what Snepp wants to say. . . . [T]heir constitutional right to listen should not be cut off by Snepp's private decision to waive his right to speak to them."[164] A "right to listen" makes sense if it refers to rights immediately associated with speech. The right to express opinions in a

---

[161] See Easterbrook, note 4 *supra*, at 783 n.39.

[162] Dworkin, note 136 *supra*, at 52.

[163] I thus find it astonishing that people can write about rights of access and rights to know without mentioning the question of the need for *constitutional* protection or the circumstances in which majority decisions may be defeated. See, *e.g.*, Lewis, *A Public Right to Know about Public Institutions: The First Amendment as Sword*, 1980 SUP. CT. REV. 1, which proceeds as if the only question for decision is whether access rights are desirable. But see Baldasty & Simpson, *The Deceptive "Right to Know": How Pessimism Rewrote the First Amendment*, 56 WASH. L. REV. 365, 383–95 (1981).

[164] Dworkin, note 136 *supra*, at 55.

public forum can be annulled if the police may round up and arrest everyone who stands and hears, even while they leave the speaker alone. But a "right to listen" is incomprehensible unless someone first possesses a right to speak and desires to do so.[165] Snepp had the desire after he quit the CIA, but he had long ago surrendered his full rights. Unless the argument about a "right to listen" is to become as circular as the argument about the "duties" in *Chiarella*, it offers no support for the proposition that Snepp's contract is invalid.

E. FROM SNEPP TO UPJOHN

The Court's treatment of *Snepp* succeeded where *Chiarella* failed. The Justices saw clearly that complete use of information may come at the expense of the appropriate incentives to produce. In *Snepp* the case for relegating the trade-off to contract is strong, and the Court thus allowed the contract to control. The First Amendment does not interfere with the contractual process.[166] A comparison of *Snepp* with *Chiarella* might suggest that cases about the value of information should be decided summarily.[167]

---

[165] In Lamont v. Postmaster General, 381 U.S. 301 (1965), the first case holding that the First Amendment protects anyone's interest in receiving information, the Court treated the listener's right as a by-product of rights possessed by willing speakers.

[166] A stronger case could be made for First Amendment protection of utterances by strangers to any original agreement. For example, a "tippee" who discovers the details of secret governmental deliberation is free to publish them. Landmark Communications, Inc., v. Virginia, 435 U.S. 829 (1978). Perhaps the same is true of tippees of trade secrets, information about tender offers, and so on. A case could even be made, although it is not persuasive, that the First Amendment allows speech that violates the copyright laws. See Triangle Publications, Inc. v. Knight-Ridder Newspapers, Inc., 626 F.2d 1171 (5th Cir. 1980). Compare *id.* at 1179–81 (Brown, J., concurring), with *id.* at 1184 (Tate, J., concurring).

[167] Professor Cox, and many who wrote in the popular press, complained that the Court denied Snepp his due by disposing of the case without briefs or argument. See note 153 *supra*, at 9–11 & n.23. The Court does so many things deserving criticism that it is a shame to assail the Justices for disposing with briefs and argument when it seems likely they will just waste everyone's time. The *Snepp* case had been fully developed in the lower courts; the petitions were filed in June 1979, and the Court did not release the opinion until February 1980. In the meantime the Court secured the full record, including the appellate briefs, from the court of appeals. The petitions and amicus briefs fully canvassed the legal arguments, as did the opinions of the lower courts. Professor Cox did not suggest any arguments that could have been made in an additional round of briefs. Even Justice Stevens, who objected to the grant of the government's cross-petition, because, he thought, the Court did not believe Snepp's petition worthy of independent consideration (444 U.S. at 524–25), did not assert that the case should have been set for full briefing and argument. Every year the Court handles approximately fifteen cases by summary disposition with opinion and another substantial group of appeals without opinion. The Justices might consider increasing the

Yet *Snepp* does not say that the use-versus-creation problem always should be resolved by contract. When the incentives of the parties to the contract cause their behavior to diverge significantly from the performance that is best for society, there is a stronger argument for intervention. The usual example of an externality is pollution, but there may be significant third party effects in the production of information as well as in the production of material goods. The last case I discuss involves such third party effects. For reasons I outline below, the use-versus-creation problems in *Upjohn* are the most difficult of any the Court faced in the past few years, and the Court, despite explicitly recognizing the problem, leaped to a premature conclusion.

IV. EVIDENTIARY PRIVILEGES

A. THE UPJOHN CASE

Upjohn apparently made "questionable" foreign payments, *i.e.*, it bribed officials of foreign governments in order to obtain sales. After Upjohn's accountants noticed the payments in January 1976, the firm dispatched its general counsel to its foreign offices to obtain additional information. The Chairman of Upjohn's board instructed all employees to cooperate with the investigation. After the general counsel had interviewed numerous employees, the firm reported some of the findings to the SEC. The Internal Revenue Service became interested in the tax consequences of the bribes and asked for the general counsel's files. Upjohn refused, asserting that the text of the interviews was covered by the attorney-client privilege and the general counsel's interview notes by the work product privilege.

As the case reached the Court, the parties disagreed about whether the attorney-client privilege reached all matters pertinent to the firm's business (the "subject matter" approach) or only those matters involving the upper echelons of the firm (the "control group" approach). They also disagreed about whether the IRS had established sufficient reasons to overcome any work product protection. Upjohn won on both counts.

---

number, relieving counsel of the (expensive) motions of briefing and arguing cases with foreordained outcomes.

Justice Rehnquist's opinion for the Court observed that the attorney-client privilege exists to make people more willing to talk to their lawyers.[168] If they know that their words will remain confidential, they will provide more information; the more they say, the more effective the lawyer can be; the more effective the lawyer, the more likely the client to comply with the law. In a corporation essential information often is held by employees outside the control group. Moreover, Justice Rehnquist observed, the lawyer's advice may be most valuable to these noncontrolling employees. Thus, the privilege must extend beyond conversations between the attorney and the control group. That was enough to require a disposition in Upjohn's favor. The IRS was free to interview the employees itself, but it would have no help from Upjohn.

Whether the privilege extends to all communications within the subject matter of the firm's business the Court would not say. Although it acknowledged that "if the purpose of the attorney-client privilege is to be served, the attorney and client must be able to predict with some degree of certainty whether particular discussions will be protected,"[169] the Court also found itself "acutely aware . . . that we sit to decide concrete cases and not abstract propositions of law."[170] It therefore announced a case-by-case approach to the limits of the privilege—an approach that "may to some slight extent undermine desirable certainty" but that "obeys the spirit" of the Federal Rules of Evidence.[171]

The work product privilege, unlike the attorney-client privilege, always has called for some balancing. The IRS argued that it needed the general counsel's notes because Upjohn's employees were scattered across the globe and because Upjohn had instructed the employees not to answer questions it considered irrelevant.[172] The Court did not decide whether such hardships would override an ordinary claim of work product privilege. Upjohn's claim was different, Justice Rehnquist explained, because an attorney's notes are likely to contain his thoughts and theories. Federal Rule of Civil Procedure 26(b)(3) provides that in allowing discovery of work

---

[168] *Upjohn*, 449 U.S. at 389–95.

[169] *Id.* at 393.

[170] *Id.* at 386.

[171] *Id.* at 397.

[172] *Id.* at 399.

product materials "the court shall protect against disclosure of the mental impressions, conclusions, opinions, or legal theories of an attorney or other representative of a party concerning the litigation." Some courts have held that this provision bars any discovery of notes containing the attorney's thoughts. The Court stopped short of such a holding, however, after concluding that the Rule requires at least a heightened showing of necessity. "[S]uch work product cannot be disclosed simply on a showing of substantial need and inability to obtain the equivalent without undue hardship,"[173] the Court wrote; Upjohn had won its second point.

B. A PUZZLE

Before reaching the Court's treatment of property rights in information, I want to discuss a statutory hurdle.[174] The statute authorizing the IRS to obtain information by summons does not mention privileges. It says, quite bluntly, that the IRS "is authorized . . . [t]o examine *any* books, papers, records, or other data which may be relevant" to the inquiry.[175] The Court paused, but only briefly, over this point, because the Solicitor General had conceded that the usual privileges apply.[176] The concession doubtless was a wise decision by the government's chief litigator; he avoids arguments doomed to rejection. But why was this one doomed?

The Court observed that the summons statute and its legislative history say nothing about privileges. If Congress had intended to override the customary privileges for summons enforcement, Justice Rehnquist reasoned, surely it would have said so. But it did not, and the Rules of Evidence and the Rules of Civil Procedure

---

[173] *Id.* at 401.

[174] There are other puzzles in the case. Why did the attorney-client privilege apply to the general counsel's interviews? There was no need for an attorney to do the interviewing; an account or any member of senior management would have done as well. If the attorney is a supernumerary, the privilege is inapplicable. Why did the work product privilege apply to interviews that apparently were not conducted in anticipation of litigation? What is the difference between work product embodying thoughts of counsel (or other agents) and work product not embodying thoughts? Does not such material embody structure or organization, if not legal musings, almost by definition? If so, what is the distinction Rule 26(b)(3) is trying to draw? I bypass these for the same reason the Court did: the parties did not pay any attention to them.

[175] 26 U.S.C. § 7602 (1976) (emphasis added).

[176] 449 U.S. at 397–99, relying in part on pp. 16, 48 of the Brief for the United States.

similarly contain no exceptions for summons enforcement cases. The reasoning tracks that of Sherlock Holmes in "The Adventure of Silver Blaze": The Court can discern the meaning of the enactment by the fact that the dog did not bark in the night.

There is a problem here, one noted by Holmes but not the Court. The dog did not bark in the night because it knew the intruder. Congress is well aware of the standard privileges. If it meant to preserve the privileges, why did it pass a statute that does not mention them? The silent legislative history offers no clues; even Sherlock Holmes would be stumped. Perhaps the Court thought that, if the question were put to the 83d Congress, which enacted the statute, it would vote to preserve the privileges. But the 83d Congress is no longer sitting, and none of its members is on the Court. Suppositions about how deceased members of Congress might answer some unasked questions are an unsatisfactory substitute for taking the language of a statute seriously. It should come as no surprise that in recent years the Court has reasoned in some cases that the statute means what it says unless legislative history indicates otherwise, and in others that the statute means what it says only if the legislative history confirms the statutory language with a reassuring: "We really mean it."[177]

C. EVIDENTIARY PRIVILEGES AS PROPERTY RIGHTS IN INFORMATION

An evidentiary privilege is a right to withhold information unless the adversary makes a concession (pays a price) worth enough to induce the privilege holder to waive (sell) his rights. The privilege is thus a species of property right in information. And it is a right against the world; it makes no difference that the Commissioner of Internal Revenue, seeking to collect taxes due, is the one who wants access. But the extent of the property right after *Upjohn* is uncertain. The Court voted for "more" rather than less but did not say how much more. The direction is more interesting than the matter

---

[177] Compare Swain v. Pressley, 430 U.S. 372, 378–79 (1977); Harrison v. PPG Industries, Inc., 446 U.S. 578, 592 (1980); and United States Railroad Retirement Board v. Fritz, 449 U.S. 166 (1981) (Rehnquist, J.), among the many cases holding that the legislative history need not repeat what is plain on the face of the statute, with NLRB v. Catholic Bishop of Chicago, 440 U.S. 490 (1979), and Watt v. Alaska, 101 S. Ct. 1673 (1981), among the many cases requiring Congress to repeat the obvious in the legislative history if it wants the statute to be enforced according to its (apparent) terms. *Swain, Harrison,* and *Fritz* all reversed decisions that had relied on the absence of "We really mean it" language in the legislative history.

of definition, and I examine the problem without elaborating on the niceties of the control group and subject matter tests.

Upjohn is an extraordinary case. The Court saw that it presented a use-versus-creation problem, and Justice Rehnquist provided a thoughtful statement of the value of property rights in information and the role of confidentiality in allowing people to realize the return from their investment in information. Litigation, like buying a house or mineral land in Ontario, is a process of negotiation. The person who knows more has an advantage. The negotiating parties can dicker not only about the house but also about the information. In litigation one party can buy information from the other by conceding on some issues or reducing his claims. He cannot have the information without paying something.

Property rights in knowledge traditionally have been modified in litigation. This is the function of compulsory process and of discovery. In its cases on compulsory process issued by government agencies, the Court has said that the agency may investigate simply to satisfy its curiosity about whether the law is being violated; the cost of compliance is, if not irrelevant, at least not of much moment.[178] In defining the extent of privileges, the Court has explicitly considered the value of the information to those seeking to use it in litigation. It has not stopped by pointing out that the information is valuable to its creator and that secrecy leads to the production of more information. Thus the press and the President alike have been told that they may not withhold information in litigation.[179] In

---

[178] See, *e.g.*, United States v. Morton Salt Co., 338 U.S. 632, 652–53 (1950); Oklahoma Press Publishing Co. v. Walling, 327 U.S. 186, 216–17 (1946); In re FTC Line of Business Report Litigation, 595 F.2d 685 (D.C. Cir.), *cert. denied*, 439 U.S. 958 (1978). *But cf.* Staats v. Bristol Laboratories Division, 101 S. Ct. 2037 (1981), *aff'g by an equally divided Court* 620 F.2d 17 (2d Cir. 1980), which had denied the Comptroller General's request for access to the records of pharmaceutical firms. See also United States v. Euge, 444 U.S. 707 (1980); United States v. LaSalle National Bank, 437 U.S. 298 (1978), which construe the summons power of the IRS broadly.

[179] See, *e.g.*, Branzburg v. Hayes, 408 U.S. 665, 682 (1972) (the press enjoys no confidential source privilege; "valid laws serving substantial public interests" may be enforced through compulsory disclosure even though that reduces the ability of the press to gather news); United States v. Nixon, 418 U.S. 683, 705–07 (1974) (although the value of confidentiality "is too plain to require further discussion," confidentiality must yield to "other values," and a privilege may not be based "on no more than a generalized claim of the public interest in confidentiality"); Herbert v. Lando, 441 U.S. 153, 170–75 (1979) (balancing the interest of the press in the confidentiality of the editorial process against the need of plaintiffs for evidence); Trammel v. United States, 445 U.S. 40 (1980) (abrogating the marital privilege against adverse spousal testimony on the ground that the privilege, although contributing to marital harmony, unduly interferes with the access of a court to evidence).

Upjohn, by contrast, there was no balancing of interests. The Court explained that secrecy would lead Upjohn to do more (and better) consulting with its lawyers, and that was that. The Court resolved the use-versus-creation problem by fiat.

One explanation for the Court's disinclination to give much weight to the value the information might have had to the government in *Upjohn* could be that in earlier cases the Court was balancing private goals served by secrecy against public goals served by disclosure in litigation. In *Upjohn*, secrecy helped improve the quality of legal advice and thus served a public function. But such a public/private distinction will not wash. The public interest is simply an aggregate term for the welfare of all. Increased "private" welfare is part of the public interest. And there was no unity of interests in *Upjohn*; the firm used its privilege to defeat a claim of access by the IRS, which presumably would have used the information to enforce the laws more accurately. The public/private distinction also cannot explain earlier cases. The public interest in formulating and enforcing rules of public law was on both sides when the Court required President Nixon to turn over the tapes of conversations with his advisers.

The Court's earlier privilege decisions offer no rule and no way of deriving a rule in any dissimilar situation. An unfocused balancing test decides nothing. It is not even a test. It just says that the Court should consider everything that turns out to be important. Nonetheless, this may well be the best way of approaching questions of privilege—at least it is best if the Court considers the right things to be important.

It is not possible to formulate an answer to the property right questions in evidentiary privilege cases without some understanding of why people invest in litigation. Litigation turns out to be a staggeringly difficult problem in the application of economic principles to law. Bargaining about stock, ore, and manuscripts is easy: the parties will bargain to move resources to higher-valued uses and invest in information to help this occur. But in litigation the parties are fighting over a sum that may be unrelated to the way in which resources are used. The IRS claims a tax of $10 million; the defendant disputes liability; the parties litigate; each party invests until its last dollar in litigation services reduces its liability (or increases the actuarial value of the case) by just one dollar. The government may follow a slightly different pattern, for it is subject to a budget constraint; it will invest until the marginal value of litigation expenditures is the same in all of its cases. Both the government and the private party will count, as part of the stakes, the value of any precedent they expect the case to generate. This value will be higher for institutional litigants such as the United States and AT&T than for people worried about their personal taxes. In some cases the value of the precedent will overwhelm the parties' other interests, but this does not happen very often. The enterprise of litigation usually is principally a fight over spilt milk. The way in which the $10 million is divided may have little or nothing to do with the way parties act in the future. The disposition of the case moves no resources to higher-valued uses.

It is possible to make the point in a more general way. Litigation is valuable for three reasons. First, some (a very few) cases lead courts to announce or alter legal rules. This is the rule-creation function. Second, courts may take existing rules as given and apply them accurately in a way that influences future behavior. The more accurate the application of the rules in particular cases, the more effect the rule itself will have in influencing behavior. The rule against bank robbery is more effective if only bank robbers are convicted than if everyone who enters a bank for any purpose has a substantial chance of being convicted. This is the rule-enforcing (general deterrence) function of litigation. Third, the court divides the stakes among the parties. This usually is done through settlements and jury verdicts that have no rule-creation value and uncertain rule-enforcing value.

The functions are not altogether separate. The process of dividing the stakes determines whether rules are being enforced accurately. The existence of compensation for victims sometimes dissuades them from taking costly precautions and thus both reinforces the rule and increases the wealth of society.[180] Sometimes the purpose of the rule is compensation, and the second and third functions merge (although the rule-enforcing function is not served unless the stakes are *properly* divided). But to the extent the

---

[180] For example, the award of damages to people who pay overcharges to monopolists makes them less likely to stop buying the monopolized good; the social cost of monopoly is precisely the reduction in quality below the competitive level, and compensation thus may prevent the occurrence of the harm that the antitrust laws seek to forestall. See Landes & Posner, *Should Indirect Purchasers Have Standing to Sue under the Antitrust Laws? An Economic Analysis of the Rule of* Illinois Brick, 46 U. CHI. L. REV. 602 (1979).

functions are separable—and they often are—society's interest in the first two greatly exceeds its interest in the third. As a rule, we would like to hold as low as possible the resources spent bickering over the distribution of a pile of money, when the distribution does not affect future conduct. Bygones are bygone.

Although society has the least interest in the stakes-dividing function of litigation, the parties find this the most important feature of the process. Because the parties' investment is influenced largely by the size of the stakes rather than by the value of the case as a precedent, they may invest far too much (as society sees things) in litigation.[181] Often one party's investment in litigation simply offsets or nullifies the worth of an investment by someone else; the defendant will match the plaintiff's expenses.[182] Sometimes, indeed, the parties' desire to obtain as much of the stakes as possible leads them to hide evidence, produce questionable evidence, or otherwise divert the outcome of the litigation from the one that maximizes society's well-being.

This means that the use-versus-creation problem, solved so easily in *Snepp* in favor of contract (and thus creation plus limited use) cannot easily be handled in *Upjohn* by deferring to the parties' decision. Making it easier for parties to litigation to keep secret the

---

[181] The observation frequently made by economic analysts of law that parties will invest too little in litigation, because they fail to take account of the value of its rule-creating function, is therefore inaccurate, if not misleading. See, *e.g.*, POSNER, note 98 *supra*, at §§ 19.1, 20.2; Landes & Posner, *Adjudication as a Private Good*, 8 J. LEGAL STUDIES 235 (1979). (I do not mean to suggest that parties invest too much in rule-creating litigation, though; because they do not capture the benefits to society of better rules, they will invest too little in this aspect of litigation. My point, rather, is that too much investment in "litigation," including the stakes-division aspect, may occur at the same time as insufficient investment in the rule-creation aspect.) See Shavell, *The Social Versus the Private Incentive to Bring Suit in a Costly Legal System* (unpublished paper, July 1981), for a discussion of the way some of these problems affect the decision to file a suit.

[182] See TULLOCK, TRIALS ON TRIAL: THE PURE THEORY OF LEGAL PROCEDURE (1980). This point is valid, however, only within a limited domain. If the parties can bargain effectively with one another they can agree not to make wasteful expenditures of this sort. Problems arise, though, in policing an agreement; once one party agrees to restrict its own expenditures, the marginal value of expenditures by the other rises, so that it has a powerful incentive to breach the agreement. One way in which the parties may agree to reduce expenses is to sign a stipulation of certain facts. But stipulations are risky; a party who signs before investigating fully may find that he did not do well on the bargain. And the entry of a stipulation on one aspect of the case might increase the marginal productivity of investments on other aspects, so that the stipulation would not ultimately reduce costs. Finally, stipulations may be set aside, and other forms of agreeing to reduce expenditures are not enforceable in court. Because litigants do not face each other frequently in disputes about the same questions, we would not expect to see many agreements even if the potential benefits were high. *Cf.* Telser, *A Theory of Self-Enforcing Agreements*, 53 J. BUS. 27 (1980).

information they generate will induce them to invest more in this activity. If information creation in litigation is useful principally to divide the stakes, then a stronger evidentiary privilege may exacerbate the problem of overinvestment while simultaneously—by denying the tribunal access to evidence—making the outcome of cases less accurate and reducing the rule-enforcement value of litigation. To say, as the Court did, that a restriction of the scope of the attorney-client and work product privileges would reduce the investment in information in litigation may be to praise that result, not to condemn it.

Society may gain or it may lose by encouraging the creation of information in litigation through broad privileges. We cannot tell without being able to determine how privileges affect (and are affected by) the value of the different functions of litigation. Tracing this web of effects is a stupefying complex task. Economists (including the game theorists) have only begun to grapple with the problems of creating and using information in litigation, and I do not have any solutions to the information questions raised by cases such as *Upjohn*.

Let us suppose that the discussion so far is enough to show that society wants to encourage the creation of information in litigation only to the extent it contributes to the rule-creation and rule-enforcement functions; otherwise we gain by a policy of maximum use of existing information at the expense of lower incentives to create it. This may not be true all of the time, but it will do for now as a standard. If we accept this premise, we may properly conclude that productive or planning information—the crafting of a strategy, the reports of experts, etc.—ought generally to be privileged, because these activities are central to the rule-creation and rule-enforcement functions.[183] On the other hand, activities that generate the particular facts of the case are of more concern to the parties' fight over the stakes than to the creation of rules. Thus most documents are discoverable; the considerations supporting discovery of case-specific facts also suggest that privileges concerning the process by which facts are gathered or deployed should be eliminated or pared back. An appropriate distinction might be between productive information and retrospective analysis. A more generous

---

[183] See Exxon Corp. v. FTC, 663 F.2d 120 (D.C. Cir. 1980) (the reports of experts hired by the FTC to evaluate its case are privileged).

scope for discovery of such factual matters—including the general counsel's interviews in *Upjohn*—discourages costly digging and prevents needless duplication of effort by the parties.[184]

This is subject to qualification. Sometimes the abrogation of a property right in information will cause people to change the way they conduct their activities. If certain writings are discoverable, people may find ways to carry on their business orally or in code. If they do, a rule granting one party access would raise the cost of litigation but give no new information to the party seeking access. It might also degrade the accuracy of the rule-enforcing function. Considerations of this sort may underlie much of the law of industrial piracy, which grants firms a right of privacy.[185] The costs of disclosure affect much litigation preparation already. Lawyers and consultants routinely withhold facts and documents from expert witnesses, because anything the expert sees is discoverable (in practice, even if not in theory). Litigation then becomes more costly (parties hire a background expert to do much of the work for a testimonial expert but shield him from documents) and more problematic (the expert's opinion may not reflect all of the facts). Yet even so, it is easy to overstate the costs of accommodating one's conduct to disclosure rules. It is unlikely that Upjohn's general counsel would have abandoned note-taking in the future if Upjohn had lost its case. Certainly the government has not abandoned memo writing, despite the Freedom of Information Act. The question ultimately is empirical, but I hazard the conjecture that the costs of more narrowly drawn privileges would not be high.

A contrary argument might run: it is remiss to consider privileges only as part of the litigation process. The attorney-client privilege helps people to comply with the law and so avoids litigation altogether. If the privilege is restricted, there will be more violations of law, more cases, and so more waste.

The response is important, but its scope is limited. Often the value of planning does not depend on confidentiality. The prospect

---

[184] See United States v. AT&T, 642 F.2d 1285 (D.C. Cir. 1980); AT&T v. Grady, 594 F.2d 594 (7th Cir. 1978), *cert. denied*, 440 U.S. 971 (1979) (the United States is entitled to documents that were discovered in a private case and deemed relevant by the parties; the turnover of the contents helps to achieve the goal of Fed. R. Civ. P. 1 to promote the "speedy" and "inexpensive" disposition of cases).

[185] See POSNER, note 5 *supra*, at 255; Kitch, note 3 *supra*.

that some day the firm might have to turn over a legal opinion in litigation probably would not dissuade it from finding out the extent to which it lawfully could bribe foreign officials. Firms frequently disclose such planning documents voluntarily in order to show that they acted in good faith with appropriate legal advice. When the value of planning turns on confidence, it may well be possible to separate compliance activities, which could be privileged, from litigation and other postviolation activities, which would not. *Upjohn* involved analysis of historical events, not planning to avoid violations.

Moreover, it is wrong to suppose that a broad privilege is needed to ensure compliance with legal rules. Firms may choose to prevent violations of legal obligations, but they also may choose to tolerate violations and pay the fines (or litigate to avoid payment). The choice between prevention and payment (or litigation) depends on the costs of each and the extent to which the two are substitutes; it also depends on the costs adversaries will incur in planning and litigating. If privileges are constricted, so that prevention becomes more expensive, this might well lead people to back away from the precipice (which they can approach closely with careful advice). Whether they do so will depend on the relative costs of fines, litigation, and altering their conduct. The higher cost of legal advice may produce more adherence to legal requirements and a net saving to society.

Just as the higher cost of prevention may lead to fewer violations, the higher effective cost of obtaining advice might lead people to spend more on that input. It all depends on the elasticity of demand for prevention.[186] Then, too, if the privilege becomes more powerful, the costs to the IRS go up. If the agency bears higher costs, it can bring fewer suits and must settle for smaller awards. The higher the costs go, the less anyone needs to worry about the legal rule, and thus the less he needs to invest in preventing violations.

---

[186] See Gould, *Privacy and the Economics of Information*, 9 J. LEGAL STUDIES 827 (1980); Pashigian, *Regulation, Preventive Law, and the Duties of Attorneys* (in preparation).

The Court's answer to the Solicitor General's argument "that the risk of civil or criminal liability suffices to ensure that corporations will seek legal advice in the absence of the protection of the privilege" (449 U.S. at 393 n.2) was that the "position proves too much, since it applies to all communications covered by the privilege . . ." (*ibid.*). The Court's answer is too glib; perhaps the Solicitor General was right, and a reexamination of the whole privilege is in order.

To take an extreme example, if all corporate information is privileged, there will be no suits, no rule enforcement, no investment in litigation.

This is hardly a conclusive retort. The upshot of the analysis I have presented here is that a broader privilege may lead to more or fewer violations of law, to more or less being spent on litigation, to more or less being spent on prevention of violations, to more or fewer cases being brought. The size and direction of these effects depend on the costs of avoiding violations and of substituting litigation for prevention. It would take subtle and sophisticated econometric analysis to show which effects predominate. The answers might be different for different legal issues and different activities. Surely one answer will not do for all time. And thus the Court was fully justified in refusing to lay down a rule in *Upjohn*, no matter what one thinks of its disposition of the case before it.

V. Conclusion

The tension between optimal use of existing information and optimal incentives to create new information pervades legal and economic problems arising out of claims to property rights in information. Although contractual agreements often may handle the tension satisfactorily, as in *Snepp*, private incentives may not be enough in every situation, as the discussion of insider trading suggests, and sometimes private incentives are positively perverse and must be adjusted by legal rules, as I maintained in discussing *Upjohn*. The analysis of information problems is difficult, and answers are elusive; much depends on empirical work that is undone or undoable.

Still, the difficulty of steering to a satisfactory resolution of the use-versus-creation problem is a poor excuse for not recognizing that there *is* a problem to address. In *Chiarella* the Justices simply missed the boat, despite a brief from the Solicitor General that discussed most of the difficult questions. In *Upjohn* the Court assumed that to state the use-versus-creation problem is to solve it; it is not, and the problem itself was far more difficult than the Court let on. Only the short, summary disposition in *Snepp* recognized the nature of the problem, and the Justices' handling of other cases does not instill confidence that their recognition in *Snepp* was deliberate.

I do not mean that the Court handled these cases poorly. The problems are hard, and, as this article shows, I might not have been able to answer the questions much better (although my answers would have been much longer). Scholars are only beginning to understand how information is created, transmitted, and used. Ideas percolate through the bar to the Court slowly. It is not out of line, though, to hope that the treatment of information problems will improve in time. The most dramatic improvement might come from grouping cases like *Chiarella, Upjohn*, and *Snepp* under the heading "information problems" rather than under "securities," "evidence," and "national security."

KENNETH W. DAM

THE LEGAL TENDER CASES

The *Legal Tender Cases* have disappeared below the surface of American constitutional law.[1] A long time has passed, both chronologically and intellectually, since a constitutional law scholar could confidently declare in 1887 that "[n]o decisions of our Supreme Court possess a more enduring interest for the student of our Constitutional History and Law than those rendered in the so-called Legal-Tender Cases."[2] In 1975 Gerald Gunther, the most historically minded of constitutional law casebook editors, dropped any mention of the *Legal Tender* decisions from his new ninth edition.[3] The Tribe treatise consigns the cases to the interior of a footnote on, of all things, the Bill of Rights.[4]

The *Legal Tender* litigation warrants great interest from a number of perspectives. Measured by the intensity of the public debate at the time, it is one of the leading constitutional controversies in American history. Then, too, *Hepburn v. Griswold*, decided in 1870,

---

Kenneth W. Dam is Harold J. and Marion F. Green Professor in International Legal Studies and Provost, The University of Chicago.

[1] The three *Legal Tender* decisions of the Supreme Court are Hepburn v. Griswold, 8 Wall. 603 (1870); Knox v. Lee, 12 Wall. 457 (1871); and Juilliard v. Greenman, 110 U.S. 421 (1884). In addition, even though they did not pass on the constitutionality of the legal tender legislation, Bronson v. Rodes, 7 Wall. 229 (1869), and Veazie Bank v. Fenno, 8 Wall. 533 (1869), were important cases throwing light on the underlying legal, political, and economic controversies.

[2] James, *Some Considerations on the Legal-Tender Decisions*, 3 PUBS. AM. EC. ASS'N 51 (1889).

[3] GUNTHER, CASES AND MATERIALS ON CONSTITUTIONAL LAW (9th ed. 1975). The seventh and eighth editions had included about one page on the subject. See, for example, GUNTHER & DOWLING, CASES AND MATERIALS ON CONSTITUTIONAL LAW 403–04 (8th ed. 1970).

[4] TRIBE, AMERICAN CONSTITUTIONAL LAW 4 n.8 (1978).

was one of the first cases to hold substantive Congressional legislation unconstitutional.[5] Yet in the next year the Court overruled itself in *Knox v. Lee*,[6] and in circumstances (involving new appointments and a strong hint of impropriety) that made the overruling "one of the most controverted matters in the history of the Court."[7]

Finally, the sequence of cases from *Hepburn* in 1870 to *Juilliard* in 1884 marks a transition in the Court's view of its role in monetary matters that was not to occur in other economic spheres until the 1930s. The sermonizing of the Chase majority opinion in *Hepburn*, characterized by the young Holmes as presenting the "curious spectacle of the Supreme Court reversing the determination of Congress on a point of political economy,"[8] gave way to the view in *Juilliard* that the constitutional issue was "a political question, to be determined by Congress when the question of exigency arises, and not a judicial question, to be afterwards passed upon by the courts."[9]

Today the student of constitutional law finds it difficult to take the *Legal Tender* cases seriously, even when he learns something about them by para-casebook means. Perhaps that is because constitutional lawyers take legal tender paper money for granted, or because they believe that the Necessary and Proper Clause is sufficiently elastic in economic cases to supply any missing constitutional foundations for the vast edifice of Congressional legislation regulating the economy. But I believe that the *Legal Tender*

---

[5] 8 Wall. 603 (1870). Between Marbury v. Madison, 1 Cranch 137 (1803), and 1865, there was only a single instance, the *Dred Scott* case, 19 How. 393 (1857), in which an Act of Congress was held unconstitutional. FAIRMAN, RECONSTRUCTION AND REUNION 1864–88, Part One (6 HISTORY OF THE SUPREME COURT OF THE UNITED STATES), 697 n.67 (1971). Of the statutes held unconstitutional by the Chase Court, the legal tender legislation was among the most important. See *Acts of Congress Held Unconstitutional in Whole or in Part by the Supreme Court of the United States*, in THE CONSTITUTION OF THE UNITED STATES OF AMERICA: ANALYSIS AND INTERPRETATION at 1597–99, Senate Doc. No. 92–82, 92d Cong., 2d Sess. (1973).

[6] 12 Wall. 457 (1871).

[7] FAIRMAN, note 5 *supra*, at 677. Fairman's chapter on the *Legal Tender* cases in his Oliver Wendell Holmes Devise History volume is the best treatment of the circumstances of the overruling. *Id.* at 677–775. This aspect of the cases is treated briefly at notes 49–52 *infra*.

[8] *Review of the Legal Tender Cases of 1871*, 7 AM. L. REV. 146 (1872–73). Holmes was the editor of the American Law Review and this unsigned article is normally attributed to him. See, *e.g.*, Thayer, *Legal Tender*, 1 HARV. L. REV. 73, 88 (1887–88). On differences of view on the *Legal Tender* cases between Holmes and Thayer, see 2 HOWE, JUSTICE OLIVER WENDELL HOLMES 53–55 (1963).

[9] 110 U.S. at 450.

cases are remote to the modern constitutional law mind simply because of a lack of knowledge of the necessary economic facts. The appointment of judges in *Marbury v. Madison*[10] and the licensing of a ferry in *Gibbons v. Ogden*[11] present factual situations that are easy to grasp. But the suspension of specie payments, the circulation of state bank notes, the requirement under the independent treasury system that all payments to the Treasury be in gold, and similar peculiarities of nineteenth-century finance make it difficult to pierce the doctrinal veneer of the opinions.

Despite all of these technicalities, the underlying economic facts have a startlingly contemporary ring in the early 1980s. Legal tender paper was issued largely because an Administration wanted to fight a war without significantly increasing taxes, an economic policy reminiscent of a twentieth-century President Johnson dealing with another civil war, though one in Vietnam. The result in the nineteenth century, rapid inflation, is even more familiar. So, too, is the floating of the dollar and its resulting depreciation against other major currencies. The hard money school's remedy for inflation, a policy of monetary restraint, is familiar as well.[12]

By mastering the financial facts underlying the *Legal Tender* cases, it is possible to penetrate beyond the level of legal analysis thus far attained. For those who want a comprehensive statement of the sequence of judicial events, Charles Fairman has provided a lengthy and superb account.[13] And James Bradley Thayer's 1887 article on the *Legal Tender* cases provides not only an excellent contemporary analysis of the doctrinal issues, but also a synopsis of the consideration by the Framers of the monetary clauses of the Constitution.[14]

Neither author, however, placed the legal tender litigation in an adequate fiscal or financial context, and both, therefore, were un-

---

[10] 1 Cranch 137 (1803).

[11] 9 Wheat. 1 (1824).

[12] What we have not experienced in recent decades is falling prices, and so it is at least intriguing to see that prices declined steadily from 1865 until close to the end of the century. See wholesale and consumer price indexes in U.S. Bureau of the Census, HISTORICAL STATISTICS OF THE UNITED STATES COLONIAL TIMES TO 1957, Series E 1–12, E 13–24, E 113–39 and E 148–56, at 115–16, 125–27. Debate over the relative contribution of hard money policies and rapidly rising productivity to the price decline finds a modern counterpart in current discussions of monetarism and supply side economics.

[13] FAIRMAN, note 5 *supra*, ch. 14; Fairman, *Mr. Justice Bradley's Appointment to the Supreme Court and the Legal Tender Cases*, 54 HARV. L. REV. 977, 1128 (1941).

[14] Thayer, note 8 *supra*.

able to come to grips with some of the most fundamental issues of constitutional law. Is it possible, for example, that the notion of a government of enumerated powers deprives the Congress of some powers essential to the nation's survival? Assuming that the Court takes the intention of the Framers seriously, what should it do if the Framers intended to withhold a power that the Court believes indispensable to meet a crisis? More generally, does the idea of a written constitution necessarily include a *force majeure* principle that permits its rules to bend in the face of overwhelming events, such as a civil or foreign war? In short, is there a necessity principle that operates, either through the Necessary and Proper Clause or by inherent power, to grant the Congress whatever power is needed?

The *Legal Tender* cases do not resolve these issues. Indeed, the various opinions do not confront them directly. They were, in fact, more directly treated in the congressional debates on the legal tender legislation. Nevertheless, the facts of the *Legal Tender* cases come as close as any cases, with the possible exception of war powers decisions, to probing these outer limits of constitutionalism.

I. What Happened?

An understanding of the *Legal Tender* cases and of the way in which they posed these larger issues of constitutionalism requires a grasp of the principal economic events leading to the issuance of legal tender paper as well as those surrounding the three leading cases. For convenience, the key facts are set forth in short compass here, with more detailed discussion of particular points deferred to the subsequent discussion of the sources of legislative power and of the question of necessity.

Salmon P. Chase was nominated Secretary of the Treasury by President Lincoln just after his inauguration in March 1861. Chase, a Cincinnati lawyer who had served as Governor of Ohio and U.S. Senator, had little knowledge of government finance or of banking. Yet he was to preside over revolutionary changes in Treasury borrowing practices in the first year of his Secretaryship. Although he had some views on how the banking system should be structured, believing in particular that a system of national banks should displace the existing structure of state banks, the impetus for change in the first year came almost entirely from the unprecedented financing needs generated by the unfolding War Between the States. The widespread belief that the war would be over in a matter of months coupled with failure to foresee the volume of expenditures required had initially encouraged the view that new taxation would not have time to take effect and would in any case be unnecessary. But as expenditures increased and as battlefield reverses induced fear of Union defeat, Chase, a believer in Jacksonian hard money, reluctantly became an advocate of paper currency.

Expenditures grew at a dizzying pace. Outlays increased from $63.1 million in 1860 to $66.6 million in 1861 and then at a bound to $474.8 million in 1862.[15] Meanwhile, tax revenues languished. The Civil War income tax, and associated excise tax measures, were not to produce significant revenue until 1863.[16] The principal source of revenue was the customs, accounting for $39.6 million out of a total of $41.5 million in revenues in 1861.[17] The Morrill Tariff Act, which became law at the close of the Buchanan Administration in March 1861, imposed a protective levy that, though increasing the level of tariffs, reduced the revenue yield.[18] Customs revenues fell by over 40 percent between the first and second quarters of 1861. Despite the stimulus war preparation gave to the Northern economy, customs revenue failed to grow with expenditures, rising to only $49.1 million in 1862.[19]

Chase chose to bridge the gap by borrowing. Though the rise in expenditures rendered some borrowing inevitable, he sought to make a virtue of borrowing in preference to taxation. He failed, for example, to implement fully an August 1861 statute imposing an income tax, because at that time he opposed such a tax in principle.[20] Taxation in any form should, he wrote as late as December 1861, be relied upon only "for *ordinary* expenditures, for prompt payment of interest on the public debt, existing and authorized, and for the gradual extinction of the principal." For *extraordinary*

---

[15] HISTORICAL STATISTICS, note 12 *supra*, Series Y 350–56 at 718.

[16] *Id.* Series Y 258–63 at 712.

[17] *Ibid.*

[18] Act of March 2, 1861, 12 Stat. 178.

[19] Report of the Secretary of the Treasury on the State of the Finances, for the Year Ending June 30, 1861, 30 (December 1861) (hereafter cited as Finance Report); MITCHELL, A HISTORY OF THE GREENBACKS, 9–10 (1903); HISTORICAL STATISTICS, note 12 *supra*, Series Y 258–63 at 712.

[20] STUDENSKI & KROOSS, FINANCIAL HISTORY OF THE UNITED STATES 141 (1952); PAUL, TAXATION IN THE UNITED STATES 7–10 (1954); HAMMOND, SOVEREIGNTY AND AN EMPTY PURSE 263–64 (1970); Act of August 5, 1861, 12 Stat. 292, 309 § 49.

expenses, "reliance must be placed on loans."[21] In short, this war was to be financed primarily by borrowing.

Borrowing, at the time Chase assumed office, took the conventional form of the sale of bonds and notes for *specie*, a term that meant gold and silver coins. Though most financial transactions between individuals were carried out in currency consisting of state bank notes and, increasingly, in checks drawn on those banks, the federal government dealt in specie. Customs duties, for example, had to be paid in gold or silver coin. And the principal and interest on bonds were also paid in coin.

In July 1861, the Treasury began borrowing not through fixed term bonds or notes but rather through demand notes. These notes, which did not bear interest, were redeemable on demand in specie. Government employees and suppliers could thus be paid not coin but pieces of paper entitling them, or whomever they assigned these "demand notes" to (say, their bank), to obtain specie from the Treasury.[22]

In August 1861, Chase decided, however, to raise the bulk of the funds needed to finance the war through conventional interest-bearing securities. Three tranches of $50 million each were proposed. In accordance with practice up to that time, it was foreseen that the bonds would be sold to the banks, who would then sell them to their customers. The banks were thus not merely commercial bankers, but, in those days long before the Glass-Steagall Act,[23] investment bankers as well. Since the banks had to pay for the bonds in specie and were not able to move them rapidly into the hands of their customers, and thereby recoup their holdings of specie, it took the Treasury most of the rest of 1861 to sell the three $50 million tranches, even though the banks were permitted to take each tranche in installments. Throughout the sale period, specie in the hands of the New York banks remained at about the $40 million level, as coin paid out by the Treasury found its way back to the banks.[24]

Before the banks could complete payment on the final $50 million

---

[21] Finance Report 1861 (December) 13, 16. (Emphasis supplied.)

[22] Act of July 17, 1861, 12 Stat. 259.

[23] HAMMOND, note 20 *supra*, at 39; Act of February 27, 1932, 47 Stat. 56.

[24] MITCHELL, note 19 *supra* at 30 (table 1). The total specie holdings of Boston and Philadelphia banks fluctuated in the $5–$8 million range. *Ibid.*

tranche, they were forced, in the wake of Union battlefield reverses and an international crisis precipitated by the forcible removal of passengers from the British steamer *Trent*, to suspend specie payments on December 30, 1861.[25] That is, they stopped redeeming their own bank notes in coin. Although the New York banks still had some $25 million in specie reserves,[26] the fall from the $40 million level revealed the onset of private hoarding of gold coin and the banks' fear that they might soon be out of specie entirely. Meanwhile, the rate of government expenditures was accelerating. The government, having failed to tax adequately, would have to borrow in 1862 even larger amounts than in the preceding half year. But how?

The alternative of selling bonds at much higher effective interest rates was discarded.[27] The alternative chosen was to issue demand notes to pay salaries and suppliers, as had been done the preceding summer.[28] But when the legislation eventually passed, there were two crucial differences. First, the new demand notes were not to be redeemable in specie but rather in 6 percent twenty-year bonds.[29] Second, and here was born the crux of the *Legal Tender* litigation, they were to be "lawful money and a legal tender in payment of all debts, public and private, within the United States."[30] These demand notes became known as greenbacks, because of their distinctive color. Some $431 million were issued and still outstanding at the end of the Civil War. However, by 1864 the Treasury was able to rely almost exclusively on taxation and the sale of bonds to finance the war.[31]

The political objection to legal tender greenbacks was that they were irredeemable in gold or silver—that they were, in Constitu-

---

[25] HAMMOND, note 20 *supra* at 123, 131–33, 157. In some states specie payments were not suspended immediately. MITCHELL, note 19 *supra*, at 146. On the banks' outstanding specie obligations to the government for the bonds, see *id*. at 40 n. 1.

[26] *Id*. at 30 (table 1).

[27] See discussion of this alternative, text *infra*, at notes 158–59.

[28] See text *supra*, at note 22.

[29] Act of February 25, 1862, § 1, 12 Stat. 345.

[30] *Ibid*. "[D]uties on imports and interest" on the public debt were excepted from the legal tender clause and thus were still payable in coin. *Ibid*.

[31] MITCHELL, note 19 *supra* at 119–31, 173. Other kinds of legal tender obligations were also issued, including compound-interest notes. *Id*. at 174–77. In Hepburn v. Griswold, Chief Justice Chase stated that these additional legal tender notes "never entered largely or permanently into the circulation." 8 Wall. at 619.

tional parlance, "bills of credit." However, because it had long been accepted that the federal government, unlike the states, could issue bills of credit,[32] the constitutional litigation centered on the legal tender provision. When the greenbacks quickly dropped to a discount against gold (or, to put it another way, gold quickly rose to a premium), reflecting the rampant inflation of the Civil War years, the groundwork for private litigation was laid. Was a debt denominated in a stated number of dollars dischargeable in an equal amount of greenbacks? Or could the creditor demand coin, or failing that, an amount in greenbacks equivalent to the gold value of the debt? If the premium on gold (which reached a high of 185 percent in July 1864[33]) was, say, 100 percent, could the creditor on a "$100 debt" require payment of $200 in greenbacks? This was a Constitutional issue, because Congress had in the legal tender clause unmistakably said that only $100 in greenbacks was required to discharge such a debt. Only if the debt was stated to be $100 in coin would the larger amount of greenbacks be required, because, as the Supreme Court held in *Bronson v. Rodes*, the statutory language did not extend to a "contract to pay a certain number of dollars in gold or silver coins."[34]

A. THE VEAZIE CASE

The crucial case of *Veazie Bank v. Fenno*[35] was decided before the validity of the legal tender legislation was passed upon by the Court. That case not only set the stage for the *Legal Tender* decisions, but the legislation it sustained is an essential chapter in the history of Civil War finance.

Up to the time of the demand note issuance in 1861, the only currency in the country other than coin was provided by notes issued by banks created under state law.[36] In 1861 notes of 1601

---

[32] "No State shall . . . emit Bills of Credit . . ." Article I, section 10, clause 1.

[33] MITCHELL, GOLD, PRICES, AND WAGES UNDER THE GREENBACK STANDARD 4 (table 1) and 6 (table 2) (1908).

[34] 7 Wall. 229, 250 (1869). Chief Justice Chase distinguished between "express contracts to pay coined dollars [which] can only be satisfied by the payment of coined dollars" and "debts," which would be satisfied by the tender of legal tender notes. *Id.* at 254. See also Butler v. Horwitz, 7 Wall. 258 (1869); Trebilcock v. Wilson, 12 Wall. 687 (1872); Thompson v. Butler, 93 U.S. 694 (1877); and Gregory v. Morris, 94 U.S. 619 (1877).

[35] 8 Wall. 533 (1869).

[36] See, however, the discussion of earlier demand note issuances, text *infra*, at note 106.

state banks circulated. Their note circulation totaled $202 million, compared to gold coin in circulation of $266 million. Bank deposits, which today would be considered part of the money supply, came to $319 million.[37] As for silver, it had disappeared from circulation entirely, except for small amounts of silver coin of less than one dollar face amount.[38] Senator John Sherman doubted whether there were 1,000 silver dollars in circulation in all of the country.[39]

State bank notes were an unsatisfactory form of national currency. The notes of many state banks traded at a discount from face value, particularly outside the community in which they were issued. Some notes were fraudulent, the supposed issuers not existing at all. With the notes of different banks freely floating against one another, commercial "banknote detector" publications grew up to permit banks and businessmen to determine current values and to spot fraudulent notes.[40]

Chase proposed a system of national banks, whose notes would be secured by reserves held in government bonds. A national banking system was in fact authorized by statute in 1863.[41] Though a number of national banks were founded, state banks continued to flourish and their notes to circulate until 1865 when a federal tax of 10 percent was levied on new state bank notes.[42] The power to tax was used with unprecedented effectiveness to destroy. State banks were left with three possibilities: to close their doors, to convert to national banks, or to stop issuing notes and rely solely on loans to sustain themselves.[43]

Veazie Bank in Maine fought extinction all the way to the Supreme Court. Secretary Chase, the father of the national banking

---

[37] HISTORICAL STATISTICS, note 12 *supra*, Series X 20–41, X 285–98 at 624–25, 649. On the money supply before the issuance of legal tender paper, see Stevens, *Composition of the Money Stock Prior to the Civil War*, 3 J. OF MONEY, CREDIT & BANKING 84 (1971).

[38] HISTORICAL STATISTICS, note 12 *supra*, Series X 285–98 at 649.

[39] 1 SHERMAN, RECOLLECTIONS OF FORTY YEARS 254 (1895).

[40] Report of The Monetary Commission of the Indianapolis Convention 197 (1898); SCROGGS, A CENTURY OF BANKING PROGRESS 160–62 (1924).

[41] Act of February 25, 1863, 12 Stat. 665. This statute was superseded by the Act of June 3, 1864, 13 Stat. 99.

[42] Act of March 3, 1865, 13 Stat. 469, § 6 at 484, reenacted in the Act of July 13, 1866, 14 Stat. 98 § 9 (bis.) at 146. See the *Veazie Bank* opinion, 8 Wall. at 538–39.

[43] By 1867 only 272 state banks (out of 1,601 in 1861) survived, and the total capital of state banks had shrunk from $430 million to $65 million. HEPBURN, HISTORY OF COINAGE AND CURRENCY IN THE UNITED STATES 336 ("statistical résumé") (1903).

system, was thus enabled, in the robes of Chief Justice Chase, to put the last nail in the coffin of state bank currency by upholding the tax. The bulk of Justice Chase's opinion in December 1869 was devoted to showing that the tax was indirect and hence not subject to attack on the ground that as a direct tax it had not been "laid . . . in Proportion to the Census" as required by Article I, Section 9.[44] In response to a second argument that the tax sought to destroy state banks, Chase went out of his way, in supporting the federal power to issue bills of credit, to remark that "[i]t is not important here, to decide whether the quality of legal tender, in payment of debts, can be constitutionally imparted to these bills."[45] This unnecessary remark provoked Justice Nelson, joined by Justice Davis, to conclude in dissent that Chase's reasoning found "no support or countenance in the early history of the government, or in the opinions of the illustrious statesmen who founded it."[46]

B. THE HEPBURN CASE

The constitutional issue had to be faced almost immediately. *Hepburn v. Griswold*,[47] decided in February 1870, was the first Supreme Court decision dealing squarely with the constitutionality of the legal tender provision. In an action brought on an $11,250, two-year promissory note due February 20, 1862, just five days before the enactment of the legal tender legislation, the Court held that the maker, Mrs. Hepburn, could not discharge the debt by the payment of 11,250 greenback dollars but would instead have to pay the greenback value of 11,250 gold dollars at the time of tender. Chase,

---

[44] 8 Wall. at 540–48. For an explanation of the direct-indirect issue, which like the *Legal Tender* cases has also been largely pushed out of the constitutional law casebooks, see Dam, *The American Fiscal Constitution*, 44 U. CHI. L. REV. 271 (1977).

[45] 8 Wall. at 548. An interesting sidelight in Chase's opinion is his reference to the denial by Congress of legal tender status to foreign coins. Under Article I, section 8, clause 5, Congress has not only the power "To coin Money" and "regulate the Value thereof" but also to regulate "foreign Coin." By the Act of February 9, 1793, 1 Stat. 300, Congress designated which foreign coins were to be legal tender and at what rates. It was not until 1857 that the legal tender quality of all foreign coins was withdrawn. Act of February 21, 1857, 11 Stat. 163, § 3. See HEPBURN, note 43 *supra*, at 47–48.

[46] 8 Wall. at 556. Justice Nelson did not single out Chase's remark about the constitutionality of the legal tender provision. This was not the first time, however, that Chase had taken an opportunity to launch *obiter* against the legal tender notes. Earlier in 1869 in Bronson v. Rodes, 7 Wall. 229 (1869), in holding that the legal tender clause did not extend to obligations denominated in coin, he pointedly opined that he did not have to reach the constitutionality of the legal tender provision.

[47] 8 Wall. 603 (1870).

writing for four of eight justices, held that Congress lacked the power to make paper money legal tender for preexisting debts. Justice Grier, a fifth member ruling against Mrs. Hepburn, found that "the legal tender clause, properly construed, has no application to debts contracted prior to its enactment," but went on to say that if it were to be construed to apply to such debts, he concurred in the opinion that it was unconstitutional.[48] A three-man minority of Justices Miller, Swayne, and Davis found the legal tender clause applicable and constitutional.

C. THE SECOND LEGAL TENDER DECISION

In May 1871 the Court decided *Knox v. Lee*,[49] which held that the legal tender legislation was constitutional as to both preexisting and subsequent obligations. It specifically overruled *Hepburn v. Griswold*.

Most of the ink that has been spilled over the *Legal Tender* cases has dealt in one way or another with the change in the composition of the Court between the two decisions. A statute increasing the Court from eight to nine members, which became effective in December 1869 (two months before the *Hepburn* decision), and the resignation of Justice Grier as of January 31, 1870 (a week before that decision), permitted President Grant to appoint two new Justices on the very day *Hepburn* was handed down.[50] These two, Strong and Bradley, not only voted with the majority in *Knox v. Lee*, creating a five to four vote for constitutionality, but Strong wrote the majority opinion and Bradley a concurring opinion.[51] These circumstances, and others well beyond the scope of this essay, led to extraordinary controversy about the Court's switch, including allegations that Grant had appointed Bradley on the understanding that Bradley would vote to sustain the legislation. Because the literature on this controversy is rich[52] and because the

---

[48] *Id.* at 626.

[49] Decided together with Parker v. Davis, 12 Wall. 457 (1871).

[50] See the chronology, apparently by Reporter Wallace, 12 Wall. at 528, and FAIRMAN, note 5 *supra*, at 716–17. Grier took part in the deliberation on Hepburn v. Griswold, although the decision was not handed down until after his resignation became effective.

[51] Chief Justice Chase and Justices Clifford and Field each wrote dissenting opinions.

[52] See particularly FAIRMAN, note 5 *supra*, at 713–63; Fairman, note 13 *supra*; and BRADLEY (ED.), MISCELLANEOUS WRITINGS OF THE LATE HON. JOSEPH P. BRADLEY 45–74 (1901).

Supreme Court voted eight to one a dozen years later in *Juilliard v. Greenman*[53] to sustain related legal tender legislation, the sordid details of that controversy can be passed over here in favor of greater attention to the substantive constitutional issues.

D. THE THIRD LEGAL TENDER DECISION

The *Juilliard* case is of particular importance, not only because it came later, and is hence decisive today, but also because a prime consideration supporting the *Knox v. Lee* majority position—the supposed necessity of issuing legal tender paper—could not suffice to justify the *Juilliard* decision. Other legislation had intervened, forbidding the Treasury from withdrawing greenbacks from circulation. It was this legislation, not simply the original 1862 statute, that was tested in *Juilliard*.

Even before the first two *Legal Tender* decisions, but after the Civil War and its financing had become history, the greenbacks had been the focus of a fierce political struggle. With the war over, the Treasury had launched itself on a policy of contraction of the money supply. The objectives were twofold. First, applying what would today be called a monetarist economic policy, the Treasury sought to reduce the money supply and thereby eliminate the inflation of the Civil War period. Although bank deposits had already become at least as important a component of the money supply as currency, devotees of the quantity theory of money in those days concentrated on currency in circulation. Hence, the Treasury sought to withdraw greenbacks from circulation.[54]

A second and longer-range objective was resumption, a term that referred to the resumption of specie payments by banks in redemption of bank notes and, to the extent there was government-issued paper currency still outstanding, by the government as well. To achieve this end, the premium on gold would have to be eliminated so that not less than a dollar's worth of gold would have to be paid out to redeem a dollar in paper currency. Another way to look at

---

[53] 110 U.S. 421 (1884).

[54] Friedman and Schwartz calculated that at the end of June 1867, bank deposits exceeded currency in the hands of the public and greenbacks constituted less than half of total currency. Thus, the greenback contraction policy was directed at only a limited portion of the money supply. FRIEDMAN & SCHWARTZ, A MONETARY HISTORY OF THE UNITED STATES 1867–1960, 17 (table 1) (1963).

resumption (though not the way it was normally viewed at the time) is to note that U.S. paper currency was floating against British sterling, which was redeemable in gold. The United States was, in short, on floating exchange rates. A return to the gold standard could have been accomplished by devaluing the dollar—that is, reducing the gold content of the dollar—but a devaluation was apparently unthinkable in that age. Consequently, resumption meant a return to the international gold standard at the dollar's pre–Civil War gold content and hence at the prewar rate of exchange.[55]

Accomplishment of these two objectives, and particularly resumption, was generally thought to entail two things. First, prices would have to fall so that the gold premium would be eliminated (and, from a different perspective, so that U.S. goods would be competitive in world markets at the prewar rate of exchange).[56] Second, the greenback would have to be withdrawn from circulation.

Treasury Secretary McCulloch announced at the end of 1865 a policy of selling bonds for the purpose of retiring greenbacks.[57] Meanwhile, prices had already begun to fall. By 1868 the median wholesale price of a list of ninety-two commodities had fallen from a peak of 216 (January 1860 = 100) to 159—in short, the median wholesale price had already fallen by over 25 percent.[58] Because wholesale prices represented incomes to manufacturers, farmers, and other economic groups, the fall in prices was not popular. The fact that retail prices also fell (though with some lag)[59] and production expanded rapidly in agriculture, mining, and manufacturing,

---

[55] *Id.* at 58–61. See generally DAM, THE RULES OF THE GAME: REFORM AND EVOLUTION IN THE INTERNATIONAL MONETARY SYSTEM, 28–29 (1982).

[56] By 1864 the median U.S. wholesale price of twenty-seven selected commodities had risen to 194 percent of the 1860 level while the median sterling price had fallen to 95 percent of the 1860 level. MITCHELL, note 33 *supra*, at 31 (table 10). In short, U.S. wholesale prices would have to fall by half or British prices double or some combination of the two price movements would be required.

[57] Finance Report, 1865, 14. The term "greenbacks" meant strictly speaking the United States notes issued in 1862 and 1863 but Secretary McCulloch also intended to retire certain interest-bearing notes that had also been given legal tender quality but were not redeemable in gold before maturity and that were known as "compound interest notes." *Ibid.*

[58] MITCHELL, note 33 *supra*, at 23 (table 4).

[59] According to Mitchell's calculations, retail prices continued to rise until 1866, whereas wholesale prices peaked in 1865. *Id.* at 76 (table 23 and chart IV).

thereby surely increasing real per capita income, tended to be overlooked.[60] Although the resulting political conflict, which centered on the withdrawal of greenbacks from circulation, has often been painted as a soft money–hard money struggle between West and East and between farmer and banker, detailed historical research has revealed a much more complicated struggle in which, for example, manufacturers were important opponents of the Treasury contraction policy.[61] Be that as it may, opposition grew until 1868, when a statute was passed prohibiting any further retirement of greenbacks.[62] Out of more than $400 million still outstanding in 1866, only $44 million had been retired.[63]

In 1875 the Resumption Act was passed providing for resumption of specie payments on January 1, 1879.[64] This legislation reflected the belief that resumption would soon be within reach in view of the fall of the gold premium to only about 15 percent and the continuing fall in price levels; wholesale prices were now more than 35 percent below the 1865 level.[65] The statute required the redemption in coin of legal tender notes thereafter presented. However, a resurgence of pro-greenback sentiment led to legislation in 1878 restricting the withdrawal from circulation of any further greenbacks, notwithstanding the 1875 Resumption Act. The statute provided that when any "United States legal-tender notes . . . may be redeemed or be received into the Treasury under any law from any source whatever and shall belong to the United States, they shall not be retired cancelled or destroyed but they shall be

---

[60] Kindahl, *Economic Factors in Specie Resumption, The United States, 1865–79*, 69 J. POL. ECON. 30, 45 (table 8) (1961). See also note 12 *supra*.

[61] SHARKEY, MONEY, CLASS, AND PARTY (1967). Sharkey concludes that "[a] careful evaluation of the evidence leads to the conclusion that the opposition to contraction on the part of the iron and steel manufacturers of Pennsylvania, New York, and the western states, and their allies was the most important single factor leading to the abandonment of that policy in 1868." *Id.* at 286.

[62] Act of February 4, 1868, 15 Stat. 34.

[63] MITCHELL, note 19 *supra*, at 174 (table 4); Finance Report 1868, lv. Compound interest notes, demand notes that were not legal tender, and so-called postage stamp currency had, however, been contracted at a much more rapid rate. Kindahl calculated that total currency outside the Treasury had contracted from $646 million in 1865 to $393 million in 1868. Kindahl, note 60 *supra*, at 44 (table 7).

[64] Act of January 14, 1875, 18 Stat. Pt. 3, 296.

[65] MITCHELL, note 33 *supra*, at 4 (table 1); and HISTORICAL STATISTICS, note 12 *supra*, Series E 1–12 at 115. The cost of living had fallen less but even that index was down about 15 percent from the 1865 level. *Id.* Series E 157–60 at 127.

re-issued and paid out again and kept in circulation."[66] The result was that the circulation of greenbacks remained fixed until 1933 at $346,681,000, the amount outstanding on the date of enactment.[67]

The Treasury interpreted the 1878 Act to permit the reissuance of greenbacks in notes of different denominations from those redeemed.[68] The *Juilliard* decision, which involved a creditor's refusal to accept greenbacks that the Court treated as having been reissued after redemption in gold coin,[69] was based on the power of Congress to issue legal tender notes in peacetime. The Court squarely held, with only Justice Field dissenting, that whether these were new or old greenbacks, issued in war or peace, for reasons of necessity or convenience, the conferring of legal tender status on irredeemable paper currency was constitutional. Indeed, the Court went so far as to state that, given the Necessary and Proper Clause as interpreted in *McCulloch v. Maryland*,[70] the issue was one for Congress rather than the courts:[71]

> [T]he question whether at any particular time, in war or peace, the exigency is such, by reason of unusual and pressing demands on the resources of the government, or of the inadequacy of the supply of gold and silver coin to furnish the currency needed for the uses of the government and of the people, that it is, as a matter of fact, wise and expedient to resort to this means, is a political question, to be determined by Congress when the question of exigency arises, and not a judicial question, to be afterwards passed upon by the courts.

The Court might well have treated *Juilliard* as simply a replay of *Knox*, since the amount of greenbacks in circulation could not exceed the amount issued in the Civil War. Moreover, the country had already returned to the gold standard in 1879, leaving the paper

---

[66] Act of May 31, 1878, 20 Stat. 87. The Panic of 1873 had unleashed expansionist pressures that led to a small additional issue of greenbacks. STUDENSKI & KROOSS, note 20 *supra*, at 183.

[67] See NUSSBAUM, A HISTORY OF THE DOLLAR 130 (1957). See FRIEDMAN & SCHWARTZ, note 54 *supra*, at 470 and 518; Act of May 12, 1933 (Agricultural Adjustment Act, Thomas Amendment), 48 Stat. 31, Title III § 43(b)(1) at 52.

[68] Argument for Plaintiff in Error, Juilliard v. Greenman, 110 U.S. at 427.

[69] *Id.* at 437–38.

[70] 4 Wheat. 316, 423 (1819).

[71] 110 U.S. at 450.

currency as a permanent and unvarying "fiduciary" issue.[72] By
nonetheless choosing to treat the issue as one of peacetime issuance
of paper money and by adopting a rule that put the constitutional
issue of future paper money issues beyond the reach of the courts,
the *Juilliard* opinion could be viewed as an advisory opinion on the
constitutionality of replacing the gold standard entirely by a fiat
money standard. It is not surprising that when the United States
left the gold standard in 1933, the *Juilliard* decision played a promi-
nent role in the ensuing gold clause litigation.[73]

II. THE ORIGINAL UNDERSTANDING

Justice Field, dissenting in *Juilliard*, relied on history for his
first point:[74]

> If there be anything in the history of the Constitution which can
> be established with moral certainty, it is that the framers of that
> instrument intended to prohibit the issue of legal tender notes
> both by the general government and by the States; and thus
> prevent interference with the contracts of private parties.

One might think that a nineteenth-century Court would have
taken the intent of the Framers seriously, especially if, as Justice
Field insisted, one could know that intent with moral certainty.[75]
Yet, as will be reviewed below, the majority's analysis of this issue
in both *Juilliard* and *Knox* was superficial at best and even indifferent to the Framers' intent. But the Framers' language, the Constitutional text, was ambiguous. Though it prohibited the states
from "mak[ing] any Thing but gold and silver Coin a Tender in
Payment of Debts," it imposed no such prohibition on Congress,

---

[72] The existence of a similar fiduciary issue was not viewed in Britain as having any
relevance to the question whether the gold standard was in effect there. DAM, note 55 *supra*,
at 26–27.

[73] See, *e.g.*, Norman v. Baltimore & Ohio Railroad Co., 294 U.S. 240, 303 (1935). The
gold clause cases did not, however, follow *Juilliard*'s political question approach.

[74] 110 U.S. at 451.

[75] On Justice Field's views and role in the *Legal Tender* cases, see SWISHER, STEPHEN J.
FIELD: CRAFTSMAN OF THE LAW 166–204 (Phoenix ed. 1969). The reasons why " 'the intent
of the Framers' is often an elusive quarry," Williams v. Florida, 399 U.S. 78, 92 (1970), and
why a court might choose not to be bound by that intent even if established are, of course,
numerous and well beyond the scope of this essay. See, *e.g.*, Wofford, *The Blinding Light: The
Uses of History in Constitutional Adjudication*, 31 U. CHI. L. REV. 502 (1964).

and therefore it could be inferred that Congress might make paper money a "Tender in Payment of Debts." But such an inference was counterbalanced by the alternative inference that since Congress was given power only to "coin Money" and to "regulate the Value thereof, and of foreign Coin," it was therefore given no similar power with respect to paper money.It was not that the issue was not discussed at the Constitutional Convention. Far from it. But the discussion as reported was somewhat confused. Still, a review of the evidence supports Field's conclusion, though hardly his "moral certainty" dictum.

The review undertaken below covers much the same ground as that covered by Thayer.[76] However, Thayer's legalistic review fails to consider adequately the economic context in which the Framers debated the future of paper money. And Thayer reaches a somewhat different conclusion, in part because he fails to examine closely the financial terms actually used by Madison in his notes on the deliberations.

The Founders certainly knew about paper money. They had seen it, and the devastating effect of issuing too much of it, in detail and profusion. The Articles of Confederation gave the "united states in congress assembled" the authority to "emit bills on the credit of the united states" upon the assent of nine states.[77] The Continental Congress did so, and at an accelerating rate, until by 1780 $100 in paper money was worth only $2.50 in specie.[78] Depreciation continued until in 1781 paper money ceased to circulate as currency—whence the phrase "not worth a continental."[79] The states, too, issued paper money, and it, too, depreciated, with Virginia currency reaching 0.1 percent of its former value by December 1781.[80] Thereafter, the Continental Congress relied almost

---

[76] Thayer, note 8 *supra*.

[77] Articles of Confederation, Article 9 §§ 5 and 6, 1 Stat. 4, 7–8.

[78] See Revolutionary War Depreciation Tables in NEWMAN, THE EARLY PAPER MONEY OF AMERICA 359–60 (1967); Amount of Continental Money Issued during the Revolutionary War, and Depreciation of the Same, in 5 AMERICAN STATE PAPERS, LEGISLATIVE AND EXECUTIVE, OF THE CONGRESS OF THE UNITED STATES . . . 1824 . . . 1828. FINANCE, at 764, 766–71 (1859).

[79] Report from Senator Levi Woodbury [New Hampshire] on Continental Currency, 1844, reprinted in 1 KROOSS (ED.), DOCUMENTARY HISTORY OF BANKING AND CURRENCY IN THE UNITED STATES 159–61 (1969).

[80] NEWMAN, note 78 *supra*, at 359–60. See STUDENSKI & KROOSS, note 20 *supra*, at 30.

exclusively on bond issues, though the bonds had to be sold in Europe.[81]

At least some of the Founding Fathers had had enough of paper money.[82] Madison said in the Federalist Papers, in commenting on the bar against state bills of credit, that the prohibition "must give pleasure to every citizen, in proportion to his love of justice and his knowledge of the true springs of public prosperity." He decried "the pestilent effects of paper money on the necessary confidence between man and man, on the necessary confidence in the public councils, on the industry and morals of the people and on the character of republican government."[83]

Madison's views on the evils of paper money were not fully shared when the issue had to do with federal bills of credit. The question arose on the floor of the Constitutional Convention in the debate on a provision in the Report of the Committee of Detail giving Congress the power to "borrow money, and emit bills on the credit of the United States."[84] Gouverneur Morris opened the debate by moving to strike out the phrase "and emit bills on the credit of the United States," arguing that "[i]f the United States had credit such bills would be unnecessary: if they had not, unjust & useless."[85]

Madison, however, asked:[86]

> [W]ill it not be sufficient to prohibit the making them a *tender*? This will remove the temptation to emit them with unjust views. And promissory notes in that shape may in some emergencies be best.

Gouverneur Morris of Pennsylvania responded that even if the words were stricken "a *responsible* minister" could still borrow

---

[81] U.S. REGISTER OF THE TREASURY, HISTORY OF THE CURRENCY OF THE COUNTRY AND OF THE LOANS OF THE UNITED STATES 17–20, 29–32 (1900).

[82] See HAMMOND, BANKS AND POLITICS IN AMERICA 95–103 (1957), for the experience of the Framers with the paper money issue in the period between the end of the Revolution and the Constitutional Convention in 1787.

[83] HAMILTON, MADISON & JAY, THE FEDERALIST, No. 44, 318 (Wright ed. 1966). Story in his Commentaries later said that making state bills a tender "entailed the most enormous evils on the country; and introduced a system of fraud, chicanery, and profligacy, which destroyed all private confidence, and all industry and enterprise." 2 STORY, COMMENTARIES ON THE CONSTITUTION, § 1371, 226–27 (1851).

[84] 2 FARRAND (ED.) THE RECORDS OF THE FEDERAL CONVENTION OF 1787 182 (1937).

[85] *Id.* at 308–09.

[86] *Id.* at 309. (Emphasis in original.)

through "notes," and in any case the "Monied interest will oppose the plan of Government, if paper emissions be not prohibited."[87] Nathaniel Gorham of Massachusetts was "for striking out, without inserting any prohibition," but George Mason of Virginia "had doubts on the subject": "Though he had a mortal hatred to paper money, yet as he could not foresee all emergencies, he was unwilling to tie the hands of the Legislature." He observed, moreover, that "the late war could not have been carried on" if paper money had been prohibited.[88]

John Francis Mercer of Maryland, "a friend to paper money," spoke against its prohibition. Although "in the present state & temper of America, he should neither propose nor approve of such a measure," still a prohibition would "stamp suspicion on the Government to deny it a discretion on this point," and it was, in any case, "impolitic also to excite the opposition of all those who were friends to paper money."[89] Connecticut's Oliver Ellsworth argued, however, that the time was ripe to "shut and bar the door against paper money" since the "mischiefs of the various experiments which had been made, were now fresh in the public mind and had excited the disgust of all the respectable part of America."[90]

Edmund Randolph of Virginia, like Madison, was cautious; "notwithstanding his antipathy to paper money, [he] could not agree to strike out the words, as he could not foresee all the occasions that might arise."[91] James Wilson of Pennsylvania and Pierce Butler of South Carolina then spoke against paper money, with Butler asserting that "paper was a legal tender in no Country in Europe." Mason, "still averse to tying the hands of the Legislature *altogether*," took exception to Butler's comparative law point, observing that "[if] there was no example in Europe as just remarked it might be observed on the other side, that there was none in which the Government was restrained on this head."[92] Two more members then spoke against the power to emit bills of credit, before a nine-to-two vote to strike the power was taken.

---

[87] *Ibid.* (Emphasis in original.)

[88] *Ibid.*

[89] *Ibid.*

[90] *Id.* at 309–10.

[91] *Id.* at 310.

[92] *Ibid.* (Emphasis in original.)

Virginia was one of the delegations voting to strike. Madison left an explanation of this vote. He said that he "became satisfied that striking out the words would not disable the Govt from the use of public notes as far as they could be safe & proper; & would only cut off the pretext for a paper currency and particularly for making the bills a tender either for public or private debts."[93]

What is one to make of this debate and its outcome? On the one hand, the vote left the Constitution without a provision one way or the other on the power to emit bills of credit. On the other, it is clear that a large majority of the states opposed giving the federal government that power. Only New Jersey and Maryland voted to retain the empowering language.[94] Only Mercer of Maryland had spoken for paper money, and his state was outvoted. Moreover, we know that at least one member of the Maryland delegation thought that since they had lost the vote, Congress would have no power to emit bills of credit. Luther Martin, one of the Maryland delegates, told the Maryland legislature that "a majority of the convention, being wise beyond every event, and being willing to risk any political evil, rather than admit the idea of a paper emission, in any *possible* event, refused to *trust* this authority to a government. . . ."[95]

A crucial question in determining the Framers' intent is whether the Virginia vote to strike should be interpreted as intended to deny the federal government the power to issue bills of credit or simply to leave the issue open. Justice Gray in *Juilliard* interpreted Madison's explanatory note as internally inconsistent:[96]

> Mr. Madison . . . "became satisfied that striking out the words would not disable the government from the use of *public notes*, so far as they could be safe and proper; and would only cut off the pretext for a *paper currency*, and particularly for making the *bills* a tender, either for public or private debts." But he has not explained why he thought that striking out the words "and emit *bills*" would leave the power to emit *bills*, and deny the power to make them a tender in payment of debts.

---

[93] *Ibid.*

[94] Gorham of Massachusetts did not want a formal prohibition but did not want to grant the power on the ground that the mere inclusion of words granting the power might "suggest and lead to the measure." *Id.* at 309. He may thus be counted as not wishing to withdraw the power.

[95] Luther Martin, *Genuine Information*, in *id.* 3:172, 206. (Emphasis in original.)

[96] 110 U.S. at 443. (Emphasis supplied.)

The italics added to this passage disclose that Madison used three separate terms—public notes, paper currency, and bills. Justice Gray treated them as synonyms. But if one parses carefully the language Madison uses, one can easily conclude that Madison sought to distinguish "notes," on the one hand, from "paper currency" and "bills," on the other. If the term "note" is interpreted to mean an interest-bearing term obligation issued when the government borrows money from private parties in contradistinction to the terms "paper money" and "bills," which clearly refer to interest-free demand paper issued in payment of an obligation, then Madison's explanation makes perfect sense. By striking the power "to emit bills," one would still leave the power "to borrow Money on the credit of the United States"[97] through interest-bearing fixed-term "public notes." Such "notes" could, in Madison's opinion, be "safe and proper," unlike "paper currency" or "bills" of credit.

The issue is thus whether Madison was thinking logically. If, at the time, the word "notes" was widely used to refer to interest-bearing fixed term obligations, then one could safely assume that Madison was thinking logically.[98] One could conclude that the Virginia delegation had decided, contrary to Justice Gray, to deny the power "to emit bills" of credit, because it did not want the government to have any power to issue paper money and *a fortiori* it wanted to exclude any power "to make them a tender in payment of debts." If, on the other hand, "notes" was solely another word for "bills," then Justice Gray was right that one cannot show any clear conclusion from the Virginia vote and hence from the Framers' deliberations as a whole.

The meaning of "bills of credit" was relatively precise. The phrase "bills of credit" was used not merely at the Constitutional Convention but throughout the Revolutionary period to refer to paper money.[99] The term "notes," on the other hand, seems to have

---

[97] Article 1, section 8, clause 2.

[98] Madison's use of "notes" in contradistinction to "bills" accords with the usage of Gouverneur Morris, who believed that the "paper emissions" could be "prohibited" while leaving "room still for *notes* of a *responsible* minister." (First emphasis supplied.) FARRAND, note 84 *supra*, at 2:309. See statement in text *supra* at note 87.

[99] See the collection of documents from the period in KROOSS, note 79 *supra*, at 1:100–52. The word "bills" was also used to refer to interest-bearing obligations, as in the Continental Congress Resolution of March 18, 1780, calling on the United States to issue "bills . . . redeemable in specie, within six years after the present, and bear[ing] an interest at the rate

been used more broadly to refer both to individual pieces of paper money and to interest-bearing fixed term obligations. In general, usage of financial terms seems to have been quite fluid, a not surprising circumstance in view of the absence of any substantial capital markets or commercial banking on the western shores of the Atlantic.[100]

Nevertheless, the distinction between "bills of credit" and "notes" seems to have been well implanted in the mind of Chief Justice Marshall. When he first interpreted the corresponding Constitutional provision prohibiting states from issuing bills of credit, he defined the term "emit bills of credit" as not applicable to "those contracts by which a state binds itself to pay money at a future day . . . for money borrowed for present use." He noted that "instruments executed for such purposes" are not "in common language, denominated 'bills of credit.' "[101] And he carefully distinguished the "bills of credit" there challenged from the private promissory "note" given in exchange for those "bills."[102]

Justice Gray's failure even to consider this natural interpretation may stem from the fact that in the Civil War period both the 1861 demand obligations and the 1862 legal tender obligations were called "notes." Perhaps this word was adopted to give them more respectability, but a simpler explanation is that the term "bills of credit" had long since disappeared from common language, as Justice Johnson had observed already in 1830.[103]

Whatever the reason for failing to interpret Madison as knowing what he was saying, it seems rather fatuous to remark, as did Justice Bradley concurring in *Knox v. Lee*, that since the "emit bills"

---

of five per centum per annum." 16 JOURNALS OF THE CONTINENTAL CONGRESS, 1774–1789 264 (1910).

[100] Madison himself appears to have used "notes" to include the concept of bills in his statement, set out in the text *supra* at note 86, that "promissory notes in that shape may in some emergencies be best." Nonetheless, the very need for the qualifying phrase "in that shape" indicates that "notes" would not otherwise be interpreted so widely as to include "bills of credit."

[101] Craig v. Missouri, 4 Pet. 410, 432 (1830).

[102] *Id.* at 424, 434–35. For a 1773 British statute distinguishing between "bills of credit" issued "in payment" and "certificates, notes, bills, or debentures" issued "as security for . . . payment," and prohibiting the colonies from declaring the former legal tender but not the latter, see 13 Geo. III. c. 57.

[103] "The terms, 'bills of credit,' are in themselves vague and general, and, at the present day, almost dismissed from our language. It is then only by resorting to the nomenclature of the day of the constitution, that we can hope to get at the idea which the framers of the constitution attached to it." Craig v. Missouri, 4 Pet. 410, 437, 441 (dissenting opinion).

language was "struck out with diverse views of members, some deeming them useless and others deeming them hurtful," the Court did not have to consider the Framers' intent.[104]

A review of the debate also reveals that the crux of concern had to do with paper money, not so much the further step of declaring it to be legal tender. Only Madison and Butler seemed concerned with the legal tender issue. Madison thought legal tender status a further evil that gave rise to the temptation to issue paper money "with unjust views."[105] And Butler, as his reference to European practice reveals, saw the distinction between the issuance of paper money and the investing of paper money with legal tender status. Although the legal tender issue thus raised fewer specific hackles than paper money as such, one could think of the intent to withhold the legal tender power as *a fortiori* established by the intent to withhold the emission power.

In short, although it may have been inconvenient to the proponents and constitutional defenders of legal tender paper money, it is difficult to escape the conclusion that the Framers intended to prohibit its use. Certainly the evidence is strong enough to force at least those constitutional lawyers who believe that the Framers' intent should be controlling to face the ultimate question of what the Court should do when it concludes that a power the Framers intended to deny has nevertheless become indispensable.

The fundamental difficulty with the foregoing analysis of the Framers' intent is quite simple. Rather soon in the life of the young Republic it came to be taken for granted that the federal government did indeed have the power to emit bills of credit. In fact, Congress did so as early as the War of 1812.[106] And if it had the power to do so, there was hardly enough to draw on in Madison's and Butler's comments to divine a constitutional distinction between the power to emit bills of credit and the further power to grant them legal tender status that would permit the former and prohibit the latter.

---

[104] 12 Wall. at 554, 559.

[105] FARRAND, note 84 *supra*, at 2:309.

[106] Justice Clifford, dissenting in *Knox*, lists twenty-one different issues of bills of credit. 12 Wall. at 587, 627–28. See also the Field dissent in the same case, 12 Wall. at 634, 636–37. The Report of the Monetary Commission, note 40 *supra*, at 398–401, summarizes the issuances of demand notes prior to 1861 and points out that none of the 1812 and little of the 1815 issuance entered public circulation as money. See also Metropolitan Bank v. Van Dyck, 27 N.Y. 400, 421–22 (1863).

The source of the power to emit bills of credit, legal tender or no, in a government of enumerated powers was not made clear. Chief Justice Chase asserted in the *Veazie Bank* case that "it is settled by the uniform practice of the government and by repeated decisions, that Congress may constitutionally authorize the emission of bills of credit."[107] It is more than a little suspicious that Chase cites none of the "repeated decisions," nor does any Justice in the various opinions in the three *Legal Tender Cases*. Justice Clifford doubtless came closer to the mark in his *Knox* dissent when he derived the power to issue bills of credit from "[e]stablished usage founded upon the practice of the government, often repeated."[108]

Whatever the source of the power to emit bills of credit, Chase had framed the constitutional issue of the *Legal Tender Cases* already in *Veazie*. Granted that Congress could authorize the emission of bills of credit, could it make them legal tender in the settlement of debts between private parties?[109] In what provision or provisions of the Constitution lay the legal tender power?

III. Sources of Legislative Power

The *Legal Tender Cases* are a ringing endorsement of a broad reading of the Necessary and Proper Clause. Justices Strong in *Knox* and Gray in *Juilliard* endorsed Justice Marshall's formulation in *McCulloch v. Maryland*: "Let the end be legitimate, let it be within the scope of the constitution, and all means which are appropriate, which are plainly adapted to that end, which are not prohibited, but consist with the letter and spirit of the constitution, are constitutional."[110] Though Justice Field dissenting in *Knox* did assert that the Necessary and Proper Clause "only states in terms what Congress would equally have had the right to do without its insertion in the Constitution,"[111] the scope of the Clause was not seriously at issue in the *Legal Tender Cases*. Rather, the inquiry was: necessary and proper to the exercise of what enumerated power granted Congress by the Constitution? Finding this core power was

[107] 8 Wall. at 548.

[108] 12 Wall. at 587, 627.

[109] 8 Wall. at 548.

[110] 4 Wheat. 316, 421 (1819), quoted at 12 Wall. at 539 and 110 U.S. at 441.

[111] 12 Wall. at 640.

the rub, and the answers given varied from opinion to opinion among those Justices affirming the constitutionality of the legal tender legislation.

The coinage power. To today's flexible legal mind, accustomed to giving Constitutional language broad readings, it might seem that the core power is the power "to Coin Money [and] regulate the Value thereof." But no member of the *Legal Tender* Courts was willing to go that far, because the Coinage Clause referred only to coin, not to paper money. As Justice Field stated in dissent in *Juilliard*, "to coin money" means "to mould *metallic* substances into forms convenient for circulation and to stamp them with the impress of the government authority indicating their value with reference to the unit of value established by law."[112] He noted that the Constitution itself distinguishes "coins" (which he defines as "pieces of metal of definite weight and value, stamped such by the authority of the government") from securities in the Counterfeiting Clause.[113] The majority in *Juilliard* agreed with this analysis in referring to the "power over a metallic currency under the power to coin money and to regulate the value thereof." So, too, Justice Strong in *Knox* had conceded that the Coinage Clause was limited to coins and merely denied that that clause contains a "lurking prohibition" that "tacitly implies a denial of all other power over the currency of the nation."[114] Granting that he was correct in rejecting any negative inference from the existence of a power over coins, the question remains as to the source of the core power to which the legal tender power could be necessary and proper.

The war powers. That amalgam of powers having to do with declaring war, raising and supporting armies, and the like might be

---

[112] 110 U.S. at 462. (Emphasis supplied.)

[113] "Congress shall have power . . . To provide for the Punishment of counterfeiting the Securities and current Coin of the United States." Article I, Section 8, Clause 6.

[114] 12 Wall. at 545. The 1930s *Gold Clause Cases*, though according Congress extremely broad powers over the currency, nevertheless continued to distinguish the Coinage Power from allied powers over paper currency: "The Constitution grants to the Congress power 'To coin money, regulate the value thereof, and of foreign coin' . . . . But the Court in the legal tender cases did not derive from that express grant alone the full authority of the Congress in relation to the currency . . . . The broad and comprehensive national authority over the subjects of revenue, finance and currency is derived from the aggregate of the powers granted to the Congress, embracing the powers to lay and collect taxes, to borrow money, to regulate commerce with foreign nations and among the several States, to coin money, regulate the value thereof, and of foreign coin, and fix the standards of weights and measures, and the added express power 'to make all laws which shall be necessary and proper for carrying into execution' the other enumerated powers" (294 U.S. at 303).

thought to support the legal tender legislation.[115] After all, Secretary Chase had agreed to the legal tender legislation only because of the urgent need for resources to fight the War between the States, and Chief Justice Chase in *Ex parte Milligan* had defined the war powers as extending "to all legislation essential to the prosecution of war with vigor and success."[116] The majority in *Knox v. Lee* did indeed debate at length the crisis conditions under which the legal tender notes were issued and even referred to Congress' pressing need "to devise means for maintaining the army and navy."[117] Still Justice Strong was unwilling to derive constitutionality directly from any war power and instead tended at times to argue some transcendent principle of necessity, preferring to stress repeatedly the "exigencies" of the situation in which the legal tender notes were issued.[118] In any case, the war powers would not necessarily suffice in *Juilliard* because of the intervening reissue of legal tender notes based on peacetime legislation.[119]

The borrowing power. A third possible source of the core power, around which a superstructure of Congressional authority might be built, lay in the borrowing power—the power to "borrow Money on the credit of the United States."[120] Surely the legal tender notes, though used to pay those who were already creditors, were an implicit form of borrowing. An argument based on the borrowing power would have to be carefully phrased, because Congress had no express power to regulate the value of borrowed money but only of coined money, as the language of the Constitution, closely read, made clear.[121]

We have already seen, however, that all sides conceded that Congress could exercise the power to borrow through the emission of bills of credit in payment of creditors. For Justice Bradley, concurring in *Knox*, that was the end rather than the beginning of the inquiry. The power to emit bills of credit "being conceded, the

---

[115] Article I, section 8, clauses 11–14.

[116] 4 Wall. at 139 (dissenting opinion).

[117] 12 Wall. at 541.

[118] *Id.* at 540–43.

[119] See discussion, text *supra*, at notes 64–73.

[120] Article I, section 8, clause 2.

[121] The 1930s *Gold Clause Cases*, building on *Veazie*, found a broad power over the currency stemming from several sources. See quotation in note 114 *supra*.

incidental power of giving such bills the quality of legal tender follows almost as a matter of course."[122] "Almost," but not quite for any other member of the Court. Aside from the possibility of some independent prohibition, to which Bradley's qualifying "almost" referred,[123] there remained the question of the logical or economic link between borrowing and the added step of legal tender status. If the borrowing could be accomplished as well without a legal tender clause, then why would the concern for strengthening the borrower-lender nexus require intrusion into relations between third parties who might treat the instrument of borrowing as money? Justice Strong's answer in *Knox* was that investing the notes with legal tender quality would make them more valuable and therefore that the premise that borrowing could be as successful without the legal tender power was false, at least in the Civil War context:[124]

> [A]s no one could be compelled to take common treasury notes in payment of debts, and as the prospect of ultimate redemption was remote and contingent, it is not too much to say that they must have depreciated in the market long before the war closed, as did the currency of the Confederate States. Making the notes legal tenders gave them a new use, and it needs no argument to show that the value of things is in proportion to the uses to which they may be applied.

Justice Strong's economics were obviously defective, since not every new use increases value. Paper money, unlike coins, may be used in the fireplace, but that possible use does not increase the value of paper money. The question is whether a new use increases the quantity demanded at a particular price. That is, of course, an empirical question, and Justice Field had an empirical answer. He observed that the $300 million of notes issued by national banks under the 1863 and 1864 national banking acts[125] "circulated equally well" with the U.S. legal tender notes even though they had no legal tender quality. "They rose and fell in the market under the same influences and precisely to the same extent as the notes of

---

[122] 12 Wall. at 560.

[123] Discussion of possible independent prohibitions, such as the Due Process Clause or the Obligation of Contracts Clause, would unduly lengthen this essay, though such possible prohibitions were extensively discussed in the *Legal Tender Cases*.

[124] 12 Wall. at 543.

[125] See discussion, text *supra*, at notes 41–42.

the United States, which possessed this quality."[126] In short, both U.S. legal tender notes and national bank notes exchanged at par and hence at one-for-one against each other. From this circumstance Justice Field inferred that the added use of the U.S. notes as legal tender among private parties did not add anything to their value in the marketplace.[127]

Although Field's evidence is compelling, it should be noted that no national bank notes were issued until the passage of the national banking act in 1863, when federal finances had immeasurably improved due to vastly increased taxation. Moreover, no legal tender notes were issued after about the time of that act's passage.[128] Justice Field also failed to consider the evidence on the market value of demand notes issued in 1861. For a time they traded at a very slight discount from legal tender notes, because not all banks were willing to take them as "current funds."[129] Perhaps to remedy that defect, legal tender quality was quickly extended to the outstanding demand notes.[130] Thereafter, the demand notes circulated at a premium over greenbacks because the demand notes, unlike the greenbacks, could be used to pay customs duties.[131]

Inherent power. Whatever the force of the contending arguments,

---

[126] 12 Wall. at 647. See the similar argument of Chief Justice Chase in *Hepburn* that the "notes which were not declared a legal tender have circulated with those which were so declared without unfavorable discrimination." 8 Wall. at 619. See text *infra*, at notes 176–78.

[127] As Justice Chase pointed out in his *Knox* dissent, the greenbacks, even without legal tender quality, would have been by statute receivable in transactions with the government. Since gold coin had stopped circulating after the suspension of specie payments, "[n]obody could pay a tax, or any [government] debt, or buy a bond without using these notes." 12 Wall. at 577. National bank notes were not receivable for these purposes under the independent treasury system.

[128] MITCHELL, note 19 *supra*, at 119–22.

[129] *Id.* at 149–54. The discount was apparently never greater than 1/5 of 1 percent. *Id.* at 153. It should be noted that the suspension by the Treasury in January 1862 of specie payments eliminated the right of a holder to redeem a demand note at par.

[130] Act of March 17, 1862, 12 Stat. 370.

[131] DEWEY, FINANCIAL HISTORY OF THE UNITED STATES 283 (9th ed. 1924). There were, of course, conceptual as well as economic arguments against Justice Strong's expanded use argument. Justice Field had argued in his *Knox* dissent that Strong's rationale proved too much because not every added use was constitutional. The government could, he said, have assured "ready acceptance of the notes" by a provision that they should serve as a "free ticket in the public conveyances of the country, or for ingress into places of public amusement, or which would entitle the holder to a percentage out of the revenues of private corporations, or exempt his entire property, as well as the notes themselves, from State and municipal taxation." 12 Wall. at 643. This quotation is a particularly striking example of a level of conceptual argument that for a late twentieth century reader mars many of the *Legal Tender* opinions.

the *Juilliard* Court, though relying on the borrowing power,[132] also elected to place its rationale on broader grounds. In part, a broader constitutional base was apparently thought necessary to support the postredemption reissuance provisions of the 1878 legislation.[133] The Court therefore chose to stress that the power to "make the notes of the government a legal tender in payment of private debts [is] one of the powers belonging to sovereignty in other civilized nations."[134] Much of the language of *Juilliard* foreshadows the claim of Mr. Justice Sutherland in *Curtiss-Wright* that the federal government has certain inherent powers simply because it became a sovereign government,[135] with the striking difference that Justice Sutherland's case involved foreign relations while *Juilliard* involved only internal economic policy:[136]

> . . . Congress has the power to issue the obligations of the United States in such form, and to impress upon them such qualities as currency for the purchase of merchandise and the payment of debts, as accord with the usage of sovereign governments. The power, as incident to the power of borrowing money and issuing bills or notes of the government for money borrowed, of impressing upon those bills or notes the quality of being a legal tender for the payment of private debts, was a power universally understood to belong to sovereignty, in Europe and America, at the time of the framing and adoption of the Constitution of the United States. The governments of Europe, acting through the monarch or the legislature, according to the distribution of powers under their respective constitutions, had and have as sovereign a power of issuing paper money as of stamping coin.

The *Juilliard* court went on to point out that the individual colonies had the disputed power, with the implication presumably that the power passed to the federation upon the entry into force of the constitution.[137] Finally, standing the issue of the Framers' intent on

---

[132] 110 U.S. at 448.

[133] See discussion, text *supra*, at notes 69–71.

[134] 110 U.S. at 450.

[135] United States v. Curtiss-Wright Export Corp., 299 U.S. 304 (1936). For a critique of the historical basis for Justice Sutherland's position in *Curtiss-Wright*, see Lofgren, *United States v. Curtiss-Wright Export Corporation: An Historical Reassessment*, 83 YALE L.J. 1 (1973).

[136] 110 U.S. at 447.

[137] *Id.* at 447–48. In this respect *Juilliard* differs from *Curtiss-Wright*, where Justice Sutherland argued that the colonies never had the foreign relations power. Still another difference between *Juilliard* and *Curtiss-Wright* includes the concentration in *Curtiss-Wright* on executive power as opposed to the power of Congress in *Juilliard*.

its head, Justice Gray sought support for his sovereignty argument from the fact that "during the Revolutionary War the States, upon the recommendation of the Congress of the Confederation, had made the bills issued by Congress a legal tender."[138]

The issue of inherent power was to arise a number of times in the ensuing century, with the Court becoming increasingly hostile to claims of such power. But what distinguishes *Juilliard* not only from the expansive *Curtiss-Wright* case but also from such restrictive cases as *Youngstown*[139] is that those cases involved the inherent power of the President. In the later cases it was assumed that if Congress delegated the Executive the power, there would be no issue of inherent power.[140] *Juilliard*, in contrast, raises the question of the inherent power of Congress and hence of the federal government as a whole. *Juilliard* thus provides a possible basis for filling any gap in the power of the federal government in times of crisis by finding an inherent power attributable to sovereignty.

Justice Gray, no doubt sensing the controversy that his sovereignty analysis might otherwise engender, took care to anchor the legal tender power in an express power, the borrowing power. In that respect the *Juilliard* opinion avoids the letter, but certainly not the spirit, of the obvious criticism of *Curtiss-Wright*, stated perhaps most simply by Louis Henkin: "The Sutherland theory . . . carves a broad exception in the historic conception, often reiterated, never questioned and explicitly reaffirmed in the Tenth Amendment, that the federal government is one of enumerated powers only."[141]

IV.. THE QUESTION OF NECESSITY

The broad-sweeping opinion in *Juilliard* was designed to end the legal tender issue once and for all, and it did so. The question of "exigency" was henceforth to be, as we have seen, "a political ques-

---

[138] 110 U.S. at 448.

[139] Youngstown Sheet & Tube Co. v. Sawyer, 343 U.S. 579 (1952).

[140] See, *e.g.*, Dames & Moore v. Regan, 101 S. Ct. 2972 (1981). *Curtiss-Wright* does, however, contain dicta to the effect that various external powers, such as the power to declare and wage war, "if they had never been mentioned in the Constitution, would have vested in the federal government as necessary concomitants of nationality." 299 U.S. at 318.

[141] HENKIN, FOREIGN AFFAIRS AND THE CONSTITUTION 24–25 (1972). In the leading gold clause case, Norman v. Baltimore & Ohio Railroad Co., 294 U.S. at 303, the Court carried the *Juilliard* approach to an extreme in seeking to find the power over money in a laundry list of Article I economic powers. See quotation in note 114 *supra*.

tion, to be determined by Congress . . . and not a judicial question."[142] Yet whether it is for Congress or for the Court, the question of necessity remains a constitutional question. Certainly the Congress that considered the 1862 legal tender legislation thought that it was debating constitutional issues, and a reader today wonders whether a late twentieth-century Congress could do as well, even with the aid of its large staff.

The factual issue of necessity presented by the *Legal Tender Cases*, whether it arises in applying the Necessary and Proper Clause or in filling an endangering gap in the panoply of enumerated powers, can be simply put: Why was the legal tender legislation necessary in the first place?

This necessity question should be distinguished from the question of the need for paper money. Paper money had overwhelming advantages over gold and silver coin for commercial purposes, and indeed a great deal of it was in use through the Civil War period, first in the form of state bank notes and then of national bank notes. Yet why was it necessary for the government itself to print paper money to pay its creditors rather than to borrow in the money markets? And if it did use the printing presses, why did it have to impress upon its paper money, unlike that of the banks, a legal tender quality? Why did it not, for example, simply continue to issue demand notes as it had done in the summer of 1861? The detailed answers are more subtle than the more obvious generalized explanations about the vast needs of the army and the failure to tax to finance the war. The more specific answers lie in the regulatory system of the time.

For an understanding of why Secretary Chase, initially a resolute opponent of the legal tender clause, was in the end forced to send a letter to the House Ways and Means Committee conceding that the legal tender legislation had become "indispensably necessary,"[143]

---

[142] 110 U.S. at 450. See fuller quotation, text *supra*, at note 71.

[143] Letter of January 29, 1862, reprinted in SPAULDING, HISTORY OF THE LEGAL TENDER PAPER MONEY ISSUED DURING THE GREAT REBELLION: BEING A LOAN WITHOUT INTEREST AND A NATIONAL CURRENCY 45–46 (1869). Although Chief Justice Chase has been widely criticized, even ridiculed, for denying as Chief Justice what he argued as Secretary, his confession of error in his *Knox* dissent places him in a not unsympathetic light. What he said in veiled language in *Knox* is essentially what history records, namely, that he would have been quite happy with another issue of demand notes but that he had to make a political compromise by acquiescing in the legal tender clause in order to obtain the requisite Congressional authorization to borrow. See 12 Wall. at 575–77; HAMMOND, note 20 *supra*, at 167–86.

the place to start is with the "independent treasury system." As an outgrowth of the antibank prejudices fed by President Jackson's war against the Bank of the United States, President Van Buren had been successful in obtaining Congressional passage of a statute separating treasury operations from the banking system.[144] Although the statute was repealed little more than a year later in the Tyler administration,[145] the independent treasury system was established once again in the Polk administration in 1846[146] and remained in place not just through the Civil War but until the creation of the Federal Reserve System in 1914.[147]

Under the independent treasury system, the federal treasury and its subtreasuries located across the country (initially in six cities) were to handle all collections and make all disbursements without assistance from any bank or other private institution.[148] Furthermore, and this is perhaps the most significant point about the system at the onset of the Civil War, treasury officers were required to deal only in specie or treasury notes.[149]

Since until the Civil War the national debt was small, and long-term bonds rather than short-term notes were often issued to finance any deficits, treasury notes were therefore not widely held.[150] And since silver was undervalued compared to gold at the mint under the statutory sixteen-to-one mint ratio and hence was more valuable as bullion than as coin, the great bulk of treasury transactions (including receipt of customs duties and payment of government salaries) was therefore carried on in gold coin.[151]

The economic historian and former Federal Reserve Board offi-

---

[144] Act of July 4, 1840, 5 Stat. 385.

[145] Act of August 13, 1841, 5 Stat. 439.

[146] Act of August 6, 1846, 9 Stat. 59.

[147] See generally KINLEY, THE INDEPENDENT TREASURY OF THE UNITED STATES AND ITS RELATIONS TO THE BANKS OF THE COUNTRY (National Monetary Commission report), Senate Doc. No. 587, 61st Cong., 2d Sess. (1910).

[148] Id. at 85. Depositories existed in still more cities, id. at 86–87, and postmasters of course collected public monies.

[149] Act of August 6, 1846, §§ 18–20, 9 Stat. 59, 64–65. KINLEY; note 147 supra, at 60. See Finance Report 1846, Appendix H at 30.

[150] In 1857, however, $52 million of one-year treasury notes were issued. KINLEY, note 147 supra, at 75. On the other hand, treasury notes were not always refinanced.

[151] Id. at 58–60; HEPBURN, note 43 supra, at 41–50. Silver "token" money (that is, coins of less than one dollar where the silver was mixed with some other metal to reduce the value of the mixture below the face value) continued to circulate.

cial Bray Hammond graphically described the operation of the independent treasury system:[152]

> [The government] was less a beneficiary of the independent Treasury arrangement than a victim of it. Had the Union Pacific Railroad Company, incorporated by Congress in 1862, been forbidden to deposit its money in banks, to accept checks or bank notes or any means of payment but coin, to pay its employees and suppliers in anything but coin, and to borrow anything but coin, the prohibitions would have seemed irrational. But, though the federal government had far greater monetary transactions than the railway, far greater receipts, far greater payments to make, far more employees, and far greater debts, still in the way most men then had of looking at it, the government's being prohibited the convenience of banking services and its being restricted to gold, which it had to keep in its own premises, seemed a fine thing, good for every one.
>
> *   *   *
>
> To keep relations between the government and the economy "pure" and wholesome, tons of gold had to be hauled to and fro in dray-loads, with horses and heavers doing by the hour what bookkeepers could do in a moment.

The independent treasury system may have been workable in peacetime, but in wartime, when the expenditures of the government were to increase sevenfold in one year,[153] the system was to prove a self-inflicted wound. It may have been "suitable for the Wars of the Roses but not for the first of modern conflicts four hundred years later."[154] Still, it provided its own relief valve by permitting transactions in treasury notes. And the issuance beginning in July 1861 of $50 million of treasury demand notes in payment of government employees and suppliers did provide some elasticity for the system.[155]

Paradoxically, the issuance of the treasury demand notes may have been the proximate cause of the suspension of specie payments by the banks in December of that year by driving the public to prefer the demand notes over the less secure state bank notes (and hence to seek redemption of the bank notes in gold) while at the

---

[152] HAMMOND, note 20 *supra*, at 22–23.

[153] See discussion, text *supra*, at note 15.

[154] HAMMOND, note 20 *supra*, at 24.

[155] See discussion, text *supra*, at note 22.

same time allowing gold to pile up in the Treasury rather than paying it out to employees and suppliers.[156] The Treasury, perhaps intending to offset public hoarding of gold, then exacerbated the problem by suspending specie payments to the extent that it refused henceforth to redeem the demand notes.[157]

In the resulting tangle the Treasury found it difficult to sell long-term bonds, at least at the same interest rate as its outstanding issues, most of which bore interest rates of about 6 percent.[158] Outstanding 6 percent bonds had fallen to a substantial discount even before the suspension of specie payments,[159] yet both the Treasury and the Congress were reluctant to sell securities at substantially higher face interest rates or to accomplish the equivalent by selling 6 percenters at a discount. A further problem lay in the requirement that bonds be paid for in specie; specie was more scarce than ever, because the suspension of specie payments led to its hoarding by private parties.

The obvious solution to the specie shortage would have been to modify the independent treasury system so that the Treasury could pay its creditors by checks drawn on the banks. Bank checks were already becoming a dominant means of payment in private transactions in large cities,[160] and the Treasury could have used a similar payment system, calling on the banks to deliver specie to the Treasury only to the extent necessary to permit the Treasury to pay interest and principal on outstanding bonds in gold coin.

Legislation had in fact been passed the previous August that most bankers thought accomplished just that objective.[161] But the actual text of the statute was narrowly drawn. Secretary Chase, an excellent if perhaps rather literal lawyer, interpreted the statute merely to permit specie to remain with the bank after sale of treasury bonds until such time as the specie was needed by the Treasury for disbursement.[162]

---

[156] HAMMOND, note 20 *supra*, at 115–18; KINLEY, note 147 *supra*, at 77–78.

[157] Finance Report 1862, at 7.

[158] In August of 1861 bonds were sold at rates as high as 7.3 percent. Finance Report 1861 (December) at 10.

[159] BARRETT, THE GREENBACKS AND RESUMPTION OF SPECIE PAYMENTS, 1862–1879 (36 Harvard Economic Studies) 46 (table 1) (1931).

[160] DEWEY, STATE BANKING BEFORE THE CIVIL WAR 215 (National Monetary Commission), Senate Doc. No. 581, 61st Cong., 2d Sess. (1910).

[161] Act of August 5, 1861, 12 Stat. 313.

[162] Indeed, the text provided nothing more. The Independent Treasury Act of 1846 was "suspended, so far as to allow the Secretary of the Treasury to deposit any of the moneys

The reluctance to sell bonds at higher interest rates than the outstanding 6 percenters warrants some explanation. Surely it was not mere prejudice against money markets. Even if there was some magic in the 6 percent rate, bonds could be sold at a discount. What price new 6 percent bonds might bring, however, was anyone's guess. Secretary Chase, using the convention of assuming that bonds would be issued bearing a 6 percent face interest rate, later declared:[163]

> Careful inquiries satisfied the Secretary that the first $60,000,000 could not be had, in coin, at better rates than a dollar in bonds for eighty cents in money; and that each succeeding loan would involve submission to increasingly disadvantageous terms. To obtain the first $60,000,000 would require, therefore, an issue of bonds to the amount of $75,000,000, and, of course, an increase of the public debt by the same sum; the next $60,000,000 would require, perhaps, $90,000,000 in bonds and debt; and the next $60,000,000, if obtainable at all, would require, perhaps, $120,000,000.

The problem was not, however, that "on this road utter discredit and paralysis would soon be reached," as Secretary Chase pretended.[164] The problem was rather that the sale of additional bonds would endanger the solvency of the banks. Chase was surely right that higher interest rates would be needed if more bonds were to be sold, particularly in view of doubts in early 1862 that the North would win the war and hence be in a position to pay principal and interest. But the catch was that as new bonds were sold, forcing interest rates higher, the market price of already outstanding bonds would surely fall to a level reflecting the effective interest rate. No one would buy outstanding bonds for more than he had to pay for new ones.[165]

---

obtained on any of the loans now authorized by law, to the credit of the Treasurer of the United States, in such solvent specie-paying banks as he may select; and the said moneys, so deposited, may be withdrawn from such deposit for deposit with the regular authorized depositories, or for the payment of public dues, or paid in redemption of . . . notes." *Id.* at § 6. In any event, the requirement that the banks be "specie-paying" restricted the usefulness of the statute after December 1861.

[163] Finance Report 1862 at 7. Congressman Thaddeus Stevens asserted that 6 percent bonds might "sell as low as sixty per cent . . . and even then it would be impossible to find payment in coin." 32 CONG. GLOBE, Part 1, at 687 (Feb. 6, 1862).

[164] Finance Report 1862 at 7.

[165] Spaulding, the chief proponent of the bill in the House, pointed out in his principal floor speech on the legal tender bill that an attempt to sell bonds "would depreciate the bonds already taken by the banks and the people." As a result, the principal value of "twenty years'

The banks were important holders of government bonds, if for
no other reason than that they were not able to sell them to investors as rapidly as they bought them from the Treasury. They
therefore held large amounts in inventory.[166] By December 1861
the New York banks' holdings of "stock," a term including government bonds, was nearly twice as high as the year before and as
their holdings of specie.[167] Meanwhile, the banks' capital strength
was weaker than in the late 1850s.[168] The refusal of the Treasury to
sell bonds to the banks as less then par, regardless of face interest
rates, may have simply worsened the banks' position by exposing
them to loss while reducing the opportunity for gain through ap-
preciation.[169]

But assuming that bonds could not be sold without endangering
the banks and therefore demand notes were to be issued, why was it
necessary to give the notes legal tender quality? Before confronting
that issue directly, it is worth investigating two grounds for the
legal tender clause that had nothing to do with necessity but that
appealed to the Congress and particularly to the chief proponent of
the legal tender clause, Congressman Spaulding, chairman of the
relevant subcommittee of the House Ways and Means Committee.
First, Spaulding saw the issuance of legal tender paper as obtaining
something for nothing. It was, to quote the subtitle of his book, "a
Loan without Interest."[170] He overlooked the fact that the issuance
of the greenbacks, at least in the volume eventually issued, would
lead to inflation and to a discount of the dollar against gold.

Second, Spaulding believed that the emission of money by the

---

six per cent bonds would, under the pressure, fall to seventy-five, seventy, sixty, and even
fifty cents" on the dollar. 32 CONG. GLOBE, Part 1, at 524 (Jan. 28, 1862).

[166] The inability of the banks to move their inventory promptly was one reason why
Treasury enlisted agents to sell the bonds to the public for the account of the banks. 2
REDLICH, THE MOLDING OF AMERICAN BANKING: MEN AND IDEAS 92, 356–57 (1968
ed.). In 1862, under the leadership of investment banker Jay Cooke, the Treasury began to
sell bonds primarily outside banking channels. LARSON, JAY COOKE, PRIVATE BANKER
116–32 (1936).

[167] Finance Report 1862 at 191. For usage of the term "stock" in the Civil War period, see,
e.g., SPAULDING, note 143 supra, at 20–21.

[168] In December 1861 the New York banks' $109 million in capital supported $198 million
in loans. Four years earlier $107 million in capital had to support only $163 million in loans.
Finance Report 1862 at 191. See also REDLICH, note 166 supra, at 2:94.

[169] The banks apparently found it hard to resell bonds above par. On the government's
refusal to sell below par, see SPAULDING, note 143 supra, at 20–21.

[170] SPAULDING, note 143 supra.

federal government was not only a privilege of sovereignty but far more dignified than the sale of bonds through the banks. He "objected to any and every form of 'shinning' by Government through Wall or State streets to begin with."[171] He was "unwilling that this Government, with all its immense power and resources, should be left in the hands of any class of men, bankers or money-lenders, however respectable and patriotic they may be. . . . Why . . . should it go into Wall street, State street, . . . or any other street begging for money?"[172] And he saw the legal tender note issue as a way to create a national currency to displace state bank notes, which were *de facto* the currency of the day. He, like Chase, may have preferred a national banking system made up of national banks issuing their own notes backed by deposits of government bonds, but such a system could not be put in place immediately.[173]

Even accepting these arguments, which are ones of convenience rather than of necessity, it must still be asked why simple demand notes without legal tender quality would not suffice? No interest would be paid on simple demand notes, and surely the government's credit was as good as the credit of the state banks, whose notes freely circulated without the benefit of legal tender legislation. The answer appears to lie in the fear that without legal tender quality a demand note would not circulate at par. On the other hand, if it were by law given this quality, then it would necessarily be worth the amount printed on its face because a holder could always discharge a debt for that amount.[174]

Much was made in the Congressional debate of the supposed injustice of paying the army in demand notes. Congressman Blake argued that only by passing the legal tender legislation could "we prevent the money sharks from robbing our soldiers of their hard earnings."[175] The subject lent itself to exaggeration, even to demagoguery, and certainly to confusion. Congressman Pike waxed grandiloquent on the misfortunes of the simple soldier:[176]

---

[171] *Id.* at 21.

[172] 32 CONG. GLOBE, Part 1, at 526. Spaulding was a banker but from Buffalo, New York, not from a major financial center.

[173] *Id.* at 524. Congressman Bingham went one step further, seeing in paper money an inescapable attribute of sovereignty. *Id.* at 637.

[174] *Id.* at 658.

[175] *Id.* at 686.

[176] *Id.* at 658.

Shall we issue to them an additional quantity of Treasury notes, when it is said here upon the floor of the House that the sutler followed the paymaster at the last pay-day, like a shark in the wake of a ship, and gobbled up batches at four dollars in gold for five dollars in notes? . . . The soldier and sailor is [*sic*] at your mercy. He cannot resign, for it is desertion. He cannot complain, for it is mutiny. He cannot refuse to serve, because it is insubordination. He must work on, and take such pay as the Government chooses to give him. The debased notes shall be reserved for his special benefit, and he may sell them to the sutler for as much as he can get for them.

The confusion in Pike's argument is obvious in retrospect. As the legal tender notes themselves subsequently depreciated against gold it became clear that demand notes had depreciated against gold because, with the departure from the gold standard implicit in the suspension by the banks and the Treasury of specie payments, the dollar was depreciating. The issuance of a large volume of legal tender paper merely contributed to that depreciation. But depreciation of the dollar against gold was quite a different matter from a discount of demand notes from par as measured in other paper money, such as state bank notes. The evidence that demand notes would be discriminated against in that sense by the "money sharks" was notably absent from the debates.

In short, a crucial, if dubious, argument in the Congress was that a legal tender note would be worth a stated amount by government fiat—whence the name "fiat money." Yet it is not obvious that a demand note without this radiating effect on legal relations between third parties would not trade at par, especially so long as it could be used at face amount to discharge obligations to the government, such as customs duties.[177] Indeed, though many state bank notes circulated at a discount, the notes of strong metropolitan banks had long traded at par, again without any legal tender quality.[178] We have already seen that Justices Strong and Field divided on this empirical issue in *Knox*.

Even if the legal tender provision were essential to circulation at par, this necessity rationale rests on a further confusion as to the

---

[177] As noted text *supra*, at note 131, demand notes circulated for a time at a premium over greenbacks precisely because they could be used, unlike greenbacks, to pay customs duties, and see note 30 *supra*.

[178] See, however, the discussion of the slight discount at which demand notes traded in early 1862, text *supra*, at note 129.

nature of a dollar. To be sure, whatever the state defines to be a dollar will be one, but governments have not proved able, as the repeated failure of price control statutes confirms, to specify for any length of time what something called a dollar will command in the marketplace. And in fact the issuance of the greenbacks led immediately both to inflation and to a discount of the dollar against gold. A demand note redeemable in gold would have kept its value in goods and services better than the irredeemable greenback. But, as we have seen, the straitjacket of the independent treasury system had already led the Treasury to suspend specie payments on outstanding demand notes.[179]

Finally, the banks preferred legal tender notes to simple demand notes. The legal tender quality of greenbacks afforded the banks several advantages. The first was that it permitted banks in some states to avoid the legal consequences of their December 1861 suspension of specie payments. Under the New York statute, for example, the holder of a bank note who sought but was denied redemption in specie might be able to cause the state to withdraw the bank's charter.[180] However, since the new notes were "legal tender for all debts, public and private," they were treated as equivalent to specie for the purpose of redeeming bank notes. The Superintendent of Banks of New York expressed his disgust at the resulting subversion of the state specie redemption requirement by the federal legal tender legislation:[181]

> It was at this time that a new element was thrown into the financial crucible. On the 20th of March, there was received at the department certain notes issued by the United States, bearing on one side the impress of a highly intellectual countenance, on the other the authoritative declaration: "This note is a LEGAL TENDER for all debts, public and private, except duties on imports and interest on the public debt." The reception of these notes released from embargo in this department nearly $30,000 of the notes of banks, under protest for non-

---

[179] See discussion, text *supra*, at notes 156–57.

[180] N.Y. Rev. Stat. c. 18, Div. II, § 4 & Div. III, § 5 (1846). See HAMMOND, note 20 *supra*, at 218–21, 240–41; Annual Report of the Superintendent of the Banking Department of the State of New-York, December 31st, 1862, reprinted in 17 BANKER'S MAGAZINE 737, 740 (1863). For the New York Bank Department's interpretation of the law, see *Bank Suspension*, 16 BANKERS' MAGAZINE 811 (1862).

[181] 17 BANKERS' MAGAZINE (1863) at 746–47. See MITCHELL, note 19 *supra*, at 147–48; McCULLOCH, MEN AND MEASURES OF HALF A CENTURY, 136–38 (1888).

redemption in specie. Is it strange that . . . the banks should have availed themselves of the immunity afforded?

The New York Court of Appeals subsequently sustained the use of legal tender notes for redemption of bank notes.[182] It was assisted in reaching that decision by the New York statute, which required redemption in "lawful money of the United States" (though at the time the statute was passed only gold and silver were "lawful money").[183] In Indiana and Vermont, the state supreme courts went even further, holding that the federal legal tender statute overrode a state statute requiring banks to redeem their bills in "gold or silver."[184]

The second advantage afforded the banks by the legal tender legislation stemmed from the power to substitute legal tender greenbacks for specie in reserves. In a number of states, banks had been required to establish a reserve for redemption of notes.[185] Before the legal tender legislation, this reserve had to be maintained in specie. But since notes could now be redeemed in greenbacks as well as specie, the usual interpretation became that greenbacks, unlike simple demand notes, could substitute for specie in bank reserves. Moreover, greenbacks could be used as reserves not only against note issue but also against deposit liabilities.[186] This was a point of great consequence for the big city banks whose profitability lay far more in their lending business than in their note circulation.

Since some portion of paper money outstanding would always be

---

[182] Metropolitan Bank v. Van Dyck, 27 N.Y. 400 (1863). See also Annual Report . . . of the Banking Department of . . . New-York, January 7, 1864, reprinted in 18 BANKERS' MAGAZINE 809, 811–13 (1864).

[183] 27 N.Y. at 401.

[184] Reynolds v. Bank of the State of Indiana, 18 Ind. 467 (1862); Carpenter v. Northfield Bank, 39 Vt. 46 (1866). See McCULLOCH, note 181 supra, at 137–38.

[185] HURST, A LEGAL HISTORY OF MONEY IN THE UNITED STATES, 1774–1970 55, 68–69 (1973). See discussion of liability reserve requirements in HOOPER, AN EXAMINATION OF THE THEORY AND THE EFFECT OF LAWS REGULATING THE AMOUNT OF SPECIE IN BANKS (1860). Hooper was a banker and a member of the House Ways and Means Committee who was particularly active in the drafting of the legal tender legislation. See HAMMOND, note 20 supra, at 159, 167ff.

[186] Id. at 194, 246, 249–50. Though there was no statutory reserve requirement in New York, New York City banks had agreed to maintain reserves equal to 25 percent of liabilities. Id. at 83. See, however, reference to a 20 percent requirement in REDLICH, note 166 supra, at 2:284, and Annual Report of the Comptroller of the Currency at xxiv (1873). For other states, see REDLICH, at 2:8–10. It is not clear that a precise statute specifically requiring "specie," such as the Massachusetts law, could have been circumvented by substituting legal tender currency. Act of March 23, 1858, 1858 Mass. Acts 54; Annual Report of . . . Bank Commissioners of the Commonwealth of Massachusetts, October 1862, reprinted in 17 BANKERS' MAGAZINE 754, 760 (1863).

in the hands of banks,[187] the legal tender quality of the greenback thus permitted the banks to have more notes and loans outstanding and thereby perhaps to increase their profitability, at least for a time. This point largely escaped notice in the Congressional debates. At least in the House, the proponents of the legal tender bill found it politically convenient to emphasize the banks' opposition to paper money.[188] Only in the Senate debate did one member, James Doolittle of Wisconsin, put his finger on the crucial point. The banks would, he pointed out, put the legal tender currency in their vaults, "like so much coin, as a basis for expanding their own currency . . . thus trebling our paper circulation."[189]

When the time came for Secretary Chase to issue his second annual report in December 1862, he complained of the diversion of the legal tender notes to the publicly unforeseen use as a substitute for specie as bank reserves:[190]

> It was only when United States notes, having been made a legal tender, were diverted from their legitimate use as currency and made the basis of bank circulation, that the great increase of [bank note circulation] began. It was purely voluntary; prompted, doubtless, by the desire of extending accommodations to business as well as by the expectation of profit.

The result, according to Chase's calculations, was a 28 percent increase in a single year in bank note circulation, and a 12 percent increase in bank loans.[191]

---

[187] Friedman and Schwartz collected data showing that of *total* currency outside the Treasury in June 1867, $247 million out of $817 million was in the hands of banks. They have no separate figure for the banks' holdings of the greenback component of total currency. FRIEDMAN & SCHWARTZ, note 54 *supra*, at 17 (table 1).

[188] The fact that most bankers, and especially the spokesman for the New York banks, James Gallatin, were publicly opposed to irredeemable paper currency has little bearing on whether banks would be relatively better off with legal tender paper currency than with demand notes. Many influential bankers considered it essential to make the new notes legal tender. HAMMOND, note 20 *supra*, at 196–200, 206, 217–18. In the Senate debates Senator Sherman read from a letter from a New York banker who asserted that New York bankers believed "almost without exception . . . that it will be fatal to pass the bill without making the notes a legal tender." 32 CONG. GLOBE, Part 1, at 790. Hammond has suggested that the supposed opposition of the banking community to the bill was partly a political concoction of Ways and Means Committee Chairman Thaddeus Stevens, who used it "for political effect" in the House debates. HAMMOND, note 20 *supra*, at 220.

[189] 32 CONG. GLOBE, Appendix, at 58.

[190] Finance Report 1862, at 15.

[191] *Id.* at 14–15. It is one of the ironies of the legal tender legislation that Chase successfully used the resulting inflationary growth in what we would today call the money supply as one of his principal arguments for the national banking system. *Id.* at 15ff. The creation of that system and the supporting *Veazie* tax on state bank notes led to the disappearance of

The evidence thus strongly suggests that the necessity at stake in
the legal tender legislation was not so much to raise funds to fight
the war but to do so in a way that preserved the solvency and
indeed the profitability of the big city commercial banks that were
at the time the principal holders and purveyors of the government's
obligations. More detailed research, state by state and indeed bank
by bank, may throw light on the relative importance of the legal
tender legislation to those objectives and on the lobbying efforts of
the banks, but the general tendency of the legislation to benefit the
banks appears undeniable. The question remains whether in the
context of the times this private benefit rose to the level of public
necessity.

V. THE LARGER ISSUES

In 1866 the Supreme Court, in deciding *Ex parte Milligan*,
had denied that there was any doctrine of necessity permitting the
setting aside of Constitutional provisions in emergencies:[192]

> No doctrine, involving more pernicious consequences, was ever
> invented by the wit of man than that any of its provisions can
> be suspended during any of the great exigencies of government.
> Such a doctrine leads directly to anarchy or despotism, but the
> theory of necessity on which it is based is false; for the govern-
> ment, within the Constitution, has all the powers granted to it,
> which are necessary to preserve its existence; as has been happily
> proved by the result of the great effort to throw off its just
> authority.

Part of the *Milligan* Court's reason for rejecting a doctrine of
necessity—that the government had "all the powers . . . necessary
to preserve its existence"—though understandable when uttered

---

many of the state banks that had benefited by the legal tender clause. Moreover, it is worth
noting that the new national banking legislation provided that the required 25 percent reserve
against notes in circulation and deposits was to be maintained in "lawful money of the United
States"—that is, in greenbacks. Act of June 3, 1864, § 31, 13 Stat. 99, 108.

[192] 4 Wall. 2, 121 (1866). See also the unreported 1863 opinion of Chief Justice Taney in
Carpenter v. United States, quoted in SWISHER, ROGER B. TANEY 567 (1936): "A civil war or
any other war does not enlarge the powers of the federal government over the states or the
people beyond what the compact has given to it in time of war. A state of war does not annul
the 10th article of the amendments to the Constitution, which declares that 'the powers not
delegated to the United States by the Constitution, nor prohibited by it to the states, are
reserved to the states respectively or to the people.' Nor does a civil war or any other war
absolve the judicial department from the duty of maintaining with an even and firm hand the
rights and powers of the federal government . . . as they are written in the Constitution."

more than a year after Appomattox, surely begs the crucial issue raised by the possibility that in another time the Court, especially if it must confront a comparable question when the survival of the nation is still in doubt, may find that the Constitution does not affirmatively extend the power it deems necessary to surmount the emergency. Indeed, the splendid cadences of *Milligan* ring somewhat hollow in view of the Court's recognition that not simply the right of habeas corpus, whose suspension is provided for in the Constitution,[193] but the right to trial by jury might have been suspended if the locus of Milligan's 1864 arrest had been not Indiana but say Virginia, then a theater of actual war.[194]

The *Legal Tender* cases present the questions whether the Constitution may indeed fail to grant affirmatively certain vital powers and whether there is nonetheless an overriding principle of necessity (whether through the Necessary and Proper Clause or through inherent power). These issues are presented in a particularly clean fashion for students of constitutional law, because the *Legal Tender* cases are free from two often confusing dimensions. Unlike the usual emergency cases such as *Youngstown*, the Court was not dealing with a question of executive power; rather the question was whether the Congress, and hence the government as a whole, had the challenged power. And unlike *Milligan*, there was no issue of individual liberties.[195]

A court may sometimes be tempted to act on the unspoken assumption that an obviously convenient and desirable power must be found in the Constitution. In *Knox*, Justice Strong yielded to that temptation in asserting that the Constitution "certainly was intended to confer upon the government the power of self-preservation."[196] Such a point of departure is surely question beg-

---

[193] Article I, section 9, clause 2.

[194] 4 Wall. at 127.

[195] Since the *Legal Tender* decisions involve federal power, they are also different from cases like Home Building & Loan Association v. Blaisdell, 290 U.S. 398 (1934), where the issue was the relation of an economic emergency to state power. There Chief Justice Hughes found that an economic emergency could furnish "a proper occasion for the exercise of the reserved power of the State," though he also insisted: "Emergency does not create power. Emergency does not increase granted power or remove or diminish the restrictions imposed upon power granted or reserved." 290 U.S. at 425, 444.

[196] 12 Wall. at 533. Justice Strong relied on the following equally faulty assumption of Chief Justice Marshall in Cohens v. Virginia, 6 Wheat. 264, 414 (1821):

America has chosen to be, in many respects, and to many purposes, a nation; and for all these purposes, her government is complete; to all these objects it is com-

ging and cannot be squared with the central concept of a federal government of enumerated powers. *Knox* thus avoided directly posing the question of necessity.

In any event, the review of the fiscal and financial circumstances undertaken here might be thought at first blush to lead inescapably to a rejection of the view that the legal tender legislation was necessary to the financing of the war and hence to the preservation of the Union. Debt securities could have been sold for specie if the Congress had been prepared to tolerate higher interest rates, and in this sense such classic critiques of Civil War finance as those of historian Henry Adams and economist Wesley Mitchell are correct so far as they go.[197]

Congress chose the legal tender alternative because legal tender currency preserved the banking system. If the necessity was then to preserve the banks rather than the Union, one might conclude that the plea of necessity was a hoax hardly deserving of constitutional consideration. But such a conclusion would be too hasty. In 1862 government bonds had to be sold through banks, and it was not until later that Jay Cooke was able to show how bonds could be sold directly to individuals through modern advertising and door-to-door promotion.[198] Even then Cooke's methods succeeded because the man in the street could pay for the bonds with greenbacks, even though principal and interest were later to be repaid in gold.[199] Collapse of the big city banks, which were in early 1862 the Treasury's indispensable link with the financial markets, might well have led to the collapse of the Union. Or at least a Court sitting in 1862 might reasonably have so feared.

In any event, Chief Justice Marshall in *McCulloch* had already established that the means chosen need not be "indispensable" in

---

petent . . . in the exercise of all powers given for these objects, it is supreme. It can, then, in effecting these objects, legitimately control all individuals or governments within the American territory.

[197] Adams, *The Legal-Tender Act*, NORTH AMERICAN REVIEW (April 1870), reprinted in ADAMS & ADAMS, CHAPTERS OF ERIE AND OTHER ESSAYS 303 (1871); MITCHELL, note 19 *supra*.

[198] 1 OBERHOLTZER, JAY COOKE, FINANCIER OF THE CIVIL WAR, 235, 239–40 (1907).

[199] So long as gold traded at a premium, the repaid principal would be of greater value than the purchase price. Similarly, payment of interest in premium gold increased the interest rate. Hence, permitting purchase with greenbacks while promising payment of principal and interest in gold raised the effective interest rate above the nominal face interest rate, at least *ex ante*.

order to be "Necessary and Proper."[200] Thus, even if the bonds could have been sold directly to the public for specie, Congress was not required to use this constitutionally less offensive method of Civil War finance. Similarly, Congress was not constitutionally required to sweep away the independent treasury system's specie requirement in order to permit the banks to buy bonds with checks and state bank notes.

The question of the core power to which the means actually chosen were ancillary is more troublesome. If the war powers have to be rejected in order to account for the sustaining of peacetime issuance in *Juilliard*, then one is left with the borrowing power. In view of the fact that the Constitutional text failed to outlaw paper money expressly, the government's long-followed practice of issuing demand notes seems sufficient to permit a late nineteenth-century Court to overcome the substantial evidence that the Constitutional Convention intended to foreclose paper money.

Nevertheless, it is hard to justify the added step of making paper money legal tender as a means of carrying out the borrowing power, particularly in peacetime. The Framers' distaste for paper money was clearly even greater when it was made legal tender. And the evidence that national bank notes circulated at par without the benefit of legal tender status should have gone far to show that that status was not necessary to circulation of paper money at par. Though the 1862 Congress, acting in the confusion of wartime, might be constitutionally excused for fearing that demand notes would trade at a discount against other nongold obligations, no such excuse can be made for the 1878 Congress that had had fifteen years of experience with national bank notes uniformly trading at par.[201] One can thus see why the *Juilliard* Court went far in the direction of saying that the legal tender power was inherent. Moreover, even if *Juilliard* can be justified as involving only the reissue of Civil War paper, rather than an independent new issuance, there remains the intriguing question of the Constitutional basis for to-day's legal tender paper. Today's fiat money, with its solemn declaration that "this note is legal tender for all debts, public and pri-

---

[200] 4 Wheat. at 411–20.

[201] For a minor departure from par in 1873 based on redemption procedures that would not apply to federal paper money, see discussion in FRIEDMAN & SCHWARTZ, note 54 *supra*, at 21–22 n.8.

vate," far exceeds in quantity the Civil War issuance, and its lineage extends back to quite different original parentage.[202]

Knox, like *Milligan*, was decided when the nation had returned to peace. That *Knox* upheld the legal tender legislation and that *Juilliard* extended the power to peacetime profoundly changed our financial history. Though the United States returned to a gold standard, the tradition of fiat money outlasted the gold standard and remains with us today. The *Legal Tender* cases deserve to live on in our constitutional consciousness as well.

---

[202] In 1979, U.S. currency and coin in circulation totaled $118.7 billion. Of this total, Federal Reserve notes accounted for $106.7 billion, and U.S. notes for only $311.6 million. Statistical Appendix to Annual Report of the Secretary of the Treasury . . . 1979, 345 (table 58). See Federal Reserve Act of December 23, 1913, 38 Stat. 251, 265 § 16.